WORKING WITH

WORD

SECOND EDITION

WORKING WITH

WORD

SECOND EDITION by Chris Kinata

The Definitive Guide to Microsoft® Word on the Apple® Macintosh™

Chris Kinata
Gordon McComb

PUBLISHED BY
Microsoft Press
A Division of Microsoft Corporation
One Microsoft Way, Redmond, Washington 98052-6399

Library of Congress Cataloging-in-Publication Data

McComb, Gordon.
Working with Word

Kinata's name appears first on the 1st edition.
Includes index.
1. Microsoft Word (Computer program) 2. Macintosh
(Computer)—Programming. 3. Word processing.
I. Kinata, Chris. II. Title.
Z52.5.M52M38 1989 652'.5 88-37284
ISBN 1-55615-185-3

Printed and bound in the United States of America.

3 4 5 6 7 8 9 MLML 3 2 1 0 9

Distributed to the book trade in Canada by General Publishing Company, Ltd.
Distributed to the book trade outside the United States and Canada by Penguin Books Ltd.

Penguin Books Ltd., Harmondsworth, Middlesex, England
Penguin Books Australia Ltd., Ringwood, Victoria, Australia
Penguin Books N.Z. Ltd., 182–190 Wairau Road, Auckland 10, New Zealand
British Cataloging in Publication Data available

Project Editor: Jack Litewka
Technical Editor: Mark Dodge

To Lydia and Jonah—bright stars both

Chris Kinata

To Eli Hollander and Jim Bierman

Gordon McComb

Contents

Acknowledgments

It's chronically amazing that so many people can lend their influence to the preparation and marketing of a book such as this. For the first edition, we owe our thanks to:

Editor Rebecca Pepper; copy editor Lee Thomas; proofreaders Marsha Wright and Mike Perry; Microsoft product-support people Sylvia Hayashi, Rob Howe, and David Dressler; reviewers among Word's development team, Chris Mason and David Luebbert; and Darcie Furlan, Becky Geisler-Johnson, and Larry Anderson of the production group at Microsoft Press.

Philip Boulding of Magical Strings for the picture of his Concert Oranmore harp, which led to the scanned image on pages 598–99; and Todd Laney, developer of the raytracing graphics routines that resulted in the wonderful PostScript image in the Introduction.

Eli Hollander, for portions of his screenplay for the movie *Out.*

For the second edition, which turned out to be nearly as significant a task as writing the entire book again from scratch, we owe great thanks to:

Editor Jack Litewka, for his untiring devotion to the ideal of shielding authors from swarms of those having sharp teeth and for his unflinching good humor when it would have been more appropriate to flinch.

Technical reviewer Mark Dodge, for the close attention he gave the manuscript. Managing editor Erin O'Connor also lent her aid in the final stages.

Proofreader Jean Zimmer (with some emergency help from Alice Copp Smith), who manifested stellar navigational talents on swelling seas of heavy prose.

Chris Mason, David Luebbert, Ray Gram, Tom Saxton, David McKinnis, and Paul Davis from the group of people at Microsoft who developed Word 4—willing and patient teachers all. We hope our incessant probing into the dark recesses of a great program was taken, in some measure, as an expression of a shared vision.

Larry Anderson, Carol Luke, Jean Trenary, Mark Souder, and Becky Geisler-Johnson of the production group at Microsoft Press, for graciously ignoring most of their finely tuned typesetting and production procedures in order to prepare this book with Word.

Introduction

Microsoft Word 4 for the Macintosh, the latest version as of this writing, is at a crossroads in the development of word-processing software. In the dark ages of word processing—perhaps seven years ago—you were restricted by the limitations of the hardware you used. There were no mice then, and so you had to use the keyboard to place markers at the beginning and end points of text you wanted to edit. Text came in only one size, and you were lucky if your combination of program and printer could produce "special effects" such as boldface and underlining.

Meanwhile, people in the publishing trade have long been working with a much more sophisticated set of parameters for measuring and formatting the text in books and other printed media. They know about kerning, letter-spacing, font families, font sizes, rules, and graphics. Moreover, they position elements on a page accurate to fractions of a point (1 point equals 1/72 inch). Unfortunately, the equipment needed to produce books, newsletters, and magazines by these methods is expensive and requires extensive training to use. So much training, in fact, that few have sufficient experience to command the entire range of tasks necessary to produce high-quality results.

Word represents a meeting place for these two realities. Many come to Word with a background colored by "traditional" word-processing programs and might not realize how far word processing has come. In fact, it helps to get another perspective on Word by considering this: Word is not a word processor.

What is it then? To the extent that you can manipulate outlines with Word, you could call it an idea processor. To the extent that you can easily enter and modify text, you could call it a text editor. You could even call it a page-layout program, using this book as evidence: Everything between its covers was printed from Word.

Word is the most successful of the new documenting environments in combining the ease of simpler word processors and the power of traditional typesetting systems. It's an environment that supports the entire range of tasks involved in creating a document, whether you're interested solely in the process of writing or charged with producing beautiful designs in print.

You can easily learn enough about Word to produce well-formatted and well-designed documents. However, to reach the outer limits of the effects you can create, you'll need to become familiar with some publishing concepts and terms. In this book we try to give you the complete range of experience you'll need to push Word to its limits—there's a lot of ground to cover!

To give you an overview of the process for creating a document in Word, Section 1, "Laying the Foundation," presents two tutorials: one for entering and editing a business letter, and one for an internal document a business might use.

Section 2, "Building the Framework," concentrates on the essentials of the Word environment, outlining, editing, and using glossaries and the spelling checker.

Section 3, "Refining the Appearance," discusses the wide range of formatting options available to you, as well as the process of printing documents.

Section 4, "Adding the Final Touches," covers embellishments you can add to your document: indexes and tables of contents, other types of tables and lists, graphics, and merge printing.

Section 5, "Blueprints for Projects," presents in detail a few projects that show what kinds of documents are possible in Word, with comments on how you might adapt them for your own needs.

Finally, Section 6, "Appendixes," contains material you might find helpful: setting up your Word disks, a table of the character sets for six fonts, a short tutorial on using PostScript in your documents, another tutorial on typesetting mathematical formulas, and a list of the huge range of defaults you can modify to customize Word.

Each chapter has the following elements:

- Where appropriate, numbered lists of steps to follow.
- Tips important for you to know, or tips of an advanced nature, which are shaded in the text to set them off from surrounding material.
- Summary sections at the end of each chapter, which outline the chapter's main points; numbered procedures and tables of mouse and key sequences are listed for future reference.

■ *Before you Continue...*

As you read through this book, keep these points in mind:

- ❑ To simplify matters, we assume you're using the mouse. If you prefer to use the keyboard, refer to the summary sections for listings of keyboard equivalents. Word has key sequences for nearly every operation and often has more than one set for a given command.
- ❑ Some menu commands are single step: You choose the command, and Word immediately carries out your request. Other commands present a set of options within a dialog box.
- ❑ Step-by-step mouse movements to select a command or complete an action are omitted. Instead, the text indicates generally what to do, such as "Choose the Find command" or "Click the Cancel button."

Before you begin to use Word, take the time to make backups of the Program and Utilities disks and arrange Word's files in a way that best suits your system. Appendix A gives details for creating working copies of your master disks. After you do this, don't be afraid to experiment. If something happens to the copy, you still have the original. After playing for a while, check out the next two chapters, which introduce the vast world of Word.

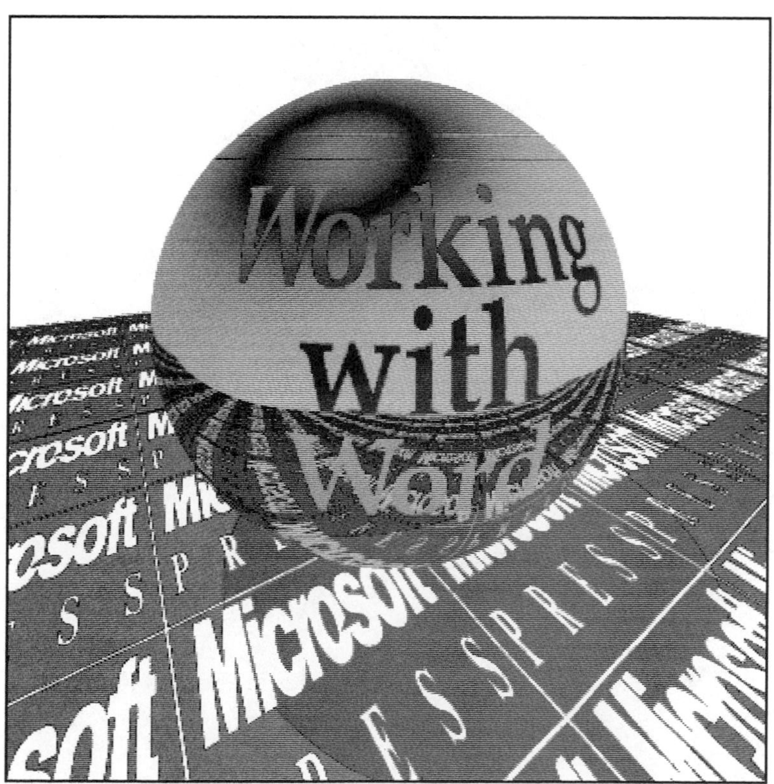

SECTION 1

Laying the Foundation

Word-Processing Concepts

Word version 4 is a sophisticated, multifeatured program that enables you to produce professional-looking documents easily and quickly. You won't master all of Word's possibilities in a few hours, of course, but you can productively use the program almost immediately with some background information and a little practice. This chapter offers both: The first half contains a primer of basic word-processing concepts and introduces some of Word's features. The second half presents a hands-on tutorial in which you'll create a simple one-page letter.

Because the Macintosh and the mouse are such natural companions, many of the exercises and explanations in this book use mouse terminology such as drag, click, and double-click. Not every writer or typist is mouse friendly, however. Many nimble-fingered keyboardists become annoyed when they have to use the mouse to perform such simple tasks as cutting and pasting. The programmers of this latest version of Word have taken great pains to please the most demanding of keyboard virtuosos. Almost every mouse-performed operation can also be accomplished with a key sequence, whether you are using a 512K Mac Enhanced, a Mac Plus, a Mac SE, or a Mac II. At the end of each chapter you'll find tables of handy keyboard shortcuts for your machine.

Start Word by double-clicking the Word icon. The Galley View window (called Document View in Word 3) appears, ready to receive text. (Figure 1-1 shows the window with a document displayed.) Drag down a command menu—for example, the Edit menu. Although you see only one set of commands, the menus in Word actually comprise two sets: Short Menus and Full Menus. (See Figure 1-2.) The Short Menus set contains commands for routine word-processing tasks; the Full Menus set contains the Short Menus commands and additional commands for more advanced tasks. If Word is in Short Menus mode, you'll see the Full Menus command at the bottom of the Edit menu—choose it to switch to Full Menus. If Word is in Full Menus, you'll see the Short Menus command on the Edit menu—choose it to switch to Short Menus. This ability to switch between modes is called *toggling*.

Now that you are acclimated to Word's basic environment, you're ready to learn about word processing in general and about Word in particular.

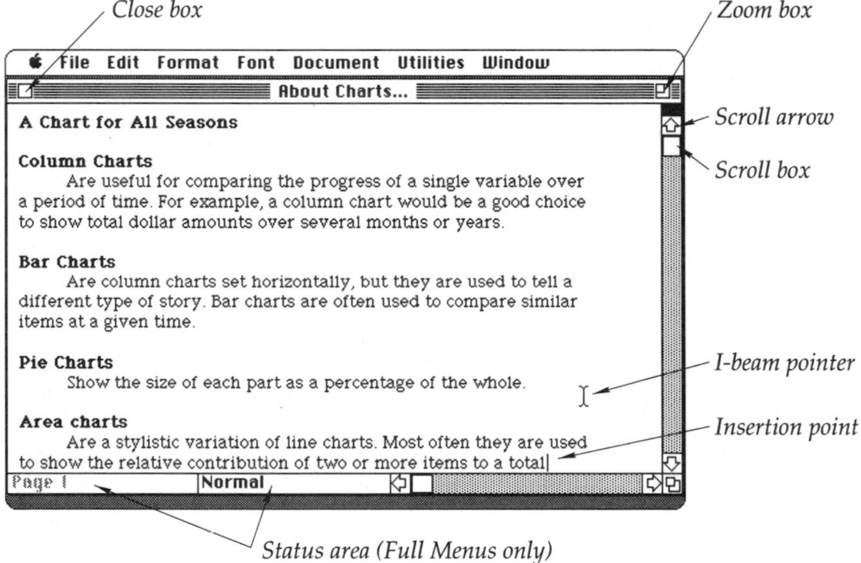

Figure 1-1

The Word desktop and a document displayed in Galley View.

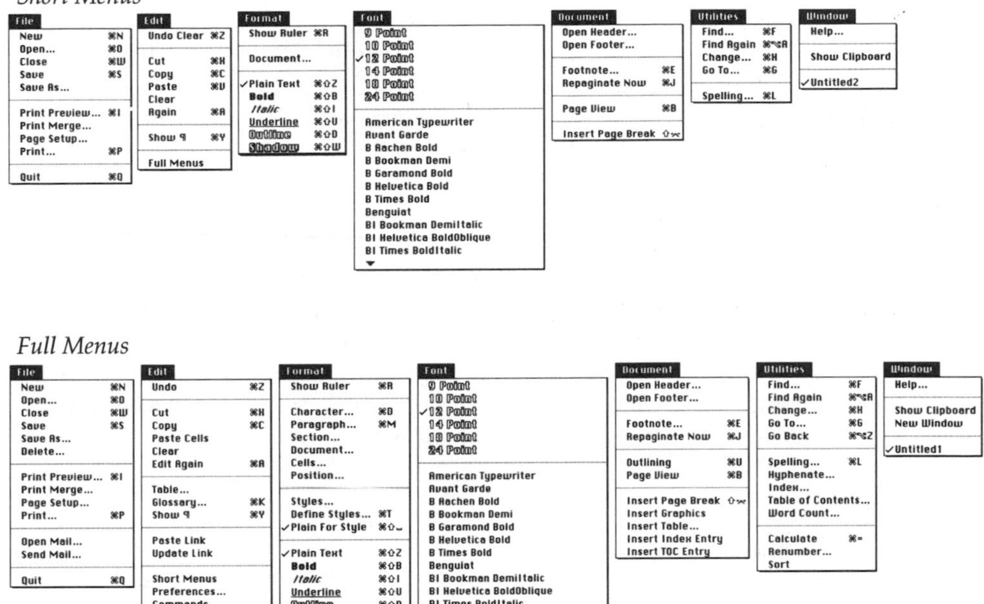

Figure 1-2
The two sets of commands: Short Menus and Full Menus.

Creating a document on a word processor involves five steps or functions: entering, editing, formatting, saving, and printing, as depicted in Figure 1-3. The first part of this chapter gives an overview of how you accomplish each of these steps in Word.

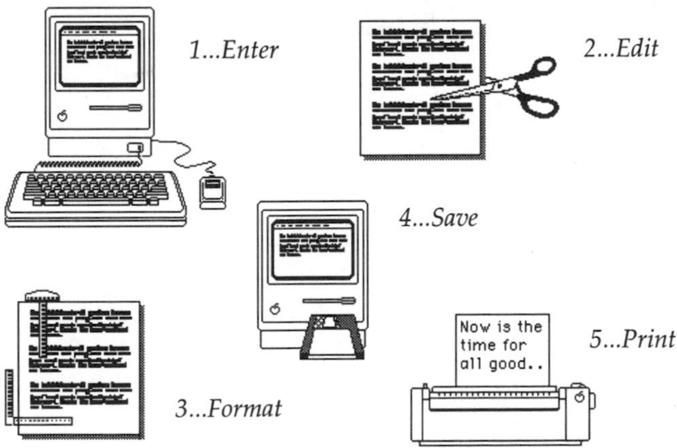

Figure 1-3
The five word-processing steps.

You won't necessarily use the entire set of steps every time you create a document, and you might not perform the functions in exactly the order presented. For a quick note to yourself, you might simply enter the text and print it. For a longer document, you might enter some text, save it, enter some more, pause to format a word (in italics, say), then edit a phrase, and so on. In Word, all five functions are available to you at all times.

■ *Entering*

The first step in creating a document is to enter text by simply typing on the keyboard. In Word, you usually enter text by typing in Galley View; however, you can create raw material for your documents in other ways as well. Among Word's features are tools to produce outlines and to insert already existing text or graphics into your work.

Outlines

When you work in *Outline View*, Word displays each heading and subheading in the familiar indented style common to outlines, as shown in Figure 1-4. This feature lets you clearly see the overall plan of a document—more clearly than when you scroll through the document in Galley View. An added benefit is that you can easily manipulate the headings in the outline. You can, for instance, move an entire heading and its associated text and graphics to another place in the document with a few clicks of the mouse button.

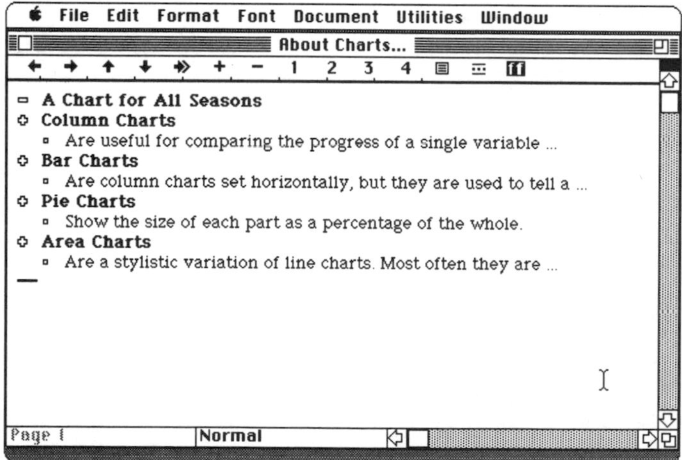

Figure 1-4
The same document as in Figure 1-1 displayed in Outline View.

Boilerplate Text and Graphics

In the old days when steam boilers were common, manufacturers found that they could use the same basic metal sheets—known as boilerplate—to construct boilers of all sizes and types. The term *boilerplate* was later used in the newspaper industry to mean any journalistic material in readily available form, usually columns or syndicated features that were already typeset.

In word processing, *boilerplate text* means any collection of characters—terms, short paragraphs, even whole documents—that you can easily insert into a document. You can save generic documents as boilerplate and then call them up as needed, or you can copy sections from a boilerplate document to the document you are creating. In Word, you can store boilerplate text in *glossaries*. A Word glossary is not a miniature dictionary; it is a collection of pieces of boilerplate text or graphics, each of which you can call up by entering the name that you assign it.

The glossary feature provides the easiest way to import boilerplate material into a document, but you can insert material in other ways, too. You can copy material to the Scrapbook and then paste it into a document, and with Word's QuickSwitch feature running under MultiFinder you can transfer material between documents even if they were made by different applications. For example, you can create an illustration in MacDraw or a table in Microsoft Excel and then insert it into a Word document. Unlike text, graphics cannot be edited in Word. You must go back to the original application used to create the graphic and edit it there. You can, however, indicate the exact placement of the graphic in the document, and you can size or crop the graphic as desired. (For more information on this subject, see Chapter 16, "Transferring Text and Graphics.")

■ *Editing*

After entering text, you can edit it: correct spelling, typographical errors, and grammar, or simply change your mind and write something else. Unlike a typewriter, a word processor lets you make changes painlessly; you don't have to commit your work to paper until you're satisfied with it. Even after printing the document, you can recall it and further alter it if you've saved it on disk. Word has two features that make the editing process even easier: a search-and-replace function and a spelling checker.

Search and Replace

Let's say you write a letter in which you consistently spell your client's name *Thomson* instead of the correct *Thompson*. You could go through the document and make each change manually, but a quicker approach is to use the Change command from the Utilities menu to replace the text. Simply enter both the old and new spellings, and Word automatically corrects each occurrence of the name. You can change phrases and complete sentences in the same way. You can also search for a word or phrase without changing it, using the Find command; at each occurrence, Word stops and displays the text.

Spelling Checker

Nothing detracts more from a professional document than misspellings and typographical errors. Other than hiring a copy editor, the best way to avoid these embarrassing mistakes is to use a spelling-check program. Word's built-in spelling checker contains a dictionary with 130,000 entries. By comparison, the typical vocabulary of a college-educated adult is roughly 20,000 words, including slang. In fact, Word's dictionary includes many slang terms, so the spelling checker helps with many kinds of writing. You can even create your own dictionaries containing a total of about 64,000 words.

■ Formatting

New users of word processors often confuse text and formatting. The difference is important. Text consists of the individual typed characters—the content of the document. Formatting is the way the content appears on the page—the "look" of the document, including type, paragraph indents, margin widths, and so on. This distinction is maintained in Word; that is, manipulating content and determining appearance require separate actions.

Like many word processors—and unlike typewriters—Word can determine much of the page and document formatting for you. For a start, it lets you enter text without concerning yourself with line endings and page endings. When a word won't fit on the current line, it is carried to the beginning of the line below; this is called *wordwrap*. The only time you press the Return key when entering text is to begin a new paragraph. When you run out of space on the current page, Word starts a new page. In practice, it's as if you were writing on a continuous scroll of paper; you might not even be aware of where the pages break until you print the document.

In Word, formatting involves five format domains: *character*, *paragraph*, *table*, *section*, and *document*. Basically, character formatting determines what the characters in your document look like; paragraph formatting controls the appearance of the lines of characters that form a paragraph; table formatting determines the size and arrangement of the cells in a table; section formatting specifies how columns of text are arranged; and document formatting determines the overall size and shape of a document. These domains are represented by commands on the Format menu (in Full Menus mode), although you can also change some characteristics of tables through the Edit and Document menus.

WYSIWYG User Interface

WYSIWYG (pronounced "wizzy-wig") is an acronym for "what you see is what you get" and refers to the faithful reproduction on screen of the text as it will appear on paper. Word is almost entirely WYSIWYG. Text appears on the screen in the same font, size, and style used for printing. Margins and text alignment are accurately reflected as well. A space of one inch on the screen translates almost exactly as a space of one inch on the printed copy.

Some formatting options, such as multiple columns, are not displayed on the screen in Galley View; but you can see the formatted result, without printing the document, in two ways. Choose Print Preview from the File menu to look at entire pages or pairs of pages, or choose Page View from the Document menu to both see your document as it will appear when printed and edit it. These commands save time and paper because you can check the layout of each page before printing.

Character Formats

Character formats affect such attributes as the font (typeface), font size, font style (for example, boldface or italic), and letterspacing. Spaces, created with the Spacebar, and tabs, created with the Tab key, are considered characters and can have formats, too. Although these characters—and thus their formats—conventionally are invisible, you can see them by choosing the Edit menu's Show ¶ command. (See Chapter 8, "Character Formatting.")

Paragraph Formats

Some formatting options, such as indents, tabs, and line spacing, affect an entire paragraph. If you make a line-spacing change to a character in a paragraph, for example, the entire paragraph is altered, not merely the character or the line that contains the character. Some paragraph formatting options appear when you choose Paragraph from the Format menu. (This command appears in Full Menus mode only.) The Word Ruler, displayed when you choose Show Ruler from the Format menu or use the Paragraph command, lets you set tabs, indention, line spacing, and alignment. (See Figure 1-5.)

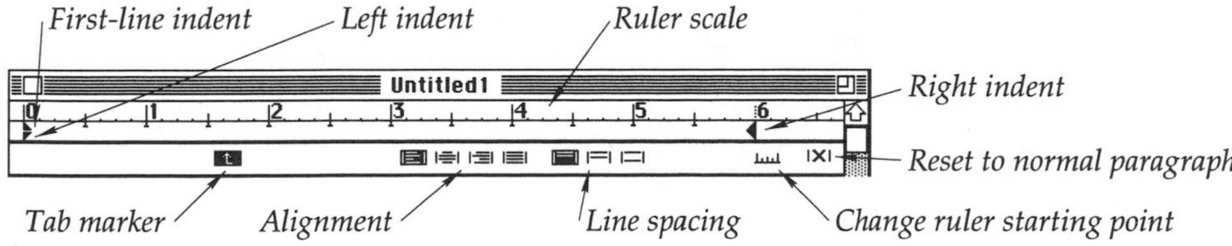

Figure 1-5
The Word Ruler, Short Menus version.

Indents

Word lets you create various kinds of paragraph indents. Many people indent the first line of each paragraph one-half inch (about five characters) from the left margin and set subsequent lines flush with the left margin. You can enter first-line indents either one by one, by pressing the Tab key, or in any number of paragraphs at once, by selecting the paragraphs and dragging the first-line indent marker (the upper of the two small triangles at the left margin in the Ruler) the desired distance to the right.

You can also create hanging indents, in which the first line of a paragraph is flush left and the rest are indented. This style of indention is often used in lists such as bibliographies. To create a hanging indent, drag to the right the lower of the two triangles in the Ruler. Figures 1-6a, 1-6b, and 1-6c show three types of paragraph indents; other types are possible. (Indenting is discussed in more detail in Chapter 9, "Paragraph Formatting.")

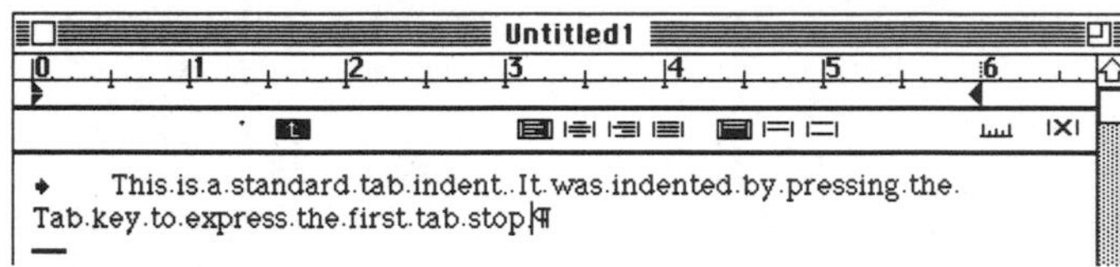

Figure 1-6a
A standard (user-entered) indent.

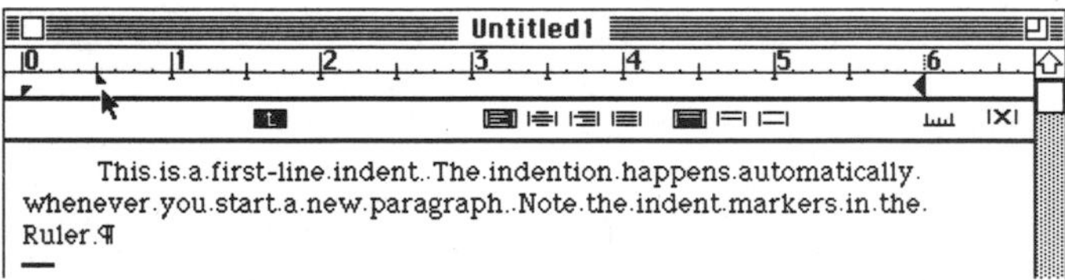

Figure 1-6b
A required (automatic) indent.

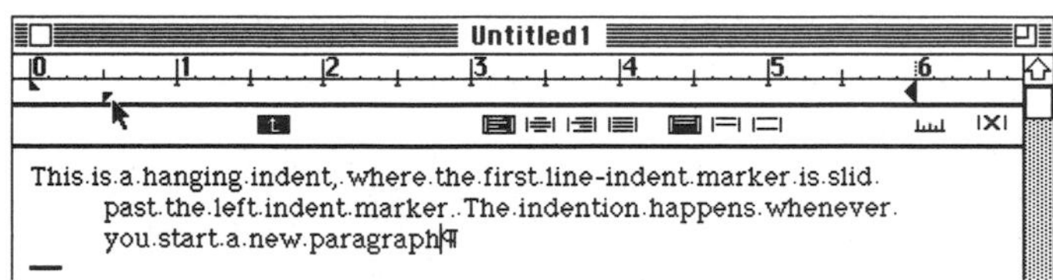

Figure 1-6c
A hanging indent.

Alignment

Alignment determines how the lines are placed between the right and left indents. Lines can be flush left (aligned on the left indent), flush right, justified (aligned on both indents), or centered between the indents. Figures 1-7a, 1-7b, and 1-7c show the same text with three different alignment formats. Notice that each paragraph is terminated with a paragraph mark, created when you press the Return or Enter key and made visible when you choose Show ¶ from the Edit menu.

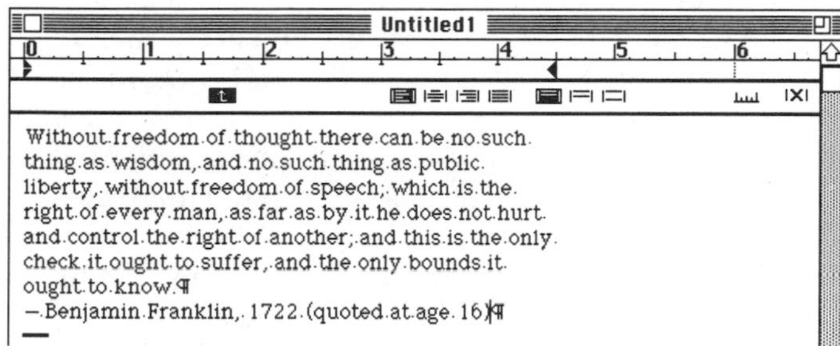

Figure 1-7a
Flush-left paragraph.

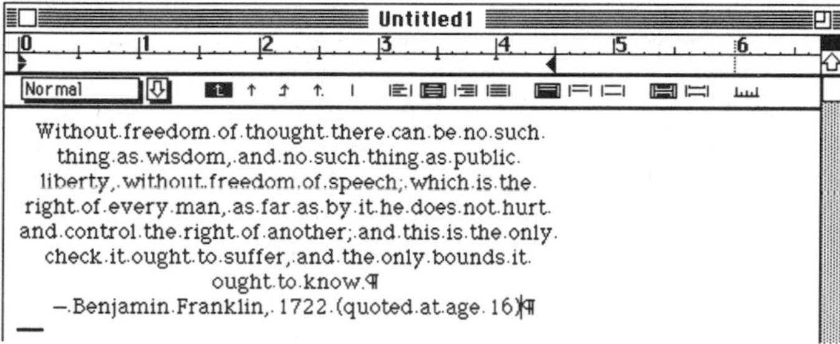

Figure 1-7b
Centered paragraph.

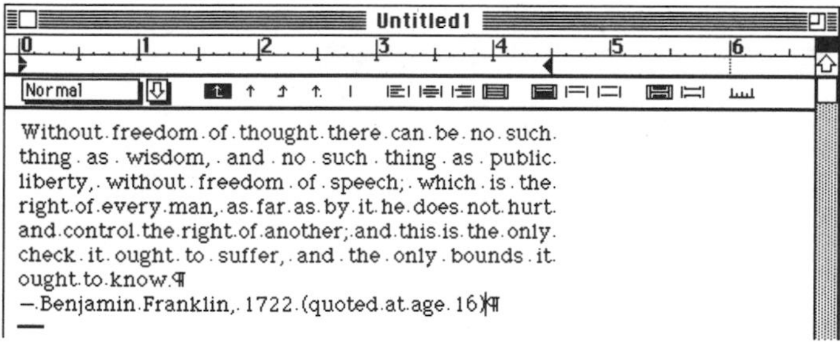

Figure 1-7c
Justified paragraph.

Styles and Style Sheets

In Word 4 the term *style* denotes a collection of character and paragraph formats that has been given a name and applied to one or more paragraphs. Format and style are closely related, but there are differences between the two. A style can be made up of a variety of character and paragraph formatting options, given a name, and applied to blocks of text using the Styles command from the Format menu. (This command is available in Full Menus mode only.) A format is a single attribute, such as line spacing or font size.

When first started, Word uses a standard block-letter style, called the *Normal* style. It calls for the 12-point New York font, indents set at the page margins, single-line spacing, and flush-left alignment. Figure 1-8 shows a document in *Normal* style.

You can alter the *Normal* style at any time, even after you enter the text. When you change a style, every paragraph that was labeled with that style changes. You can even group styles to form style sheets, a powerful feature unique to Word. When you want to reformat a document, you simply edit the style sheet or import a style sheet from another document, and the document instantly takes on a completely new look. You're saved the time and trouble of going through the text and reformatting it paragraph by paragraph. Best of all, once you get the hang of it, the style sheet feature is easy to use.

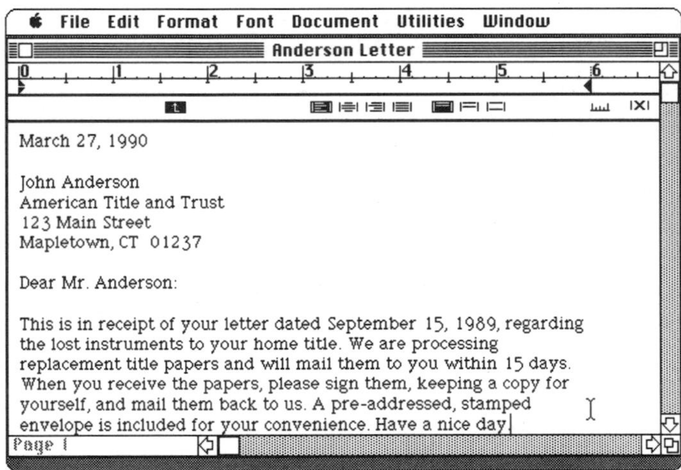

Figure 1-8
Word's *Normal* style.

Table Formats

Laying out pieces of text in columns and rows is more complicated than formatting text in only one column, because the number of possible formats is much larger. Previous versions of Word offered the Side-By-Side paragraph format and multiple-column sections. Word 4 presents a new type of structure, the table, in which you can set up a rectangular grid of cells, each cell of which becomes a small window containing a number of paragraphs. Figure 1-9 shows an example.

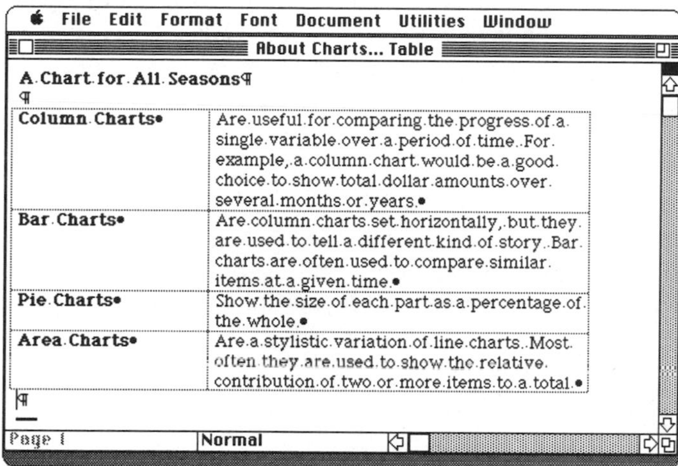

Figure 1-9
A typical table, shown in Galley View.

Section Formats

Section formatting lets you determine certain overall layout features for any text that you define as a separate part of your document—that is, as a section. A good analogy for sections are the chapters in a book. For example, you might format one part of a document in two columns and leave the rest in one column, or you might create a running head that appears on every page of the document except the first page of each chapter. If a document has only one section—the default condition—Word applies the section formats you set to the entire document.

Headers, Footers, and Footnotes

Word greatly facilitates the use of headers and footers—repeating text that appears at the top (head) or the bottom (foot) of every page or of pages within desired sections. You need enter the text only once; Word then prints it on every designated page. Word also prints footnotes at the bottom of the appropriate page or at the end of a section or document, as you request, and even keeps track of the numbering for you. For example, if you insert a new footnote, the program renumbers all subsequent notes and their in-text references.

Columns

Newsletters, brochures, menus, and many other types of documents are conventionally set up in two or more columns. Word lets you format a document with as many columns as there are characters on a line, but the practical maximum for a vertical 8.5-by-11-inch page is four columns. The columns do not appear alongside one another as you enter the text in Galley View (and therefore are not WYSIWYG), but they do appear this way when you use Print Preview or Page View.

Auto Numbering

Certain documents, such as outlines, legal documents, screenplays, and technical manuals, use numbering to identify lines and paragraphs. Word can number lines and paragraphs, freeing you from this time-consuming task. The program can also renumber lines and paragraphs if you move, add, or delete blocks of text.

Document Formats

The fifth format domain, that of the document itself, controls the overall shape of each page, including attributes such as page size, the placement of footnotes, and page margins (although you can use paragraph formatting to change the "margins" for particular paragraphs—in Word these are called indents). You can change document formatting options in typical Macintosh style by choosing Page Setup from the File menu. When the Page Setup dialog box appears, click the Document button to access the Document dialog box. Or you can arrive at the same dialog box by simply choosing Document from the Format menu.

■ *Saving*

You probably already know that all files that you intend to keep must be saved on a disk. Once saved on disk, files can be recalled for subsequent editing or printing. When you save a file in Word with the Save or Save As command from the File menu, it is not erased from the screen, and thus you can continue working with it. This is useful because with Word, as with most other Macintosh programs, you should save each document at frequent intervals (every 15 minutes or so), as well as before you close the document's window or quit a session. Turning off the machine without saving the document erases all your work.

Word lets you save documents in various data formats. You'll probably save most Word files in regular Word 4 format, but you can also save files so that they can be read directly by Word version 1, Word 3, Microsoft Write, MacWrite, and Microsoft Works (all for the Macintosh) and by Word for the IBM PC. Finally, you can save files in RTF interchange format (used by some

Mac, IBM PC, and UNIX applications) and in ASCII (text only) format, with or without line breaks. This range of options lets you more easily export data for use with other applications, telecommunicate your Word documents to other Macs, and transfer them between the IBM PC and the Macintosh.

■ *Printing*

Although technology pundits have long foreseen a paperless world in which all letters and other documents are distributed electronically, printed documents are still the norm rather than the exception. Word has several major features that help you get your work on paper the way you want it.

Print Preview and Page View

As you work on a document, it is often helpful to see exactly what it will look like when printed. Word's Print Preview command, on the File menu, and the Page View command, on the Document menu, provide this view of your document. In Print Preview mode, an example of which is shown in Figure 1-10, you can adjust the positions of headers (also called running heads), the width of margins, and the placement of page numbers. You can also change *page breaks* so that important headings appear at the top of a page.

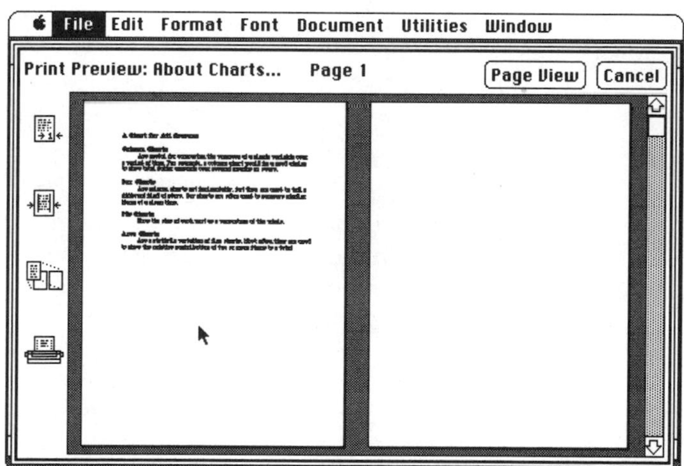

Figure 1-10
The same document used in Figures 1-1 and 1-4 in Print Preview mode.

Page View provides another way of looking at your document. Instead of seeing a reduced view of an entire page as it looks when printed, when you choose Page View from the Document menu you see the full-scale version, as shown in Figure 1-11 on the following page. You can edit and format text in this view exactly as you can in Galley View. You might decide that you prefer working with documents from this view; if you do, you can tell Word to open documents in Page View by choosing Preferences from the Edit menu and clicking the appropriate button in the dialog box that appears. However, there is a cost: Every action you take in Page View is displayed more slowly than in Galley View because of the larger number of calculations Word must perform to display the document.

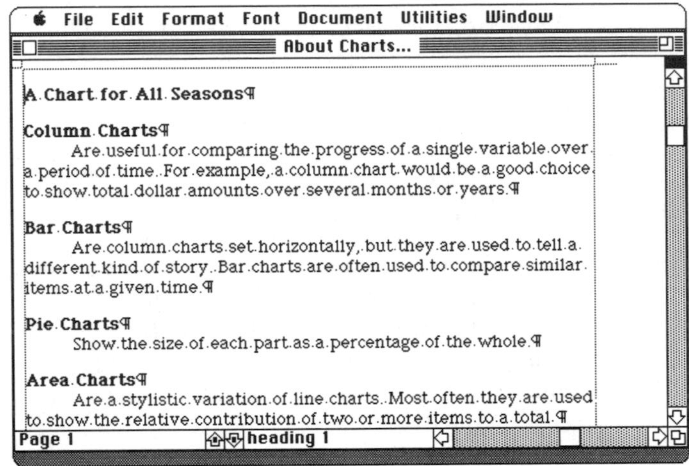

Figure 1-11
The same document shown in Page View.

Pagination

Pagination is the process of breaking text into pages and of numbering them. Word can break pages for you, or you can do it manually. Word can number pages; you can specify on which page to begin the numbering, where on the page to place the number, and what kind of numbering to use: Arabic numerals, Roman numerals (uppercase or lowercase), or letters.

Hyphenation

Word's built-in hyphenation feature, accessible from the Hyphenate command on the Utilities menu (Full Menus mode only), lets you correctly hyphenate almost every word in the English language. Hyphenation can improve the appearance of your copy by helping you avoid particularly unequal line lengths in ragged-right (flush-left) text and unsightly word spacing in justified text.

You can have Word hyphenate the entire document automatically or have Word pause before each word it wants to hyphenate so that you can confirm the placement of the hyphen. With the latter method, when the program encounters a word that is too long to fit on the current line but can be hyphenated, the word is displayed in a dialog box and marked at one or more proper hyphenation points. (See Figure 1-12.) You can then decide if and where the hyphenation is to occur.

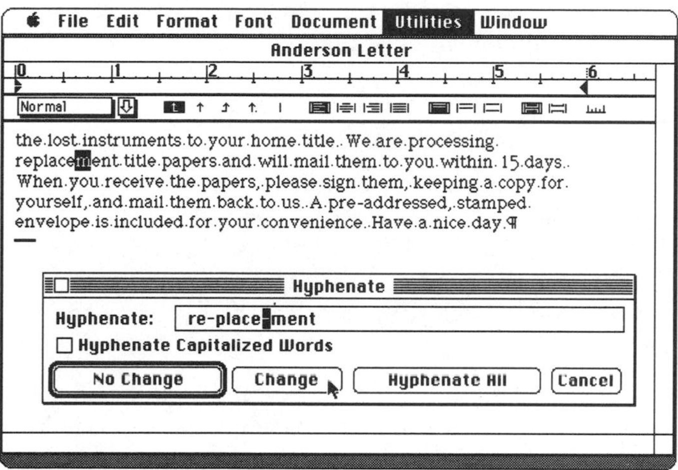

Figure 1-12
The hyphenation feature.

Merge Printing

The process of merge printing, often simply referred to as merging, is similar to using boilerplate or glossary text. You simply merge the main document (containing the form letter) with a data document (containing names, addresses and other "personalizing" information). Word then prints a different version for each chunk of data in the data document: With a form letter, it prints a different copy for each name. (See Figure 1-13.)

October 15,	October 15,	October 15,	October 15, 1990
Joan Foxwor 1025 Maple Moretown, N	Robert Temp 15-23 Expre Niagara Fall	Jessica Stu 634 Flower Granger, MN	Melvin Crooks, CPA 876-A Main Del Mar, CA 92014
Dear Joan:	Dear Bob:	Dear Aunt Je	Dear Mel:
We're movin larger accon Island and w new phone n of November	We're movin larger accon Island and w new phone n of November	We're movin larger accon Island and w new phone n of November	We're moving again! We've outgrown our larger accommodations. We've found a be Island and will be moving there by the 10 new phone number are listed below. I'll t of November, and I hope you can come!
Best,	Best,	Best,	Best,
Alex, Beth, a	Alex, Beth, a	Alex, Beth, a	Alex , Beth, and Mikey

Figure 1-13
Merge printing.

■ *Concepts into Action: Creating a Letter*

Theory goes only so far. In this section, you'll learn how to apply the five basic word-processing steps—entering, editing, formatting, saving, and printing—to create a basic one-page letter, using only the Short Menus commands. But first, you need to set up your program so that what you see on the screen matches the descriptions in this tutorial.

Setting Up

If you haven't already started Word, do so by double-clicking its icon. A blank Galley View window appears. Word will store your settings (such as Short Menus versus Full Menus) from session to session so that you don't have to reconfigure the program to your liking each time you start it. Thus, before beginning the tutorial, do the following to ensure that your settings are the same as the ones used here:

1. **Choose the Short Menus mode.** Pull down the Edit menu. If the Short Menus command shows near the bottom of the Edit menu, choose it. You are now in Short Menus mode. If the Full Menus command appears at the bottom of the Edit menu, you are already in Short Menus mode.
2. **Hide the formatting marks.** Pull down the Edit menu. If the Hide ¶ command is near the bottom of the menu, choose it. Word now hides all formatting marks. If Show ¶ appears instead, the formatting marks are already hidden.
3. **Display sizes in inches.** Choose the Show Ruler command from the Format menu. The Ruler should be graduated in inches, as shown at the top of Figure 1-14. If the Ruler shows centimeters, points, or picas, change it:

   ❶ Choose Full Menus from the Edit menu.

   ❷ Choose Preferences from the same menu.

   ❸ In the dialog box that appears, select the Inch option from the drop-down list. Then click OK.

   ❹ Choose Short Menus from the Edit menu.

   ❺ Choose Hide Ruler from the Format menu.

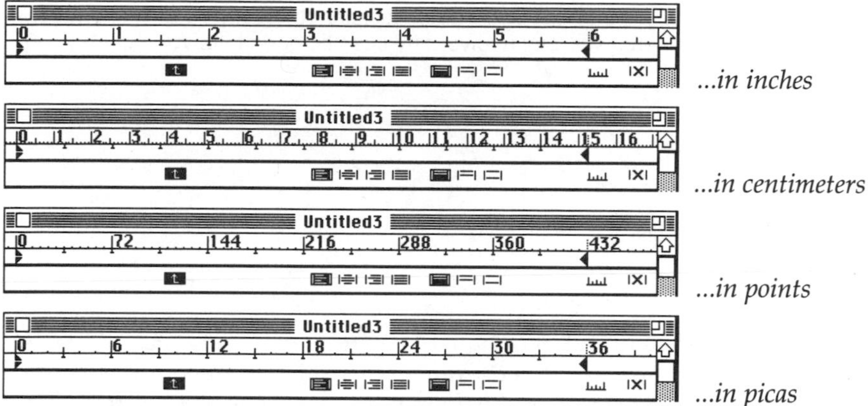

Figure 1-14
The four types of Ruler graduations.

If you were to quit Word right now, these settings would be saved. You would not need to repeat the procedure of setting them up unless someone changed them on your working copy of Word. In Chapter 5, "Writing and Editing Techniques," you will learn more about setting preferences and saving them in the Word Settings file.

Entering the Text

Type the following text into the blank window. (When you see ¶, press the Return key.) Notice that you don't have to press the Return key after each line. Word places ("wraps") words that won't fit on the current line onto the next line. If you make a typing mistake, press the Backspace key (the Delete key on some keyboards) to erase characters to the left of the blinking insertion-point marker.

January 15, 1990¶
¶
Michael Fox, Associate Editor¶
MOTHER-OF-INVENTION NEWS¶
5690 Sunset Drive¶
Hollywood, CA 91500¶
¶
¶
Dear Mr. Fox:¶
¶
Thank you for your letter concerning our new line of high-impact plastic gears. We understand that you would like samples and product sheets for an article on designing with gears in an upcoming issue of Mother-of-Invention News. I've enclosed a merchandise request form. Once we have the form, we can send the samples to you.¶
¶

Please don't hesitate to write or call if you need assistance. I can, if you wish, put you in touch with our engineers, who can answer any specific questions you may have.¶
¶
Sincerely,¶
¶
¶
¶
David A. Buxton¶
Public Relations Specialist¶
¶
Enc.¶

The text of the letter might not fit in one window on the screen. You can scroll back to the beginning of the document by dragging the scroll box on the right side of the window or by clicking the up arrow in the scroll bar, as shown in Figure 1-15. Similarly, you can use the horizontal scrolling feature to pan back and forth to see all of an extra-wide document.

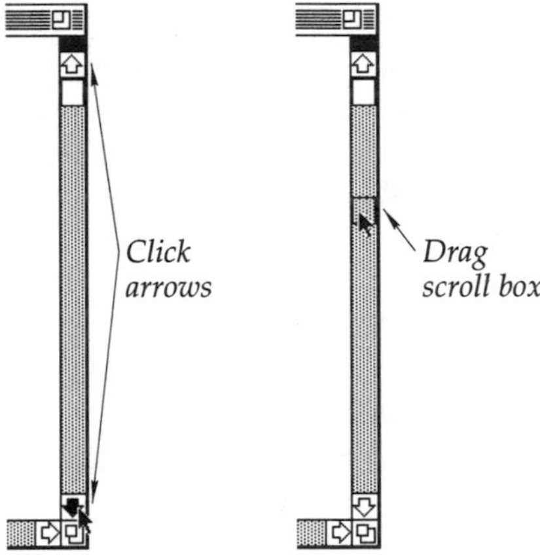

Figure 1-15
Vertical scrolling in a document.

Editing the Text

You can add characters, words, or sentences to the body of your letter. Add some text after the sentence *I've enclosed a merchandise request form* by following this procedure:

❶ Set the insertion point immediately to the right of the period at the end of the sentence by moving the I-beam pointer there and clicking the mouse button.

❷ Press the Spacebar once (or twice if you prefer two spaces between sentences).

❸ Type this text:

Please complete it and send it back to me at your convenience.

As you add the new text, Word pushes the characters beyond the insertion point to the right. Repeat the procedure to add a single word in the next paragraph:

❶ Set the insertion point immediately after the word *specific* in the second paragraph.

❷ Press the Spacebar once.

❸ Type the word *technical.*

If the two words run into each other, set the insertion point between them and press the Spacebar. If too many spaces occur between the words, set the insertion point immediately to the left of the second word and press the Backspace key to delete each unwanted space.

Adding Paragraphs

Once you have typed the letter, you can go back and add any amount of text anywhere you like. Add more text to the letter by following this procedure:

❶ Set the insertion point after the last period of the second paragraph, at the end of the sentence ending *questions you may have.*

❷ Press the Return key twice to start a new paragraph and insert a blank line.

❸ Type this text:

As you may know, we have been making high-grade gears for more than 50 years. In the early years, Anderson Gear had three employees: John Anderson, his wife Loretta, and his younger brother Ted. The company now employs more than 220 people and has sales offices around the world. In addition to the new line of affordable high-impact plastic gears, Anderson Gear manufactures and markets a complete line of stock gears made with brass, nylon, steel, aluminum, and fiber-reinforced plastic.¶

Editing Words in Page View

To see what the letter looks like as a printed page, choose Page View from the Document menu. What you see should match Figure 1-16 on the following page. Dotted lines surround the body of the text to show you where the margins are, if the Show Text Boundaries in Page View option is set in the Preferences dialog box. To return to Galley View, you would choose Page View again, but for now let's stay in Page View to edit the letter.

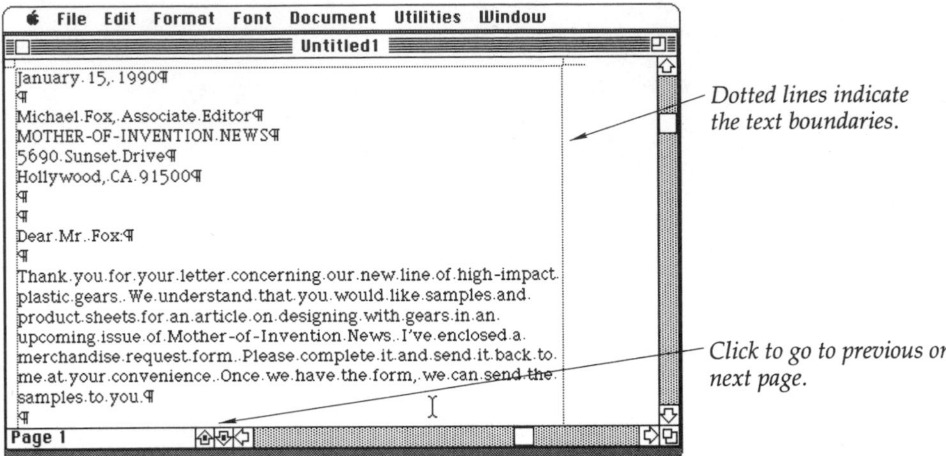

Figure 1-16
Using Page View.

If you scroll around on the page, you'll see that Word displays the margins and edges of the paper, showing you where the text appears relative to the page edges. Also, notice the set of arrows near the left end of the horizontal scroll bar. When you click one of these, Word switches to a view of the previous or next page. If you do this now, however, Word beeps because the document consists of only one page.

Now change a word in the letter. Locate the term *high-grade* in the first sentence of the third paragraph. "High-grade" sounds like crude oil, not a precision-machined part, so change it to *fine-grade.*

❶ Set the insertion point immediately to the left of the hyphen.

❷ Press the Backspace key four times to delete the word *high.*

❸ Type the word *fine.*

That was easy. Now try a different method to change a word. Locate the word *people* in the middle of the third paragraph (in the sentence *The company now employs...*).

❶ Place the pointer on *people* and double-click. (You don't need to set an insertion point first to select an entire word.)

❷ Without doing anything else, type *men and women.* Word replaces the selection (*people*) with the new text (*men and women*).

Moving Paragraphs Within the Document

In the original text, the paragraph beginning *Please don't hesitate to write or call* closed the letter. Because you added a paragraph to the end of the text, however, this closing statement moved to the middle of the letter. Instead of retyping the paragraph, cut and copy it using the Clipboard.

1. Scroll the window so that the *Please don't hesitate to write or call...* paragraph is in view.
2. Place the I-beam pointer on the paragraph, and slowly move the pointer to the left. Just beyond the left edge of the text, the pointer changes to a right-pointing arrow, as shown in Figure 1-17. The pointer is now in the *selection bar*, an invisible strip that runs along the left edge of the window in Galley View and is just to the left of the left margin in Page View. The selection bar is useful for selecting lines, paragraphs, and even the entire document.

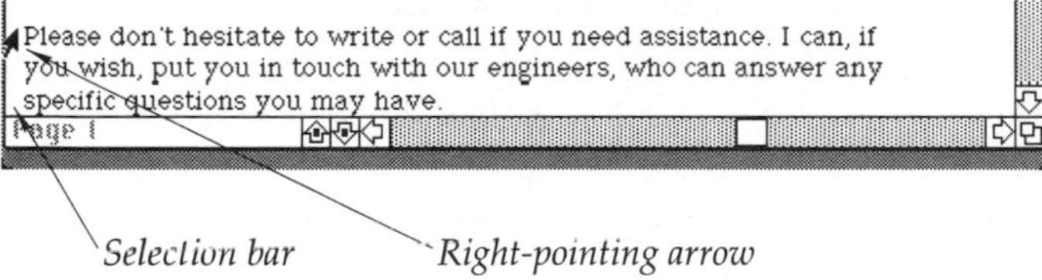

Figure 1-17
The pointer points to the right when in the selection bar.

3. Double-click in the selection bar to select the paragraph. The entire paragraph should become highlighted. If not, go back to Step 2 and try again.
4. Choose Cut from the Edit menu. Word removes the selected text from the document and places it on the Clipboard.
5. Press the Backspace key (the Delete key on some keyboards) once to remove the extra line between the paragraphs.
6. Set the insertion point on the line after the paragraph ending *fiber-reinforced plastic*. Press the Return key once.
7. Choose Paste from the Edit menu. Word inserts the previously cut selection at the insertion point.

Checking for Errors

Word's built-in spelling checker scans your documents, looking for words that you misspelled or typed incorrectly. Word knows how to spell about 130,000 words and, if you want, presents the correct spelling for you, saving you from having to look up entries in the dictionary. You can also enter the correct spelling from the keyboard and have Word use it to replace the incorrect text. You have full control over when and where Word alters the spelling of text. To check the letter for spelling:

1. Set the insertion point at the beginning of the document.
2. Choose Spelling from the Utilities menu. The dialog box shown in Figure 1-18, on the following page, appears.

3. Start the spelling check by clicking the Start Check button or pressing the Return key. (You can always select bordered buttons in Macintosh dialog boxes by pressing the Return key.)
4. Word may present another dialog box asking you to verify your choice. Answer by clicking the OK button.
5. The first suspect word in the letter is *Michael*—that is, if you didn't make any mistakes before that word. It is shown after Unknown Word in the Spelling dialog box and is also highlighted in the text. This word is spelled correctly, but the spelling checker has noted it because it isn't in Word's dictionary. (Nor are any proper nouns, although you can add them—as well as other words—to your own dictionary file, as explained in Chapter 2.) Click the No Change button and proceed.
6. Assuming that you haven't made any typographical errors, the next suspect word is *Loretta.* Again, the word is spelled correctly but isn't in Word's dictionary. Click No Change to skip past it.
7. If a word is flagged as suspect and is indeed spelled incorrectly, change it by entering the proper spelling in the Change To box. Then click the Change button or press the Return key.

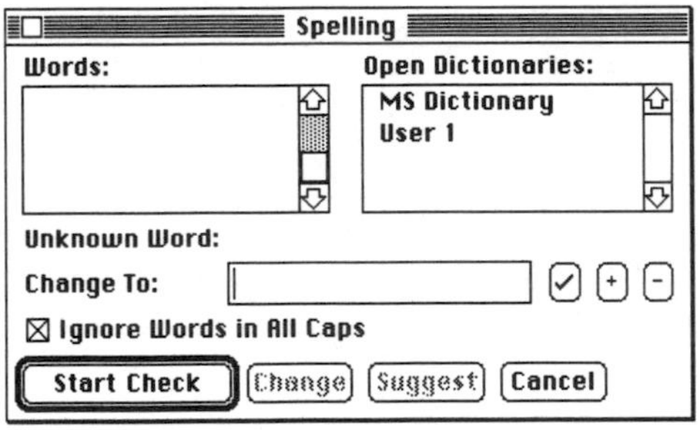

Figure 1-18
The Spelling dialog box.

8. Continue through the rest of the letter, clicking the No Change button for properly spelled words and entering the new text and clicking the Change button for improperly spelled words.
9. After the letter has been checked, Word presents a dialog box saying *End of document reached.* Click OK. (If you started the spelling check at a point other than the beginning, Word asks if you want to start over at the beginning. In this case, click OK to check the entire document.)

You can have Word analyze a suspect word and come up with a list of potential correct spellings by clicking the Suggest button. Alternative spellings appear in the Word list box. (See Figure 1-19.) The first word in the list is highlighted and also appears after Change To. Scroll down the list if necessary, click on the suggestion you want, and then click the Change button.

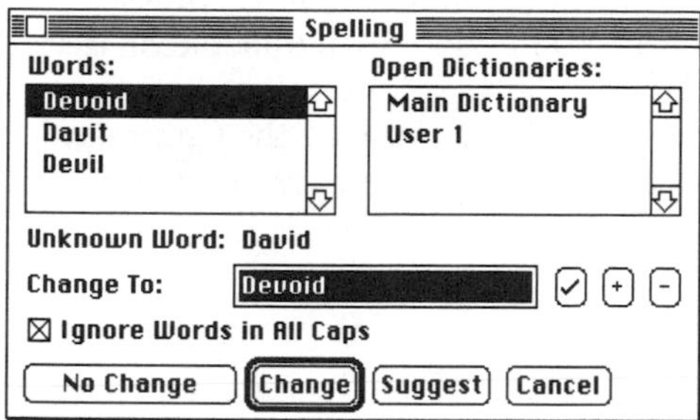

Figure 1-19
Using the Suggest feature.

Formatting the Text

Formatting in Word is a fascinating and complex subject; in fact, several later chapters are devoted to the topic. This exercise gives you only a glimpse of the possibilities.

Formatting Characters

You can change the font, font size, and style of any character in a Word document. For now, try underlining a few words. In the first paragraph, locate the text *Mother-of-Invention News*. (Remember that Word should still be in Page View.)

❶ Select the text as follows: Move the pointer just to the left of *Mother*. Press the mouse button and, holding it down, drag the mouse until the pointer is after the *s* in *News*. (Don't select the period.) Then release the mouse button. The phrase *Mother-of-Invention News* should be highlighted.

❷ Choose Underline from the Format menu. The text becomes underlined.

❸ Click anywhere in the document window to deselect the text.

Font styles can be mixed and matched. You can combine underlining with boldfacing, for example, or you can combine shadow, outline, and italic styles in the same text. The effect isn't always pretty, but you can experiment until you get the look you want. To combine styles, select the text and then choose each style. A check mark appears beside the styles you have activated. You can cancel any style by choosing it again. (The check mark goes away.) To return to regular text, select the text and choose Plain Text.

Creating a Letterhead

The sample letter is designed for use with preprinted letterhead stationery. You can incorporate a standard letterhead into the document and print it with the rest of the text. The letterhead can consist of text or graphics.

First, you can "shrink" the document a bit to make room for the letterhead. Word normally starts up with the 12-point New York font. Reduce the letter in size by changing the font to 12-point Times (pick another font if Times isn't installed): Select the entire document by pressing the Command key and clicking in the selection bar, and then choose Times from the Font menu. Deselect the document by clicking anywhere in the window.

Text Letterhead

You can type the letterhead text directly at the top of the document.

❶ Set the insertion point at the very beginning of the document, before the *J* in *January*. Press the Return key once, then click in the new first line to set the insertion point there.

❷ Choose Show Ruler from the Format menu, as well as Show ¶.

❸ Click the Center icon in the ruler (the second icon from the left in the alignment icons; see Figure 1-5). The text you enter will now be centered between the left and right indents.

❹ Type this text. (Remember to press the Return key where you see a ¶.)

Anderson Gear Company¶
121 Pike Avenue South¶
Urbaneville, NJ 01111¶
(201) 555-1265¶
¶

You can make the name of the company stand out by selecting it and choosing Bold from the Format menu. Scroll around on the page to see how the document looks. It should resemble Figure 1-20.

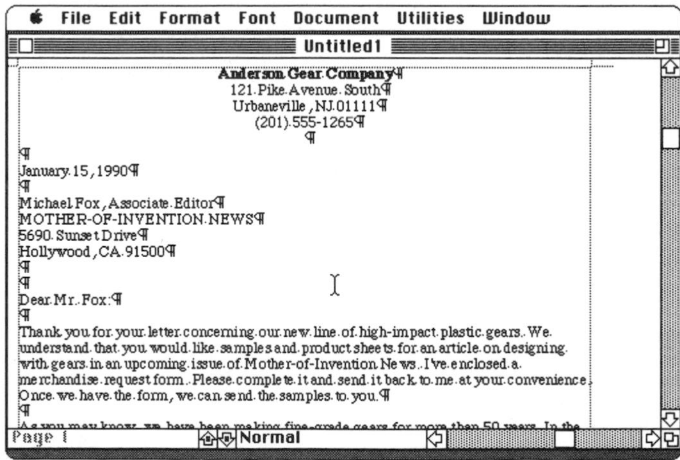

Figure 1-20
Letter with text letterhead, in Page View.

Notice that the date is too close to the letterhead. To correct this:

1. Position the insertion point immediately to the left of the *J* in *January.*
2. Press the Return key twice. Each time, the text moves down one line.

Saving Your Work

You'll probably want to save most of the documents you write with Word. To save the letter:

1. Choose Save As from the File menu.
2. Enter *Reply Letter* as the name of your sample letter, and click Save.

If you want to save the letter on a disk other than your Word Program disk (the name of the disk appears in the upper right corner of the Save dialog box), click the Eject and Drive buttons, as you do in most other Macintosh applications.

Note that the letter remains in the window so that you can continue working with it. When you are through making changes to a document, save it and then close the window by clicking the close box. If you forget to save the changes before closing the window, Word reminds you by displaying a dialog box.

The times you need to use the Save As command are when you are saving a new file for the first time, when you want to save an existing file under another name, or when you want to save the file on another disk or in another file format. Otherwise, you can simply choose the Save command or press Command-S. Word then saves the file under the old name. If the disk that contains the document is not in a drive, Word asks you to insert it.

It's a good idea to save your documents at frequent intervals as you work with them. Otherwise, if a power outage or other problem should occur as you're writing, your work would be lost. By saving often and regularly, you decrease the chance of having to redo a document from scratch.

Previewing and Printing the Letter

Printing is one of the more straightforward tasks you do with Word. Before printing, however, check the document's layout in Print Preview to be sure it looks all right. Choose Print Preview from the File menu; the letter appears in miniature form, as shown in Figure 1-21 on the following page. Note the four icons at the left side of the window. Here's how they work:

- ❑ Page Number: Click the icon, and then click on the page to set the position for the page number.
- ❑ Margin Set: Click to set page-specific margins and page breaks.

- ❑ One-page display: Click to switch between one-page and two-page display. In a one-page display, the image is somewhat larger.
- ❑ Printer: Click this to bring up the Print dialog box. Enter a page range in the To and From fields, or leave the fields empty to print the entire document.

You can't edit the document while in Print Preview, but you can change margins and set the position of the page numbers. (These techniques are explained in depth in later chapters.) Also, although Galley View and Page View occupy only the space on the screen you've given the window, the Print Preview window has the form of a dialog box and takes up the entire screen, regardless of which model of monitor you're using.

To return to Galley View (if that was the mode currently in effect), click the Cancel button in the upper right corner of the Print Preview window, or press Command-(period). To return to Page View, click the Page View button in the upper right corner of the Print Preview window, or double-click anywhere on the displayed page.

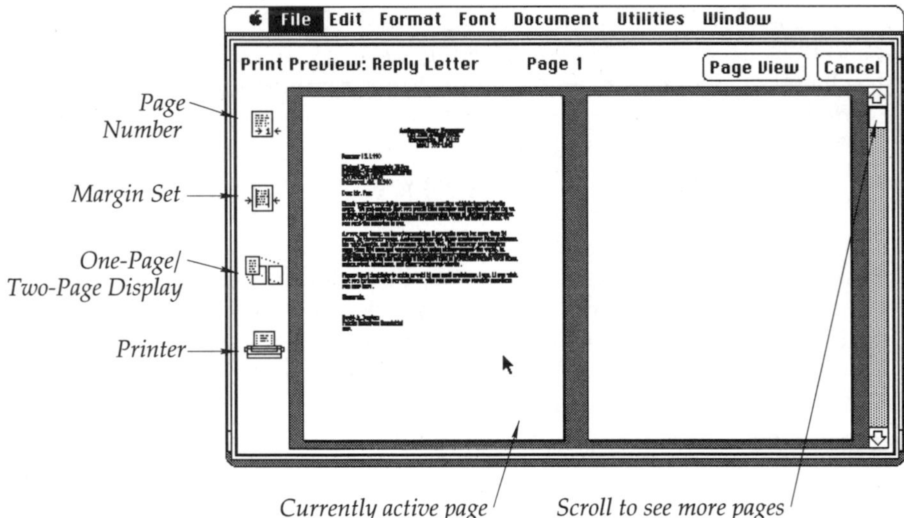

Figure 1-21
Print Preview of letter.

Now you can print the letter. Be sure the printer is turned on and on line; if you're using an ImageWriter, the SELECT light should be glowing. And of course, be sure the printer is loaded with paper and connected to the Macintosh. (Refer to your printer's instruction manual for details on setting it up and connecting it to the Macintosh.) To print the letter:

1. Choose Print from the File menu.
2. Select the appropriate options in the dialog box that appears for the printer, as shown in Figure 1-22.
3. Click OK or press the Return key.

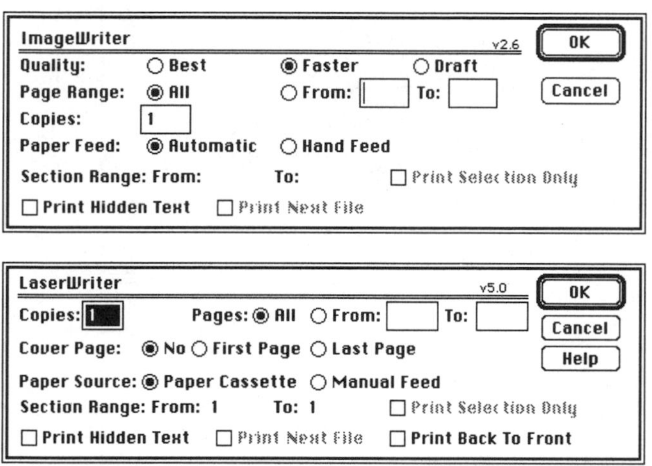

Figure 1-22
The Print dialog boxes for the ImageWriter and LaserWriter.

You can stop printing at any time by clicking the Cancel button in the dialog box that appears during printing, or in the case of the ImageWriter, you can temporarily freeze printing by clicking the Pause button. Figure 1-23 on the following page shows how the letter looks when printed on the LaserWriter.

Anderson Gear Company
121 Pike Avenue South
Urbaneville, NJ 01111
(201) 555-1265

January 15, 1990

Michael Fox, Associate Editor
MOTHER-OF-INVENTION NEWS
5690 Sunset Drive
Hollywood, CA 91500

Dear Mr. Fox:

Thank you for your letter concerning our new line of high-impact plastic gears. We understand that you would like samples and product sheets for an article on designing with gears in an upcoming issue of Mother-of-Invention News. I've enclosed a merchandise request form. Once we have the form, we can send the samples to you.

As you may know, we have been making fine-grade gears for more than 50 years. In the early years, Anderson Gear had three employees: John Anderson, his wife Loretta, and his younger brother Ted. The company now employs more than 220 men and women and has sales offices around the world. In addition to the new line of affordable high-impact plastic gears, Anderson Gear manufactures and markets a complete line of stock gears made with brass, nylon, steel, aluminum, and fiber-reinforced plastic.

Please don't hesitate to write or call if you need assistance. I can, if you wish, put you in touch with our engineers, who can answer any specific questions you may have.

Sincerely,

David A. Buxton
Public Relations Specialist
enc.

Figure 1-23
Final LaserWriter printout of letter.

Points to Remember

- The five basic steps in word processing are entering, editing, formatting, saving, and printing. You will not always go through all of these steps for every document, and you may want to vary their order from document to document.
- Word provides two sets of menus: Short Menus and Full Menus. Choose the Short Menus or the Full Menus commands from the Edit menu to toggle between the two. Full Menus mode offers many more features and is thus more useful once you know your way around in Word.
- Formatting in Word involves five format domains.

  Character formats determine what the characters in your document look like (the font and font style, for example).

  Paragraph formats control the appearance of the lines of characters that form a paragraph, including line spacing, alignment, and the positions of tab stops within a paragraph.

  Table formats set up special gridlike structures for arranging text in rows and columns.

  Section formats determine the appearance and arrangement of sequences of paragraphs, such as the number of horizontal columns on a page, and the location and content of running headers and footers.

  Document formats specify the overall defaults for the document (the size of the page, the position of margins on the page, and the placement of footnotes, for example).
- Word provides four ways to view a document.

  Galley View is the way you normally view a document—it shows how the text itself looks, with line breaks and character and paragraph formats in place. However, some parts of the document, such as headers and footers, are not displayed.

  Outline view collapses the document into an outline form so that you can see and manipulate the list of topics.

  Page View lets you both see your document as it looks when printed, and edit the document.

  Print Preview lets you check the layout of a document in reduced size and change certain aspects of a document such as margins and page breaks.
- A style is a collection of character and paragraph formats that describe a given paragraph or group of paragraphs. Styles can be grouped together to form style sheets that apply to an entire document.
- The selection bar is an invisible strip that runs along the left edge of the window in Galley View or Page View. It lets you select lines and paragraphs quickly. When you see a right-pointing arrow, your pointer is in the selection bar.

Techniques

Basic Skills

Scroll in a document

1. Click the appropriate arrow in the vertical scroll bar.

Select text

1. Move the pointer to one end of the text.
2. Press the mouse button, drag the pointer to the other end of the text, and release the mouse button. (See also the shortcuts in the following section.)

Deselect text

1. Click anywhere in the document.

Editing

Insert text

1. Position the pointer and click to set the insertion point.
2. Type the new text.

Replace text

1. Select the text to be replaced.
2. Type the new text.

Move text

1. Select the text to be moved.
2. Choose Cut from the Edit menu to move it to the Clipboard.
3. Set the insertion point where you want to move the text.
4. Choose Paste from the Edit menu.

Check spelling

1. Set the insertion point where you want the spelling check to begin.
2. Choose Spelling from the Utilities menu, and press the Return key.
3. Click Suggest to have Word list potential correct spellings for an unknown word.
4. Select the correct spelling from the list Word offers, or enter the correct spelling in the Change To field.

❺ Click the Change button to change the spelling.

Formatting

Display or hide formatting marks

❶ Choose Show ¶ or Hide ¶ from the Edit menu.

Display or hide the Word Ruler

❶ Choose Show Ruler or Hide Ruler from the Format menu.

Change graduations in Ruler

❶ Choose Preferences from the Edit menu. If you are in Short Menus mode, choose Full Menus first.

❷ In the dialog box that appears, click the button for the type of graduation you want.

❸ Click OK.

Change a character attribute

❶ Select the text to be changed.

❷ Choose a character format from the Format menu.

Or,

❶ Select the text to be changed.

❷ Choose Character from the Format menu.

❸ Select the formatting options you want.

❹ Click OK.

Change the font and point size

❶ Select the text to be changed.

❷ Choose a font from the Font menu.

❸ Change the point size of selected text by choosing a point size from the same menu.

Center text

❶ Set the insertion point within the paragraph to be centered, or select a block of text to be centered.

❷ Display the Word Ruler, and click the Center icon. Any text you type while the Center icon is selected is centered.

Preview a document before printing

❶ Choose Print Preview from the File menu.

To return to Galley View from Print Preview, either click the Cancel button in the upper right corner of the window or press Command-(period).

Preview a document and edit it

❶ Choose Page View from the Utilities menu. If you are in Print Preview, click the Page View button or double-click anywhere on a displayed page.

To return to Galley View from Page View, choose Page View again.

Saving

Save a new document

❶ Choose Save As from the File menu.

❷ Type a filename, and select the folder or disk to which you want to save the document.

❸ Press the Return key.

Save an existing document

❶ Choose Save from the File menu.

You'll see the progress of the save expressed as a percentage in the lower left corner of the window in Galley View or Page View.

Printing

Print a document

❶ Choose Print from the File menu.

❷ Check the settings.

❸ Press the Return key.

Keyboard and Mouse Shortcuts

To	Do this
Show/Hide ¶	Command-Y (toggles)
Show/Hide Ruler	Command-R (toggles)
Copy	Command-C
Cut	Command-X
Paste	Command-V
Select a word	Double-click on the word.
Select a paragraph	Double-click in the selection bar next to the paragraph.
Select the entire document	Click in the selection bar while pressing the Command key, or press Option-Command-M.
Print the document	Command-P
Save the document	Command-S

Word Fundamentals: Creating a Two-Page Document

The exercise presented in this chapter begins where the letter tutorial in Chapter 1 left off. Now that you've worked in Short Menus mode to produce a standard block-format letter, you are ready to create a different, more elaborate kind of document while exploring Full Menus mode. Along the way, you will use some of Word's more advanced features: You'll learn how to work with outlines, add words to a personal dictionary, and create style sheets, as well as how to take fuller advantage of the Ruler and formatting commands. By the end of the chapter you will have transformed two pages of raw text into a polished piece of work.

■ *Entering the Text*

If Word isn't already up and running, start it from the desktop. Check the menu and preference settings, as described in Chapter 1. This tutorial assumes that:

- ❑ Full Menus mode is in effect.
- ❑ Format marks are not displayed.
- ❑ The unit of measurement is inches.

Making an Outline

Your first step in creating a document might be to stop and think about what you want to say. Suppose that you are a senior account representative for Garrett & Associates, a public relations firm doing promotional work for the New York entertainment industry. Because the company's accounts are growing at a rate that fast outstrips the staff's ability to handle them, you recently hired a new crop of junior account representatives to fill the gap. Before they can hope to succeed in the trade, however, they need to master the common jargon; toward this end, you must create a vocabulary list.

Start by using Word to organize your thoughts. When you choose Outlining from the Document menu, you see a blank window in Outline View, as shown in Figure 2-1. We will explore Outline View in detail in Chapter 4, "Organizing Through Outlining," but for now, let's use only enough of Word's outliner to rough out our document.

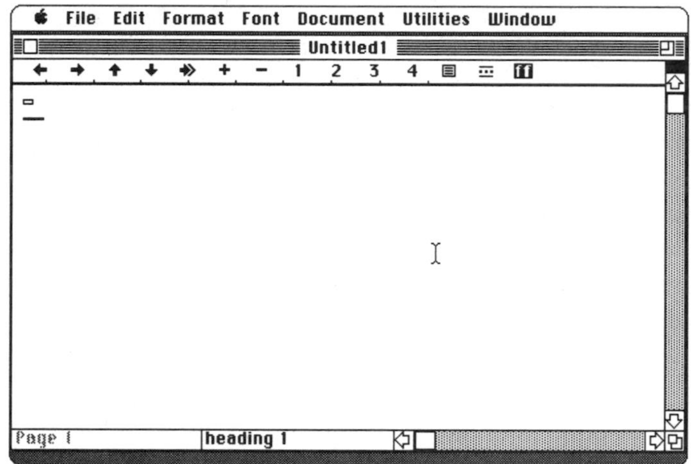

Figure 2-1
A blank window in Outline View.

You decide that first you need an introduction, then the list of jargon terms, and finally a cute closing remark. Type these three headings in your document; where you see the ¶ symbol, press the Return key.

Introduction¶
Jargon Terms¶
Cute Closing Remark¶

As you enter these headings, Word displays the level of each in the lower left corner of the window, in an area called the *status box*. You can change the level of a heading very easily by clicking one of the first two icons in the Outline icon bar. Do this with the list of jargon terms that you enter next.

❶ Place the insertion point at the end of the *Jargon Terms* heading by clicking anywhere to the right of the line.

❷ Press the Return key to start a new line. The status box gives the level of the new heading as *heading 1*. (In previous versions of Word, this would read *level 1*.)

❸ Click the right arrow icon in the Outline icon bar. The insertion point moves to the right, and the status box now says *heading 2*. Anything you type will now be a subheading under the level 1 heading.

❹ Enter these terms:

Boffo¶
Wipe¶
Big Dance in Newark¶
Tasty¶
RAP¶
Tenay Deejays¶
Angel¶
Breather¶
Zzz¶
Bally¶
Brodie¶
Gig¶
Four & Three¶
HIP¶
Nope¶

You typed the terms as they might have occurred to you, but they really should be in alphabetical order. No problem—simply use the Sort command while in Outline View:

❺ Select the list of terms by moving the pointer to the left margin of either the first or last line of the list. Move the pointer in the margin (the selection bar) until the I-beam pointer turns into a right-pointing arrow. Hold down the mouse button and drag the mouse to the other end of the list to select only the terms.

❻ While the words are selected, choose Sort from the Utilities menu to reorder the list instantly. Click anywhere in the document to deselect the list.

If you made a mistake—selected the wrong text, for instance—merely choose Undo Sort from the Edit menu before you do anything else, and try again. The Undo command is remarkably handy: The phrase you see when you display the Edit menu reflects the last operation performed. The outline should now look like Figure 2-2 on the following page, with every heading formatted in 12-point New York. If the headings are formatted in Helvetica or Geneva and are in boldface, click the icon at the right end of the Outline icon bar. This toggles the display of the default character formats assigned to the various levels of headings, discussed a little later in this chapter.

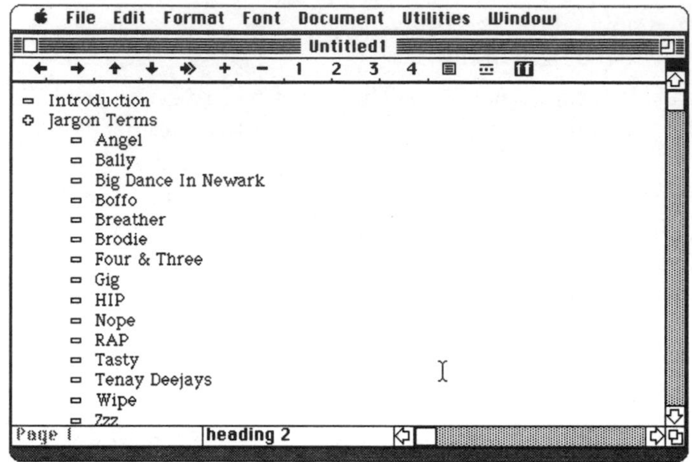

Figure 2-2
The terms after being sorted.

Editing the Outline

While you're in Outline View, change the major headings so that they more fully describe their purpose:

❶ Select the first heading, *Introduction*, by clicking in the selection bar to the left of it.

❷ Type the following text, which replaces the text you selected (don't press the Return key after you type it):

Show Biz Buzzwords

Now change the second and third headings:

❸ Select the *Jargon Terms* heading, and replace it with this text:

The Lingo

❹ Select the *Cute Closing Remark* heading, and replace it with this text:

In Closing...

Now that you have edited the outline, you can move on to work with the body of the text. The finished outline is shown in Figure 2-3.

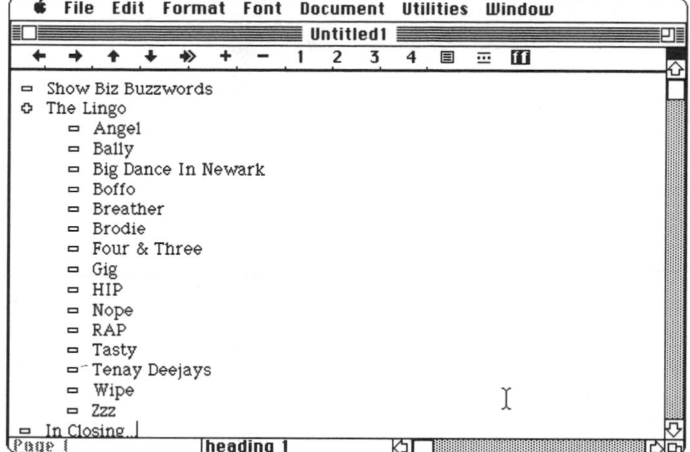

Figure 2-3
The finished outline in Outline View.

TIP

Don't Press the Return Key After You Retype a Heading in Outline View
Doing so inserts an extra paragraph mark in the style for that heading. This can cause problems when you later try to insert body text on the line after the heading. Any text you type in front of one of these extra paragraph marks will be in the same style as the heading, instead of in the *Normal* style you expect. This happens because the style attached to the paragraph mark determines the style of the entire paragraph.

To return from Outline View to Galley View, again choose Outlining from the Document menu. What you now see depends on whether or not you have the 12-point Helvetica font installed in your System file. If you do, Word uses it as the default font for your base style, as shown in Figure 2-4 on the following page. If you don't, Word uses 12-point Geneva as the default font. To see the complete list of fonts available, choose Character from the Format menu. The Font menu lists only a few of the more common fonts (unless you've already added some fonts to it).

Now, before you enter the rest of the text, save the document by choosing Save As from the File menu. Name the document *Buzzwords*, and click Save.

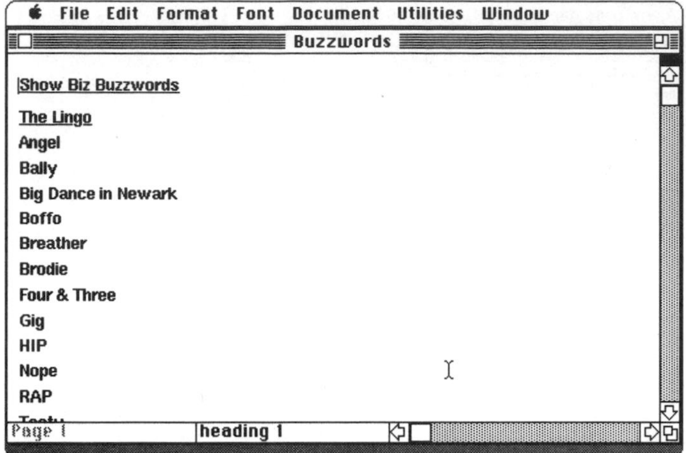

Figure 2-4
The finished outline in Galley View.

Using Styles

Notice that when you return to Galley View, all the headings and jargon terms you entered are there, but their formatting is a little different from when you entered and edited them in Outline View. The text is in boldface, and the level 1 headings seem to have a little more space above them than before and are underlined. If you set the insertion point in any of the headings, the name of the level you assigned to that heading becomes visible in the status box. This is the name of the style you attached to the text when you entered the topic in Outline View and assigned it a heading level. Every level of heading you create in Outline View has a style name, from *heading 1* to *heading 9*, even though you see icons in the Outline icon bar only for levels 1 through 4. (We'll discuss how to access the other heading levels in Chapter 4, "Organizing Through Outlining.")

Let's investigate this further. Click anywhere in the first heading, *Show Biz Buzzwords*, and choose Define Styles from the Format menu. A dialog box like the one in Figure 2-5 appears.

Listed are four items. Ignore the *New Style* item for now, and click on *heading 1*. When you do this, the style's name pops up in the Style field, and a list of the style's formatting attributes appears below the name. Currently, the *heading 1* style definition should read *Normal + Font: Helvetica, Bold Underline, Space Before 12 pt*. This means that the *heading 1* style is based on the *Normal* (default) style, that it is displayed in boldface with an underline, and that an extra 12 points of line spacing is inserted before the heading to set it off from the preceding text. (Font sizes and line spacing are specified in Word in points. A point is a conventional unit of measure equal to $1/72$ inch, so 12 points of extra line spacing is equal to $1/6$ inch.) When you click the Show

Formatting icon in the Outline icon bar, Word toggles the display of the headings between their formatted and unformatted versions. Each item in the Define Styles list box is a style, and the collective list is called the style sheet for that document. Word stores a style sheet within each document you create.

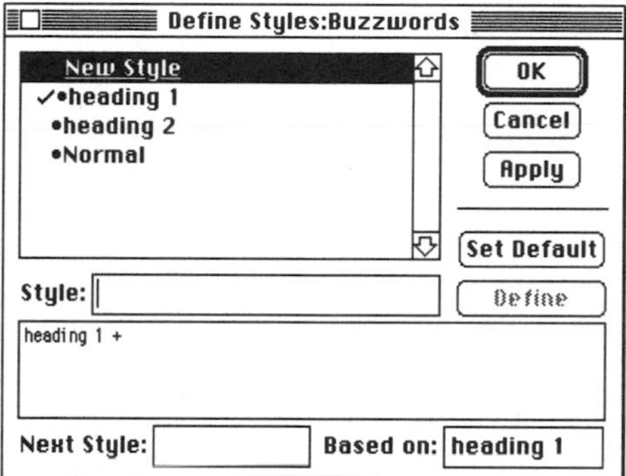

Figure 2-5
The Define Styles dialog box.

You might have noticed in looking at the *heading 1* style definition that formats for two of the four format domains—character and paragraph—are represented. The boldface attribute is a character format; the extra line spacing is a paragraph format. Style definitions can contain both types of formats, but when you apply a style to some text, the formats that make up the style affect the entire paragraph that contains the text. If, for example, you change the font, font size, font style (such as bold or italic), line spacing, space before or after a paragraph, or alignment in a style definition, the change is reflected in every paragraph to which you attached the style. Thus, you can't use a style to change the format of a single word within a paragraph.

Play a bit with the *heading 1* style definition so that you can see how changing the style changes your document. While the Define Styles dialog box is displayed and the *heading 1* style is selected, choose Italic from the Format menu. *Every heading in your document that has the heading 1 style changes at the same time.* The style definition also changes to reflect the new attribute. This is why the style feature in Word is so powerful: It allows you to establish a consistent design for a document and to refine that design until it's exactly the way you want it, without having to hunt for and reformat every piece of text. The care and feeding of style sheets is discussed later in this chapter and throughout this book, but for now make a few adjustments to the heading styles so that you can enter the rest of the text. With the *heading 1* style still selected:

❶ Choose Italic again from the Format menu to return paragraphs having the *heading 1* style to the unitalicized typeface. (This is one of the commands in Word that toggle: Choose it once to turn it on; choose it again to turn it off.)

❷ Click the Define button in the dialog box, and then click OK.

Now change the definition of the *heading 2* style, which is attached to the jargon words in the document:

❸ Click on any of the jargon words.

❹ Choose Define Styles from the Format menu.

❺ Select the *heading 2* style.

❻ Choose Bold from the Format menu to toggle off the boldface format.

❼ Choose Italic to italicize all the jargon words.

❽ Click the Define button, and then click OK.

At this point, your document should look like Figure 2-6. The next step is to enter the introductory paragraph, the jargon definitions, and the closing paragraph.

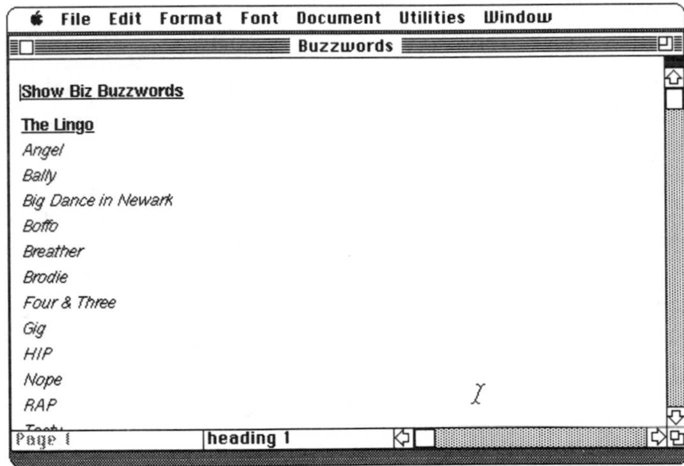

Figure 2-6
The document after redefining the styles.

Entering the Body Text

The body of the document consists of three distinct portions: an introductory paragraph, then a series of smaller paragraphs for the definitions, and, finally, the closing paragraph.

The Introductory Paragraph

Place the insertion point at the end of the *Show Biz Buzzwords* heading by clicking anywhere to the right of the line, and press the Return key. Type the following text:

Garrett & Associates Public Relations serves more than a dozen entertainment-industry clients, from a three-person circus act to a multibillion-dollar-a-year record company. Like all fields, the entertainment industry has its own peculiar lingo: colorful words and phrases used in conversation, news releases, and even newspaper and magazine articles. Here is a short list of some of the more common show biz terms you'll need to know in your new position as junior account representative.

At some point as you typed this text, you might have noticed that the style name in the status box for the text you entered is *Normal*. Take a quick look at the definition of this style by choosing Define Styles again and then selecting the *Normal* style. This is the style assigned to your text in the absence of any other style definition. Many people who use Word without learning about style sheets use this style constantly without ever being aware that it exists. Yet by changing the definition of this style, you can reformat all the body text in your document in one stroke (well, maybe one stroke and a couple of mouse clicks). Click Cancel to close the dialog box.

The Jargon Definitions

Each definition of a term is a separate paragraph following its heading in the *heading 2* style: Enter each definition by placing the insertion point at the end of a term, pressing the Return key, and typing the definition. Don't type the terms again, only the definitions.

Angel:

The backer of the show. During the Roaring Twenties, the term angel was used by con men to describe the victims of their swindles, so use the term carefully!¶

Bally:

A free show. Used most often in connection with a carnival sideshow to promote the main attraction inside the tent. The bally often ended up being more interesting than the real show, which is probably why the term is often used today to describe a show that promises more than it delivers.¶

Big Dance in Newark:

Everyone loves your show—the producers, the backers, the critics, even the stagehands. So why isn't anyone in the audience? There must be a big dance in Newark!¶

Boffo:

A success through and through. The word probably sprang from the phrase "good box office." See brodie.¶

Breather:

A film that has little going for it except atmosphere: the mood created by the lighting, set decoration, and camera angles.¶

Brodie:

A turkey. The term was first coined in dubious recognition of Steve Brodie, perhaps the greatest belly flopper of all time. Disgruntled by his lack of success, poor Steve tried to end it all in 1886 by jumping off the Brooklyn Bridge. He flopped on that one, too: He survived the attempt and went on living for another 40 years. See boffo.¶

Four & Three:

A theatrical company not located in New York City. The term's origins lie with the small New York-based repertory troupes, whose casts comprised four men and three women.¶

Gig:

In the music industry, an engagement to perform.¶

HIP:

Short for high-impact priority. Any record album called a HIP hit is slated for a multimillion-dollar advertising campaign.¶

Nope:

Short for no promotion. If a record company doesn't think an album has a chance, the album is marked as a nope (usually with a hole drilled in the corner of the cover), given no advertising, and sent to the cutout bins of cheap department stores.¶

RAP:

Short for radio airplay.¶

Tasty:

In the record industry, the current in word for "the greatest." Generally replaces boss, groovy, heavy, and mellow.¶

Tenay Deejays:

Radio station deejays who play only the Top Ten.¶

Wipe:

Being fired before the show ends.¶

Zzz:

A G-rated film.¶

Part of the document, with the definitions typed in, is shown in Figure 2-7.

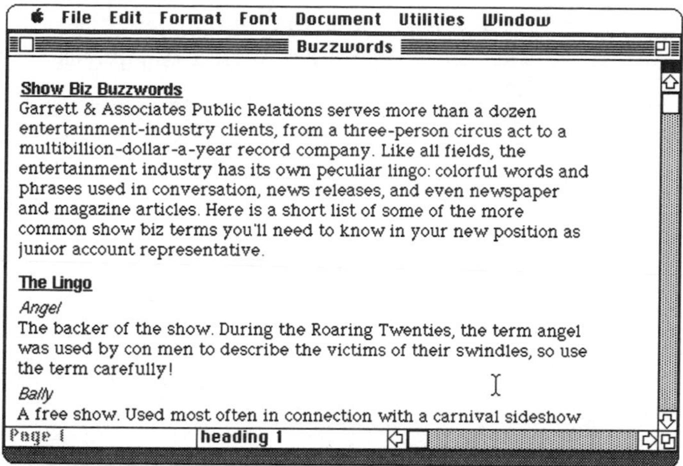
File Edit Format Font Document Utilities Window

Buzzwords

Show Biz Buzzwords

Garrett & Associates Public Relations serves more than a dozen entertainment-industry clients, from a three-person circus act to a multibillion-dollar-a-year record company. Like all fields, the entertainment industry has its own peculiar lingo: colorful words and phrases used in conversation, news releases, and even newspaper and magazine articles. Here is a short list of some of the more common show biz terms you'll need to know in your new position as junior account representative.

The Lingo

Angel

The backer of the show. During the Roaring Twenties, the term angel was used by con men to describe the victims of their swindles, so use the term carefully!

Bally

A free show. Used most often in connection with a carnival sideshow

Page 1 heading 1

Figure 2-7
Portion of document after entering the definitions.

The Closing Paragraph

Now wrap up this production by entering the closing remarks. Place the insertion point at the end of the last heading, *In Closing*, press the Return key, and type this text:

Be a boffo representative of Garrett & Associates! If you pull a brodie and don't please your angel by giving these tasty terms some RAP, we'll mark you nope, and you might even need a HIP promotional to land another gig (undoubtedly with a Four & Three) after you get wiped!

■ *Editing the Text*

For the purpose of this tutorial, we'll assume that you are an inspired writer and need make no changes to your document other than to correct a few misspelled words. If you think you made a few mistakes other than incorrect spelling, take a moment to scroll through the document and make changes using the methods you learned in Chapter 1.

Even if you're an expert typist, it's still a good idea to use Word's spelling checker to locate misspelled words. This time, however, try adding words to a personal dictionary.

Creating a Personal Dictionary

The entertainment-lingo document contains numerous words not found in Word's main dictionary, which is stored in a file named *MS Dictionary*. In your role as senior account representative, you might use some of these words in future documents, in which case you should add the specialized words to a personal dictionary. (You cannot add to or edit the main dictionary.) Adding words to a personal dictionary is a straightforward task:

❶ Save the document again before using the spelling checker: Choose Save from the File menu.

❷ Set the insertion point at the beginning of the document (immediately before the *S* in *Show*), and choose Spelling from the Utilities menu. A small dialog box appears briefly, telling you that the MS Dictionary is being loaded.

When the Spelling dialog box appears, note that the Open Dictionaries list box shows MS Dictionary and User 1. User 1 is a personal dictionary that Word creates for you. Later you will learn how to create other dictionaries. Both the MS Dictionary and your personal dictionaries (User 1, User 2, and so on) are loaded automatically when you choose the Spelling command if the dictionaries are in the same folder as Word when you launch the program. Otherwise, you may see a dialog box asking where they are. (Refer to Appendix A for recommendations on arranging your Word files.)

❸ Click the Start Check button.

❹ Unless you somehow misspelled *Show*, the first unknown word should be *Biz*. Click the + button to add the word to your personal dictionary.

❺ Click the Continue Check button. The next suspect word should be *Garrett*. Skip this one by clicking the No Change button.

❻ Continue checking until you reach the end of the document. Notice that the spelling checker differentiates between uppercase and lowercase letters: The program stops at *biz*, even though you previously added *Biz* to the dictionary. Later in this book, you'll learn how to check both uppercase and lowercase versions of words, adding only the lowercase version. When you reach the end, a dialog box appears, saying *End of document reached*. Click OK.

Reopen the Spelling dialog box by choosing the Spelling command one more time. Click on User 1 in the Open Dictionaries list box. The words you added are shown in the Words list box. If you discover that you added a word you don't want, select it and click the – (minus) button.

Saving the Dictionary

Like documents, your dictionaries should be saved before you quit Word. The easiest way to save your User 1 dictionary is simply to quit Word when you are ready to end your session; a dialog box appears, giving you the opportunity to save both your document and the User 1 dictionary:

❶ Choose Quit from the File menu.

❷ Word asks if you want to save your Buzzwords document. Click Yes.

❸ Word asks if you want to save your User 1 dictionary. Click Yes.

❹ The Spelling dialog box appears as Word verifies that it's a dictionary you're saving; then a Save As dialog box appears in front of the Spelling dialog box. Word assumes that you want to save the User 1 dictionary in the same folder as your document, but instead save it in the same folder as Word. Then, the next time you start Word and do a spelling check on another document, Word will be able to access this dictionary without having to ask you where it can be found. After you switch to the correct folder, click Save. Your User 1 dictionary is now recorded on disk.

If you or someone else used the program's spelling checker before, the actual sequence of steps may differ from that presented here. For example, if the User 1 dictionary is already in the Word folder, Word will simply ask you if you want to save the changes to User 1 rather than presenting the Save As dialog box. Click Yes to update the dictionary.

■ *Formatting the Text*

With all the text entered and corrected, now you can play with designing and formatting the document. The styles you used earlier will make this process a breeze. After you adjust the design of the document, you will finish the formatting by changing the characteristics of individual words. You can always alter the font, font size, and font style while you're writing, of course, and you will probably do this often, but for the sake of simplicity this exercise separates the entering and editing process from the formatting process.

Establishing a Design Through Styles

You can establish an overall design for the document by working with the style sheet. Start Word again, and open the Buzzwords document. The first step is to adjust the style for the first and second levels of headings:

❶ Choose Define Styles from the Format menu, and select the *heading 1* style.

❷ Choose Character from the same menu. The Character format dialog box appears.

❸ In the upper left corner a drop-down list displays the names of all the fonts that have been installed in your System file, when you click on the box or the arrow to the right of the box. Select Times from the list; when you do, all the font sizes installed for that font appear in the drop-down field just to the right, when you click on the arrow. Select the 18-point font. If either or both of these options aren't available, simply choose another font and point size from the options available, or click in the field and enter another size.

❹ In the lower left corner of the dialog box, the Bold typeface option is selected. The 18-point font is visible enough without boldfacing, so click in the Bold check box to toggle off the format. Also, notice that the Underline drop-down list reads *Single*. Finally, click OK.

❺ In the lower right corner of the Define Styles dialog box, the contents of the Based On field read *Normal*. This means that if you did not set a specific format (for the font, for instance) for the *heading 1* style, then that format is taken from, or based on, the *Normal* style. This topic is explored in depth later; for now, simply double-click on the word *Normal* and press the Backspace key. (On some keyboards this key is called the Delete key.) This makes the *heading 1* style independent of the *Normal* style so that the changes you will make to the *Normal* style a little later will not affect this style. Click in the style definition area or in the style name edit field to update the definition.

❻ The *heading 1* style definition now reads *Font: Times 18 point, Underline, Flush Left, Space Before 12 pt*. All the first level headings in your document have changed to reflect the modified style. Click Define.

❼ Now select the *heading 2* style, and choose the Character command again.

❽ Change the font to Times (or whatever font you chose in Step ❸), and leave the 12-point size option as is. Leave the italic typeface, but add boldface; then click OK. The *heading 2* style definition should read *Font: Times 12 point, Bold Italic, Flush Left, Space Before 6 pt*. Select and delete the contents of the Based On field, as you did for the *heading 1* style.

❾ Now click Define and Cancel. (Clicking Define and OK would define the style and then apply it to the paragraph containing the insertion point. Clicking Define and Cancel redefines the style without applying it.)

Thus, without having to search for each heading and repeat the same steps over and over, you simply and elegantly established a design for most of the document. If you used the Times font for the headings, your document should look like the one in Figure 2-8.

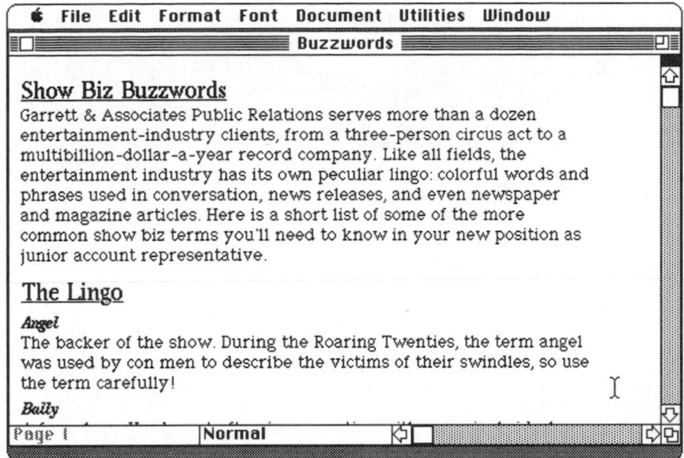

Figure 2-8
Portion of document showing reformatted headings

Now work with the body text. This time you'll change not only the character formatting (the font and size) but also the paragraph formatting.

❶ Choose Define Styles again. Select the *Normal* style. The current style definition should read *Font: New York 12 point, Flush left.*

❷ Choose the Character command. Select Palatino 10 point (or any other suitable font and size). Click OK.

❸ Choose Show Ruler from the Format menu. The Ruler appears at the top of the document window, as shown in Figure 2-9 on the following page.

❹ Change the position of the left indent, a paragraph format. Position the pointer over the left indent marker (the lower of the two small triangles in the Ruler), press the mouse button, and drag the marker half an inch to the right. Both triangles will move. The left indent of the body text (but not of the headings) changes to reflect the new indent.

❺ Click the Justified alignment icon (the last of the alignment icons in the Ruler). If the alignment icons are obscured by the Define Styles dialog box, drag the dialog box out of the way by its title bar. In the Define Styles dialog box, click Define and Cancel.

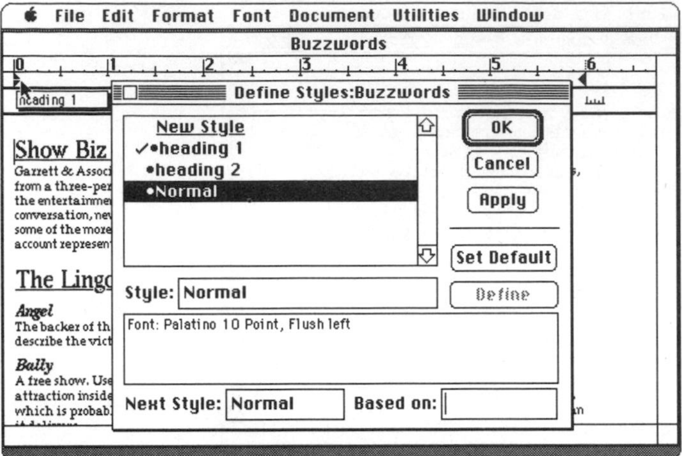

Figure 2-9
Ruler with pointer positioned at left indent marker.

Making Final Formatting Adjustments

Now that the overall design is set, you need to reformat a few words. Under the *Boffo* heading, look for the words *See brodie*, double-click on *brodie*, and choose Italic from the Format menu. Under the *Brodie* heading, look for the words *See boffo*, double-click on *boffo*, and choose Italic again. In the final paragraph, italicize the words *boffo, brodie, angel, tasty, RAP, nope, HIP, gig, Four & Three*, and *wiped*. Standard style recommends using italic for the punctuation following an italicized word. Also, you might notice that the I-beam pointer, the insertion point, and the highlight showing the selection all slant to the right over italicized material—a new feature in Word 4. (For better word spacing after the italicized words, you could add an extra space, but spacing in italicized words almost always looks better on paper than on the screen, especially on PostScript printers.)

Adding a Footer and Page Number

Your document should now be approximately 1½ pages long—that is, long enough to have a header or footer and page numbers. To see exactly where the page break occurs, choose Repaginate Now from the Document menu. The page break—a dotted line, as shown in Figure 2-10—should be within the *Tasty* definition. The Print Preview and Page View commands also repaginate the current document. Notice that the page break occurs between the term and its definition; we'll fix this in Print Preview in a moment.

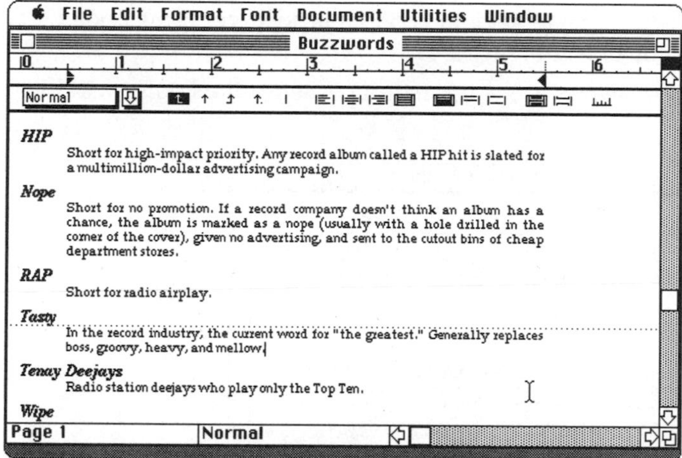

Figure 2-10
A page break produced by repagination.

To create a footer containing the page number:

❶ Choose Open Footer from the Document menu. The Footer window appears at the bottom of the screen. Choose Show Ruler from the Format menu to see the type and placement of the default tabs in the Footer window. The status area in the lower left corner of the Footer window says *footer* because the text you type in this window has this style, which is another of the automatic styles. (If you chose Define Styles now, you would see this style added to the other so-called *automatic* styles in the list box.)

❷ Type the text *Garrett & Associates* into the Footer window. Press the Tab key twice to move past the center-aligned tab stop to the right-aligned tab stop superimposed over the right indent marker. Type *Page*. Press the Spacebar once to put a space after the word.

❸ Click the Page Number icon in the upper left corner of the Footer window. The numeral *1* or *2* appears, depending on which page contains the insertion point when you choose the Open Footer command. Choose Show ¶ from the Edit menu for a moment: A dotted box surrounds the number. When you clicked the Page Number icon, you inserted a special character into the footer that Word increments for each new printed page. Choose Hide ¶ to hide the formatting marks, and choose Hide Ruler to hide the Ruler.

❹ Press the Return key to move the insertion point to the start of the next line, and type *4321 5th Avenue, New York, NY 10011.*

❺ Select both lines, and choose Italic and then Bold from the Format menu to set them off a little from the body text. Choose the 12 Point option from the Font menu to make the footer text a little larger. Your footer should look like the one in Figure 2-11.

❻ Now click in the close box in the upper left corner of the Footer window to save the footer.

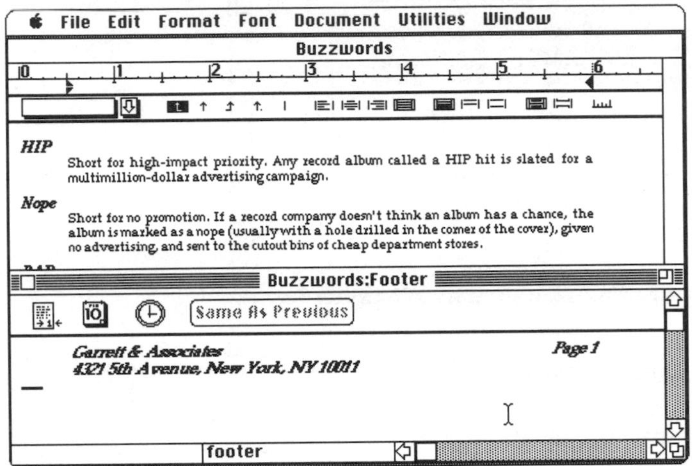

Figure 2-11
The completed footer.

■ *Previewing and Printing the Document*

In Word, looking at your document in Print Preview and Page View modes is a great way to avoid printing draft copies repeatedly. You can get immediate feedback on the overall appearance of your document, zoom in to take a closer look, and adjust margins, page breaks, and header and footer placement. Let's use Print Preview to check the layout of the Buzzwords document.

When you choose Print Preview from the File menu, you see the entire Buzzwords document in miniature. Play around a little in this mode to get a taste of how to make final adjustments to your document before printing. Click the second icon from the top, the Margins icon. A set of guidelines appears on the second page, showing the placement of the margins and the footer for both pages of the document, as in Figure 2-12.

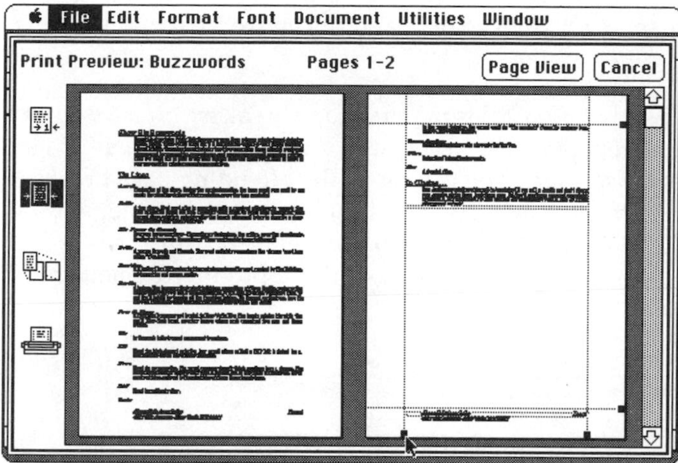

Figure 2-12
The document in Print Preview mode, showing the margin and footer guidelines.

To adjust the left margin, place the pointer on the handle of the left margin guideline (see the arrow pointer near the bottom of Figure 2-12), and drag it to the right. As you do this, the area to the left of the Page View button displays the width of the left margin. Set the left margin to 1.5 inches. To have Word update the screen image using the new margin, click the Margins icon again. You can also click anywhere else on the screen except within the page that shows the guidelines. Now move the right margin toward the left so that it is set to 1.5 inches as well.

Take a look at your screen now to see how the page number in the footer turned out. The page number is now positioned a little to the right of the right indent of the body text. This happened because the position of the page number in the Footer window is determined by a tab stop, and tab stops are measured relative to the left indent of the paragraph. (If you want, you can go back to the Footer window later to realign the page number.)

Before you print this document, adjust the page break so that the *Nope* definition moves to the top of the next page:

❶ Click the Margins icon, and then click anywhere in the first page. The guidelines will move to the first page of the displayed document.

❷ Move the pointer to the page-break line, a broken line just above the line for the bottom margin. You can tell the page-break line from the bottom margin because the page-break line appears between the side margins only, whereas the bottom margin runs across the entire page. You'll know the pointer is in the right place when the arrow pointer changes to a cross-hair pointer.

❸ Press the mouse button when you see the cross-hair pointer, and drag the page-break line up until it is above the heading *Nope*. When you release the button, the display will be updated, and the entire *Nope* definition will appear on page 2.

Note that Word will not adjust this manual page break if you later edit the document and then repaginate it. As a result, you may end up with page breaks in odd places. If necessary, you can move the offending page breaks out of the way in Print Preview mode or simply select and delete them in Galley View. Figure 2-13 shows that this type of page break, called a *manual* or *forced* page break, looks different from those produced when you repaginate a document.

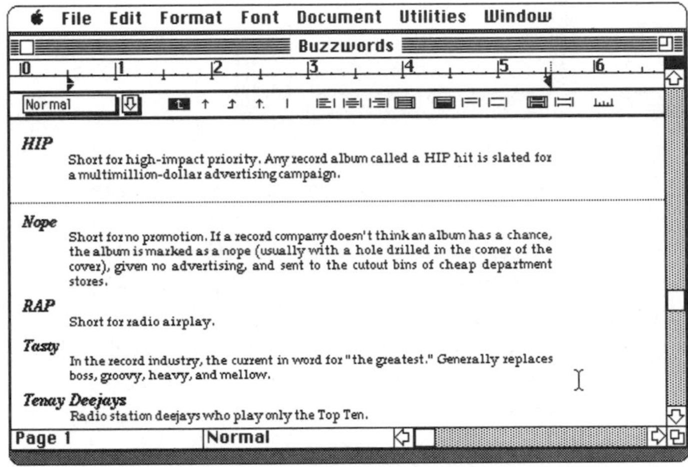

Figure 2-13
A manual page break inserted in Galley View.

The document requires no special print settings, so print it in the usual way:

❶ Choose Print from the File menu. You can print while you are in Print Preview mode.

❷ Be sure the printer is on and is loaded with paper.

❸ Click the OK button.

If you need to stop the printing process during printing, press Command-(period), if you're using a LaserWriter. If you're using an

ImageWriter, you can also click the Pause or Cancel buttons. The printed document should look like Figures 2-14a and 2-14b on this and the following page, which were printed on a LaserWriter.

Show Biz Buzzwords

Garrett & Associates Public Relations serves more than a dozen entertainment-industry clients, from a three-person circus act to a multibillion-dollar-a-year record company. Like all fields, the entertainment industry has its own peculiar lingo: colorful words and phrases used in conversation, news releases, and even newspaper and magazine articles. Here is a short list of some of the more common show biz terms you'll need to know in your new position as junior account representative.

The Lingo

Angel

The backer of the show. During the Roaring Twenties, the term angel was used by con men to describe the victims of their swindles, so use the term carefully!

Bally

A free show. Used most often in connection with a carnival sideshow to promote the main attraction inside the tent. The bally often ended up being more interesting than the real show, which is probably why the term is often used today to describe a show that promises more than it delivers.

Big Dance in Newark

Everyone loves your show—the producers the backers, the critics, even the stagehands. So why isn't anyone in the audience? There must be a big dance in Newark!

Boffo

A success through and through. The word probably sprang from the phrase "good box office." See *brodie*.

Breather

A film that has little going for it except atmosphere: the mood created by the lighting, set decoration, and camera angles.

Brodie

A turkey. The term was first coined in dubious recognition of Steve Brodie, perhaps the greatest belly-flopper of all time. Disgruntled by his lack of success, poor Steve tried to end it all in 1886 by jumping off the Brooklyn Bridge. He flopped on that one, too: He survived the attempt and went on living for another 40 years. See *boffo*.

Four & Three

A theatrical company not located in New York City. The term's origins lie with the small New York-based repertory troupes whose casts comprised four men and three women.

Gig

In the music industry, an engagement to perform.

HIP

Short for high-impact priority. Any record album called a HIP hit is slated for a multimillion-dollar advertising campaign.

Garrett & Associates
4321 5th Avenue, New York, NY 10011

Page 1

Figure 2-14a

First page of the printed document.

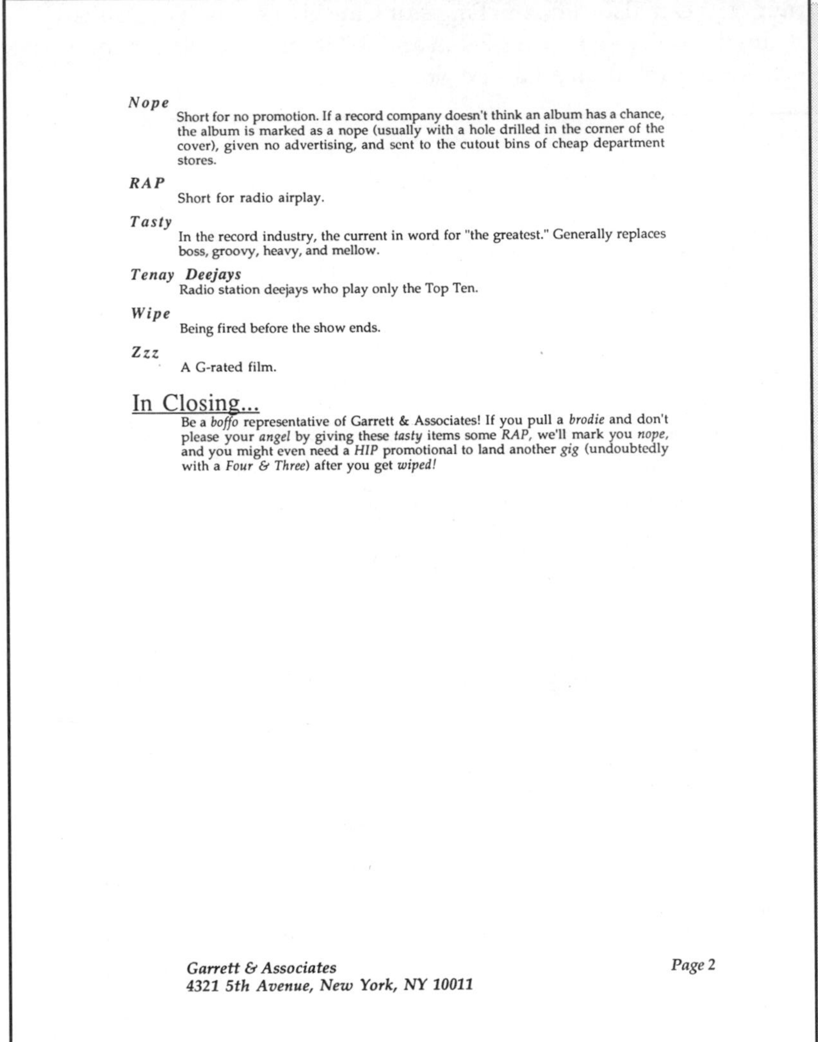

Nope
Short for no promotion. If a record company doesn't think an album has a chance, the album is marked as a nope (usually with a hole drilled in the corner of the cover), given no advertising, and sent to the cutout bins of cheap department stores.

RAP
Short for radio airplay.

Tasty
In the record industry, the current in word for "the greatest." Generally replaces boss, groovy, heavy, and mellow.

Tenay Deejays
Radio station deejays who play only the Top Ten.

Wipe
Being fired before the show ends.

Zzz
A G-rated film.

In Closing...

Be a *boffo* representative of Garrett & Associates! If you pull a *brodie* and don't please your *angel* by giving these *tasty* items some *RAP*, we'll mark you *nope*, and you might even need a *HIP* promotional to land another *gig* (undoubtedly with a *Four & Three*) after you get *wiped!*

Garrett & Associates
4321 5th Avenue, New York, NY 10011

Page 2

Figure 2-14b
Second page of the printed document.

You've now learned the basics of creating documents with Word. You have also begun to appreciate how easy the program is to use and have gained some sense of the variety and depth of its features. When you're ready to take fuller advantage of Word's power, turn to Section 2, "Building the Framework."

Points to Remember

Many of these techniques and topics are covered in much greater detail in later chapters.

- ❑ The text you see in Outline View resembles a traditional outline. The different levels of headings are indented, and you can toggle the display of character formats in the text by clicking the Show Formatting button.
- ❑ You can have up to nine levels of topics in an outline, but the Outline icon bar contains icons for displaying only up to level 4. (See Chapter 4, "Organizing Through Outlining," for tips on displaying the other five heading levels.)
- ❑ The status box in the lower left corner of the window shows, among other items, the name of the style assigned to the paragraph containing the insertion point. If no other style has been assigned, the *Normal* style is used.
- ❑ A style applies to an entire paragraph. You cannot apply a style to part of a paragraph, and you can assign only one style to a paragraph. In Word, a paragraph is defined as any amount of text followed by a paragraph mark (shown as a ¶ when Show ¶ is in effect). It is possible to change the format of individual characters in a paragraph. Simply select the text to be changed and choose the attributes you want from the Font and Format menus.
- ❑ Word maintains a personal dictionary named User 1 for you. You can add words to and delete words from your own personal dictionaries, but you cannot change entries in Word's MS Dictionary.
- ❑ The first time you save a personal dictionary, be sure to put it in the same folder as the Word program so that Word will be able to find it. Otherwise, Word will save the dictionary in the same folder as the document, which may not be the right one.

Techniques

Basic Skills

Undo the previous command

❶ Choose Undo from the Edit menu.

The words that appear after Undo vary depending on the previous command.

Outlining

Enter Outline View

❶ Choose Outlining from the Document menu.

Return to Galley View

❶ Choose the Outlining command again.

Enter outline headings

❶ Type your headings, and press the Return key after each one.

❷ Click the right arrow icon in the Outline icon bar to begin typing subheadings.

❸ Click the left arrow icon to return to the next higher level of heading.

The status box in the bottom left of the window shows the level of the current heading.

Change the level of an outline heading

❶ Set the insertion point on the heading to be changed.

❷ Click the left arrow icon in the Outline icon bar to promote the heading, or click the right arrow icon to demote the heading.

Replace an outline heading

❶ Select the heading to be replaced.

❷ Type the new heading.

Do not press the Return key after you type the new heading.

Enter body text into an outline

❶ Return to Galley View.

❷ Set the insertion point after the appropriate heading.

❸ Press the Return key, and type the text.

Sorting

Arrange a group of lines in alphabetical order

❶ Select the lines to be sorted.

❷ Choose Sort from the Utilities menu.

Working with Styles

Display the definition of a style

❶ Choose Define Styles from the Format menu.

❷ Select the style from the list box. Its definition will appear below the Style field.

❸ Click Cancel when you are through.

Alter the character attributes of a style

❶ Choose Define Styles from the Format menu.

❷ Select the style you want to alter from the list box.

❸ With the Define Styles dialog box open, choose from the Format menu the attributes you want to assign to the style (Bold, Italic, Underline, and so on). Alternatively, choose the Character command to select options from the Character dialog box, and click OK when done.

❹ Click Define, and then click Cancel.

Alter the left indent of a style

❶ With the Define Styles dialog box displayed, choose Show Ruler from the Format menu.

❷ Drag the left indent marker (the lower of the two triangles on the left) to the new indent position. (Both triangles will move.)

❸ Click Define and Cancel in the dialog box.

Alter the alignment of a style

❶ Follow the steps for adjusting the left indent, but click one of the alignment icons in the Ruler instead of moving the left indent marker.

Using a Personal Dictionary

Add a word to a personal dictionary

❶ During a spelling check, click the + button in the Spelling dialog box to add the highlighted word to your User 1 dictionary.

❷ Click Continue Check to check the rest of the document.

Remove a word from a personal dictionary

❶ Click on the name of a dictionary in the Open Dictionaries list box.

❷ The list of words in that dictionary appears in the Words list box.

❸ Select the word you want to delete, and click the – button.

Page Formatting

Add a footer with a page number

1. Choose Open Footer from the Document menu.
2. Type any text that is to appear at the bottom of every page. Text you type at the center-aligned tab stop in the *footer* style will be centered.
3. Place the insertion point where you want the page number to appear.
4. Click the Page Number icon to have Word insert page numbers.
5. Format the footer as you like.
6. Click in the close box to save the footer.

Adjust margins in Print Preview mode

1. Click the Margins icon to display the margin guidelines.
2. Drag the handle of the margin you want to move to the new location.
3. Click outside the page to update the screen.
4. Click the Margins icon again to remove the guidelines.

Adjust page breaks in Print Preview mode

1. With the margin guidelines displayed, drag the page-break line (the dotted line stretching from the left margin to the right margin near the bottom of the page) to the new location. The display updates when you release the mouse button.
2. Click on a page to move the margin guidelines to that page, if necessary.

This process inserts a manual page break that will not be changed when Word repaginates the file.

SECTION 2

Building the Framework

The Word Environment

Getting around in the Word environment, as powerful as it is, can be a bit disorienting for first-time users. Although your document has only one appearance when printed, when writing and editing in Word you learn to view a document in more than one way, and to navigate between views, as well as within documents, menus, and dialog boxes. Word also offers a great degree of freedom in the way you set up your working environment: If you want, you can move almost any command to any menu, or you can assign your own key sequences for invoking the various commands available. Once you've set the environment up the way you want, you can save the configuration in the form of a Settings file, so you can return to the same environment established in a previous session or even create and switch between different versions of the environment customized for specific purposes.

■ *Navigating in Word*

You've already encountered all four of Word's views on a document in Chapters 1 and 2—Galley View, Page View, Outline View, and Print Preview. Each of these views on a document has its purpose, and as you explore the farthest reaches of Word, you'll find yourself flipping easily from one to another. Word also presents a plethora of ways for you to divide and conquer the windows on your desktop and to use them to find your way around in a document. Finally, you can also use the keyboard to call up Word's menus and dialog boxes and to choose from among their options without having to use the mouse.

Word's Views on a Document

Older typesetting systems produce long rolls of text, called *galleys*, containing paragraphs printed one after another. Professional layout people would cut these galleys into pieces and paste them onto boards in the arrangement each page was to have. Word's first view, Galley View, shown in Figure 3-1, is similar because it displays paragraphs in the actual order they occur in the document. Galley View offers the fastest mode available in Word for writing, editing, and adding most character and paragraph formats to text.

In Galley View complicated formats such as Side-by-Side paragraphs, page headers and footers, footnotes, and so on, do not appear in their final positions as they do when printed but are arranged one after the other. Multiple-column text appears in only one column, and to enter and format headers, footers, footnotes, and page numbers you must open a separate window or switch to another view. When you repaginate, Word draws dotted lines across the screen to indicate the page breaks.

Word usually starts up in Galley View, but you can make Word start up in Page View by choosing Preferences from the Edit menu and setting in the dialog box the Open Documents in Page View option.

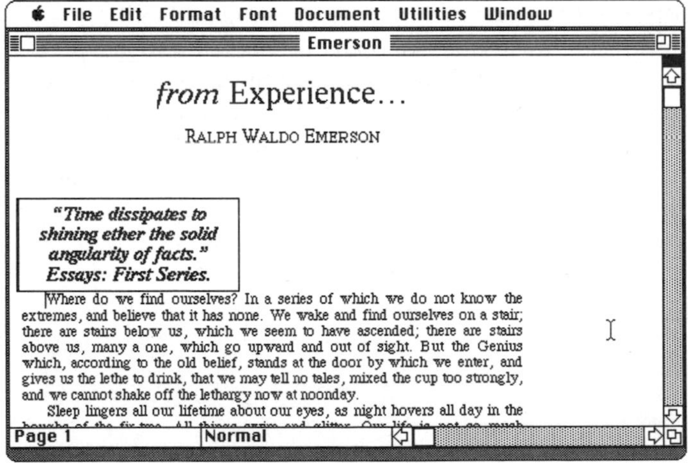

Figure 3-1
A document displayed in Galley View.

Page View, new in Word 4, lets you write, edit and format your document almost as it will appear when printed, although more slowly than in Galley View. You can edit and reformat text, and you can see headers, footers, page numbers, and footnotes on screen. In Page View you can see an actual representation of each page, as shown in Figure 3-2. Complex formats such as Side-by-Side paragraphs and multiple-column text appear on screen in the same way they do when printed. To edit headers, footers, and footnotes, you simply move to the appropriate location on the page instead of opening another window as in Galley View.

Because it takes Word longer to recalculate and update the screen in Page View than in Galley View, you're usually better off doing the bulk of your writing and editing in Galley View and then switching to Page View when you want to refine the document's appearance. The actual order of the paragraphs in a document can be difficult to discern in Page View, because you can place paragraphs in fixed positions relative to other paragraphs, the text column, or the page. You can see the extent of each block of text by pressing Command-Y or setting the Show Text Boundaries in Page View option in the Preferences dialog box (which causes Word to draw dotted lines around each block of text).

Because an image of each page is created, there's no need to indicate page boundaries by dotted lines (as in Galley View). When you scroll off of one page or click one of the paging icons in the status area, Word jumps to the next or previous page.

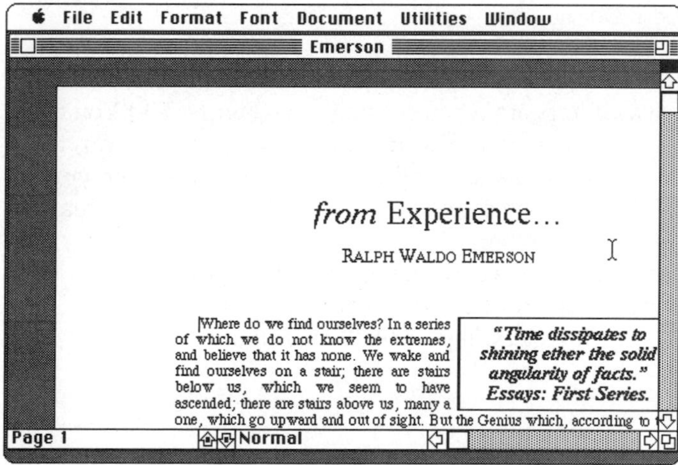

Figure 3-2
The document displayed in Page View.

Outline View, shown in Figure 3-3, lets you work with the structure of the document, apart from the presentation of the document on the page. In Word 4, you can also see the character formats of the text if you want. You can enter blocks of text, assign headings, and rearrange the sequence of thoughts in your documents simply by pressing a few keystrokes. For more information on working in Outline View, see Chapter 4, "Organizing Through Outlining."

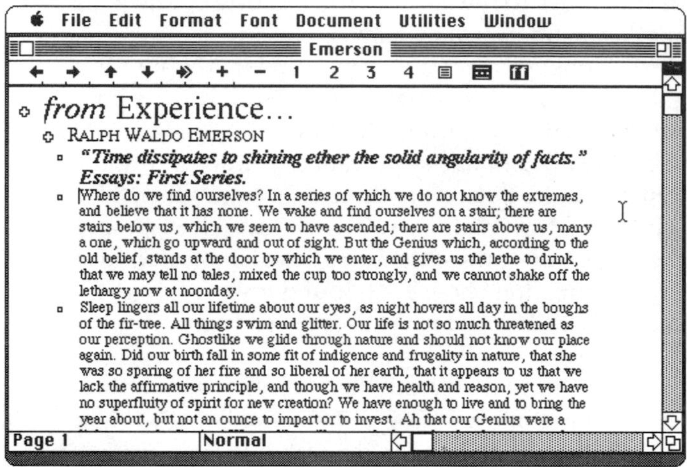

Figure 3-3
The document displayed in Outline View.

You can use the fourth view, Print Preview, to check the layout of whole pages of the document as it appears when printed. (See Figure 3-4.) You can't edit in Print Preview—page images appear in a dialog box, and you can't choose any of Word's menu commands while in this mode. However, you can make a few types of formatting changes, such as adjusting the placement of headers, footers, and page numbers.

You can also adjust the margins and set page breaks by dragging guidelines with the mouse. For additional information on using Print Preview to refine page layouts, see Chapter 14, "Document Formatting and Printing."

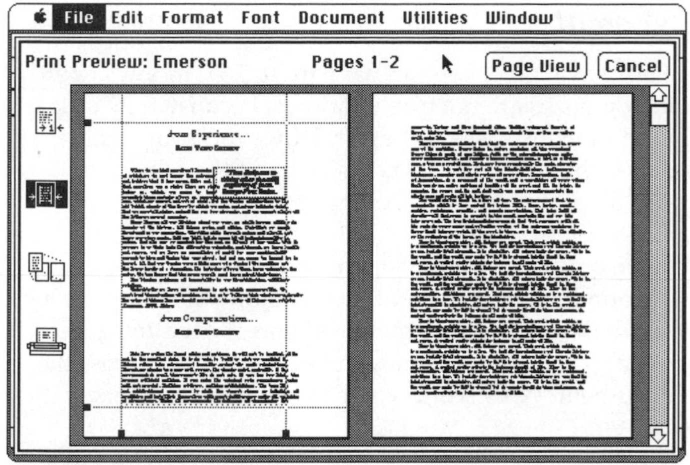

Figure 3-4
The document displayed in Print Preview.

The process of switching between views is fairly straightforward, although you'll encounter a few quirks. The following table shows how you can switch to almost any view from any other view. For example, repeatedly choosing Page View from the Document menu alternates between Page View and Galley View. To switch to Outline View, choose Outlining from the Document menu. However, if the prior view was Page View and you choose Outlining again, Word switches to Galley View; instead, choose the Page View command to switch to Page View.

To go from	To	Do this
Galley View	Page View	Choose Page View (Command-B).
	Outline View	Choose Outlining (Command-U).
	Print Preview	Choose Print Preview (Command-I).
Page View	Galley View	Choose Page View again (Command-B).
	Outline View	Choose Outlining (Command-U).
	Print Preview	Choose Print Preview (Command-I).
Outline View	Galley View	Choose Outlining again (Command-U).
	Page View	Choose Page View (Command-B).
	Print Preview	Choose Print Preview (Command-I), but the preview you see is of the outline.
Print Preview	Galley View	If the prior view was Galley View, click Cancel (Command- .).
	Page View	Click the Page View button, press Command-B, or double-click on page. If the prior view was Page View, you can also click Cancel (Command- .).
	Outline View	Not available—if you press Command-U, Word beeps.

Window Management

Depending on the memory available, you can have up to 23 windows open at the same time. Most dialog boxes are not true windows, because they lack a close box, scroll bars, and in many cases a title bar. However, some dialog boxes behave like windows in many ways, and so some of the window-management techniques discussed here can be applied to certain dialog boxes as well.

Usually you will have only one window open, and it will fill the screen. You can move around in the document by using any of the techniques discussed so far, but you will probably use the scroll bars most often. (See Figure 3-5.) The horizontal scroll bar lets you scan back and forth across the printable area of the document. With Word, you can create documents that are up to 22 inches wide.

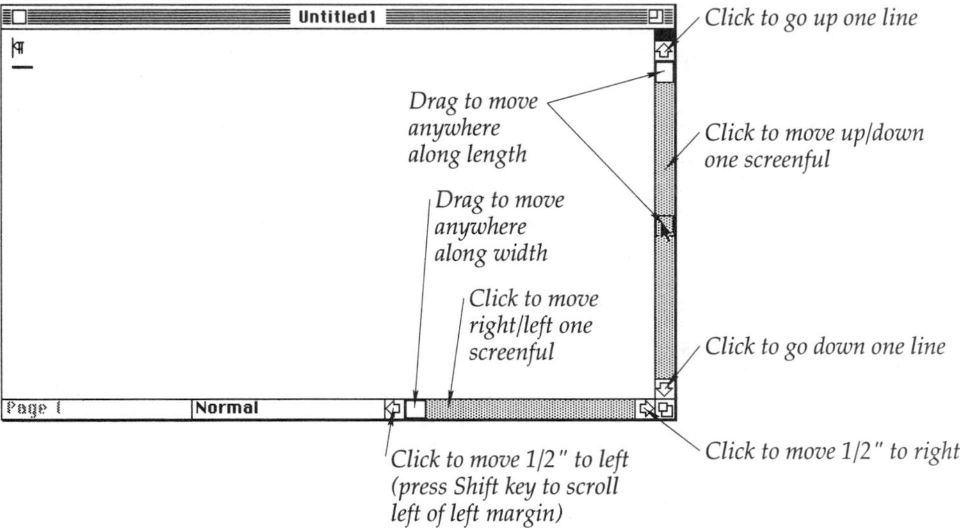

Figure 3-5
Using the scroll bars.

Resizing and Relocating Windows

Whether you have one window on the screen or many, you can freely resize and move them. Word 4 saves the size and placement of a window with the document, making it easy to maintain special locations for documents on screen.

- ❑ To expand or shrink a window, drag the size box (in the lower right corner).
- ❑ To move a window around the screen, drag it by its title bar. You can't push the entire title bar off the screen. To drag an inactive window without first making it active, press the Command key while you drag it.

- To quickly expand or shrink a window, double-click in the size box or title bar, or single-click in the zoom box in the upper right corner. These actions toggle the window between a full-screen display and its previous size and location. This is handy if you need to keep a collection of windows on the screen; when necessary, you can zoom one out to take over the screen and then send it back to its original dimensions when you are finished with it.

Many dialog boxes with title bars can be moved around on the screen like windows, although they can't be resized or scrolled. To move a dialog box when you want to see the text underneath, simply click on the title bar and drag it out of the way. To move the box back so that you can work with it, double-click on the title bar. Every time you double-click, the dialog box reverts to its previous position. Word saves the positions of dialog boxes in the Word Settings file when you quit, so they'll be in the same place when next invoked.

Handling Multiple Windows

Only one window is active at a time. Commands you choose and characters you type affect or go into the active window only. You can always identify the active window: It's the only one in which the scroll bars and title bar are visible. To make a window active, click anywhere in it. The active window is always on top; others might be hidden behind it.

Another way to activate a window is to choose it from the list that appears in the Window menu. (See Figure 3-6.) Each window is listed by document name. Windows that haven't been saved yet are named Untitled1, Untitled2, and so on. To activate a window, select it from the list.

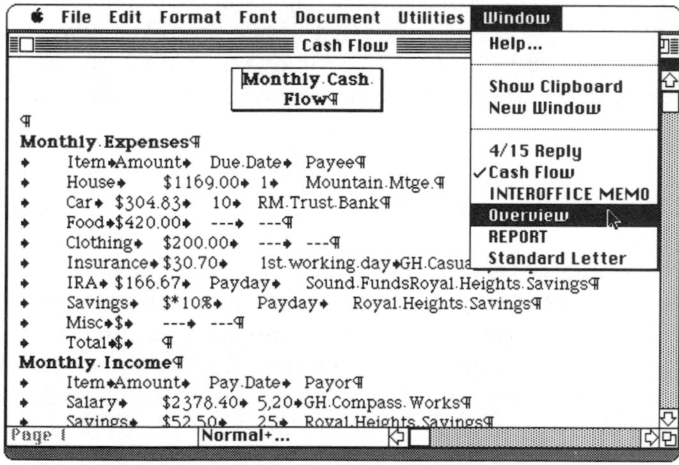

Figure 3-6
Windows listed in the Window menu.

You can also open more than one window on the same document, by choosing the New Window command on the Window menu. The title bar of each new window displays both the document's name and its number. Each time you choose the New Window command, Word adds a new window and increments the number appended to its name in the title bar. To remove a second window, click its close box. This feature of Word is particularly useful when you want to work at two or more locations in a document, or in more than one view at a time. For example, you can put the entire outline of a document in a second window while you edit the document's text in the first.

Split Windows

All windows in Galley View, Page View, and Outline View can be split horizontally into two *panes* (in Full Menus mode only). The top and bottom panes have their own scroll bars so that you can selectively view any part of the document in either one. Split windows are most often used to view two separate portions of the same document—the beginning and end of a report, for example, to see how well the closing remarks summarize the rest of the document.

You can't display a different document in each pane, but you can display the same document in a different view in each pane. This can be tremendously helpful when, for example, you'd like to enter and edit text in a pane set to Galley View, but instantly see the effects of formats as printed in a pane set to Page View. Another use, discussed in Chapter 4, is to put one pane in Galley View and the other in Outline View, so you can enter and edit text—and at the same time keep track of the overall structure of the document.

To split a window, drag the split bar (the black bar immediately above the vertical scroll bar) downward, or press Option-Command-S. You can vary the proportion of the panes by positioning the split bar exactly where you want it. As with windows, only one pane is active at a time. The active pane is the one containing the insertion point. To remove the split, drag the split bar all the way up or down; the view in the lower of the two panes takes over the screen.

Other Ways to Find Your Way

Word offers you a multiplicity of ways to find your way around in a document. You can use synchronized scrolling with a split window, one pane of which is in Outline view. You can also use the Find command, discussed in Chapter 5, "Writing and Editing Techniques," to jump to the location of a significant phrase. If you're working on a document and need to quit for the day, you can type a unique string, such as @@@, to mark your place and to use as the search string the next day.

You can also go to a specific page, jump to any of the last few places you edited using the Go Back command, or arrange your windows so that you can see more than one part of your document at a time.

The Go To Command

Choose Go To from the Utilities menu to jump to a specific page in your document, or click in the left half of the status area, where the current page number is normally displayed. Keep these facts in mind when using the Go To command:

- ❑ The document must be paginated.
- ❑ If changes were made to the document since it was paginated, the page numbers in the status box will be dimmed. You can still use the Go To command, but the page numbering might not be accurate.
- ❑ If you specify a number larger than the number of pages in the document, Word takes you to the last page.
- ❑ If your document has more than one section, you can enter a section as well as a page number. For example, you can enter *2s3* to go to the second page in the third section, but only if the Restart At 1 option is set for that section. (See Chapter 12, "Section Formatting.") You can also enter a section number alone, such as *s3*, to go to the page beginning that section.

The Go Back Command

The Go Back command is one of Word's most convenient features, yet it's one of the least known. The idea is simple: Word remembers the locations of the last few places where you entered or edited text. To move the insertion point to the last place you edited, choose Go Back on the Utilities menu, press Option-Command-Z on the keyboard or the 0 key on the keypad. Use it again to go to the location before that, and so on. By using the command repeatedly, you can cycle through the locations over and over again. Word remembers as many as four locations, although the actual number of locations is often only two or three, depending on what you did last. Every time you make a change at a different place, the location of the oldest edit is forgotten.

You can use this feature when you want to paste something into your document and then continue typing at the beginning of the pasted text rather than at the end. After you paste something into a document, the insertion point moves to the end of the pasted material. If you then use the Go Back command, the insertion point jumps back to the beginning of the pasted text, where you first placed the insertion point. Using it again takes you to the place you edited before that, and eventually the insertion point ends up back at the end of the material you pasted.

Another good use for this feature is when you want to move a section out of the area in which you are working and then continue editing in that area. Simply select and cut the material, scroll to the new location, paste it, and use the Go Back command twice. The insertion point jumps first to the beginning of the pasted text and then to the place from which the material was cut so that you can continue working.

Finally, you can use the Go Back command if you've scrolled away from the area in which you were working and you simply want to return there. In this case, Word returns first to the location of the insertion point and then to the location of the last edit.

Navigating by Keystroke

Continuously reaching for your mouse to invoke one of Word's many editing and formatting effects can sometimes be frustrating. So you start memorizing the key sequences that call up the effects, which helps keep your fingers on the keys and off the mouse. But you soon discover that the number of assigned key sequences runs into the hundreds—nearly 300 commands are available in the Commands dialog box (discussed later in this chapter), and most of these can have one or more assigned key sequences. Your Mac and Word have enough memory to keep track of them, but you might not. Fortunately, Word provides a number of key sequences for moving among menus and activating the various components of dialog boxes. This convenient feature allows you to develop a general technique for invoking effects without having to remember specific sets of keystrokes.

Moving Among Menus

To activate a menu item without touching the mouse, press the period key on the keypad. Word highlights the menu bar at the top of the screen to signal that it's ready for your impending choice of a menu. Next, either press the number of the menu, counting from left to right (the Apple menu is 0, the File menu is 1, and so on), or press the first letter of the menu. The menu having that number or beginning with that letter drops down. If you use a letter and want to go beyond the first menu starting with that letter—using *f* to go to the Format menu, for instance—press the Shift key first. Pressing *f* repeatedly, while holding the Shift key down, cycles the selected menu among the File, Format, and Font menus. You can also use the left and right arrow keys to lower the menus in turn, starting with the File menu.

To choose a command on a menu once the menu is displayed, press the first letter of the command. Word highlights the first command beginning with that letter. If you continue pressing the key, Word cycles through all the commands on the menu beginning with that letter. Alternatively, you can use the up and down arrow keys to move the highlight one command at a time; if the command is near the bottom of a menu, it's often easier to press the up arrow key to move the highlight up from the bottom. When the command you want is highlighted, press Return to execute the command.

If you make a mistake or change your mind about choosing the command, press Command-(period), the Escape key (if your keyboard has one), or the Backspace key to cancel the operation. Also, the keypad exhibits an interesting behavior: The first press of the 4 key or the 6 key drops the menu having that number, but subsequent presses move the opened menu to the left or right in the same way that the arrow keys do.

Moving in a Dialog Box

Once you've called up a dialog box, you can use various sequences of keystrokes to move among and activate the various objects in it—buttons, check boxes, radio buttons, edit fields, list boxes, drop-down lists, and drop-down fields. Figure 3-7 shows the Character dialog box and the Save As dialog box, which between them contain most of of the standard objects you're liable to find.

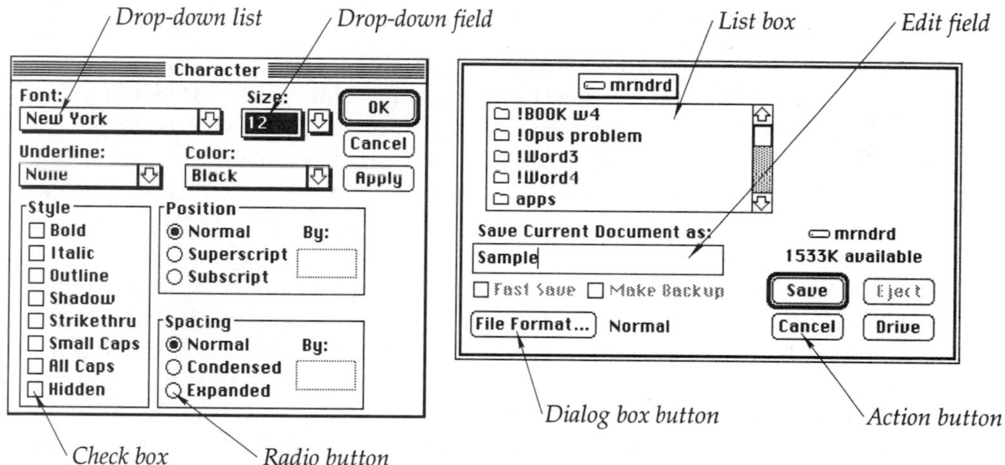

Figure 3-7
The objects found in dialog boxes.

Experienced Mac users usually know that pressing the Return key or the Enter key has the same effect as clicking OK or, in general, as clicking the button surrounded by the thick line. Similarly, pressing Command-(period) is the same as clicking the Cancel button. Slightly more complicated key sequences exist in Word for activating the other items in a dialog box, as discussed in the following paragraphs.

You can also assign a key sequence to a specific feature, option, or command that you access frequently, through the Commands dialog box, discussed later in this chapter. The names of all commands available in Word are listed at the end of each chapter and again in Appendix E, "Word's Preset Defaults." To reproduce complicated combinations of key sequences, try using a macro-recording program such as MacroMaker, Automac III, or Tempo to automatically open the dialog box and move to the desired group or option.

Edit Fields

Use the Tab key to move the insertion point from one edit field to the next, in roughly a top-to-bottom order within the dialog box. If you press Shift-Tab, the insertion point moves in a bottom-to-top order. The text in the field is selected; when you begin to type, the new text replaces it. If an edit field is not active, the insertion point skips over the field. If you first activate the field, repeatedly pressing the Tab key eventually moves the insertion point to the field. For example, if the Normal option is set in the Spacing group of the Character dialog box, the By field is dimmed. If you then select the Condensed option, the By field becomes activated, and pressing the Tab key moves the insertion point to the field.

List Boxes

If the dialog box contains a list box, pressing the up arrow or down arrow key moves the highlighted selection. If a folder name in the list box is selected, you can press Command-down arrow, Return, or Enter to open the folder. If a filename is selected, pressing Command-down arrow moves the selection downward to the next file or folder. Similarly, you can shift to the next higher folder (that is, close the currently open folder) by pressing Command-up arrow.

In the Open and Delete dialog boxes, you can make the highlight jump to a specific file by typing the first few letters of the file's name. If you type the first few letters in a dialog box that has an edit field as well as a list box, such as in the Save As dialog box, the letters you type appear in the field rather than select a name. Unfortunately, this trick doesn't work in list boxes other than those displaying filenames, such as the list box in the Styles dialog box.

Selecting by Letter

If you press Command and the first letter of the option you want to change, the effect is often as if you had clicked the check box, radio button, drop-down list, or action button with the mouse. Predicting the precise effect in any given dialog box requires experience, because this technique chooses only the first option in the dialog box that begins with the letter. For example, pressing Command-B in the Character dialog box selects the Bold option in the Style group. Check boxes have an additional property—you can press Command-B again in the Character dialog box to deselect the Bold option. However, pressing Command-E selects the Expanded option in the Spacing group. If you want to return the text to Normal spacing, pressing Command-N won't work because the key sequence selects the Normal option in the Position group!

You can also open drop-down lists and drop-down fields in the same manner. In the Character dialog box, pressing Command-F opens the Font drop-down list and leaves it on the screen. You can then use the up and down arrow keys to move the highlight up and down in the list, but a more efficient way to select a font is to type the first letter of its name. If you do this, the highlight jumps to the first option that begins with the letter.

If you keep pressing the letter, the highlight cycles through all the options beginning with that letter. Press Command-(period) to cancel the drop-down list, or press Return to accept the selected option.

Finally, selecting an item by letter also works with action buttons such as OK, Cancel, and Apply. In the case of the Character dialog box, this works only with the Apply button, because Command-C opens the Color drop-down list, and Command-O toggles the Outline option in the Style group.

Selecting by Item

The most general way to select options in a dialog box from the keyboard is simply to move from one option to the next and do the keyboard equivalent of clicking on the option to select it. When you press Command-Tab or the period key on the keypad, Word displays a dotted underline under an option, usually the Cancel button in the dialog box. The dotted underline blinks at roughly the same rate as the insertion point. Use the Control Panel to change the rate, as discussed later in this chapter.

If you keep pressing either key sequence, the dotted underline moves among the various items in the dialog box in generally a top-down or left-to-right fashion. If you simultaneously press the Shift key, the dotted underline moves in the opposite direction. When the dotted underline moves to the option you want to activate, whether it be a check box, radio button, drop-down list, drop-down field, or action button, press Command-Spacebar or the 0 key on the keypad to activate the item. Pressing either of these two key sequences is the same as if you had clicked on the item with the mouse.

Finally, you can press the right arrow and left arrow keys to quickly move the underline to the first option in each of the option groups in the dialog box. For example, pressing the right arrow key in the Character dialog box cycles the dotted underline among the Style, Position, and Spacing groups—Word briefly underlines the title of each group to draw your attention to the group. After the dotted underline has moved to the first option in the group, use Command-Tab or the period key on the keypad to highlight the specific option you want.

Getting Help

Word offers several ways to get help. If Word isn't running, you can double-click the icon of the Help file from the Finder's desktop to both launch Word and access the Help feature. If Word is already running, you can choose About Word from the Apple menu and then click the Help button, or you can choose Help from the Window menu. Either way, Word displays the Help dialog box: Scroll in the list of topics, and double-click the topic you want to read about.

You can obtain what is called context-sensitive help by first pressing Command-? (strictly speaking, you actually press Command-/) and then clicking on the option, choosing the command, or using the key sequence for which you want help. Word opens the Help dialog box, shown in Figure 3-8, and presents the relevant topic. For example, you can display the dialog box containing the topic shown in the figure by pressing Command-/ to request context-sensitive help, then pressing Command-/ again to get help on Help itself! A page reference in the dialog box leads you to a page in the documentation where the topic is discussed in more detail.

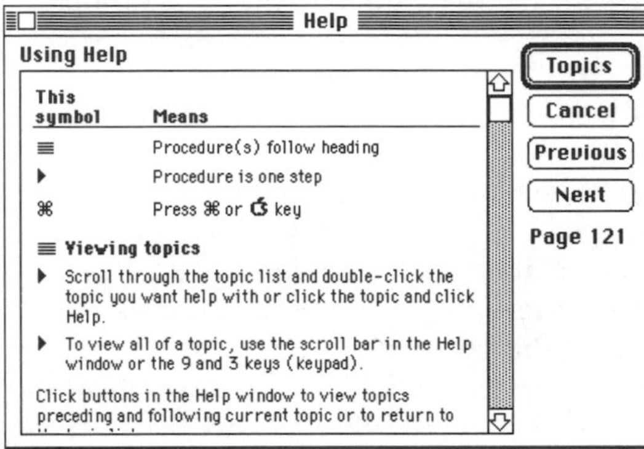

Figure 3-8
Word's Help dialog box.

TIP

Opening the Help File as a Document
One fascinating feature of the Help file (which Word uses to present the Help dialog box) is that it's a document like any other you might create in Word 4. This has two implications. The first is that you can make a copy of the file, and then you can open the copy to reformat and print it as a quick reference guide. This lets you review or quickly find hard-copy summaries for the most important features of Word. The second implication is that you can edit the Help file by changing parts of it, adding new text to existing topics, or creating new topics.

Be careful when experimenting with the following advanced procedure, however; work with a copy of the Word Help file from the original Utilities disk, in case the file becomes unusable. You also need a copy on hand of ResEdit (or any utility that can change file types). Let's assume you want to add a new Help topic called *My Notes*, to be listed just after the *Using Help* topic in the list of topics that appears when you first choose Help.

❶ Duplicate the Word Help file. Change the name of the original file to *Word Help ORIG* (or a similar name). Change the name of the duplicate file to *Word Help*.

❷ Launch Word 4 and open Word Help.

❸ Insert a new topic under the line that begins *Using Help*. Enter the name of the new topic: *My Notes*. You might notice at this point that you can enter page references for the topic by following the format of the other entries—turn on Show Hidden Text in the Preferences dialog box first, because the page references have the Hidden character format.

❹ The material for each help topic is in its own section, delimited by section marks. Insert a new section between *Using Help* and *Product Support*.

❺ Enter your notes. You can use the style sheet that belongs to the Help document. If you want to use symbols found in other topics, copy and paste them.

❻ Save the file (turn Fast Save off first) and quit Word.

❼ Start ResEdit, select the changed Word Help file, and choose Get Info from the File menu. In the File Type edit field, replace *WDBN* with *WHLP*. Quit ResEdit. (You aren't limited to ResEdit; you can use any utility that permits changing the file type of a file.)

When you launch Word again and choose Help, either through the About Word dialog box or by choosing Help from the Window menu, you'll see that the title of the new topic, *My Notes*, appears in the expected place, immediately under the *Using Help* title. Double-clicking *My Notes* opens the relevant topic.

■ *Customizing Word*

As you plumb the depths and scale the heights of serious writing and editing with Word, you might find it convenient to adapt the Word environment to your particular needs. You can do this in three ways:

- ❑ By making changes in the Control Panel. These changes are stored within your Macintosh and apply to all the programs you use.
- ❑ By changing Word's default settings for characteristics such as the current unit of measurement, the arrangement of commands on menus, the key sequences used to activate commands, size of margins, number of text columns, and so on. Word 4 typically stores these defaults in a file called *Word Settings (4)*, but you can create and easily switch between Settings files having other names, containing defaults for a variety of working environments.
- ❑ By adding your own PostScript operators to the Word program itself. This is an advanced procedure, described in Appendix C, "Using PostScript."

The Control Panel

The Control Panel desk accessory, shown in Figure 3-9, controls several characteristics of the Macintosh keyboard and screen display. You can alter these characteristics with the Word startup disk or any startup disk on which the Control Panel desk accessory is installed. The changes to the Control Panel are stored in the Mac's parameter RAM and are kept fresh by the Mac's battery; they remain in effect until you change them again or until the battery fails or is removed. Because the Control Panel is part of the Macintosh system software, any changes you make to the Control Panel affect not only Word but also any other program you work with. (Be sure you have the latest versions of the Mac system software.)

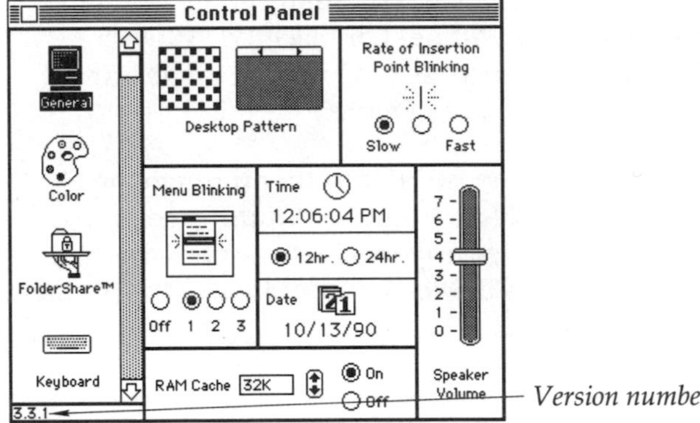

Figure 3-9
The Control Panel.

The Control Panel options of primary interest are:

- Key repeat rate (displayed when you click the Keyboard icon): Sets the rate at which the character keys repeat when they are held down. Touch typists often prefer to set the key repeat at fast or moderately fast; others should set it at slow or moderately slow.
- Delay until repeat (displayed when you click the Keyboard icon): Sets the time interval after which the keys start to repeat. Touch typists can choose a short delay; others do best with a moderate delay.
- Double-click speed (displayed when you click the Mouse icon): Sets the interval between successive clicks that the Mac interprets as a double-click. Keep it at the slow setting if you're new to double-clicking. If you're comfortable with the mouse, you might prefer the fastest setting.
- Mouse tracking (displayed when you click the Mouse icon): Sets the tracking ratio of the mouse and pointer. When you select one of the tracking options, the pointer moves in a variable ratio depending on the speed of the mouse—the faster the mouse moves, the farther the pointer travels. If you choose the tablet option, the pointer moves in a constant

1:1 ratio with the mouse, regardless of speed. Choose this setting if you're using a graphics tablet or if you're having trouble positioning the pointer accurately.

- Rate of insertion-point blinking (displayed when you click the General icon): Sets the rate at which the insertion point blinks. It's difficult to locate a slowly blinking insertion point in a full screen of text. Choose the medium or fast speed to enhance visibility of the insertion point.
- Menu blinking (displayed when you click the General icon): Sets the number of times a chosen menu item blinks before the command is carried out. Most people set this at one blink to save a little time.
- If you're using a Mac II with a color monitor, you'll probably find it helpful to reduce the number of colors displayed (displayed when you click the Monitors icon). Scrolling speed in Word (as well as in most other programs) is greatly affected by the number of color levels set here. Scrolling when using 16 or 256 colors is much slower than when using only black and white, particularly when you've set the Fractional Widths option in the Document dialog box (discussed in Chapter 14, "Document Formatting and Printing").

Changing Word's Defaults

No word processor can please all the people all the time. Word is extremely accommodating, however, letting you personalize certain operating parameters to make life easier. Your preferences are usually recorded in a file called Word Settings (4), which you can see in the System Folder on the Finder's desktop. You can also create a series of settings or configuration files with different names, each containing defaults that customize Word for different purposes, and easily switch from one settings file to another. If the Word Settings (4) file is erased or damaged, Word reverts to the "preset" settings, which are hard-wired into the Word program itself. To see the complete set of these defaults, see Appendix E, "Word's Preset Defaults."

You can change defaults from several places in Word:

- By choosing Preferences from the Edit menu and setting options in the dialog box that appears.
- By clicking the Set Default button in the Define Styles, Section, and Document dialog boxes. (Additional details on choosing new defaults are provided in the chapters that deal with these topics.)
- By taking a variety of other actions, such as setting Full Menus or Short Menus, moving Word's dialog boxes around on the screen, or changing the number of pages shown in Print Preview—even turning on the NumLock key, for those having Extended keyboards.
- By choosing Commands from the Edit menu to bring up a dialog box where you can assign commands to menus or assign your own keystroke

sequences to these commands. You can also add the names of documents, glossary items, and style names to the Work menu, without using the Commands command.

Appendix E, "Word's Preset Defaults," contains a table that lists the categories of defaults that a Settings file stores (Word's default settings) and lays out some of your options. If you're reading this book for the first time, front-to-back, some of these options might be cryptic. Never fear—refer back to the table as you read on.

Setting Preferences

To set default options, such as the unit of measurement and whether text formatted with the hidden character format is visible on screen, choose Preferences from the Edit menu. The dialog box shown in Figure 3-10 appears, listing various options.

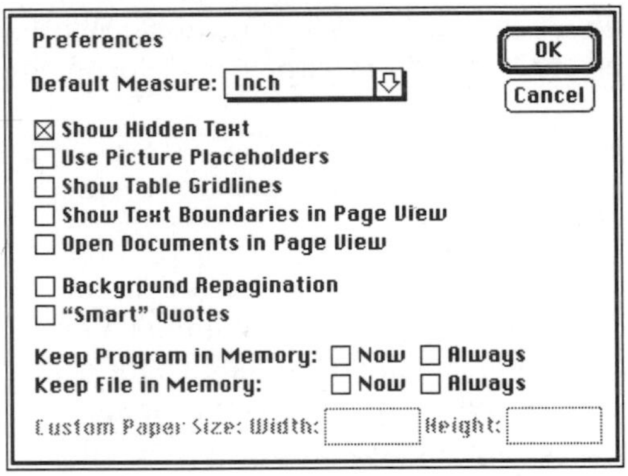

Preferences
Default Measure: Inch
OK
Cancel
☒ Show Hidden Text
☐ Use Picture Placeholders
☐ Show Table Gridlines
☐ Show Text Boundaries in Page View
☐ Open Documents in Page View
☐ Background Repagination
☐ "Smart" Quotes
Keep Program in Memory: ☐ Now ☐ Always
Keep File in Memory: ☐ Now ☐ Always
Custom Paper Size: Width: Height:

Figure 3-10
The Preferences dialog box.

Unit of measurement

Click in the drop-down list and drag to choose a unit of measure—inches, centimeters, points (1/72 inch), or picas (1/6 inch, or 12 points). The units displayed for measurement in many text fields (as well as on the Ruler) change to the new choice. In other fields, such as the Line Spacing field in the Paragraph dialog box, the point unit is always used. You can also express a measurement in another unit, and Word converts it to the current preference the next time you display the dialog box. To enter a measurement, use the abbreviations *in*, *cm*, *pt*, and *pi*. Regardless of the unit used, all measurements in Word are accurate to 1 point.

Show Hidden Text

If you format text with the Hidden character attribute, the text won't appear in the document when printed (unless you set the Print Hidden Text option in the Print dialog box). It also disappears from the screen version of the document—unless you've set the Show Hidden Text option. When you make hidden text visible, Word indicates it by putting a dotted line under the material. The Dotted Underline character format looks exactly the same on screen, so be careful when using both formats in the same document.

The space that visible hidden text takes on screen affects repagination. Be sure to turn off Show Hidden Text when you get to the point of working with the layout and page breaks in the document. The page numbers in an extracted table of contents or an index, however, aren't affected by visible hidden text, because Word turns off the option before the extraction.

Use Picture Placeholders

Scrolling through a passage in a document containing many bitmap-type graphics often requires patience. If you're using a Mac II with a color monitor, scrolling through color bitmaps can be maddeningly slow. When you set the Use Picture Placeholder option, Word represents graphics as gray rectangles, permitting fast scrolling regardless of the size or type of the graphic. This option is an excellent candidate for placement on a menu or for calling via a key sequence of your choice, if you find yourself flipping frequently back and forth between displaying and not displaying graphics. On the other hand, once you've inserted graphics into a document, you generally don't need to see them again until the document is printed. (Setting the option doesn't affect the way graphics are printed.)

Show Table Gridlines

Without seeing the extent of each cell in a table, it can be difficult to know where to place the pointer for selecting lines and paragraphs. Selecting the Show Table Gridlines option facilitates editing in tables by marking the edges of the rows and columns in the table with a dotted line. These lines are visible in both Page View and Galley View. (For a discussion of Word 4's table format, see Chapter 11, "Formatting Tables and Lists.")

Show Text Boundaries in Page View

Editing in Page View can be a little tricky if, for example, you've set up complicated structures of Side-by-Side formatted paragraphs and you're not quite clear where one paragraph ends and another starts. Setting this option helps here. When the option is set, Word draws dotted lines on the boundaries of each paragraph. Setting the option also helps to lay out your pages; you can more easily see the page as an arrangement of blocks of text. However, you can duplicate the effect of both this option and the Show Table Gridlines option by using the Show ¶ command, which also displays boundaries as dotted lines.

Open Documents in Page View

Setting this option tells Word you want every newly opened document to appear in Page View instead of Galley View. The cost of working in Page View is speed—slower editing, scrolling, and formatting speeds—because

Word makes more time-intensive calculations to present material with complex formats than it does in Galley View.

Background Repagination

In previous versions of Word, you had to repaginate manually—by using the Repaginate command, by switching to Page Preview (now Print Preview), or when extracting a table of contents or index. Word 4 repaginates dynamically when the Background Repagination option is set, by waiting for moments when you aren't using the keyboard or mouse. The cost of background repagination is a small decrease in responsiveness.

"Smart" Quotes

One of the most telling ways to determine the level of expertise used in desktop publishing is to notice whether quotes are represented by the correct characters. To typographers and others in the publishing industry, the common ' and " symbols are foot and inch marks, not quotes. On the Macintosh, you can enter standard single (‘ ’) and double (“ ”) quotes, both opening and closing, by pressing combinations of the Shift, Option, and the [or the] key. Unfortunately, it's hard to embed these key sequences in one's unconscious without practice. Word makes using correct opening and closing quotes easy when the Smart Quotes option is set—all you do is type either the ' or the " key, as usual. Word then scans the surrounding text and inserts the appropriate character. If a space precedes the quote, Word inserts an opening quote; in all other cases, Word inserts a closing quote. This is particularly handy for apostrophes, which are represented by single closing quotes.

Custom Paper Size

If you've chosen one of the ImageWriters as the current printer, you can set up a custom paper size that becomes one of the paper size options in the Page Setup dialog box. If you've chosen a LaserWriter, the Custom Paper size options are dimmed and unselectable.

The Memory-Management Options

What exactly is memory management? Normally, Word loads only parts, or *segments*, of itself into memory as needed. When a segment is no longer needed, it remains in memory until Word needs to use the memory for another segment. Similarly, Word loads only part of your document at a time. As you scroll through the document, Word loads additional parts of the document while returning other parts to disk.

This memory-management system makes sense if your Mac has little memory to spare, but all the loading and unloading of program and file segments can slow the program's operation. If you like, you can tell Word to load nearly all the program into memory at once. (Word will still load its printing and file-conversion segments only when they are needed.) When you launch the program, it takes a little longer for the blank document window to appear, but thereafter Word runs briskly. And you can further instruct Word to load and keep an entire document in memory. Again, you will notice a delay as a long document loads, but subsequent operations are speeded up, because Word doesn't need to access the disk drives as often.

You can even open multiple documents at once—theoretically as many as 23—and load each one entirely into memory (as long as there is enough free memory to accommodate them). Word uses a few of the slots that are available for opening files for its own purposes, such as for opening the Glossary and for maintaining headers and footers, so at times it might seem that the limit is less than 23 files. If you really need to open as many documents as possible, try quitting Word to close every file (whether or not the file was opened by you), and launch Word again to clear the slate.

Word lets you specify whether you want to load the program or files into memory for the current session only or for all sessions; if you choose the latter, Word records the change in the current Settings file when you quit.

- To load all of Word or the current document (the frontmost document on Word's desktop) for the current session only, select the appropriate Now option.
- To load all of Word or the current document for all sessions, select the appropriate Always option.

TIP

Using Memory-Management Options with One Disk Drive
You can particularly benefit from the memory-management options if you have only one disk drive. Normally, Word would keep asking you to swap disks in and out of the drive as you work with your documents. With both Word and the documents in memory, however, you can minimize disk swapping and thus make your work go much faster.

How well the memory-management options work depends on how much memory is available to Word. The options fare better with a Macintosh Plus, SE, or II than with a 512 KB Mac, because the first three machines have more memory. Running under MultiFinder can also cramp Word. If you select the icon for the Word program from the Finder's desktop, and then choose Get Info, you'll see two areas called Suggested Memory Size and Application Memory Size. Word runs well when given at least 1024 KB of RAM—give it more (for example, 1536 KB) if you often work with very large documents. In addition, memory-gobbling utilities and desk accessories, such as the DeskPict INIT file (a utility that permits replacement of the usual patterned background with an image of your choice), eat into the space otherwise used by Word's memory-management options and make them less effective.

Interestingly, although these memory-management options make the program more responsive, they don't affect the overall length of your editing session. This is because Word reserves a block of memory for keeping track of the changes you make to a document, and the size of this block never varies. Preloading the program into memory affects the responsiveness of the program when you issue a command, and preloading a document affects the speed of operations such as scrolling and searching and replacing. In Word 4, the amount of memory available for editing is less of a concern, because the size of this area in memory is much larger than in earlier versions.

TIP

Using Disk Caching with Word's Memory-Management Options
The Macintosh system software lets you control an aspect of memory management through a technique called *disk caching,* in which you set aside some of the Mac's memory to store frequently accessed blocks of the documents you work with; this memory is then unavailable for the program. (See the RAM Cache option in the Control Panel shown in Figure 3-9.) Because Word does a good job of managing memory, it's usually counter-productive to have both disk caching and the memory-management options set at the same time. Usually, you'll benefit most from using Word's memory-management preferences alone.

Creating Custom Menus and Key Sequences

Word is one of the few Macintosh programs to let you change the contents of its menus—in effect to create custom commands! You can change menus in Word in two ways. First, you can quickly add formats to the Format menu and documents, glossary items, and style names to the special Work menu by using a special key sequence and selecting what you want to add. (We'll discuss this method next.) Second, through the Commands command, Word 4 offers an almost frightening degree of freedom in assigning commands to menus and in assigning key sequences to these commands.

Changing Menus Without the Commands Command

Simply press Option-Command- + (actually the = key—not the plus key on the keypad), and then select the font, format, document, or whatever you want to add. Experiment by adding a document to the Work menu:

1. Press Option-Command- +. The pointer changes to a large plus sign.
2. Choose Open from the File menu, and double-click on the filename you want to add. A new menu name, Work, appears in the menu bar, and the menu bar blinks to signal that the item has been added. Note, however, that Word doesn't actually open the document.
3. Pull down the Work menu; the first item on it is the name of your document. Choosing the new "command" opens the document.

The Work menu is convenient for documents that you use frequently or need quick access to, such as boilerplate text or a list of ideas that you add to throughout the day. Later chapters describe how to add glossary items and styles to the Work menu. Adding to the Font and Format menus is also easy. To add a character format, for example, simply press Option-Command- +, choose Character from the Format menu, and click on the option.

You can even add many items to a menu at the same time. Begin by calling up the appropriate dialog box—the Character dialog box, for instance. Then press Option-Command- +, click on the font or format you want to add, and repeat these two steps as many times as you want while the dialog box is displayed. Each time you add an item, the menu bar blinks. If you wish, you can also hold the Shift key down as you click on a series of items to add. If you try to add an item that's already on the menu, you'll hear a beep, but no harm will be done. Click Cancel when you're finished. Resist the temptation to add every conceivable option to the menus, for the amount of free memory decreases with each addition.

Removing options that you don't use from these menus is simple: Press Option-Command- – (hyphen), pull down the appropriate menu, and choose the option you want to delete. The pointer is a large minus sign when you're in the delete mode. You can delete more than one item by holding down the Shift key as you remove menu items.

Changing Menus and Key Sequences with the Commands Command

Using the Option-Command- + key sequence is perhaps the easiest way to add documents, glossary items, and styles to the Work menu, but it isn't the most powerful way. The reason is that Word makes assumptions about where you want the item to appear on the Work or Format menu. Through the Commands dialog box, you can add, move, or remove almost all of Word's commands to or from any of Word's menus. You can also assign or reassign the preset key sequences for Word's commands.

Customizing menus and key sequences is also important because only a few of the total number of commands available in Word are assigned to menus when you first start the program, in either Short Menus or Full Menus mode. (For a complete list of Word's commands and what they mean, refer to Appendix E, "Word's Preset Defaults.") For example, in the Outline View of Word 3, you could selectively display up to nine levels of outline headings by clicking the appropriate icon in the outline icon bar. In Word 4, the outline icon bar reveals icons for displaying only up to four levels. However, the commands for displaying up to the ninth level still exist but aren't assigned to either icons in the Outline icon bar or commands on any menu, so you can access them by adding them to a menu or by assigning them a set of key sequences. Similarly, if you use the Side-by-Side paragraph format (formerly an option in the Paragraph dialog box of Word 3), you can add a command for it to the Format menu.

When you choose Commands from the Edit menu, Word displays the Commands dialog box, shown in Figure 3-11 on the following page. On the left side of the dialog box is a list box displaying almost every menu command, action, or dialog box option available in Word. On the right side are areas for adding a selected command to a menu and for assigning a key sequence to the command. At the bottom is an area for saving and loading sets of default configurations.

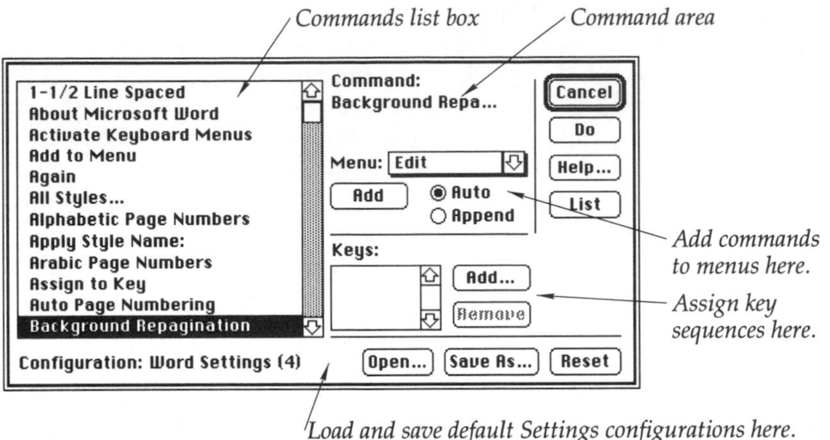

Figure 3-11
The Commands dialog box.

Let's add a command to the Format menu—and assign it a key sequence as well. The Use Picture Placeholders option in the Preferences dialog box is a good one to add: It doesn't appear on any menu, it doesn't have an assigned key sequence, and yet it's the type of feature you might want to easily toggle on and off.

❶ Choose the Commands command.

❷ Scroll in the list box, and select the Use Picture Placeholders command. Its name appears under the Commands heading at the top of the dialog box, and the drop-down list underneath is activated.

❸ To add the command to the Edit menu at the position suggested by Word, simply click the Add button under the Menu drop-down list. To append the command below whatever other commands have already been added to the menu you've selected, click the Append button. (If you select a command that already exists on a menu, the name of the menu appears at the top of the Menu drop-down list but is dimmed, and the Add button changes to Remove. Click the Remove button first, and then add the command to the menu you want.)

❹ To assign a key sequence to the command, click the Add button in the Keys group. Word displays a dialog box requesting the key sequence you want to add. For this example, press Shift-Option-Command-p (for Picture). The dialog box disappears, and symbols representing each of the keys you pressed appear in the Keys list box. If you use a key sequence that has already been assigned to another command, Word displays a dialog box telling you this and gives you the options of replacing the previous assignment or canceling the operation.

❺ Click Cancel.

Some of the command names are a bit cryptic. If you select a command and click the Help button, Word displays a dialog box containing a sentence or two of explanation. If you click the List button, Word creates a list of all the key assignments for the current menu. If you want a list of all the commands, not only those having menu or key assignments, press the Shift key as you click the List button. Appendix E, "Word's Preset Defaults," contains tables listing the keyboard symbols that Word uses as well as each of the commands available in the dialog box, its meaning, and the default key sequence assigned to it.

Several types of commands are listed in the Commands dialog box, and the way you handle each varies with its type:

- Standard menu commands such as Open from the File menu, and Page View from the Document menu. These already have a place on a menu but might not have a corresponding key sequence. You can remove the command and add it to another menu, or you can assign a key sequence to it.
- Options normally found in dialog boxes, such as the Small Caps character format, the Page Break Before paragraph format, or the Use Picture Placeholders option in the Preferences dialog box. These commands generally don't have either a menu or a key sequence assignment.
- Options that normally have a key sequence but generally aren't found on a menu. An example is the Activate Keyboard Menus command, which you use when pressing Command-Tab or the period key on the keypad to select a menu command from the keyboard, as discussed earlier this chapter. Some of these options can't be added to menus or removed from the menu where they reside, such as the About Microsoft Word command, which must remain on the Apple menu. Another example is the Backspace command—when you select it in the list box, a menu name doesn't appear in the drop-down list, and Word doesn't let you add the command to any menu. You can, however, assign another key sequence to it or change its existing key sequence.
- Using a command followed by an ellipsis (...) brings up the appropriate dialog box. The options you choose in the dialog box determine the effect produced. For example, you can add the Paragraph Borders command to the Format menu and thereby avoid having to click the Borders button in the Paragraph dialog box each time you want to create a paragraph border effect.
- Selecting a command followed by a colon displays a drop-down list in the Command area that allows you to add more than one form of the command. For example, selecting the Apply Style Name command brings up a drop-down list containing the names of all styles defined in the current document and offers the Work menu as the place to store them. In this case you could add all style names in the drop-down list to the Work menu—or, for that matter, to any other menu.

When you add a name listed in the drop-down list, Word adds a diamond bullet before it to verify that you've added the option as a menu command. If you select one of the style names in the drop-down list, you can specify a key sequence for it, but Word doesn't indicate that a key sequence has been added until you reselect both the Apply Style Name command and that style name in the drop-down list. To see the complete list, click the List button to create a table.

The current arrangement of menus and key sequences is stored in the Word Settings file specified at the bottom of the Commands dialog box. The buttons in the Configuration area of the dialog box affect the menu assignments, as discussed in the next section.

TIP

Combining Custom Key Sequences with Macros
Assigning your own key sequences to commands is particularly effective with macro recording programs such as Tempo from Affinity Microsystems and AutoMac III, which is shipped with the Word 4 utility disks. Most macro recording programs work better when recording keystrokes rather than mouse movements, because key-sequence commands generally take effect relative to the position of the insertion point, while mouse movements are generally made relative to some position on the screen. It's much easier to predetermine the position of the insertion point with key commands than by positioning the pointer.

Also, macros recorded from keystrokes typically work more quickly than those recorded from mouse movements, because Word permits entering dialog box commands, for instance, ahead of the actual appearance of the dialog box.

Loading, Saving, and Resetting Settings Files
Once you've spent time setting up a custom configuration of menus and key sequences, you can save the configuration in a Settings file under a name that reflects its purpose. As mentioned earlier, these Settings files contain all of Word's defaults, not merely those set through the Commands command. The complete list of defaults stored in a Settings file is presented in Appendix E. Customized configurations have many uses:

- The Short Menus configuration offers one set of menu commands, and the Full Menus another. You can set up menu configurations that are between Short and Full Menus in complexity, adding commands to menus as you learn about and use them.
- If you're used to working with another word processor, you can change the key commands to ones you've already learned.
- You can create Settings files for different purposes. For example, you could customize Word for working on a newsletter, and then change to a different configuration for correspondence.

- Different users working on the same Mac can create their own menu and key-sequence configurations.

When you launch Word by double-clicking its icon, settings from the file named Word Settings (4) are loaded. You can also locate a Settings file on the Finder's desktop and double-click it to start Word. Word uses these settings as it loads. Whichever Settings file is loaded becomes the current Settings file for that session. Any preference changes you make during the session are recorded in that Settings file when you quit Word.

At any time during the course of a session, you can save the current state of the Settings file under any name you choose. When you click the Save As button at the bottom of the Commands dialog box, Word presents a version of the Save As dialog box for saving the Settings file under the same name or under a new name. The System Folder is the best place to save Settings files, because it's the same place that Word stores the Word Settings (4) file when you first launch Word.

To switch to a new Settings file, first open the Commands dialog box and save the current state of the Word environment in the Settings file you've been using. Next, click the Open button; Word displays a form of the standard Open dialog box, showing only the names of folders and valid Settings files. Simply double-click the name of the Settings file to load it.

Clicking the Reset button in the lower right corner of the Commands dialog box has various effects, depending on whether you press the Shift key or the Option key as you click the button.

- If you've changed the configuration of the currently loaded Settings file and want to return it to the state it was in when first loaded, simply click the Reset button. Word responds with a dialog box requesting *Are you sure you want to revert to configuration file settings?* Click OK to reset the current Settings file.
- If you want to return the current Settings file back to the preset defaults set by Microsoft for the Word Settings (4) file, press the Shift key while clicking the Reset button. Word responds with a dialog box requesting *Are you sure you want to revert to default settings?* Remember that all custom menu arrangements, key assignments, the style sheet, and other defaults stored in the Settings file revert to the preset defaults, not only the keyboard and menu assignments.
- Pressing Option and clicking the Reset button is more for fun than for anything else, because it adds all the commands that can be added to the suggested menus. When you do this, Word asks *Are you sure you want to add all commands to menus?* The menus (predominantly the Edit, Format, Document, and Utilities menus) grow to dozens of items each, forming a very impressive array when demonstrating your knowledge of Word to your associates! Unlike using the Shift key, resetting the menus with the Option key doesn't affect the other items stored in the current Settings file.

■ *Saving Your Work*

If you've ever had something go wrong while you were working at a computer and realized in horror that a lot of hard work had disappeared forever, you know the importance of saving files regularly—*and* of making backup copies. If this has never happened to you, don't learn this lesson the hard way. It's a good idea to save your work after every page or so. That way, if something happens, you stand to lose only the last page, not the entire manuscript. To save your document, do the following:

1. Choose Save from the File menu.
2. If the document hasn't been saved before, Word asks for a name. Type a suitable name into the Save Current Document As field.
3. Click the Save button.

Names can be up to 31 characters long, but you should keep your names short so that you can read them easily on the Finder's desktop. A name can contain any character except the colon (:). To save the file on a different disk, click the Drive or the Eject button, as usual. To save it in a different folder, select the folder you want from the list box and then click Save.

The only time you have to provide a name for a document is the first time you save it. After that, when you choose Save, Word assumes that you want to use the same name and record the document on the same disk.

Replacing a File

If the name you give a document has already been used for another document in that folder, you have three choices:

1. Choose another name.
2. Save it on another disk or in another folder.
3. Save it on the current disk with the name provided.

The first two choices leave the old file alone. The third erases the old file and replaces it with the new one—so be sure that this is what you want to do. Word provides a safety feature to help you avoid accidentally erasing files. If you use a name that already exists in that folder, Word beeps and displays a dialog box. Click No if you don't want to replace (and therefore erase) the old file; click Yes if you do.

Doing a Fast Save

Word stores in memory a list of the edits you make rather than altering the original text of the document. This is one of the secrets of Word's editing speed—it doesn't take the time to actually rearrange the text every time you make a change. What you see on the screen is a combination of the original draft and the list of corrections.

If the Fast Save option is selected when you click the Save button, the document itself isn't updated; only the most recent corrections are added to the file. Fast saves are faster because it takes less time to update the list of corrections than to reorder the entire document. If you do a fast save when this list gets too long, Word rewrites the entire document anyway to empty the list and speed up subsequent editing. This complete reordering is called a *full save*. You can tell when Word is doing a full save because the status box displays what percentage of the document has been saved, and it increments more slowly for full saves than fast saves.

Other than when you deselect the Fast Save option manually, Word also deselects the option when you save the document for the first time, when you change the name of the document, or when you save it to another disk.

TIP

When Not to Use the Fast Save Option
You may want to turn off the Fast Save option under two exceptional circumstances. First, if you need to make a large number of changes to a document (perhaps by using the Change command), do a full save first to empty the edit list. This gives Word more memory to store the impending changes. Similarly, when the document is very large, you may find that Word runs out of memory more frequently. Doing full saves rather than fast saves preserves as much memory as possible for your document. Second, some programs that can read Word files, such as PageMaker from Aldus Corporation, require that you do a full save of the document before they can successfully read the file.

Making Backup Copies

Often it's a good idea to preserve the last version of an important document as a backup, in case you make a mistake you can't undo and want to revert to the earlier version. You can make a copy from the Finder's desktop, but Word lets you make a backup copy without leaving the program.

❶ Choose Save As from the File menu.

❷ Click the Make Backup option.

❸ Click the Save button.

The backup is named *Backup of* (filename). Whenever you save the document from this point on, Word saves the previous version of the document as the backup and the edited version as the actual file. However, when you use this feature, it overrides the Fast Save option and does a full save every time.

Saving in Different Formats

Word normally saves documents in Word 4 format, but you can also save your document in other file formats. For example, you can save a document in Text Only format so that it can be read by another word processor or transferred to a spreadsheet. To save in a format other than Word 4 (in Full Menus mode only):

1. Choose the Save (for a first save) or Save As command. Before providing a name and clicking the Save button, click the File Formats button. A list of formats appears in a dialog box, as shown in Figure 3-12. Click the format you want. The available formats are as follows:

   Normal: Stores the file in Word 4 format.

   Text Only: Creates an ASCII file. Files in this format contain text characters only, without formatting. For use with other word processors and some telecommunications programs.

   Text Only with Line Breaks: The same as Text Only, but Word inserts a paragraph mark or carriage return at the end of each line.

   Microsoft Word 1.0/Microsoft Works: Stores the file in the format used by Word 1.0 for the Macintosh. This format is also used by Microsoft Works. When you open a document created with Word 1.0 or Microsoft Works, Word converts it to Word 4 format.

   Microsoft Word 3.0/Microsoft Write: Stores the file in the format used by Word 3 for the Macintosh. This format is also used by Microsoft Write. When you open a document created with Word 3 or Microsoft Write, Word converts it to Word 4 format.

   Microsoft Word (MS-DOS): Stores the file in the format used by Microsoft Word for MS-DOS computers. Of course, you must first transfer the file to a disk that is compatible with the MS-DOS computer.

   MacWrite: Stores the file in the format used by Apple's MacWrite (compatible with both the RAM-based and disk-based versions). When you open an existing MacWrite document, Word converts it to Word 4 format.

   Interchange format (RTF): RTF stands for Rich Text Format, a format used by programs that run on the IBM PC, the Macintosh, and XENIX/UNIX computers. An RTF file contains both text and English-like formatting instructions. Word can convert an existing RTF file into Word 4 format.
2. Click the OK button in the Format dialog box.
3. Provide a name for the document.
4. Click Save.

If you select a file format other than Normal, Word activates the Default Format For File check box at the bottom of the dialog box. If you select this option, Word always converts the file to that format when saving. This can be helpful, for instance, when working with Text Only files, and you don't want Word to save a style sheet with the text.

When you convert a Word 4 file to another format, be aware that many formats have no analog in the formats supported by other word processors. Converting between various formats will surface again in Chapter 16, "Transferring Text and Graphics," which discusses the problems involved in transferring files between programs and from one machine to another.

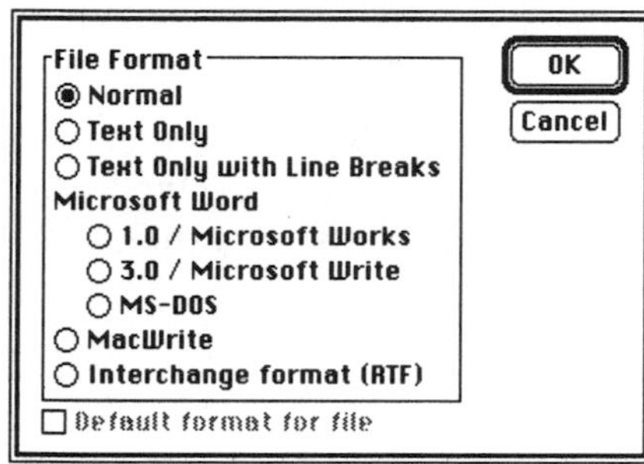

Figure 3-12
The File Format dialog box.

■ Points to Remember

- ❑ Word offers four views on a document. Galley View is for rapid writing, editing, and formatting, but doesn't display such formats as side-by-side paragraphs and multiple-column text. In Page View you can write and edit documents as they will appear when printed, but screen updating is slower than in Galley View. Outline View displays the overall structure of a document, so you can rearrange its parts easily. Print Preview displays entire pages of a document, allowing you to check the layout of pages and to change certain document formats such as margins and page breaks.
- ❑ You can have as many as 23 windows open at one time, including those for documents, headers, footers, and dialog boxes. You can open more than one window on a document, or split a window into two panes, each of which contains a different view.
- ❑ The status box in the lower left corner of a document window usually contains the current page number. In the following situations, the page number is replaced with other information:

  After an Open, the number of characters in the document is briefly displayed.

  If you open a locked file, you can read it but not change it, and the status box displays the message *Locked File.*

  During a time-consuming operation, such as a Save, the percentage of the task completed is displayed. After a Save, the number of characters in the file is displayed.

  When you enter a temporary mode, a prompt is displayed. For example, after you press Shift-Command-S to assign a style from the keyboard, the status box reads *Style.*

  During certain graphics and Page Preview operations, sizes and the pointer position are displayed.

  During repagination, printing, and table-of-contents or index generation, the page currently being processed is displayed.
- ❑ Many ways exist to navigate among Word's views on a document, among menu commands, and within dialog boxes. If you want, you can operate Word almost solely from the keyboard.
- ❑ The Control Panel, available from the Apple menu, lets you control characteristics of the mouse, keyboard, and screen display.
- ❑ Word maintains the Word Settings (4) file to store your preferences from session to session so that you don't have to set them each time you start Word. You can have more than one settings file and switch between them. To start Word with a settings file other than Word Settings, double-click on the settings file you want to use or load it through the Commands dialog box.

- If you have enough memory, Word will run faster when you load the entire program and any open documents into memory. To change this and other operating preferences (such as the current unit of measurement and custom page sizes), choose Preferences from the Edit menu and set the appropriate options.
- The Work menu is a user-defined menu to which you can add documents, glossary entries, and styles that you use frequently.
- You can add unlisted commands and options to any menu in Word, and you can remove and change their location on menus. You can also assign one or more key sequences to most of the commands and options in Word using the Commands command.
- A document name can be 31 characters long, but short names are easiest to read in the Open and Save As dialog boxes and on the Finder's desktop.

Techniques

Navigating Among Views on a Document

To switch from one view on a document to any other, use the commands in the following table. For alternate key sequences, see the Commands table at the end of the Summary.

To go from	To	Do this
Galley View	Page View	Choose Page View (Command-B).
	Outline View	Choose Outlining (Command-U).
	Print Preview	Choose Print Preview (Command-I).
Page View	Galley View	Choose Page View again (Command-B).
	Outline View	Choose Outlining (Command-U).
	Print Preview	Choose Print Preview (Command-I).
Outline View	Galley View	Choose Outlining again (Command-U).
	Page View	Choose Page View (Command-B).
	Print Preview	Choose Print Preview (Command-I), but the preview you see is of the outline.
Print Preview	Galley View	If the prior view was Galley View, click Cancel (Command- .)
	Page View	Click the Page View button, press Command-B, or double-click on page. If the prior view was Page View, you can also click Cancel (Command- .).
	Outline View	Not available—if you press Command-U, Word beeps.

Managing Windows

Move a window

❶ Drag the title bar.

Close a window

❶ Click the close box at the left end of the title bar.

Change the size of a window

❶ Drag the size box (in the lower right corner).

Split a window into two panes

❶ Drag down the split bar (the black bar above the vertical scroll bar) or press Option-Command-S.

❷ Drag it up or down to restore the window to one pane.

Toggle between a small and a full-size window

❶ Click the zoom box at the right end of the title bar, or double-click in the title bar or the size box in the lower right corner.

Shrink two full-screen windows to half-screen size

❶ Double-click the size box of each window.

The first is placed in the upper half of the screen, and the second is placed in the lower half.

Open a new window for the document in the active window

❶ Choose New Window from the Window menu.

The title bar of each new window on the same document contains the document's name and ends with a distinguishing sequence number. Changes made in one window appear in all others belonging to the same document.

Scrolling

Scroll a line at a time

❶ Click the arrows at the ends of the scroll bars.

Scroll a screenful at a time

❶ Click the gray part of the scroll bar, above or below the scroll box, depending on whether you want to scroll forward or backward.

Scroll quickly in the document

❶ Drag the scroll box to the corresponding position.

The current page number appears in the status box, dimmed after the point where you've edited the document, to indicate that it's an estimation.

Scroll back to a previous selection or insertion point

❶ Press the Go Back key (Option-Command-Z or 0 on the keypad on the keyboard).

Pressing the key repeatedly cycles through the last several edit locations.

Scroll horizontally to left of left margin

❶ Hold down the Shift key and click on the left arrow in the horizontal scroll bar.

Scroll to a specific page

❶ Choose Go To from the Search menu, or double-click the left half of the status area.

❷ Type the number of the page you want.

❸ Click OK.

The page numbers refer to the last repagination of the document. If each section of your document begins with page 1, you must also specify a section number. For example, *1s2* indicates page 1 of section 2. You can also use the scroll box to go to a page by following the display of page numbers in the status box as you drag the scroll box.

Customizing Menus

Add a command to a menu

❶ Press Option-Command- + (on the keyboard). The cursor changes to a plus sign. Click on the item you want to add. Use Shift-click to add more than one item.

You can add	To this menu	Items to add
Formatting options	Format or Font	Any item from the Character or Paragraph dialog boxes or from the Ruler.
Documents	Work	Any document in the Open dialog box or on the title bar of a window.
Glossary entries	Work	Any entry in the Glossary dialog box.
Styles	Work	Any style name in the Styles or Define Styles dialog box.

Delete a command from a menu

❶ Press Option-Command-- (hyphen).

❷ Choose the command you want to delete from the Format, Font, or Work menu.

❸ Use Shift-click to delete more than one item.

Add a command through the Commands dialog box

❶ Choose Commands from the Edit menu.

❷ Select the command you want to add in the list box. Its name appears under the Commands heading at the top of the dialog box, and the drop-down list underneath is activated.

❸ To add the command to the menu at the position suggested by Word, click the Add button under the Menu drop-down list. To append the command below whatever other commands have already been added to the menu you've selected, click the Append button. (If you select a command that already exists on a menu, the name of the menu appears at the top of the Menu drop-down list but is dimmed, and the Add button changes to Remove. Click the Remove button first, and then add the command to the menu you want.)

❹ Click Cancel.

You can display a brief summary of the meaning of a command by selecting it and clicking the Help button. You can get a list of the current menu and key assignments by clicking the List button. If you want a list of all the commands, not only those having menu or key assignments, press the Shift key as you click the List button. The tables in the Summary section of each chapter list these commands, as does the table in Appendix E, "Word's Preset Defaults."

Add a key sequence to a command

❶ Choose Commands from the Edit menu.

❷ Select the command to which you want to assign a key sequence. Its name appears under the Commands heading at the top of the dialog box.

❸ Click the Add button in the Keys group. Word displays a dialog box requesting the key sequence you want to add. Enter the key sequence. The dialog box disappears, and symbols representing each of the keys you pressed appear in the Keys list box. If you use a key sequence that is already assigned to another command, Word displays a dialog box telling you this and gives you the options of replacing the previous assignment or canceling the operation.

❹ Click Cancel.

Saving

To save a document, glossary, or personal dictionary; rename a document; make a backup copy; save on a different disk; or save a document in a different file format for use with other programs:

1. Choose Save As from the File menu.

   Save Current Document As: Type the document name. If the document is already named, Word proposes the current name. Click Save to accept the proposed name, or type a new document name.

   Fast Save: Saves your documents much faster but creates longer files that take up more disk space. When edits to a document accumulate, Word disables this option automatically and does a full save to consolidate changes.

   Make Backup: Creates a backup copy of the last version you saved under the name *Backup of* (filename).

   File Format: Lists options for saving your document in different file formats. After clicking this button, you can choose among the following:

File format option	Saves as this
Normal	Word 4 format.
Text Only	Creates an ASCII file without Word formatting; use for transferring the document to other programs.
Text Only with Line Breaks	Creates an ASCII file without Word formatting but with carriage-return characters at the end of each line.
Microsoft Word 1.0/Microsoft Works	Saves in Microsoft Word 1.0 format (for working with external programs that read only Microsoft Word 1.0 format, such as Microsoft Works).
Microsoft Word 3.0/Microsoft Write	Saves in Microsoft Word 3 format; also used by Microsoft Write and certain other programs.
Microsoft Word (MS-DOS)	Saves in PC Word format (for transferring files from your Macintosh to a PC).
MacWrite	Saves in MacWrite format.
Interchange format (RTF)	Converts all formatting, the style sheet, and graphics into the RTF interchange format and saves as a text file.

■ *Command and Keyboard Shortcuts*

Manipulating Windows

To	Keyboard press
Make next window active	Option-Command-W
Zoom window	Option-Command-] (toggles)
Split window	Option-Command-S (toggles)

Choosing Commands with the Period Key on the Keyboard

❶ Press the period on the keypad (or Command-Tab) to enter into menu-selection mode. The menu bar is highlighted. In this mode, you can do any of the following from the keyboard:

To	Keyboard press	Keypad press
Choose a menu	First letter of menu, or Shift-letter to choose next menu starting with that letter, or right and left arrow keys	Number of menu—0 for Apple menu, 1 for File menu, and so on. Once menu is selected, use the 4 and 6 keys to move left and right.
Choose a command	First letter of command, or up and down arrow keys	2 and 8
Execute a command	Return or Enter	
Cancel a command	Backspace (delete), Command-(period)	

Navigating in Dialog Boxes

To move	Keyboard press	Keypad press
To next text field	Tab	
To previous text field	Shift-Tab	
Up in list box	Up arrow	
Down in list box	Down arrow	
To next group of options	Right arrow	
To previous group of options	Left arrow	
To next option	Command-Tab	. (Decimal point)
To previous option	Shift-Command-Tab	
Select the current option	Command-Spacebar	0
Select an option directly	Command-first letter of option, or only the letter if only buttons are present	

Commands

See the table in Appendix E, "Word's Preset Defaults," for a table describing the key icons used in the following table.

Command name	Meaning, menu	Standard keyboard	Keypad	Extended keyboard
About Microsoft Word	Identifies version of Word and provides access to online help.			
Activate Keyboard Menus	Activates menu bar so that you can choose menu commands using keys.			
		⌘⇥	▦.	
Add to Menu	Adds the selected command to its predefined "home" menu. Mouse pointer changes to +.			
		⌘⌥= or ⌘⇧⌥=		
Assign to Key	Assigns a key combination to a command. Mouse pointer changes to ⌘.			
		⌘⌥←	⌘⌥▦+	
Background Repagination	Toggles option to automatically repaginate a document during pauses in typing and editing.			
Cancel	Stops current command action.			
		⌘.	⌧	
Close	Closes active document.			
	File	⌘W		
Commands...	Creates and opens customized keyboard and menu configurations.			
	Edit			
Context Sensitive Help	Displays Help information for open command dialog box or a command you subsequently select from a menu.			
		⌘/		help
Delete...	Deletes an unopened document.			
	File			
Fast Save Enabled	Toggles option to save a file more quickly but with less efficient use of memory.			
Find Again	Repeats search for text or format you specified when you last chose Find or Find Formats command.			
	Utilities	⌘⌥A		
Find...	Searches for text and/or special characters.			
	Utilities	⌘F		
Go Back	Displays previous selection or returns insertion point to its previous position.			
	Utilities	⌘⌥Z	▦0	
Go To...	Displays indicated page if document has been paginated.			
	Utilities	⌘G		

Command name	Meaning, menu	Standard keyboard	Keypad	Extended keyboard
Help…	Displays list of online Help topics.			
	Window			
Hide ¶	Toggles display of Word's normally invisible characters, such as spaces, tabs, and paragraph marks. If the characters aren't visible, the command reads *Show ¶* and appears in the list box after Show Text Boundaries.			
		⌘R		
List All Fonts	Lists all installed fonts on Font menu.			
Load File into Memory	Toggles option to load as much as possible of open file into memory for current session.			
Load Program into Memory	Toggles option to load as much as possible of Word program into memory for current session.			
Make Backup Files	Turns on and off the option to make a backup copy of a saved document.			
More Keyboard Prefix	Amplifies extent of subsequent keyboard action; e.g., right arrow key moves to next paragraph instead of next character.			
		⌘⌥'		
Move Down One Text Area	Moves insertion point to text area below text area containing insertion point (in Page View) or to cell below cell containing insertion point (within a table).			
			⌘⌥⌨2	
Move Left One Text Area	Moves insertion point to text area left of text area containing insertion point (in Page View) or to cell at left of cell containing insertion point (within a table).			
			⌘⌥⌨4	
Move Right One Text Area	Moves insertion point to text area right of text area containing insertion point (in Page View) or to cell at right of cell containing insertion point (within a table).			
			⌘⌥⌨6	
Move to Bottom of Window	Places insertion point after last character visible in window.			
				end
Move to End of Document	Places insertion point after last character in document.			
			⌘⌨3	⌘*end*
Move to End of Line	Moves insertion point to end of current line.			
			⌨1	
Move to First Text Area	Moves insertion point to first text area visible in window (in Page View) or to first cell visible in window (within a table).			
			⌘⌥⌨7	
Move to Last Text Area	Moves insertion point to last text area visible in window (in Page View) or to last cell visible in window (within a table).			
			⌘⌥⌨1	

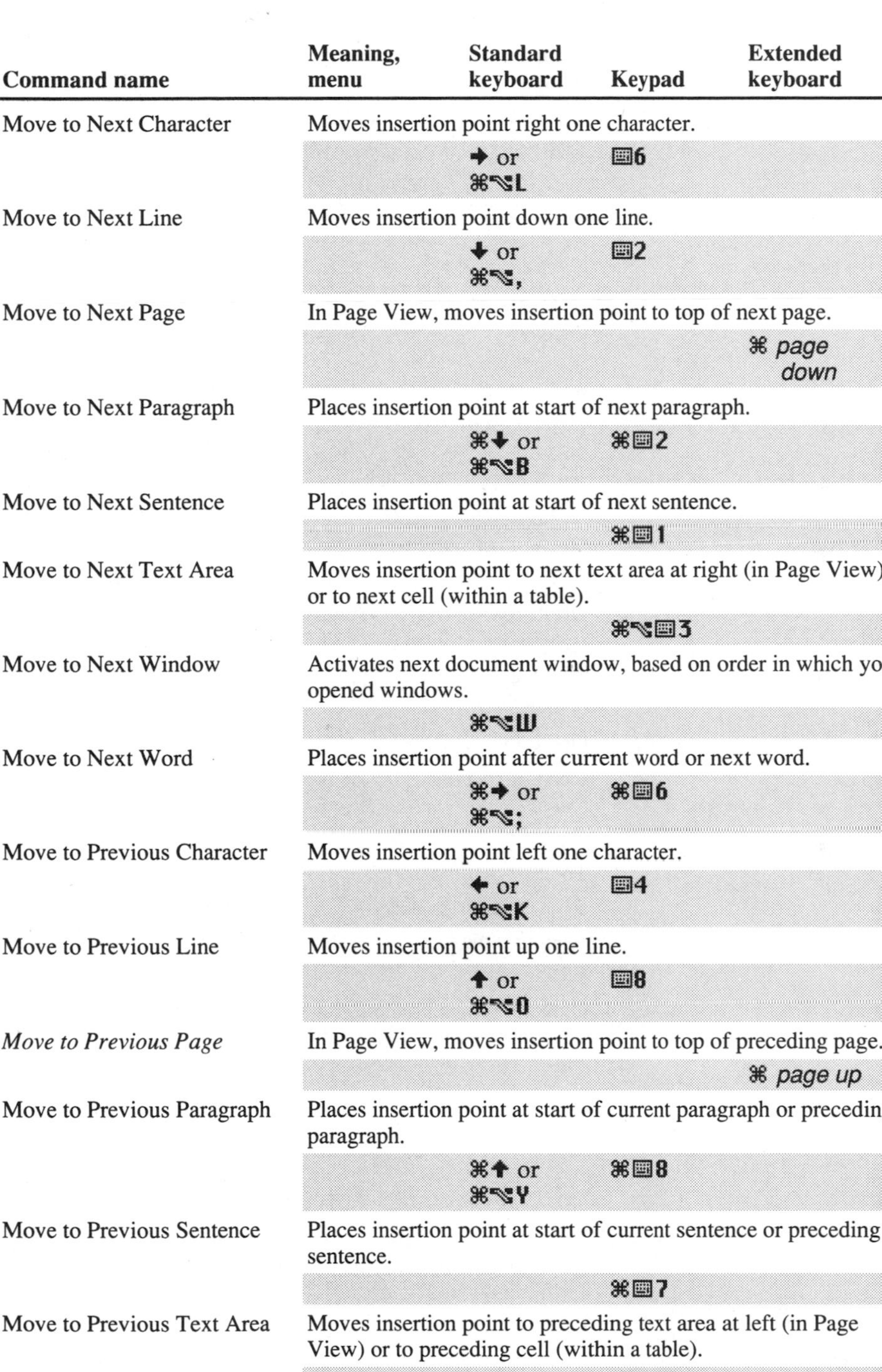

Command name	Meaning, menu	Standard keyboard	Keypad	Extended keyboard
Move to Next Character	Moves insertion point right one character.	→ or ⌘⌥L	▤6	
Move to Next Line	Moves insertion point down one line.	↓ or ⌘⌥,	▤2	
Move to Next Page	In Page View, moves insertion point to top of next page.			⌘ *page down*
Move to Next Paragraph	Places insertion point at start of next paragraph.	⌘↓ or ⌘⌥B	⌘▤2	
Move to Next Sentence	Places insertion point at start of next sentence.		⌘▤1	
Move to Next Text Area	Moves insertion point to next text area at right (in Page View) or to next cell (within a table).		⌘⌥▤3	
Move to Next Window	Activates next document window, based on order in which you opened windows.	⌘⌥W		
Move to Next Word	Places insertion point after current word or next word.	⌘→ or ⌘⌥;	⌘▤6	
Move to Previous Character	Moves insertion point left one character.	← or ⌘⌥K	▤4	
Move to Previous Line	Moves insertion point up one line.	↑ or ⌘⌥O	▤8	
Move to Previous Page	In Page View, moves insertion point to top of preceding page.			⌘ *page up*
Move to Previous Paragraph	Places insertion point at start of current paragraph or preceding paragraph.	⌘↑ or ⌘⌥Y	⌘▤8	
Move to Previous Sentence	Places insertion point at start of current sentence or preceding sentence.		⌘▤7	
Move to Previous Text Area	Moves insertion point to preceding text area at left (in Page View) or to preceding cell (within a table).		⌘⌥▤9	

Command name	Meaning, menu	Standard keyboard	Keypad	Extended keyboard
Move to Previous Word	Places insertion point before current or preceding word.			
		⌘← or ⌘⌥J	⌘▦4	
Move to Start of Document	Places insertion point before first character in document.			
			⌘▦9	⌘*home*
Move to Start of Line	Moves insertion point to beginning of current line.			
			▦7	
Move to Top of Window	Places insertion point before first character visible in window.			
			⌘▦5	*home*
Move Up One Text Area	Moves insertion point to text area above text area containing insertion point (in Page View) or to cell above cell containing insertion point (within a table).			
			⌘⌥▦8	
New	Opens a new untitled document.			
	File	⌘N		F5
New Window	Opens a new window for active document.			
	Window			⇧F5
Open Documents in Page View	Toggles option to open documents in Page View rather than Galley View.			
Open File Name:	Opens indicated document.			
Open…	Opens a document. Dialog box lists all Word files and files in formats recognized by Word.			
	File	⌘O		F6
Page View	Toggles Page View.			
	Document	⌘B		F13
Preferences…	Brings up the Preferences dialog box.			
	Edit			
Quit	Quits Word and prompts you to save changes to open documents, glossaries, and dictionaries.			
	File	⌘Q		
Remove From Menu	Removes a selected command from a menu. Mouse pointer changes to ▬.			
		⌘⌥-		
Save	Saves active document under its current name.			
	File	⌘S		F7
Save As…	Renames document, saves it in a different format, or saves it in a different drive or folder.			
	File		⇧F7	
Screen Test	Displays graphics to test display monitor. Click the mouse to stop.			

Command name	Meaning, menu	Standard keyboard	Keypad	Extended keyboard
Scroll Line Down	Scrolls first line in window out of view, displaying one more line at bottom of window.			
		⌘⌥/	▦*	
Scroll Line Up	Scrolls last line in window out of view, displaying one more line at top of window.			
		⌘⌥[	▦+	
Scroll Screen Down	Displays next screenful (based on window size) of document.			
		⌘⌥.	▦3	*page down*
Scroll Screen Up	Displays preceding screenful (based on window size) of document.			
		⌘⌥P	▦9	*page up*
Select Whole Document	Selects entire document. Same as pressing the Command key while clicking in the selection bar.			
		⌘⌥M		
Select Window:	Activates indicated document window.			
Short Menus	Switches between Full Menus and Short Menus.			
	Edit			
Show Clipboard	Displays contents of Clipboard.			
	Window			
Show Hidden Text	Toggles display of hidden text, indicated with a dotted underline.			
Show Menu Function Keys	Toggles display of extended keyboard function keys assigned to menu commands.			
Show Table Gridlines	Toggles display of nonprinting gridlines in a table.			
Show Text Boundaries	Toggles display of nonprinting boundary lines of text areas in Page View.			
Show ¶	Displays screen symbols such as ¶ (paragraph mark).			
	Edit	⌘Y		
Smart Quotes	Toggles option to use “ ” and ‘ ’ instead of " and ' when you press the standard quote key.			
Split Window	Splits active window.			
		⌘⌥S		
Undo	Reverses latest command action if possible.			
	Edit	⌘Z		F1
Use Picture Placeholders	Toggles display of gray rectangles in place of graphics.			
Zoom Window	Switches active window between its full size and an alternate size.			
		⌘⌥]		
---Separator---	Inserts a dashed line at bottom of selected menu (used to separate groups of commands).			

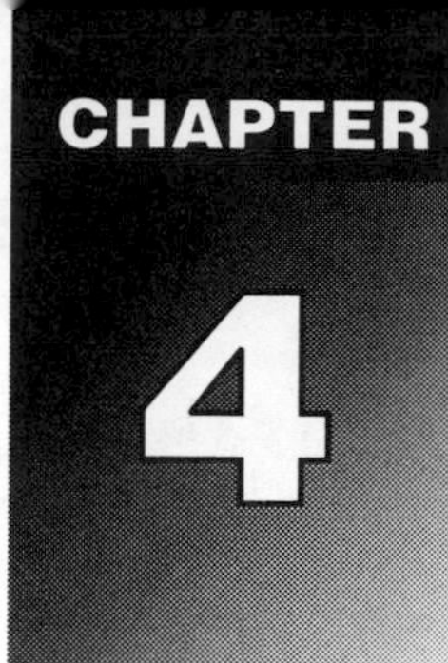

Organizing Through Outlining

Whether you're writing a business letter, preparing an important speech, or churning out a spy thriller, Word's built-in outlining feature can help you transform your thoughts into a complete, well-organized document. The feature serves not only as a planning aid—that is, as a means to create a conventional outline—but also as a powerful writing and editing tool. In fact, you can use it to reorganize an entire document, freely moving blocks of text with a few clicks of the mouse.

To enter Outline View, be sure that you are in Full Menus mode, and then choose Outlining from the Document menu. If you are starting a new document, the outline window is empty. If you already entered some text in Galley View or Page View, however, it appears in the window (although you might see only the first line of each paragraph). This occurs because Outline View presents a different view of the same document, not a different document. Thus, any change you make to an outline is reflected in the Galley View or Page View text, and vice versa.

■ *Creating and Manipulating Outline Text*

Across the top of the outline window, Word displays the Outline icon bar (shown in Figure 4-1), which contains the tools you use to work with outlines. Most menu commands are accessible in Outline View and operate the same as they do in Galley View and Page View, but the Footnote, Spelling, and Hyphenate commands, for example, are unavailable and dimmed. In Word 3, many commands on the Format and Font menus were also unavailable, but in Word 4 you can access them if the Show Formatting icon is selected in the Outline icon bar. Let's examine the function of each icon.

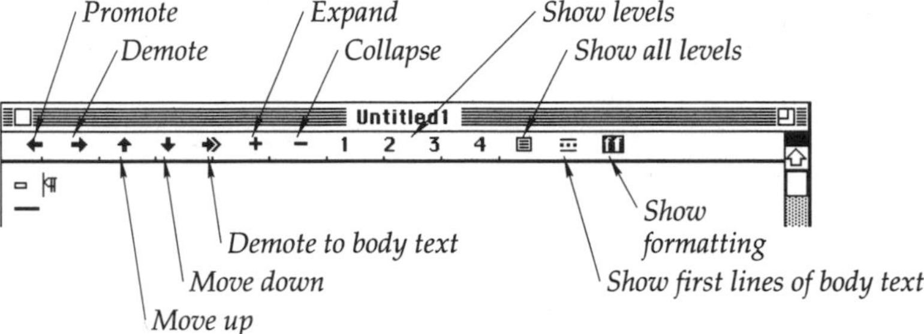

Figure 4-1
The Outline icon bar.

Setting Levels and Promoting and Demoting Headings

Like conventional outlines, Word outlines are organized by heading level, with each level distinguished from the others by the amount of indention. The main, or level 1, headings appear near the left margin; level 2 headings are indented one default tab stop (set in the Document dialog box) to the right; level 3 headings are indented an additional tab stop; and so on. Any paragraph that isn't a heading is called body text, is indented half a default tab stop to the right of its heading, and is preceded by a small square, as shown in Figure 4-2. Subtext is any text that falls under a heading, including subordinate headings and body text. Headings that have subtext are preceded by a plus sign; those that don't have subtext are preceded by a minus sign.

In typical Word 4 fashion, many ways exist to manipulate headings and body text in Outline View. As described in Chapter 2, to establish the level of a heading, you can select some text or start a new line and click the Promote icon (←) or the Demote icon (→). The left arrow "promotes" the heading to the next higher level; the right arrow "demotes" the heading to the next lower level. You can use the Promote and Demote icons before or after you enter headings or other text in the outline.

You can use the mouse in an intuitive way to drag a heading or body text paragraph to a new level or position in the document. If the pointer is over any of these icons, it becomes a four-headed arrow. You can drag the heading to the left to promote the heading, to the right to demote it, up to move the heading toward the beginning of the document, and down to move it toward the end of the document. If you click on a plus icon, all associated subtext becomes selected, too. If you hold down the Option key and click, only that heading becomes selected. When you drag the material to the left or right to change its level, the pointer changes to a pair of arrows pointing left and right, and Word draws a dotted vertical line at that heading level on the screen. Dragging the pointer and the line to the left, for example, promotes the headings in the selected material—when you release the mouse button, Word promotes the headings in the material, but leaves the body text as is.

If your keyboard has arrow keys, you can also establish heading levels by pressing the left or right arrow key. Don't try to establish levels by pressing the Tab key, however. As in Galley View, it simply inserts a tab character and indents the line to the next tab stop. This means that your heading will not be associated with the appropriate style. If you think that you may have absentmindedly used the Tab key in an outline, choose Show ¶ from the Edit menu to make the tab characters visible.

The current level is displayed in the status box in the lower left corner of the window, as illustrated in Figure 4-2, and names the style of the paragraph in the selected text. Once a level has been established, you can either type some text or edit text you already entered. If the text extends beyond one line, the characters on subsequent lines are indented when the text wraps. When you finish a heading, press the Return key; the heading then becomes a separate paragraph. The insertion point stays at the same heading level. If you want to change levels, simply click the Promote or Demote icon again.

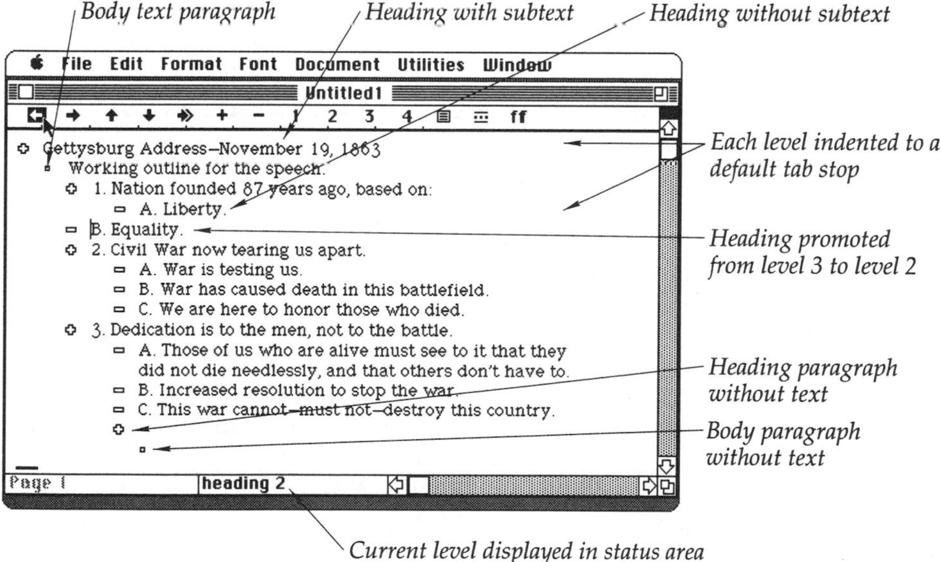

Figure 4-2
The outline window.

You insert new levels between existing ones the same way that you insert new paragraphs in Galley View. Click at the end of the line above where you want to insert the new line, and press the Return key. The space you open for the new entry has the same level as the heading above it, as shown in Figure 4-3. Click the icons or press the left or right arrow key to promote or demote the new heading.

Word's outlining feature is extremely flexible: You can enter headings and establish levels in a variety of ways. For example, you can enter all the level 1 headings first, without having to switch between level settings, and then go back and insert the level 2 headings. Or you can simply type in the entire outline and then establish levels afterward. To speed up the latter approach, you can promote or demote a number of adjacent headings at the same time, even if they are on different levels, by selecting them as a group and clicking the appropriate icon, or dragging them with the mouse. This shortcut is also handy if you want to make room for new levels or place existing headings under a newly created heading.

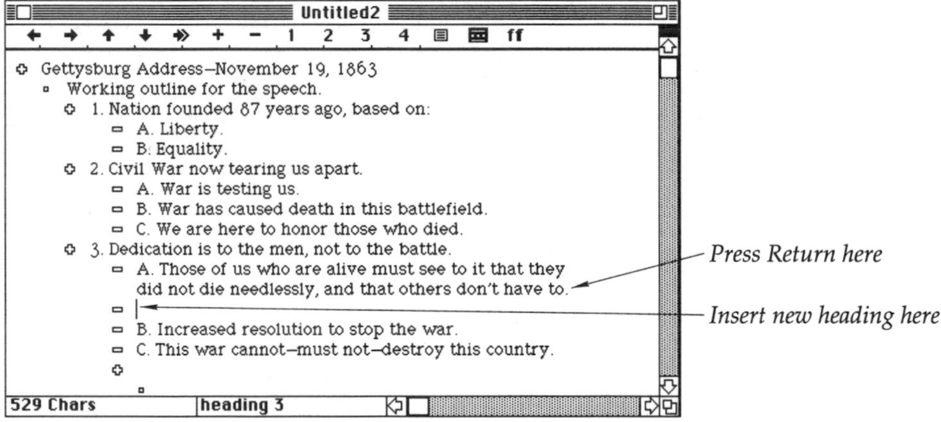

Figure 4-3
Inserting a new heading.

Moving Headings Up and Down ↑ ↓

The Move Up (↑) and Move Down (↓) icons in the Outline icon bar let you rearrange headings and the body text beneath them. Simply select the material you want to move, and click the appropriate icon. If you select two or more headings, they all move at once. If you select the first line of a paragraph of body text, the entire paragraph moves. The Move Up and Move Down icons do the same job as the Cut and Paste commands (which are also available in Outline View), but they do it more quickly. You can also use the up and down arrow keys if your keyboard has them.

You can move material within an outline in one of two ways: selecting by line or by heading. For either way, you can click the appropriate icon or use the arrow keys on the keyboard. You can also use the mouse to drag the selected material up a number of lines—when you do this, the pointer changes to a pair of arrows pointing up and down, and Word draws a dotted horizontal line across the screen. Dragging the pointer up moves the line up a heading at a time—when you release the mouse button, Word inserts the material there.

Selecting by Line

Suppose you want to reverse the order of two headings, neither of which has any subheadings or body text. You can accomplish this most easily with a technique called *line selection*. Simply click anywhere within the first heading and then click the Move Down icon (or click within the second heading and click the Move Up icon). For example, if you select heading 2 in the outline shown in Figure 4-3 and click the Move Down icon, the heading moves down one line, as shown in Figure 4-4. The level of the headings remains the same, even if the two headings you are reversing are on different levels.

You can also select single lines by clicking once in the selection bar next to the line to be moved or by holding down the Option key as you click the icon to the left of the line.

If you select two or more adjacent lines, you can move them as a group. (To select multiple lines, drag in the selection bar or drag over the lines themselves.) In Outline View, Word selects the entire heading, even when you click in the middle of it.

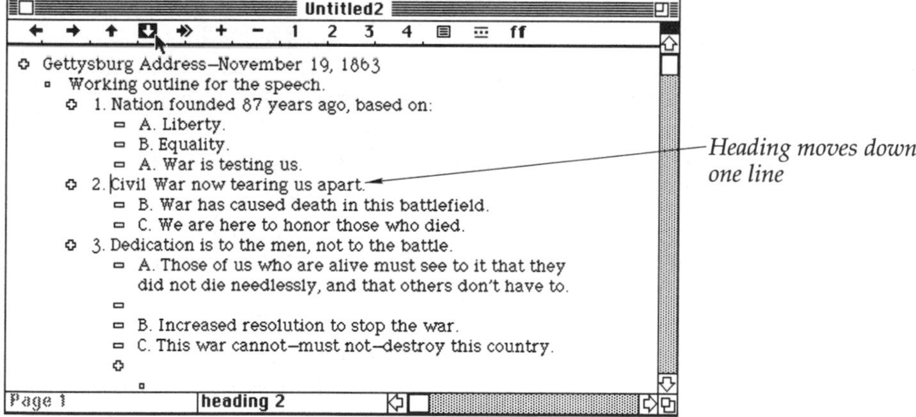

Figure 4-4
Moving a heading one line at a time.

Selecting by Heading

Moving selected lines one line at a time is useful for fine-tuning an outline, but often you'll want to rearrange your document more radically, for example, by placing all of part 3—the major heading, its subheadings, and all body text paragraphs—before part 2. You do this with a technique called *heading selection.*

To select a heading and all its associated subtext, double-click in the selection bar next to the heading, or simply click on the icon to the left of the line. Clicking the Move Up icon now moves the selected heading and its subtext up one line.

Demoting a Heading to Body Text ➾

Normally, the text you type in Outline View consists of headings of varying levels. Sometimes, however, you may want to enter a short paragraph of body text within an outline and format it in the *Normal* style, like regular text entered in Galley View. (In Outline View, *body text* is any paragraph that is not formatted as a heading; it is indented half a default tab stop to the right of its heading.) One method is to enter the text as an outline heading (level 1 for maximum line length), and then select anywhere within the text and click the Demote to Body Text icon (➾). To continue entering headings, simply start a new line and click the Promote or Demote icon.

You can also change body text to an outline heading by selecting anywhere within the text and clicking the Promote or Demote icon or by dragging the icon of the body text to the desired level in the outline.

Collapsing and Expanding Subtext + –

Word lets you collapse and expand the subtext under a heading so that you can view only what you want to see. There are two ways to do this. The first way is to collapse all the text under the heading. When you either double-click the heading's icon or click in the selection bar to the left of the heading and click the Collapse icon (–), the material underneath disappears. A dotted line appears under a collapsed heading to indicate the hidden material. The Expand icon (+) does the reverse: When you select a heading in the same way and click the Expand icon, the subtext reappears. Or double-click the heading's icon again.

The second way is to collapse successive levels of body text and headings; only the body text paragraphs first, then the lowest level of subheadings, and so on, until only the main heading remains. To do this, either click the heading's icon once or place the insertion point within it, then click the Collapse icon once for every level you want to collapse.

Word does not print collapsed text, so if you want to print the entire outline, be sure all levels are expanded. If you do print an outline with some text collapsed, the dotted line representing collapsed text does not appear in the printed version.

TIP

Moving a Main Heading by Collapsing and Moving It
In addition to the heading-selection method described above, you can also move a main heading along with all its subtext by selecting the main heading, clicking the Collapse icon, and then clicking the Move Up or Move Down icon. Word treats the heading and its subtext as one group.

Showing Specific Levels 1 2 3 4

The Expand and Collapse icons work on only those headings you've selected; the number icons, on the other hand, collapse and expand one or more heading levels for the entire outline. For example, if you click the number 2 in the icon bar, the outline displays levels 1 and 2; any higher numbered levels are collapsed. (See Figure 4-5.) When you use the number icons, regular text paragraphs are always collapsed, so if you want to see all heading levels without body text, simply choose an icon number higher than the number of heading levels in your outline. And because Word does not print collapsed levels, you can use the number icons to create a simplified outline for distribution to others while maintaining a complete version for your own use. (An alternative is to extract a table of contents from the outline, a subject covered in more detail in Chapter 15, "Creating a Table of Contents and Index.")

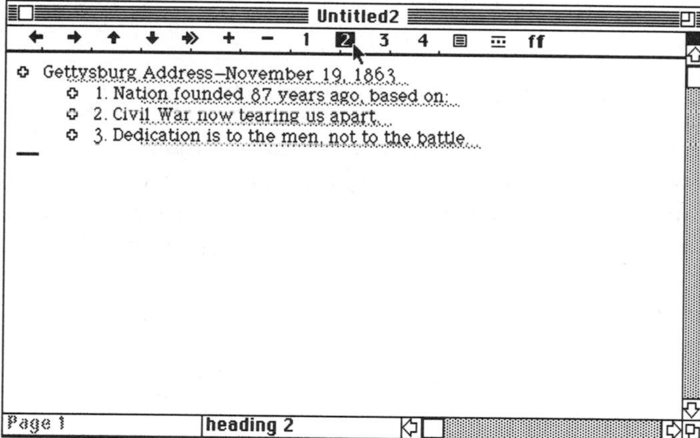

Figure 4-5
Headings collapsed by clicking the 2 icon.

The Outline icon bar in Word 4 has level icons only up to level 4. To display levels 5 through 9, you can press Option-Command-T and enter the number of the level you want to display. For example, to display heading levels 1 through 5, press Option-Command-T. The word *Outline* appears in the status area. When you press the number 5 on the keyboard, Word expands or collapses the outline to that level. You could also use the

Commands command to add the desired Show Level command to a menu of your choice. (The default is the Document menu.) Or you can assign your own key sequence to the command, such as Command-5 for displaying through heading level 5. Chapter 3, "The Word Environment," describes how to use the Commands dialog box.

Showing All Text ▤

The Show All icon (▤) to the right of the number icons works like a switch. Click it once to collapse only the body text while displaying all heading levels. As with collapsed levels, collapsed body text is indicated by a dotted line on the screen. You can click it again to display all heading levels and the body text.

Showing Body Text

Normally, Word displays only the first line of each body text paragraph. If the body text is longer than one line, an ellipsis (...) appears at the end of the line. If you want to expand all body text paragraphs to their fullest extent, simply click the Show Body Text icon ( ). Word highlights the icon. Click the Show Body Text icon again to collapse body text paragraphs to their first lines.

Displaying the Character Formats of Headings **ff**

It's often helpful to see the formats of the headings in an outline as they appear in Galley View. Click the Show Heading Formats icon (**ff**) to see the formats; click again to remove the formats. This function displays only the character formats—if the paragraph formats were displayed, the logical structure of the outline might well become unrecognizable.

TIP

Changing the Format of Headings in a Document
In Outline View, text is normally shown in either the character formats for the *Normal* style or the character formats for the styles assigned to each paragraph. Clicking the Show Formats icon toggles the display of these character formats. The look produced by the default definitions for the *heading* styles becomes visible when you go to Galley View or Page View, where you see that the *heading* styles are approximately the same as the *Normal* style, except that they call for the Helvetica font, boldface, and add a little space before each heading. See Appendix E, "Word's Preset Defaults," for the preset definitions of the *heading* and other automatic styles.

To change a *heading* style, you can go through the text and format each instance manually, but it is far easier to change the format of all instances of each style by using style sheets. Simply choose Define Styles from the Format menu, click on the name of the *heading* style you want to change, then choose the formats you want from the appropriate menus, and click Define and Cancel, as you learned in Chapter 2. See Chapter 10, "Working with Style Sheets," for a thorough discussion of this topic.

■ *Numbering*

You can use the Renumber command from the Utilities menu to number or renumber an outline of up to nine levels. The command affects all selected headings; if no text is selected, Word renumbers the entire document. To select all the outline except its title—which you probably don't want to number—use the Shift-click method: Click at the beginning of the desired selection and, while holding down the Shift key, click at the end.

Once the headings are selected, choose the Renumber command; the dialog box shown in Figure 4-6 appears. Click the All button beside the Paragraphs label. The Start At field probably contains a 1. If it doesn't, the first paragraph selected will start with a number other than 1. If you want to start at a number other than what Word proposes, simply select the contents of the field and enter the number.

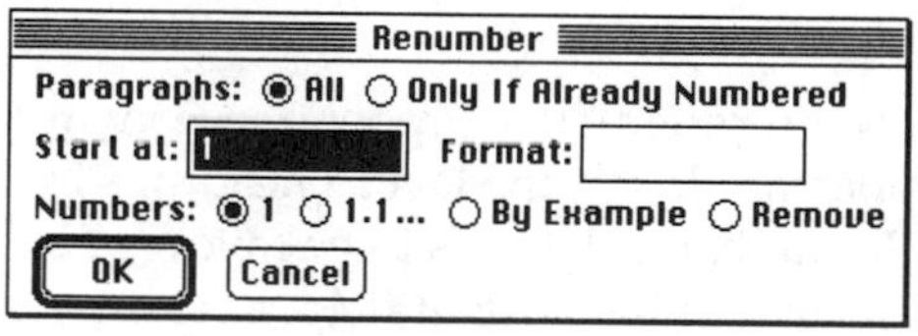

Renumber
Paragraphs: ◉ All ○ Only If Already Numbered
Start at: 1 Format:
Numbers: ◉ 1 ○ 1.1... ○ By Example ○ Remove
OK Cancel

Figure 4-6
The Renumber dialog box.

Unless you specify otherwise, Word numbers each level starting with numeral 1. The numbering is repeated for each set of levels, producing a result like that shown in Figure 4-7 on the following page. (If you want to try this with the sample outline we've used in this chapter, remove all the numbers first.)

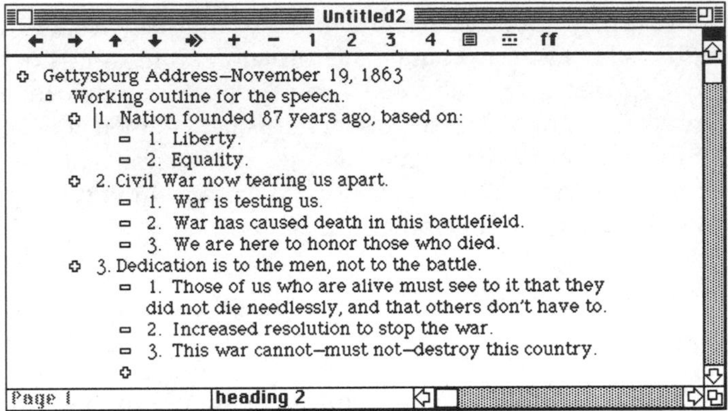

Figure 4-7
Portion of a numbered outline.

Word provides a large range of numbering formats. In addition to Arabic numerals, you can use uppercase or lowercase Roman numerals, uppercase or lowercase letters, or any combination of these. Furthermore, you can follow the numbers or letters with a period, comma, parenthesis, or any other nonalphanumeric character.

For example, suppose you wanted to number a five-level outline using this standard format:

I.A.1.a.i.

That is, the level 1 headings are to be preceded by an uppercase Roman numeral, the level 2 headings by an uppercase letter, the level 3 headings by an Arabic numeral, and so on; and each number or letter is to be followed by a period. You would enter the desired format in the Format field, as shown in Figure 4-8a, and click OK. The resulting outline would resemble Figure 4-8b.

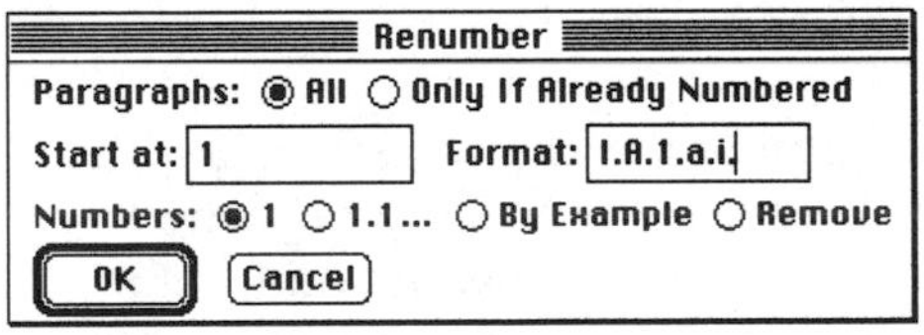

Renumber
Paragraphs: (•) All ( ) Only If Already Numbered
Start at: 1 Format: I.A.1.a.i.
Numbers: (•) 1 ( ) 1.1... ( ) By Example ( ) Remove
OK Cancel

Figure 4-8a
A numbering style specified in the Format field.

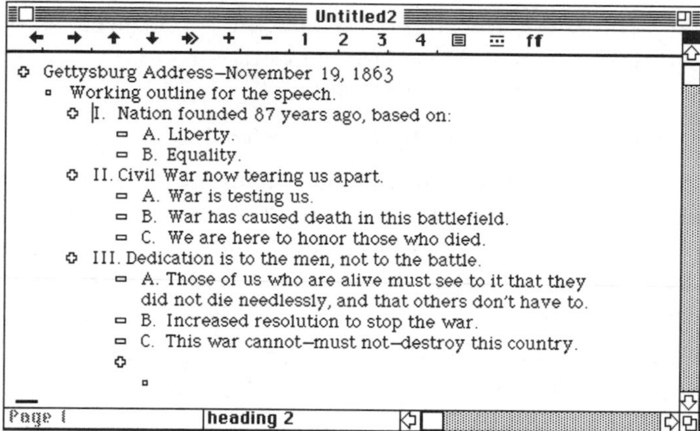

Figure 4-8b
The result after renumbering.

To have each heading reflect both its own level and the levels above it, select the 1.1 option in the Numbers field. In the outline shown in Figure 4-8b, for example, this option would cause the B section of part I to be numbered *I.B.* instead of merely *B.*

Whether you use the 1.1 option or the 1 option, you can easily rearrange and then renumber headings by repeating the numbering process. Simply select the affected text, choose the Renumber command, specify the number format, and click OK.

As you can see, the numbering function is not only flexible but easy to use. If you experiment further with the Renumber command, however, you'll find that it reveals some complexities and, occasionally, offers frustrations. For example, although you might never use this information, it's interesting to know that you can have a character precede as well as follow your outline numbers. Word inserts a *starting character* before each entry if the first character you enter in the Format field is nonalphanumeric—a parenthesis, for example. Such a character is optional, as is an *ending character* such as the last period in the Format field of Figure 4-8a. But beware: If you dispense with an ending character—a period, for example—no period will appear after Arabic numerals in your outline, but one will still follow all letters and Roman numerals. Word does this to prevent confusion in a case such as the following:

A A New Way to Number Outlines

A word of warning: The Renumber command sometimes produces results that initially surprise you. Simply experiment until you get the look you want. A few more instructions and tips follow:

- The Start At option works only for the first heading level.
- To create an alphabetical sequence, starting with a letter other than *A*, use the letter's corresponding number in the Start At field and either the *A* or *a* format in the Format field. For example, to start the numbering with D-1, enter *4-1* in the Start At field and *A-1* in the Format field. Roman numbering works similarly.
- To remove outline numbering, double-click the Remove option in the Renumber dialog box. Double-clicking any of the radio buttons is the same as selecting it and clicking OK.
- If you change the order of part of the outline after numbering it, select the text and the first heading level above it that still has correct numbering. When you choose the Renumber command, the By Example option is selected, and the Start At field displays the number of the first selected paragraph. Word assumes that you want to use the numbering format of the first paragraph you selected unless you specify otherwise.
- If you want to number only some headings in an outline, place a number (any number will do) beside those headings as you create the outline. When you are done, select the entire outline and click on the Only If Already Numbered option. Headings without numbers are skipped.
- If you follow the numbering format with a space, Word follows each number in the outline with a space instead of the customary tab character. However, first remove the numbering before using this format.
- You can change the numbering manually and then use the Sort command from the Document menu to reorder your outline. (See Chapter 11, "Formatting Tables and Lists," for more information on the Sort command.)
- You can use the Renumber command on any set of paragraphs, not only outlines. Lawyers use this feature, but prefer the Line Numbering paragraph format, which permits numbering every line in a paragraph. The Line Numbering format is discussed in Chapter 9, "Paragraph Formatting," and in Chapter 12, "Section Formatting."

■ *Using Outlining as an Editing Tool*

You can use Word's outlining feature as an editing tool in two ways. First, you can navigate in a document very easily in Outline View—much more easily than by scrolling manually or by searching for key words in Galley View. Second, you can rearrange large sections of text more efficiently with outlining icons than with the Cut and Paste commands.

Navigating with Outline View

In Word, you can manually scroll through a document to find what you're looking for, you can use the Find command to look for key words, or you can use the Go To command from the Search menu to go to a specific page. None of these methods can take you directly to the beginning of a section of text, but the outlining feature can, through a method called *synchronized scrolling*. The procedure is simple. Display the document in Outline View, and then click in the vertical scroll bar until the heading you want is the topmost line in the window. Now return to Galley View. That heading appears at the top of the window.

Synchronized scrolling works even better when you split a window into two panes with one pane in Outline View and the other in Galley View. Starting in Outline View, for example, divide the window by dragging down the solid black bar (the split bar) at the top of the scroll bar. Then click in one pane, and press Command-U to switch to Galley View. Now scroll a bit through the pane containing the outline; the topmost heading in the Galley View pane changes as you scroll. This synchronization makes it easy to work on the structure of a document in one pane and on the body text in the other. To remove the split from the window, drag the split bar to the top or bottom of the window; the bottom pane takes over the window. (See Chapter 3, "The Word Environment," for more information on split-screen techniques.)

Moving Paragraphs

You've already seen how to use the Move Up and Move Down icons to move headings around in an outline. You can also use this feature to move entire paragraphs within a document without having to carefully select text, cut it out, set a new insertion point, and paste it in again. Simply select the paragraphs and click the appropriate icon. (See Figure 4-9.) When you return to Galley View, you see that all characters in the selected text are transported, including blank lines and forced page breaks. You can remove these if they adversely affect the layout of the document.

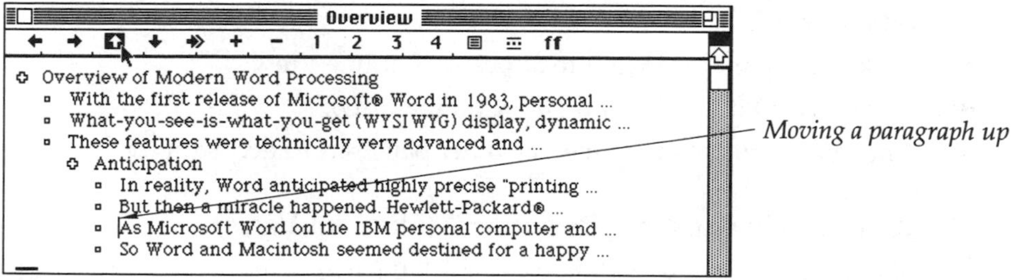

Figure 4-9
Moving a paragraph within an outline.

Points to Remember

- In Outline View, any change to the outline changes the document itself.
- Outlines can contain two kinds of paragraphs: headings, which are assigned styles *heading 1* through *heading 9*, and body text, which is any other style of paragraph. The subtext of a heading consists of all the subordinate headings and body text under that heading.
- The way in which you select a heading determines how the Move Up and Move Down icons work. If you double-click in the selection bar, the icons move the selected heading and its associated subtext up or down one line. With line selection, the icons simply move the selected block up or down one paragraph.
- The way in which you select a heading also determines how the Expand and Collapse icons work. If you click in the selection bar or otherwise select the entire heading , the icons collapse or expand all the subtext at once. If instead you select only part of the heading or merely set the insertion point somewhere in it, each click on the icons collapses or expands one subheading level at a time.

Techniques

See "Mouse and Keyboard Shortcuts" later in this summary for an overview of the icons in the Outline icon bar.

Scroll to a specific section (synchronized scrolling in one pane)

1. Enter Outline View.
2. Scroll until the section you want to see is at the top of the window.
3. Return to Galley View.

Show Outline View in one pane and Galley View in the other

1. Drag down the split bar (the black bar at the top of the vertical scroll bar) as far as you want.
2. Click in the pane you want to appear in Outline View.
3. Choose the Outlining command (Command-U).
4. When you scroll in one pane, the other pane scrolls accordingly.

Select a heading and all its subtext (Outline View)

1. Double-click in the selection bar, or click the icon that precedes the heading.

Promote or demote a group of adjacent headings

1. Select the block to be affected and click the appropriate icon.

Promote body text to a heading

1. Select the paragraph to be promoted and click the Promote icon, or drag its icon to the heading level you want.

Move a heading and its subtext, or a body paragraph, up or down

1. Select the entire heading by double-clicking in the selection bar to the left of the heading, or click the heading's icon.
2. Click the Move Up or Move Down icon, or drag the selected material to the new location.

Or,

1. Collapse all levels beneath the level of the heading you want to move.
2. Select the heading and click the Move Up or Move Down icon, or drag the collapsed material to the new location.

Print a simplified outline

1. Collapse the outline to show only the heading levels you want to print.
2. Choose Print from the File menu.

Number or renumber an outline

1. Select the text to be renumbered. (If none is selected, the command affects the entire document.)
2. Choose Renumber from the Document menu.
3. Specify the options you want to use.

   The 1.1 option precedes the number for a heading with the numbers of the headings above it (for example, *1.2.1.*).

   The By Example option causes Word to use the numbering format of the first selected paragraph.
4. Click OK.

Specify a numbering format

1. Unless you indicate otherwise, Word uses Arabic numerals followed by periods.
2. Enter the format you want to use in the Format field of the Renumber dialog box (for example, *I.A.i.*).

Remove outline numbering

1. Click Remove in the Renumber dialog box.
2. Click OK.

■ *Mouse and Keyboard Shortcuts*

In Outline View, as in Galley View, the keypad keys are available for moving the insertion point.

To	Mouse click	Keyboard press	Keypad press
Promote heading	←	left arrow	
Demote heading	→	right arrow	
Move heading up	↑	up arrow	
Move heading down	↓	down arrow	
Demote heading to body text	⇛	Command-right arrow	
Collapse next lower heading or text	−		–
Expand subtext	+		+
Collapse selected heading			Command- –
Expand selected heading			Command- +
Display up to level 4	1 2 3...		
Display levels 5 through 9		Option-Command-T, then the number.	
Display all levels and body text (toggles)	▤		*
Display all lines in body text	⋯		=
Display character formats of headings	ff		/

To manipulate the outline while in Galley View or Page View, press Option-Command-T and then press the key(s) indicated below:

To	Keyboard press	Keypad press
Promote heading	left arrow or K	4
Demote heading	right arrow or L	6
Move heading up	up arrow	8
Move heading down	down arrow	2
Demote heading to body text	Command-right arrow	

Commands

Command name	Meaning, menu	Standard keyboard	Keypad	Extended keyboard
Collapse Selection	In Outline View, hides selected outline headings and/or body text regardless of heading level.			
Collapse Subtext	In Outline View, hides all subordinate levels or the next higher level subordinate to the selected outline heading, depending on whether the entire heading is selected.			
Demote Heading	Lowers selected heading paragraph to next lower outline level.			
Expand Subtext	In Outline View, displays all subordinate levels or the next lower level subordinate to the selected outline heading, depending on whether the entire heading is selected.			
Make Body Text	Makes selected paragraph the body text of preceding outline heading.			
Move Heading Down	Moves selected outline heading or body text below next visible paragraph in outline.			
Move Heading Up	Moves selected outline heading or body text above preceding visible paragraph in outline.			
Outline Command Prefix	Sets the prefix enabling you to promote, demote, and move outline paragraphs in Galley View or Page View by pressing a key.			
		⌘⌥T		
Outlining	Toggles Outline View.			
	Document	⌘U		⇧F13
Promote Heading	Raises selected heading paragraph to next higher outline level.			
Renumber…	Automatically numbers or renumbers selected paragraphs in specified sequence.			
	Utilities			⌘F15
Show All Headings	In Outline View, displays headings of all levels and body text.			
Show Heading 1	In Outline View, displays only heading level 1.			
Show Heading 2	In Outline View, displays only heading levels 1 and 2.			
Show Heading 3	In Outline View, displays only heading levels 1–3.			
Show Heading 4	In Outline View, displays only heading levels 1–4.			
Show Heading 5	In Outline View, displays only heading levels 1–5.			
Show Heading 6	In Outline View, displays only heading levels 1–6.			
Show Heading 7	In Outline View, displays only heading levels 1–7.			

(continued)

Command name	Meaning, menu	Standard keyboard	Keypad	Extended keyboard
Show Heading 8	In Outline View, displays only heading levels 1–8.			
Show Heading 9	In Outline View, displays heading levels 1–9.			
Show/Hide Body Text	In Outline View, switches between display of all body text and first line only.			
Show/Hide Formatting	In Outline View, turns on and off display of character formatting.			
Sort	Sorts entire document or selected paragraphs, columns, or lines in ascending order (A–Z or 1–9) according to leftmost character.			
	Utilities			
Sort Descending	Sorts entire document or selected paragraphs, columns, or lines in descending order (Z–A or 9–1) according to leftmost character.			

Writing and Editing Techniques

With Word, the process of writing, or entering text, is nearly indistinguishable from rewriting, or editing. Letters, words, and entire phrases can be added easily, deleted, or moved around, even during the initial writing stages. In this chapter, therefore, writing and editing are generally treated as one concept. Here, we'll examine in greater detail some of the features and techniques introduced in Chapters 1 and 2, and you'll cover some new ground. More specifically, you will learn about entering standard and special characters, selecting text you want to manipulate, moving text within a document, and finding and changing text.

■ *Discovering Word's True Characters*

On your Macintosh keyboard, you'll find represented the alphabetic, numeric, and punctuation characters that appear on a typewriter keyboard. However, Word supplies many characters that a typewriter, or even other word processors, don't. And some familiar characters work, in Word, in unfamiliar ways. This section provides a brief overview of some of the program's character features. For a thorough discussion of fonts, see Chapter 8, "Character Formatting."

Special Font Characters

Almost every Mac comes with several fonts, or typefaces, that comprise standard characters as well as some additional ones. To see the standard characters in a given font, choose the Key Caps desk accessory from the Apple menu and choose the font you want to see from the Key Caps menu in the menu bar. (See Figure 5-1. In Key Caps desk accessory versions before 3.0, you can view the Chicago font only.) To see the characters available with different key combinations, hold down the Shift key, the Option key, the Shift-Option combination, or the Control key on some keyboards. Each time you press one of these, the Key Caps keyboard displays the set of characters produced when you hold down that key and press the keys on the keyboard. When you type on the Mac keyboard or click on the Key Caps keyboard, text appears in the field above the keyboard. You can cut or copy the text to paste it into a Word document; the text is transferred, but not the font.

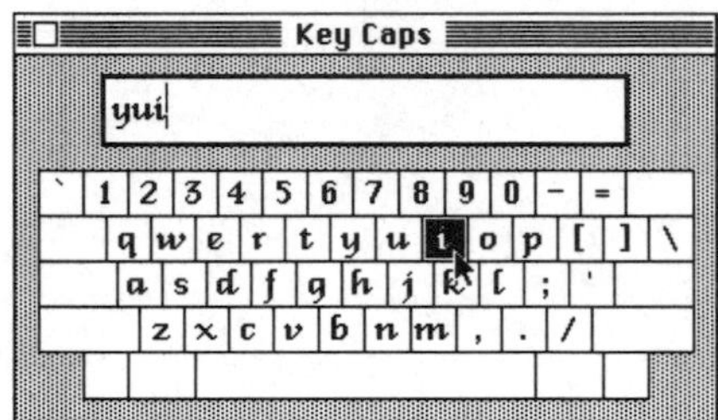

Figure 5-1
Key Caps with the Venice font.

Word is an international program that lets you add accent (diacritical) marks to characters by pressing the following key combinations. The accent is added to the next character typed; pressing the Option-key combination twice creates only the accent character.

Press	To get
Option-`	` (grave accent)
Option-e	´ (acute accent)
Option-i	^ (circumflex)
Option-n	~ (tilde)
Option-u	¨ (umlaut)

You can also buy fonts that have special zero-width characters. Typing one of these characters produces a symbol that overlays the next character typed—useful for creating obscure accented or combined letters. And you can use font-editor programs such as Fontographer from Altsys Corporation to make adjustments to one of Word's fonts. Unless the font editor supports the LaserWriter and PostScript, however, the font changes you make might not appear when you print the document on a PostScript printer.

Almost all fonts contain not only text characters but graphic characters as well. The chart in Figure 5-2 shows some of the characters found in common fonts. To see one example of a graphic character, press Shift-Option-` (grave accent); as the chart indicates, the current font and point size determine which character is entered. Use the Key Caps desk accessory to find the key sequences for other graphic characters, such as the bullet (•, Option-8) and the paragraph mark (¶, Option-7).

You can also use fonts containing nonalphabetic images such as Cairo, Taliesin, Symbol, and Zapf Dingbats. (The last two are high-resolution fonts that print well on the LaserWriter.) The Symbol font has a special significance: Word uses it to construct equations in its formula-translation feature. See Appendix D, "Mathematical Typesetting," for more information.

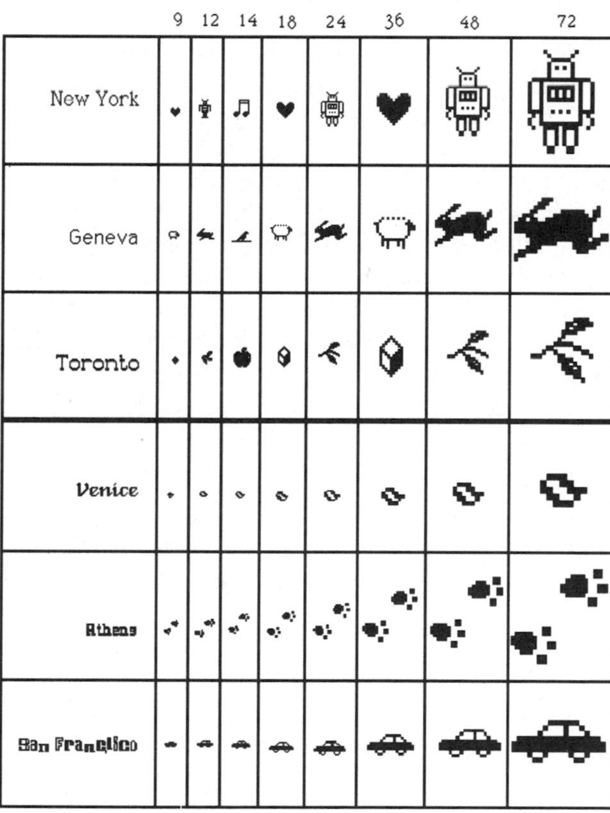

Figure 5-2
Some graphic characters available in Word fonts.

Hyphens, Dashes, and Spaces

Use hyphens to join words together, to make a compound word or phrase, such as *built-in* or *state-of-the-art*. When you press the hyphen key (located to the immediate right of the zero key), you create what is termed a *normal* hyphen. If a hyphenated word or phrase appears at the end of a line, Word may break (wordwrap) the line at the hyphen, like this:

built-
in

or this:

The new toy is a three-
wheeled cart.

If you then edit the text in a way that affects the wordwrap, Word rejoins the compound word on one line.

If you don't want Word to break a line at a hyphen, you can enter a required, or *nonbreaking*, hyphen by pressing Command- ~ (actually, the Command key and the ` key). If you want a word to be hyphenated only if it falls at the end of a line, enter an *optional* hyphen by pressing Command- - (the Command key and the hyphen key). Optional hyphens have no width and usually don't appear on the screen unless the word breaks at the end of the line. Word inserts optional hyphens when you choose Hyphenate from the Utilities menu. To display optional hyphens (whether inserted by you or by Word), choose Show ¶ from the Edit menu. Figure 5-3 shows the appearance of the three types of hyphens when Show ¶ is on. (For more information on hyphens and the Hyphenate command, see Chapter 14, "Document Formatting and Printing.")

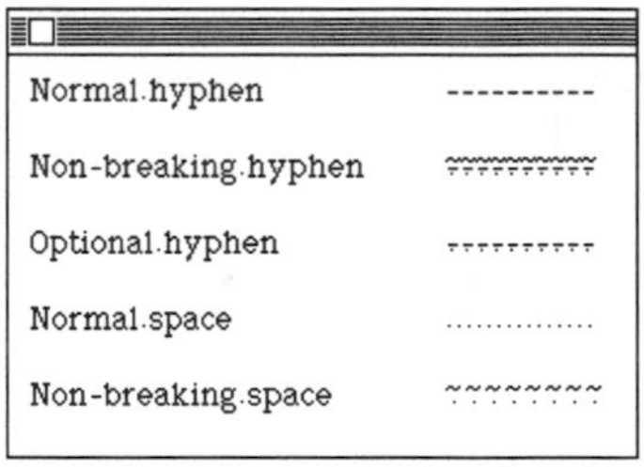

Normal·hyphen ----------
Non-breaking·hyphen
Optional·hyphen
Normal·space ....
Non-breaking·space

Figure 5-3
The three types of hyphens and two types of spaces.

Similar to hyphens are the less frequently used *en* (–) and *em* (—) dashes, created by pressing Option- - and Shift-Option- -. The em dash is the typesetter's equivalent of two hyphens—the common alternative—used when you want to indicate a break in thought, for example. The en dash, which is a bit wider than a hyphen, is used primarily with ranges of numbers, as in *1987–88* or *pp. 18–24*. The en dash is also used to join two terms when one of them consists of two separate words or a hyphenated word (for example, New York–based, first-in–first-out accounting). Word will break at these dashes if they occur at the end of a line.

With Word, as with a typewriter, pressing the Spacebar creates a blank space. In Word, however, this space is a nonprinting character, appearing as a small dot when Show ¶ is on. Actually, you can produce two kinds of spaces. When you press the Spacebar alone, you insert a *normal space*; Word understands that it can break a line at the space and that it can adjust the width of the space in justified paragraphs. When you press Option-Spacebar, Word inserts a *nonbreaking space,* at which it will not break the line (see Figure 5-3). You might use a nonbreaking space to keep compound words, names, or addresses on the same line. You can also insert this character after the numbers in a numbered list when you're using justified alignment. That way, when Word adjusts the width of the spaces within each line, the space after each number remains unchanged. Use this type of space judiciously; too many nonbreaking spaces will make the right edge of your text look very ragged or, if you are using justified alignment, will cause unacceptably wide spaces between words.

ASCII Codes and Characters

A little-known but useful feature of Word is its dual ability to report the ASCII code of any selected character in a document and to enter any character into a document when you type its ASCII code. ASCII—the American Standard Code for Information Interchange—assigns a number for every letter, number, punctuation mark, and symbol so that different computers and different programs on the same computer can (at least theoretically) read one another's text. The letter *A,* for instance, is assigned the code 65. A complete set of ASCII codes for some common fonts, including Symbol and Zapf Dingbats, is given in Appendix B.

You can find the ASCII code for any character by selecting the character and pressing Option-Command-Q. The code for that character appears in the status box in the lower left corner of the screen. If you type the ASCII code for a different character, the new code replaces the old in the status box; when you press the Return key, the new character replaces the old in text.

To enter a character without replacing another, place the insertion point where you want the character to appear and press Option-Command-Q. The word *Code* appears in the status box, and the character assigned to the number you type is entered in the document when you press the Return key. You can cancel this operation by pressing Command-(period) or by clicking in the window. Also, if you need to enter another character by its ASCII code, you can simply click in the status box without first pressing Option-Command-Q. The word *Code* appears again and you can then enter the ASCII code for the character.

■ *Basic Editing*

Of the basic actions required to enter and edit text, three of the most basic are creating paragraphs, backspacing to erase text, and selecting text before otherwise manipulating it. You practiced these actions in Chapters 1 and 2; this section gives you some additional information.

Creating Paragraphs

Pressing the Return (or Enter) key both completes a paragraph—leaving behind a paragraph mark, which is visible with Show ¶ on—and starts a new line and paragraph; this is called a *hard return*. Many of Word's formatting options, such as alignment and margins, apply to an entire paragraph; that is, the lines of text preceding the paragraph mark conform to the formatting options you chose for that paragraph. See Figure 5-4 for an example of this.

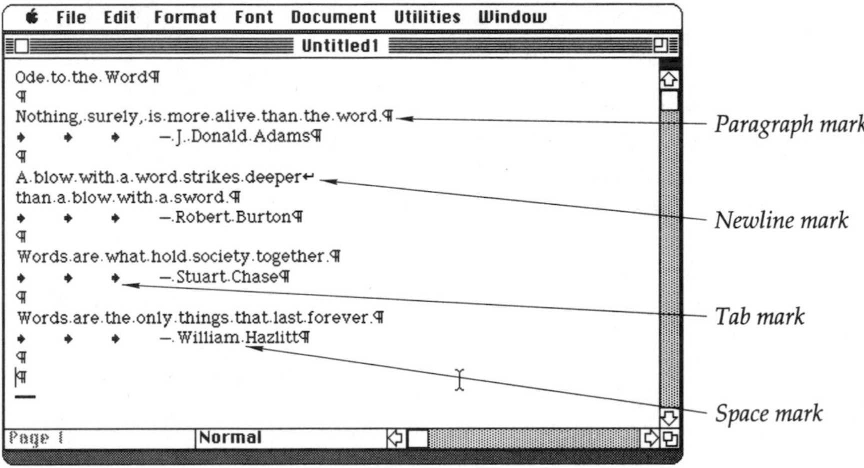

Figure 5-4
Sample text with formatting marks.

If you want to finish a line without starting a new paragraph, press Shift-Return to enter a *soft return*, also known as a *newline mark*. You can use soft returns when you want to handle a series of lines as one paragraph. The paragraph formatting commands then apply to all the lines.

Finally, if you want to end a paragraph but not move the insertion point to the new line, press Option-Command-Return. This action is useful if you want to break a paragraph in the middle and then start typing at the end of the first paragraph.

Backspacing over Text

As you've learned, pressing the Backspace key (or the Delete key) deletes the character to the immediate left of the insertion point. If you try to backspace from one paragraph to another that has a different format, however, Word beeps when you reach the paragraph mark and refuses to backspace over it. It does this to keep you from losing any formatting. To delete the paragraph mark, you must select it (by double-clicking on it as though it were a word—although you can also double-click to the right of the paragraph mark) and then press the Backspace key.

Selecting Text

In Word, as in most other Macintosh applications, you first select the text you want to manipulate, and then you specify what you want to do with it. Most word processors for other types of computers require you to work in reverse: Choose the action first and then select the text. The latter method isn't as intuitive, and it usually requires you to reselect the same text block again and again if you want to perform a number of actions on it. Word lets you select text in a variety of ways. Some of these ways call for you to click in the *selection bar*; this is an invisible strip that runs along the left edge of the document window. The pointer becomes a right-pointing arrow when it is in the selection bar.

To select	Do this
An insertion point	Click at the desired spot.
One or more characters	Drag over them.
A whole word	Double-click on the word.
One sentence	Press the Command key, and click anywhere in the sentence.
One line	Position the pointer in the selection bar next to the line, and click.
One paragraph	Double-click in the selection bar next to the paragraph.
A range of text	Position the pointer in the selection bar at one end of the section, and drag to the other end of the section. *or* Click at one end of the section; Shift-click at the other end of the section.
The entire document	Press Option-Command-M. *or* Position the pointer in the selection bar, and Command-click.
A column of text (also called *block selection*)	Press the Option key, and drag through the column. (See Figure 5-5, following.)

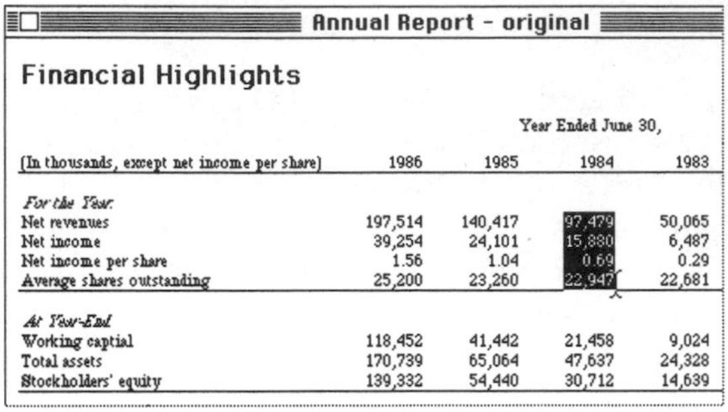

Annual Report - original

Financial Highlights

	Year Ended June 30,			
(In thousands, except net income per share)	1986	1985	1984	1983
For the Year:				
Net revenues	197,514	140,417	97,479	50,065
Net income	39,254	24,101	15,880	6,487
Net income per share	1.56	1.04	0.69	0.29
Average shares outstanding	25,200	23,260	22,947	22,681
At Year-End				
Working captial	118,452	41,442	21,458	9,024
Total assets	170,739	65,064	47,637	24,328
Stockholders' equity	139,332	54,440	30,712	14,639

Figure 5-5
Selecting a column of text.

There is also a huge variety of ways to use the keyboard to move the insertion point and select text. The commands and key sequences for effecting them can be found in tables at the end of this chapter and in Appendix E, "Word's Preset Defaults."

Shift-Clicking and Other Methods

Shift-clicking is one of the easiest ways to select text. You click once to set a starting point, or *anchor*, and then click again—this time holding down the Shift key—at a second point either before or after the anchor.

To see how this works, click within some text to set an anchor point, press the Shift key, click again at some other point (either before or after the anchor point), and then drag the mouse. Note that the selection is anchored where you first clicked the mouse button. When you release the mouse button after clicking the second time, the selection is set.

Another way to select text is a unit at a time. You can select text one word at a time by double-clicking on the first word and then dragging over the other words you want to select. Only whole words are added to the selection. If you press the Command key, click in a sentence, and then drag, the selection proceeds a sentence at a time. If you double-click in the selection bar and drag, you select one paragraph at a time, and clicking once in the selection bar and then dragging causes text to be selected one line at a time.

When you use this method, the unit selected becomes the anchor. For example, if you double-click in the selection bar and then drag, the entire paragraph you clicked in is always part of the selection, regardless of the direction in which you drag the mouse.

This technique can be very useful, but it can also be a bit frustrating if, for example, you are selecting paragraphs and then decide you want to end the selection in the middle of a paragraph. You won't be able to do it without deselecting the text and starting over using the Shift-click method.

Extending or Reducing a Selection

Once you have selected some text, you can extend or reduce the selection. The basic technique for doing this is to press the Shift key before you click. To extend the selection, move the pointer to the end of the text you want to add and Shift-click. To reduce the selection, move the pointer to the beginning of the text you want to deselect and Shift-click.

The original anchor that you set with your first mouse click is used as a reference point when you extend or reduce the selection. Thus, you can extend a selection in only one direction: the same direction as the original selection. If you try to extend it in the opposite direction, the text from the anchor to the new selection boundary will be selected, but text on the other side of the anchor will no longer be selected. Think of the selection as revolving around the anchor.

The unit of text that is added to or removed from the selection depends on the method you use to make the original selection. If you select text by dragging over it or by using the Shift-click method, you can Shift-click on a given character and extend or reduce the selection exactly to that character. If you double-click to select a word and then Shift-click in the middle of another word, the whole word will be added to the selection. Similarly, if you double-click in the selection bar to select a paragraph and then extend the selection by Shift-clicking in the middle of the next paragraph, the entire paragraph will be added. This also works for sentence and line selection.

■ *Copying and Moving Text*

Word gives you two ways to copy and move text. You can use the Cut, Copy, and Paste commands (all in the Edit menu), which use the Clipboard, or you can use the Copy To and Move To keyboard commands, which bypass the Clipboard. If you copied graphics into your document from another source, you can move or copy them with these commands; the procedure is the same as for text.

Both these methods let you move or copy text within a Word document or from one Word document to another. However, both files must be open if you want to use the Move To or Copy To command to transfer text between documents. This is not necessary with the Cut, Copy, and Paste commands.

It is also possible to use the Cut, Copy, and Paste commands to move or copy text to or from another Macintosh application, such as Microsoft Excel or Microsoft Works. This is discussed in Chapter 16, "Transferring Text and Graphics."

Using the Cut, Copy, and Paste Commands

To move or copy with the Edit menu commands:

1. Select the block of text to be cut or copied.
2. Choose Copy or Cut from the Edit menu.
3. Indicate a new location for the text by selecting an insertion point (in the current document or another document).
4. Choose the Paste command to enter the block at the insertion point. (See Figure 5-6.)

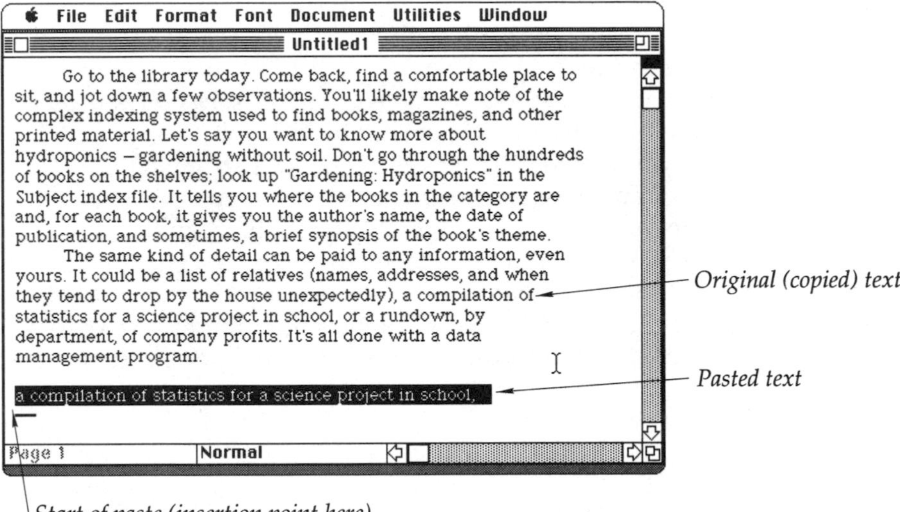

Figure 5-6
Pasted text.

Viewing the Clipboard

From time to time, it's helpful to view the contents of the Clipboard to see what you are pasting into the document. To do this, choose Show Clipboard from the Window menu. A short Clipboard window appears on the bottom of the screen. To see more of the window, enlarge it by dragging the title bar upward and then dragging the size box in the lower right corner until the window is the size you want, or expand it to full size by clicking in the zoom box in the upper right corner. Click in the close box when you are through.

Using the Move To and Copy To Keyboard Commands

Word includes two shortcut commands that bypass the Clipboard: the Move To and Copy To keyboard commands. In addition to saving time, these commands let you duplicate or relocate blocks of text without disturbing the contents of the Clipboard and work with large documents when free memory is scarce. To copy text:

1. Select the text you want to duplicate.
2. Press Option-Command-C. Note that the status box in the lower left corner of the window reads *Copy to.*
3. Scroll or move to the spot in the document where you want to copy the text block, and click. A dotted insertion point appears, as illustrated in Figure 5-7.
4. Press Return to copy the block. The original text block is unaffected.

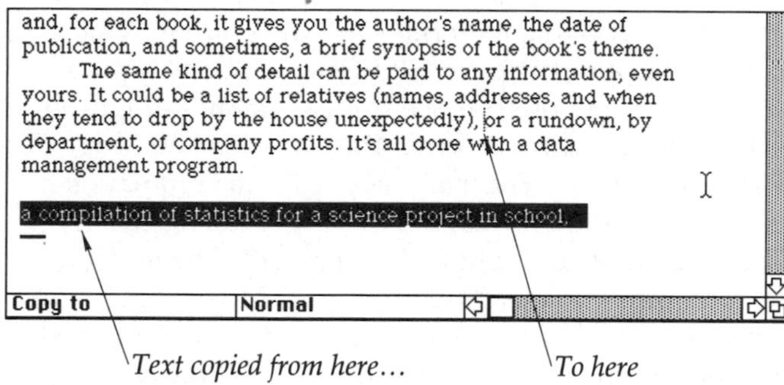

Figure 5-7
Copying text with the Copy To command.

If you change your mind or discover that you selected the wrong material, you can press Command-(period) to cancel the operation before you press Return. Also, instead of simply clicking an insertion point for the destination, you can select text for replacement using any of the methods described above. You'll see a dotted underscore rather than the normal highlight, and the selected text is replaced by the copied text.

The process of moving text is nearly identical:

1. Select the text you want to move.
2. Press Option-Command-X. Note that the status box reads *Move to.*
3. Scroll or move to the spot in the document where you want to move the text block, and click. A dotted insertion point appears. (See Figure 5-8 on the following page.)

❹ Press the Return key to move the block. The original text block is deleted and appears in the new location.

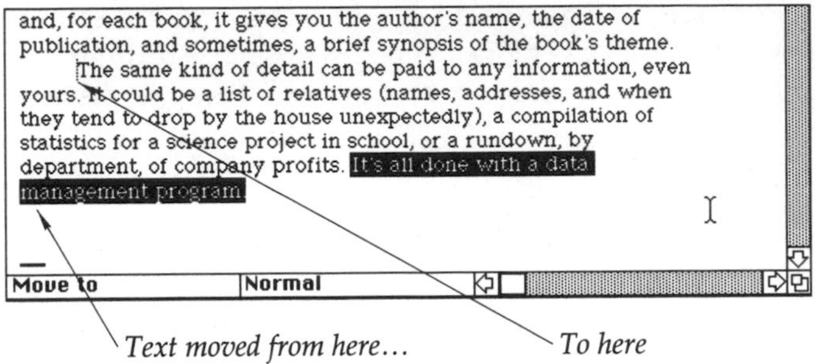

Figure 5-8
Moving text with the Move To command.

All this is fine for moving or copying material from the place in which you're working in a document to another place. But what if you're typing and suddenly decide to grab a phrase or sentence from a distant paragraph and enter it at the insertion point? It turns out that the Copy To and Move To commands magically become the Copy From and Move From commands if no text is selected when you issue the command. Simply set the insertion point and press Option-Command-C or Option-Command-X. The insertion point stops blinking, and the status box reads *Copy from* or *Move from*. Select the material you want to copy or move; as you do so, it will be underscored with a dotted line. Press the Return key after selecting the material to complete the command.

■ *Finding and Changing Text*

Want to find all occurrences of the word *halcyon* in your latest manuscript? If the document is any size at all, you'll spend a lot of time if you have to hunt down every last one. But Word can do it in a flash. And if you want to replace *halcyon* with another, easier-to-understand word, such as *tranquil* or *peaceful*, Word can do that, too.

Finding Text

Word can search a document for any character or group of characters. You can enter a part of a word, an entire word, or a phrase, and Word will find every occurrence of it. To find a word, you usually start by clicking at the beginning of the document to set the insertion point there. The search then starts from the beginning. Then do the following:

1. Choose Find from the Utilities menu. A dialog box, like the one in Figure 5-9, appears.
2. Enter the word or words (hereinafter called a *string*) into the Find What edit field.
3. Set the Whole Word and Match Upper/Lowercase options, as desired. (See below.)
4. Click the Start Search button. If Word finds a match, it stops and selects the string in the document.
5. To find the next occurrence, click the Find Next button.

When you are finished, click Cancel or click in the Find window's close box.

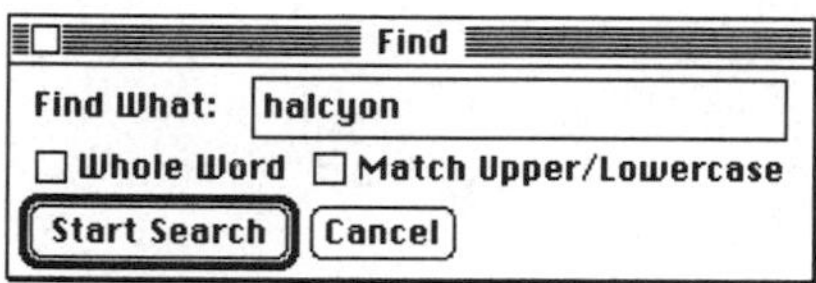

Figure 5-9
The Find dialog box.

Word helps you avoid finding matches that are not what you want by letting you set two options, Whole Word and Match Upper/Lowercase.

With Whole Word, the program selects only text strings that stand on their own, with a space on either side. When searching for *hyper*, for instance, Word normally flags *hyper, hyperbole, hyperspace,* and all other words that have *hyper* anywhere in them. Click Whole Word, and the program flags only *hyper*.

Leave the Whole Word option off when you are searching for both the root and derivations of a word. Searches work best when the root is an uncommon word. The search string *the* will select a lot of words (*these, other, their, thesis,* and so forth); the search string *magnet* narrows the field to only a few similar words: *magnetize, electromagnetic, magneto,* and so on.

The Match Upper/Lowercase option specifies that you are looking for words that are capitalized (or not capitalized) in a certain way. If this option is off, Word would find a word like *Eschew* in all its possible capitalizations: *eschew, ESCHEW, esChew,* and so forth. With the case option on, Word would flag only *Eschew*.

If you want, you can also copy text from a document and paste it into the Find What field. Word enters the text, removing any formatting it had.

Changing Text

To replace a text string, you usually start by clicking at the beginning of the document to set the insertion point there. Then do the following:

1. Choose the Change command from the Utilities menu. A dialog box, like that shown in Figure 5-10, appears.
2. Enter the text to be replaced in the Find What field.
3. Type the replacement text in the Change To field.
4. Set the Whole Word and Match Upper/Lowercase options as desired.
5. Click the Start Search button. If Word finds a match, it stops and selects the string. Click the Change button to replace the string, or click No Change to leave the string as it is and continue the search.
6. If you want Word to change all occurrences of the string without having you verify them, click the Change All button instead of Start Search.

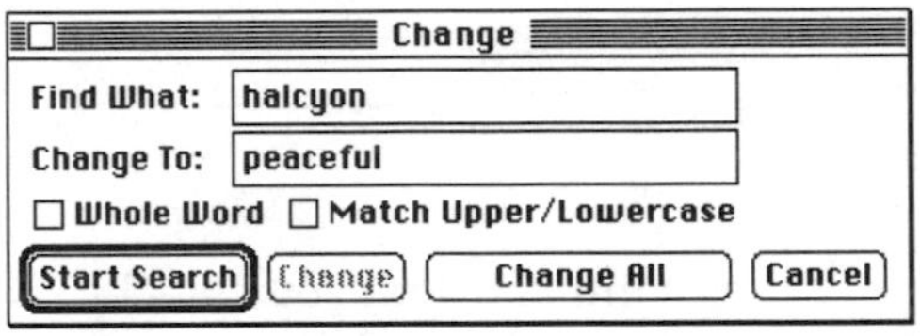

Change
Find What: halcyon
Change To: peaceful
Whole Word Match Upper/Lowercase
Start Search Change Change All Cancel

Figure 5-10
The Change dialog box.

The Change Selection button makes the change in the currently selected text and stops the search. This button has two uses. For one, you can use it to replace at once all occurrences of the search string in a selected block of text. To do this, select the block, choose Change, enter the text you want to find and replace, and click Change Selection. Because Word selects the search string when it finds it, you can also use this button to change the current occurrence of the string and then discontinue the search. Simply click Change Selection when the program stops at a word. Word will change the selection and leave the Change dialog box on the screen so that you can enter a new Find What or Change To string and begin another search.

Wildcard Searches

In card games, a wildcard is a chameleon; it can assume the identity of any card in the deck. In Word, a wildcard is a special character that assumes the identity of one or more characters in a search (Find What) string. You use wildcard characters to find variations in spelling and so forth. You cannot, however, use wildcard characters in the Change To field.

Word supports one wildcard character: the question mark (?). The question mark substitutes a single character in that position in the search string. Here are some examples:

Type	To find
Budget?	*Budget1*, *Budget2*, *Budget3*, and other words that start with *Budget* and have one other character (won't find *Budget10*).
sep?rate	*separate*, *seperate*, and other spellings in which the fourth character is different.

Searching for and Replacing Special Characters

Word lets you search for special characters, including format marks, page breaks, and tabs. To make it easier, first display the space, tab, paragraph, and newline marks by choosing the Show ¶ command. You enter the circumflex (^) character by pressing Shift-6.

Type	To find
^*w*	"White" space (as seen with paragraph formatting symbols off). It finds all formatting marks, including nonbreaking spaces, paragraph marks, tabs, newline marks, optional hyphens, section marks, and page breaks. If several marks are together, Word selects them all when found.
^*s*	A nonbreaking space.
^*t*	A tab mark.
^*p*	A paragraph (hard return) mark.
^*n*	A newline (soft return) mark.
^-	An optional hyphen.
^~	A nonbreaking hyphen.
^*d*	A section mark (including required page breaks).
^?	A question mark.
^\	A formula character.
^^	A caret.

Interesting Facts About Finding and Changing Text

Interesting Fact 1. Unless Match Upper/Lowercase is on, Word retains the capitalization when replacing text. This means that capitalization at the beginning of sentences is kept. For example, if you entered *hello* in the

Find What field and *howdy* in the Change To field, they would come out in your document as follows:

Original word	Changed to
hello	howdy
Hello	Howdy
HELLO	HOWDY

Interesting Fact 2. The Find What and Change To fields can each contain up to 24 visible characters, but you can type as many as 255 characters in each field. The runoff text in the field scrolls left as you type.

Interesting Fact 3. You can replace a block with text that is longer than 255 characters by first copying the new string into the Clipboard (select it and choose Copy) and then typing *^c* in the Change To field. This code does not work in the Find What field: To search for text that matches the contents of the Clipboard, simply copy the text and paste it into the Find What field.

Interesting Fact 4. The text strings that you enter in the Find What and Change To fields remain there until you change them or until you quit Word. This saves you from having to retype the text if you use the same string over again. Further, the Find What fields of the Find and Change dialog boxes are shared. For example, if you type *dimethylnitrosamine* in the Find What field of the Find dialog box, the same word will appear if you then display the Change dialog box.

Interesting Fact 5. To search for a string with a question mark in it, precede the question mark with a circumflex character (^). Here is an example:

To find	Type
What is this thing called love?	*What is this thing called love^?*

Interesting Fact 6. To search for a string with a circumflex (^) in it, precede the character with a second circumflex; you would enter *40^^6* to find *40^6*.

Interesting Fact 7. To find any ASCII character, whether you can type it directly from the keyboard or not, enter the ASCII code for that character by typing *^n*, replacing *n* with the ASCII code number you want, from 0 to 255. You can use this technique in the Change To field as well. See Appendix B, "Table of Character Sets," for a complete list of the codes for each special character. Interestingly, if you enter the code for a letter and don't have the Match Upper/Lowercase option selected, Word will find both uppercase and lowercase letters.

Why is this so useful? Because some formatting characters and special graphic characters exist that you can't type directly from the keyboard or enter as one of the special characters described in the previous section. Specifically, you can use the ASCII code numbers to look for the following:

To find	Type
Graphics	*^1*
Page number character from header	*^2*
Current date character from header	*^3*
Current time character from header	*^4*
\ (used in formulas) and footnote separator	*^6*
Footnote continuation separator	*^7*
Page break	*^12*
Required hyphen	*^30*
Space character	*^32*

Other ASCII codes produce characters that either can be typed directly from the keyboard or are undefined, but undefined characters appear as small rectangles (□).

TIP

Removing Undefined Characters from Imported Text Files
Often, when you capture a file with a modem or transfer a file from a PC, strange characters appear in your document. The linefeed character, ASCII 10, is probably the most common of these. If you choose Show ¶, often all you see is the standard Mac symbol for an undefined character, a small rectangle (□). If all you can see is this generic character, how can you search for it and replace it with nothing?

Simply select the mystery character, find its ASCII code by pressing Option-Command-Q, and enter that decimal ASCII code in the Find What field of the Change dialog box, leaving the Change To field blank. See Chapter 16, "Transferring Text and Graphics," for more information on importing text files.

■ *The Undo and Again Commands*

Mistakes happen to everyone, but when you're hurrying to perfect a term paper, report, or magazine article, accidentally deleting a paragraph you really want to keep or fouling up the formatting of an entire page can be frustrating and nerve-racking. Word lets you undo almost any action, including typing, editing, deleting, and formatting.

To undo the previous command, choose Undo from the Edit menu immediately. Word remembers only one action at a time, and thus you can undo only the last action or command. When you are typing, Word remembers all the characters you entered since the last command.

The Undo command is context sensitive—that is, it describes the command that can be undone, as shown in Figure 5-11. For example, if you typed some text, the command reads Undo Typing. If you did a paste, the command reads Undo Paste. If the previous command is one that can't be reversed, the command reads Can't Undo and is dimmed.

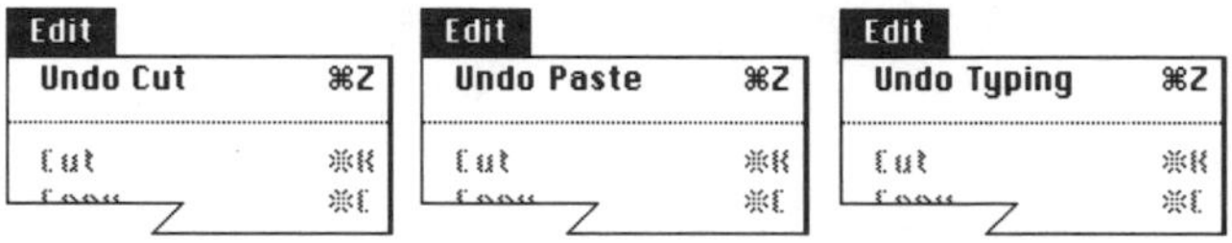

Edit		Edit		Edit	
Undo Cut	⌘Z	Undo Paste	⌘Z	Undo Typing	⌘Z
Cut	⌘X	Cut	⌘X	Cut	⌘X
Copy	⌘C	Copy	⌘C	Copy	⌘C

Figure 5-11
Examples of the Undo command.

TIP

Using the Undo Command to Experiment
You can use the Undo feature to test the look and feel of formatting, editing, or some other change in the document. Make the change, and then look over the document. If you like the way it looks, keep it. If you don't, undo the change and start over. When you've undone something, the Undo command changes to Redo. You can undo and redo changes easily by pressing Command-Z.

Word doesn't have Undo commands for the actions listed in the table below. Fortunately, however, they can be reversed by clicking a Cancel button in a dialog box if it appears, by choosing the command again, or by some other action. To stop a command that is in progress, try pressing Command-(period).

To reverse	Do this
Starting Word	Quit Word (use Command-Q).
About MS Word	Click the OK button.
New	Close the new window.
Open	Click the Cancel button.
Close	Click the Cancel button (or reopen the document).
Save As	Click the Cancel button.
Delete	Click the Cancel button.
Page Preview	Close the Page Preview window.
Merge Print	Click the Cancel button.
Page Setup	Click the Cancel button.
Print	Click the Cancel button.
Quit	Click the Cancel button (or restart Word after you reach the Desktop).
Show/Hide ¶	Choose the command again.

To reverse	Do this
Preferences	Click the Cancel button.
Short/Full Menus	Choose the command again.
Go To	Click the Cancel button.
Show/Hide Ruler	Choose the command again.
Outlining	Choose the command again.
Spelling	Click the Cancel button.
Window menu commands	Close the window (for Show Clipboard, or New Window), or reactivate the desired window.

On the other hand, there will be times when you want to use the same command repeatedly. You can do this with the Again keyboard command. Simply press Command-A to repeat your last command. To repeat the last Find command, press Option-Command-A. The Again command can save you a good number of keystrokes. Here are a few other ways to use it:

- After replacing text by typing over it, you can replace other text with the same phrase by selecting the text and pressing Command-A.
- After a copy operation done without the Clipboard (Option-Command-C), you can copy the same text to another place by setting the insertion point in another location and pressing Command-A.
- After making a set of formatting changes using a dialog box, the Ruler, or the Copy Formatting command (Option-Command-V), you can apply the changes to another selection.
- You can repeat a Print command and use the same options.
- You can mix repeated find operations with general editing, repeated text-replace commands, or formatting changes.

■ *Counting Words in a Document*

Word 4 has a very convenient feature for professional writers and others who need to keep track of their progress when writing. The Word Count feature scans through the current document and counts characters, words, lines, and paragraphs in the body of the document and its footnotes, but not headers or footers. If you've selected a range of text, Word counts only the items in the selection. Make sure the Show Hidden Text option in the Preferences dialog box is turned off before starting the count, unless you want text having the Hidden character format to be scanned as well. (The Hidden character format is discussed in Chapter 8, "Character Formatting.") When you choose Word Count from the Utilities menu, the dialog box in Figure 5-12 on the following page appears.

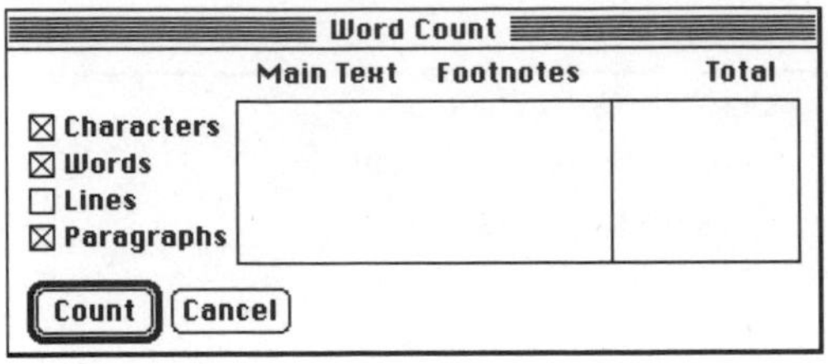

Word Count
Main Text Footnotes Total
☒ Characters
☒ Words
☐ Lines
☒ Paragraphs
Count Cancel

Figure 5-12
The Word Count dialog box.

In the dialog box, select the items you want to count—the Lines option is not selected by default, because the number of lines in a document varies with the way it's formatted, but the number of characters, words, and paragraphs do not. Next, click the Count button; as it counts Word displays the percentage of the document or selection that has been read. Click the Cancel button when done to dismiss the dialog box or to abort the count before Word has finished.

Points to Remember

- ❑ Use the Key Caps desk accessory to view characters that constitute a font. You can copy special characters from Key Caps to paste into a document.
- ❑ Word has three types of hyphens: normal hyphens, which are always visible; nonbreaking hyphens, which are always visible but are never broken at the end of a line; and optional hyphens, which are only visible at the end of lines. Don't confuse these hyphens with the en dash (Option- –) and the em dash (Shift-Option- –).
- ❑ Word supports two types of space character—the normal space and the nonbreaking space (Option-Spacebar). Word does not break a nonbreaking space if it occurs at the end of a line. In justified text, Word doesn't expand nonbreaking spaces.
- ❑ You can find the ASCII code of a selected character, and enter a character by its ASCII code, by using the Option-Command-Q key sequence.
- ❑ Word supports normal end-of-paragraph marks (which you create by pressing the Return key) and soft returns, or newlines (which you create by pressing Shift-Return).

Techniques

View the contents of the Clipboard

❶ Choose Show Clipboard from the Window menu.

❷ Click the close box when you're through.

Repeat the previous command (the Again key)

❶ Press Command-A.

To repeat the last Find command, press Option-Command-A.

Undo the previous command

❶ Choose Undo from the Edit menu.

Entering formatting characters

To enter	Press
End of paragraph	Return or Enter
Nonbreaking space	Option-Spacebar
Nonbreaking hyphen	Command- ~

(continued)

To enter	Press
Optional hyphen	Command- – (hyphen)
End of line (newline)	Shift-Return
New page	Shift-Enter (on keypad)
New section	Command-Enter (on keypad)
Formula character	Option-Command- \
Paragraph mark after insertion point	Option-Command-Return

Entering accented characters

❶ Press the keys for the accent desired from the following table.

❷ Enter the character to be accented.

To enter	Press
Grave accent (`)	Option-`
Acute accent (´)	Option-e
Circumflex (^)	Option-i
Tilde (~)	Option-n
Umlaut (¨)	Option-u

Entering other characters

To enter	Press
En dash (–)	Option- – (minus)
Em dash (—)	Shift-Option- – (minus)
ASCII character codes (see Appendix B)	Option-Command-Q, then enter the character's ASCII code and press the Return key

View characters available with different key combinations

❶ Choose Key Caps from the Apple menu.

❷ Select a font from the Key Caps menu.

❸ Hold down the Shift key, the Option key, or the Shift-Option combination to see the characters available from the keyboard.

If you want,

❶ Type the characters you want.

❷ Choose the Copy or Cut commands.

❸ Paste them into the Word document.

❹ Format them in the font you desire.

Selecting Text

To	Do this
Select an insertion point	Point to where you want to insert, and then click.
Select a character	Drag over it.
Select a word	Double-click anywhere in it.
Extend a selection by words	Double-click and drag.
Select a sentence	Command-click anywhere in the sentence.
Extend a selection by sentences	Command-click and drag.
Select a line of text	Click in the selection bar to the left of the line.
Extend a selection by lines	Drag in the selection bar.
Select a paragraph	Double-click in the selection bar to the left of the paragraph.
Extend a selection by paragraphs	Double-click in the selection bar and drag.
Select any block of text	Drag across the text, or click at one end and Shift-click at the other end.
Select the entire document	Command-click in the selection bar, or press Option-Command-M.
Select a graphics frame	Click inside the frame. A solid frame and three handles will appear.

Copying Text

Copy text using the Clipboard

❶ Select the text and choose Copy from the Edit menu.

❷ Position the insertion point where you want to place the text.

❸ Choose Paste.

Copy text without using the Clipboard

❶ Select the text and press Option-Command-C. *Copy to* appears in the status box.

❷ Set the insertion point where you want to copy the text.

❸ Press the Return key.

You can also start with an insertion point placed where you want to put the text:

❶ Press Option-Command-C. *Copy from* appears in the status box.

❷ Select the text you want to copy.

❸ Press the Return key.

You can cancel this command by pressing Command-(period).

Moving Text

Move text using the Clipboard

❶ Select the text you want to move.

❷ Choose Cut from the Edit menu.

❸ Position the insertion point at the new location.

❹ Choose Paste.

Move text without using the Clipboard

❶ Select the text, and press Option-Command-X. *Move to* appears in the status box.

❷ Position the insertion point where you want to move the text.

❸ Press the Return key.

You can also start with an insertion point:

❶ Press Option-Command-X. *Move from* appears in the status box.

❷ Select the text you want to move.

❸ Press the Return key.

You can cancel this command by pressing Command-(period).

Finding Text

Search for text

❶ Choose Find from the Utilities menu to search for text and select it.

❷ Enter up to 255 characters in the Find What field, and set options from the list at the top of the following page. To find a special character, enter a code from the following table:

To find	Type
Any single character	*?*
A question mark	^*?*
White space	^*w*
A nonbreaking space	^*s*
A tab mark	^*t*
A paragraph mark	^*p*
A newline mark	^*n*
An optional hyphen	^-
A nonbreaking hyphen	^~
A section mark or page break	^*d*
A caret (^)	^^
Any character by its ASCII code	^ *ddd*, where *ddd* is its ASCII code

Whole Word: Finds whole words only—not those embedded in other words.

Match Upper/Lowercase: Finds only the arrangement of uppercase and lowercase characters you specify. If this option is turned off, the search string will be matched regardless of capitalization.

❸ Click one of the buttons in the following list:

Start Search: Starts the search at the insertion point or the beginning of the selection.

Find Next: Continues the search.

Cancel: Stops the search.

❹ If you started the search at some place other than at the beginning of the document, when Word reaches the end, it asks if you want to continue the search from the beginning of the document. Click Yes or No.

Finding and Changing Text

Search for and replace text

❶ Choose Change from the Utilities menu.

❷ Enter the text to be found in the Find What field. See "Finding Text" on the previous page for a list of special characters you can use in this field.

❸ Enter the replacement text in the Change To field. If you leave this field blank, Word deletes the search text. To specify a special character, type the appropriate entry from the following table:

To replace with	Type
A nonbreaking space	^*s*
A tab mark	^*t*
A paragraph mark	^*p*
A newline mark	^*n*
An optional hyphen	^-
A nonbreaking hyphen	^~
A page break	^*d*
A caret (^)	^^
The contents of the Clipboard	^*c* (must be used by itself)
Any ASCII character	^*ddd*, where *ddd* is its ASCII code

Whole Word: Finds and changes whole words only—not characters embedded in words.

Match Upper/Lowercase: Finds and changes only the arrangement of uppercase and lowercase characters you specify. If this option is turned off, the search string will be matched regardless of capitalization, and replacement text will be adjusted to match the capitalization of found text.

❹ Click one of the buttons from the following list:

Start Search: Starts the search at the insertion point or the beginning of the selection.

No Change: Leaves the selected text unchanged and finds the next occurrence.

Change: Changes the selected text and finds the next occurrence.

Change All: Changes all occurrences of the search text throughout the document.

Change Selection: Changes all occurrences of the search text within the selection and cancels the search.

❺ If Word reaches the end of the document, it asks if you want to continue the search again from the beginning of the document. However, if you started at the beginning of the document, Word simply says it has reached the end of the document. Click Yes or No.

Find and change text in a footnote or header

❶ Open the Footnote window by pressing Shift-Option-Command-S, by pressing the Shift key while dragging down the split bar, or by choosing Open Header or Open Footer from the Document menu.

❷ Choose Change, and search for and replace the text as you would normally.

■ *Mouse and Keyboard Shortcuts*

To delete	Mouse click	Keyboard press
Previous character		Backspace (Word stops at paragraph marks that separate paragraphs with different formats.)
Previous word		Option-Command-Backspace
Next character		Option-Command-F
Next word		Option-Command-G
Block of text	Select text and press	Backspace
Block of text and move it to Clipboard	Select text, choose Cut, or press	Command-X
Block of text and replace with new text	Select text and	Type replacement text

■ *Commands*

Command name	Meaning, menu	Standard keyboard	Keypad	Extended keyboard
Again	Repeats latest command or editing action.			
	Edit	⌘A		
Backspace	Deletes selection or character left of insertion point.			
Change…	Finds and replaces text with replacement text you specify.			
	Utilities	⌘H		
Clear	Deletes selection from document without placing it on Clipboard.			
	Edit			
Copy	Copies selection to Clipboard.			
	Edit	⌘C		F3
Copy as Picture	Copies selection as a MacDraw graphic onto Clipboard.			
		⌘⌥D		
Copy Text	Copies current selection to new location or copies subsequent selection to current position of insertion point.			
		⌘⌥C		⇧F3
Cut	Deletes selection from document and places it on Clipboard.			
	Edit	⌘H		F2
Delete Forward	Deletes character to right of insertion point.			
		⌘⌥F		⌦
Delete Next Word	Deletes word (or part of word) to right of insertion point.			
		⌘⌥G		
Delete Previous Word	Deletes word (or part of word) to left of insertion point.			
		⌘⌥⌫		
Extend to Character	Extends selection (highlighted area) to character you type.			
		⌘⌥H	⌨ -	
Find Again	Repeats search for text or format you specified when you last chose Find or Find Formats command.			
	Utilities	⌘⌥A		
Find…	Searches for text and/or special characters.			
	Utilities	⌘F		
Hide ¶	Toggles display of Word's normally invisible characters, such as spaces, tabs, and paragraph marks. If the characters aren't visible, the command reads *Show ¶* and appears in the list box after Show Text Boundaries.			
		⌘A		
Insert Formula	Inserts formula code (\ ).			
		⌘⌥\		

(continued)

Command name	Meaning, menu	Standard keyboard	Keypad	Extended keyboard
Insert Index Entry	Inserts index entry codes, formatted as hidden text, before and after selected text or on either side of insertion point. **Document**			
Insert Line Break	Breaks a line of text without starting a new paragraph. Inserts newline character (displayed as ↵ with Show ¶ on).	⇧↩		
Insert New Paragraph	Terminates current paragraph and inserts a paragraph mark.	↩ or ⌤		
Insert Nonbreaking Hyphen	Inserts a hyphen preventing a line break within a hyphenated word that occurs at end of a line. Hyphen is displayed as ¬ when Show ¶ is on.	⌘`		
Insert Nonbreaking Space	Inserts a space preventing a line break on either side of space. Space is displayed as ˜ when Show ¶ is on.	⌥␣ or ⌘␣		
Insert Optional Hyphen	Inserts a hyphen that is printed only when a word is broken at the hyphen. Hyphen is displayed as ˜ when Show ¶ is on.	⌘ -		
Insert Page Break	Inserts a manual page break at insertion point. **Document**	⇧⌤		
Insert Tab	Inserts tab character, displayed as ➔ when Show ¶ is turned on.	⇥ or ⌥⇥		
Insert Table…	Inserts a table having specified number of rows and columns at insertion point. **Document**			
Insert TOC Entry	Inserts table-of-contents entry codes, formatted as hidden text, before and after selected text or on either side of insertion point. **Document**			
Move Text	Moves current selection to new location or moves subsequent selection to current position of insertion point.	⌘⌥X		⇧F2
Move to Bottom of Window	Places insertion point after last character visible in window.			*end*
Move to End of Document	Places insertion point after last character in document.		⌘▦3	⌘*end*
Move to End of Line	Moves insertion point to end of current line.		▦1	

(continued)

Command name	Meaning, menu	Standard keyboard	Keypad	Extended keyboard
Move to Next Character	Moves insertion point right one character.	→ or ⌘⌥L	▦6	
Move to Next Line	Moves insertion point down one line.	↓ or ⌘⌥,	▦2	
Move to Next Paragraph	Places insertion point at start of next paragraph.	⌘↓ or ⌘⌥B	⌘▦2	
Move to Next Sentence	Places insertion point at start of next sentence.		⌘▦1	
Move to Next Word	Places insertion point after current word or next word.	⌘→ or ⌘⌥;	⌘▦6	
Move to Previous Character	Moves insertion point left one character.	← or ⌘⌥K	▦4	
Move to Previous Line	Moves insertion point up one line.	↑ or ⌘⌥O	▦8	
Move to Previous Paragraph	Places insertion point at start of current paragraph or preceding paragraph.	⌘↑ or ⌘⌥Y	⌘▦8	
Move to Previous Sentence	Places insertion point at start of current sentence or preceding sentence.		⌘▦7	
Move to Previous Text Area	Moves insertion point to preceding text area at left (in Page View) or to preceding cell (within a table).		⌘⌥▦9	
Move to Previous Word	Places insertion point before current or preceding word.	⌘← or ⌘⌥J	⌘▦4	
Move to Start of Document	Places insertion point before first character in document.		⌘▦9	⌘*home*
Move to Start of Line	Moves insertion point to beginning of current line.		▦7	
Move to Top of Window	Places insertion point before first character visible in window.		⌘▦5	*home*
Numeric Lock	Toggles Num Lock so that you can type numbers using numeric keypad.		▦⌧	

(continued)

Command name	Meaning, menu	Standard keyboard	Keypad	Extended keyboard
Paste	Inserts Clipboard contents at insertion point or in place of current selection.			
	Edit	⌘V		F4
Paste Special Character	Inserts a special font character indicated by decimal code you type.			
		⌘⌥Q		
Select Whole Document	Selects entire document. Same as pressing the Command key while clicking in the selection bar.			
		⌘⌥M		
Show Clipboard	Displays contents of Clipboard.			
	Window			
Undo	Reverses latest command action if possible.			
	Edit	⌘Z		F1
Word Count…	Displays number of characters, words, paragraphs, and lines in a document or selection, excluding headers and footers.			
	Utilities			⌥F15
"Smart" Quotes	Toggles option to use " " and ' ' instead of " " and ' ' when you press the standard quote key.			

Automatic Text Entry with Glossaries

Microsoft Word has many features aimed at automating the writing process. One of the most important of these is its support for *glossaries*. If you've ever found yourself thinking, as you typed the same text over and over, that there must be a better way, or if you've ever wished that you could insert a letterhead at the top of a document quickly and easily, the glossary feature is for you. It allows you, with a few keystrokes, to insert a predefined block of text or a graphic anywhere in any of your documents.

In Word, a glossary is not a list of terms and their definitions but a file containing blocks of text and graphics. Each block is called a glossary entry, and each glossary entry has a name that you use when you want to insert it into a document. With glossaries you save time, not to mention many keystrokes.

Suppose that you are a lawyer or a lawyer's assistant and that you often prepare contracts for clients. Most contracts contain small chunks of standard text. Instead of typing these chunks each time you draw up a contract, you can record them as separate glossary entries. Then, when you want to insert one into a contract, you press a few keys in the proper sequence, and the text appears automatically.

This chapter shows how to use glossaries to drastically reduce the time you spend typing text. You'll learn how to create a glossary entry, call it up at a moment's notice, delete or edit it, as well as how to manage glossary files.

■ *Anatomy of a Glossary*

As illustrated in Figure 6-1, each block of text or graphic is a single entry. Glossary entries are similar to the cuttings you might keep in the Scrapbook desk accessory, but you can access glossary entries much more quickly.

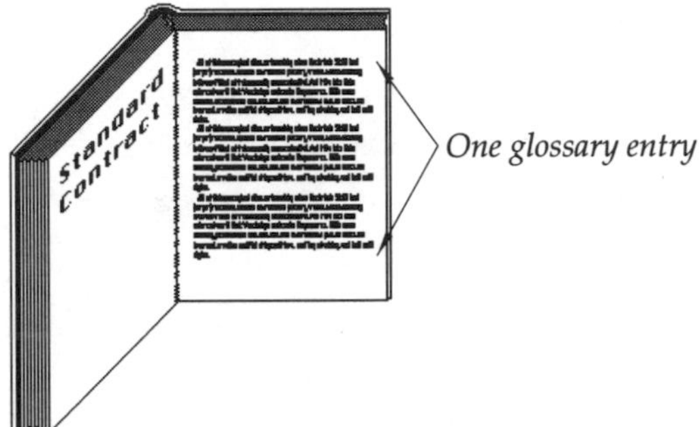

Figure 6-1
A glossary is similar to the Scrapbook.

You already saw how a glossary could make assembling a legal contract easier and faster. Here are a few other items that are perfectly suited to be glossary entries:

- ❑ Letterheads (text, graphics, or both).
- ❑ Your name and return address.
- ❑ Often-used mailing addresses of friends and business associates.
- ❑ Account numbers.
- ❑ Telephone numbers.
- ❑ Names or long words, such as *Santiago de los Caballeros* and *phenylalanine.*
- ❑ Text with unusual formatting, such as the Zapf Dingbat *o* followed by a tab character, which we use for the shadowed boxes in this list.
- ❑ Headers and footers that you use regularly.
- ❑ Graphic elements, such as gray rules from MacDraw or digitized logos.
- ❑ PostScript graphics elements.
- ❑ Character names, scenes, and camera directions in screenplays.
- ❑ Samples of long mathematical formulas. (See Appendix D, "Mathematical Typesetting.")

- ❑ The complimentary close in business letters, such as:

Sincerely,¶
¶
¶
¶
David A. Buxton¶
Public Relations Specialist¶
¶
enc.¶

Word comes with a glossary file called Standard Glossary. Inside this file are a number of default glossary entries, each marked by a bullet in the Glossary dialog box, for inserting the time and date in various formats, for inserting the current page number, and for using Word's print merge commands. The time and date entries are of two types: static and dynamic. When you enter a static item into your document, Word inserts the appropriate text but does not continuously update it. When you insert a dynamic time or date, Word updates it when you print the document. Static entries contain the word *now*, and dynamic entries contain the word *print*. You can either add to the Standard Glossary or create your own glossary files. The Standard Glossary is accessed every time you start Word. Unlike style sheets, which are linked to a single document, glossaries can be shared among all your Word documents.

■ *Creating a Glossary Entry*

The first step in creating a glossary entry is to select a graphic or a block of text to use. You can also paste the contents of the Clipboard into a glossary, if it is more convenient to do so. Of course, the number and size of your entries determine the size of the glossary file, and the larger the file the less room there will be on your work disk for other files. Most of your glossary entries will be a sentence or two in length, and the graphics will be relatively small. However, Word doesn't restrict the size of an entry—you could store a blank business-letter template, for example. To add an entry to the glossary:

❶ Select the text or graphic in the normal way, or copy or cut something to the Clipboard.

❷ Choose Glossary from the Edit menu. The Glossary dialog box appears. (See Figure 6-2 on the following page.)

❸ Think of a name for the glossary entry. The shorter the name the better, but it should be fairly descriptive. Type the name into the Name field.

❹ If you want to use the contents of the Clipboard as the glossary entry, choose the Paste command and skip to ❻. (Pasting something from the Clipboard automatically defines the entry.)

5. Click the Define button. The item, whether selected or on the Clipboard, is recorded as an entry in the current glossary, with the name you provided.
6. Close the Glossary dialog box by clicking the Cancel button or the close box.

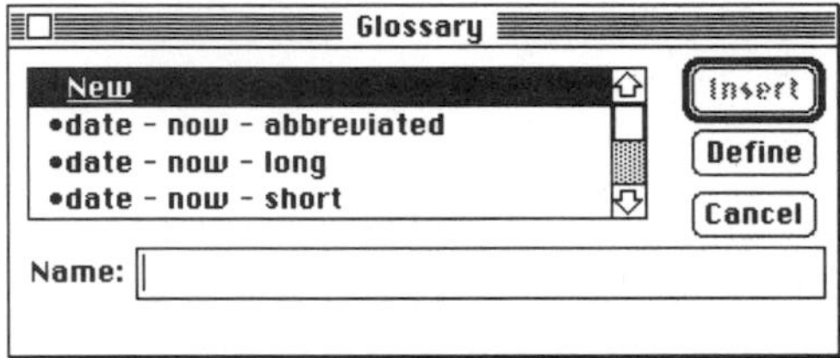

Figure 6-2
The Glossary dialog box.

If you click the Define button without providing a name, Word names the glossary entry for you. The first name assigned is *Unnamed1*, the second is *Unnamed2*, and so forth. You can change the name of a glossary entry by selecting the name you want to change in the list box, typing a new name in the Name edit field, and then clicking Define.

Like any other Word document, a glossary must be saved or any changes and additions you have made will be lost. If you don't save the glossary, Word will prompt you to do so when you quit the program. If you add several entries to the glossary, it is a good idea to save them right away, rather than waiting until the end of your Word session. However, you don't need to save a glossary in order to use entries you've just added. To learn more about your options for saving a glossary, see "Working with Glossary Files," later in this chapter. If you simply want to save your new entries in the Standard Glossary file, display the Glossary dialog box and choose Save As from the File menu. Be sure that the filename is *Standard Glossary*, and then click Save.

■ *Inserting a Glossary Entry*

You can insert a glossary entry into your document in three ways: by choosing the Glossary command, by accessing the glossary from the keyboard, or by choosing a glossary entry that you have added to the Work menu. (See Chapter 3, "The Word Environment," for more about the Work menu.)

Regardless of the method you use, you must first set the insertion point where you want the entry to appear. If, instead of merely placing the insertion point, you select a graphic or a block of text, the glossary entry will replace the selection.

Choosing the Glossary Command

To insert an entry using the mouse and the Glossary command, do the following:

❶ Choose the Glossary command. The Glossary dialog box appears.

❷ Scroll through the list box and click on the entry you want to use.

❸ Click the Insert button, or simply double-click on the entry name.

The entry is placed at the insertion point, as shown in Figure 6-3, or it replaces the previously selected text or graphic. If you decide not to use a glossary entry, click the Cancel button or the close box. If you make a mistake and need to undo the entry, choose Undo Insert Glossary Text from the Edit menu.

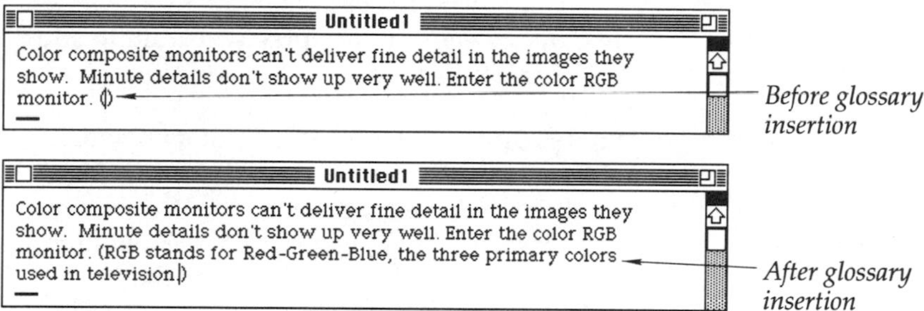

Figure 6-3
Before and after inserting a glossary entry.

Using the Keyboard

If you remember the name of the glossary entry, you can insert it more quickly by using the keyboard. Simply place the insertion point, or select the material you want to replace with the entry, and then do the following:

❶ Press Command-Backspace. As Figure 6-4 on the following page shows, the status box in the lower left corner of the window reads *Name.*

❷ Type the name of the entry. You can use uppercase or lowercase letters; Word doesn't care. Keeping your entry names short helps make this process more convenient.

❸ Press the Return key when you're finished typing. The entry is placed at the insertion point or replaces the previously selected material.

If you misspell the entry, the program will beep at you. To cancel the insertion, press Command-(period) or click anywhere in the document.

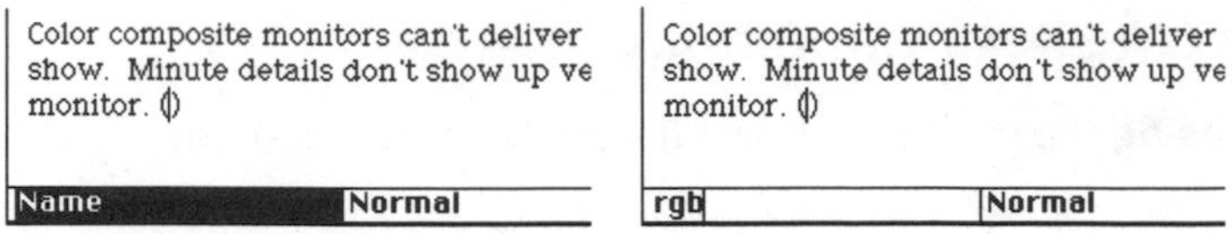

Color composite monitors can't deliver show. Minute details don't show up ve monitor. ¶

Name | Normal

Color composite monitors can't deliver show. Minute details don't show up ve monitor. ¶

rgb | Normal

Figure 6-4
The status box during entry insertion from the keyboard.

Using the Work Menu

The third way to insert a glossary entry is to create an item for it on the Work menu and then simply choose that menu item when you want to insert the entry. To add a glossary entry to the Work menu, do the following:

1. Press Option-Command- +. The pointer changes to a large plus sign.
2. Choose the Glossary command, and click on the entry you want to add to the Work menu. The menu bar blinks to confirm the addition.

To test the new Work menu item, place the insertion point somewhere in your document, and then choose the new glossary menu item. It couldn't be easier. You may want to add all your glossary entries to the Work menu in this way, but restrain yourself. Once you begin using the Work menu to add documents, glossary entries, and style names, you'll realize that selecting items from a huge menu can take longer than going through the Glossary dialog box.

Formats Within Glossary Entries

Any glossary entry you create contains, in addition to text or graphics, any character or paragraph formats the material may have. If the selected or copied material for the entry contains a paragraph mark, the paragraph formats that are attached to it (such as line spacing, indention, and style information) remain with the entry in the glossary. For this reason, unless you specifically want the paragraph formats to travel with the entry, select only the text inside a paragraph and not the entire paragraph before you create the glossary entry. If you do this, only the character formats of the selected material remain with the entry.

Any styles attached to the material at the time you create the entry are also recorded in an invisible glossary style sheet. These formats and styles are carried over when you insert an entry into a document, even if it is not the same document from which the entry originally came. If a style name attached to the entry already exists in the document, Word uses the document style to format the inserted entry. On the other hand, if a style attached to the entry does not exist in the document's style sheet, then Word adds it from the style sheet hidden in the glossary.

For example, let's say that a book you are working on has a heading called *For Further Reading* at the end of each chapter, listing the bibliographic references for the chapter, and that it has the *heading 2* style. In addition to using the *heading 2* style that you developed (say, 14-point Palatino bold with 20 points Space Before), you manually added italics to the *For Further Reading* heading. Then, suppose that you select this heading and create a glossary entry called *head/biblio*.

If you opened a blank document and inserted this glossary entry, you would see the italic formatting of the original but not the 14-point Palatino bold style you defined in the first document, because the *heading 2* style is an *automatic* style, meaning that it is automatically predefined for every blank document. Because the default definition for the *heading 2* style is the *Normal* style font in bold, with 6 points Space Before, you would see these formats plus the italic you added manually. In all probability, this is not what you expected or wanted.

This behavior may seem awkward to you, but there is a reason for it that applies to other aspects of Word as well. When you copy a style into a document—whether by inserting a styled glossary entry or by copying and pasting styled material from one document to another—the styles of the document, not of the inserted material, take precedence. This approach preserves the information contained in the document until you decide to change it. If it were otherwise, a style attached to an inserted paragraph could overwrite a style in your document's style sheet, causing all the text in that style to be changed. In other words, you can add a style that wasn't in your document before, but Word won't let you replace a style without making a conscious choice.

If you want the *heading 2* styles in the two documents to match, it's easy enough to copy the styles from the source document to the new document. Simply choose Define Styles while the new document is active; then choose Open and open the source document's style sheet. All the styles defined in the source overwrite the styles of the same name in the new document. See Chapter 10, "Working with Style Sheets," if you want to copy only a few of the styles to the new document.

The behavior of not transferring a style definition that already exists in a document when you insert a glossary entry also holds for a glossary itself. This is a consequence of the fact that a glossary has only one hidden style sheet. For example, suppose that you define a new entry in the current glossary for a paragraph having a style called *letterhead*. Suppose you now close the document from which this entry came and open a new document. In the new document you create a definition for the *letterhead* style that is different from that in the first document. If you now create a new glossary entry for a paragraph having the *letterhead* style of the new document, the new definition does not stay with the entry in the glossary because the glossary's hidden style sheet already contains a definition for that style.

TIP

Opening a Glossary as a Document

Here is an experiment for the stouthearted to demonstrate that glossaries do indeed have hidden style sheets. Note that the average user will never need to open a glossary in this way; it is easy to make almost any change to a glossary using the standard methods described in the next section.

First, close every open document for safety's sake. Then open a new document and choose the Glossary command. Next choose Save As, naming the glossary *Glossary Test*, in order to create a copy of the glossary for your experiments. Once you've done this, quit and restart Word; this is necessary because Word lets you open a glossary as a document only if it's the first time it is being opened for any reason during that session. Now hold down the Shift key while choosing Open Any File from the File menu. A dialog box appears, listing every file in the current folder, regardless of whether it's a Word document or not. Open *Glossary Test* as a document.

You see a list of every entry in your glossary, each ended by a paragraph mark (invisible unless Show ¶ is on). You can carefully change the material in this document—editing within an entry, reformatting text, and so on—but be careful not to delete an entry. If you do, glossary entries may no longer match their correct names or the glossary may become totally unusable.

Choose the Define Styles command to see the list of styles attached to the glossary. You can do many things with the glossary's style sheet: change style definitions, delete styles that are no longer attached to glossary entries, and even open a style sheet belonging to another document to merge its styles into the glossary's style sheet.

When you have finished editing the glossary document, save it. A Fast Save preserves the file type attached to the glossary so that you can open it as a glossary again without problems. However, if you made many edits, have many documents open (remember the suggestion to close all open documents?), or repaginated the glossary document (although you should never need to do this), Word does a Full Save and changes the document's file type and icon to those of a standard Word document.

If this happens, don't worry; you can still open the document as a glossary if you haven't changed the file too much. To do this, restart Word, choose the Glossary command, and press the Shift key while choosing Open from the File menu. When the Open dialog box appears, open *Glossary Test*. If all goes well, your edited glossary document will be reopened as a glossary. To complete the process, immediately save this glossary under a third name, such as *New Glossary*, so that Word will change the file type and icon back to those of a glossary.

Any time you open a glossary in this way, test carefully any changes you make before using it with an important document.

This technique can be helpful if for some reason you suspect that your glossary has been damaged and you want to recover its contents. Simply open the glossary as a document using the steps outlined above, and copy its contents into a blank document. You can then reconstruct the glossary.

■ *Modifying a Glossary Entry*

You can change the contents, format, and name of any glossary entry except the standard entries (those preceded by a bullet in the Glossary dialog box). You can also delete any glossary entry you no longer need (again, with the exception of the standard entries).

Editing an Entry

Often, after creating a glossary entry, you will decide that you need to make a few changes in it. Start by inserting into a document the entry you want to change. Use a new, blank document window if necessary, to avoid messing up the one in which you are currently working. Then redefine the contents of the entry as follows:

❶ Make the desired changes in the contents and format of the material you inserted.

❷ Select the edited material.

❸ Choose the Glossary command.

❹ Select in the list box the entry to be replaced, and click the Define button.

❺ Click Cancel to resume editing.

Another way to accomplish the same end is to copy the edited entry, open the Glossary dialog box, select the entry, and then choose the Paste command.

TIP

Editing Graphics Stored in the Glossary
Word cannot edit graphics imported from programs like MacPaint or MacDraw. If you need to edit a graphic stored as a glossary entry, open the Glossary dialog box, select the entry, and choose the Copy command. Then go back to the drawing program, paste the graphic, change it, and cut or copy the new version to the Clipboard. Finally, restart Word, open the Glossary dialog box again, select the entry name, and choose the Paste command to replace the entry with the contents of the Clipboard.

Changing the Name of an Entry

To change the name of a glossary entry without changing its contents, do the following:

❶ Choose the Glossary command.

❷ Select in the list box the entry to be renamed.

❸ When you click on a glossary entry, the name appears selected in the Name field. Enter the new name.

❹ Click the Define button.

❺ Click Cancel to resume editing.

Even though you may have selected or copied something in your document, when you change an entry name, Word assumes that you don't want to store the selected or copied material under the new name. If you change your mind and decide you do want to create a new entry with the selected or copied material, click Cancel and create the new entry as described earlier.

Deleting an Entry

To delete a glossary entry you no longer need, do the following:

❶ Choose the Glossary command.

❷ Select in the list box the entry to be deleted.

❸ Choose the Cut command.

❹ Word double-checks to be sure you really want to delete the entry. Click Yes if you do or No if you don't.

❺ Click Cancel to resume editing.

Once you have cut an entry, you may find it helpful to paste its contents into a document you called, for instance, *Glossary Heap*, so that you can recover it if you need it again.

■ *Working with Glossary Files*

Glossaries have many applications. You can, if you want, store full paragraph formatting with glossaries so that when entries are inserted in text, they use their own special formatting characteristics, rather than the characteristics of the surrounding text. You can also store only the text of a paragraph, without its paragraph formatting but retaining its character formatting. You can also print glossaries so that you have a record of the name and definition of each entry.

You are by no means limited to a single glossary. Custom glossaries are ideal for storing text and graphic entries for specialized applications. One glossary file might contain entries for use with the LaserWriter and PostScript, another might contain entries for use with business correspondence, and still another might include entries for technical and scientific papers. You can use one glossary file at a time, or you can combine them in any way you want, by cutting and pasting entries between them or by incorporating all the entries from one glossary into another.

Once you have set up glossaries to your liking, you can print them so that you have a record of the name and definition of each entry.

Word opens the Standard Glossary file the first time you choose the Glossary command. This file is included on the Word master disk and should be kept in the same folder as the Word program. If, when it starts, Word cannot find a Standard Glossary file on the disk (see Appendix A, "Setting Up Word," for the list of where Word looks for files), it creates a new one. Of course, you can generate your own custom glossary files and store them on any disk.

Probably the most important thing to understand about glossaries is the relationship between the Standard Glossary and the current glossary. The *current glossary* is a working area within Word; it is simply a block of memory. The Standard Glossary is a file that actually exists in your Word folder. When you choose the Glossary command for the first time in a session, Word opens the Standard Glossary file and adds its entries to the current glossary. If you add entries to the current glossary from your documents and then quit Word, Word asks if you want to save the current glossary and prompts you with the Standard Glossary filename if you haven't opened any other glossaries in the meantime.

To begin exploring glossary files, try saving any entries you've added to the current glossary in the Standard Glossary file. The easiest and the most common way of doing this is simply to quit Word and have it ask whether or not you want to save the changes to the glossary. However, often you will want to save changes you made and either begin a new glossary or open one that you already created. To save the current glossary as the Standard Glossary, do the following:

❶ Choose the Glossary command.

❷ Choose Save As from the File menu. A dialog box appears, requesting a filename for the current glossary.

❸ If you haven't cleared the current glossary or opened one with a different name, Word suggests the obvious, *Standard Glossary*, as the filename. If that name doesn't appear, type it in.

❹ Click Save. Word asks you to confirm that you want to replace the existing Standard Glossary file. Click Yes.

❺ Click Cancel in the Glossary dialog box.

Note that saving a glossary does not affect the contents of the current glossary.

Clearing the Current Glossary

Every time you open a glossary file, you add its contents to all the other entries in the current glossary. To avoid this, you can explicitly clear the current glossary of entries beforehand. You should also do this when you want to create a new glossary so that you start with a clean slate before adding new entries.

For example, suppose that you start Word and begin using the glossary. The current glossary would then consist of the entries in the Standard

Glossary, which Word opened when you chose the Glossary command. If you choose Glossary again and open a different glossary, you would add the contents of the second glossary to the current glossary, which already contains the entries in the Standard Glossary. Later, when you quit Word and save the current glossary under the same name as that of the second glossary you opened, all the entries, including those in the Standard Glossary, would be saved in the file. As you can see, it is important to clear the current glossary before opening or creating another if you want to keep the entries separate.

To clear the current glossary, you open the Glossary dialog box and choose New from the File menu, as follows:

❶ Choose Glossary from the Edit menu.

❷ Save any changes you made to the current glossary, if you want to keep them.

❸ Choose New from the File menu. The dialog box shown in Figure 6-5 appears, to verify that you want to clear the contents of the current glossary. Click Yes.

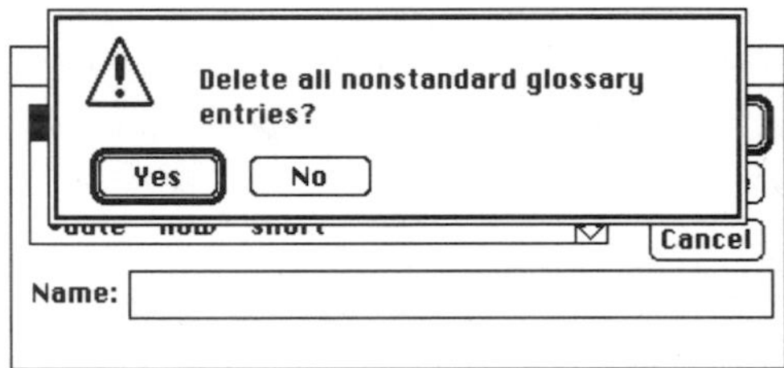

Figure 6-5
Word verifies that you want to clear the glossary.

At this point, the current glossary is empty of entries other than the standard items. You can now either create a new glossary or open another glossary stored on disk. To start a new glossary, select each piece of boilerplate text in turn, and enter it into the current glossary with a suitable name. When you're finished, save the current glossary with an appropriate title, or quit and let Word lead you through the process.

You can also clear the current glossary and create a new entry at the same time. Simply select the material (text, graphics, or both), open the glossary, clear it, name the new entry, and click the Define button.

Opening a Glossary

Once you've created a custom glossary, you need to know how to open it so that you can use it in your documents and add, delete, or modify its entries.

❶ Choose the Glossary command to open the Glossary dialog box.

❷ Choose the New command to clear the current glossary.

❸ Choose the Open command. A list of available glossary files appears in the list box. Click the Drive and Eject buttons if you want to view glossary files on other disks. The Standard Glossary file is exactly the same as any other (except that it is the one opened by default), so you can open or reopen it if you want.

Repeat the process for as many glossary files as you like. Remember, however, that the entries from each file will be added to the others in the current glossary. If you would rather delete entries in the current glossary before opening another one, choose the New command first.

If you want, you can start Word and open a glossary file at the same time by double-clicking on the icon of the glossary file.

Combining and Extracting Glossary Entries

Because opening a glossary without clearing the current glossary first adds the glossary's contents to the current glossary, you can combine entries from many smaller glossaries into larger glossaries. Combining glossaries lets you share entries across many disks. However, because glossary entries are stored by name, trouble can arise if you merge an entry into a glossary that already has an entry of the same name. When this happens, Word gives preference to the merged glossary item, and the entry with that name in the current glossary is replaced.

To remove one or more entries that you don't want included in the combined glossary, select each entry and choose the Cut command. Word verifies your choice with a dialog box; click Yes or press the Return key to delete the entry. When you have deleted all the entries you don't want, save the current glossary under a new name.

If you mistakenly delete an entry you want to keep, don't panic. The entry isn't permanently gone; it still exists in the original glossary file on disk, and it may even exist in the Clipboard, if you haven't replaced it with other material. Choose Show Clipboard from the Window menu to see if it is still there. If it is, paste it back as though you were creating a new entry. You can also get an entry back by opening its glossary again. This will merge all the deleted entries back into the combined glossary, so if you don't want some entries, you will have to delete them again.

Another way to recover an entry or to move or copy an entry from one glossary file to another is to save the current glossary under a new name, clear it, open the old glossary, and cut or copy entries from the old glossary to the new one. To do this, first save the current glossary, and then do the following:

❶ Choose the New command to clear the current glossary.

2. Choose the Open command and open the glossary from which you want to copy the entry.
3. Select the entry you want to copy.
4. Choose the Copy command to place the entry in the Clipboard.
5. Choose the New command again to clear the current glossary.
6. Choose the Open command and open the glossary to which you want to copy the entry.
7. Choose the Paste command to add the entry to the current glossary.

Before you go on to other tasks, it is a good idea to save your combined glossary. Otherwise, your hard work may be lost. If you neglect to save the glossary, Word will remind you to do so when you quit the program.

TIP

Moving Groups of Glossary Entries
If you need to move more than one glossary entry at a time, you might try a few tricks. The first trick is simply to insert all the entries you want to move from the source glossary into a document, clear the current glossary, open the destination glossary, and then add the entries to it. The second trick is to save a copy of the source glossary under a temporary name, such as *My Glossary/trash*, and then delete all the entries you don't want to move. With this modified glossary as the current glossary, open the destination glossary to merge the two sets of entries.

The third trick, not for the fainthearted, is to make a duplicate of the source glossary, clear the current glossary, open the destination glossary, and then open the copy of the source glossary *as a document* by pressing the Shift key while choosing the Open Any File command. You can then scroll through the entries, selecting and reentering them as needed. Delete the copy of the source glossary when you're done, as it might no longer be a usable glossary file.

Printing the Current Glossary

Names of glossary entries can be as difficult to remember as names of styles. Fortunately, you can print the name and definition of every currently loaded glossary entry. A printed list of available glossary entries can serve as a helpful reference while you are working.

To print the entries in a particular glossary file, first clear the current glossary and open the glossary you want to print. If you simply want to print the entries in the current glossary, you need not bother to do this. Then do the following:

1. Choose the Glossary command to display the Glossary dialog box, if it's not already on the screen.
2. Choose the Print command.

❸ Select the desired options, and then click OK.

If you'll be printing more than one glossary file, remember to clear the slate each time before you open the next glossary file, or all the entries will be merged into one huge glossary.

The glossary entries are printed in alphabetical order. The printout includes the name of each entry and its contents. (See Figure 6-6.)

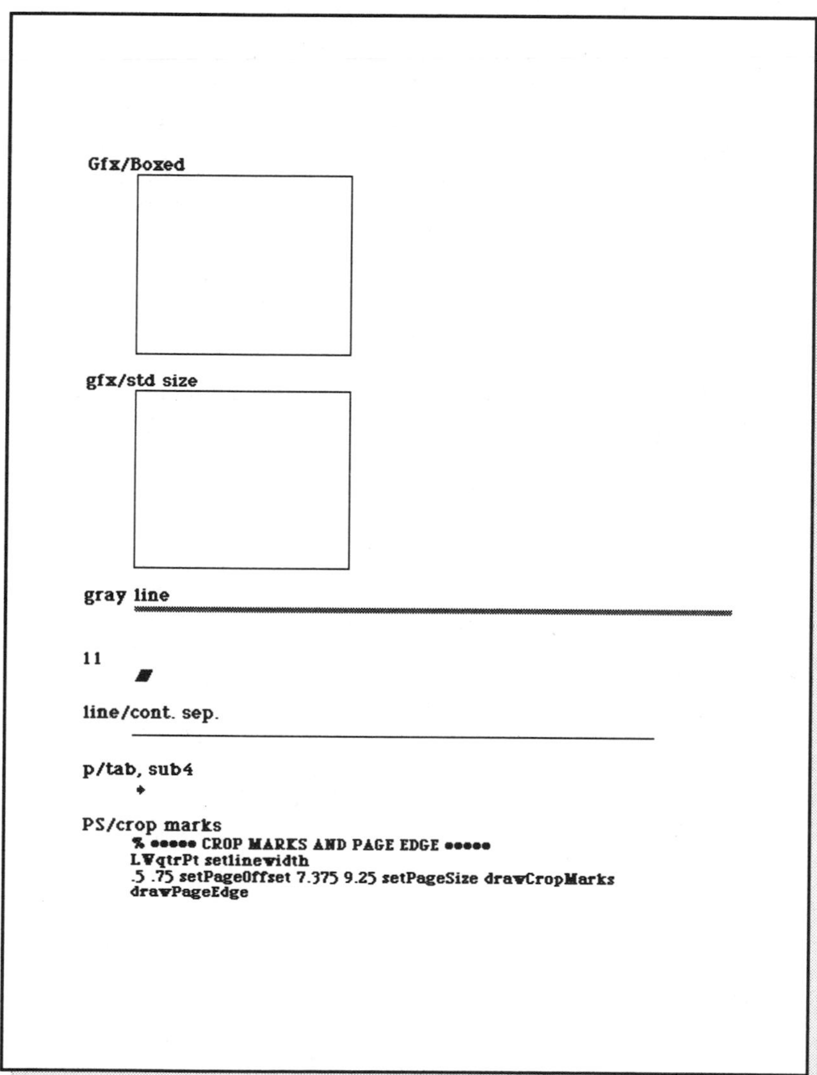

Gfx/Boxed

gfx/std size

gray line

11

line/cont. sep.

p/tab, sub4

PS/crop marks

% ●●●●●● CROP MARKS AND PAGE EDGE ●●●●●●
LWqtrPt setlinewidth
.5 .75 setPageOffset 7.375 9.25 setPageSize drawCropMarks
drawPageEdge

Figure 6-6
A page from a printed glossary.

■ *Points to Remember*

- ❑ A glossary is a collection of entries, each with a name, that you can insert into your documents quickly and easily. An entry can consist of text, graphics, or both.
- ❑ Unless you specify otherwise, Word stores your glossary entries in a file called the Standard Glossary. This file is provided on your Word disk and must be in the same folder as the Word program.
- ❑ Word loads the Standard Glossary when you first choose the Glossary command or otherwise access a glossary entry in a given session.
- ❑ All glossary files contain the following standard entries, which you cannot modify or delete (although you can change the format of time entries from 12-hour to 24-hour format through the Control Panel):

Glossary entry	Type	Format of entry
date - now - abbreviated	static	Fri, Jan 5, 1990
date - now - long	static	Friday, January 5, 1990
date - now - short	static	1/5/90
date - print - abbreviated	dynamic	Fri, Jan 5, 1990
date - print - long	dynamic	Friday, January 5, 1990
date - print - short	dynamic	1/5/90
page number	dynamic	(current page number)
print merge	static	«»
time - now	static	7:01 AM
time - now - with seconds	static	7:01:03 AM
time - print	dynamic	7:01 AM
time - print - with seconds	dynamic	7:01:03 AM

- ❑ Each glossary entry retains the style, character formats, and paragraph formats that were attached to the text when the entry was created. However, if the document into which an entry is inserted contains a style with the same name as a style attached to the entry, the inserted entry is formatted according to the document style, not the glossary style. If no style exists by that name, the glossary style is used.
- ❑ The current glossary is a work area that contains the entries belonging to the glossaries which have been opened. Each time you open another glossary, its contents are added to the current glossary. If you want to remove the current entries before you open another glossary, you must do so explicitly by choosing the New command.

Techniques

Working with Glossary Entries

Create a glossary entry

1. Select the text or graphic you want to use.
2. Choose the Glossary command.
3. Type a name for the entry.
4. Click Define.

Insert a glossary entry into a document

1. Place the insertion point.
2. Choose the Glossary command (Command-K).
3. Select the name of the entry to be inserted.
4. Click Insert, or simply double-click the entry name.

Or,

1. Place the insertion point.
2. Press Command-Backspace. (The status box displays the prompt *Name.*)
3. Enter the name of the glossary entry you want to insert.
4. Press the Return key, or cancel by pressing Command-(period).

Display an entry

1. Choose the Glossary command.
2. Select an entry name.
3. The first part of the entry text appears at the bottom of the dialog box.

To see the entire entry, insert it in your document, read it, and then choose Undo (Command-Z) to remove it.

Replace an entry

1. Select the replacement material in your document.
2. Choose the Glossary command.
3. Select the name of the entry to be replaced.
4. Click Define.

The text from the document replaces the previous entry; the first part of the new entry appears at the bottom of the dialog box.

Delete an entry

❶ Choose the Glossary command.
❷ Select the name of the entry to be deleted.
❸ Choose the Cut command.
❹ Click Yes in the dialog box that appears.

The entry will be moved to the Clipboard.

Rename an entry

❶ Choose the Glossary command.
❷ Select the entry to be renamed.
❸ Type the new name.
❹ Click Define.

Add a glossary entry to the Work menu

❶ Press Option-Command- +.
❷ Choose the Glossary command.
❸ Click on the entry you want to add.

This lets you insert the entry simply by choosing it from the Work menu.

Working with Glossary Files

Save the current glossary

❶ Choose the Glossary command.
❷ Choose the Save As command.
❸ Type the name of the glossary to be saved.
❹ Click Save.

Clear the current glossary

❶ Save the current glossary first if it contains changes you want to keep.
❷ Choose the Glossary command.
❸ Choose the New command.
❹ Click Yes in the dialog box that appears.

Open a custom glossary

❶ Choose the Glossary command.
❷ Clear the current glossary, if you want.

❸ Choose the Open command.
❹ Select the glossary file you want to open.

Copy an entry from one glossary file to another

❶ Choose the Glossary command.
❷ Open the source glossary.
❸ Copy the appropriate entry to the Clipboard.
❹ Clear the current glossary.
❺ Open the destination glossary.
❻ Paste the entry into the glossary.

Print the current glossary

❶ Choose the Glossary command.
❷ Choose the Print command.
❸ Click OK.

■ *Commands*

Command name	Meaning, menu	Standard keyboard	Keypad	Extended keyboard
Glossary Entry:	Inserts indicated glossary entry at insertion point.			
Glossary…	Inserts or defines a glossary entry.			
	Edit	⌘K		
Insert Date	Inserts current date glossary entry (m/d/y).			
Insert Glossary Text	Prompts you to type a glossary entry name and inserts glossary entry text at insertion point or in place of selection.			
			⌘⌧	
Insert Page Number	Inserts automatic page number glossary entry.			
Insert Time	Inserts print time glossary entry.			

Using the Spelling Checker

Word's built-in spelling checker is a boon to anyone who makes typing mistakes or sometimes forgets how to spell a word—and who doesn't? Because the spelling checker is built into Word, you don't have to quit the program and start up another application in order to check spelling. This means that you can call up the spelling checker at a moment's notice and quickly check text, even a single word.

This chapter discusses the nuances of the spelling checker. You'll learn how to do basic tasks, such as adding words to and deleting words from one or more personal dictionaries, as well as more advanced techniques, including how to manipulate personal dictionary files.

■ *Doing a Spelling Check*

You can run a spelling check at any time, but for most documents, you'll want to wait until most of the writing and editing is done. Checking a document too early in the creative process doesn't guard you against spelling and typographical errors later on.

If you have any text in hidden format in your document, be sure it's visible before you start the spelling check: Choose Preferences from the

Edit menu, and click Show Hidden Text in the dialog box if the option is not already on. Word won't check hidden text unless it's visible. (Hidden text is discussed in Chapter 8, "Character Formatting.") Then, to check an entire document:

1. Click at the beginning of the document to place the insertion point there. (Word begins checking from the insertion point.)
2. Choose Spelling from the Utilities menu. After a short wait while Word loads the dictionary (when this is the first time in the session that you use the spelling checker), the dialog box shown in Figure 7-1 appears. If Word can't locate the MS Dictionary file, it presents a dialog box asking you to find the folder or insert the disk containing the file.
3. Click the Start Check button to begin the spelling check.

When Word finds a word that isn't in its dictionary, it selects the word and displays it after Unknown Word, and the Start Check button now reads *No Change.* Your options at this point include any of the following:

- Correct the word.
- Have Word suggest an alternate spelling.
- Add the word to a personal dictionary.
- Both correct the word and add it to a personal dictionary.
- Do none of the above—neither correct the word nor add it.

These options are described at length in the sections that follow. If you want to get on with your work now and learn the details later, you can use the spelling checker at its most basic level by doing one of the following: Click No Change to continue the spelling check without changing the word; type the correct spelling after Change To, and then click Change to correct the word and continue the spelling check; or click Suggest to have Word display a list of proposed spellings for the word, select one, and click Change.

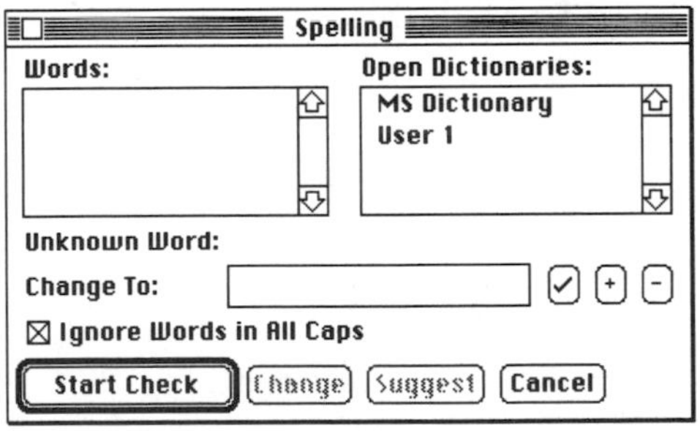

Figure 7-1
The Spelling dialog box.

You don't have to check the entire document; you can also check single words and blocks of selected text by selecting the text before you choose the Spelling command. If you select only one word, Word checks that word. When it has finished checking the selection, Word displays a dialog box that says *Finished checking selection*. Click OK (or press the Return key), and you are back to editing.

You can use this feature to check the spelling of single words as you type. After entering a word that you suspect may be spelled incorrectly, double-click on it to select it, and then choose the Spelling command. If the word is spelled correctly, Word displays its *Finished checking selection* message. Press the Return key to resume editing. If the word is spelled incorrectly, Word flags it as an unknown word.

If you start a spelling check anywhere but at the beginning of a document, Word displays the message *Continue checking from beginning?* when it reaches the end. Click Yes to have Word check from the beginning of the document, or click Cancel to resume editing.

Ignoring Words in All Caps

Acronyms are words formed from the initial letters within a term and are usually capitalized. Because of their specialized nature, acronyms are not included in Word's dictionary. If you write or edit a document that is loaded with acronyms, the spelling check will stop every few words, making the whole process a hindrance rather than a help.

For this reason, Word lets you ignore words that are capitalized. If you want to skip over acronyms and other words that are all caps, be sure that the Ignore Words in All Caps option is on (on is the default setting) before you start the spelling check. If you want to check capitalized words, click the box to turn off the option.

Correcting a Word

If you're like most people, your most common mistake will be mistyping words that you know how to spell. For example, you might have typed *adding the term to adictionary* and want only to separate the correctly spelled words. To do this, you can either type the correct word (or words), or you can edit it.

To retype the entire text:

❶ Click in the Change To edit field and type the correct spelling (*a dictionary* in the example above).

❷ Click the Change button. Word replaces the text and continues checking your document.

To edit the text:

❶ Click on the word displayed next to the Unknown Word label. The term appears in the Change To edit field.

❷ Click in the Change To field to deselect the word and set the insertion point.

❸ Edit the word. When you're finished, click Change to change the word in the document and continue the check.

Having Word Suggest a Spelling

If, while checking a document, Word finds an unknown word that you're not sure how to spell, don't reach for your printed dictionary yet. You can access Word's internal dictionary by clicking the Suggest button. The program then presents a list of words that it believes are close to the one you want, in order of its estimation of the probability. (See Figure 7-2.) These suggestions come from the MS Dictionary only, not any of your personal dictionaries. If it can't find any alternatives, Word displays a message telling you this. Then you can grab your Webster's.

If many words are displayed in the list box, scroll to find the one you want. When you spot the right word, select it, and then click the Change button or simply double-click on the word in the list box. If you click the Suggest button by accident after Word has presented the list, you may see a dialog box that says *Word is already spelled correctly*. This happens because the program is reading the word in the Change To field, which is the word currently selected in the Words list box, and that word is spelled correctly.

Getting a suggestion for a word you typed can be very efficient, sometimes even more efficient than taking the time to remember how to spell it correctly and edit it manually. Simply double-click on the word, choose the Spelling command, click the Suggest button, and double-click on the correct spelling to replace the word in your document.

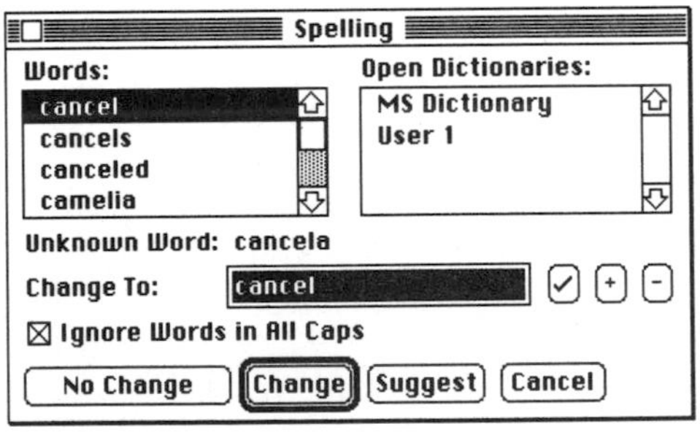

Figure 7-2
A list of suggested words.

If you don't find the word you're looking for in the list of suggestions, try this: Enter a different (probably incorrect) spelling of the word in the Change To field, and then click the check mark (√) button located immediately to its right. Clicking this button asks Word to search for the Change To word in its dictionary. If the word is spelled correctly this time, a dialog box appears telling you so. If the word isn't found in the dictionary, the program displays it as the Unknown Word. To list a set of alternatives for the new entry, click the Suggest button again, and see if the correct word is provided in the Words list box.

Adding Words to a Personal Dictionary

Often, a term that Word stops on is spelled correctly but is not in the MS Dictionary. The word might be a proper noun or a specialized term used in your field or profession. If the word is one that you're likely to use again, you'll probably want to add it to one of your personal dictionaries. The words you add are recognized in subsequent spelling checks, and you usually don't have to worry about them anymore.

The MS Dictionary, which is shipped with Word, cannot be altered. The internal format of the file is designed for maximum efficiency—adding words to it would slow down the checking process. Instead, words are added to personal, or User, dictionaries. You can create and use any number of personal dictionaries, although having a large number of dictionaries open at the same time can also slow down the checking process. A good rule of thumb is to keep fewer than 1,000 words in each of five open dictionaries.

For example, you can create a dictionary filled with legal terms for use when you write and edit legal documents. Another dictionary can hold contractors' terms, for writing and editing home-building specifications. The smaller the dictionary, the faster the spelling checker works. It's better to have many small dictionaries and use them as needed than to have one very large personal dictionary.

Creating a personal dictionary and adding words to it is simple. Word assumes that you want to use the MS and User 1 dictionaries whenever you use the spelling checker, so Word opens them when you choose the Spelling command. (See Appendix A, "Setting Up Word," for a list of the folders Word checks to find the MS and User dictionaries.) The Open Dictionaries list box shows the dictionary files that are currently open. (See Figure 7-3 on the following page.) Unless you've already added words to it, the User 1 dictionary is empty.

To add a word to User 1 or another personal dictionary, assuming that the Spelling dialog box is displayed and the unknown word is selected:

❶ If you have more than one personal dictionary open, click on the name of the dictionary to which you want to add the term. This step is optional if only the User 1 and Main dictionaries are open, because Word assumes you want to add terms to the User 1 dictionary. If more than one personal dictionary is open, Word assumes that you want to add the term to the dictionary you selected last, unless you specify otherwise.

❷ Click the plus (+) button, as shown in Figure 7-3. The word is added to the selected dictionary, the contents of which appear in the Words list box. (If more than four words are in the dictionary, you may have to scroll in the Words list box to see the word you just added.)

❸ Repeat the process for each additional word that you want to add to the selected dictionary.

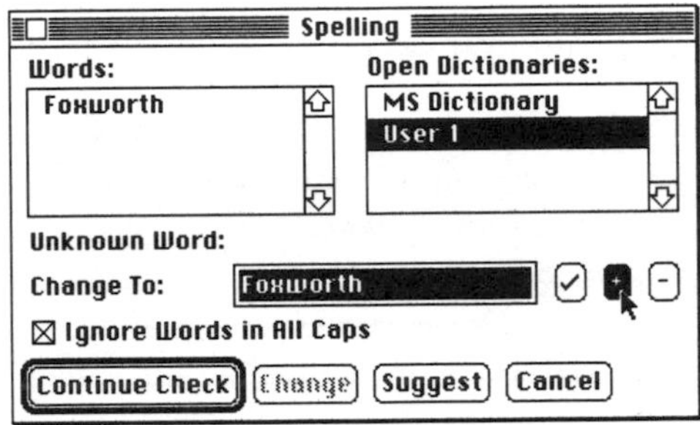

Figure 7-3
Adding a word to the User 1 dictionary.

Correcting a Word and Adding It to a Dictionary

Of course, nothing prevents you from both changing the word and adding it to a personal dictionary. You can accomplish this as follows:

❶ Click on the name of the dictionary to which you want to add the word.

❷ Click in the Change To field and enter the correct spelling, or click on the unknown word to enter it into the Change To field, and edit it.

❸ Click the + button to add the word to the selected dictionary.

❹ Click the Change button. Word replaces the text.

Beware of trying to add more than one word at a time when you click the + button, as you might when separating two words joined by a typing mistake. If you do this, unpredictable results can occur; for example, the words you add might not show up in the list for the dictionary you selected.

Skipping Past Words

Very often, Word's spelling checker will stop on a person's name, a company name, a street name, or another word that you don't want to add to a personal dictionary. The easiest thing to do in this situation is to click the No Change button and continue. Once you've done this for a given word, the program remembers it, and for the rest of that session, it skips past the word, pausing on it only long enough to let you know the word might still be suspect.

However, what if you change your mind and decide to add the word or name to a dictionary after all? Because Word only pauses on the words you have skipped over, it doesn't seem as though you have the opportunity any longer. If you double-click on the word and choose the Spelling command to check its spelling, Word responds that the word is spelled correctly. The program assumes that you knew what you were doing when you skipped over the word and that, therefore, it must be spelled correctly.

Word offers two ways to get around this and add a word to a selected dictionary once you've skipped over it. The first is to set an insertion point in the document, choose the Spelling command, type the word into the Change To field, and click the + button.

The second way involves a trick. If you press the Shift key while choosing the Spelling command, you'll see that the Spelling command has changed to the Reset Spelling command. If you choose the Reset Spelling command, Word forgets its list of skipped words and stops on each one again, allowing you to correct it or add it to a dictionary. Therefore, to add a word, double-click on it to select it and then press the Shift key while choosing the Spelling command. This time Word doesn't tell you that the word is spelled correctly, but instead presents the Spelling dialog box. Simply select the dictionary to which you want to add the word, and click the + button.

Removing Words from a Dictionary

Sooner or later, you'll need to delete a word from one of your personal dictionaries. You might decide that you no longer need a word you previously added, or you might find out that *zephir* is spelled with a *y* instead of an *i* and want to remove the mistake. Here's how to do it:

1. Select the dictionary from the Open Dictionaries list box. The words in that dictionary appear in the Words list box.
2. Select the word to be deleted in the Words list box.
3. Click the minus (–) button to delete the word.

Moving a Word from One Dictionary to Another

To move a word to another dictionary, you must remove it from the source dictionary and then add it to the destination dictionary. The Change To field makes this process simple:

1. Select the source dictionary in the Open Dictionaries list box.
2. Select the word to be moved in the Words list box. The word appears in the Change To field.
3. Click the – (minus) button to delete the word from the dictionary.
4. Select the destination dictionary in the Open Dictionaries list box.
5. Click the + (plus) button to add the word to the dictionary.

■ Working with Dictionary Files

Using dictionary files is much like using any other file; you can open them, close them, and rename them with the commands on the File menu while the Spelling dialog box is active. You can replace the MS Dictionary with one more suited to speakers of the King's English: the UK Dictionary. You can even transfer groups of words from one dictionary to another or convert a dictionary from another word processor into one that Word can use, although these procedures are only for experimentalists.

Saving Dictionaries

Dictionaries, like documents, must be saved on a disk, or their contents will be lost. Word opens the MS and User 1 dictionary files whenever you start the first spelling check in a session. If you want your most frequently used personal dictionary opened for you each time you use the spelling checker, have it be the one named User 1, and store the file in the folder that contains the MS Dictionary.

To save the User 1 dictionary, select it, and then choose the Save command while the Spelling dialog box is active. Click the Save button in the dialog box that appears. (If you've already used the dictionary and created a User 1 dictionary, Word simply saves the file under that name without presenting the dialog box.) The file is saved on the disk as *User 1*. If you neglect to save the dictionary, Word reminds you to do so when you quit the program. If this happens, click the Yes button to save the dictionary.

Alternatively, you can save the dictionary under a different name, on a different disk, or in a different folder. With the User 1 dictionary selected, choose the Save As command and type the new name, as illustrated in Figure 7-4. Note that the Save dialog box looks and behaves like the one you see when saving a regular document, except that you can't specify a file format or make backup copies of the dictionary file. Click the Drive or Eject button if you want to place the dictionary on another disk. A dictionary can have any name, but to help keep things straight on your desktop, why not add *Dict* to the end of its name, to differentiate it from the other documents you have on the disk?

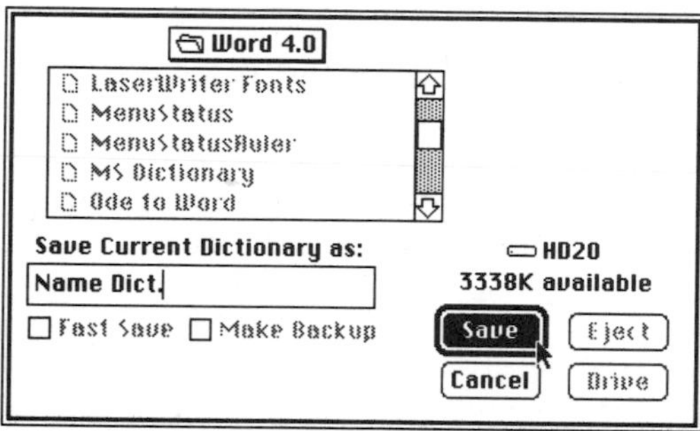

Figure 7-4
The Save Dictionary dialog box.

Creating a New Dictionary

Adding words to the User 1 dictionary is by far the most convenient approach to take if you want all your words in one place. However, if you work with documents from many different fields, you might find that your User 1 dictionary contains so many terms that the speed of the spelling check degrades. (Each personal dictionary works best when kept to fewer than 1,000 words.) You might also find it convenient to keep proper names in one dictionary (called Name Dict, for instance), standard words not in the MS Dictionary in the User 1 dictionary, and special jargon in yet another (such as Apiarian Dict). To start a new dictionary:

1. Choose the Spelling command.
2. Choose New from the File menu. The name of the new dictionary appears in the Open Dictionaries list box. If the only dictionaries open are MS Dictionary and User 1, the new name is User 2.
3. Choose the Save As command to rename your new dictionary, if you like.

After you've created a new dictionary, add your terms to it and save the changes when you quit Word.

Opening and Closing Dictionaries

To open a previously saved dictionary:

1. Choose the Spelling command.
2. Choose the Open command.
3. A list of dictionaries in the current folder is shown in the dialog box. Select and open the dictionary you want.

Open dictionaries are displayed in the Open Dictionaries list box. They remain open until you close them or quit Word. To close a dictionary:

1. In the Open Dictionaries list box, select the name of the dictionary you no longer want to use.
2. Choose the Close command from the File menu. If you've made any changes to the dictionary, Word displays a dialog box asking whether you want to save the dictionary first. Click Yes to save it and close it.

Remember: Keep open only those dictionaries that you need. Your spelling checks are faster that way.

Changing the MS Dictionary to the UK Dictionary

If you live in the British Isles or Canada, you'll probably be interested in spelling words the British way: *theatre, humour, realise,* and so on. You can do this from the Finder by substituting the UK Dictionary (found on the Word Utilities disk) for the MS Dictionary. Simply change the name of the MS Dictionary file to another name, such as *US Dictionary,* and then change the name of the UK Dictionary to *MS Dictionary.* Reverse the process to switch back.

Advanced Work with Dictionaries

The normal way of adding words to a dictionary is to enter each individually as you check a document. This can be time-consuming if you want to create a dictionary from a word list or convert a dictionary from another word processor or spelling-check program to a Word dictionary.

Adding a Word List to a Personal Dictionary

The procedure for adding a large group of words to a dictionary without using tricks is straightforward. Simply open the document containing your word list, choose the Spelling command, start the check, and for each word that Word selects, click the + button (or press Command- +) and then press the Return key. If you're working with more than one dictionary, first select the dictionary to which you want to add the word. Otherwise, Word assumes that you want to add all words to the last dictionary selected.

Converting a Non-Word Dictionary to a Word Dictionary

The process just described can be time-consuming for lists containing hundreds of words. A shortcut exists for converting a word list to a dictionary, but proceed with caution: Damaged dictionary files might result. Make copies beforehand of every dictionary you use, and revert to the duplicate if you damage a dictionary file. You can copy a file by quitting Word and using the Duplicate command from the Finder's File menu.

The document containing the list of words you want to convert to a dictionary must be stored as a text-only file. First be sure that the words in the document are in the proper format. Each word must be on a line of its own and should end with a paragraph mark (a Return). No extra spaces should appear before or after any word, as shown in Figure 7-5. (The best way to check this is to choose Show ¶ from the Edit menu.) The words should not have capital letters in them unless you want to require that a given word (such as a proper name) be capitalized.

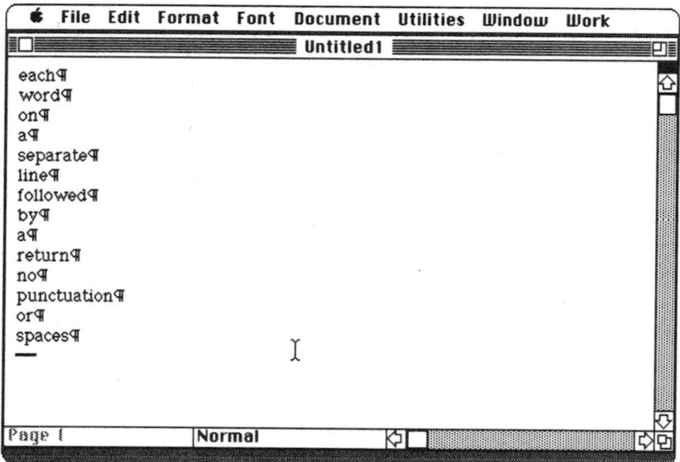

Figure 7-5
The format for converting a word list to a dictionary.

Next, organize the words into three groups, with all-capped words (such as acronyms) first, then initial-capped words (such as proper names), and finally lowercase words. Then select one group at a time and choose the Sort command. The words in each group are sorted from A through Z. When you have sorted the list, be sure there are no blank lines anywhere, including the paragraph mark at the end of the document. (Word does not let you remove the last paragraph mark in a document, so remove the one at the end of the line before it to close up the blank line.) Save the document as a text-only file.

(Choose Save As, click the File Formats button, and click on the Text Only option.) Then close the document. So far, so good.

To convert the document into a personal dictionary, do the following:

1. Choose New from the File menu to open a blank document.
2. Choose the Spelling command. The Spelling dialog box appears.
3. Press the Shift key and choose the Open Any File command. (Use the mouse, not Shift-Command-O, which is the keystroke sequence for inserting open space in a paragraph.)
4. Open the previously saved document by double-clicking on its name in the list box that appears. The document's name will appear in the Open Dictionaries list box.
5. Select the dictionary's name in the list box (if it's not already selected).
6. Choose the Save As command. Type a new name, or keep the old name. When using the old name, Word asks you to verify that you want to replace the old file; click Yes.

Word converts the file into a personal dictionary, which can be used like any other dictionary. You can add words to it, delete words from it, open it (in the same way you open other dictionaries), close it, and more.

Converting a Dictionary to a Regular Document

You can open any dictionary other than the MS Dictionary as a normal document. You might want to do this, for instance, when using a Word dictionary with another spelling-check program (on the Macintosh or some other computer). The other spelling program must accept word lists that have one word per line, each line ending with a paragraph mark.

You can also use this technique if you want to print a list of the words in a personal dictionary, because Word currently doesn't offer a way to print a dictionary file. In addition, you can open more than one personal dictionary and combine, split, or transfer groups of words at a time.

To convert a dictionary to a regular Word document:

1. Make duplicates of the dictionary files you want to convert, in case something goes wrong. Do this by quitting Word and using the Duplicate command on the Finder's File menu.
2. Restart Word. If you try to open a dictionary as a document after choosing the Spelling command in a session, Word will present a dialog box saying *Not a valid Word document.*
3. Press the Shift key and choose the Open Any File command. The names of all the documents in the current folder are shown. Open your personal dictionary file as a document. Do this for every duplicated dictionary file with which you want to work.

Avoid the temptation to open anything other than regular Word documents and personal dictionary files, unless you're opening a duplicate of the file. Even if Word can successfully open a file (such as the Finder), doing so might cause Word to fail or, worse, might disrupt and permanently damage the file if you try to save it.

❹ Edit the lists; cut, copy, or paste between them; or format and print them. If you want to prepare a text-only document to be converted back into a dictionary, however, be sure that each word list you create conforms to the pattern described in the previous section.

❺ When you're finished, save each word list. If you want to convert a word list back into a dictionary, save it in Text Only file format.

Once you've opened and converted a dictionary in this way, you should quit and restart Word before using it with the spelling checker. You can then open the word lists you created as dictionaries if you want, using the methods described earlier in this section. If you don't restart the program, Word will insist that any dictionaries you converted are still open, even if you've closed all document windows.

Points to Remember

- You cannot change entries in Word's MS Dictionary, but you can create your own personal, or User, dictionaries. Each personal dictionary can have as many as 64,000 entries, and you can have as many as 16 dictionaries open at once, but for speedy spell-checking, limit your entries to 1,000 per dictionary, and don't have more than five dictionaries open at one time.
- The spelling checker will not check text that is in hidden format unless it is visible. The Preferences dialog box controls the display of hidden text.
- Word opens the MS Dictionary and the User 1 dictionary when you choose the Spelling command. You must open other dictionaries you want to use.
- When you click the No Change button for an unknown word during a spelling check, Word ignores that word for the rest of the session. To have Word "forget" its list of No Change words, press the Shift key while you choose the Spelling command.
- If you need to, you can convert a document to a dictionary file or open a dictionary file as a document. However, always be sure to make copies of any files you manipulate in this way, in case one should become damaged.

Techniques

Check Spelling

The Spelling dialog box	Action
Words list box	After you click Suggest, shows possible correct spellings; after you select a personal dictionary, shows the words in that dictionary.
Open Dictionaries list box	Shows the names of the open dictionaries.
Unknown Word area	Shows the word that caused the spelling checker to stop.
Change To field	Contains the word that is to replace the unknown word or that is to be added to the selected dictionary.
Ignore Words in All Caps option	Indicates whether Word should ignore uppercase text and acronyms.
√ button	Checks the spelling of the word shown in the Change To field.

The Spelling dialog box	Action
+ button	Adds the unknown word or the word in the Change To field to the selected personal dictionary.
– button	Removes the selected word from the selected dictionary.
Start Check or Continue Check button	Starts or continues a spelling check.
Change button	Replaces the unknown word with the word in the Change To field.
No Change button	Skips past the word for the rest of the session.

Start a spelling check

1. Position the insertion point where you want to begin the spelling check, or select specific text. (Double-click on a word to check its spelling alone.)
2. Choose Spelling from the Utilities menu. Word checks first the word containing the insertion point or to the left of it.
3. Click Start Check, or press Return.

When a word is not found in a dictionary, it appears in the Unknown Word area. If you start a check in the middle of a document, when Word reaches the end, it asks if you want to continue checking from the beginning of the document. Click OK to continue or Cancel to stop.

Add the unknown word to a personal dictionary

1. Select the dictionary.
2. Click the + button, or press Command- +.

Correct the unknown word

1. Type the replacement in the Change To field, or click on the unknown word to display it in the Change To field and then edit it.
2. Click the Change button, or press Return.

Correct the unknown word and add it to a dictionary

1. Type the replacement in the Change To field, or click on the unknown word to display it in the Change To field and then edit it.
2. Select the dictionary to which you want to add the word.
3. Click the + button, or press Command- +.
4. Click the Change button, or press Return.

Have Word suggest a spelling for the unknown word

1. Click the Suggest button, or press Command-S.
2. Select the correct word.
3. Click the Change button, or press Return.

Do nothing to the unknown word

1. Click the No Change button, or press Return. Word will not stop on that word again during the current session.

Remove a word from a dictionary

1. Choose the Spelling command.
2. Select the dictionary by clicking on its name in the Open Dictionaries list box.
3. Select the word to be removed from the Words list box, or type it in the Change To field.
4. Click the – button, or press Command- –.

Working with Dictionary Files

Create a new dictionary

1. Choose the Spelling command.
2. Choose New from the File menu.
3. In the Change To field, type each word you want to add and click the + button after each. Be sure to type words as they should appear in the document; for example, type all proper names with an initial capital letter.

You can also run a spelling check on a document containing the words you want to add.

Open a dictionary

1. Choose the Spelling command.
2. Choose Open from the File menu.
3. Open the desired dictionary file.

The name of the dictionary appears in the Open Dictionaries list box.

Save a dictionary

❶ Choose the Spelling command.

❷ Select the dictionary you want to save.

❸ Choose the Save command.

❹ If you haven't saved the dictionary before, Word will ask you to specify a name. Do so, and then click Save.

Close a dictionary

❶ Choose the Spelling command.

❷ Select the dictionary you want to close.

❸ Choose Close from the File menu.

Move a word from one dictionary to another

❶ Choose the Spelling command.

❷ Select the source dictionary and select the word to be moved. The word appears in the Change To field.

❸ Click the – button to delete the word.

❹ Select the destination dictionary.

❺ Click the + button to add the word to the selected dictionary.

Use the UK Dictionary

❶ Give the MS Dictionary another name, such as *US Dictionary*.

❷ Change the name of the UK Dictionary file to *MS Dictionary*.

Reverse the process to go back to using the MS Dictionary.

■ *Commands*

Command name	Meaning, menu	Standard keyboard	Keypad	Extended keyboard
Reset Spelling	Clears list of spelling corrections Word remembers for current session.			
Spelling…	Checks a document or selected text for incorrect spelling.			
	Utilities	⌘L		F15

SECTION 3

Refining the Appearance

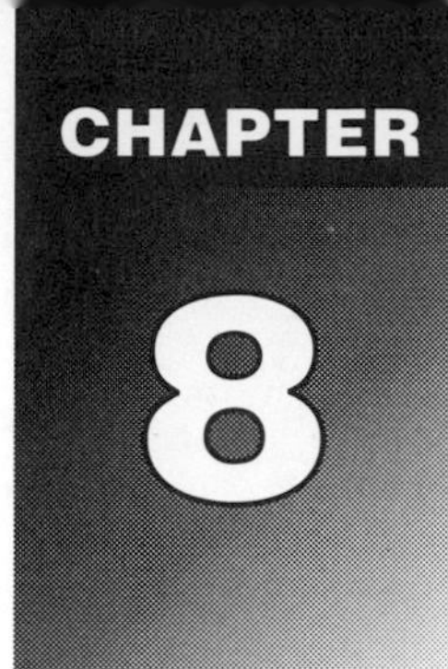

Character Formatting

When you spend a lot of time getting the wording in a document just right, you want it to look good on paper. A well-designed document presents text in a format that is attractive, readable, and easy to follow. It invites the reader to delve into its pages. A document that is not formatted or that is poorly designed is likely to turn away potential readers. Reading such a document is distracting because the design elements that should serve as guideposts for readers are inconsistent or missing altogether. A poor design can intrude upon and detract from the message you are trying to get across.

Microsoft Word provides many features for enhancing the look, style, and readability of your written communications. These capabilities allow you to do much more than construct simple paragraphs or italicize a word here or there. Word's formatting features enable you to personalize your documents and make them special with little extra work on your part.

With Word, you can format your documents almost any way you like. For example, Word lets you freely adjust tabs, margins, line spacing, and character attributes. With only a handful of commands, you can precisely control the location of every character on every page. In the next several chapters, you'll learn about controlling the look of your text and the shape of each paragraph, numbering pages in a variety of styles and formats, creating tables, breaking documents into sections, and more.

■ *An Overview of Document Design*

Look at the sample documents in Chapter 18, "Blueprints." They were developed not to represent the ultimate in modern graphic design but to give you an idea of the range of effects you can achieve in Word and to show you how to go about creating similar designs for your own documents. As you read the next few chapters, keep in mind the following principles of good design.

Your primary goal is a document that is attractive and readable. The font you use must be easy to read, and the relationship of the font used for body text to the fonts used in headings, headers, and footers should be harmonious and balanced. The lines of text should be short enough for you to read without losing your place. You should be able to find the major sections in a document, but the design elements that give the document its order and structure should not be overwhelming or distracting.

The appearance you develop for a document should be consistent. Readers use design elements (the style of headings, for example) to orient themselves. If a main heading and a subtopic look too much alike, or worse, if the same level of heading is in a different style in two places, the reader may become confused as to the logic and structure of your thesis. Style sheets in Word are a tremendous aid for establishing a consistent design. With this feature you can attach styles to the different elements of your document and fine-tune the design before, during, and after the writing of text. When you make a change to a style definition, every instance of that style in the document changes as well.

The design you develop for a document should also be appropriate to its subject. Poetry, for example, doesn't consume much space on a page, and so you can be freer with margins and line spacing, and you might arrange to have each poem printed on the right side of the page, with a graphic on the left. A scientific treatise might have four or five heading levels, because its purpose is not so much to provide an aesthetic experience as to communicate information clearly.

Of course, more than anything else, you want the design of your document to present your topic clearly. After all, unless you write for yourself alone, you are writing to communicate with the reader. Every element in a document—the content as well as the appearance—should support that clarity. The reader should not have to work to extract meaning from the material you present.

The need for clarity and consistency is of such importance that in many fields documents must be formatted according to specific requirements, or they are rejected out of hand. Doctoral dissertations, for example, must be prepared using a strict set of manuscript preparation rules; the same applies to screenplays, government bids and reports, and application forms. Often you can get style guides from writer's manuals, from the editorial offices of the publication for which you are writing, or from the department where you expect to get your doctorate. Once you have received a style guide, you must then translate its rules into a set of specifications—page dimensions and margins, font choices, style sheet definitions, placement of footnotes, and so on—in Word.

The Five Format Domains

In Word, you apply formatting and design decisions by making changes within one of the five format domains. These range in scope from the smallest unit your document can contain—the character—to the largest possible—the document itself.

Character Formats

A character to Word is like an atom to a chemist; in a Word document, there is no smaller unit. You can change the appearance of almost all 256 elements in the ASCII character set by changing their *font*. Some fonts, such as Zapf Dingbats, contain few or no alphabetic letter shapes, but instead consist of geometric shapes, border patterns, specialized icons, and so on. You can change the point size, or *font size*, of characters, and you can also change their attributes, or *font style* (not to be confused with styles on a style sheet), by making them bold or underlining them. Finally, you can adjust the placement of characters on a line by superscripting or subscripting them, or by expanding or contracting the spacing of characters. These topics are covered in this chapter.

Paragraph Formats

A paragraph is any collection of characters that is delimited by the paragraph mark, which is entered when you press the Return key. The paragraph attributes you can change in Word include margins, indention, location and type of tab stops, alignment and spacing of lines, and space before and after each paragraph. You can also draw lines around paragraphs as well as change their placement on the page—printing them side by side, starting them at the top of a page, or making sure that two paragraphs are kept together on one page. The next chapter covers this subject.

You can collect a set of character and paragraph formats, give it a name, and store it in a style sheet with other style definitions. When you apply a style, you apply it to one or more whole paragraphs; each paragraph in a document is assigned a style. When you make adjustments to a style, the changes are reflected in every paragraph to which that style has been applied. Styles are discussed in detail in Chapter 10, "Working with Style Sheets."

Table Formats

The Table format domain is a new feature in Word 4. It fulfills many of the purposes of both the Side-by-Side paragraph format and the multicolumn section formats. It has the advantage of being much more intuitive than either method for arranging text and graphics in rows and columns. You can create a table by choosing Insert Table from the Document menu and specifying the number of rows and columns the table is to have. Or you can transform a selected series of paragraphs into a table. For example, if you want to put a series of twelve paragraphs into a grid of three columns by four rows, simply select them, choose Insert Table, and enter the appropriate numbers in the Insert Table dialog box. Each cell in the table becomes a "minidocument" having its own selection bar, indents, and spacing. You can create even more complex structures by entering more than one paragraph in a given cell.

Once you've created a table, you can add, subtract, and merge rows, columns, and cells through the Table command, found on the Edit menu. You can also alter the spacing within the table and add borders with the Cells command, found on the Format menu, and by making adjustments in the Ruler. We'll go into tables more deeply in Chapter 11, "Formatting Tables and Lists."

Section Formats

Sections are collections of paragraphs that are separated by the double-dotted line that appears when you press Command-Enter. Sections are perhaps most easily compared to chapters in a book: You can have a chapter always start on a right-hand page, or you can use a running head that is different from the chapter before it, and you can specify that footnotes be printed at the end of each chapter. In a more generic sense, sections control some of the larger design elements in a document. For example, you can change from three-column text to one-column text and back again within one page of a newsletter by defining each of the areas as a different section. Chapter 12, "Section Formatting," covers this topic, and Chapter 13, "Headers, Footers, and Footnotes," deals with more of these large-scale design elements.

Document Formats

The largest unit in your document is the document itself, composed of one or more sections. Some of the parameters that pertain to the document as a whole include the size of the paper on which you want to print your document, the overall margins of the page, whether you want to print vertically or horizontally, and whether footnotes should fall at the end of the document or at the end of sections within the document. You can change these attributes by choosing Document from the Format menu, by manipulating the document while in Print Preview mode, and by making adjustments in the Ruler. Document formatting, Print Preview, and all preparations for printing are covered in Chapter 14, "Document Formatting and Printing."

■ *Working with Character Formats*

Characters consist of the letters, numbers, symbols, and punctuation marks you write with in Word. You can vary the shape, size, style, and placement of characters individually or throughout an entire document. Character formats in Word consist of the following:

- ❑ Font: You are limited only by the number and variety of fonts installed in the System file on the Word disk.
- ❑ Font size: The size of a font can range from 2 points to 127 points. The Macintosh follows typesetting standards and displays 72 points per inch on the screen.
- ❑ Font style or attribute: Choose from among underline, outline, **bold**, *italic*, and more—or combine them as you see fit. You can bury comments, editorial notes, and so on in your documents by using the Hidden character attribute.
- ❑ Position: In addition to their normal position on the baseline, characters can be either above it (as a superscript) or below it (as a subscript).
- ❑ Spacing: You can s t r e t c h or shrink the spacing of characters.
- ❑ Color: You can change the color of text, and see the color when the text is displayed on a color monitor. However, colored text always prints in black, even on a color printer.

You establish a character format primarily through the Character dialog box, although you can also access some formats from the Format and Font menus. Text can be formatted either after you've entered it or as you type it. In the first case, you simply select the text and choose one or more character formats. In the second, you set the insertion point and choose a new character format. Every character you type after that reflects the new format.

When you replace text, the characters you type retain the format of the original text. Suppose you underlined one word in a document. If you double-click on the word to select it and then start typing, the new text will be underlined. If you backspace over the word to delete it, the insertion point is still set for the underlining attribute, even after you delete the last character. Any new text you type in that spot will be underlined.

This behavior can be a little confusing; you probably don't expect to see underlining after you've deleted the word. However, Word assumes that you've just placed the insertion point there and chosen that set of formats in preparation for inserting some text. A good trick for getting around this is simply to backspace one character past the beginning of the underlined word to reset the insertion point to plain text.

When you choose Character from the Format menu, you see a dialog box like the one shown in Figure 8-1 on the following page. It is divided into groups of options that reflect the character formats you can apply to text.

You can move this dialog box, as you can move the others that have a title bar, by dragging it to a new position. Double-clicking in the title bar toggles the dialog box between its original position and the new position so that you can reveal the text beneath it. For your convenience, Word records in the current Word Settings file the position the box is in when you quit the program.

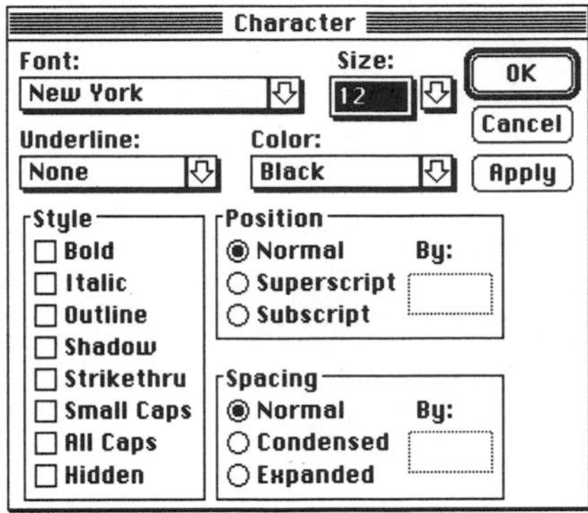

Figure 8-1
The Character dialog box.

The Character dialog box is the control center for all character formats; you can see what formats your text has by placing the insertion point and displaying this dialog box.

By definition, the insertion point is always between two characters. The format of text you type at the insertion point is almost always determined by the preceding character. The exception is when the preceding character is one of the special characters Word uses for such items as footnote references and the page and date elements in the Header and Footer windows. In these cases the format is taken from the text immediately preceding the special character. The reason for this should be obvious: You want any text you insert after a footnote reference to have the same format as the rest of the text, rather than the format of the footnote reference. If for some reason you have more than one of these special characters in a row (for example, the time and date elements in a Header window), Word reverts to plain text instead of taking the format from the text preceding the special characters.

Changing the Font

Word uses the 12-point New York font when you first start typing in the *Normal* style (if you haven't yet redefined the style), but you can choose a new font for any text in the document.

Fonts, sometimes called *typefaces*, are stored as resources in the System file on the Word disk. The Character dialog box displays the names and point sizes of all the fonts that are currently installed. All startup disks have their own System file, each of which can contain a different set of font resources. Use the Apple Font/DA Mover to install or remove fonts (as well as desk accessories). The amount of space a font consumes is not trivial, especially if you install a range of point sizes. The larger the point size of a font, the more disk space it uses. It is best to install only fonts you will use regularly. Alternatively, if you don't have a hard disk, you can use more than one System disk, each with its own System file and font assortments, for special occasions when you need an unusual or special typeface.

Choosing Fonts from the Character Dialog Box

Word displays fonts in the Font drop-down list in the Character dialog box and on the Font menu. To choose a new font from the list box:

❶ Choose the Character command. The dialog box appears.

❷ Select the font you want from the Font drop-down list.

❸ Click OK.

Instead of clicking the OK button, you can click the Apply button to see the effect of your font choice in the document without dismissing the dialog box. Clicking Cancel after using the Apply button does not cancel the font change; to do that, you must choose Undo Formatting from the Edit menu.

Choosing Fonts from the Font Menu

To choose a new font from the Font menu, simply pull down the menu and select the one you want. If the font isn't there, you must access it through the Character dialog box. In both Short Menus and Full Menus, all the installed fonts are normally listed on the Font menu.

If fonts you use regularly are not on the Font menu, you can add them as follows: First choose the Character command; then, for each font you want to add, press Option-Command- + and click on the font name. Similarly, you can remove a font name by first pressing Option-Command- – and then selecting the name from the Font menu.

The Font, Format, and Work menus in Word 4 are no longer limited to 31 items each. If you've added more fonts than your screen can display at one time, you see a triangle at the bottom of the menu. Drag the pointer below the end of the menu to scroll the menu and display the items at the bottom of the list. When you do this, the first few items on the menu are replaced with another triangle, which signals that more items are listed above the top of the menu. Unfortunately, you cannot choose these "hidden" menu items from the keyboard; use the mouse instead.

Choosing Fonts from the Keyboard

You can also set a font from the keyboard. Press Shift-Command-E; the word *Font* appears in the status box of the window. Type the first few letters of the name of the font you want—enough to establish it as unique—and press the Return key. To change the font again, simply click in the status area. The word *Font* appears again, and you can type a new font name.

TIP

Font ID Numbers
Instead of typing the font name in the status box when you are using the Shift-Command-E key sequence, you can type the ID number for the font. The Macintosh system and some programs know each font both by a number assigned to it and by its name. This table lists some common font ID (FID) numbers:

FID	Name	FID	Name
0	Chicago	13	Zapf Dingbats
1	Geneva	14	Bookman
2	New York	15	Helvetica Narrow
3	Geneva	16	Palatino
4	Monaco	18	Zapf Chancery
5	Venice	20	Times
6	London	21	Helvetica
7	Athens	22	Courier
8	San Francisco	23	Symbol
9	Toronto	24	Mobile
10	Seattle	33	Avant Garde
11	Cairo	34	New Century Schoolbook
12	Los Angeles		

Word, however, uses only the font ID number, and not the font name, to keep track of your fonts internally. This can cause occasional problems, because the Font/DA Mover is capable of changing this number if you install a font that has the same number as a font already installed in the System file. Suspect that you are having this problem if you create a document under one System file and find that, when you reopen it under another, a font used in the document seems to have been replaced with another, even though that font is also installed in the second System file. (If a font used in your document doesn't exist in the System file, Word substitutes another font, usually New York or Geneva.)

For example, the Boston and Zapf Dingbats fonts may collide if your System file originally had Boston in it and you added Zapf Dingbats later. If you create a document containing some dingbats on another Mac and then open the document under this System file, all the Zapf Dingbats in your document change to characters in the Boston font. To correct this situation:

1. Launch the Font/DA Mover, and open the System file's fonts.
2. Remove the Zapf Dingbats and Boston fonts.
3. Reinstall the Zapf Dingbats font from a copy of the original disk containing the LaserWriter Plus fonts. (If you don't have the disk, try installing the font from another System file that doesn't have

Boston on it.) The original font ID number is preserved this time, because no collision occurs.

4. Reinstall the Boston font. Because the Zapf font has already been installed, the ID number of the Boston font in the System file changes instead of that of the Zapf font.
5. Quit the Font/DA Mover.

Because the Macintosh font-numbering conventions no longer strictly require that each font have a unique ID number, you might run into this problem more frequently with special fonts obtained from sources other than Apple.

If you don't have the option of removing and adding fonts to the System file of the Mac which prints your document, you can also try saving the file in the Rich Text Format (RTF) on the Mac that you've used to create the document. When you do this, Word encodes the fonts used in the document both by name and by font number. Then, when you want to print the document on the Mac having a different arrangement of fonts, simply open the file from Word on that Mac to convert the RTF file back to Word format. In fact, to see the ID numbers attached to the fonts in your System file, you can save any file—even an empty document—in RTF and then open the file as text, without converting the file into a Word document. A table listing the fonts and the font numbers appears at the beginning of the RTF file. (For more information on RTF files, see Chapter 16, "Transferring Text and Graphics.")

Changing the Font Size

Fonts come in different point sizes, usually ranging from 9 to 24 points. You can actually use any point size from 2 to 127 (in whole numbers); if the specific point size you want is not installed on the disk, Word scales the font to fit your request. Scaled fonts typically look jagged and uneven, as depicted in Figure 8-2, because the scaling is not always perfect. For speed and appearance, choose only font sizes that are installed on the disk. If you are using a LaserWriter, the scaling issue is not as important, because fonts are scaled smoothly when printed, regardless of what you see on the screen.

This is text in 12-point Geneva.

This is text in 21-point Geneva.

Figure 8-2
A normal font and a scaled font.

Note that when you choose a font from the Font menu, some of the sizes are outlined and others are plain. In Figure 8-3, the outlined font sizes are the ones installed in the System file for the font preceded by a check mark in the lower part of the menu. The nonoutlined sizes are not installed; if you choose one of these, Word scales the font from one of the sizes that are available.

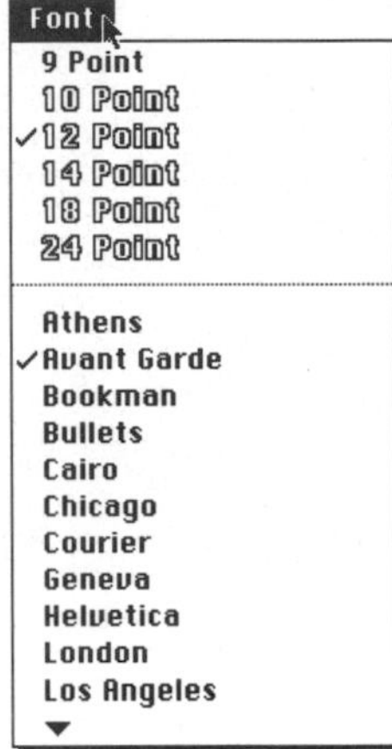

Figure 8-3
Font menu for Avant Garde sizes.

If you must pick a font size that is not installed in your System file, try for one that's exactly twice as large as an outlined font size. Text scaling in Word—and in other Macintosh applications, for that matter—works better when performed in even multiples of an installed font. A 12-point font scaled up to 24 points looks better than the same font scaled to 18 points.

Choosing a Font Size from the Character Dialog Box

You can choose a font size at any time, whether you pick a new font or not. Like fonts, font sizes can be selected from within the Character dialog box or from the Font menu. To change the font size from the Character dialog box, do the following:

❶ Choose the Character command.

❷ The Font Size drop-down field (to the right of the Font drop-down list) lists the point sizes installed on the disk for the selected font. If you see the size you want, select it. Otherwise, type the new point size in the Size field. (The number displayed in the field is the currently selected size.)

Remember that scaled fonts slow down the Mac and might look jagged and uneven onscreen and remain so when you print the document on a dot-matrix printer such as the ImageWriter. If you print on a PostScript printer such as the LaserWriter this is not as important a consideration, because they can scale fonts much more smoothly.

Choosing a Font Size from the Font Menu

To pick a new font size from the Font menu, pull down the menu and select the one you want. Like fonts, font sizes can be added to and removed from this menu. For example, if you are doing a newsletter and use 36-point Bookman for the titles of your articles (commonly called the *display font*, as opposed to the *text font* for your document), you would add the 36-point size to the Font menu as follows:

❶ Choose the Character command.

❷ Press Option-Command- +. The mouse pointer changes to a plus symbol.

❸ Because the Size field is already selected, type *36*, replacing the previous contents of the field.

❹ Click on the entry in the Size field. The menu bar blinks, signaling that the item has been added to the Font menu.

❺ Click Cancel to dismiss the dialog box.

To remove a size from the Font menu, press Option-Command- – and select the size from the menu.

Choosing a Font Size from the Keyboard

You can't set a specific font size from the keyboard, but you can easily increase or decrease the current size. Simply select some text or set an insertion point, and press either Shift-Command- > to increase the size or Shift-Command- < to decrease the size. Word displays the new point size in the status box of the window, choosing the next size from a list of the most common font sizes (7, 9, 10, 12, 14, 18, 24, 36, 48, 60, and 72 points). Keep increasing or decreasing the size until you have what you want.

Changing Character Styles

All characters can be assigned various styles, such as boldface or underlining. Do not confuse these with paragraph styles, which are discussed in Chapter 9, "Paragraph Formatting." These styles are listed in the Style option group in the Character dialog box and in the Underline drop-down list above. Most character styles can be mixed—that is, you can both boldface and underline text if you want. Do this with caution, however; too many character styles can spoil the brew. Figure 8-4 on the following page shows Plain Text (for comparison) and the 12 possible character styles and how they look on the screen. (See "Removing Character Formats" later in this chapter.)

Plain Text – ABCDEFabcdef1234567890
Bold – ABCDEFabcdef1234567890
Italic – ABCDEFabcdef1234567890
Underline – ABCDEFabcdef1234567890
Word Underline – ABCDEFabcdef1234567890
Double Underline – ABCDEFabcdef1234567890
Dotted Underline – ABCDEFabcdef1234567890
~~Strikethru – ABCDEFabcdef1234567890~~
Outline – ABCDEFabcdef1234567890
Shadow – ABCDEFabcdef1234567890
SMALL CAPS – ABCDEFABCDEF1234567890
ALL CAPS – ABCDEFABCDEF1234567890
Hidden – ABCDEFabcdef1234567890

Figure 8-4
Plain Text plus the 12 character styles.

When every character of a block of text you've selected has exactly the same set of character styles (a *homogeneous* set of character styles) and you choose the Character command, you see those styles checked in the Style group of the dialog box. If some of the characters in the selected text have different formats, you see all the check boxes filled with gray. The check boxes are also gray if you've selected a large amount of text, roughly 500 characters if you are selecting by characters or 40 paragraphs if you are selecting by paragraphs.

If you are experienced with Microsoft Excel, you might expect Word to use a similar convention for the display of style options in the dialog box: checked if all selected text has the format and gray if only some of the text has the style. However, there are so many possible combinations that it would take Word too long to analyze the text you've selected and display the information in the dialog box. Instead, Word shows every check box filled with gray.

A similar condition exists in the lower half of the Format menu. If you select text that has a homogeneous set of character styles and then pull down the menu, you see those styles checked on the menu. If you select text that does not have a homogeneous mixture of character styles (or if too much text is selected), not one of the menu items is checked.

Choosing Character Styles

You can set a character style in one of three ways. First, you can choose Character from the Format menu and select options from the dialog box that appears.

The second way is to choose an option from the lower half of the Format menu. You can add character styles to the Format menu by first choosing the Character command and then pressing Option-Command- + and clicking on every character style you want to add to the menu. When you're finished adding the styles, click Cancel to avoid changing anything in your document. Similarly, you can remove a character style by pressing Option-Command- – and selecting the relevant menu item.

The third way to set a character style is to press a sequence of keys from the keyboard. You might better remember these sequences if you keep in mind that Word uses Shift-Command combinations for formatting operations and Option-Command combinations for editing operations. The complete set of key sequences you need to achieve these effects is presented at the end of this chapter. Don't forget that you can assign your own key sequences to the character style commands through the Commands dialog box.

All these methods for setting a character style toggle. For example, if you select a word and underline it, you remove the underlining by using the same command or set of keystrokes again. If the text you select does not have a homogeneous set of styles, the style you choose will be applied to all the text. Using the same command again will then remove the style from every character in the text.

Now let's take a tour through Word's range of character styles.

TIP

Undoing Style, Position, and Spacing Formats
While the Character dialog box is displayed and before you click Apply, you can return certain options in a changed format to their original states without resetting other options you want to keep—like a partial Undo command. Each group in the Character dialog box is surrounded by a line and has a title: Style, Spacing, and Position. (The font and font size aren't marked in this way and don't work like this.) If you selected a set of changes to the options in a particular group and want to return them to their original states, simply click on the title of that group. For example, to revert to the previous character style settings, you would click on the Style title in the dialog box.

The Bold, Italic, Outline, Shadow, and Strikethrough Styles

The bold, italic, outline, shadow, and strikethrough character styles are quite straightforward. To set one of these styles, simply select the text and apply the format by using one of the methods described in the previous section.

The outline and shadow formats (as well as the underline, subscript and superscript formats discussed below) are unusual in that using them often changes the line spacing for the lines in the paragraph containing the formatted text. For example, if you outline a word in a paragraph, you might notice that the following line moves down a bit. This happens because the format has changed the dimensions of the text in the paragraph, and Word pushes down the subsequent lines to accommodate the change.

Usually you don't want this to happen, as it detracts from the appearance of your document. Choose the Paragraph command from the Format menu and check the Line field in the Spacing group; when the line spacing is set to Auto or to a number close to single spacing, Word makes adjustments to the line spacing. The remedy is either to set the line-spacing number high enough to provide room to spare if a format increases the vertical dimension of the text, or to use a negative number in the Line field. A negative line-spacing number tells Word to use that line spacing regardless of the dimensions of the text in the line. This is discussed in more detail in the next chapter, "Paragraph Formatting."

Underlining Text

Word supports five forms of underlining, only one of which can be selected at a time:

- None: Choose this when you've underlined text and want to remove the underlining.
- Underline: A standard underline. Underlines all characters, including spaces.
- Word Underline: Underlines complete words and punctuation marks only; spaces, nonbreaking spaces, and tabs are not underlined.
- Double Underline: Places a double underline below all characters and spaces.
- Dotted Underline: Places a dotted underline below all characters and spaces. When printed on the LaserWriter, a dotted underline looks more like a gray bar than a series of dots.

If you are experienced with earlier versions of Word, you might have used its tab leader feature to draw horizontal lines in your documents for elements such as dotted lines in contracts or page-number references in tables of contents. This feature exists in Word 4, but you don't have to use it as much because of the new version's wider range of underline attributes (as well as a wider range of paragraph border formats). When you underline text containing tabs, the tabs are underlined as well. If you want to underline only text—the headings in a table, for instance—use the Word Underline format.

Capitalizing Text

You can choose SMALL CAPS or ALL CAPS but not both. Small caps are commonly used for the abbreviations A.M., P.M., B.C., and A.D., for acronyms that might be obtrusive if presented in full-size capital letters, or to give a distinctive look to display text (such as article titles). You type lowercase letters, which in small-capped format are converted to capital letters in the next smaller font size.

These formats are interesting in that they don't really convert lowercase letters to uppercase letters; only the appearance of the text changes. If you type lowercase letters in one of these formats, you see uppercase letters as though you had pressed the Caps Lock key. However, if you then remove the formats, the text returns to whatever case you originally typed.

Using Hidden Text

The hidden format affects characters in one of two ways: When the Show Hidden Text option is turned on in the Preferences dialog box (displayed from the Edit menu), characters formatted as hidden appear with a dotted underline, as shown in Figure 8-5. This is easy to confuse with the dotted underline format—in fact, text can have both formats at the same time. When Show Hidden Text is turned off, the text disappears from view. The Show Hidden Text option affects the visual display of characters only; a similar option in the Print dialog box controls whether or not hidden text is printed.

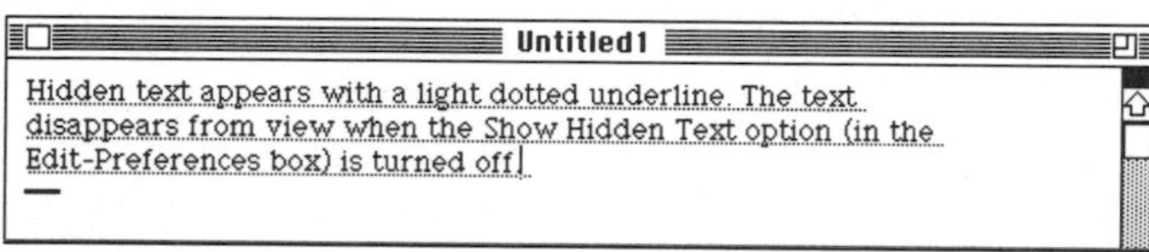

Figure 8-5
Hidden text as it appears on the screen.

Hidden text can be considered the ultimate formatting option because you can control whether text with this format is visible or invisible. The main uses for hidden text are as follows:

- ❏ To bury comments in a document. This is useful for documents created or edited by more than one person. You can pass remarks from person to person without changing the apparent content of the document.
- ❏ To hide PostScript commands in a document. (See Appendix C, "Using PostScript.")
- ❏ To indicate markers for tables of contents and index entries. (See Chapter 15, "Creating a Table of Contents and Index.")
- ❏ To bury a filename before material transferred with Word's QuickSwitch feature. (See Chapter 16, "Transferring Text and Graphics.")

Hidden text has a few properties that make it different from the other character attributes. When you do a spelling check, for instance, Word does not check the spelling of hidden text while it is invisible. To check the spelling of hidden text, first turn on the Show Hidden Text option. Similarly, you usually do not want to repaginate or hyphenate hidden text, and so you should make it invisible before repaginating or hyphenating your document. Also, you can print the hidden text regardless of whether or not it's visible on screen when you select the Print Hidden Text option in the Print dialog box.

TIP

Adding Show Hidden Text to the Format Menu
You can add the Show Hidden Text option to the Format menu by choosing Preferences from the Edit menu, pressing Option-Command- +, and clicking on the Show Hidden Text option. The menu bar blinks to signal that the option has been added to the menu. To remove the option, press Option-Command- – (minus), and choose Show Hidden Text from the menu.

Changing the Position of Text

The various characteristics of characters have been given names over time; Figure 8-6 shows some of them. Word usually prints and displays characters with their baselines aligned, even when more than one font, size, or character style is on a line. You can move text up or down relative to this baseline with the Position options in the Character dialog box.

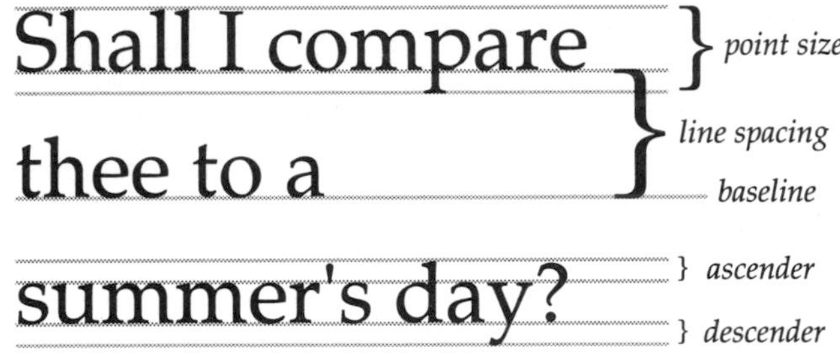

Figure 8-6
Character anatomy.

The superscript format is often used to place numbers or special graphic characters (often called dingbats) a little above the text for such purposes as marking footnote references. In fact, if you look at the automatic style definition for footnote references, you'll see that it uses the superscript position format. Here are some of the characters that frequently appear as superscript:

Character	Name	Key sequence
*	asterisk	Shift-8
™	trademark	Option-2
®	registered trademark	Option-R
§	section mark	Option-6
†	dagger	Option-T
‡	double dagger	Shift-Option-7

You can use the Key Caps desk accessory to find other special characters. Another use for superscripts and subscripts is for exponents and for the indices of subscripted variables:

$$r_{(n+1)}^2 = x^2 + y^2$$

Look closely at the Mac's screen and you'll see that it is composed of many lines, each of which is made up of tiny dots, or *pixels*. The standard Macintosh screen contains 342 lines with 512 dots per line (or a screen resolution of 512 by 342 pixels). Each pixel on the standard screen is 1 point, or 1⁄72 inch, on a side.

In Word, you can specify both superscripts and subscripts in increments of 1 point, from 0.5 to 63.5 points (about 7⁄8 inch). Measurements *as they are reported by Word* are rounded to increments of a point, regardless of the measurement you enter. It may seem extreme to have a superscript that is as much as 63 points above the baseline, but it isn't when you consider that in some mathematical applications superscripts themselves can have superscripts and that large font sizes might need high superscripts to achieve the right effect.

To raise text by 1 point, select it and choose the Character command. Click the Superscript option in the Position group. Word offers the default positioning, 3 points. Change the number to 1 point and click OK. Figure 8-7 shows the effect of superscripted and subscripted text moved 2, 4, and 6 points above and below the baseline.

The key sequence for superscripting, Shift-Command- +, raises the selected text 3 points above the baseline. Interestingly, it also reduces the font size to the next lower size, as if you had pressed Shift-Command- < as well. The key sequence for subscripting, Shift-Command- –, works similarly.

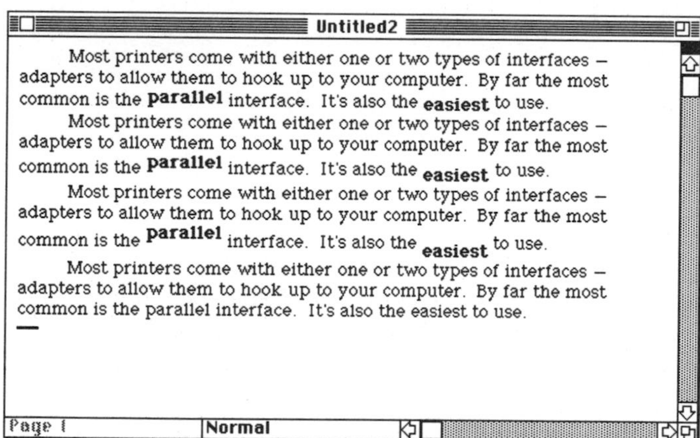

Figure 8-7
Subscripted and superscripted text (the boldface is for emphasis).

Changing the Spacing of Text

Most fonts for the Macintosh are known as *proportional fonts*—that is, the *i*'s and *l*'s take up less horizontal space than the *m*'s and *w*'s. Characters in fixed-width, or *monospace,* fonts, including Monaco and Courier (the latter is used with the LaserWriter), are evenly spaced on the screen and on paper. The spacing properties of a font are built into it when the font is created. You can extend or contract this spacing with the Spacing options. The process of adjusting the spacing between letters or throughout a font is called *kerning* in the publishing and graphic-arts trades.

To increase the spacing between characters, choose the Character command, click Expanded in the Spacing group, and enter the number of points by which you want to increase the spacing. Word always adds the space after the character, not before. You can expand the spacing by as much as 14 points. However, as is the case with the Position formats, the spacing is rounded to increments of 1 point when printed. To decrease the spacing, click Condensed and enter a measurement from 0 to 1.75 points; because Word rounds to increments of one point, the only value that works here is 1 point. Figure 8-8 shows some examples of expanded and condensed text.

Expanded 0.0 points
Expanded 0.5 points
Expanded 1.0 points
Expanded 1.5 points
Expanded 2.0 points

Condensed 0.0 points
Condensed 0.5 points
Condensed 1.0 points
Condensed 1.5 points
Condensed 1.75 points

Figure 8-8
Expanded and condensed text.

Generally you kern text for three reasons: to adjust specific letter pairs, to stretch or contract an entire font, and to achieve special typographic effects.

Kerning Pairs of Letters

Often, a pair of letters does not fit together pleasingly when printed, leaving either an unsightly gap or no space at all. Consider the following examples:

Unkerned	Kerned	Effect used
VA	VA	Condensed, 1 point
RT	RT	Condensed, 1 point
wC	wC	Expanded, 1 point
$400	$ 400	First character expanded, 3 points

At a quick glance, these differences might seem subtle, but they can have a significant impact on the aesthetics of your documents, particularly in large display text such as titles of articles or sections in a document.

To kern a pair of letters, select the first letter, choose the Character command, and enter an appropriate spacing. Because the spacing is measured from the end of each letter selected and you want to adjust the gap between two letters, be sure to select only the first letter in the pair.

TIP

Kerning Tables in Word

A kerning table in typography consists of a list of selected pairs of letters and a specification for each pair describing how much space to remove (or add) between them. Word doesn't support kerning tables yet, in that it can't look for specific pairs of letters and adjust their spacing automatically, but with some work you can achieve a similar effect. To create a "kerning table" in a certain font at a specific point size (such as that established in a style definition), do the following:

1. In a blank area of your document, type each pair of letters that needs kerning. Select the first letter in each pair, and set its spacing.
2. When you've finished, go back to the beginning of the list and copy (don't cut) the first pair to the Clipboard.
3. Choose Change from the Search menu, and enter that pair in the Find What edit field and enter ^*c* in the Change To field. This allows you to replace the pair with the contents of the Clipboard.
4. Search through the document, replacing each match in that font and font size with the kerned pair. Because the spacing characteristics of two letters depend on whether the letters are in uppercase or lowercase, you may want to create new pairs for uppercase and lowercase combinations.

This can be an involved task if carried to extremes, so it's best to limit the kerning replacements to obvious cases. You can also use macro-recording software—such as AutoMac III, Apple's MacroMaker, or Tempo from Affinity Microsystems—to make this process more automatic.

Finally, note that you can use Word's mathematical typesetting feature to position characters relative to each other at intervals beyond condensing by 1 point or expanding by 14 points. See Appendix D, "Mathematical Typesetting," for more information.

Kerning a Font

The phrase *kerning a font* properly refers to the process of establishing a kerning table, often containing hundreds of character pairs, and slowly refining it until the spacing is perfect (to a typographer's eyes, which are more sensitive than those of mere mortals). Here the term describes the act of expanding or condensing every character of a font by a certain amount of space; this is known as a *tracking adjustment*.

Because a style sheet definition specifies at most one font per style, you can use this feature to stretch or compress all text in a given style. Simply choose Define Styles from the Format menu, select the style you want to adjust, choose the Character command, and alter the spacing. Click OK to add the spacing format to the style definition. If you use this method to adjust the spacing between the characters in a font attached to a style, remember that it will also apply to any text within a paragraph having that style, not only the font the style specifies.

Expanding or Contracting Selected Text for Effect

The third major use of spacing adjustments is purely for artistic effect. Consider these typographic elements:

T H E J U P I T E R

□□□□□□□□□□□□□□□□□□□□□□□□□□□□□□□□□□□

Wolfgang Amadeus Mozart

GETTING STARTED

Configuring Your Word Disk

As you can see, you can change the spacing of text in your document for reasons that have nothing to do with the legibility of the text. Simply select the text to be affected, choose the Character command, and enter the spacing you want to use. Click Apply or OK to put the spacing into effect.

TIP

Adding Position and Spacing to the Format Menu

You can add position and spacing formats to the Format menu, but the method for doing so is a little different from that for adding other character formats. To add a 2-point superscript to the menu, choose the Character command, select the Superscript option, and enter *2 pt* in the edit field. Then press Option-Command- +, click on the Superscript option again, and click Cancel. When you pull down the Format menu, you will see, toward the bottom, the *Superscript 2 pt* option. You can add a collection of formats, say 1-point, 2-point, and 3-point superscripts, to the menu. Incidentally, you can add the Normal Spacing and Normal Position options to the menu as well.

Changing the Color of Text on the Screen

If you select a color from the options on the Color drop-down list, the selected text changes to that color on the screen. Currently, only seven colors (other than black) are available: blue, cyan, green, magenta, red, yellow, and white. Unfortunately, if you print a document containing colored text, the text prints in black, even if the printer is capable of printing color. However, using colored text in documents does benefit you in that it lets you mark text for editing or to indicate on screen who has entered what text when more than one person works on a document.

Setting text to a color works even if your Mac or monitor isn't capable of displaying color. Simply select the text and give it the desired color attribute. When the document is viewed on a Mac II with a color monitor, the text appears in the color you've set.

Using colored text does have one drawback. On-screen scrolling is dramatically slower when more than two colors are displayed on a Mac II—the more colors displayed, the slower the scrolling becomes. (You set the number of colors displayed by opening the Control Panel, selecting the Monitor icon, and setting the desired number of colors.) Scrolling is even slower when you've also set Fractional Widths in the document—as much as six times slower than when scrolling in black-and-white. If you need to use color, you might try restricting its use to writing instead of editing and to when you aren't using the scroll bars as much.

Removing Character Formats

Once you've established a set of formats for the characters in your text, how do you go about selectively removing them if you need to? The most obvious way to remove a specific character attribute is to call up the Character dialog box and deselect the option. Remember that, depending on the amount of text selected when you choose the Character command and whether it contains a homogeneous set of formats, some options in the Style group of the dialog box might be selected and some or all of the options might be gray. The Character dialog box is like a master control panel for the character formats in the selected text. Clicking on a gray attribute option fills the box with an X and sets that format for all the selected text. Clicking on the option again clears the box and removes that format from the text.

To remove one of the position or spacing formats, simply click the Normal radio button in the appropriate group of the dialog box. Of course, because these groups use an edit field to specify the amount of spacing change for the format, you can't return a 3-point superscript, for example, to a previously established 2-point superscript without typing the number in the field.

Sometimes you will want to remove *all* the character attributes without affecting the font, spacing, and position formats in your text. One way to do this is to deselect the options in the Character Style group one by one, as has been discussed. An easier way is to choose Plain Text from the Format menu, or press Shift-Command-Z. This command deselects every option in the Style group of the Character dialog box, leaving the font, position, and spacing unchanged. It works even if these character attributes are part of a style definition assigned to the text; selecting the text and using this command removes the attributes.

If you work with styles, you will often find that it's convenient to return selected text in a paragraph to the base character formats defined for the style assigned to that paragraph, removing any additional formats (attribute, font, position, or spacing) you've added. You can accomplish this by selecting the text and choosing Plain Text for Style from the Format menu, or press Shift-Command-Spacebar.

Testing New Character Formats

The Character dialog box has three buttons: OK, Cancel, and Apply. Clicking the OK button tells Word to implement your formatting choices and close the dialog box. The Cancel button aborts your changes (as long as you haven't yet clicked Apply) and closes the dialog box. The Apply button, however, lets you test the new format without closing the dialog box. When you click this button, any selections you made in the Character dialog box are applied to the selected text without dismissing the dialog box. (See Figure 8-9.) You can move the dialog box out of the way if it covers the selected text. (Double-click on the title bar to toggle it between the two positions.) The Apply button is a time-saver when you're experimenting with a new format. Use it when you're having trouble making up your mind or simply trying out an option.

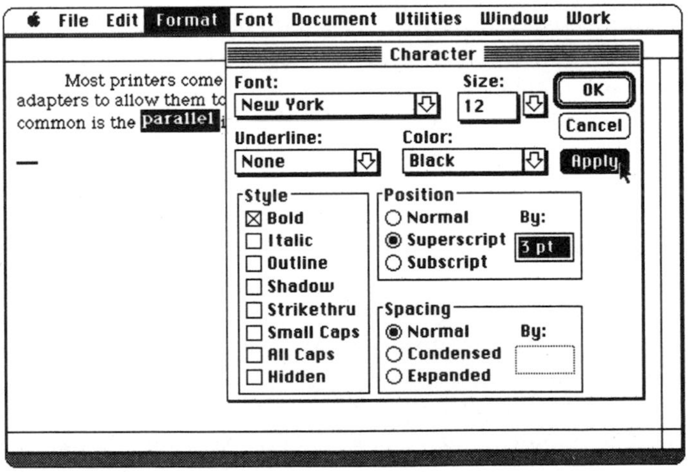

Figure 8-9
Applying a new format.

If, after experimenting with the Apply button, you want to return your text to its original state, simply click OK and then choose Undo from the Edit menu. Clicking Cancel won't remove the formats you've added with Apply.

■ *Points to Remember*

- ❑ A well-designed document is attractive and readable. Use a design appropriate to your subject matter.
- ❑ To implement the design of your document in Word, you work with five format domains: character, paragraph, table, section, and document. The character domain, the subject of this chapter, controls font, font size, character attributes (boldface, italic, and so on), letter-spacing, and the position of characters with respect to the baseline. The other domains are described in detail in later chapters.
- ❑ The Character dialog box, displayed when you choose Character from the Format menu, is the main vehicle for altering character formats, although you can also issue certain commands from the Font menu, the Format menu, and the keyboard.
- ❑ The Character dialog box shows the formats in effect for the selected text or for the text containing the insertion point. If all the selected characters don't have the same attributes or if you've selected a large amount of text, the boxes in the Style group are gray, and the drop-down lists appear blank.
- ❑ The Hidden character format lets you create hidden text. Text in this format doesn't appear when Show Hidden Text in the Preferences dialog box is turned off, and it isn't printed when Print Hidden Text in the Print dialog box is turned off. When hidden text is invisible, it isn't hyphenated, repaginated, or checked for spelling.
- ❑ Even though you can make formatting adjustments in Word of fractions of a point, all measurements as reported by Word are rounded to increments of a point when the document is printed.

■ *Techniques*

The Character Dialog Box

Option	Action
Font information group	Sets the font and font size.
Font drop-down list	Shows the names of the fonts currently installed in your System file. The font selected is the current font.
Size drop-down field	Shows the current font size. You can select another from the list of available sizes, or you can enter a different font size (from 2 points to 127 points). If you specify a size that is not available, Word scales the font to match the size you requested.

Option	Action
Style settings	Adds or removes character styles.
Underline drop-down list	Sets an underline format: None, Single, Word, Double, and Dotted.
Color drop-down list	Sets the color of text on-screen: Black, Blue, Cyan, Green, Magenta, Red, Yellow, and White. Colored text prints in black, even with printers capable of color.
Style group	Sets other character styles for text: Bold, Italic, Outline, Shadow, Strikethru, Small Caps, All Caps, Hidden.
Position group	Positions characters relative to the baseline. Enter values from 1 to 63 points, in 1-point increments.
Normal button	Places text on the baseline.
Superscript button	Places text above the baseline; defaults to 3 points.
Subscript button	Places text below the baseline, defaults to 2 points.
By field	Specifies how many points above or below the baseline to position text.
Spacing group	Sets the spacing between characters (kerning).
Normal button	Uses the default spacing.
Expanded	Increases the space between characters by up to 14 points.
Condensed	Reduces the space between characters by up to 1 point when printed.
By field	Specifies number of points to add to or subtract from the normal spacing between characters. Enter values in multiples of 1 point.
Buttons	
OK	Implements the selected formats and closes the dialog box.
Cancel	Closes the dialog box without implementing the selected formats.
Apply	Implements the selected formats without closing the dialog box.

Change the character format of existing text

❶ Select the text.

❷ Choose Character from the Format menu.

❸ Make the desired changes in the dialog box.

❹ Click OK.

(If the formats you want appear in the Font or Format menu, simply select the text and choose the desired options.)

Change the character format before typing text

❶ Set the insertion point where the text is to appear.

❷ Choose Character from the Format menu.

❸ Make the desired changes in the dialog box.

❹ Click OK.

(If the formats you want appear in the Font or Format menu, simply set the insertion point and choose the desired options.)

Undo a formatting change

❶ Choose Undo Formatting from the Edit menu immediately after you make the change.

Add a font to the Font menu

❶ Choose the Character command.

❷ Press Option-Command- +.

❸ Click on the font you want to add.

Add a font size to the Font menu

❶ Choose the Character command.

❷ Select the font for which you want to add the font size.

❸ Select the font size in the list box, or type it in the Size field.

❹ Press Option-Command- +.

❺ Click on the font size.

Add a character attribute to the Format menu

❶ Choose the Character command.

❷ Press Option-Command- +.

❸ Click on the attribute you want to add.

Add a position or spacing format to the Format menu

❶ Choose the Character command.

❷ Select the option you want to add, and enter the amount of the spacing in the By field.

❸ Press Option-Command- +.

❹ Click on the option to be added.

Remove a format from the Format or Font menu

1. Press Option-Command- – (minus).
2. Pull down the menu from which the option is to be removed.
3. Choose the option to be removed.

Remove all character attributes from selected text

1. Choose Plain Text, or press Shift-Command-Z.

Restore selected text to the base style for the paragraph

1. Choose Plain Text for Style from the Format menu, or press Shift-Command-Spacebar.

Keyboard Shortcuts

Changing the Font

To	Press
Set the font for selected text	Shift-Command-E, enter first letters of font name or font ID number, and then press Return.
Insert a Symbol font character	Shift-Command-Q, then type the character.

Use the Key Caps desk accessory to view font character sets. You can copy characters you type in Key Caps and paste them in your document. The new text takes on the style of the surrounding text, but new paragraphs are formatted in the *Normal* style.

Changing the Font Size

To	Press
Increase the font size	Shift-Command- >
Decrease the font size	Shift-Command- <

The new font size appears in the status area.

Changing Character Styles

These key sequences toggle; use the same keystrokes to set and remove the format.

For	Press
Bold	Shift-Command-B
Italic	Shift-Command-I
Underline	Shift-Command-U
Word underline	Shift-Command-]
Double underline	Shift-Command-[
Dotted underline	Shift-Command-\
Strikethrough	Shift-Command-/
Outline	Shift-Command-D
Shadow	Shift-Command-W
Small caps	Shift-Command-H
All caps	Shift-Command-K
Hidden text	Shift-Command-X

Changing the Position

For	Press
3-point superscript, reduced font size	Shift-Command- + (plus)
2-point subscript, reduced font size	Shift-Command- – (minus)

Removing Formats

To	Press
Return to the character attributes defined for that style	Shift-Command-Spacebar
Remove character attributes only	Shift-Command-Z

■ Commands

Command name	Meaning, menu	Standard keyboard	Keypad	Extended keyboard
Black	Toggles black character color.			
Blue	Toggles blue character color.			
Bold	Toggles bold character format.			
	Format	**⌘⇧B**		**F10**

Command name	Meaning, menu	Standard keyboard	Keypad	Extended keyboard
Caps	Toggles capitals character format.			
		⌘⇧K		⇧F10
Change Font	Changes current font to font you indicate by typing font name and pressing Return.			
		⌘⇧E		
Character…	Changes character formatting of current selection.			
	Format	⌘D		F14
Condensed:	Reduces space between characters by specified number of points.			
Copy Formats	Copies character or paragraph formatting of selection (depending on whether entire paragraph is selected) and applies it to subsequently selected text.			
		⌘⌥V		⇧F4
Cyan	Toggles cyan character color.			
Dotted Underline	Toggles dotted underlining.			
		⌘⇧\		⌥F12
Double Underline	Toggles double underlining.			
		⌘⇧[		⇧F12
Expanded:	Increases space between characters by specified number of points.			
Find Formats	Searches for character or paragraph formats matching that of selected text, depending on whether an entire paragraph is selected.			
		⌘⌥R		
Font Name:	Applies specified font to selected text or to text typed at insertion point. A drop-down list appears at the top of the dialog box, where you can select a font to add to the Font menu. You can also assign a key command to the selected font.			
	Font			
Font Size:	Applies specified font size to selected text or to text typed at insertion point. A drop-down field appears at the top of the dialog box, where you can select a font size to add to the Font menu or enter an unlisted font size. You can also assign a key command to the selected font size.			
	Font			
Green	Toggles green character color.			
Hidden Text	Toggles hidden text character format.			
		⌘⇧V	⌘⇧H	⌥F9
Italic	Turns italic character format on and off.			
	Format	⌘⇧I		F11

(continued)

Command name	Meaning, menu	Standard keyboard	Keypad	Extended keyboard
Italic Cursor	Toggles slanted insertion point and mouse I-beam pointer in italic text.			
Larger Font Size	Increases font size to next larger size.			
		⌘⇧. or ⌘⇧>		
List All Fonts	Lists all installed fonts on Font menu.			
Magenta	Toggles magenta character color.			
Normal Position	Applies normal character position (relative to text baseline) to selected text or text you type at insertion point.			
Normal Spacing	Applies normal character spacing to selected text or text you type at insertion point.			
Outline	Toggles outline character format.			
	Format	⌘⇧D		F11
Plain Text	Removes character formatting that can be turned on and off, such as bold, italic, and underlining.			
	Format	⌘⇧Z		⇧F9
Red	Toggles red character color.			
Shadow	Turns shadow character format on and off.			
	Format	⌘⇧W		⌥F11
Show Hidden Text	Toggles display of hidden text, indicated with a dotted underline.			
Small Caps	Turns small capitals character format on and off.			
		⌘⇧H		⌥F10
Smaller Font Size	Decreases font size to next smaller size.			
		⌘⇧<	⌘⇧,	
Strikethru	Turns strikethrough character format on and off.			
		⌘⇧/		
Subscript:	Lowers characters below baseline by specified number of points and reduces font size to next smaller size.			
		⌘⇧-		
Superscript:	Raises characters above baseline by specified number of points and reduces font size to next smaller size.			
		⌘⇧=		
Symbol Font	Applies Symbol font to current selection.			
		⌘⇧Q		
Underline	Turns single continuous underlining on and off.			
	Format	⌘⇧U		F12
White	Toggles white character color.			
Word Underline	Toggles word underlining.			
		⌘⇧]		⌘F12
Yellow	Toggles yellow character color.			

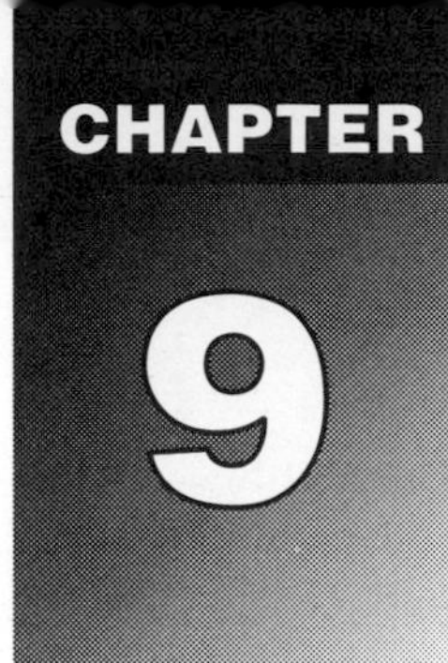

Paragraph Formatting

Chapter 8 discussed the types of formatting you can do within the character format domain, Word's smallest level of detail. This chapter explores the next horizon, the paragraph format domain. Paragraph formats control these characteristics:

- Indention.
- Alignment.
- Line spacing.
- Space before and after the paragraph.
- Type and location of tabs.
- Graphic treatment of paragraphs—lines, boxed paragraphs, and so on.
- Grouping and placement of paragraphs on a page.
- Whether the lines of the paragraph are numbered when printed.

■ *Working with Paragraphs*

Previous chapters have defined a paragraph, but it's worth repeating. In Word, a paragraph is any block of text that precedes a paragraph mark, which is created by pressing either the Return key or the Enter key. A paragraph can have one letter in it or hundreds. It can even be a blank line.

If you want to see the boundaries of paragraphs, you can do so by choosing Show ¶ from the Edit menu. With Show ¶ in effect, you see all the characters that are usually invisible, including paragraph marks, newline marks, tabs, and spaces.

To see how the paragraph mark acts as the boundary of a paragraph, type two paragraphs of sample text, and then select and delete the first paragraph mark. It's relatively easy to select a paragraph mark when it's visible; when it's not visible, a good trick is to position the mouse pointer just to the right of the last line of the paragraph and double-click. You'll see a black rectangle representing the selected paragraph mark. When you delete the mark, the two paragraphs fuse into one.

Before launching into a full-scale exploration of paragraph formatting, you should know a few techniques for working with paragraphs.

- ❑ You can join two paragraphs by selecting the paragraph mark between them and pressing the Backspace key. If you try to backspace through a paragraph mark to delete it, and the preceding paragraph has different paragraph formats, Word beeps and does not delete the paragraph mark. Word does this to decrease the likelihood of your deleting paragraph formats unintentionally.
- ❑ Pressing Option-Command-Return inserts a paragraph mark after the insertion point instead of before it. This is useful when you want to both break a paragraph and continue typing at the end of the first paragraph.
- ❑ Changes to the paragraph formatting of existing text affect only the selected paragraphs. If you set the insertion point or select only part of a paragraph, the formatting within all that paragraph, and in that paragraph alone, changes.
- ❑ If you alter paragraph formats while typing, you change the formatting for any paragraphs you type after that. (This might not apply if you use the Next Style feature of Word's style sheets, discussed in the next chapter.)
- ❑ Pressing Shift-Return starts a new line but does not end the paragraph. These *newlines*, also called soft returns, are helpful when you need to start a new line but want Word to consider the lines as one paragraph. The uses of the newline character are discussed in this and later chapters. Note that its mark (with Show ¶ on) looks like a bent arrow instead of the proofreader's paragraph mark, as shown in Figure 9-1 on the following page.

¶ *Paragraph mark*

↵ *Newline mark*

Figure 9-1
Paragraph and newline marks.

Changing Paragraph Formats

To change a paragraph format in a document, first select one or more paragraphs, and then do one of the following:

- Choose Show Ruler from the Format menu, and click one of the icons in the Ruler icon bar. You can also change some document properties (such as page margins) from the Ruler.
- Choose Paragraph from the Format menu, and make changes within the Paragraph dialog box. You can also call up the Paragraph dialog box by double-clicking any of several items in the Ruler: the indent markers, the scale in the Ruler bar itself, or any of the line-spacing or paragraph-spacing icons in the icon bar. (Double-clicking the tab icons brings up the Tabs dialog box.)
- Choose an option you've added to the Format menu or another menu.
- Use a key sequence to make the change.
- Set a style by choosing it from the Style drop-down field in the Ruler, by choosing Styles or Define Styles from the Format menu, or by choosing a style you've added to the Work menu. (The next chapter is devoted to this subject, so we won't cover it here.)

Some formats are not accessible by every method. You can set alignment, for example, from the Ruler, from the Format menu (after you have added its options), and from the keyboard, but not from the Paragraph dialog box. Each of these methods is discussed briefly here and in more detail where we explore each of the paragraph formats.

TIP

Styles and Paragraph Formats
Changing paragraph formats through the style sheet is much easier than hunting down each instance of a text element and reformatting it manually. See Chapter 10, "Working with Style Sheets," for more information.

The Ruler

Word's Ruler controls the position of indents and tabs, text alignment, and spacing between lines and paragraphs. Through the Ruler you can also change some document and table formats. For example, you can change the margins of the document and the width of columns in tables. Many of these functions are also available through other commands in Word, but the Ruler makes them more accessible. The Ruler must be visible for you to use it. If it is not displayed at the top of the window in Galley View or Page View, choose Show Ruler from the Format menu. Conversely, to remove the Ruler, choose the Hide Ruler command. You can also display the Ruler in the following windows:

- ❏ The Header window.
- ❏ The Footer window.
- ❏ The Footnote window, as well as the Footnote Separator, Continued Separator, and Continued Notice windows (all of which concern footnotes).

The Ruler is shown in Figure 9-2, with labels for the various icons and markers. The unit of measure shown in the Ruler reflects the current Default Measure setting in the Preferences dialog box.

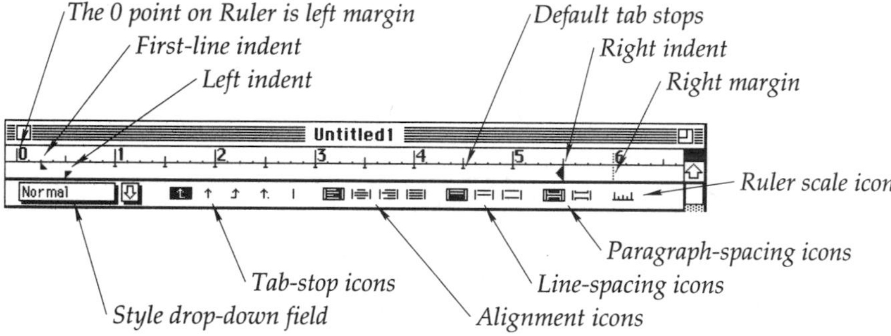

Figure 9-2
The Ruler, showing the normal scale.

Clicking the Scale icon toggles among three types of scale in the Ruler. If you are using a split window and choose Show Ruler, the Ruler appears at the top of the active pane. Regardless of its location, the Ruler changes to reflect the formats of the currently selected text, whether the text is in the top or bottom pane or even if it has scrolled off the screen. The formats reported, and the settings you change within the Ruler, depend on which of the three types of scale is visible—paragraph in the normal scale, document in the page scale, or table in the table scale. This effect differs from that of the character formats, which you can apply to a single character if you want. You can make changes from the Ruler while you type your document or while you edit it.

In the *normal* scale, discussed in this chapter, you can place tab markers and change the position of indents. The 0 point is placed at the left edge of the text column (which is the same as the left margin for one-column text), the left edge of cells in tables, or the left edge of the text column in multi-column sections.

In the second type of scale, called the *page* scale, the 0 point is placed at the left edge of the paper, and you can drag the bracket-shaped margin markers relative to the edges of the page. If you're using more than one column in the current section, you can also set the column width and the spacing between columns. Section formats are discussed in Chapter 12, "Section Formatting," and document formats are discussed in Chapter 14, "Document Formatting and Printing."

The third type of scale, called the *table* scale, appears only if the currently selected text is in a table. In it you can change the left indent of the table and the relative widths of cells in the table. Tables are discussed in Chapter 11, "Formatting Tables and Lists."

Clearing the Ruler

If you make many alterations in the Ruler and then change your mind, you can reset the paragraph formats in several ways. You can choose Undo from the Edit menu to remove all the formats you've added in the Ruler since the last nonformatting operation. For example, if you click the right-alignment icon in the Ruler, choose the Character command, click Cancel, click the double-space icon in the Ruler, and then choose Undo, both the right-alignment and the double-spacing formats are undone.

Another way to reset the paragraph formats for text is to reapply the style assigned to the text. To reapply a style, select the paragraph, click in the style field in the Ruler, and press Return. Word displays a dialog box asking if you want to reapply the style to the selected text. Click OK or press Return. A faster way to do this is to assign a key sequence to the Styles command. (In Word 3, this was Command-B, but pressing this in the default key assignment now switches to and from Page View.) When you press the key sequence you've assigned, the Styles dialog box appears with the style of the paragraph highlighted in the the list box. Press Return to reapply the style. Because you can issue commands at a faster rate than Word processes them, you can press the key sequence and immediately press Return: If you do this quickly, Word reassigns the style without displaying the Styles dialog box.

The Paragraph Command

Just as the Character dialog box is the master control panel for the character formats, the Paragraph dialog box is the primary means of controlling the layout of paragraphs. Choose the Paragraph command to bring up the dialog box shown in Figure 9-3 on the following page.

The Ruler accompanies the dialog box (if it is not displayed already), as if you had chosen both the Show Ruler and Paragraph commands at the same time, and you can make adjustments in either the Ruler or the dialog box.

The Paragraph dialog box is divided into six basic sections: the Indents option group, the Spacing option group, a series of check boxes that control options for grouping paragraphs relative to one another, and three buttons that bring up dialog boxes for setting tabs, drawing borders, and positioning paragraphs.

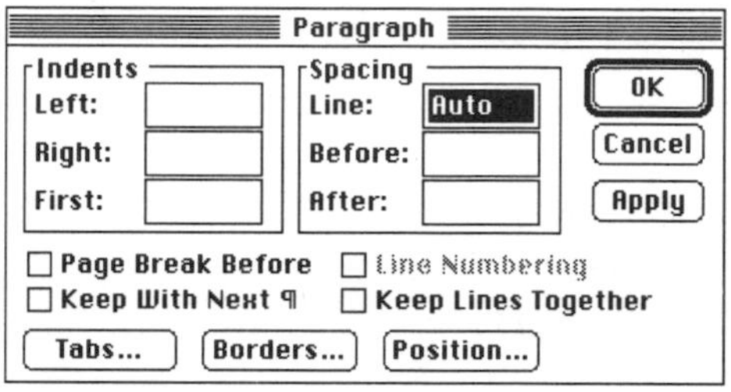

Figure 9-3
The Paragraph dialog box.

The Paragraph dialog box also has three control buttons: OK, Cancel, and Apply. These work exactly like the buttons in the Character dialog box. OK indicates that you're through fiddling with the formats and you want to implement the changes you made and get back to the document. Cancel means that you've decided not to make any changes after all.

The Apply button lets you audition format changes without closing the Paragraph dialog box. This works best when you are changing the format of previously typed text; you can't readily see the change in a blank document.

To use the Apply button, select the paragraphs to be changed, display the Paragraph dialog box, and click the options you want. Drag the box by the title bar if it obscures the text you want to see. (Double-click in the title bar to alternate between the two positions.) Click the Apply button to audition the changes. The dialog box stays open, but the text changes to the new format. Continue choosing new formats and applying them for as long as you like. When you leave the dialog box, use the Undo command if you want to revert to the format that existed before the last Apply. Clicking Cancel doesn't undo an Apply.

If you need to see the effect of a massive formatting change and are afraid you might mess up the document or forget how it was originally formatted, save the document before the test. Then, if the experiment goes awry, you can close the document without saving it and reopen the original.

Adding Paragraph Formats to the Format Menu

So far in your exploration of Word, you've seen how to add documents, glossaries, font names and styles to Word's menus. You can also add all the paragraph formats to the Format menu by pressing Option-Command- + and clicking the desired paragraph format in either the Ruler or the Paragraph dialog box, but you can't add any tab-stop formats. By using the Commands command, you can assign formats to menus other than the Format menu, and you can add or change the key sequences attached to Word's formatting commands. As we'll see later, there are some paragraph formats that you *must* add to a menu or assign a key sequence in order to use, such as the command for the Side-by-Side format, discussed later in this chapter.

■ *Working with Paragraph Formats*

Now that you've learned the various methods for using the paragraph formats, let's consider each format in turn. Figure 9-4 shows a typical paragraph and some of the formats you can change.

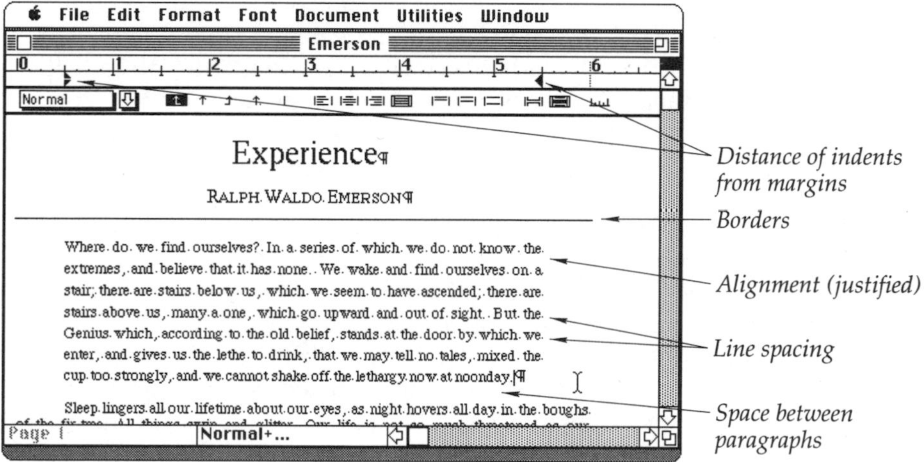

Figure 9-4
A typical paragraph. (Note the insertion point at the end of the first body paragraph.)

Indents

Setting an indent is not the same as setting a margin, and many people are confused on this point. You set the margins by changing the contents of the Margins edit fields in the Document dialog box (available from the Format menu), in Print Preview, or by clicking the Scale icon in the Ruler and dragging the margin markers to a new position. You set indents by dragging an indent marker in the Ruler in the normal scale or by specifying an indent in the Left, Right, or First edit fields in the Paragraph dialog box.

What is the difference between an indent and a margin? The Margins settings in the Document dialog box apply to your document as a whole; they specify the default boundaries of the text on the page, whether the text is in the *Normal* style, in another style, or in a header, footer, or other element. Until you change the margins, Word establishes them at 1 inch from the top and bottom of the page and 1.25 inches from the left and right edges of the page.

Indents, on the other hand, are a way of temporarily changing the left and right margins for selected paragraphs in your document. The three types of indent are left, right, and first line. If you haven't explicitly changed the left or right indents (the first-line indent will be discussed in a moment), Word assumes you want your text to run to the margins.

Indents are measured from the left and right edges of the text column for the currently selected paragraphs. For normal single-column text, the text column is the same as the distance between the left and the right margins. For multiple-column text, the text column is the same as the width of one column. For cells in a table, it's the width of a cell. The left edge of the text column is the 0 point on the Ruler, and the position of the left indent (the lower of the two triangles at the left edge of the Ruler) is relative to this point. If you change the left margin (and thus change the 0 point), the left indent changes too, remaining the same distance from the 0 point as before. Similarly, the position of the right indent is relative to the right edge of the text column, which appears as a dotted vertical line in the Ruler. (See Figure 9-2.)

Besides the left and right indents, you can control the first-line indent (the upper of the two triangles at the left edge of the Ruler). This indent applies only to the first line of the paragraph. The first-line indent is measured relative to the left indent rather than to the 0 point on the Ruler, and the left and first-line indents are normally linked together so that moving the left indent also moves the first-line indent. (To move the left indent independently of the first-line indent, hold down the Shift key as you drag the left-indent marker.) The most common use of the first-line indent is to offset the first line of a paragraph, but its range of applications is much wider, as you will see in the next section.

A Small Gallery of Indention Effects

This section gives you a quick tour through the range of effects that you can achieve through different placements of the left, right, and first-line indents relative to one another in your documents.

To provide a reference point for this discussion, Figure 9-5 shows the standard format for normal paragraphs. The left and right indents are at the same location as the left and right margins, and there is no first-line indent. Many people use a tab to indent the first line of a paragraph; whether you do this or use the first-line indent is not important as long as you achieve the results you want.

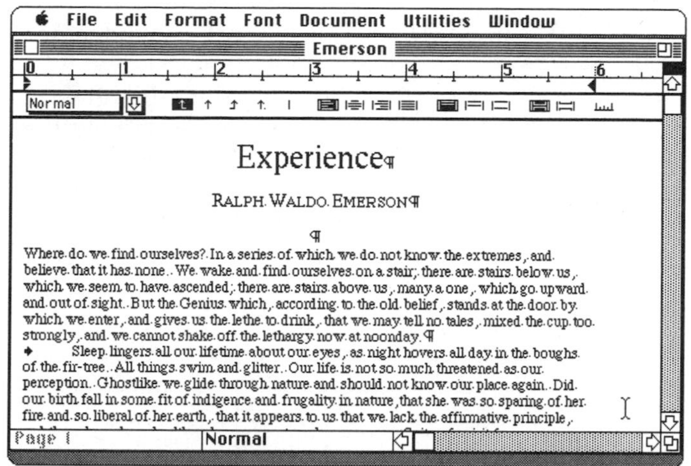

Figure 9-5
Normal paragraph indention.

You can create another indention pattern, called *nested indention*, by moving the left and right indents toward the center and away from the margins, as shown in Figure 9-6. Nested indents are often used for quotations or to set off captions for figures.

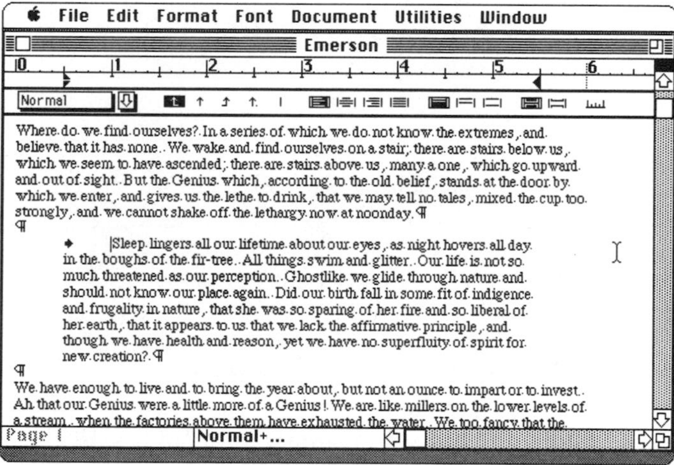

Figure 9-6
Nested paragraph indention.

A *hanging indent* occurs when you place the first-line indent to the left of the left indent, as shown in Figure 9-7. Hanging indents are very useful for lists and are often used in bibliographies. The numbered procedures in this book, each paragraph of which is preceded by Zapf Dingbat characters such as ❶ (ASCII characters 182 through 191), are called *numbered lists* and use hanging indents. The unnumbered lists in this book, each paragraph of which is preceded by the Zapf Dingbat character ❑ (lowercase *o*), are called *bulleted lists*. In both cases, a tab mark is used within the hanging indent to make the number or bullet stand out from the body of text.

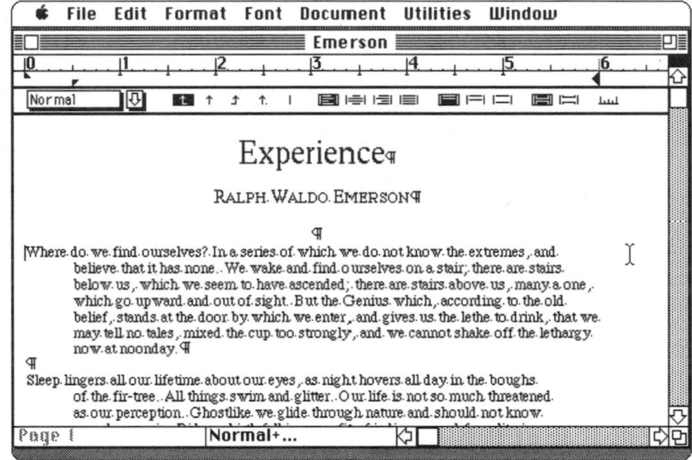

Figure 9-7
Hanging indents.

Finally, Word lets you place any of the indent markers outside the limits of the page margins. Negative indents are particularly good for the headings in a document. Such indents are called *negative indents* because they must be measured in negative numbers; otherwise, they would be confused with normal indents. (See Figure 9-8.) Because Word does not display the edges of the printable area of the page in the Ruler, when you use negative indents you risk having your text run off the page. You can use Print Preview, or you can click on the Ruler scale icon to switch to the page scale (which does show the left and right edges of the page, although your printer might not actually print to the page edge) to check for this problem. Also, because negative left indents run to the left of the left margin, Word may not show them in Galley view. To shift the screen to the right, as shown in the figure, press the Shift key while clicking the left arrow in the horizontal scroll bar.

You can combine these indention patterns in any way you want. For example, you can create negative hanging indents or use a nested indent for the left edge of the text and leave the right indent at the right margin.

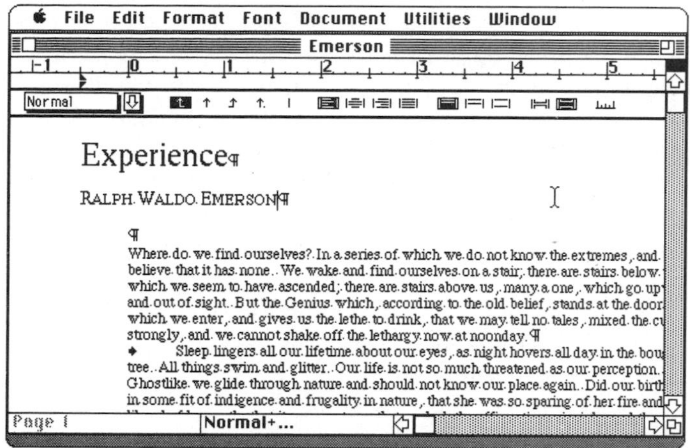

Figure 9-8
Negative indention.

Setting Indents from the Ruler

To set indents with the Ruler, first choose Show Ruler from the Format menu and select the paragraphs to be affected. If you are changing only one paragraph, simply click in it: Because indention is a paragraph format, this will cause the new indents to be applied to the entire paragraph. When you click in a paragraph, the Ruler in the normal scale displays the current placement of the three indent markers. If you select more than one paragraph and those paragraphs use different formats or have been assigned different styles, the Ruler is filled with gray and the markers reflect the indents of the first paragraph selected.

Once you've specified the text, drag the appropriate indent marker in the Ruler to the location of the new indent. To move the first-line and left-indent markers together, drag the lower triangle. If you drag only the upper triangle, you'll move only the first-line indent. To move only the left indent, press the Shift key and then drag the lower triangle. The position of the first-line indent is always linked to that of the left indent. Even if the two indents are in different positions, moving the left indent causes a corresponding change in the position of the first-line indent. The Shift key uncouples the markers so that you can drag them separately.

Indents can be positive or negative with respect to the left and right edges of the text column. You normally start the text at the 0 point on the Ruler, but you can also start it farther to the left or right. This 0 point is normally locked at the left edge of the screen, but you can drag the first-line or left-indent marker (or both) past the edge of the screen. After a delay of about one second, the scale in the Ruler and the contents of your document slide to the right, revealing the negative indent positions. Alternatively, you can Shift-click the left arrow in the horizontal scroll bar to move the document to the right, and then you can move the indent markers.

Setting Indents from the Paragraph Dialog Box

When you choose the Paragraph command, the Ruler appears, so everything discussed in the previous section applies here as well. However, the Ruler limits the precision with which you can specify an indent. As elsewhere in Word 4, the Ruler uses minimum increments of 1 point (1/72 inch), converted into the unit you've chosen in the Preferences dialog box—multiples of 0.014 inches, 0.035 centimeters, or .083 picas. By using the Left, Right, or First edit field in the Paragraph dialog box, you can specify indents with an accuracy of 1 point, again converted to the current unit of measure.

Suppose you have set inches as the unit of measure in the Preferences dialog box. If you want to set a left indent of 1 pica (1/6 inch, or 0.1667 inch), you need to use the Left edit field, as follows:

1. Select the text you want to format.
2. Choose the Paragraph command. The Ruler and the Paragraph dialog box appear.
3. Click the first-line indent marker. The position of the left indent is displayed in the Left field.
4. Enter the position of the indent—*0.1667 in*, *12 pt*, or *1 pi*. Or you can drag the marker and watch the value in the Left edit field change accordingly—of course, if you've set picas as the default unit of measurement in the Ruler, it's much easier to set the indent to 1 pica. Click OK to implement the indent.

Remember that first-line indents are measured relative to the left indent, not the left page margin. If you want to set a hanging indent, enter a negative number.

TIP

Checking Special Indent Values

An interesting problem can occur when you want to check an indent value (or a tab value, for that matter) that you have set to an intermediate position (that is, a position between two Ruler increments). If you open the Paragraph dialog box and click on an indent marker set to a special value, it pops to the nearest interval (1/16 inch if you're using inches), and the corresponding edit field shows the new position, not the original value.

To read the value associated with an indent or tab marker without changing it, you can pretend that you want to create a new style and choose the Define Styles command. The *New Style* item in the list box is selected automatically; the definition displayed underneath describes the formats contained in the selected text, including the position of the marker.

If the selected text already has a style attached, the definition simply names the style and does not list its definition. In such cases, delete the contents of the Based On field and then click in the Style field. The complete definition for the selected text appears, as though you were starting from scratch, and you can find the position of the marker in the definition. Click Cancel when you're ready to close the dialog box.

Paragraph Alignment

The Ruler alone controls the alignment of lines within each paragraph; no alignment options are available from within the Paragraph dialog box. You can choose from four types of paragraph alignment, as shown in Figure 9-9:

- Left aligned ("flush left"). Lines are even with the left indent, and their right edge is ragged.
- Centered. Lines are centered over the midpoint between the left and right indents.
- Right aligned ("flush right"). Lines are even with the right indent, and their left edge is ragged.
- Justified. Lines are even with both the left and right indents. Word expands the spaces between words to push the ends of lines to the left and right indents.

To set alignment, select some paragraphs (or set the insertion point if only one paragraph is to be affected) and click one of the alignment icons in the Ruler. To indicate the alignment of a paragraph you are about to type, set the insertion point and then click the appropriate icon.

A lone figure stood among the brick buildings, a figure accustomed to the dankness of the night and the glare of the street lamps. The eyes of the figure slowly scanned up and down the avenue, but the rest of the body was awkwardly still, as if the wetness and clinging coldness had paralyzed it. *Left aligned*

A lone figure stood among the brick buildings, a figure accustomed to the dankness of the night and the glare of the street lamps. The eyes of the figure slowly scanned up and down the avenue, but the rest of the body was awkwardly still, as if the wetness and clinging coldness had paralyzed it. *Centered*

A lone figure stood among the brick buildings, a figure accustomed to the dankness of the night and the glare of the street lamps. The eyes of the figure slowly scanned up and down the avenue, but the rest of the body was awkwardly still, as if the wetness and clinging coldness had paralyzed it. *Right aligned*

A lone figure stood among the brick buildings, a figure accustomed to the dankness of the night and the glare of the street lamps. The eyes of the figure slowly scanned up and down the avenue, but the rest of the body was awkwardly still, as if the wetness and clinging coldness had paralyzed it. *Justified*

Figure 9-9
The four types of paragraph alignment.

Line Spacing

Word can separate lines by almost any distance that you'd like. In typesetting, the term *line spacing* refers to the distance from the baseline of one line of text to the baseline of the next or preceding line. Word does not use the same convention, but for most purposes the effects are similar. You'll learn more about this in a moment, but first let's work with setting line-spacing formats from the Ruler.

Setting Line Spacing from the Ruler

The Ruler provides three line-spacing settings: single space (or *auto* line spacing), one-and-one-half space (18 points), and double space (24 points). This lets you set the three most common line spacings quickly, without calling up the Paragraph dialog box. To change the line spacing for a selected paragraph, click the desired line-spacing icon just to the right of the alignment icons. The effects of the three line spacings are shown in Figure 9-10. Like the other paragraph formats, the line-spacing setting affects the entire paragraph.

When you use the default single spacing, Word adjusts the line spacing to the point size of the text in the paragraph. Clicking this option is the same as calling up the Paragraph dialog box and entering *auto* in the Line Spacing edit field. For example, if a paragraph is in a 10-point font, the automatic line-spacing format sets the line spacing to about 12 points. (The actual *auto* line spacing varies with the font, and is usually two or three points more than the font size.) If you insert a character (or graphic) that is taller than 10 points, the spacing around that line opens up a bit to accommodate the oversized element. This happens frequently when you use more than one font or point size in a line of text, use the outline or underline character formats, or have subscripts or superscripts in your text. If you want the line spacing to remain constant at a certain setting, regardless of the size of the elements within the line, you must set it with the Paragraph command, discussed in the next section.

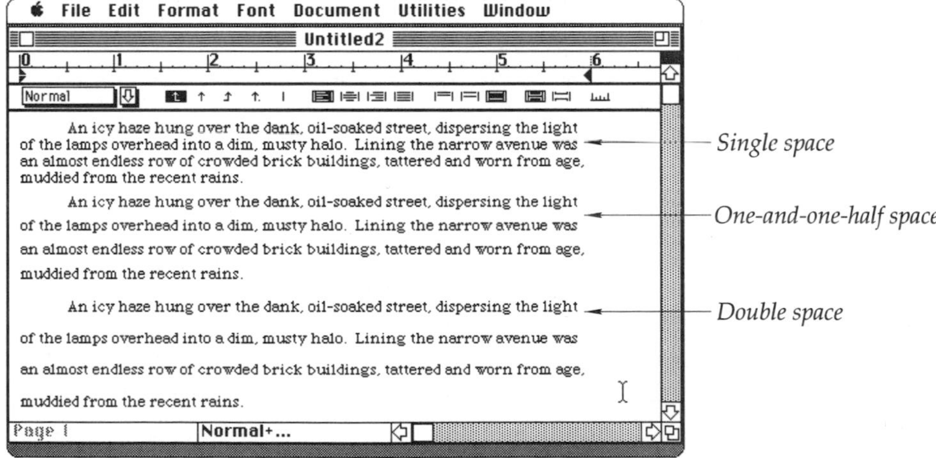

Figure 9-10
The three types of line spacing available from the Ruler.

The one-and-one-half-space option sets the line spacing to 18 points per line, but Word will open up the line spacing if something in a line is larger than 18 points. The double-space option works in the same way but sets the spacing to 24 points per line. Actually, both these spacing options are misnamed: The only font size for which 24 points really is double spaced is, of course, a 12-point font. If you use the double-space option with an 18-point font, you still get 24 points of space, not 36 points.

Setting Line Spacing from the Paragraph Dialog Box

You can get much more control over the line spacing in your text by using the Line field in the Spacing group of the Paragraph dialog box. It lets you specify line spacing in the following measurements:

- Points. Enter *12 pt,* for instance, to single-space a 12-point font.
- Inches. If you require a spacing of 1 inch between lines, for example, enter *1 in* in the Line field.
- Centimeters. To specify a spacing of 2 centimeters between lines, enter *2 cm* in the Line field.
- Picas. Even though the pica unit of measurement isn't commonly used to specify line spacing, you could, for example, enter *2 pi* to space lines 2 picas apart.
- Lines. You can set line spacing in multiples of lines. To triple-space your text, for example, enter *3 li* in the Line edit field. Word interprets a line as 12 points.

You can express any measurement in fractions, but the next time you open the Paragraph dialog box, Word converts the measurement into multiples of 1 point. To express a fractional measurement, use a decimal value (for example, *1.13 in* or *2.5 pi*). Enter the word *auto* or the number *0* to have Word adjust the line spacing automatically for the font size, which is what Word enters if you've previously clicked the single-space icon in the Ruler.

As was mentioned earlier, some character formats or font sizes can produce text elements that extend higher or lower than the rest of the characters in a line of text, causing Word to add extra space above or below the line. This can happen regardless of the line spacing, given an extreme enough combination of character formats. Whenever the Line edit field contains a measurement expressed as a positive number, Word adjusts the actual line spacing to accommodate oversized elements. To prevent this behavior and force a specific line spacing regardless of the dimensions of the text, enter the line-spacing distance as a negative number: Word then uses the absolute value of the number.

TIP

Line Spacing in Word

Word does not follow the standard publishing convention of measuring line spacing from baseline to baseline. Instead, it calculates the spacing from descender to descender. (See Figure 9-11.) You may recall from Chapter 8 that a descender is the part of a character that extends below the baseline of text, such as the tails of the lowercase letters *y*, *g*, and *q*. The descender-to-descender distance is often the same as the baseline-to-baseline distance.

You can see the space allotted for a line by selecting it and observing the upper and lower limits of the highlight, as shown in Figure 9-11. To illustrate this point, the size of a word containing a descender has been increased to accentuate the effect. The highlight extends from the top of the highest character in the line (or, in some fonts, a point or two higher than the highest character) to the bottom of the lowest character. Notice that the highlight touches the descender of the line above it.

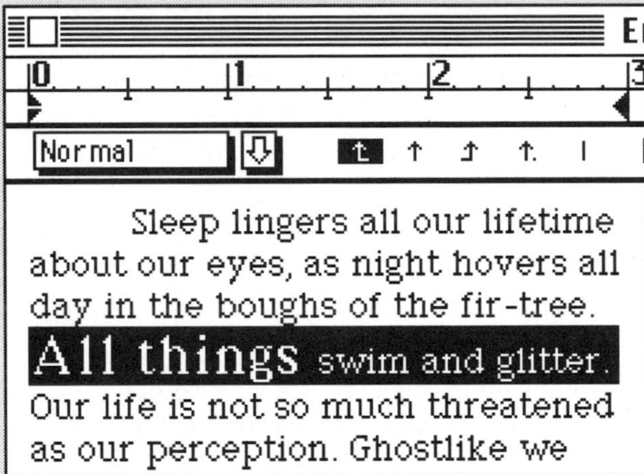

Figure 9-11
Line spacing is actually measured from descender to descender.

When you set automatic line spacing by entering *auto* in the Spacing field of the Paragraph dialog box, the spacing of each line is determined by the distance from the top of the highest ascender to the bottom of the lowest descender. If a given line doesn't contain characters with descenders, the space for the descender is still reserved. Similarly, space is also reserved for the ascender height of a font even if a given line doesn't contain characters with ascenders.

When you increase the line spacing to more than that set by automatic spacing, the extra space appears above each line in the paragraph, even the first line in the paragraph. This behavior can lead to some tricky problems if you're aiming for highly accurate paragraph formatting in a document. This is particularly true when two successive paragraphs have different line-spacing formats.

For example, the distance between level headings and the first paragraph under them will vary if the font sizes of the various types of headings are different, yielding descenders of different lengths. If the body text under each heading is in the *Normal* style with automatic line spacing, the distance between the baseline of a heading and the baseline of the first line in the paragraph depends solely on the font size of the heading, not the line spacing. To adjust the actual baseline-to-baseline distance between paragraphs with different line-spacing formats, experiment with setting negative line-spacing formats and with the Before and After paragraph formats discussed next.

Paragraph Spacing

A second type of spacing within the paragraph format domain is used to separate a paragraph from the ones before and after it. The Space Before format adds space above the top edge of the interval set by the line spacing in the paragraph, and the Space After format adds space below the lowest descender in the last line of the paragraph. Figure 9-12 shows how these formats work together. The paragraph containing the title of the essay and the name of the author are separated by the title's Space After format, not a blank line. The first and second paragraphs of the essay are separated by the Space Before format of the second paragraph, as indicated by the highlight.

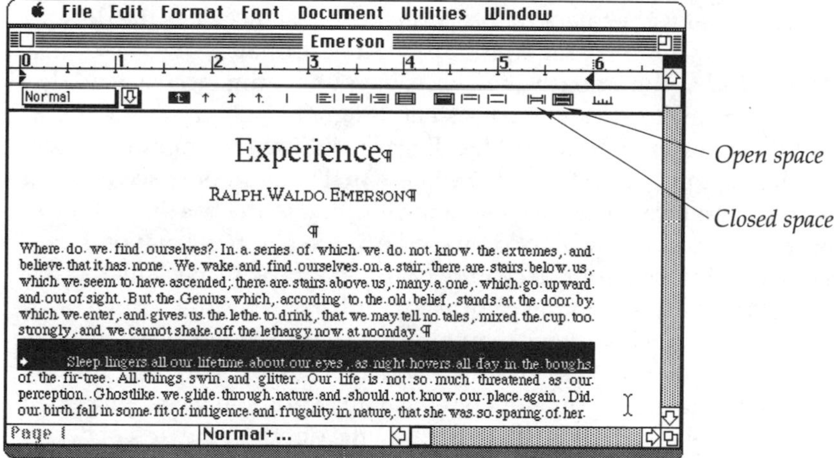

Figure 9-12
The Space Before format in relation to a typical paragraph.

The Space Before and Space After formats are useful for setting off body text, indicating a pause in the flow of a document, or setting off the headings in a document. The Space Before format is used in the default *heading 1* and *heading 2* styles. (Again, using the style sheet to establish space around text elements is a powerful means for developing a consistent design in a document.)

Setting Paragraph Spacing from the Ruler

The Ruler offers only two paragraph-spacing options: either no extra space (the Closed Space icon) or 12 points of space before each paragraph (the Open Space icon, which was used in Figure 9-12). If you want paragraphs to be separated by the same amount of space as the lines, click the Closed Space icon. If you want extra space between paragraphs, click the Open Space icon. You can also get to the Paragraph dialog box by double-clicking any of the line-spacing or paragraph-spacing icons.

Setting Paragraph Spacing from the Paragraph Dialog Box

Use the Before and After fields in the Spacing options of the dialog box to set the spacing before and after each selected paragraph. Like the Line edit field, these fields accept spacing in inches, centimeters, points, or lines, although Word always displays the measurements in points when you reopen the dialog box. To remove extra spacing before or after a paragraph, you must enter *0 pt* in the appropriate field; simply deleting the entry won't work.

TIP

Paragraph Spacing in Word

Like line spacing, paragraph spacing is not measured from baseline to baseline. Technically, the Space Before format (for instance) sets the distance to the bottom of the prior paragraph's Space After format.

This can lead to some confusing effects in your document, particularly when you are trying to achieve a consistent design. In a good design, the treatment of elements such as level headings, including the amount of space before each one, must be consistent. Yet the actual amount of space before a heading, measured from the baseline of the heading to the baseline of the previous paragraph, depends not only on the Space Before format of the heading, but on both the font size of the prior paragraph (especially the length of its descenders) and the prior paragraph's Space After format.

However, you can take steps to minimize this type of inconsistency. The most obvious strategy is to use either the Space Before or Space After format in your design. That way, you will know that any variation in the placement of design elements is caused by differences in the depth of the descenders in the prior paragraph, a function of the font size used.

The next step is to realize that the design elements in a document usually follow one another in regular patterns. For example, body text almost always follows a heading. Generally, you want to add extra space not only before the heading but after it as well. In such cases, it's better to set both Before and After spacing formats for the headings so that you don't have to locate the first paragraph of body text after each heading and to manually set a Space Before format for it. By analyzing your document, you can determine which elements follow one another and adjust your formats accordingly.

Finally, you can create special spacing elements that consist of nothing more than a paragraph mark to which you have assigned an appropriate style. For example, you can use a style called *Std. Line Space* with a specific line spacing to regularize the spacing around figures and around numbered and bulleted lists. You can store the paragraph mark in a glossary; when you insert it, if that style name exists in your document, Word uses its definition; if not, Word copies the style from the style sheet hidden in the glossary.

You can even create a complete set of spacing elements, each with its own special style, for removing the spacing inconsistencies between any two design elements in your document. In other words, you can create a spacing element for all possible pairs of paragraphs, for example:

Sp/Norm-Level1
Sp/Norm-Level2
Sp/Norm-Level3
Sp/Fig-Level1
Sp/Fig-Level2
Sp/Fig-Level3
Sp/Norm-NumList (before a numbered list)
Sp/NumList-Norm (after a numbered list)

Then, after you've placed all the spacing elements (hopefully by inserting elements from the Glossary) and you're ready to fine-tune the design of the document, you can adjust the spacing throughout by changing the style definitions for these elements. This is the method used to implement the design of this book. Obviously, this can lead to very complicated style sheets and is only for the most demanding of document designs.

Tabs

Tabs are characters that you can use to align text in columns without laboriously adding and deleting spaces. Tabs are invisible, but you can use the Show ¶ command to make them appear. When you press the Tab key (or Option-Tab when working within a table), the insertion point moves to the next tab stop. If you haven't changed the default tab stops in the Document dialog box, Word assumes that you want them placed evenly at ½-inch intervals. The four different types of tab stops, shown in Figure 9-13 on the following page, are:

- ❑ Flush left. Aligns the left edge of the text with the tab stop. This is the default tab stop.
- ❑ Centered. Centers the text over the tab stop.
- ❑ Flush right. Aligns the right edge of the text with the tab stop.
- ❑ Decimal aligned. Aligns the decimal point with the tab stop.

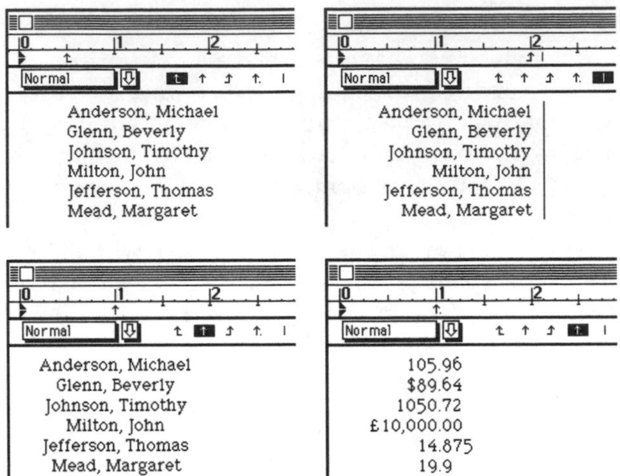

Figure 9-13
The different types of tab stops.

You will often use centered and flush-right tab stops to create smart-looking tables. The decimal tab stop is ideal for presenting numbers in an orderly fashion. You can have any number of digits to the right and left of the decimal point, yet all the decimal points line up at the tab stop. If the number doesn't have a decimal point, the tab stop acts like a flush-right tab stop.

A fifth icon in the Ruler is next to the four tab-stop icons. The vertical line is not really a tab stop, but it is often used to draw lines in tables and so is grouped with them. It draws a line that you can use as a separator or border. You simply select the icon and click in the Ruler where you want a line to appear; you don't need to enter any characters to create the line, and the insertion point skips past the line when you press the Tab key. The line continues down the page through each paragraph that has this format. This feature can be used for other types of formatting as well, especially multiple-column documents. The flush-right tab-stop example in Figure 9-13 shows how you can use this tab stop with the vertical line format.

You can set tab stops in several ways in Word 4:

- ❑ Change their default positions from the Document dialog box.
- ❑ Select a tab icon in the Ruler, and drag a tab marker to the desired position.
- ❑ Specify new positions in the Tabs dialog box, which you can call up by clicking the Tabs button in the Paragraph dialog box, by double-clicking any of the Tab icons, by adding the Tabs command to a menu, and by assigning a key sequence to the Tabs command in the Commands dialog box.

Changing the Default Tab Stops

Word's default tab stops are set at ½-inch intervals along the length of the Ruler. The positions of the default tab stops are marked by tiny, upside-down T icons in the Ruler. Technically, these default tab stops are not in the paragraph format domain but are part of a document level format that belongs to every paragraph in the document. Even if you set some tab stops, the default tabs will remain to the right of those you've set unless you completely clear all default tab stops.

Tab markers take precedence over the default tabs, so if you place a tab marker on the Ruler, the default tab stops to the left of it disappear. To change Word's default tab stops or to eliminate them completely, do the following:

❶ Choose the Document command from the Format menu.

❷ Double-click in the Default Tab Stops field, and enter a new number. The measurement can be in inches, centimeters, or points. The smallest default tab stop you can set is 1 point, converted to the current unit of measurement; the largest is 22 inches. (Enter *22 in* if you want to remove all the default stops.)

❸ Click OK to set this tab-stop interval for the current document only. Click Set Default to store the new default tabs in the current Settings file and use them for all subsequent documents you create under that Settings file.

Setting Tabs Stops from the Ruler

As with indents, nondefault tab stops can be set in two ways: from the Ruler alone or from the Tabs dialog box. To set a tab stop from the Ruler, do the following:

- ❑ To place a tab stop on the Ruler, drag the icon for the type of tab you want to the desired location on the Ruler. You can also simply click the icon for the type of tab you want and then click at the desired location in the Ruler.
- ❑ To move a tab stop, drag its marker along the Ruler to the new position.
- ❑ To remove a tab stop, drag its marker off the Ruler and release the mouse button.

If you're moving a tab stop and you click near but not directly over it, the marker moves with the pointer (even though the pointer isn't directly over the marker). This can be a problem when you are positioning tab stops close to one another or close to an indent marker—instead of adding a new marker, Word assumes you want to move the old marker. To avoid this, click somewhere else in the Ruler to add the tab marker and then drag it to the correct position. If a tab marker is positioned directly over an indent marker and you click over both, moving the pointer moves the tab, not the indent.

Often it's helpful to drag more than one tab marker at a time. If you press the Shift key before dragging the first tab marker, all the markers to the right move with it, retaining their relative positions.

If you select several paragraphs having different tab settings, the Ruler is filled with gray and shows the tab markers for the first paragraph only. Because any paragraph can have up to 50 tab stops set within it, when you add a tab stop to a Ruler filled with gray, you add that tab stop to every paragraph selected. The new tab stop replaces an old one only if they are in the same position. To remove the tab stops from every paragraph and add new ones, you first have to remove all the tab markers from each paragraph. You can then reselect the paragraphs and establish the new tab stops.

Note: The Ruler is also filled with gray if any of the other paragraph formats vary among the selected paragraphs. However, because the other paragraph formats permit only one option each (for instance, a paragraph can have only one left indent and only one line spacing format), changing such a format replaces that format in all the paragraphs selected.

Setting Tab Stops from the Paragraph Dialog Box

Tab stops are easily set from the Ruler. Like indents, however, they can be set more precisely from the Position field in the Tabs dialog box. The minimum increments for tabs set from the Ruler are the same as those for indents set from the Ruler: 1 point, converted to the current unit of measure. Also, the dialog box offers several tab leaders (discussed in the next section). To set a tab stop using the Tabs dialog box:

❶ Select the paragraphs you want to format.

❷ Choose the Paragraph command. The Paragraph dialog box appears, as does the Ruler if it isn't already visible. Click the Tabs button (or use any of the methods to call up the Tabs dialog box described earlier). The Tabs dialog box appears.

❸ Drag the desired tab stop onto the Ruler. The Position field displays the current position of the tab marker.

❹ Enter a position for the tab stop, click OK, and press the Return key (or click Set to set the tab stop and keep the Tabs dialog box open).

To remove a tab stop, either drag it off the Ruler or select it and click the Clear button. If you place a number of tab stops, make mistakes, and want to start again from scratch, you can clear all the tab stops from the Ruler by clicking the Clear All button. However, if you have set tab stops in a style and want to remove only those you've added to a paragraph beyond those set in the style definition, you must reapply the style. Click the Clear All button to remove all tab stops, even those set in a style definition.

TIP

A Hanging Indent Sets the First Tab Stop Automatically
If you create a hanging indent by setting the first-line indent to the left of the left indent, Word sets the first tab stop at the position of the left indent. For example, the numbered and bulleted lists in this book use a default tab stop of 18 points, or 0.25 inch. Because the first line of the text for each item in the list begins at the left indent (for example, *Drag* in ❸ on the previous page), we didn't establish an additional tab-stop format for the first line.

Tab Leaders

Tab leaders are extra characters that Word uses to fill blank spaces before a tab stop. You can use a tab leader, for example, when preparing a table of contents, as shown in Figure 9-14. The tab stop on the right, for the page number, has a dotted leader. When you press the Tab key to move to the tab stop, Word inserts the leader in the line. The three styles of leader are dots, dashes, and underlines. You can assign a different tab leader to each tab stop you place on the Ruler.

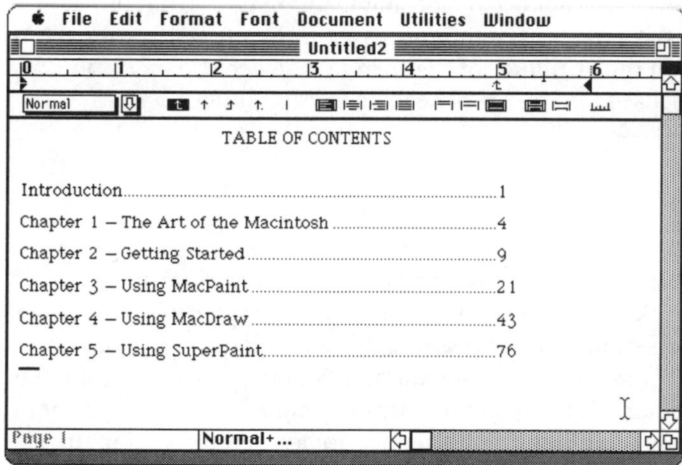

Figure 9-14
Dotted tab leaders in a table of contents.

A leader fills the space before the tab stop to which it is assigned. To assign a tab leader to a tab stop:

❶ Select the paragraphs you want to format, and call up the Tabs dialog box.

❷ Drag the type of tab you want from the icon bar onto the Ruler at the position you want.

❸ Click the leader you want in the Leader option group. Click OK to resume editing.

To add a leader to an existing tab stop, display the Tabs dialog box, click the tab marker to receive the leader, and then click on the type of leader you want. Click Set or OK to implement the leader. Word adds a dot to the left of the marker in the Ruler to indicate that you've assigned a leader to the tab stop. Remember that tab leaders, like tabs, are in effect only for those paragraphs that are so formatted. If you want tab leaders to apply to all paragraphs in your document, either specify them before you start writing, select all the paragraphs and choose the tab leader for them at the same time, or add the leader to one or more style definitions.

TIP

Checking Tab Leaders
You can check the type of tab leader assigned to a tab and change it if you want, by clicking the tab marker in the Ruler (with the Tabs dialog box displayed). When you do so, the option for the tab leader assigned to that marker is selected. Click another option if you want to change the leader. Click the tab marker carefully, without moving the mouse—or you might have to reassign its position.

You can also check tab leaders by choosing Define Styles from the Format menu to see the proposed definition, as though you were going to create a style based on the attributes of the currently selected paragraph. This technique is discussed in the tip "Checking Special Indent Values" earlier in this chapter.

Borders

The Border options allow you to draw lines, often called *rules*, around paragraphs. When you click the Borders button in the Paragraph dialog box, the Paragraph Borders dialog box appears, as shown in Figure 9-15 on the following page. (Of course, you can also call up the dialog box by adding the Paragraph Borders command to a menu or by creating a key command for it.) The border formats were originally intended to be used for setting up tables; they are considerably enhanced in Word 4. In fact, the border formats in Word 4 take two forms, one for paragraphs and one for the cells in tables. Tables are discussed in detail in Chapter 11, "Formatting Tables and Lists"; for now, we will limit the discussion to an overview of the various effects you can achieve with borders in paragraphs.

The four types of border format, shown in Figure 9-16 on the following page, are Plain Box, Shadow Box, Outside Bar, and Custom. When you set up a box format, you will see changes in the tiny schematic in the center of the dialog box, which represents two paragraphs. Any of the four border types can be drawn in 1-point lines, 2-point lines, double 1-point lines, 1-point dotted lines (actually gray when printed on a PostScript printer), and hairlines (½-point lines when printed on a PostScript printer and 1-point lines otherwise). Finally, the Spacing field lets you adjust the distance between the border and the material in the paragraph.

Paragraph Borders
OK
Cancel
Plain Box
Shadow Box
Outside Bar
Custom
Spacing:

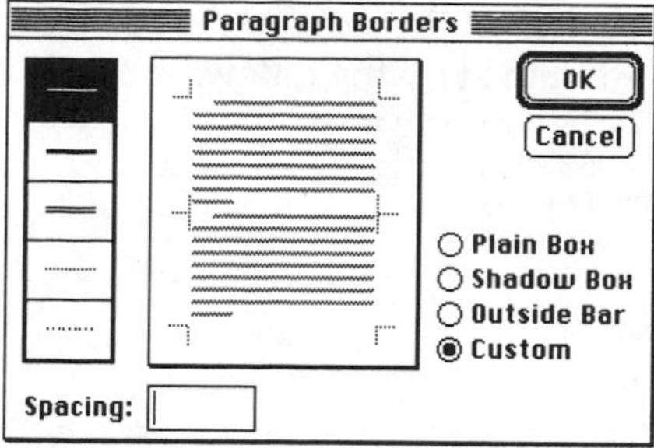

Figure 9-15
The Paragraph Borders dialog box.

In addition to the borders created with this feature of Word, you can create effects with the Vertical Bar icon next to the Tab icons in the Ruler, with the tab leader characters, with any of the various underlining character formats, with lines and other shapes copied from drawing programs such as SuperPaint or MacDraw, or by inserting PostScript operators before the paragraph.

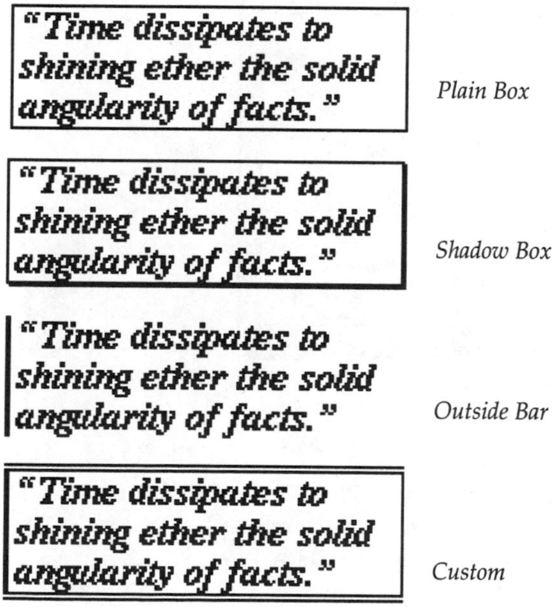

"Time dissipates to shining ether the solid angularity of facts."
Plain Box
"Time dissipates to shining ether the solid angularity of facts."
Shadow Box
"Time dissipates to shining ether the solid angularity of facts."
Outside Bar
"Time dissipates to shining ether the solid angularity of facts."
Custom

Figure 9-16
The four types of paragraph border boxes.

Plain and Shadow Boxes

The Plain Box option draws a line around the limits of the selected paragraphs. The Shadow Box option is the same as the Plain option, except that 1-point lines are added to the bottom and right edges of the box, regardless of the border style used. The placement of the sides of the box, apart from the use of the Spacing field, is determined by the following parameters:

Side	Controlled by
Left	Left or first-line indent, whichever is leftmost.
Right	Right indent.
Top	Highest ascender in first line of paragraph.
Bottom	Lowest descender in last line of paragraph.

Figure 9-17 shows an example of this format. You might think that the upper and lower limits of the box would be set by the Space Before and Space After formats, but this is not the case. Use these paragraph-spacing formats instead to set off boxed text so that the lines do not run too close to the preceding or succeeding paragraph.

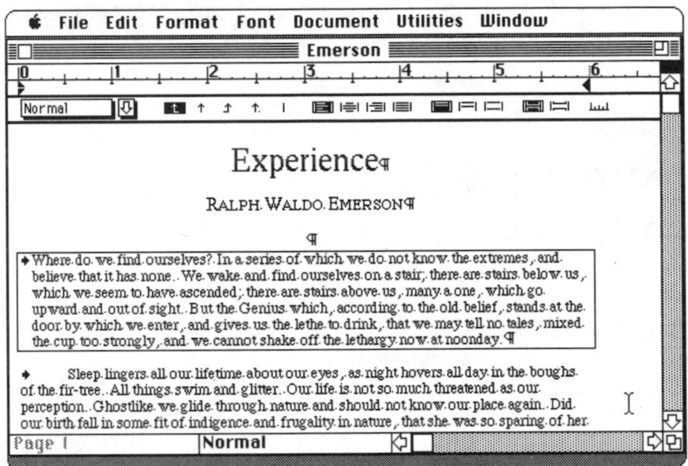

Figure 9-17
The Plain Box border effect.

Probably the easiest way to create a simple Plain Box effect for a series of paragraphs is to select them, bring up the Paragraph Borders dialog box, and double-click the Plain Box option. (However, you can also use the Commands command to add to a menu the command with the daunting name *TLBR Single Paragraph Border*.) All the box options, except Custom, toggle when you click them, so to remove a box you simply click the option again. The borders in the tiny two-paragraph schematic disappear. In Word 4, the boundary between two paragraphs is free of a border unless you put one there with the Custom format.

In Word 4, it's easy to add space between the text in the paragraph and the border: To set uniform spacing around the text, you click in the Spacing field, enter a number in points (entering *pt* to specify points is optional, although you can use other units of measurement as well), and click the Plain Box option. When you do this, Word reduces the size of the mock paragraphs in the schematic to reflect the amount of space added. (The drawing would be more representative if the paragraph remained the same size and the borders enlarged.) The default spacing distance is 2 points: you can add between 0 and 31 points of space to that, but Word doesn't let you use negative numbers to shift the border within the indents. The added space extends to the left and right of the indents that you've set and is added to the Space Before and Space After settings established in the Paragraph dialog box.

Outside Bars

Ordinarily, the Bar option causes Word to draw a vertical line to the left of the paragraph. Like the other box formats, bars are placed 2 points to the left of the leftmost indent. However, if you turn on the Mirror Even/Odd Margins option in the Document dialog box, Word places the bar on the left side for left-hand (even-numbered) pages and on the right side for right-hand (odd-numbered) pages.

Custom Boxes and Other Border Effects

Word 4's border feature really shines when you're creating custom border formats. When you select the Custom box option, you can click in the approximate areas of the top, bottom, left side, and right side of the schematic to place borders there. You can also click on the boundary between the two mock paragraphs to establish the border to be used between paragraphs. If you select a line weight (thickness) before clicking on a side, that line weight is used. If you enter a spacing distance before clicking on a side, the spacing separates that border from the text. Word updates the schematic to reflect all selected options.

You can place rules above or below a paragraph in Word 4 by clicking only the top or bottom border in the schematic. The placement of lines above and below a paragraph follows the rules for boxes: The leftmost indent (left or first-line) determines the left end of the line, and the rightmost indent sets the right end.

If you happen to create a Custom box format that you could have created by setting the Plain Box option, you'll see that Word selects it for you when you next call up the Paragraph Borders dialog box or look at the definition of the style in the Define Styles dialog box.

Figure 9-18 on the following page presents a small gallery of custom border effects; we've added ¶ symbols to make the end of each paragraph more apparent.

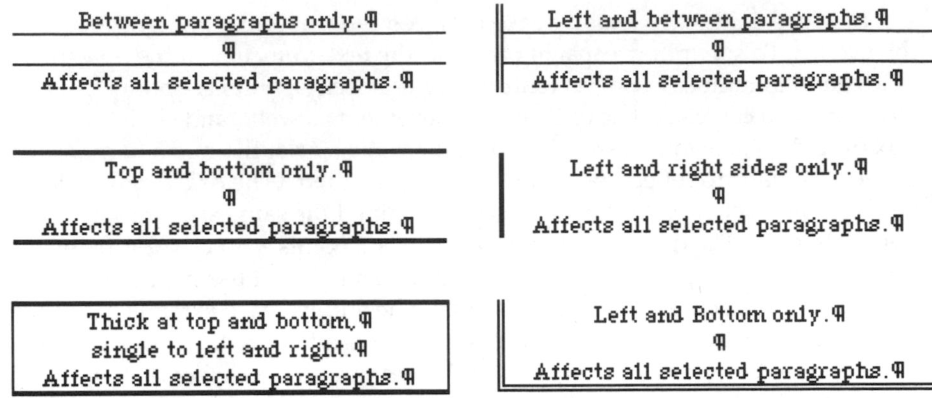

Figure 9-18
A sampling of custom border effects.

TIP

Special Border Effects

You have two ways of establishing designs for the elements in your documents: You can work within the normal range of the software to see what effects you can create, or you can start out with an idea and experiment to see how that design might be implemented. The first method is generally easier, whereas the latter method yields richer results at a greater expense of time. Working with the border formats in Word is no different, and to that end here is a potpourri of suggestions for special border effects:

- ❑ Remember that you can use alignment on a hanging first-line indent to set the left edges of boxes and rules. You can then set a tab stop to set the actual starting position of the first line.
- ❑ You can construct boxes from underlined tabs, tab leaders, and vertical bars, in addition to using the border formats.
- ❑ You can combine vertical bars with the paragraph border formats. The vertical bar will extend to the edge of the relevant border. This is particularly useful for setting up tables. (See Chapter 11.)
- ❑ You can use newline marks (Shift-Return) and tabs to create extra space between borders and the paragraph text. If you're using justified alignment, a newline mark causes the text in that line to spread out to the right indent (if the line contains more than one word). This can happen when you use a newline mark to simulate the end of a paragraph in a series of paragraphs that you want to surround with one box. If this occurs, insert a tab character just before the newline mark to force left alignment of the last line in the paragraph.

- You can create rules and other graphic elements in MacDraw, MacPaint, or another drawing program and copy them into your document. You can then format the graphic with any of the border formats, vertical bars, and so on. The glossary is a good place to store these elements when you have perfected them.
- You can turn the formatted image of a set of paragraphs into a graphic by selecting the paragraphs, pressing Option-Command-D, and pasting the image back into the document. You can then assign the Outline character format to the image to put a border around it. This border can be stretched until it is placed correctly with respect to the text. After doing this, format the original paragraphs as hidden text so that you can edit the text if you need to. See Chapter 16, "Transferring Text and Graphics," for more information on using this technique.
- Instead of using the document itself to experiment with exotic border elements, open a new, blank document and copy material from the document. Or you can save a copy of the document under a different name, such as *Test*, and experiment with the copy instead.
- You can use a macro-recording desk accessory, such as AutoMac or Tempo, to standardize complicated formatting operations.
- Finally, you can create nearly any effect you want by adding PostScript commands before the paragraphs. This topic is covered in Appendix C, "Using PostScript."

Options for Paragraph Layout

The spatial arrangement of paragraphs on the pages of most documents is straightforward. Each paragraph you type typically follows the one you've typed previously, and a paragraph that doesn't end at the bottom of a page spills over to the top of the next. More complex structures, however, are much harder to conceptualize and implement in software.

If pixels and phosphor were type on paper, arranging text or graphics would be easier—simply cut the paper, stick the material anywhere on the page, and arrange the text around it accordingly. Unfortunately for the paper-and-scissors method, positioning one piece of text according to the design rules for the document doesn't mean you've positioned all such pieces of text in the document, as you can by using styles in Word. And if the design rules change, someone must pull all the sticky pieces of paper off the board and start over.

Word 3 offered several approaches for grouping and arranging paragraphs in the traditional sequential format, whether they contain text, graphics, or both. These approaches are supported in Word 4 through the Paragraph dialog box:

- You can use the Page Break Before format to ensure that one selected paragraph, or all paragraphs assigned a style having the format, are placed at the top of a page.
- You can use the Keep With Next ¶ option to ensure that a heading and the text it heads, for example, are never separated by a page break.
- If you want a given paragraph always to appear in one block, you can use the Keep Lines Together option.
- Although not properly a page-layout option, you can establish the numerical sequence of paragraphs by using the Line Numbering option in conjunction with the Line Numbering section format.

When faced with the task of laying out paragraphs in patterns other than strict sequential chains, you could use other features of Word 3—all of which are supported in Word 4:

- You can use tab stops in conventional tables to separate items of text, discussed earlier in this chapter as well as in Chapter 11, "Formatting Tables and Lists."
- You can use section formats to flow text into more than one column on a page. (See Chapter 12, "Section Formatting.")
- Finally, you can use the Side-by-Side paragraph format to overlap paragraphs or arrange them horizontally within a column of text.

Although Word 4 supports tabbed tables, multiple columns, and the Side-by-Side format, two new features—the Table format and the Position paragraph format—reduce the need for them. You can use the Table format to create gridlike structures consisting of columns and rows of cells, each of which can contain paragraphs of text to which you've added character, paragraph, and style formats. We cover the Table format in Chapter 11.

The Position paragraph format goes far in solving the sticky problem of creating arbitrary arrangements of paragraphs. With positioned paragraphs, you can take a given paragraph out of the standard one-after-another sequence and put it anywhere on the page, in much the same way you could with scissors, paper, and layout wax. In fact, you can place the paragraph not only by entering measurements and settings options in the Position dialog box, but also by dragging the positioned object around on the page in Print Preview, almost as if it really were a floating rectangle of paper. When you position paragraphs in this way, Word 4 displays a surprising ability to wrap the text belonging to the other paragraphs on the page around the positioned object to make space for it.

Because the Table format and the Position paragraph format replace most of the uses for Side-by-Side paragraphs, the Side-by-Side format is no longer represented by an option in the Paragraph dialog box. To apply the Side-by-Side paragraph format, you must create a key sequence for it or add it to a menu through the Commands command. Nevertheless, this format is still the best one to use for certain effects, such as drop caps—an example of which you can see in the first paragraph of each chapter in this book.

We'll discuss the paragraph version of the Position format (a version also exists for tables) in this section, followed by an excursion into the fading glories of the Side-by-Side format. But first, let's consider the simpler methods for controlling the arrangement of paragraphs on a page.

Page Break Before

The Page Break Before option tells Word to start the paragraph on a new page. You might use this feature at the beginning of a full-page chart or to start a chapter of a book on a new page. (This can also be done with section formats.) In most cases, you'll preview page breaks before printing. To set the page-break format, select the paragraph, choose the Paragraph command, click on the Page Break Before option, and then click OK. This is often an easier way to force a page break than entering a manual page break through Page Preview or pressing Shift-Enter. You can add the Page Break Before format to a menu, assign it a special key sequence through the Commands command, or attach it to a style such as the *heading 1* style.

If you have already used Word 3, you might have noticed the interaction between page breaks and the Space Before format. If you manually created a page break—by entering a required page break (entered with Shift-Enter), by using the Page Break Before format, or by entering a section mark—Word 3 began the new page with the Space Before distance of the paragraph. On the other hand, if Word created the page break through repagination, the Space Before format was ignored. Now, Word 4 always uses the Space Before format, regardless of how the page break was created.

Keep With Next ¶

Use the Keep With Next ¶ option to group two or more paragraphs on one page. You can use this feature to keep a heading with the text it heads, a caption with a graphic, or the name of a character in a screenplay with the dialogue that follows. Note that Word is still free to chop either paragraph in two to start a new page, but it will never break the page between the two paragraphs. To keep a series of paragraphs together, simply select all but the last paragraph. (Because the format keeps the paragraph to which it is assigned with the one that follows it, you don't need to select the last paragraph.) Then choose the Paragraph command, and select the Keep With Next ¶ option.

You can remove paragraphs from the series at any time by selecting one or more of the paragraphs and turning off the Keep With Next ¶ option.

Line Numbering

The Line Numbering option is dimmed unless you have turned on the Line Numbering option in the Section dialog box. When you set the Line Number section format, Word turns on the Line Numbering paragraph format, and you have to turn it off for the paragraphs you don't want numbered. This feature is covered in more depth in Chapter 12, "Section Formatting."

When the Line Numbering format is set for a paragraph, you don't see the numbers in Galley view, but they appear in Print Preview and when you print the document. Line numbering has its own automatic style, but it doesn't support some paragraph formats, such as tabs and first-line indents. Word doesn't use these formats, even if you do add them to the definition for the *line number* style. Also, line numbering doesn't appear in side-by-side paragraphs or in headers and footers.

Keep Lines Together

The Keep Lines Together option keeps an entire paragraph on one page, preventing Word from breaking it in the middle. Use this option with Keep With Next ¶ if you need to create an unbroken block of text.

A practical limit exists to the amount of text that can fit on one page. If you tell Word to keep lines together, yet the paragraph is longer than one page, Word fills the first page with as much text as it can and then puts the remainder on a fresh page, rather than insisting that the job can't be done.

The Position Dialog Box

The easiest way to experience the power of the Position paragraph format is to work through an example. Let's say you have a quotation that you want to position on the right side of the opening paragraph in a newsletter article, with the text of the first paragraph wrapped around the left and bottom sides of the quote. Start by entering the quote immediately before the first paragraph in the article: We have increased the font size to 14 points, added the italic and bold character formats, and centered the text between the indents. Figure 9-19 shows how the quote and the rest of the text might look in Page View before turning the paragraph containing the quote into a positioned object.

To make the boundaries of the paragraph more obvious, select the paragraph containing the quote, call up the Paragraph Borders dialog box, and select the Plain Box format. Then add a little space between the border and the top and bottom lines in the quote; enter *4pt* in the Spacing field of the Border dialog box, and click on the upper and lower edges of the border schematic. (Notice that the border type changes to Custom when you do this.) Finally, click OK to apply the border format.

Figure 9-19
The text of the article and the quote in Page View.

Now add the Position paragraph format and see what happens in Page View. With the paragraph still selected:

❶ Choose the Position command, or choose the Paragraph command and click the Position button. This command has its own entry on the Format menu because you can position tables as well as paragraphs, as discussed in Chapter 11, "Formatting Tables and Lists." The Position dialog box appears, as shown in Figure 9-20.

❷ The Paragraph Width field should read *Auto*. Select this entry and replace it with *2.25 in*. The Distance From Text field should read *.125in*, (1/8 inch).

❸ From the Horizontal drop-down field, select the Right option to align the right edge of the paragraph on the right side of the column. Leave the default contents of the Vertical drop-down field *In line* as is for now.

❹ Click OK.

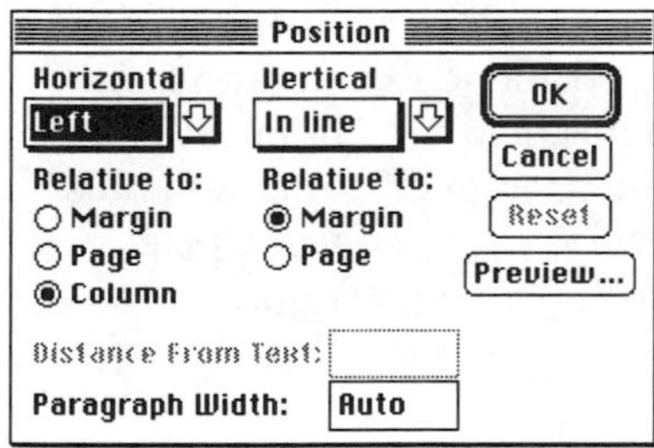

Figure 9-20
The Paragraph Position dialog box.

Figure 9-21 shows the result as it might appear in Page View. The text of the first paragraph wraps around the quote, and both paragraphs align on their upper boundaries. The quote fits into an area 2¼ inches wide, as set in the Paragraph Width field. It helps to think of this field as setting synthetic margins against which the indents of the paragraph are aligned. When the field contains the default setting, *Auto,* the width of the positioned area corresponds to the distance between the left and right edges of the text column. This example contains a single column of text, so the left and right edges of the column correspond to the left and right margins.

Notice the small box near the upper left corner of the quote in Page View—visible when Show ¶ is also on. If you double-click this mark, called the paragraph properties mark for that paragraph, the Position dialog box appears, enabling you to refine the position of a paragraph without having to choose the Position command again.

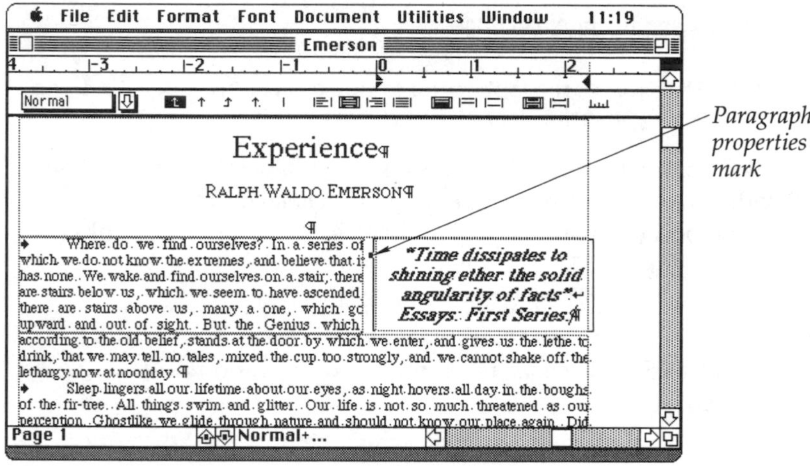

Figure 9-21
The quote in Page View, after formatting as a positioned paragraph.

When you replace the *Auto* entry in the Paragraph Width field with a new value, Word activates the Distance From Text field. This field adds space (the default is 0.125 inch) to separate the positioned paragraph from the text that wraps around it. If you play with this field for a moment, you'll see that if the upper or lower limits of the positioned paragraph plus the value entered in the Distance From Text field intrude even one pixel into a line of the text wrapping around the quote, the nonpositioned text wraps to a new line. This space extends out from all sides of the paragraph that contact text; sides touching the margin, for instance, aren't separated from the quote by the Distance From Text value.

TIP

Another Way to Distance Text from Positioned Paragraphs
The value you set in the Distance From Text field also extends above and below the positioned paragraph, often combining with the way the non-positioned text wraps to produce unsightly gaps at the top or bottom of the positioned material. You can work around this by setting the distance to *0* and using the indents within the positioned material to create gaps on the left and right sides. When you click in a positioned paragraph with the Ruler displayed on the screen, the 0 point on the Ruler shifts to the left edge of the positioned paragraph as established by the Paragraph Width value, as the Ruler in Figure 9-21 shows. Because the added space starts from the limits of "synthetic margins" established by the Paragraph Width value and not from the position of the indents, you can use indention to place the paragraph anywhere within the positioned area.

Similarly, you can use the Line Spacing, Space Before, and Space After paragraph formats to adjust vertically the placement of the paragraph within the positioned area.

Positioned paragraphs offer a variety of options for placement relative to the prominent features on a page. In the example discussed above, selecting the Right option from the Horizontal drop-down field tells Word to align the right edge of the quote on the right edge of the text column, because the Relative To option in the Horizontal group was set to Column. By selecting options from the Horizontal and Vertical drop-down fields, you can determine how the positioned object is aligned with the area set in the Relative To options. If you select the contents of the Horizontal field and enter a number, the left edge of the positioned object is positioned relative to the left edge of the area selected from the Relative To options. The Vertical field works similarly, except that the vertical position is determined from the top edges of the positioned object and either the margin or the page.

By selecting the appropriate Relative To options in either the Horizontal or Vertical group, you can align an edge of the positioned object on an edge of the overall page margins, an edge of the page, or an edge of the text column. The 18 Horizontal positioning formats and 9 Vertical positioning formats can create a total of 162 different arrangements of positioned paragraphs. The table on the following page shows the combinations possible for each orientation.

	Margin	Page	Column
Horizontal Options			
Left	Left edge aligns on left margin.	Left edge aligns on left edge of page.	Left edge aligns on left edge of current column.
Center	Centered between left and right margins.	Centered between left and right edges of page.	Centered between left and right edges of current column.
Right	Right edge aligns on right margin.	Right edge aligns on right edge of page.	Right edge aligns on right edge of current column.
Inside	On right-hand (odd) pages, left edge aligns on left margin.	On right-hand (odd) pages, right edge aligns on left *margin.*	On right-hand (odd) pages, left edge aligns on left edge of current column.
	On left-hand (even) pages, right edge aligns on right margin.	On left-hand (even) pages, left edge aligns on right *margin.*	On left-hand (even) pages, right edge aligns on right edge of current column.
Outside	On right-hand (odd) pages, right edge aligns on right margin.	On right-hand (odd) pages, left edge aligns on right *margin.*	On right-hand (odd) pages, right edge aligns on right edge of current column.
	On left-hand (even) pages, left edge aligns on left margin.	On left-hand (even) pages, right edge aligns on left *margin.*	On left-hand (even) pages, left edge aligns on left edge of current column.
Absolute	Left edge measured relative to left margin.	Left edge measured relative to left edge of page.	Left edge measured relative to left edge of current column.
Vertical Options			
In Line	Relative To settings have no effect here. Top edge aligns with top edge of the Space Before setting of the first nonpositioned paragraph following it. If more than one in-line paragraph occurs in a chain, the first paragraph top-aligns with the top edge of the first nonpositioned paragraph after the chain, and each additional in-line paragraph starts at the bottom of the one before it.		
Top	Top edge aligns on top margin.	Top edge aligns on top edge of page.	(Not available.)
Center	Centered between top and bottom margins.	Centered between top and bottom edges of page.	(Not available.)
Bottom	Bottom edge aligns on bottom margin.	Bottom edge aligns on bottom edge of page.	(Not available.)
Absolute	Top edge measured relative to top margin.	Top edge measured relative to top edge of page.	(Not available.)

The distinction between the Absolute entries and the others in the first column of the table merits some discussion. You can select the contents of either the Horizontal or Vertical drop-down fields and enter a number to set an absolute distance from the desired boundary. Another way to accomplish this is to assign a Position format to the paragraph and then to click the Preview button in the Position dialog box to switch to Print Preview. If you click the Margins icon, a set of guidelines appears, delimiting the various features of the page. You can drag these guidelines to adjust the placement of these features. We'll discuss the adjustments you can make in Print Preview to your document in Chapter 14, "Document Formatting and Printing," but for now, notice the dotted guidelines surrounding the quote. If you place the pointer within the rectangle, the pointer changes to a cross, signifying that you can drag the positioned object to a new position on the page.

When you move a positioned object in this way, Word usually replaces the previous contents of the Horizontal and Vertical fields with numbers representing the absolute location of the object from the top and left edges of the page. However, this is not always the case: If one of the edges of a positioned object corresponds to one of the natural boundaries you might have chosen in the Position dialog box, Word might take the liberty of selecting it for you. However, if you place the top edge of a positioned paragraph on what might be considered its In Line alignment, Word doesn't select the option for you.

This approach has one drawback. Let's say you've set up the Right Relative to Margin and the In Line formats, and then you switch to Print Preview to adjust the placement slightly. Word will probably convert the placement of the paragraph relative to the original body text to its absolute placement on the page. If you then switch back to Galley View and add more text above the spot where the paragraph is located in Galley View, the positioned paragraph stays in the same location on the page—even if you might have wanted the paragraph to move down with the body paragraph. For this reason, unless you have a need to place a paragraph in a specific location on the page, use the In Line option rather than placing the paragraph by dragging it in Print Preview.

TIP

Electronic Posted Notes, Marginal Annotations, and Sidebar Boxes

You can set up a convenient style for entering editing notes or marginal annotations in a document by using the Position paragraph format. An example of a marginal annotation is shown in Figure 9-22.

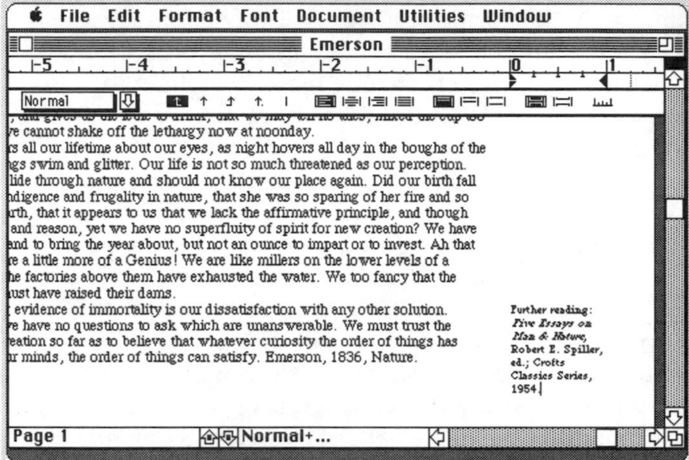

Figure 9-22

A marginal annotation created with the Position paragraph format.

To create this style, first select a paragraph containing a note to which you want to attach the style. Formatting the text in a small, dense point size (such as 9-point Times) might be a good idea. Next, display the Ruler if it isn't visible, and apply Position formats to the note by following these steps:

❶ In the Horizontal drop-down field, select the Right option. Also, select the Page option in the Horizontal group. As mentioned in the table above, this puts the positioned object in the right margin, with the right edge of the positioned object aligned relative to the right edge of the page.

❷ From the Vertical drop-down field, select the In Line option. (The Relative To setting is irrelevant.)

❸ Enter a Paragraph Width value that will allow the positioned text to fit between the right margin and the right edge of the paper: If it's too wide, some text will drift into the left edge of the body text, causing the body text to wrap around the note. For this example, let's say the distance between the right margin and the right edge of the page is 1½ inches; therefore, enter *1 in*.

❹ Set the Distance From Text value to *.25 in* to separate the note from the right edge of the page. You might have to increase the Distance From Text value if your printer can't print closer to the edge of the page than this.

❺ Click OK.

❻ Finally, click in the Style drop-down field in the Ruler, enter *note* or a similar name, and press Return. Word presents a dialog box asking *Define style "note" based on selection?*. Click OK to define the new style.

A variation on this theme exists that is better suited for creating sidebar boxes than for creating posted notes. Use the same settings as in the example, but select the Outside format instead, to make the left edge of the note align on the right margin, distanced from the text by 1/4 inch. Finally, don't forget that you can add a boxed border format to make the sidebar text stand out from the body of the document.

TIP

A Miscellany of Positioning Tips

- Normally, you can bring up the Paragraph dialog box by double-clicking the paragraph properties mark visible when Show ¶ is on. (See Figure 9-21.) For positioned paragaphs, double-clicking brings up the Position dialog box.
- Positioning a paragraph determines only the paragraph's position on the page, not the page number on which the object appears. Whether or not a positioned object will appear on a given page depends on its sequence in Galley View.
- Setting the Background Repagination option in the Preferences dialog box helps when you're working with paragraph formats such as the Position format, because you'll see more quickly the effects of new formats on screen.
- If the interval available for wrapping text around a positioned object is less than 1 inch wide, Word doesn't try to fill the space with text; instead, it leaves the area blank.
- You can gain a clearer understanding of the way the various paragraph formats interact by setting the Show Text Boundaries in Page View option in the Preferences dialog box.
- Because positioning unlinks the connection between paragraph order in Galley View and its final position on the page, you can better navigate around complicated layouts by splitting the window into two panes, one in Galley View and the other in Page View.

Side-by-Side

The Side-by-Side paragraph format is similar to the Position format. However, instead of permitting the placement of paragraphs anywhere on the page, regardless of their actual sequence in Galley View, the paragraphs are placed next to each other in a controlled manner. The paragraphs to be placed side by side follow one another in the document and are meant to be grouped horizontally. You can use the Side-by-Side format for design elements such as the following:

- Two-column scripts, although the Table format might be easier to use.
- Marginal annotations, references, or graphics and captions arranged horizontally, although the Position format is usually better for this purpose.
- Drop caps—as mentioned in the section on the Position format earlier. It's easier to use the Position format, but duplicating the same effect through the Side-by-Side format gives you more control over the placement of the drop cap.

You can format Side-by-Side paragraphs as you write, or you can select and format them after you've entered them. Most of Word is WYSIWYG (what you see is what you get), but this is not really the case with Side-by-Side paragraphs. Instead, in Galley View the paragraphs appear one after the other, properly indented so that they will not overlap when printed side by side. However, once you've set up paragraphs in this format, it's a simple matter to use the Print Preview command to see what they will look like when printed. Unfortunately, the Page View feature of Word 4 doesn't support displaying Side-by-Side paragraphs as well as it does the Position format; often the paragraph having the format becomes invisible when you switch to Page View. Also, as mentioned earlier, the Paragraph dialog box in Word 4 doesn't contain an option for the Side-by-Side format: To use this option, use the Commands command to add it to the Format (or to another) menu, or assign a key sequence. For the following discussion, we'll assume you've added the Side-by-Side command to the Format menu.

Setting up Side-by-Side paragraphs involves two steps: assigning the Side-by-Side format to the paragraphs you want to group and then adjusting the indents for the paragraphs so that they are placed the way you want them. The order of the steps doesn't really matter. Be sure that each pair of paragraphs to be formatted in this way touch. It won't work if you've inserted a paragraph mark between the two paragraphs to create a blank line.

Let's take the simplest case first—two paragraphs that are to be arranged horizontally on the page, as shown in Figure 9-23. First, assign them the Side-by-Side format:

❶ Select both paragraphs.

❷ Choose the Side-by-Side command.

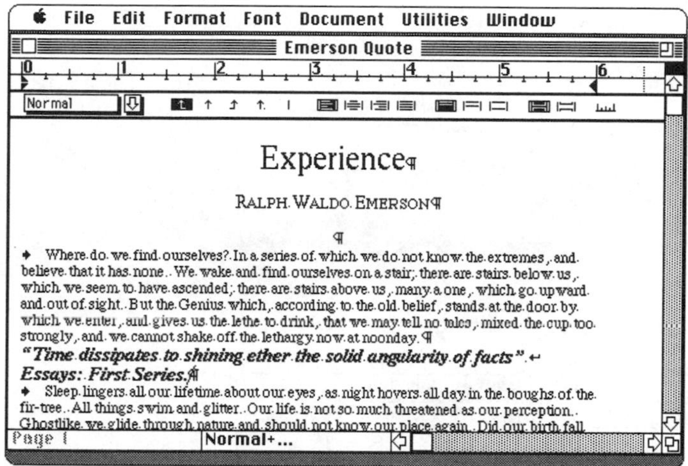

Figure 9-23
The two paragraphs to be set side by side.

At this point you don't see a visible difference on the screen. Next, indent each paragraph in turn, one on the left and one on the right:

❸ Select the first paragraph by clicking in it.

❹ Display the Ruler.

❺ Set the left and right indents for the first paragraph. You want the first paragraph on the left side of the page, and the left indent is undoubtedly already at 0 inches, so simply drag the right indent marker to 3 ½ inches.

❻ Select the second paragraph.

❼ Set a ¼ inch interval between the paragraphs by dragging the left indent of the second paragraph to 3 ¾ inches.

You can also set the indents in the Indents group of the Paragraph dialog box. The screen should now look like Figure 9-24 on the following page. To check your work, view it in Page View or Print Preview. (See Figure 9-25.) Alternatively, you can print the experimental paragraphs alone: Select the paragraphs, choose the Print command, select the Print Selection Only option, and then click OK.

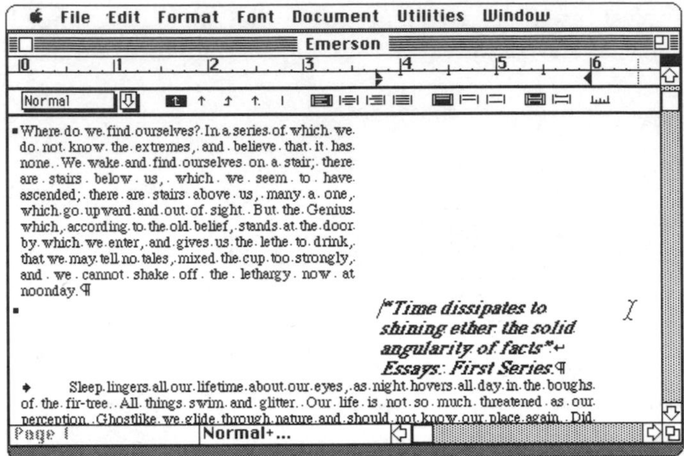

Figure 9-24
The paragraphs after Side-by-Side formatting in Galley View.

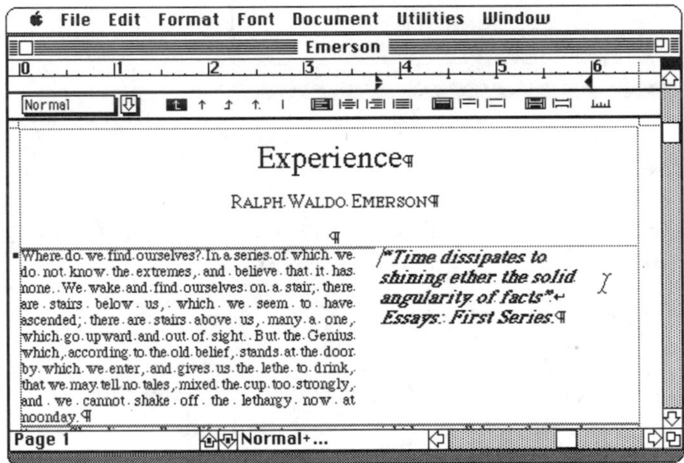

Figure 9-25
The same paragraphs in Page View.

TIP

Using the Style Sheet to Set Indents
Going back and forth between two or more indent settings can be a chore, but you can almost eliminate the trouble by using the style sheet feature. Simply define two styles on the style sheet, one for the left paragraphs and one for the right paragraphs. You can then assign either style with a few keystrokes. See Chapter 10, "Working with Style Sheets," for more information.

Now let's consider a more complicated case, one that reveals the inner logic of the Side-By-Side format. Suppose you're preparing a newsletter in a single-column format but want to place a graphic in the center of the page with notes arranged around it, as shown in Figure 9-26. (The attribution of tribe names to these artifacts is whimsical.) Figure 9-27 shows the original sequence of the paragraphs. (Incidentally, the graphic is an arrangement of full-screen images digitized with ThunderScan and compressed to 50 percent of their original sizes, using a technique described in Chapter 16, "Transferring Text and Graphics.")

1. Kwakiutl oil lamp, discovered by George MacDonald during his field study of North American Indian energy usage.

2. Samish woven basket, circa 1921, now in our Indian Works in the Twentieth Century exhibit.

3. Burnished Salish clay pot, discovered in our Columbia River digs, found by Judith Lindsay.

4. Tlingit seal-oil lamp, found by a summer intern on MacDonald's field study.

❑ If you'd like more information on this fascinating study, contact the Museum's Patron Relations Office. Intern, vacation, and summer-study programs are also available.

Figure 9-26
A more complex side-by-side arrangement.

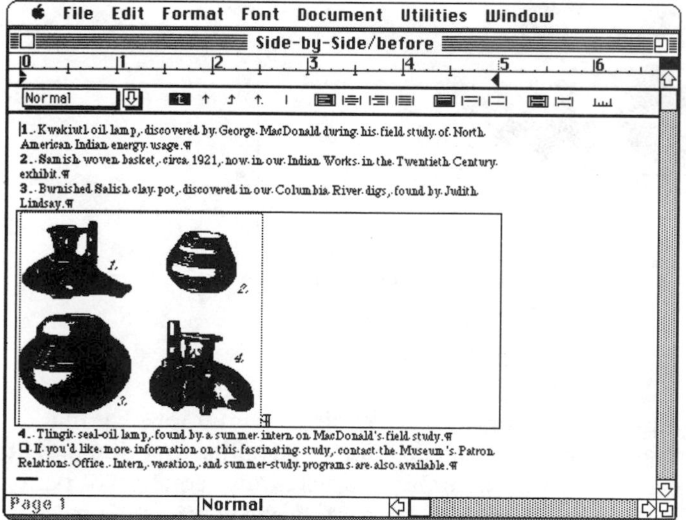

Figure 9-27
The paragraphs before being formatted.

To re-create this arrangement of paragraphs, enter the paragraphs listed in the figure. Select all the paragraphs (including the graphic), and set the Side-by-Side format. Then, for each paragraph, set the left and right indents according to the following table.

Element	Left indent	Right indent
Paragraphs 1 and 2	0 inches	1 inch
Paragraph 3 and graphic	1 1/8 inches	3 7/8 inches
Paragraphs 4 and 5	4 inches	5 inches

When you're done, the paragraphs should look like Figure 9-28. To make the group look better, add 4 points of space after each text paragraph. Also, paragraphs 1 and 2 are right aligned, paragraph 3 is justified, and the paragraph containing the graphic is centered and has a box border format.

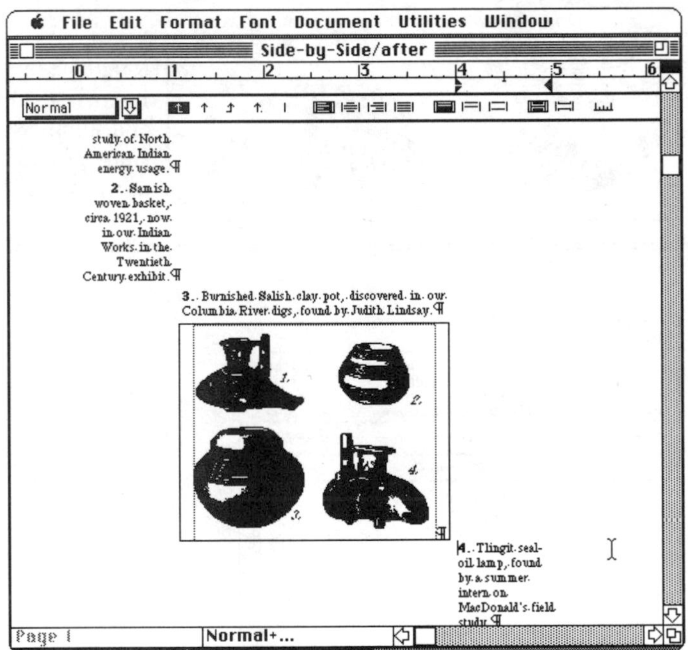

Figure 9-28
The formatted paragraphs in Galley View.

Word actually places each paragraph in a chain of paragraphs having the Side-by-Side format according to the position of its left or first-line indent alone, whichever is leftmost. (A chain of paragraphs is any sequence of paragraphs that is preceded by and succeeded by paragraphs not in the Side-by-Side format.)

The rules for the placement of paragraphs in the Side-by-Side format are as follows:

- If the paragraph's leftmost indent is the same as the one before it, Word places the paragraph in the same column as the one before it.
- If the leftmost indent of a paragraph is greater than (to the right of) the leftmost indent of the one before it, Word starts a new column. The new column starts at the beginning of the Space Before setting for the first paragraph in the chain having a left indent less than that of the new column.
- On the other hand, if the paragraph's leftmost indent is less than the one before it, Word places the paragraph in a new row. The new row starts just below the longest column in the row above it.

In the example, the first and second paragraphs are in the same column because they have the same leftmost indents. The third paragraph starts a new column because its leftmost indent is greater than that of the one before it; it is aligned with the beginning of the first paragraph. The paragraph containing the graphic goes below the third paragraph because they have the same leftmost indents. The fourth paragraph starts a new column because, again, its leftmost indent is greater than that of the graphic and paragraph 3. Finally, the fifth paragraph has the same leftmost indent as the fourth one. Because no paragraph has a leftmost indent less than the one before it, no new rows were started.

TIP

Experimenting with the Side-by-Side Format

Set up the following three styles to play with this feature of Word:

Style and alternate name	Indents
Column1, c1	0 and 2 inches
Column2, c2	2 and 4 inches
Column3, c3	4 and 6 inches

Assign the Side-by-Side format and the Plain Box format to each. The Plain Box format will make it easier to see the limits of each paragraph. Create a series of about six short paragraphs of different lengths, and number them as in the example so that you can see where they'll go. Then you can assign a column style to a paragraph by clicking in it, pressing Shift-Command-S, entering the alternate name (c1, c2, c3) of the style you want to give to the paragraph, and then pressing the Return key. Use Print Preview or print the page to see how assigning styles in different patterns changes their arrangement with respect to one another.

TIP

Drop Caps

A drop cap is a typographic element that consists of a large capital letter at the beginning of a paragraph—usually at the start of a chapter or major section in a document—that is brought down (or dropped) below the baseline of the first line in the paragraph. You can create drop caps like the one shown in Figure 9-29 (shown as text rather than as a screen dump, because Word doesn't display side-by-side drop caps in this case) in a few steps. After typing the paragraph:

1. Type the capital letter by itself in a new paragraph before the paragraph in question. Set a larger font size for the capital letter, and give it and the paragraph it belongs to the Side-by-Side format.
2. Move the left indent of the paragraph containing the capital a bit (about 1/4 inch) to the left of the body paragraph. This makes the body paragraph start a new column to the right of the capital. Word draws overlapping paragraphs as though they were transparent—a side effect of the Side-by-Side format and one of the few advantages that Side-by-Side has over the Position format—so neither obscures the other. In this way, you can create elements you couldn't create with Word's standard range of features.
3. Insert tabs at the beginning of the first few lines of the text paragraph to create a space for the capital, and insert a tab before the capital to position it flush left with respect to the left indent of the body paragraph.
4. Use Print Preview to see the effect. You can lower or raise the drop cap by adding space before or after it in the Paragraph dialog box. Figure 9-30 shows the formats used to create the drop cap in Figure 9-29.

Where do we find ourselves? In a series of which we do not know the extremes, and believe that it has none. We wake and find ourselves on a stair; there are stairs below us, which we seem to have ascended; there are stairs above us, many a one, which go upward and out of sight. But the Genius which, according to the old belief, stands at the door by which we enter, and gives us the lethe to drink, that we may tell no tales, mixed the cup too strongly, and we cannot shake off the lethargy now at noonday.

Figure 9-29

A Side-by-Side drop cap (the letter *W*).

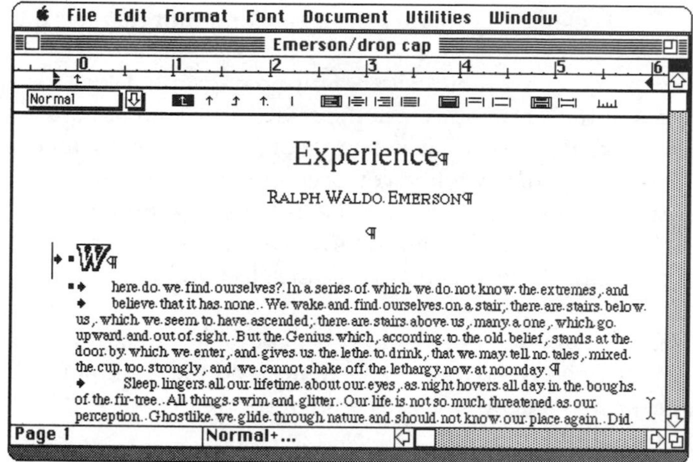

Figure 9-30
The Ruler settings for the drop cap in the previous figure.

■ *Formatting Tricks and Tips*

This section consists of a collection of useful tips you can use while formatting your documents.

Searching for and Replacing Formats

You can search for and select text that has the same formats as the text you have just selected by using the Option-Command-R key sequence. Use this feature, along with the Again commands (discussed in a moment), to find and change all text with a specific set of formats.

What you find depends on what you have selected. For example, to find all occurrences of a particular set of paragraph formats, select a paragraph having those formats by double-clicking in the selection bar. (However, if Show ¶ is on and you double-click in the first line of a paragraph that contains a paragraph properties mark, Word displays the Paragraph dialog box or the Position dialog box.) Then press Option-Command-R. If Word finds any paragraphs after that with the same formats, it selects them, stopping at the end of the last paragraph with that set of formats.

Similarly, if you set an insertion point and use the Option-Command-R key sequence, Word selects every character beyond that point having the character formats of the character preceding the insertion point, up to the first character having a different format. Incidentally, if the selection stops at the end of a paragraph when you do this, it's because the (usually) invisible paragraph mark doesn't have the same formats. If you set an insertion point in plain text (that is, text with no additional character formats) and search for formats in this way, Word selects all text after the insertion point that has the same font.

If you select more than one word but not an entire paragraph, Word searches for the formats of the last character in the selection. The main use for this technique is to systematically replace one set of formats (character or paragraph) with another, particularly when you aren't using style sheets. However, once you have changed the formats for a given paragraph or set of characters, how do you search for further occurrences of the old formats? There is no text nearby in the old format that you can select and use as a pattern for a new search.

Simply press Option-Command-A (Again) to repeat the original format search. Notice the similarity between this key sequence and the Command-A sequence used to repeat the last action. These commands are designed to work together, as follows:

1. Select the text having the formats you want to find and change. Press Option-Command-R to find the next segment of matching text.
2. When Word selects the matching text, change its formats as needed.
3. Press Option-Command-A to repeat the format search.
4. When Word selects more matching text, press Command-A to repeat the format change.
5. Repeat steps 3 and 4 throughout the rest of the document. If no matching text is found, when Word reaches the end of the document it asks if you want to continue from the beginning. Click Yes if you do, or click No if you don't. If you're changing all of a certain set of formats, you probably should click Yes, because the text upon which you based your original search has not yet been changed.

Using the Again Command for Ruler Format Changes

When using the Ruler to make formatting changes to a paragraph, you can use the Command-A key sequence to repeat the last set of format changes collectively. For example, you can set justified alignment, a range of tab stops, and double spacing in one paragraph and then repeat the entire set of formats in another paragraph by clicking in it and pressing Command-A.

Transferring Formats Quickly

You can easily transfer the formats of a paragraph to others without using style sheets, if need be. You use one paragraph as the master paragraph and copy its formats to the others. This trick relies on the fact that Word connects the formats for a given paragraph to its paragraph mark. When you replace the paragraph mark of a paragraph with that of another, you also replace its paragraph formats.

First, select the paragraph mark for the master paragraph by double-clicking in the space just to the right of it (turning Show ¶ on beforehand makes this easier), as Figure 9-31 illustrates. Press Command-C to copy it to the Clipboard. Next, select the paragraph mark for the paragraph you want to change and press Command-V to replace it with the one in the Clipboard.

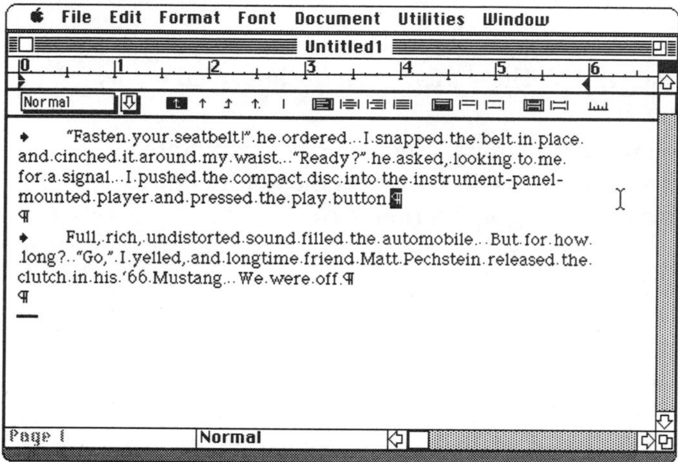

Figure 9-31
A selected paragraph mark.

You can replace a group of paragraph marks at once by first copying the master paragraph mark to the Clipboard and then selecting the range of paragraphs you want to change. Next, choose the Change command; in the Find What field enter *^p*, and in the Change To field enter *^c*. Click OK to replace the paragraph marks. One final observation: The style assigned to a paragraph is also tied to the paragraph mark, so you can use this technique to assign a style to a selected range of paragraphs.

Formatting Glossary Entries

Most of the time, text you select for use as a glossary entry will not include the paragraph mark. Text without the paragraph mark is stored without paragraph formatting. If you insert that text into the middle of a paragraph, it takes on the formats of the paragraph.

However, if you specifically want to store the paragraph formats as well—for a company letterhead, for example—select both the text and the paragraph mark before creating the new glossary entry. You can even store the paragraph mark only, without the text.

Copying Character and Paragraph Formats

You can copy either character or paragraph formats from a sample without having to repeat a complicated set of formatting steps. Whether you copy paragraph or character formats depends on what you have selected—a series of characters or an entire paragraph.

❶ Select the sample text or paragraph.

❷ Press Option-Command-V. The status box in the lower left corner of the screen reads *Format To*.

❸ Select the text you want to reformat. The selection has a dotted underline. When all the text is selected, press the Return key to transfer the character or paragraph formats.

Points to Remember

- A paragraph is any block of text that precedes a paragraph mark (¶). It can even be a blank line. Paragraph marks are visible only when Show ¶, from the Edit menu, is in effect.
- The paragraph format domain controls tabs, indention, alignment, line spacing, the spacing before and after paragraphs, the presence of rules or boxes around paragraphs, the grouping and placement of paragraphs on the page, and the numbering of lines in paragraphs.
- Paragraph formats are attached to the paragraph mark. Deleting the paragraph mark removes the formats. (The paragraph then merges with the one that follows it.) Replacing the paragraph mark changes the paragraph formats to those attached to the new paragraph mark.
- The Paragraph dialog box and the Ruler, displayed when you choose Paragraph from the Format menu, are the primary means by which you alter paragraph formats. You can display the Ruler alone by choosing Show Ruler from the Format menu, and you can also add paragraph formats to menus through the Commands command.
- The Ruler and the Paragraph dialog box show the paragraph formats in effect for the selected paragraphs or for the paragraph containing the insertion point. If the selected paragraphs have different formats, the Ruler and the boxes for the paragraph layout options in the Paragraph dialog box are filled with gray.
- The unit of measure shown in the Ruler reflects the current unit of measure set in the Preferences dialog box, available from the Edit menu. You can choose inches, points, picas, or centimeters.
- The Indents group in the Paragraph dialog box and the Tabs dialog box allow you to set indents and tabs more precisely than you can with the Ruler. The minimum interval for each in the various units of measure is 1 point, converted to the current unit of measurement:

Unit of measure	Accuracy in edit field
Inches	0.014 inch (in)
Centimeters	0.035 centimeter (cm)
Points	1 point (pt)
Picas	0.083 pica (pi)

- Indents are not the same as margins. Margins are in the document format domain and apply to your document as a whole; you set them with the Document dialog box, available from the Format menu. Indents apply to individual paragraphs and are used to override the margin to achieve a particular effect in your document. On the Ruler, the 0 point represents the left margin, and a dotted vertical line shows the location of the right edge of the column: If one column exists, the dotted line also corresponds to the right margin.

- ❑ Setting a tab stop removes all default tab stops to its left.
- ❑ Specifying a tab stop for selected paragraphs adds a new tab stop to the ones already there and replaces an existing tab stop only if set at exactly the same position.

■ *Techniques*

The Ruler

Icon	Name	Action
Indent markers		
◣	First line indent	Sets the indent for the first line of the paragraph.
◤	Left indent	When you drag the left-indent marker, the first-line indent moves with it. To move the left-indent marker alone, press Shift and drag the marker.
◀	Right indent	Sets the right indent.
Default tab stops		
2	Default tab stop	Defined in the Document dialog box.
Style drop-down field		
Normal ⇩	Style drop-down field	Sets the style, or redefines the style by example.
Tabs		
↑	Flush left tab	Characters begin at the tab stop.
↑	Flush right tab	Characters end at the tab stop.
↑	Centered tab	Characters are centered over the tab stop.
↑.	Decimal aligned tab	Decimal points are aligned on the tab stop.
|	Vertical line	Draws a vertical line in the paragraph. Not a true tab stop.

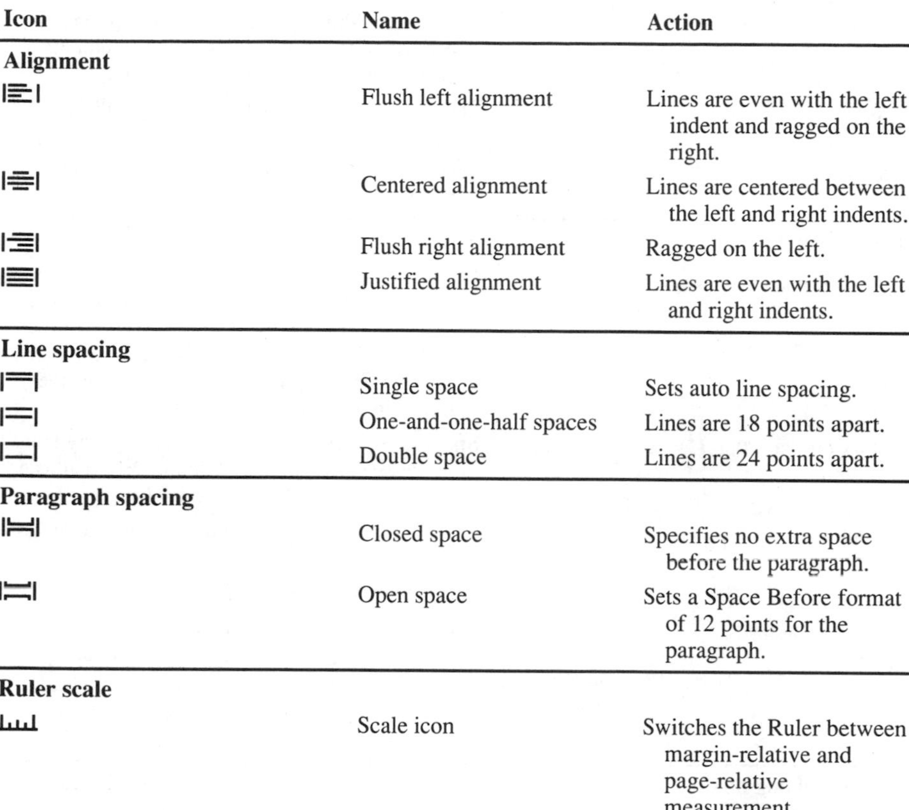

Icon	Name	Action
Alignment		
	Flush left alignment	Lines are even with the left indent and ragged on the right.
	Centered alignment	Lines are centered between the left and right indents.
	Flush right alignment	Ragged on the left.
	Justified alignment	Lines are even with the left and right indents.
Line spacing		
	Single space	Sets auto line spacing.
	One-and-one-half spaces	Lines are 18 points apart.
	Double space	Lines are 24 points apart.
Paragraph spacing		
	Closed space	Specifies no extra space before the paragraph.
	Open space	Sets a Space Before format of 12 points for the paragraph.
Ruler scale		
	Scale icon	Switches the Ruler between margin-relative and page-relative measurement.

The Paragraph Dialog Box

Indents group	Shows or sets the position of the indent marker. Measurements can be in inches (in), centimeters (cm), points (pt), or picas (pi).
Left field	Sets the left indent. Measured from the left edge of the text column.
Right field	Sets the right indent. Measured from the right edge of the text column.
First field	Sets the first-line indent. Measured relative to the left indent.
Spacing group	Determines the spacing before, within, and after the paragraph. Specify spacing in inches (in), centimeters (cm), points (pt), picas (pi), or lines (li). Fractional values are acceptable; values with more than two decimal places are truncated.
Line	Specifies spacing between lines in a paragraph. Auto (the default) sets the spacing automatically; spacing varies with the font size. The

	spacing within a paragraph varies, when necessary, to accommodate larger elements. Enter a negative value to prevent this.
Before	Specifies the spacing before a paragraph. Enter *0 pt* to remove the extra space.
After	Specifies the spacing after a paragraph. Enter *0 pt* to remove the extra space.
Tabs dialog box	Sets various types of tabs for paragraphs.
Type option group	Specifies the type of tab stop. Decimal aligns text on the first internal period within it; if there is no period, text aligns on the right edge of the text. Bar draws a 1-point vertical line, not a true tab stop; pressing the Tab key expresses the insertion point through the bar.
Leader option group	Specifies the type of tab leader: periods, hyphens, or underscored space characters. Word adds a dot to the left of the tab marker having a leader.
Set button	Sets the tab format without dismissing the dialog box.
Clear button	Clears the selected tab stop.
Clear All button	Clears all nondefault tab stops.
Position field	Click on a tab stop in the Ruler, and the entry changes to reflect its position. Enter a new value, click Set or OK, and the position changes.
Borders dialog box	Draws various types of borders around paragraphs. Select a border type and a box type, or click on the boundaries in the paragraph schematic at the center of the dialog box. The four sides are determined by the leftmost indent, the right indent, the highest ascender in the first line, and the lowest descender in the last line.
Border type group	Sets the type of border to be drawn.
Box type option group	Sets the type of box drawn. Plain Box draws a border around the perimeter of a chain of selected paragraphs. Shadow Box is similar, but draws a thicker line at the bottom and right edges. Outside Bar draws a vertical bar 2 points to the left of the left indent or on the outside indent if Mirror Odd/Even Pages is set in the Document dialog box.
Spacing field	Adds space beyond the 2-point space separating the border from the text in the paragraph. To set a different spacing on a certain side, enter the spacing value, and then click on the desired boundary in the schematic.
Paragraph layout options	Establish various spatial arrangements for paragraphs.
Page Break Before option	Starts the paragraph on a new page.

Keep With Next ¶ option	Does not permit a page break after the paragraph. Word is still free to place a page break within any paragraph having this format.
Line Numbering	Adds or removes line numbering in a paragraph. This option is dimmed unless the Line Numbering option in the Section dialog box is turned on.
Keep Lines Together	Does not permit a page break anywhere in the paragraph.
Position dialog box	
Horizontal drop-down field	Sets the type of horizontal alignment to the boundary set in the Relative To group below. Aligns the left or right edges of the paragraph on the left, right, inside, or outside edge of the selected boundary; or centers the paragraph between the left and right edges of a boundary.
Vertical drop-down field	Sets the type of vertical alignment to the boundary set in the Relative To group below. In Line aligns the top edge of the positioned paragraph with the top edge of the first nonpositioned paragraph following. You can also align the paragraph on the top edge, bottom edge, or centered between the top and bottom edges of a boundary.
Relative To groups	Sets the vertical and horizontal boundaries on which the paragraph is to be positioned: margins, page edges, or the left and right edges of the current text column.
Distance From Text field	Sets the space between the synthetic margins set by the Paragraph width value and the body text wrapped around the positioned object.
Paragraph Width field	Sets synthetic margins against which the indents of the positioned paragraph are measured.
OK button	Implements the selected position formats and closes the dialog box.
Cancel button	Closes the dialog box without implementing the selected formats.
Reset button	Converts a positioned paragraph into a nonpositioned paragraph.
Preview button	Switches to Print Preview for you to check the placement or to drag the positioned object after clicking the Margins icon.
Paragraph dialog box buttons	
OK button	Implements the selected formats and closes the dialog box.
Cancel button	Closes the dialog box without implementing the selected formats.
Apply button	Implements the selected formats without closing the dialog box.

Working with Paragraphs

Merge two paragraphs into one

1. Choose Show ¶ from the Edit menu to display the paragraph marks.
2. Select the paragraph mark between the two paragraphs.
3. Press the Backspace key.

Start a new line without ending the paragraph

1. Press Shift-Return.

Insert a paragraph mark after the insertion point

1. Press Option-Command-Return.

Copy paragraph formats from one paragraph to another

1. Select the paragraph mark of the paragraph whose formats are to be copied, and copy it to the Clipboard.
2. Select the paragraph mark for the paragraph to be changed.
3. Paste the paragraph mark from the Clipboard to the document, replacing the selected paragraph mark.

You can also use this technique to copy styles among paragraphs.

Copy character or paragraph formats from one place to another

1. Select the text whose formats are to be copied. If the selection includes a paragraph mark, the paragraph formats are copied.
2. Press Option-Command-V. The status box reads *Format To.*
3. Select the text to be reformatted, and press the Return key.

Specifying Text to Be Formatted

Format one paragraph

1. Set the insertion point in the paragraph.

Format several sequential paragraphs

1. Select the paragraphs.

Format text you are about to type

1. Set the insertion point where you plan to enter the text.

Setting Indents

Set an indent from the Ruler

❶ Select the paragraphs to be indented.
❷ Choose Show Ruler from the Format menu.
❸ Drag the appropriate marker to the location of the indent.

If you move the left-indent marker (the lower of the two left triangles), the first-line indent moves with it. To move the left indent only, press Shift and then drag the left-indent marker.

Set the left or first-line indent to the left of the page margin

❶ Drag either or both indents past the 0 point on the Ruler.
❷ After a 1-second delay, the window scrolls to the right.

You can also scroll to the left of the 0 point by pressing the Shift key as you click the left scroll arrow.

Set an indent

❶ Select the paragraphs to be indented.
❷ Choose Paragraph from the Format menu.
❸ Click in the First, Left, or Right edit fields, and enter the position of the indent in inches, centimeters, points, or picas .
❹ Click OK.

You can also drag an indent marker in the Ruler; the value of the indent appears in the appropriate field in the Indents group.

Setting Line and Paragraph Spacing

Set line spacing or paragraph spacing from the Ruler

❶ Select the paragraphs to be affected.
❷ Display the Ruler.
❸ Click the appropriate icon.

Set line or paragraph spacing with the Spacing options

❶ Select the paragraphs to be affected.
❷ Choose the Paragraph command.
❸ Enter the new spacing in the Line, Before, or After field.
❹ Click OK.

Setting Tabs

Change Word's default tab stop interval

❶ Choose Document from the Format menu.
❷ Double-click in the Default Tab Stops field.
❸ Enter a new tab-stop interval in inches, centimeters, points, or picas.
❹ Enter 22 *in* to remove all default tab stops.
❺ Click OK.

You can set up to 50 tab stops in a given paragraph.

Set tab stops from the Ruler

❶ Select the paragraphs to be affected.
❷ Choose Show Ruler from the Format menu.
❸ Drag the appropriate tab icon to the desired location on the Ruler.

Set tab stops from the Tabs dialog box

❶ Select the paragraphs to be affected.
❷ Choose the Paragraph command, and click the Tabs button.
❸ Drag the icon for the type of tab you want onto the Ruler. The setting for the tab stop appears in the Position field.
❹ Enter the new position of the tab stop in the Position field.
❺ Click OK.

Delete a tab stop

❶ Drag the tab marker off the Ruler, or select the tab marker and click the Clear button in the Tabs dialog box.

Move a tab stop

❶ Drag the marker on the Ruler, or click on the marker and specify a new position in the Position field.

Place a vertical line in the paragraph

❶ Select the paragraphs to be affected.
❷ Choose Show Ruler from the Format menu.
❸ Drag the Vertical Line icon to the desired location.

Assign a tab leader to a tab stop

❶ Select the paragraphs to be affected.

❷ Choose the Paragraph command, and click the Tabs button. The Tabs dialog box appears.

❸ Set a new tab, or click on an existing tab.

❹ Click the option you want in the Leader option group. Click None to remove an existing tab leader from the stop.

❺ Click OK.

Adding Borders

Adding a Plain Box, Shadow Box, or Outside Bar

❶ Select the paragraphs to be affected.

❷ Choose the Paragraph command, and click the Borders button. The Borders dialog appears.

❸ Select a line style: Single, Thick, Double, Dotted, or Hairline. On a PostScript printer, the Dotted line type prints in a 50 percent gray, and the Hairline is 1/150 inch thick (about 1/2 point). On a non-PostScript printer, the Hairline width is 1 point.

❹ Enter a positive number in the Spacing field to add more than the 2-point minimum space between the border and the text. Borders are measured from the leftmost and right indents of the paragraph and from the upper and lower limits of the Line Spacing setting.

❺ Select the Plain Box, Shadow Box, or Outside Bar options. The Outside Bar prints on the left side of the paragraph or on the outside edge of the paragraph if you've set the Mirror Even/Odd Margins option in the Document dialog box.

❻ Click OK.

Double-clicking anywhere on the outer edge of the schematic sets the Plain Box type. Clicking in the center of the schematic adds a border between every two paragraphs having that format.

Adding a Custom border

❶ Select the paragraphs to be affected.

❷ Choose the Paragraph command, and click the Borders button. The Borders dialog box appears.

For each border added:

❸ Select a line style, as for the standard boxes.

❹ Enter a positive number in the Spacing field to add more than the 2-point minimum space between the border and the text of the paragraph.

❺ In the schematic, click on the paragraph boundary that is to have the border. If the Custom box type isn't already selected, clicking on one of the paragraph boundaries automatically selects it.

❻ When you've finished specifying borders, click OK.

Clicking in the center of the schematic adds a border between every two paragraphs having that format. To determine the line style on a given boundary, press the Option key and click on the border. The icon for that line style becomes selected. Two clicks, a moment apart, (not double-clicking) on a boundary that has a border deletes the border. Otherwise, clicking on a boundary that has a given line style toggles the border on and off.

Specifying Paragraph Layout Options

Force a page break before a paragraph

❶ Select the paragraph to be affected.

❷ Choose the Paragraph command.

❸ Click the Page Break Before option.

❹ Click OK.

Disallow page breaks in or between paragraphs

❶ Select the paragraphs to be affected.

❷ Choose the Paragraph command.

❸ Click the Keep With Next ¶ or Keep Lines Together option (or both).

❹ Click OK.

Remove line numbering from a paragraph

The Line Numbering option is dimmed unless you have turned on the Line Numbering option in the Section dialog box. When you do this, all lines are numbered automatically. To remove the line numbers from certain paragraphs:

❶ Select the paragraphs to be affected.

❷ Choose the Paragraph command.

❸ Click the Line Numbering option.

❹ Click OK.

Create positioned paragraphs

❶ Select the paragraph to be affected.

❷ Choose the Position command, or click the Position button in the Paragraph dialog box.

3. Set the desired horizontal and vertical alignment options relative to the desired boundary of the left, right, top, or bottom margins or page edges, or set them to the left and right boundaries of the current text column.
4. Enter a number in the Paragraph Width field other than the default *Auto* to establish synthetic margins against which the indents of the positioned paragraph are measured.
5. Enter a value in the Distance From Text field to add space between the positioned object and the body text wrapped around it, if any.
6. Click OK.

If you click in the positioned paragraph and the Ruler is visible, the 0 point on the Ruler shifts to the left edge of the boundary set by the Paragraph Width value.

Set paragraphs side by side

This format doesn't appear in the Paragraph dialog box of Word 4. You must add it to a menu or create a key sequence for it through the Commands dialog box.

1. Select the paragraphs to be affected.
2. Choose the Side-by-Side command or use the key sequence.

Next, indent the paragraphs so that they will fit beside one another in the arrangement you want, according to the position of their left or first-line indents (whichever of the two indents is leftmost). You can preview Side-by-Side arrangements in Print Preview but often not in Page View.

- ❑ If the leftmost indent of a paragraph is greater than (to the right of) that of the paragraph above it, the paragraph goes to the right of the preceding paragraph on the same row.
- ❑ If the leftmost indent of a paragraph is less than that of the preceding paragraph, it starts a new row below the preceding paragraph.
- ❑ If the two leftmost indents are the same, the second paragraph appears underneath the one before it and in the same column.

Other Techniques

Change the alignment of text

1. Select the paragraphs to be affected.
2. Choose Show Ruler from the Format menu.
3. Click the icon for the type of alignment you want.

Return the selected paragraphs to the Normal style

❶ Press Shift-Command-P, or choose the Normal style from the drop-down field in the Ruler, or press Shift-Command-S and type *Normal*.

Display a list of the formats for the current paragraph

❶ Choose Define Styles from the Format menu.

❷ If the current formats are not listed, delete the contents of the Based On field and click in the Style field.

❸ Click Cancel when you are finished.

Add paragraph formats to a menu

❶ Press Option-Command- +.

❷ Choose Paragraph from the Format menu.

❸ Click on the option you want to add in the Ruler or dialog box.

Or, add the desired commands through the Commands dialog box.

Search for and replace paragraph formats

❶ Select text having the formats you want to search for.

❷ Press Option-Command-R. Word selects the next block of text with those formats.

❸ Change the formats as needed.

❹ Press Option-Command-A to search for the next occurrence of the formats.

❺ Press Command-A to repeat the format change.

■ *Commands*

Command name	Meaning, menu	Standard keyboard	Keypad	Extended keyboard
1 1/2 Line Spaced	Sets one-and-one-half-line spacing (18 points) for selected paragraphs.			
Centered	Centers text of selected paragraph between left and right indents.			
		⌘⇧C		
Change Ruler Scale	Cycles among the three ruler scales: normal, page, and table scales.			

(continued)

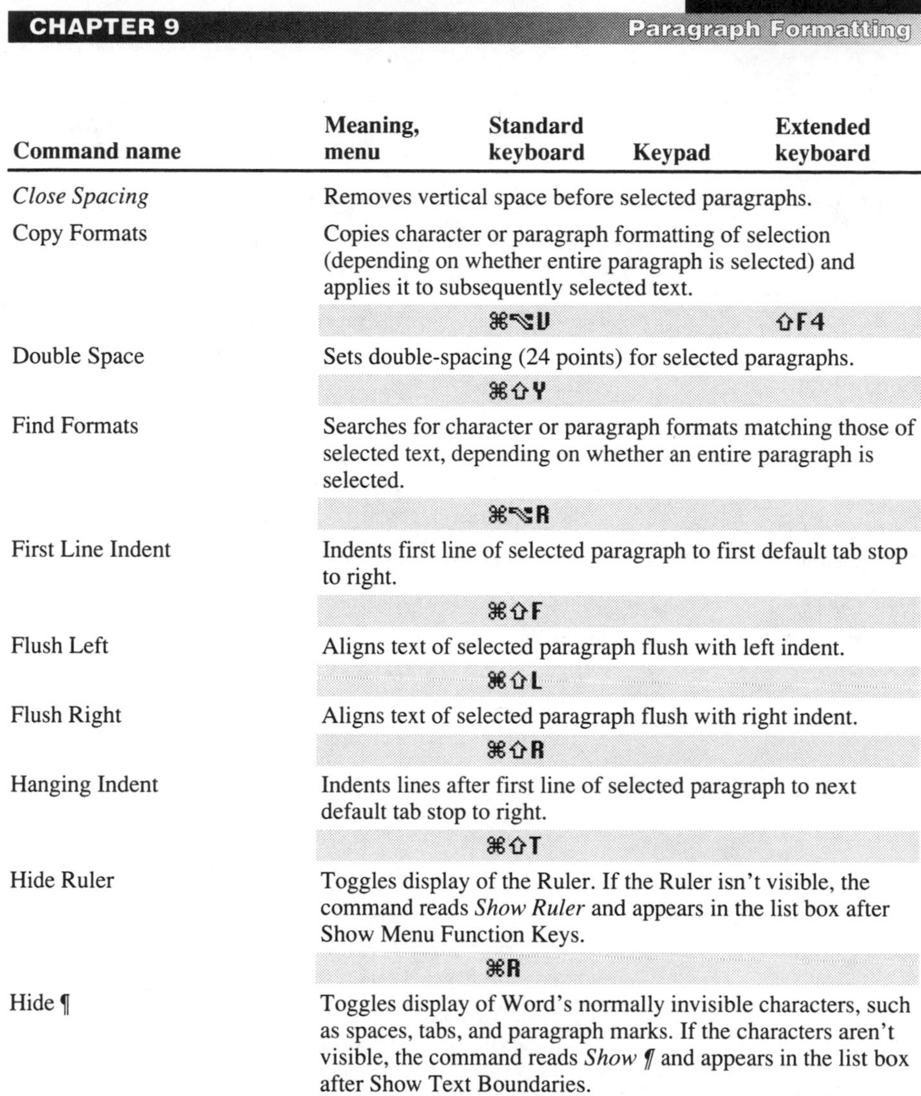

Command name	Meaning, menu	Standard keyboard	Keypad	Extended keyboard
Close Spacing	Removes vertical space before selected paragraphs.			
Copy Formats	Copies character or paragraph formatting of selection (depending on whether entire paragraph is selected) and applies it to subsequently selected text.			
		⌘⌥V		⇧F4
Double Space	Sets double-spacing (24 points) for selected paragraphs.			
		⌘⇧Y		
Find Formats	Searches for character or paragraph formats matching those of selected text, depending on whether an entire paragraph is selected.			
		⌘⌥R		
First Line Indent	Indents first line of selected paragraph to first default tab stop to right.			
		⌘⇧F		
Flush Left	Aligns text of selected paragraph flush with left indent.			
		⌘⇧L		
Flush Right	Aligns text of selected paragraph flush with right indent.			
		⌘⇧R		
Hanging Indent	Indents lines after first line of selected paragraph to next default tab stop to right.			
		⌘⇧T		
Hide Ruler	Toggles display of the Ruler. If the Ruler isn't visible, the command reads *Show Ruler* and appears in the list box after Show Menu Function Keys.			
		⌘R		
Hide ¶	Toggles display of Word's normally invisible characters, such as spaces, tabs, and paragraph marks. If the characters aren't visible, the command reads *Show ¶* and appears in the list box after Show Text Boundaries.			
		⌘R		
Insert New Paragraph	Terminates current paragraph and inserts a paragraph mark.			
		↵ or ⌤		
Justified	Justifies text of selected paragraph between left and right indents.			
		⌘⇧J		
Keep Lines Together	Prevents a page break within selected paragraph.			
Keep with Next ¶	Prevents a page break between selected paragraph and following paragraph.			
Nest Paragraph	Shifts left indent of selected paragraph to next default tab stop to right. First-line indent is relative to new left indent position.			
		⌘⇧N		

(continued)

Command name	Meaning, menu	Standard keyboard	Keypad	Extended keyboard
New ¶ After Ins. Point	Inserts a paragraph mark after insertion point without moving insertion point to next line.			
		⌘⌥↩		
No Line Numbers in Paragraph	Turns off line numbering for selected paragraph. Available if line numbering option is on for current section.			
Normal Paragraph	Applies *Normal* style to paragraph.			
		⌘⇧P		
Open Spacing	Adds 12 points of vertical space before selected paragraphs.			
		⌘⇧O		
Paragraph Border:	Applies specified type of border to selected paragraph.			
Paragraph Borders…	Applies and removes paragraph borders.			
Paragraph…	Changes paragraph formatting of selected paragraph(s).			
	Format	⌘M		⇧F14
Position…	Positions selected paragraphs on current page.			
	Format			
Show Ruler	Toggles display of ruler at top of document, footnote, or header/footer window.			
	Format	⌘R		
Show Styles on Ruler	Displays list of styles from ruler style selection box.			
Show ¶	Displays screen symbols such as ¶ (paragraph mark).			
	Edit	⌘Y		
Side by Side	Applies Side-by-Side format to selected paragraphs.			
Single Line Spaced	Sets single-spacing (12 points) for selected paragraphs.			
Tabs…	Sets and clears tabs for selected paragraph(s). Controls tab alignment and type of tab leader.			
Unnest Paragraph	Shifts left indent of selected paragraph to next default tab stop to left. First-line indent is relative to new left-indent position.			
		⌘⇧M		

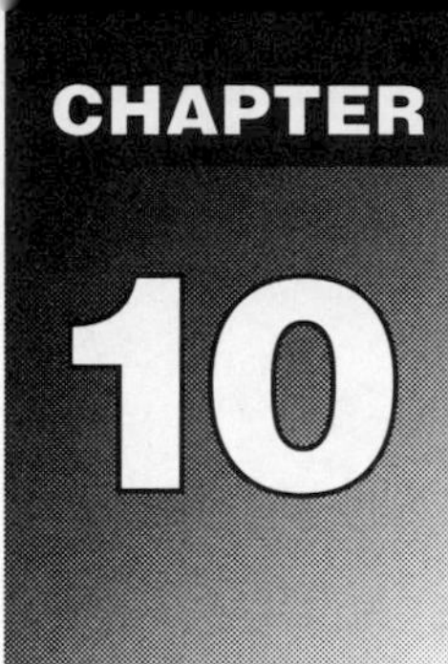

Working with Style Sheets

The style sheet might well be Word's most powerful feature, yet it is also the least understood. Although styles can be used to produce complex effects, the basic concept behind them is quite simple: A style is merely a group of character and paragraph formats that you've given a name; a style sheet is all the styles one document contains.

You've already encountered styles many times in this book. In Chapter 2, you learned how to create an outline and use the *heading* styles to establish a consistent design for the heads in a sample document. You've also seen numerous allusions to the fact that using styles is easier than repeating a complicated series of formatting operations for each element in a document. Finally, it should be clear by now that every document uses styles, even if you haven't assigned any explicitly, because Word assigns the *Normal* style to the text you enter in the absence of any other style.

The most important principle behind the concept of styles is that nearly every document consists of repeating design elements, such as:

- Level headings (assigned one of the *heading* styles)
- Body text (assigned the *Normal* style)
- Headers
- Footers

- ❏ Figure captions
- ❏ Tables
- ❏ Lists
- ❏ Side-by-side text in columns
- ❏ Marginal annotations

Without styles, you would have to maintain a detailed list of the font, font size, line spacing, alignment, and other character and paragraph formats for each element. Experimenting with the design for a document would be difficult, as you would have to make each formatting change individually.

With styles, all you have to do is identify the unique design elements in a document and define and name each element. You can then attach a style to an element simply by selecting the element and specifying the style; the character and paragraph formats contained in the style definition are applied to the text at once. If you want to play with the appearance of a document, you merely have to modify a style, and every paragraph assigned that style changes instantly.

Moreover, once you've taken the time to work out a well-balanced and good-looking set of styles for one document, you can easily transfer the style sheet to another document. In this way, you can build on your efforts rather than repeat them. In addition to letting you transfer styles between documents, Word also supports standard operations such as the cutting, pasting, and deletion of style entries.

■ *Style Sheet Basics*

As was mentioned earlier, a style is a collection of character and paragraph formats that has a name. More specifically, a style can contain any formatting instruction available in the Character dialog box, the Ruler, and the Paragraph dialog box. Section and document formats set in the Section dialog box, Document dialog box, and elsewhere cannot be stored in a style.

Each style sheet can contain a maximum of 255 styles. Many of these styles are so common that they are predefined as *automatic styles*; there are 34 of these, including the *Normal* style. You've already encountered the *heading* styles in Chapter 2; others include the *header* style for headers, the *footer* style for footers, and the *page number* style, which controls the format of the page number you can place in Page Preview. That leaves 221 empty slots for your design elements. By comparison, this book uses 52 styles, 14 of which are automatic styles.

Styles affect an entire paragraph at a time and therefore might better be termed paragraph styles. The style assigned to a paragraph is tied to its paragraph mark, as was mentioned in the previous chapter. You can't, for example, double-space half a paragraph and single-space the other half. Once you assign a style to a paragraph, you can selectively alter the format for any character within the paragraph. If a style calls for bold text, for instance, you can still remove the boldface from any portion of the text. Similarly, you can override any paragraph format in a style definition by manually applying another format.

However, once you have created a style, you should generally alter the formats of text having that style through the style sheet, rather than by making extensive manual adjustments. As Figures 10-1a and 10-1b illustrate, if you change the definition of a style, all text formatted with it changes instantly.

Unlike a glossary, which can be shared by all documents, a style sheet is considered a part of a particular document. You can, however, copy style sheets from one document to another, as you'll see later in this chapter.

You do not need to save your style sheets on disk, as you do personal user dictionaries, glossaries, or documents. Because the style sheet is a part of the document, it is saved when you save the document.

Word keeps the preset definitions for the automatic styles in a default style sheet, stored in the current Word Settings file. You can change the preset definitions of these styles and even add more styles to the list so that any new document you create starts with the new defaults. This, too, is discussed later in the chapter. First, you have to learn how to define and use styles.

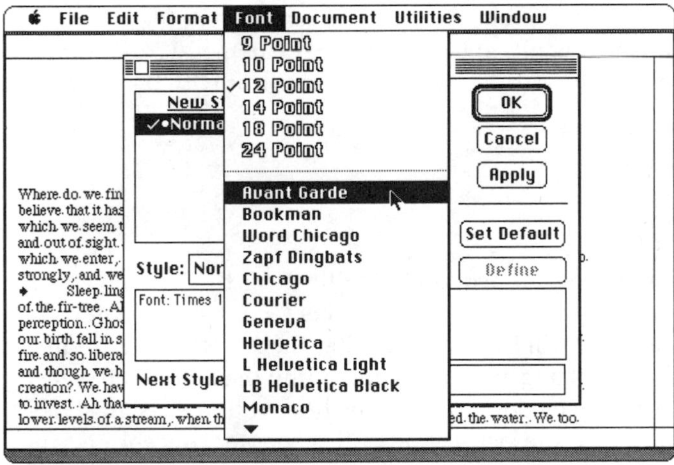

Figure 10-1a
Changing the font format through the style sheet.

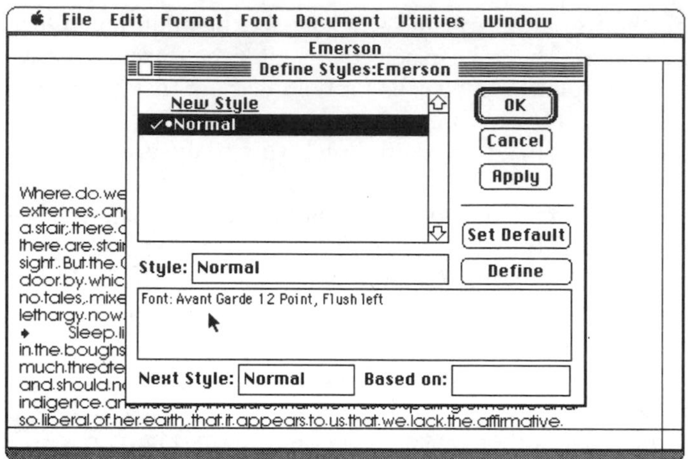

Figure 10-1b
After the style has changed.

TIP

Multiple Word Settings Files and Default Style Sheets
Although this was mentioned in Chapter 3, it bears repeating in this context: You can create different settings files for different purposes (giving each a different name, of course). To start Word with one of these settings files, double-click its icon from the Finder, or call it up in the Commands dialog box. In this way you can set up different environments, each with its own default style sheet. When you double-click a document icon or the Word icon, the program uses the defaults specified in the file named Word Settings. If no Word Settings file exists, Word creates one and fills it with the preset defaults.

■ *Defining Styles*

You will probably want to become acquainted with styles by defining a few of your own and applying them in a document. This section and the next describe how to do this. You will learn how to alter the *Normal* style, define your own styles, and make changes to styles, including the automatic styles. Once you know these basic techniques, you'll see how you can assign styles to paragraphs of text. Finally, the last section of this chapter concentrates on more advanced techniques for manipulating styles.

Redefining the Normal *Style*

The easiest way to begin learning about styles, and probably the most common use for styles, is to redefine the *Normal* style, one of the 34 automatic styles that Word supports. When you choose New from the File menu and start typing, this is the style Word assigns to your text. The preset definition for the *Normal* style is as follows:

- ❑ Character formats: 12-point New York. If the New York font is not installed in your System file, Geneva is used instead.
- ❑ Paragraph formats: Single-line spacing, flush-left alignment, no tabs other than the defaults established in the Document dialog box, closed paragraph spacing, paragraph indents even with the left and right margins.

Each new Word document starts with the *Normal* style. The style that is assigned to the first paragraph of text you selected (or the paragraph containing the insertion point) appears in the right portion of the status box, located near the lower left corner of the window. (See Figure 10-2.) When you open a new document, the box always reads *Normal*.

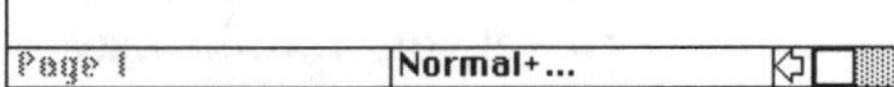

Figure 10-2
The style name in the status box.

Try redefining the *Normal* style by changing its font from New York to Helvetica and specifying double-spaced lines. Start by making a copy of a short document for your experiments. You can do this from the Finder by selecting the file and choosing Duplicate from the File menu, or from Word by opening the file and saving it under a different name.

Now start Word if you haven't already, open the file, and save it as Text Only by choosing Save As from the File menu, clicking the File Format button, selecting the Text Only option, clicking OK, and then clicking Save. This step removes all character and paragraph formats from your document and converts it to *Normal* style text.

Next, choose the Define Styles command, or double-click the style-name portion of the status area. The Define Styles dialog box appears, as shown in Figure 10-3 on the following page.

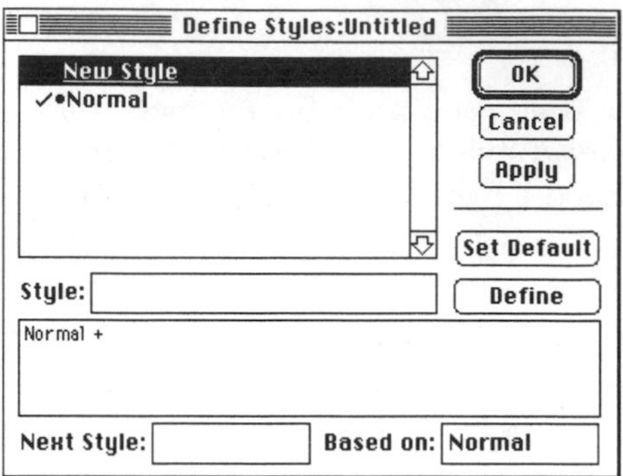

Figure 10-3
The Define Styles dialog box.

The list box showing all the styles currently defined in your document contains only two entries: *New Style* and *Normal*. The name *Normal* is preceded by a check mark, indicating that it is the style of the currently selected paragraph, and a bullet, indicating that it is one of the automatic styles. The automatic styles appear in this list box only when you use them in a document. For example, when you look at the styles for a document created with the outlining feature, you see a style name for every level your outline uses.

Notice that the *New Style* entry is underlined; this means it really isn't a style per se but a "dummy" style. Word assumes when you call up the dialog box that you want to create a new style rather than modify an old one, and so instead of highlighting the name of the style of the selected text, it highlights *New Style*.

❶ Click on *Normal* in the list box. The current definition of the *Normal* style appears in the lower part of the dialog box.

❷ Choose Character from the Format menu. Select Helvetica (or any other font) and click OK. Notice that all the text in your document changes to the new font.

❸ Press Command-R to display the Ruler. (Or choose Show Ruler from the Format menu.)

❹ Click the double-space icon in the Ruler. The text in your document changes to the double-space format. (Incidentally, this is a great way to set double spacing for printing the rough drafts of your document. You can change it back to single spacing when you're ready to print the final version.)

❺ Click the Define button to redefine the *Normal* style, and then click Cancel. If you want to both redefine the style and apply it to the currently selected text, click Define and OK (however, simply clicking OK alone also defines it). If you want to cancel the operation, click Cancel without clicking Define.

If you want, you can redefine the *Normal* style for all new documents by clicking the Set Default button just above the Define button. Both buttons redefine the style, but the Set Default button also changes the definition in the current Word Settings file. The Define button changes the style for the current document alone.

Defining a New Style by Command

You saw how to redefine the *Normal* style by command. Defining a new style by command involves a similar process, except that you work with the *New Style* item instead of the *Normal* entry in the list box of the Define Styles dialog box. Here is the procedure:

❶ Choose the Define Styles command. When the dialog box appears, the *New Style* item is selected.

❷ Enter a name in the Style edit field. Style names can contain any character except the comma. Word is case sensitive when it comes to styles: It maintains a distinction between uppercase and lowercase letters. Keep this in mind when you assign style names. Also, even though you can enter names up to 254 characters long, only 24 characters fit into the Define Styles list box.

❸ Choose the character and paragraph formatting commands you want to define for the style from the Format and Font menus, or use the key sequences for the formats. As you set the formats, they appear in the definition area of the dialog box. (See Figure 10-4.)

❹ When you're done, click the Define button; then click OK to apply the new style to the currently selected paragraph or Cancel to define the new style without applying it.

It is possible to assign alternate names to a style by separating the names with commas. This is useful if you want to assign short codes that are easy to enter from the keyboard. Alternate style names are discussed in more detail later in this chapter, in the section on assigning styles from the keyboard.

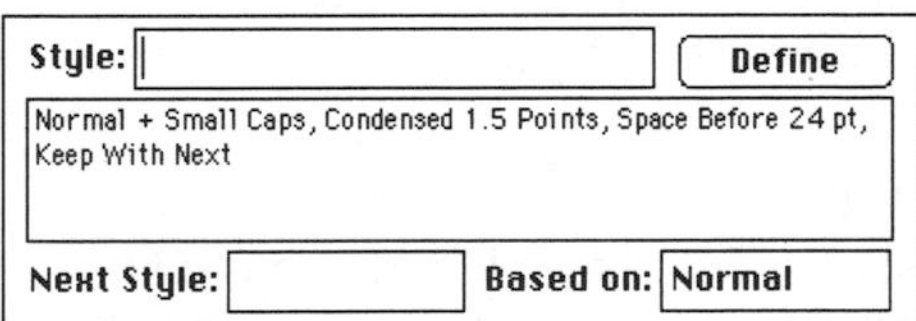

Figure 10-4
Styles in the definition area.

Defining a New Style by Example

Defining a new style by example is like defining one by command, but instead of choosing a series of formatting commands, you base the style on a sample of text that has the character and paragraph formats you want.

This technique is useful if, for example, you make some paragraph formatting changes to text in the *Normal* style and then decide to save these formats as a separate style so that you can use them again. When you change the formats in a paragraph of normal text, you see *Normal* + in the status box. You can interpret this as "This paragraph uses the *Normal* style, with some additional paragraph formats applied manually." When you display the Define Styles dialog box, the formatting changes you have made are listed in the definition area.

You can define a style by example in two ways: through the Define Styles dialog box and from the Ruler (a much easier way available in Word 4).

Defining by Example Through the Define Styles Dialog Box

Here's how to define these formats as a style through the Define Styles dialog box. After you create the combination of character and paragraph formats you want to use as a template:

❶ Choose Define Styles from the Format menu. The *New Style* item is selected in the dialog box, and the current definition of the selected paragraph appears in the lower part of the dialog box. (If you selected more than one paragraph, you see the paragraph formats of the first paragraph and the character formats of the first character of the selection. If you only set the insertion point, you see the character formats of the first character after the insertion point.)

❷ Click in the Style edit field, and type the name of your new style. Do not use commas in the name. (See the previous section for more information on style names.)

❸ Click the Define button, and then click OK to apply the new style to the currently selected paragraph, because you undoubtedly want to assign the style to the paragraph you used to create the style.

The name of the new style appears in the status box.

Defining by Example from the Ruler

Using the Ruler to define formats as a style is far easier than using the Define Styles dialog box. After you create the effects you want to record in the style and select the paragraph:

❶ Choose Show Ruler from the Format menu. (If you selected more than one paragraph, you'll be adding the paragraph formats of the first paragraph and the character formats of the first character of the selection. If you only set the insertion point, you'll be adding the character formats of the first character after the insertion point.)

2. Click in the Style drop-down field, and then type the name of the new style. Do not use commas in the name. (See the previous section for more information on style names.)
3. Press Return. Word displays a dialog box, asking whether you want to define a style having the name you've entered, based on the formats in the selected paragraph. Click Define or press Return again. (If you're sure you want to define the style, it's much faster simply to press the Return key quickly twice—when you do this, Word doesn't display the dialog box.)

   Word adds the name of the new style to the others on the drop-down field.

TIP

Creating a Work Area for Styles in a Document
A good way to experiment with styles, while minimizing the effect of formatting on the actual text of the document, is to create a work area at the end of the document, as follows:

1. Copy a sample of each design element to the end of the document. For example, copy an example of each level of heading—one for the body text, a sample of each type of table or list, and so on.
2. Place the insertion point at the beginning of each paragraph, and enter the name you will give to the style when you define it.
3. Format each element until you have what you want.
4. Use each formatted sample to define the style for it by example, as was just described.

Using a work area is also a good way to get all the design elements in one place so that you can see how they work together.

Assigning Styles to Paragraphs

Once you've named and defined a style, you can apply it before or during the typing of a paragraph or any time after you type it. When you apply a style, the selected paragraphs take on the defined formats, as though you had manually set an entire range of character or paragraph formats at once.

You apply a style in one of five ways: by choosing a style from the Styles drop-down field in the Ruler, by choosing the Styles command or the Define Styles command from the Format menu, by choosing a style that you've added to the Work menu, or by using a key sequence to call up the style by name. Also, if certain styles tend to follow each other, you can have Word assign them as you write.

Applying a Style from the Ruler

This is perhaps the easiest way to attach a style to a paragraph. Assuming the Ruler is visible, select one or more paragraphs and choose the style from the Style drop-down field.

If the first paragraph in the selection already has the style you want to apply, Word responds with a dialog box, asking if you want to reapply the style to the paragraph. This is useful when you've applied a paragraph format that doesn't belong to the definition for the style. (You can tell this is the case when the style name in the status area has an appended plus sign and ellipsis.)

Using the Styles or Define Styles Command

The technique for applying styles is basically the same for the Styles and Define Styles commands. Either command works well for this purpose. Simply select some text, choose either command, select a style, and click OK to assign the style to the text. If you choose the command while typing or if you place the insertion point in a paragraph, the style is applied to the paragraph containing the insertion point.

You're already familiar with the Define Styles dialog box. The Styles dialog box, shown in Figure 10-5, is an abbreviated version of the Define Styles dialog box. It contains a list box showing all the styles on the style sheet. (Remember that only the automatic styles you're actually using appear in the box.) The definition of the highlighted style appears in the lower part of the dialog box. Finally, you see the familiar OK, Cancel, and Apply buttons on the right side of the box. You might find it more convenient to use this dialog box for applying styles, once you've defined them with the Define Styles dialog box.

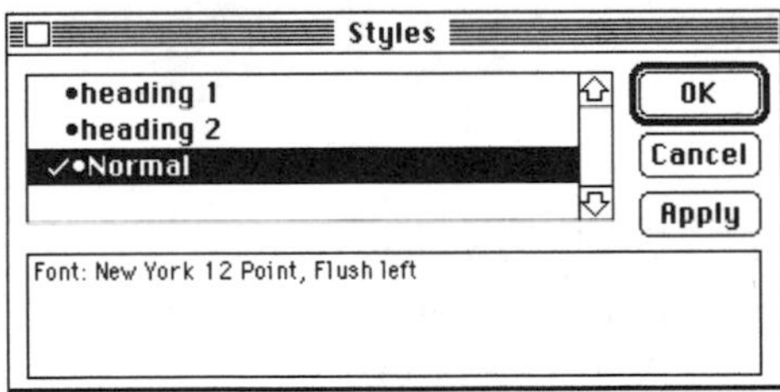

Figure 10-5
The Styles dialog box.

Applying Styles from the Work Menu

Once you're comfortable with styles, adding them to the Work menu makes applying them within your documents very convenient. The process is simple: Choose the Styles or Define Styles command, press Option-Command- +, and click on a style name in the list box. The menu bar blinks to signal the addition. If you've already added that style to the menu, the program beeps. Once you've added a style to the Work menu, you can apply it simply by placing the insertion point in a paragraph or selecting some text and then choosing the style from the menu as though it were an ordinary Word command.

As was mentioned earlier, style sheets are kept with their documents. However, Word stores the Work menu in the current Word Settings file and makes the same menu available to any document you work with. If you choose a style from the Work menu that doesn't exist in the document, Word merely beeps and does nothing.

This situation suggests two approaches you can take when working with styles that you have added to the Work menu. The first approach, and by far the most powerful, is to standardize the names you give your styles. The definition assigned to a given name can vary from document to document. Remember that Word is sensitive to case in style names, so be careful to keep capitalization consistent. You can even share styles among documents you use to promote this consistency. (This topic is explored later in this chapter.)

The other approach is to maintain a series of different Settings files and start Word by double-clicking on the Settings file you want to use for that session or by loading the Settings file from the Commands dialog box. This approach is a bit more cumbersome than standardizing the style names but can be very useful when you work with widely varying types of documents.

Applying Styles from the Keyboard

Using the keyboard to assign styles saves you from reaching for the mouse and pulling down menus. You might prefer the keyboard method once you get used to style sheets and want to work as quickly as possible from the keyboard alone. The keyboard approach does require that you know your styles by name, because you must enter their names from the keyboard.

1. Set the insertion point or select the text to be affected by the new style.
2. Press Shift-Command-S. Note that the status box now reads *Style*.
3. From the keyboard, type the name of the style you want to use, and press the Enter key or the Return key.

You do not need to type the entire name of the style you want, only enough to distinguish it from the rest of the styles in the style sheet. Also, although Word is case sensitive when you are defining styles and invoking them from the Work menu, here you can enter the name in lowercase letters if it will not conflict with another style name.

For example, suppose you wanted to apply a style the you've named *Special*. None of Word's automatic styles start with *S* and, assuming that none of the styles you've created start with an *S* (whether uppercase or lowercase), you can simply press Shift-Command-S, type the letter *s* and press the Return key. Word will understand which style you want to use.

However, suppose now that you have another style called *Specification*. Both *Special* and *Specification* start with the same five letters, so to differentiate between the two, you must type at least the first six letters of the style you want to use, either *specia* or *specif*.

If you change your mind about applying the style after using this shortcut, you can abort the command by pressing Command-(period) or clicking anywhere in the document window. Word also aborts the command if you take longer than about 20 seconds to enter a style name in the status area.

A Shortcut for the Keyboard Command

If you are assigning styles to text you've already entered, you will probably use the mouse to scroll through the document and select insertion points. After you've used the Shift-Command-S keyboard routine once, you can merely click in the status box to display the *Style* prompt. (See Figure 10-6.) Then type the first few letters of the style name and press the Return key.

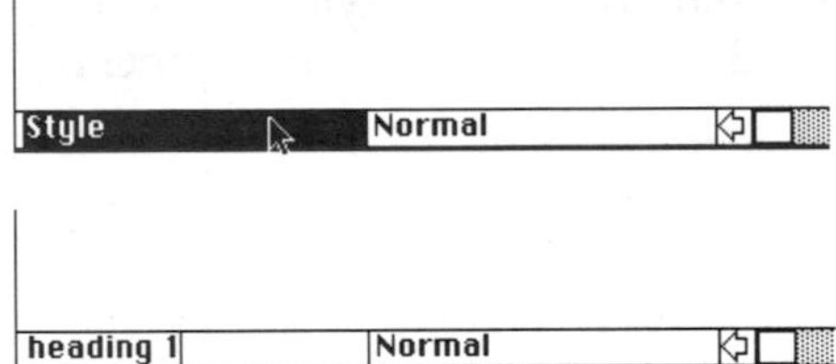

Figure 10-6
Clicking in the status box.

The status box also displays prompts for other options, including font selection and the entry of ASCII code characters. To recall the *Style* prompt after using any other of these commands, press Shift-Command-S again.

Alternate Style Names

When you enter a name for a style you're defining, you can give the style one or more alternate names separated from one another by commas. The best use for these alternate names is to create code names that are easy to remember and easy to enter from the keyboard.

For example, suppose you are writing a screenplay and have created different styles for the various parts of the document, such as for the character name, dialogue, and action. The names and codes you use for these styles might resemble the ones in Figure 10-7. You can apply the *dialogue* style by pressing Shift-Command-S and typing the entire word *dialogue* to differentiate it from the *dialogue list* style, or you can simply type *dg*. You can add the code when you first define, or later redefine, the style.

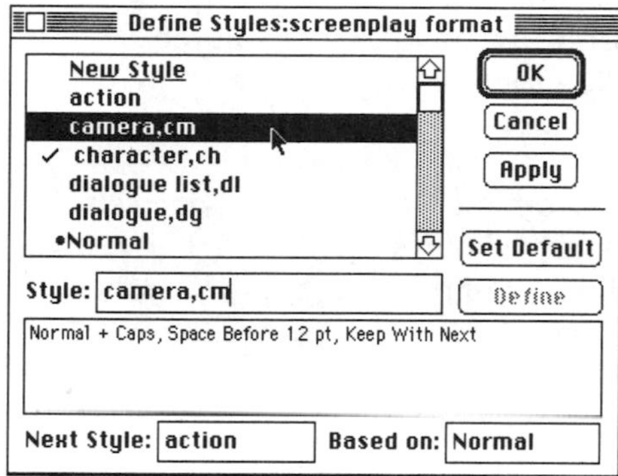

Figure 10-7
Style names and their alternates in the Define Styles list box.

Remember that the rules about entering a unique style name when using Shift-Command-S apply to alternate names as well as full names. For example, if in Figure 10-7 the style *dialogue* had the alternate name *dia*, and the style *dialogue list* had the alternate name *dial*, you would not be able to access the *dialogue* style by entering *di* alone, because *di* is shared by two alternate names.

TIP

Applying Styles with the Again Key
In Word, Command-A is the Again command; it repeats the previous command. You can use this command to apply the same style repeatedly to different paragraphs within your document. First, apply to some text the style you want to use. Then, set the insertion point where you want to apply the style again and press Command-A.

The Next Style Option

The Next Style option is a great help when you're entering the text for a document and expect certain styles to follow one another in a logical progression.

For example, body text usually follows a heading in a document. If you are using one of the *heading* styles for the heads and the *Normal* style for the body text, this means you want to start typing in *Normal* style text after you've entered the heading and pressed the Return key.

Without the Next Style feature, you would have to change the style for the body text to *Normal* manually. However, if you enter *Normal* in the Next Style edit field when you define the style for each level of heading, Word switches automatically to the *Normal* style when you press the Return key after typing a heading.

The automatic *heading* styles are preset to use *Normal* as the Next Style. For other styles, the style itself is the default; that is, text you type after pressing the Return key continues in the same style. For an example of how this feature of Word might be used in a document, take a look at the screenplay document in Chapter 18, "Blueprints."

TIP

Overriding the Next Style
If a style has a Next Style entry different from the name of the style itself, and if you want to continue in the style instead of proceeding to the Next Style, then press Command-Return at the end of the paragraph. Word ignores the Next Style and continues in the same style as that of the preceding paragraph.

Applying Styles and Pre-existing Character Formats

Suppose you have been writing in the *Normal* style and have put some text in italics, as shown in Figure 10-8a. Later, you decide you'd like to create a style for quotes that contains the italic character attribute. If you go back and apply the style to the entire paragraph, you'll see every word in the paragraph become italicized *except* the quoted text, which returns to the un-italicized (often called *Roman*) typeface. Figure 10-8b on the following page shows how this might look.

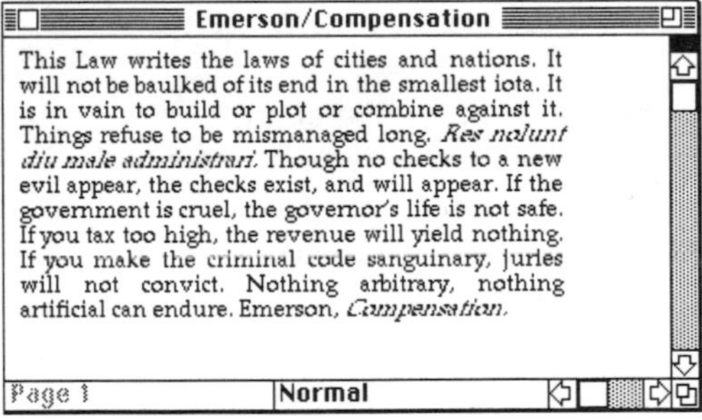

Figure 10-8a
The text as it might appear if you add italics manually.

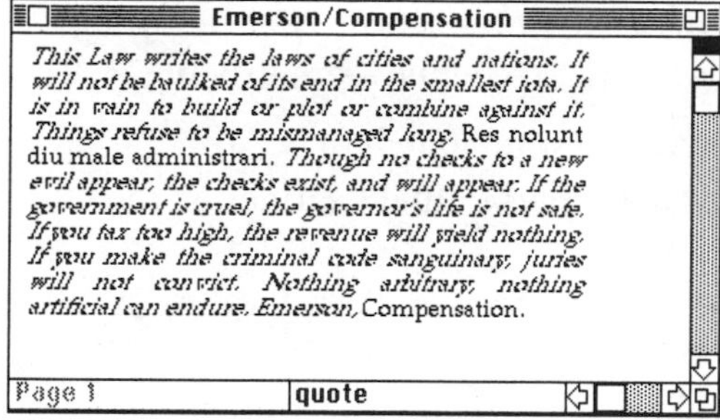

Figure 10-8b
The text as it appears if you apply a style containing the italic character attribute.

Why does this happen? In most cases, you change the typeface of text to emphasize it or to convey a certain quality. When you apply a style containing the character format you've previously added to text in a paragraph, Word preserves the distinction between the words you've altered and those you haven't by *toggling* the character format you've added.

This can be confusing when you have formatted all the text in a paragraph with a certain character format and then decide to create a style for the paragraph containing the same character format. When you apply the style to the paragraph you've formatted manually, it appears as if the character format you added has disappeared.

For example, suppose you put a heading in boldface to make it more visible, redefine a *heading* style for it, and then add the boldface attribute to its definition. When you apply the style back to the heading, the boldface attribute that was already there toggles, and the boldface goes away.

To reset the character formats for the heading to those defined in the style, do the following:

❶ Select the text, either by selecting only the text you want to reset or by double-clicking in the selection bar next to the heading to select the entire paragraph.

❷ Choose the Plain Text command, or press Shift-Command-Z.

■ *Redefining Styles*

You can use the technique you learned for redefining the *Normal* style, presented earlier in this section, to alter any style you want, including the automatic styles. Any change you make to an automatic style affects the current document only; the default styles are not changed. (You'll learn how to reset the defaults later in this chapter.) You can redefine an existing style in two ways: through the Style drop-down field in the Ruler and through the Define Styles dialog box.

Redefining a Style from the Ruler

If the Ruler is visible, this is the easiest way to redefine a pre-existing style:

1. Select a paragraph having the style you want to redefine.
2. Modify its character and paragraph formats until it's formatted the way you want the style to look.
3. Choose that style name from the Style drop-down field. Or click in the field, type the name, and press Return.
4. Word displays the dialog box, asking if you want to reapply or redefine the style.
5. Select the Redefine option and click OK.

Redefining a Style Through the Define Styles Dialog Box

The advantage of using the Define Styles dialog box is that you can edit a series of style definitions more easily by working with each in turn, instead of using the Ruler to redefine an example of each style in the document. This method also works better if the style sheet contains a style that isn't assigned to any text in the document. Here is the basic procedure for redefining an existing style through the dialog box:

1. Choose the Define Styles command, and select the style you want to redefine. The definition of that style appears in the definition area.
2. Make the desired changes in the style by choosing commands from the Format and Font menus or by using their keyboard equivalents.
3. Click the Define button, and then click Cancel, because you probably want to redefine the style without applying it to the currently selected paragraph.

If you change your mind about redefining the style and you haven't yet clicked the Define, OK, Apply, or Set Default buttons, you can restore the style to its original definition by clicking on another style name or clicking the Cancel button.

Renaming a Style

To assign a different name to a style, do the following:

1. Choose the Define Styles command. Scroll through the styles in the list box and click on the one you want to rename.
2. Edit the name in the Style edit field, and then click the Define button.
3. Word double-checks to verify that you want to change the name. Click OK.
4. Click OK or Cancel to resume writing or editing.

Note that if you try to rename one of the automatic styles, Word simply assigns the new name as an alternate name. You can use this technique to assign all paragraphs in one style to another style. Suppose, for example, that you've created two styles, called *styleA* and *styleB*, formatted a series of paragraphs with each style, and then discovered that you really want to group both sets of paragraphs under *styleA* and not use *styleB* at all. You might think you'd have to find each instance of *styleB* and change it to *styleA*, but there's a better way. You can merge all the paragraphs in *styleB* into *styleA* by doing this:

1. Choose the Define Styles command and select *styleB*. Its name appears in the Style edit field.
2. Change the name to *styleA*, and click Define.
3. Word asks *Name matches style. Merge with styleA?* You want to assign *styleA* to all the paragraphs now in *styleB*, so click OK. The Define Styles dialog box reappears, and *styleA* is selected in the list box.
4. Click Cancel because you probably don't want to apply *styleA* to the currently selected text.

Also, if both styles that you merge have short names, both sets of short names remain. For example, suppose *styleA* has the short name *a*, and *styleB* has the short name *b*. If you merge *styleB* into *styleA*, the resulting entry in the list box will appear as *styleA, a, b*.

Transferring Formats with Cut, Copy, and Paste

You can copy character and paragraph formats both between styles in a style sheet and from sample text to a style in the same document. Doing so replaces the definition of the style receiving the copied formats.

To use sample text as a template for a style, select it, choose Define Styles, select a style name from the list box, and choose the Paste command. (After selecting the template text, you could choose the Copy command, but in this case it's necessary only to select the text.) Click Define to record the new definition. Instead of pasting the text you've selected (or copied), the command transfers only the formats of the text to the style, replacing the prior definition. This is similar to the process of defining a new style by example, but this method is better when you've already defined a style and want to replace its definition with another.

Similarly, you can cut or copy a definition from one style to the Clipboard and use it to replace the definition of another style. If you choose Cut instead of Copy, Word asks you to verify that you want to delete the style. After the style is in the Clipboard, select another style in the list box and choose the Paste command to replace its definition. Then be sure to click Define to define the new style. Note that you can't use this technique to transfer styles from one document to another.

When a dialog box is active on the screen, Word lets you click the buttons in it by pressing the Command key and the first letter of the text that shows in the button. This causes conflicts with the standard key commands for editing; for instance, the key command for Cancel is Command-C, the same as the keyboard equivalent of the Copy command. The dialog box takes precedence; therefore, in this case you have to use the mouse to choose the Copy command. However, because no button in the dialog box starts with the letter V, you can use Command-V to paste a style definition if you want.

TIP

Resetting a Style to the Definition of the *Normal* Style
An easy way to reset the definition of a style to that of the *Normal* style is to select the name of the style in the Define Styles dialog box, choose the Show Ruler command if the Ruler isn't visible, and then press Shift-Command-P, the key sequence for resetting paragraphs to the *Normal* style.

Redefining the Automatic Styles

You can redefine the automatic styles just like you can redefine any of the styles that you create. You can also change the defaults for these styles. If you don't like the way Word formats indexes, for example, you can change the automatic index styles to your liking and use the modified styles as the new defaults.

To see an automatic style listed in the Styles or the Define Styles dialog box, choose the Define Styles command and enter its name in the Style edit field. Also, you can force Word to show all its automatic styles by pressing the Shift key while choosing the Define Styles command. A bullet precedes each of the automatic styles in the list box.

To change an automatic style, do the following:

❶ Select the automatic style you want to modify.

❷ Change the style definition by command or by copying and pasting formats from another style or from some sample text.

❸ If you want to redefine the style without setting a new default, click the Define button and then click Cancel. If you want to use the definition as the default, click Set Default. Word asks you to verify that you want to record the style in the default style sheet. Click OK, and then click OK or Cancel in the Define Styles dialog box, depending on whether or not you want to assign the style to the current paragraph.

When you click Set Default, the new default style is stored in the Word Settings file.

To return to the original, or *preset,* definitions for the automatic styles, rename the Word Settings file and start Word again by double-clicking the Word program icon. When you do this, Word uses the preset definitions stored within the program itself. (Refer to Chapter 3 for more information on the Word Settings file.)

The following table, repeated in Appendix E, "Word's Preset Defaults," lists the formats for Word's automatic styles. You can change any of the definitions to suit your needs.

Style name	Definition
footer	Normal + Tab stops: 3 in Centered; 6 in Right Flush
footnote reference	Normal + Font: 9 Point, Superscript 3 Point
footnote text	Normal + Font: 10 Point
header	Normal + Tab stops: 3 in Centered; 6 in Right Flush
heading 1	Normal + Font: Helvetica, Bold Underline, Space Before 12 pt
heading 2	Normal + Font: Helvetica, Bold, Space Before 6 pt
heading 3	Normal + Bold, Indent: Left 0.25 in
heading 4	Normal + Underline, Indent: Left 0.25 in
heading 5	Normal + Font: 10 Point, Bold, Indent: Left 0.5 in
heading 6	Normal + Font: 10 Point, Underline, Indent: Left 0.5 in
heading 7 through *heading 9*	Normal + Font: 10 Point, Italic, Indent: Left 0.5 in
index 1	Normal +
index 2 through *index 7*	Normal + Indent: Left (in multiples of 0.25 in)
line number	Normal +
Normal	Font: New York 12 Point, Flush left
page number	Normal +
PostScript	Normal + Font: 10 Point, Bold Hidden
toc 1	Normal + Indent: Right 0.5 in, Tab stops 5.75 in …; 6 in Right Flush
toc 2 through *toc 9*	Normal + Indent: Left (in multiples of 0.5 in), Right 0.5 in, Tab stops: 5.75 in …; 6 in Right Flush

Don't use these names for your own styles unless you want to replace their definitions. In addition, avoid names that begin with the same letters as any of these names. The more diverse the name, the easier you can call it up with the Shift-Command-S key sequence.

Some automatic styles have unusual characteristics that affect the way you use them.

- *Line number, page number:* These two styles are based on the *Normal* style with no additional formatting. You can set more character formats for them, but Word ignores any paragraph formats you set. The reason is that Word locks the position of line numbers on the line, and page numbers are placed in the location you specify in Page Preview.

- *PostScript:* If you intend to use PostScript in your documents, you must assign this style to each line of PostScript code in your document. You can change any format in the definition for this style, except that it must have the Hidden format. See Appendix C, "Using PostScript," for more information.
- *Footnote reference:* This is the style used for footnote reference marks in your documents. It is unusual in that you can set it for text that appears within a paragraph. This is the sole exception to the rule that a style must be attached to an entire paragraph; a paragraph can have a style and also contain a footnote reference that has its own style. For this reason, the *footnote reference* style has been called a *semicharacter style*, whereas all the others are true paragraph styles. When you redefine this style, the formats of all the footnotes you entered previously do not change; this style affects only those you enter after you redefine the style. To reformat the footnote references you entered before changing the style, you must go back and reenter each footnote reference mark.

The Based On Field and Style Families

The Based On edit field in the Define Styles dialog box represents an option that you don't need to use when learning about styles but is tremendously useful when you want to use styles to their fullest. The Based On field lets you base one style on another and add formats to the dependent style.

The Based On option in the Define Styles dialog box allows you to define styles that are based on other styles. When you change the "parent" style, all the dependent styles change accordingly.

Good design practice typically requires the use of two or three fonts in a document. More fonts than this tends to confuse the reader and results in a cluttered graphic style. On the other hand, most documents do have more than a few design elements. For example, in a book you might have:

- Three or four levels of headings.
- A running head style.
- A body text style.
- A figure-caption style.
- A chapter title style.
- A style for marginal notes or annotations.
- A style for formatting figures.

Document designers commonly divide fonts into two classes: display fonts, such as those used for chapter titles and level heads, and body fonts, such as those used for footnotes and the body text itself. Imagine putting each style in the list above into one category or the other and being able to play with various combinations of fonts to see how they work together without having to redefine each style manually.

This is the principle behind the Based On option. With this feature you can create two parent styles called *DisplayFont* and *BodyFont*, for instance, and base each style in the list on one style or the other. Each parent style contains one or more format specifications; in this case, each would contain only the font you wanted to use for that type of style. Each dependent style would then refer to its parent for the font to use and add the other character and paragraph formats you specified in its definition.

An Example

Let's consider a typical use for the Based On option. Suppose you wanted all the headings in a document to use the same font but want to wait to decide on a font until after you've entered the text. You'd like to vary the *heading* styles by using different point sizes for each and making them bold to distinguish them from the body text. A good way to do this is with the work area technique presented in the tip "Creating a Work Area for Styles in a Document," earlier in this chapter. First, create a style called *DisplayFont*:

❶ Go to the end of the document, start a new paragraph, and press Shift-Command-P to reset all paragraph formats for it to the *Normal* style.

❷ Without moving the insertion point, type *DisplayFont Sample*.

❸ Double-click in the selection bar next to the paragraph to select it, and give it the display font you'd like to start with. (The whole point of styles is that you can change your mind as often as you like without having to reformat everything.) Use Avant Garde or any sans serif font such as Helvetica or Geneva.

❹ With the paragraph still selected, choose the Define Styles command.

When the dialog box appears, the *New Styles* item is highlighted, and you can see the current definition of the selected sample paragraph: *Normal + Font: Avant Garde*. The Based On edit field reads *Normal*. Leave *Normal* as the parent style—it's useful to base all other styles in a document on the *Normal* style. Then, if you need to apply a format across every style at once, you can apply it to the *Normal* style.

For example, you could double space your entire document by setting the double-space format in the *Normal* style. All styles based on the *Normal* style are then double spaced unless you have set new line-spacing formats in the definitions of the dependent styles. You could then change all styles back to single-spacing for the final version by redefining the *Normal* style to use the single-space format. Now define the style:

5. Enter *DisplayFont* in the Style edit field.
6. Click Define. Because you also want to apply this style to the sample text, click OK. The style area in the status box now reads *DisplayFont*, as you can see in Figure 10-9.

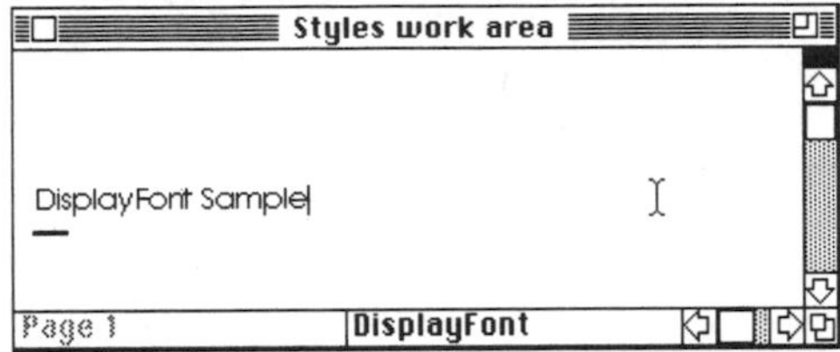

Figure 10-9
The *DisplayFont* sample after the style is defined.

Next, redefine the *heading* styles, much as you did in Chapter 2 when you created the show biz document. This time, however, base the definition for the *heading* styles on the display font defined in the *DisplayFont* style:

1. Select and copy the *DisplayFont* sample paragraph to the Clipboard. Set an insertion point about two lines down, and press Command-V to paste the line back into the document.
2. Replace the name *DisplayFont* in the new sample with *heading 1*.
3. Choose the Define Styles command. Figure 10-10 shows the dialog box that appears.

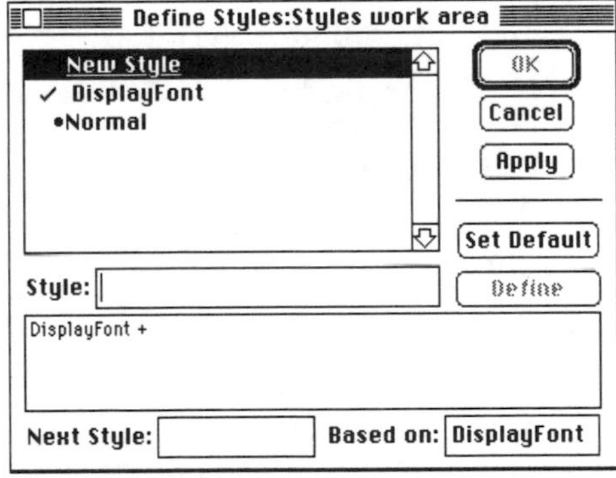

Figure 10-10
The Define Styles dialog box before a new *heading* style is defined.

The *New Style* entry in the list box is selected. The Based On edit field now reads *DisplayFont*, because the paragraph containing the insertion point has been assigned that style. The definition reads *DisplayFont +*, reiterating its dependence on that style.

❹ Enter *heading 1* in the Style edit field to name the style.

❺ Choose 18 Point from the Font menu, and choose Bold and Underline from the Format menu to add these formats to the *heading 1* style. Choose the Paragraph command, set the Before field to 20 points, and click OK.

The definition now reads *DisplayFont + Font: 18 point, Bold Underline, Space Before 20 pt*, reflecting the changes you've made. This means that the *heading 1* style uses the font defined for *DisplayFont* but in the 18-point size, boldfaced, and underlined; in addition, paragraphs in this style are set off from the preceding text. If you change the font specification in *DisplayFont*, the definition shown for *heading 1* doesn't change, although *heading 1* will use the new font.

❻ Click Define.

❼ Word responds with the message: *Style is automatic. Change its definition to match New Style?* You'll see this message because, even though the *heading 1* style does not appear in the list box, it is an automatic style and therefore still defined for the document. Click Yes.

❽ To assign the redefined *heading 1* style to the currently selected sample text, click OK.

When you click OK, the dialog box goes away, the sample text takes on the formats of the new *heading 1* style, and the status box reads *heading 1*, as shown in Figure 10-11.

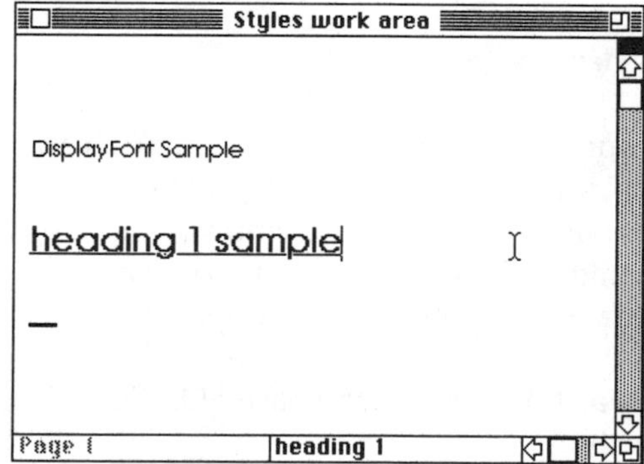

Figure 10-11
The work area after the *heading 1* style is redefined.

Use the same process to redefine the *heading 2* and *heading 3* styles. Because you want to base their definitions on the *DisplayFont* sample, copy and paste it again for each of the two styles. Change the names in the samples to *heading 2* and *heading 3*. Then, for each style, do the following:

❶ Select the sample text and choose the Define Styles command. The Based On edit field reads *DisplayFont*.

❷ Enter *heading 2* or *heading 3* in the Style edit field.

❸ Set appropriate formats for each style from this table:

Style	Formats
heading 2	14 Point, Bold, 14 points Space Before
heading 3	12 Point, Bold, 8 points Space Before

❹ Click Define, and then click OK when Word asks if you want to redefine the pre-existing style.

❺ Click OK to apply the style to the sample text.

When you're done, the Style work area should look like Figure 10-12.

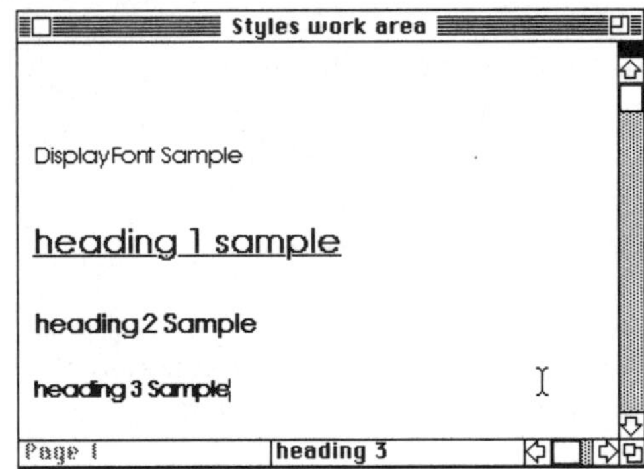

Figure 10-12
The work area after the *heading* styles are defined.

This may seem like a lot of work, but it will save you time later. You can format the headings in your document by assigning the appropriate style, and when you are ready to refine the design for your document, you can do so without searching for and reformatting each head. Finally, if you want to change the font for the headings, you have to redefine the *DisplayFont* style only once.

Note that you can also simply type a style name in the Based On field if you choose not to use the work area technique.

Style Sheet Strategies

If you extend the hierarchy implied by the previous example you might get a structure like that shown in this table:

Style name	Definition
Normal	Palatino 10 Point, Flush Left
DisplayFont	Normal + Font: Avant Garde
header	DisplayFont + Font: 10 Point, Bold, Border: Line Below
footer	DisplayFont + Font: 10 Point, Bold, Border: Line Above
heading 1	DisplayFont + Font: 18 Point, Bold, Space Before 20 pt
heading 2	DisplayFont + Font: 14 Point, Bold, Space Before 14 pt
heading 3	DisplayFont + Font: 12 Point, Bold, Space Before 8 pt
(other styles based on *DisplayFont*)	
BodyFont	Normal +
BodyText	BodyFont + Line Spacing -12 pt
footnote reference	BodyFont + Font: 9 Point, Superscript 3 Point
footnote text	BodyFont + Space After 3 pt
Table/2 column	BodyFont + Space After 4 pt, Tab stops: 0.13 in; 2.25 in; 2.38 in
Table/3 column	BodyFont + Space After 4 pt, Tab stops: 0.13 in; 2 in; 3.38 in; 3.5 in
(other styles based on *BodyFont*)	

The *Normal* style is at the top level, followed by the two font styles, *DisplayFont* and *BodyFont*. Based on the *DisplayFont* style are the *heading* styles you just redefined, as well as the *header* and *footer* styles. Stemming from the *BodyFont* style is a style called *BodyText* for the main body text, as well as the various styles for footnotes, tables, index entries, and so on.

Word supports these dependent relationships through the Based On field to a depth of nine styles, including the *Normal* style. This means that if *Style1* is based on the *Normal* style, *Style2* is based on *Style1*, and so on, with the deepest style you can define being *Style8*. With a total of 255 styles and a depth of 9 styles, Word's style sheet can handle nearly any structure you can imagine.

An interesting fact about this structure is that no text in the document is actually formatted in the *DisplayFont* or *BodyFont* styles, other than the samples in the work area. These styles are used only to enhance the consistency of the document's design and make it easier to adjust and maintain.

Your own style sheets don't have to follow this pattern if it does not suit your documents. The table of preset style definitions presented earlier in this chapter and in Appendix E, "Word's Preset Defaults," lists what is probably the most common way of arranging the dependencies in a style sheet. This is the structure Word supplies if you ignore the Based On field completely. All styles, including the automatic ones, are based on the *Normal* style. When using this arrangement, you typically enter the body text in the *Normal* style and define all other styles in relation to it. This arrangement is easy because you can create and maintain it with no special effort and because you can use the commands that reset the style of selected paragraphs, such as the Shift-Command-P key sequence, to return the text to the *Normal* style.

Occasionally it's useful to minimize the interactions between the styles on a style sheet. You might find it helpful to do this when you're first learning about style sheets, for instance. If you remove the entry in the Based On edit field for a style, the style retains the formats of the former parent style but is no longer linked to it. You can see the definition of the style change in the Define Styles dialog box when you delete the contents of the Based On field; the definition of the parent style is added to the definition of the style that was once dependent.

A similar result occurs when you change the parent of a dependent style by entering the name of the new parent style in the Based On field. If *styleA* is the name of the first parent style and *styleB* is the name of the second, the definition of the dependent style changes from *styleA* + *(formats)* to *styleB* + *(formats)*.

Subtracting Formats from Dependent Styles

If you think about the syntax of a style definition in the Define Styles dialog box, you might notice that it usually says something like *Normal* + *Font:*, and so on. The definition of a dependent style is either additive or replaces a format in its parent's definition. What do you do if a parent style specifies a format that you don't want in the dependent style definition?

For most character and paragraph formats, one format merely replaces another. For example, if you don't want a font, you set a different font. But the tab-stop paragraph formats are different, because you can specify a list of various types of tab stops in the definition for the style. In this case, you can actually subtract a paragraph format without replacing it with another.

For example, let's say the parent definition sets a tab stop at 2 inches. When you define the dependent style, you'll see the tab stop at the expected location in the Ruler. If you drag the tab stop off the Ruler, you'll see the words *Not at 2 in* appended to the definition of the dependent style. This tells you that even though the parent style sets a tab stop, that specification doesn't hold for the dependent style.

TIP

Resetting Character and Paragraph Formats
If you've set paragraph and character formats for text to which you've assigned a style (even if you haven't, the text still has the *Normal* style), you can return either the paragraph or character formats to the base definition for the style. First, select the text. To return the text to the base character formats for the style, press Shift-Command-Spacebar. To return the text to the base paragraph formats for the style, reapply the style.

■ *Sharing Style Sheets Among Documents*

Every new document you create has its own style sheet. This can be both a hindrance and a help. You benefit from this because you can create many kinds of formats for a variety of documents—from reports, manuscripts, and outlines to screenplays, proposals, and letters—and work with only those styles that are used with the specific kind of document. The disadvantage is that sharing a common style among many documents is a little more difficult. However, Word gives you four ways of doing this:

- ❑ Merge the style sheet of another document into the current document.
- ❑ Transfer styles when you copy styled text from one document to another.
- ❑ Add styles to Word's default style sheet stored in the Word Settings file, and update a document's style sheet from that one.
- ❑ Add the styles kept with an entry stored in the glossary when you insert that entry.

Merging a Style Sheet from Another Document

You can copy an entire style sheet from another document; any styles in the current document that have the same name are replaced with the ones being copied. Here's what to do:

1. Choose the Define Styles command.
2. While the dialog box is active, choose Open from the File menu.
3. Select and open the document containing the style sheet you want to import.

The document itself won't be opened, but Word will add the styles in it to the style sheet for the current document, as illustrated in Figure 10-13 on the following page. When two styles have the same name, the style being merged replaces the one in the destination document. If a style in the source document doesn't exist in the destination document, Word adds it to the destination document. If a style in the destination document has a name that doesn't exist in the source document, its definition remains intact. Therefore, if you want to preserve a style that has the same name as a style in the source document, change the name before you merge the style sheets.

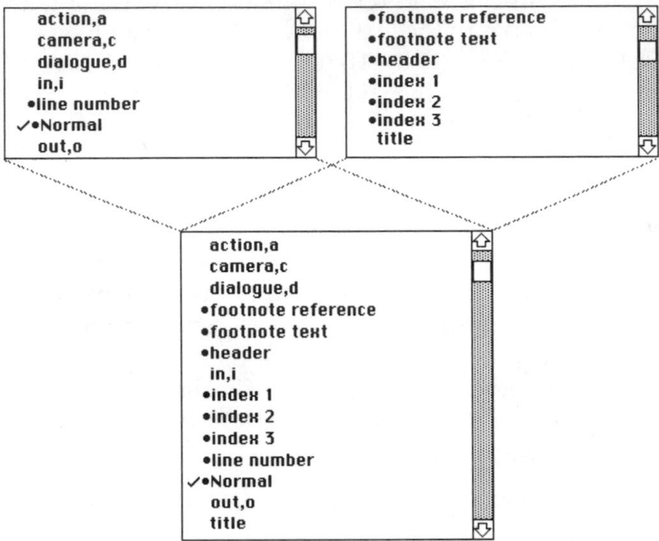

Figure 10-13
Merging style sheets.

The greatest use for merging style sheets is when you want to maintain a consistent style across many documents. You can create and maintain a reference document, or template, containing the styles that establish the design. In this document, keep at least one sample of text formatted with every style in the style sheet so that you can see how the styles work together.

This method is similar to the technique described earlier of using a style work area at the end of your document, except that you keep this work area in a separate document. You can even develop families of template documents, each of which expresses a highly refined design.

You can use these templates in two ways to create new documents:

- ❑ Make a copy of the template file and type your new document into it. This leaves the original template document unchanged.
- ❑ Start a new document and merge the template style sheet into it, using the instructions given above.

If you enter text directly into the template document, you run the risk of accidentally saving it without first renaming it. You can avoid the extra trouble this causes by being sure you have a backup of the template in case anything happens to the original.

TIP

Protecting Template Style Sheets
If you've invested much time in developing a complex style sheet for a design, you might try locking the template document while you are in the Finder's desktop. Do so by clicking the icon for the document and choosing the Get Info command. Then click the Locked check box. This prevents the template from being accidentally thrown away or resaved. To turn the protection off, open the Get Info box again and click the Locked check box once more. If you try to save a locked document, Word offers you the chance to provide a different name.

Transferring Styles by Copying Text

When you copy styled text from one document into another, and that text has a style that is not on the destination document's style sheet, Word transfers that style and its definition. If the destination document has a style with the same name as the copied text, the pasted text takes on the formats of the same style in the destination document.

You can use this behavior to selectively transfer a few styles from a sample instead of all of them. Select a paragraph in the source document that is formatted with the style you want, copy it to the Clipboard, and paste it into the destination document. You can then delete the copied text if you want; the style will remain in the destination style sheet even if the text is removed.

Beware, however, of copying too many styles at once with this method. If you copy more than 51 paragraphs in one operation, Word will decide to copy all the styles to the destination document. This can be confusing, but you are not in any danger of losing style information in the destination document; when styles are copied into a document in this way, the definitions of the styles in the destination document are not replaced by those of the same name in the source document.

Updating Styles from Word's Default Style Sheet

You've already seen how to add styles to the default style sheet stored in the Word Settings file. Every time you create a new document, Word uses this default style sheet to establish formats for the design elements in it. However, when you change one of the automatic styles, the new style does not affect previously typed documents.

To update the style sheet of an existing document after you've changed the default styles in the Word Settings file, first create a new document. The new document uses the default style definitions. Then, copy into the blank document the contents of the document you want to update, in pieces if you want. Those styles in the pasted text having the same names as ones in the default style sheet take on the formats of the new default styles. Don't forget to copy the contents of the Header, Footer, and Footnote windows as well.

Using the Glossary to Insert a Style

Chapter 6 mentioned that the glossary contains its own style sheet for glossary entries that have styles attached. An entry can contain more than one style. When you insert a glossary entry into a document, it's as though you had pasted it into the document; the styles in the destination document take precedence. Therefore, this method works only for styles that don't already exist in the document's style sheet.

You can have glossary entries that consist of nothing more than paragraph marks to which styles are attached. Give these style glossary entries the same name as the style itself.

■ *Printing Style Sheet Definitions*

While the Define Styles dialog box is active, you can choose Print from the File menu to print a complete list of the styles you are using in a given document. Having a list of styles in front of you makes designing a system of styles easier and also reminds you of their names. Further, the definition area in the dialog box doesn't have quite enough room for complicated style definitions, such as those you might create for a table with many tabs. Word prints the styles in alphabetical order by name; the definition appears on the next line.

■ Points to Remember

- ❑ A style is a named collection of paragraph and character formats. A style sheet is the collection of styles for a document and is saved with the document. If no other style has been assigned to a paragraph, it defaults to the *Normal* style. A style sheet can have as many as 255 styles.
- ❑ Word includes a set of 34 automatic styles that are assigned by operations such as specifying a header, placing a footnote, or using the outlining feature. You can redefine automatic styles. A style sheet shows only the automatic styles used in the document. To see all 34 automatic styles, press the Shift key while choosing Styles or Define Styles.
- ❑ Only one style can be assigned to a given paragraph and is tied to its paragraph mark. Some styles, such as *footnote reference*, *page number*, and *line number*, have special characteristics.
- ❑ You can override the formats in the style assigned to a paragraph by manually specifying new formats.
- ❑ A style can have more than one name; separate names by commas. You can use a second, shorter name to make the key sequence for assigning a style (Shift-Command-S) easier to execute.
- ❑ Use the Define Styles command to create new styles and modify existing ones. When the Define Styles dialog box is displayed, all menu and keyboard formatting commands, including the Ruler, are available and apply to the style selected in the list box. Use the Define Styles or the Styles command from the Format menu to apply styles.
- ❑ You can add style names to the Work menu, but the definitions for the styles are not attached to the names; any styles you assign from this menu must already be defined in your document.

■ Techniques

The Define Styles dialog box

(The Styles dialog box is an abbreviated version of the Define Styles dialog box and thus will not be described separately.)

Item	Description
Styles list box	Lists all styles defined for the document. A bullet precedes automatic styles. A check mark precedes the style assigned to the currently selected paragraph. Any action you perform while this dialog box is displayed affects the highlighted style.

(continued)

Item	Description
Style edit field	If *New Style* is highlighted in the list box, this field lets you enter a name for the new style. If some other style name is selected in the list box, this field lets you enter a new name for that style. A style name can contain any character except the comma. You can assign more than one name to a style by separating them with commas.
Definition area	Shows the formats used in the currently selected style or in the currently selected paragraph.
Based On edit field	Lets you define a new style by starting with an existing style as its base. Any changes to the base, or parent, style affect the dependent style. Deleting the name from the Based On field removes this link without altering either style.
Next Style edit field	Lets you specify the style that will follow by default any paragraph entered in the style you are defining. The change of style takes place during text entry only, when you press the Return key or the Enter key with the insertion point immediately in front of the paragraph mark. This doesn't work when the window is in Outline view.
Buttons	
OK button	Applies the highlighted style to the currently selected paragraphs and closes the dialog box.
Apply button	Applies the highlighted style to the selection in the document without closing the dialog box.
Define button	Creates a new style, renames an existing style, or records changes to the formats of a style.
Set Default button	Adds the selected style to Word's default style sheet in the Word Settings file. If the style name already exists in that style sheet, the new definition replaces the old.

Working with Styles

Assign a style to text using the Ruler

❶ Select the paragraphs to which you want to assign the style, or set the insertion point where you'll begin typing in the style.

❷ If the Ruler isn't visible, choose Show Ruler from the Format menu.

❸ Select the style you want to assign from the Styles drop-down field.

If the first paragraph in the selection already has that style, Word presents a dialog box asking if you want to reapply the style.

Assign a style to text using the Styles command

1. Select the paragraphs to which you want to assign the style, or set the insertion point where you will begin typing in the style.
2. Choose Styles from the Format menu.
3. Select the style you want to assign.
4. Click OK or Apply.

Assign a style to text from the keyboard

1. Select the paragraphs to which you want to assign the style, or set the insertion point where you will begin typing in the style.
2. Press Shift-Command-S.
3. Enter enough of the name of the style to distinguish it from any other style, and press the Return key.

Define a style by command

1. Choose Define Styles from the Format menu.
2. Be sure the *New Styles* item is selected.
3. Type the name for the style in the Style field.
4. Choose the character and paragraph formats for the style. Each format you choose appears in the definition area of the dialog box.
5. Click Define to define the style.
6. Click OK or Cancel.

Define a style by example through the Ruler

1. Select the paragraph containing the formats you want to use in the style.
2. Click in the Style field in the Ruler. Type a name for the style in the Style field, and press Return.
3. Word presents a dialog box, asking if you want to define the style based on the selection. Click Define or press Return.

A quick way to add styles by this method is to enter the new style name and press the Return key twice quickly.

Redefine a style by command

1. Choose the Define Styles command.
2. Select the style you want to redefine.
3. Change the formats in any way you like.
4. Click Define, and then click Cancel.

Redefine a style by example

❶ Select a paragraph having the style you want to redefine.

❷ Change its character and paragraph formats until it's the way you want it to look.

❸ Click in the Style field in the Ruler, and press Return.

❸ Word presents a dialog box asking if you want to reapply or redefine the style based on the selection. Select the redefine option and click OK or press Return.

Rename a style

❶ Choose the Define Styles command.

❷ Select the style you want to rename.

❸ Type the new name in the Style field.

❹ Click Define, and then click OK in the dialog box that appears.

❺ Click Cancel.

Add an alternate name to a style

❶ Choose the Define Styles command.

❷ Select the style you want to rename.

❸ Click at the end of the style's name in the Style edit field, type a comma, and then type the alternate name.

❹ Click Define, and then click Cancel.

Delete a style

❶ Choose the Define Styles command.

❷ Select the style you want to delete.

❸ Choose Cut from the Edit menu. Word asks for confirmation.

❹ If the style also appears in the default style sheet, Word asks if you want to delete the style there too.

Any text having the deleted style reverts to the *Normal* style.

Delete a style and assign text in that style to another style

❶ Choose the Define Styles command, and select the style to delete.

❷ In the Style edit field, replace the name of the style being deleted with the name of the style to be used instead.

❸ Click Define, and then click OK in the dialog box that appears.

❹ Click Cancel.

Transfer selected styles from another document

❶ Select text having the styles to be copied, and copy it to the Clipboard.

❷ Open the document to receive the styles, and set the insertion point.

❸ Choose the Paste command to copy the text and its accompanying styles from the Clipboard. Any styles not already defined in the destination document are added to its style sheet.

Note: This works only if the styles being copied do not have the same names as styles already in the destination document.

Insert a style attached to a glossary entry

❶ Insert the glossary entry into the document. Any styles not already defined in the document are added to its style sheet.

Note: This works only if a style with that name is not already defined in the document. A glossary maintains only one common style sheet for all entries, so if you create a glossary entry for text having a style that is already defined in the glossary, the new glossary entry uses the previously defined style.

Remove a style from a glossary's style sheet

❶ Press the Shift key while choosing the Open command.

❷ Select and open the glossary. The glossary opens as a Word document.

❸ Choose the Define Styles command.

❹ Select the style you want to remove from the glossary's style sheet.

❺ Choose the Cut command. Click OK when Word asks if you want to delete the style.

❻ Click the Cancel button in the Define Styles dialog box.

❼ Save and close the glossary.

Any glossary entries having the deleted style revert to the *Normal* style.

Merge a style sheet from another document

❶ Choose the Define Styles command.

❷ Choose the Open command.

❸ Open the document containing the style sheet you want to copy.

The opened style sheet is merged with the style sheet of the active document. In case of conflict, the definition in the opened style sheet prevails.

Transfer formats between styles in a document

❶ Choose the Define Styles command.
❷ Select text having the formats you want to transfer.
❸ Choose the Copy command to copy the definition to the Clipboard.
❹ Select the style to which the definition is to be transferred.
❺ Choose the Paste command.
❻ Click Define, and then click Cancel.

Copy formats from text to an existing style within a document

❶ Select the text whose formats you want to copy. (You don't need to choose the Copy command to copy the formats to the Clipboard.)
❷ Choose the Define Styles command, and select the style receiving the formats.
❸ Choose the Paste command.
❹ Click Define, and then click OK or Cancel.

Add an automatic style or change an automatic style's defaults

❶ Choose the Define Styles command. (Hold down Shift and choose Define Styles to view all the automatic style definitions.)
❷ Select the automatic style you want to modify, or type the name of a new style that you want to add.
❸ Choose the character and paragraph formats to be used in the style.
❹ Click Set Default, and then click OK in the dialog box that appears.
❺ Click OK or Cancel.

Print a style sheet

❶ Choose the Styles or Define Styles command.
❷ Choose the Print command.

This is especially useful if you've created a complex style sheet or styles with complex definitions that don't fit in the Styles dialog box or the Define Styles dialog box.

Add a style to the Work menu

❶ Choose the Styles or Define Styles command.
❷ Press Option-Command- +.
❸ Click on the name of the style you want to add. If you want to add more than one style, press the Shift key while clicking on the style names.
❹ Click Cancel to close the dialog box.

■ *Commands*

Command name	Meaning, menu	Standard keyboard	Keypad	Extended keyboard
All Styles...	Applies a selected style to selected paragraph(s). Dialog box lists defined styles and all automatic styles.			
Apply Style Name:	Applies indicated style to selected paragraph.			
Change Style	Changes style of selected paragraphs to style you indicate by typing style name and pressing Return.			
		⌘⇧S		
Define All Styles...	Defines, modifies, and applies styles. Dialog box lists defined styles and all automatic styles (even if you haven't explicitly defined them).			
Define Styles...	Defines, modifies, and applies styles. Dialog box lists defined styles and automatic styles used in your document.			
	Format	⌘T		
New ¶ with Same Style	Starts a new paragraph with same style as current paragraph. Overrides Next Style indicated in Define Styles dialog box.			
		⌘↩		
Plain For Style	Removes all character formatting not defined in the current style from selected text. Restores font, font size, and other character formats defined for style of a paragraph.			
	Format	⌘⇧␣		F9
Plain Text	Removes character formatting that can be turned on and off, such as bold, italic, and underlining.			
	Format	⌘⇧Z		⇧F9
Show Styles on Ruler	Displays list of styles from ruler style selection box.			
Styles...	Applies a selected style to selected paragraph(s). Dialog box lists defined styles and automatic styles used in your document.			
	Format			

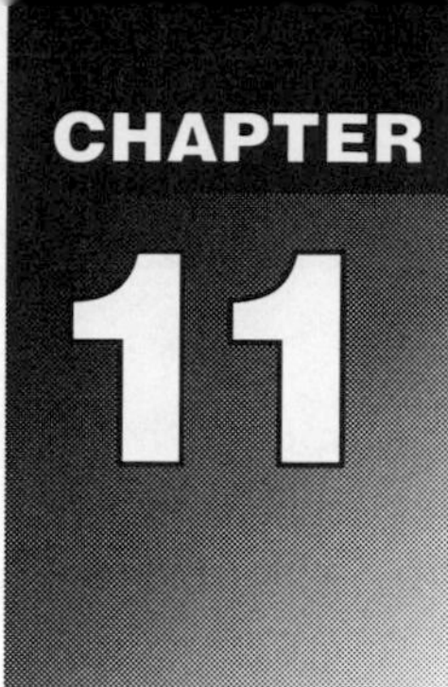

Formatting Tables and Lists

In the past, using a word processor to format financial, statistical, and mathematical data was a formidable, if not impossible, task. Tables and lists were best presented by using a spreadsheet program such as Microsoft Excel or Multiplan. Microsoft Word version 4 changes all this. You can directly format tables and lists to prepare multicolumn ledger sheets, invoices, statistical tables, and more. Word even has a calculation feature that you can use to add, subtract, multiply, and divide groups of numbers.

You can set up three main types of tables in Word:

- The "traditional" tabbed table, in which columns of text are separated by tab characters, as shown in Figure 11-1 on page 331. You can enter the tabs yourself, or you can copy the table from a spreadsheet program such as Microsoft Excel. When you paste a range of cells copied from a spreadsheet program, you'll find that the tabs have been automatically inserted. A paragraph mark ends each row. A list is a variation of this kind of table, consisting of one column of entries with a paragraph mark at the end of each line.
- Tables created in the Table format, new in Word 4, as shown in Figure 11-7 on page 339. You can create a table before you enter text, or you can convert a series of paragraphs or columns delimited by tabs to a table, by using the Insert Table command.

- A more obscure way to create tables, by formatting paragraphs with Side-by-Side or Position paragraph formats, as shown in Figure 11-34 on page 369. This method can be useful in certain cases—we discuss it here because many users of Word 3 were accustomed to creating tables with the Side-by-Side format.

To distinguish these ways of structuring tables, we'll call them *tabbed tables, cell tables,* and *Side-by-Side* or *Position paragraph tables.*

You can also use other, more obscure, types of tabular arrangements to place paragraphs of text in columns and rows. For example, you can arrange text in one or more columns with the Section command, discussed in Chapter 12, "Section Formatting." Multicolumn sections don't preserve the horizontal placement of elements customary in standard tables, so we won't discuss them in this chapter.

You can even edit and format a table in a program such as Microsoft Excel, and then copy an image of the table and paste it into Word as a graphic. (For more information on moving tables prepared with a spreadsheet program to Word, see Chapter 16, "Transferring Text and Graphics.")

You can even create complex, hybrid types of tables containing tables within tables, or lists within tables; for example, you could put a small tabbed table inside one cell of a larger cell table, or a list within a cell in a cell table. Word also gives you the ability to convert tables from one type to another.

We'll discuss all three types of tables in this chapter. We'll also present other information related to the care and feeding of tables and lists, such as sorting the items in tables and lists, renumbering them, adding various types of borders, and using Word to perform simple mathematical calculations.

■ *Working with Tabbed Tables*

The new cell table format in Word 4 is preferred for most purposes. However, traditional tabbed tables are better for certain applications. One reason is that the cell table format doesn't support styles, so if a document contains many tables that have a common style—in particular those that don't contain wrapped lines—you're often better off using the simpler tabbed-table format. Because most people have some familiarity with tabbed tables, we'll discuss this type of table first.

Editing and Formatting Tabbed Tables

The most rudimentary form of tabbed table contains only numerical data or text formatted in the *Normal* style. It consists of a series of lines in which entries (typically numbers) are separated by tab characters. The tabs align the entries according to the tab stops you set so that the table is easier to read. A sample of this type of table is shown in Figure 11-1, both without and with

Show ¶ turned on, so you can see more clearly where the tabs have been placed. Notice the insertion point at the beginning of the first line in the body of the table; the Ruler reflects the positions of the tabs established for that line. We've also used the newline mark, entered when you press Shift-Return, to break the lines in the table's title and in the table headings.

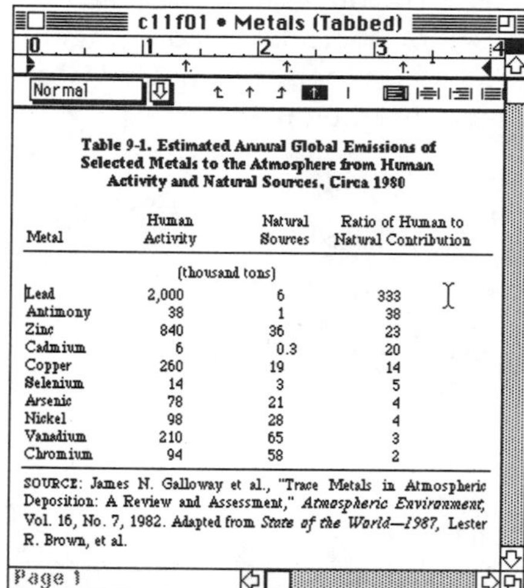

c11f01 • Metals (Tabbed)

Normal

Table 9-1. Estimated Annual Global Emissions of Selected Metals to the Atmosphere from Human Activity and Natural Sources, Circa 1980

Metal	Human Activity	Natural Sources	Ratio of Human to Natural Contribution
	(thousand tons)		
Lead	2,000	6	333
Antimony	38	1	38
Zinc	840	36	23
Cadmium	6	0.3	20
Copper	260	19	14
Selenium	14	3	5
Arsenic	78	21	4
Nickel	98	28	4
Vanadium	210	65	3
Chromium	94	58	2

SOURCE: James N. Galloway et al., "Trace Metals in Atmospheric Deposition: A Review and Assessment," *Atmospheric Environment,* Vol. 16, No. 7, 1982. Adapted from *State of the World—1987,* Lester R. Brown, et al.

Page 1

c11f01 • Metals (Tabbed)

Normal

Table 9-1. Estimated Annual Global Emissions of Selected Metals to the Atmosphere from Human Activity and Natural Sources, Circa 1980

Metal Human Activity Natural Sources Ratio of Human to Natural Contribution
(thousand tons)
Lead 2,000 6 333
Antimony 38 1 38
Zinc 840 36 23
Cadmium 6 0.3 20
Copper 260 19 14
Selenium 14 3 5
Arsenic 78 21 4
Nickel 98 28 4
Vanadium 210 65 3
Chromium 94 58 2

SOURCE: James N. Galloway et al., "Trace Metals in Atmospheric Deposition: A Review and Assessment," Atmospheric Environment, Vol. 16, No. 7, 1982. Adapted from State of the World—1987, Lester R. Brown, et al.

Page 1

Figure 11-1

A simple table, shown without and with Show ¶ turned on.

As was discussed in Chapter 9, "Paragraph Formatting," Word supports four types of tabs, all of which are suited for tabbed tables: right-aligned, left-aligned, centered, and decimal. You can also use the vertical-line "tab stop" to format this type of table. The vertical line isn't actually a tab stop because it doesn't force text to align at a particular distance from the left margin, but it works well with the other tab markers for creating vertical borders within tabbed tables.

Of the four types of tab markers, the decimal tab is most frequently used with numeric data. (See Figure 11-1.) With a decimal tab, the decimal points are aligned vertically, regardless of the number of digits that precede or follow the point. Right-aligned and left-aligned tabs are most often used to present textual data. You can, of course, mix tab types on a line.

You can arrange tab stops either before or after you enter the data for a tabbed table. If you enter the data before setting tab stops, Word assumes that you want to use the default tabs, which are placed at intervals along the Ruler. You can change this default tab-stop interval in the Document dialog box. To enter the data, type each number or piece of text, and then press the Tab key to move the insertion point to the next default tab stop.

Once you've entered the data, select the lines for which you want to add tab stops, and choose Show Ruler. For each column of data, select the desired tab icon, click in the Ruler to establish an initial position away from any other tab marker, and then drag the icon to its final position. Every time you add a tab stop, the default tab stops to the left of it disappear. (Several other ways of setting tab stops were described in Chapter 9.) If you need to reposition any tab stops, remember to select all the lines in the table before adjusting the tab stops. (See Figure 11-2.) Otherwise, you'll end up changing only the tabs in the selected lines or in the line containing the insertion point.

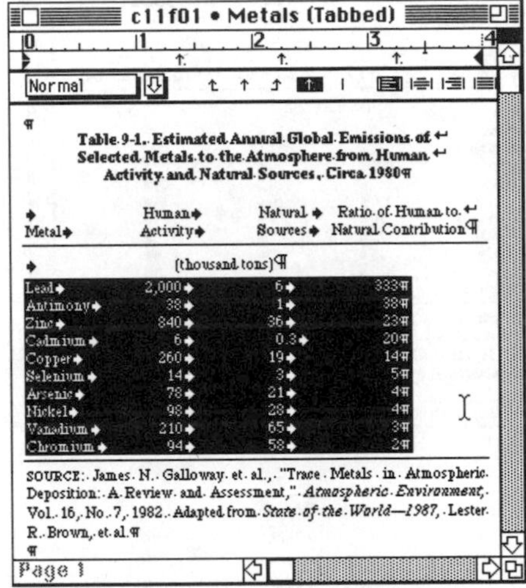

Figure 11-2
Adjusting the tab stops in the entire table.

Editing a tabbed table is only slightly more difficult than editing regular text. The point to remember is that tab characters separate the items on each line, and if you delete one of these characters, all the items to the right of it slide one tab stop to the left. You can delete the item itself if you want to have a blank space in the table, but leave the tab before it in place. It might help to display the tab characters by choosing the Show ¶ command before you prepare or edit the table. (A side note: If an entry contains no periods, you can select the entire entry by pressing the Command key and clicking anywhere in it.)

You can also wrap lines in tabbed tables, continuing the entries in each row of the table on one or more lines, while preserving the structure of one "record" per carriage return. This type of format is useful for telephone lists, an example of which is shown in Figure 11-3.

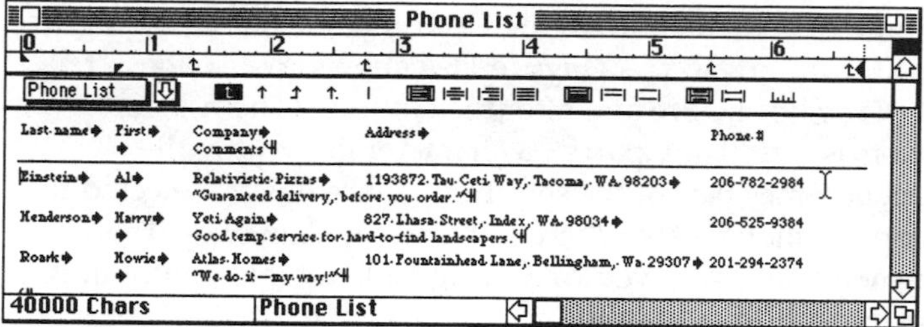

Figure 11-3
A two-line phone list.

TIP

Using Styles to Format Tabbed Tables
You might recall from Chapter 9 that if you've set different paragraph formats for some paragraphs in the selected text, the Ruler might be filled with gray. This can lead to minor difficulties when setting tabs, because you might see only those set for the first line of text in the selection, and no others. If you add a tab stop to the selected text, Word doesn't remove the other tab stops unless you actually replace one that was there before. Word also fills the Ruler with gray if all the tabs in the selection are the same, but you've added any other paragraph format to some but not all lines in the selection. To determine the formats that have been set in the text, often it becomes necessary to click in each line to discover which line has the differing paragraph formats.

One way to deal with inconsistent paragraph formats in a table is to return all the selected text to the *Normal* style and start over. However, instead of setting tab stops manually, you can define a style that has the tab stops you want and apply it to all the lines in a tabbed table. Then, if you need to adjust the table at any time, you redefine the style instead of manually reformatting the lines in the table. This technique is particularly handy when you have many tabbed tables in a document that are formatted in the same way.

Cutting and Pasting Data in Tabbed Columns

Word normally treats the characters in a document like one long string of beads, connecting the end of one line to the beginning of the next. When you select text in the document, you select a string of characters that starts at one point in the text and stops at another point.

Word also lets you select a portion of two or more lines, rather than all the characters between two points. That is, you can select one column of text in a multicolumn tabbed table and leave alone the remainder of each line.

To select a column of text, hold down the Option key while dragging over the column you want to select. As Figure 11-4 shows, Word doesn't select the portions of the line before and after the column. (The rule for selection of characters is this: If any part of a character lies within the highlighted block, it becomes part of the selection.) Once you've selected the column, you can copy or move it elsewhere or format it all at once. This feature can be a tremendous timesaver for editing tabbed tables; without it you would have to move each item in the column individually.

Note that if you select the tab characters along with the data in the table and then choose the Cut command, the columns to the right of it slide to the left. You might not want this to occur. Also, if the widths of the text in a column vary greatly or if you're using the left-aligned or centered tab stop for the column, you might find it necessary to adjust the positions or type of tab stops for the table so that you can select the material correctly. You can also drag from any corner of the intended selection. Once the column is in the Clipboard, you can paste it anywhere, even to another program such as Microsoft Excel or Microsoft Chart. If you paste it into Excel, for example, the tabs are removed, and each item goes into a separate cell in the spreadsheet.

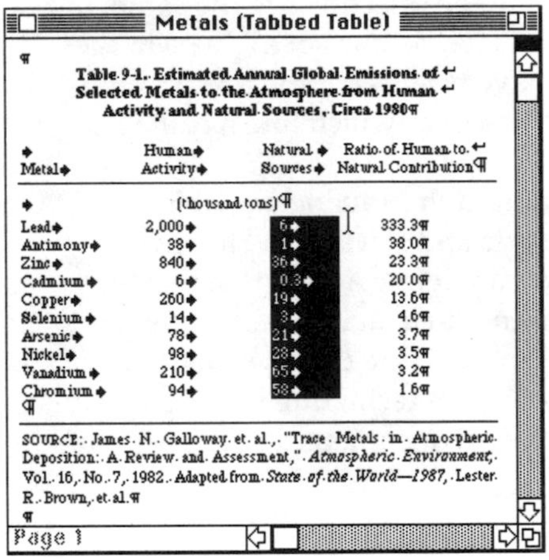

Metals (Tabbed Table)

Table 9-1. Estimated Annual Global Emissions of Selected Metals to the Atmosphere from Human Activity and Natural Sources, Circa 1980

Metal	Human Activity	Natural Sources	Ratio of Human to Natural Contribution
	(thousand tons)		
Lead	2,000	6	333.3
Antimony	38	1	38.0
Zinc	840	36	23.3
Cadmium	6	0.3	20.0
Copper	260	19	13.6
Selenium	14	3	4.6
Arsenic	78	21	3.7
Nickel	98	28	3.5
Vanadium	210	65	3.2
Chromium	94	58	1.6

SOURCE: James N. Galloway et al., "Trace Metals in Atmospheric Deposition: A Review and Assessment," *Atmospheric Environment*, Vol. 16, No. 7, 1982. Adapted from *State of the World—1987*, Lester R. Brown, et al.

Page 1

Figure 11-4

Selecting a column by holding down the Option key while dragging up and to the right from the lower left corner of the column.

You can use this method for selecting blocks of text to move a column or to switch the order of two columns in a tabbed table. Suppose, for example, you have a four-column table and you want to reverse the order of the second and third columns. Here's what you could do:

1. Press the Option key and select the third column. You also want to select the tab characters preceding the items in the third column, so start at the right edge of the first item in the second column, and drag down to just beyond the right edge of the third column.

❷ Press Command-X to cut the third column and place it in the Clipboard.

❸ Place the insertion point immediately to the right of the first item in the first column.

❹ Press Command-V to paste the column back into the table. The columns on the right move to the right to make room for it.

Of course, you could also select and cut the second column instead of the third.

If you are pasting an extra column into a table, be sure that an extra tab marker is present to accommodate the new column. If you try to insert a fifth column into a table that has tab markers for only four columns (that is, only three tab markers per line), Word might paste in the new column without separating it from the column to the left. Remember that you can undo the Paste command if the results aren't what you expected. If the extra tab characters aren't in the column copied to the Clipboard, you should add them to the table before you paste in the column.

This process isn't as easy if you want to copy or move a column to the far right of a tabbed table, because each line of the table ends with a paragraph mark rather than with a tab character. One way to deal with this is to select and cut the tab characters preceding the text in the column instead of those following. Another way is to add a tab character at the end of every line before you paste in the new column. You can insert a tab character at the end of each line of the last column, before the paragraph mark, by searching for the paragraph marks and replacing each with a tab character and a paragraph mark, as follows:

❶ Select every line in the table.

❷ Choose Change from the Search menu.

❸ Enter ^*p* in the Find What field.

❹ Enter ^*t*^*p* in the Change To field.

❺ Click the Change Selection button. Close the Change dialog box when the program finishes.

❻ Cut the column, place the insertion point between the newly inserted tab mark and the paragraph mark at the end of the first line, and paste in the column.

Enhancing Tabbed Tables

Basic, unadorned tabbed tables are fine for routine work, but for a touch of pizzazz, you can enhance them by adding horizontal and vertical lines and boxes. Chapter 9, "Paragraph Formatting," discusses these formats at length. This brief recap explains how to use them with tabbed tables.

Adding Vertical Lines

You can use the vertical-line tab icon in the Ruler to separate columns. With the Ruler visible, select the entire table and place a vertical line tab at each spot along the Ruler where you want a column separator to appear. Figure 11-5 shows a tabbed table to which a vertical line has been added.

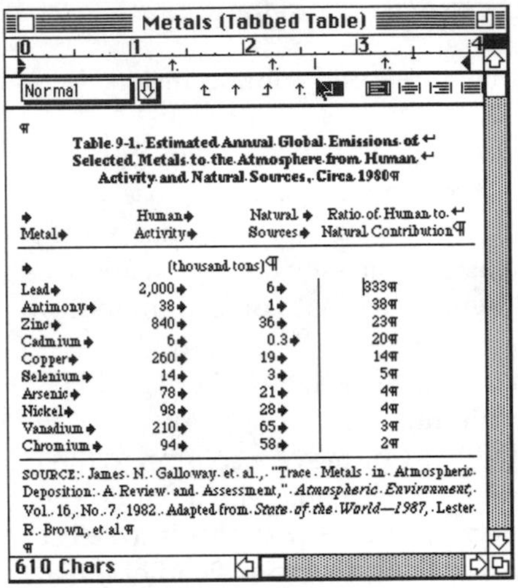

Metals (Tabbed Table)

Normal

Table 9-1. Estimated Annual Global Emissions of Selected Metals to the Atmosphere from Human Activity and Natural Sources, Circa 1980

Metal	Human Activity	Natural Sources	Ratio of Human to Natural Contribution
	(thousand tons)		
Lead	2,000	6	333
Antimony	38	1	38
Zinc	840	36	23
Cadmium	6	0.3	20
Copper	260	19	14
Selenium	14	3	5
Arsenic	78	21	4
Nickel	98	28	4
Vanadium	210	65	3
Chromium	94	58	2

SOURCE: James N. Galloway et al., "Trace Metals in Atmospheric Deposition: A Review and Assessment," *Atmospheric Environment*, Vol. 16, No. 7, 1982. Adapted from *State of the World—1987*, Lester R. Brown, et al.

610 Chars

Figure 11-5
A vertical line used as a column separator.

Remember that the vertical-line marker isn't a true tab stop. When you press the Tab key, the insertion point skips past the vertical line to the next true tab stop. Thus, adding vertical lines doesn't affect the overall positioning of the items in a tabbed table.

Adding Horizontal Borders

As discussed in Chapter 9, horizontal borders stretch from the leftmost indent to the right indent of the paragraph to which you add the border. You might use such borders, for example, to separate column headings from the data underneath them. To draw a line under column headings, for example, do the following:

1. Select the line containing the tabbed table's column headings.
2. Choose the Paragraph command, and click the Borders button. (It's convenient to add the Paragraph Borders command to the Format menu and then to choose the new menu command. Adding commands to menus is discussed in Chapter 3, "The Word Environment.")
3. Select a line type, and click in the area below the paragraph template in the Border dialog box.
4. Click the OK button.

In Figure 11-5, for example, we added a border 3 points below the headings in the table by setting the appropriate options in the Paragraph Borders dialog box, and we added 3 points of Space Below to separate the heading and borders from the text beneath. Adjust the right and left indents, as needed, if the line stretches too far.

Boxing a Table

Boxing a table isolates it on the page. If you're familiar with Word 3 you might remember that if you wanted one box to surround the whole table, you had to replace the paragraph marks at the end of all but the last line in the table with newline marks (created when you press Shift-Return). This made one paragraph of the entire table, to which you could then add a box format.

In Word 4, however, the task of drawing one box around the entire table becomes almost trivial. To have Word draw a simple box around a tabbed table, do the following:

1. Select every line in the table.
2. Choose the Paragraph command and click the Borders button, or choose the Paragraph Borders command.
3. Select a line weight and the Plain Box option.
4. Click OK.

Select other options in the Paragraph Borders dialog box to change line types or the spacing between the border and the text. You can mix line types and the spacing along the various boundaries to create special effects, as discussed in Chapter 9, "Paragraph Formatting." Figure 11-6a and Figure 11-6b (on the following page) present a small gallery of box formats for a typical tabbed table. (You can also combine vertical-line tabs from the Ruler with border formats, as shown in the fourth example in the figure.)

Table 9-1. Estimated Annual Global Emissions of Selected Metals to the Atmosphere from Human Activity and Natural Sources, Circa 1980

Metal	Human Activity	Natural Sources	Ratio of Human to Natural Contribution
	(thousand tons)		
Lead	2,000	6	333
Antimony	38	1	38
Zinc	840	36	23
Cadmium	6	0.3	20
Copper	260	19	14
Selenium	14	3	5
Arsenic	78	21	4
Nickel	98	28	4
Vanadium	210	65	3
Chromium	94	58	2

SOURCE: James N. Galloway et al., "Trace Metals in Atmospheric Deposition: A Review and Assessment," *Atmospheric Environment*, Vol. 16, No. 7, 1982. Adapted from *State of the World—1987*, Lester R. Brown, et al.

Table 9-1. Estimated Annual Global Emissions of Selected Metals to the Atmosphere from Human Activity and Natural Sources, Circa 1980

Metal	Human Activity	Natural Sources	Ratio of Human to Natural Contribution
	(thousand tons)		
Lead	2,000	6	333
Antimony	38	1	38
Zinc	840	36	23
Cadmium	6	0.3	20
Copper	260	19	14
Selenium	14	3	5
Arsenic	78	21	4
Nickel	98	28	4
Vanadium	210	65	3
Chromium	94	58	2

SOURCE: James N. Galloway et al., "Trace Metals in Atmospheric Deposition: A Review and Assessment," *Atmospheric Environment*, Vol. 16, No. 7, 1982. Adapted from *State of the World—1987*, Lester R. Brown, et al.

Figure 11-6a
Box border variations.

Table 9-1. Estimated Annual Global Emissions of Selected Metals to the Atmosphere from Human Activity and Natural Sources, Circa 1980

Metal	Human Activity	Natural Sources	Ratio of Human to Natural Contribution
	(thousand tons)		
Lead	2,000	6	333
Antimony	38	1	38
Zinc	840	36	23
Cadmium	6	0.3	20
Copper	260	19	14
Selenium	14	3	5
Arsenic	78	21	4
Nickel	98	28	4
Vanadium	210	65	3
Chromium	94	58	2

SOURCE: James N. Galloway et al., "Trace Metals in Atmospheric Deposition: A Review and Assessment," *Atmospheric Environment,* Vol. 16, No. 7, 1982. Adapted from *State of the World—1987,* Lester R. Brown, et al.

Table 9-1. Estimated Annual Global Emissions of Selected Metals to the Atmosphere from Human Activity and Natural Sources, Circa 1980

Metal	Human Activity	Natural Sources	Ratio of Human to Natural Contribution
	(thousand tons)		
Lead	2,000	6	333
Antimony	38	1	38
Zinc	840	36	23
Cadmium	6	0.3	20
Copper	260	19	14
Selenium	14	3	5
Arsenic	78	21	4
Nickel	98	28	4
Vanadium	210	65	3
Chromium	94	58	2

SOURCE: James N. Galloway et al., "Trace Metals in Atmospheric Deposition: A Review and Assessment," *Atmospheric Environment,* Vol. 16, No. 7, 1982. Adapted from *State of the World—1987,* Lester R. Brown, et al.

Figure 11-6b
Box border variations.

■ *Working with Cell Tables*

The cell table structure is the most flexible way to arrange text in rows and columns of elements. You can put almost anything into a cell—as much as a standard page of text and graphics, formatted with collections of character and paragraph formats. You can even update the contents of a cell, or update the entire table, by establishing a link to a document created in a program other than Word (as discussed in Chapter 16, "Transferring Text and Graphics"). Cell tables have other uses as well. For example, you can use a cell table as a data document (as discussed in Chapter 17, "Merge Printing").

Cell tables have one drawback over traditional tabbed tables—Word doesn't permit setting up styles for them. However, you can add styles to the text within a cell in a table, and you can create glossary entries for tables that contain table elements which conform to standard design rules for documents.

Think of a cell in a table as a "mini-document" that has its own selection bar, and has its own top, bottom, left, and right margins, set by the limits of the cell boundaries. A typical cell table is shown in Figure 11-7. Notice that one of the major advantages of the cell table structure is that you can wrap text within cells, without having to break lines and insert tabs between columns (as is necessary in the tabbed table structure).

As shown in the figure, the cells in a table can form regular arrangments of cells in a rectangular grid. Cell tables can also form irregular arrangements in which a cell (for example, the one containing the name of the table in the figure above) can stretch across one or more columns. A cell can contain more than one paragraph, each formatted with a different style, if desired. Each cell is a unit: If a cell doesn't fit at the bottom of one page, Word moves the cell to the top of the next page rather than break the cell into two pieces. If a cell is too long to fit entirely on one page, Word cuts it off at the bottom of the page without running the text onto the top of the next page.

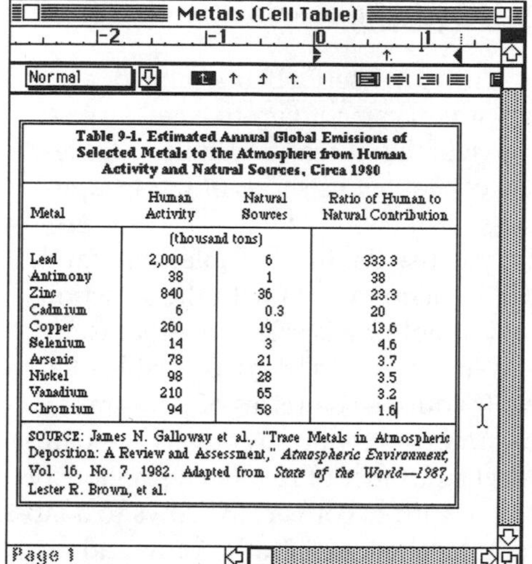

Table 9-1. Estimated Annual Global Emissions of Selected Metals to the Atmosphere from Human Activity and Natural Sources, Circa 1980

Metal	Human Activity	Natural Sources	Ratio of Human to Natural Contribution
	(thousand tons)		
Lead	2,000	6	333.3
Antimony	38	1	38
Zinc	840	36	23.3
Cadmium	6	0.3	20
Copper	260	19	13.6
Selenium	14	3	4.6
Arsenic	78	21	3.7
Nickel	98	28	3.5
Vanadium	210	65	3.2
Chromium	94	58	1.6

SOURCE: James N. Galloway et al., "Trace Metals in Atmospheric Deposition: A Review and Assessment," *Atmospheric Environment,* Vol. 16, No. 7, 1982. Adapted from *State of the World—1987,* Lester R. Brown, et al.

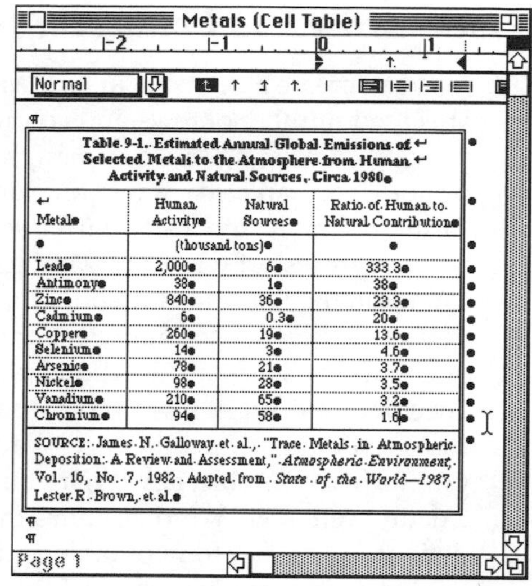

Figure 11-7
A typical cell table.

When you turn Show ¶ on, Word displays dotted lines around each cell, called *table gridlines,* and ends the material contained in the cell with a large dot, called the *end-of-cell* marker. This marker also ends each row. You don't see standard paragraph marks at the end of each snippet of text in the figure; the end-of-cell marker fulfills the same purpose, but you can't select (or copy or paste) the mark as you can paragraph and section marks.

Most of your work with cell tables is done with three commands: Insert Table on the Document menu, Table on the Edit menu, and Cells on the Format menu. You choose the Insert Table command to insert an empty table grid into a document or to change a series of previously entered paragraphs into a filled cell table.

Once the table is created, you can add or delete rows, columns, or selected ranges of cells with the Table command, found on the Edit menu. With the Table command you can also merge the contents of two or more cells together or split cells that have been previously merged.

Finally, you can use the Cells command to alter the width, height, indention, and alignment of the cells in a table, although you can also change the width and indention of cells from the Ruler.

You can add borders to individual cells, to ranges of cells, or to the entire table by clicking the Borders button in the Cells dialog box, or by adding the Cell Borders command to the Format menu and choosing it. You can also set the placement of cells and rows in a table through the Position dialog box, in much the same way that you can with standard paragraphs, as discussed in Chapter 9, "Paragraph Formatting."

Creating and Converting Cell Tables

You can create a cell table in two ways. You can insert a blank table of a specified number of rows and columns, or you can convert to a cell table a previously existing series of paragraphs (whether it was originally a table or not). You can also convert an existing cell table to a series of paragraphs formatted in the more standard format.

Regardless of what you want to do, you use the Insert Table command, found on the Document menu. The specific action varies with the selection you made before choosing the command. If nothing is selected—that is, if you simply clicked an insertion point—Word inserts a blank cell table of a specified number of rows and columns. If you select a series of paragraphs that aren't already a cell table, Word assumes you want to convert the paragraphs to a cell table. Finally, if you select a number of rows in a previously existing cell table, Word assumes that you want to convert the rows to a tab-delimited or other form of table and replaces the Insert Table command on the Document menu with the Table to Text command.

Throughout the following discussion, you might find it convenient to use the Commands dialog box to add commands found at the end of this chapter to an appropriate menu. To avoid confusion, use the menu placement Word suggests until you become more familiar with this type of table.

Inserting a Blank Cell Table

To insert a new, empty cell table, do the following:

❶ Place the insertion point where you want the table.

❷ Choose Insert Table from the Document menu. The dialog box in Figure 11-8 appears. Notice that the options in the Convert From group at the bottom of the dialog box are dimmed, verifying that you aren't converting previously existing text to a table.

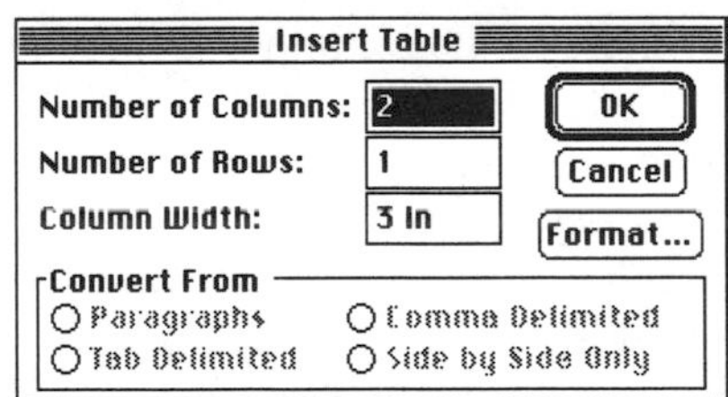

Figure 11-8
The Insert Table dialog box.

❸ Initially, Word uses values which create a table consisting of two columns and one row. You can create tables of up to 31 columns, and a theoretically unlimited number of rows. Enter the number of columns and the number of rows you want in the two edit fields. For this example, enter *3* in the Number of Columns field, and enter *5* in the Number of Rows field.

❹ Word sets the initial width of each column of cells to half the width of the current text column—for one-column text, this would be the same as the distance between the margins. You can change the width of selected columns later, either from the Ruler or through the Cells command, found on the Format menu. The default values for the Left and Right margins, set in the Document dialog box, are 1.25 inches, leaving a text column width of 6 inches. In this example, Word divides this by 3, for the three columns of the proposed table, and displays the result, *2 in*, in the Column Width field. Leave the suggested column width as is.

❺ Click OK to insert the table. Figure 11-9 shows the resulting empty table, displayed with Show ¶ on.

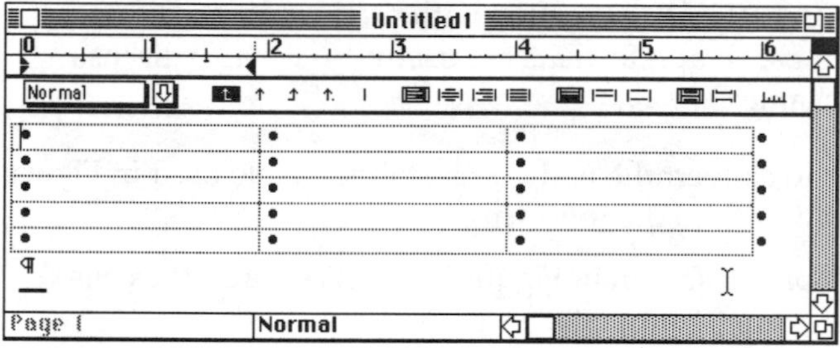

Figure 11-9
The new table, with Show ¶ on.

As you can see in the figure, Show ¶ displays both the end-of-cell markers and the edges of the cells in the table. You can also choose Preferences from the Edit menu and select the Show Table Gridlines option, which displays the dotted lines in the table, but not the end-of-cell markers. Each cell is 2 inches wide, and the indent markers in the Ruler reflect the "pseudo-margins" established by the cell boundaries.

The width of a table doesn't change if you later change the margin settings, and (as mentioned earlier) you can't establish styles for tables, so you should be fairly certain your margins won't change before creating a large number of tables in a document. Otherwise, you have to go back and reformat the column widths for each table you've entered in the document.

If you click the Format button in the Insert Table dialog box, Word inserts a table corresponding to the values you've entered and immediately brings up the Cells dialog box, just as if you had clicked OK and then chosen Cells from the Format menu. (We'll discuss the Cells command a bit later in this chapter.)

Converting a Series of Paragraphs to a Table

If you're familiar with Word before version 4, you've probably created tables from columns of entries separated by tab characters, as discussed earlier in this chapter. Word lets you convert this type of table (as well as others) to the cell table structure. Simply select the table and choose the Insert Table command. You can convert four types of traditional tables to cell tables:

- ❏ Tables consisting of a series of paragraphs.
- ❏ Tables constructed from tabbed columns.
- ❏ Tables constructed from entries separated, or *delimited*, by commas. Word's merge data documents are good examples of this. Many database programs also generate text files in this format.
- ❏ Tables constructed from paragraphs having the Side-by-Side paragraph format in Word 3. Because the cell table structure fulfills this need well, you can convert this older type of table to a cell table. (Occasionally, however, tables formatted with the Side-by-Side and the related Position paragraph formats are useful, so we also discuss these later in this chapter.)

Let's say you want to convert the body of the tabbed table used in Figure 11-1 to a cell table. To do this, do the following:

❶ Select the tabbed table, as shown in Figure 11-10. (We'll add the cells for the title and source reference later.)

❷ Choose the Insert Table command. The dialog box in Figure 11-11 appears.

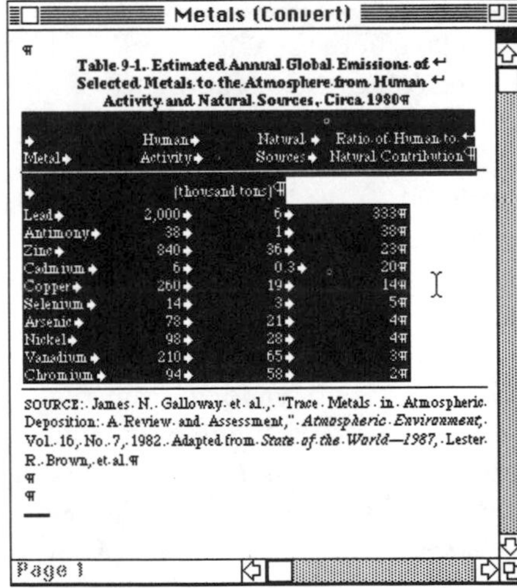
Metals (Convert)

Table 9-1. Estimated Annual Global Emissions of Selected Metals to the Atmosphere from Human Activity and Natural Sources, Circa 1980

Metal	Human Activity	Natural Sources	Ratio of Human to Natural Contribution
	(thousand tons)		
Lead	2,000	6	333
Antimony	38	1	38
Zinc	840	36	23
Cadmium	6	0.3	20
Copper	260	19	14
Selenium	14	3	5
Arsenic	78	21	4
Nickel	98	28	4
Vanadium	210	65	3
Chromium	94	58	2

SOURCE: James N. Galloway et al., "Trace Metals in Atmospheric Deposition: A Review and Assessment," *Atmospheric Environment*, Vol. 16, No. 7, 1982. Adapted from *State of the World—1987*, Lester R. Brown, et al.

Page 1

Figure 11-10
The tabbed table with the body of the table selected.

Insert Table

Number of Columns: 4

Number of Rows: 13

Column Width: 1 in

OK

Cancel

Format...

Convert From

Paragraphs

Comma Delimited

Tab Delimited

Side by Side Only

Figure 11-11
The Insert Table dialog box after selecting the tabbed table in Figure 11-10.

Notice that Word has made a good guess about the type and structure of the table from what has been selected. It proposes *4* columns and *13* rows—one row for each line ending in a paragraph mark and an extra line for the column headings, because the first line ends in a newline mark. The Number of Rows field is dimmed because, for the number of entries selected, the number of rows created depends solely on the number of columns specified. Word has also calculated the width of each column by dividing the number of columns into the width of the current text column. In this case, the text column in 4 inches wide, so the suggested column width is 1 inch. Notice also that Word has selected the Tab Delimited option in the Convert From group.

❸ Click OK to convert the tabbed table to the cell table format. The result is shown in Figure 11-12 on the following page. Each line of the rightmost three column headings in the tabbed table appears in its own cell. We'll combine the entries later, when we discuss editing the contents of cells.

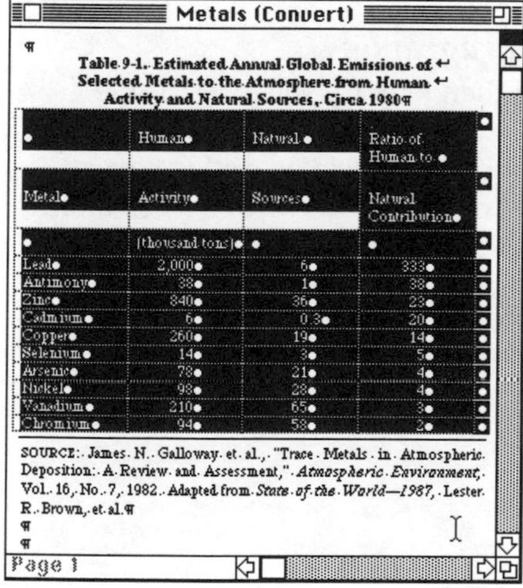
Metals (Convert)

Table 9-1. Estimated Annual Global Emissions of Selected Metals to the Atmosphere from Human Activity and Natural Sources, Circa 1980

	Human	Natural	Ratio of Human to
Metal	Activity	Sources	Natural Contribution
	(thousand tons)		
Lead	2,000	6	333
Antimony	38	1	38
Zinc	840	36	23
Cadmium	6	0.3	20
Copper	260	19	14
Selenium	14	3	5
Arsenic	78	21	4
Nickel	98	28	4
Vanadium	210	65	3
Chromium	94	58	2

SOURCE: James N. Galloway et al., "Trace Metals in Atmospheric Deposition: A Review and Assessment," *Atmospheric Environment*, Vol. 16, No. 7, 1982. Adapted from *State of the World—1987*, Lester R. Brown, et al.

Page 1

Figure 11-12
The resulting cell table after conversion from the tabbed format.

If the selected text has a very complex arrangement, the precise effect of a conversion can be hard to foretell. For example, if you select a series of paragraphs in which the entries in each row are separated by commas instead of tab characters, Word suggests the Comma Delimited option in the Convert From group. However, if you selected the text in the table above and selected the Comma Delimited option instead of the suggested Tab Delimited option, Word changes the number of suggested columns to 2. Why? Because Word scans the selected text, finds the single comma in the second column after the row starting with the word *Lead,* and determines that this divides the row (and therefore the table) into two columns. If you clicked OK with the proposed formats, Word would separate the 2 and the *000*. With both the Tab and Comma Delimited formats, Word scans each row in the selection—the row containing the greatest number of tabs or commas determines the number of columns suggested.

Similarly, if you select a series of paragraphs, call up the Insert Table dialog box, and select the Paragraphs option in the Convert From group, Word tries to determine the number of rows and columns to suggest by trying to evenly divide 2 or 3 columns into the number of paragraphs in the selection and then presents the resulting number of rows. If the number of paragraphs you're trying to convert isn't divisible by those numbers, Word gives up and waits for you to enter the desired number of rows and columns.

Finally, if you've constructed a table from paragraphs having the Side-by-Side paragraph format, Word converts the selected paragraphs in much the same way it does when the Paragraph option is selected, but removes the Side-by-Side format, even if it's part of the style definition for those paragraphs. Also, Word translates the indention for the paragraphs into approximately the same column widths as in the selection.

Converting a Table to a Series of Paragraphs

If you select a series of rows in a table and then look for the Insert Table Command on the Document menu, you'll see that the Insert Table command has changed to the Table To Text command. The associated dialog box is shown in Figure 11-13. Word gives you the option of converting a cell table to a series of paragraphs, a tabbed table, or a series of rows, each item of which is separated by a comma and a space character.

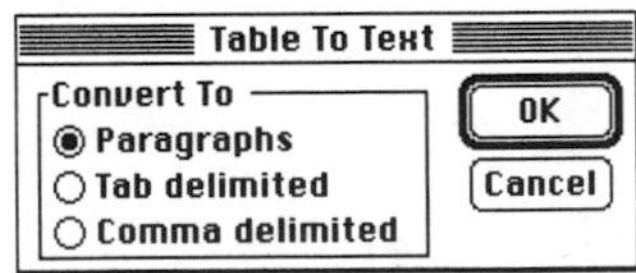

Figure 11-13
The Table To Text dialog box.

If you select the Paragraphs option, Word creates a series of paragraphs consisting of the contents of the first cell in the first row, then the contents of the second cell in the first row, and so on. If you select the Tab Delimited option, Word creates a paragraph of each row but inserts tab characters between each column entry. If you choose the Comma Delimited option, Word creates a paragraph of each row, as with the Tab Delimited option, but separates entries with a comma and a space character instead.

Word doesn't support converting a table to a Side-by-Side series of paragraphs. However, you can convert a cell table to a simple series of paragraphs and then add the Side-by-Side format and the appropriate margin formats, as discussed in Chapter 9, "Paragraph Formatting."

To convert a cell table to one of these standard formats, do the following:

1. Select the table. To select the entire table, press the Option and Command keys, and double-click anywhere in the table.
2. Choose the Table To Text command. The dialog box in Figure 11-13 appears.
3. Select the type of paragraphs to which you want to convert the table.
4. Click OK.

What happens if you've entered more than one paragraph into a given cell? A good way to think of the conversion process is to imagine that Word converts each end-of-cell marker to a paragraph mark, a tab character, or a comma-and-space, depending on which you've selected. The paragraph marks that existed in the original cell table are untouched by the conversion.

Editing Tables

Once you've created a cell table or converted one from another format, you can edit the contents of cells in tables or alter the arrangement of the cells in a table. To do this, you need to know how to select the text in cells and ranges of cells in a table and how to move the insertion point around in a table. You can use the Copy, Cut, and Paste commands on the Edit menu to rearrange the text in cell tables. You can also use the Table command to change the order of cells in a table, to insert new rows and columns, and to merge the contents of two or more cells into one cell stretching across more than one column.

Selecting in Tables

The rules for selecting text in a cell table are a little different than for selecting normal text. For example, in normal text, you can select a line by clicking in the selection bar next to the line. In tables, each cell has its own selection bar—if you click in a cell selection bar, however, you select the entire cell.

Similarly, double-clicking in the selection bar of any cell in a row selects the row—not the paragraph. You can also double-click anywhere to the left of the leftmost cell boundary. To select a paragraph within a cell, you must explicitly drag from the beginning of the paragraph through the paragraph mark at the end.

To select an entire column, move the pointer to the top border of the topmost cell in that column. You'll see the pointer change to a downward-pointing arrow. You can achieve the same effect more easily by pressing the Option key and clicking in a column. To select the entire table, press the Option key and double-click in any column.

The reasons for selecting text in a cell, and ranges of cells in a table, are the same as anywhere else in a document—for editing text and for applying formats. For example, you can apply a tab-stop format to an entire column at once by selecting the column and applying the tab format, either from the Ruler or through the Tabs dialog box.

In the same way that clicking in a paragraph selects the entire paragraph for paragraph formatting, selecting any text in a cell (or simply clicking in a cell) selects the cell for formatting through the Cells dialog box, discussed later in this chapter.

Moving in Tables

The easiest way to move the insertion point from cell to cell within a table is to press the Tab key. This behavior is meant to simulate the use of the Tab key in spreadsheet programs such as Microsoft Excel. To enter a tab character in a table, press Option-Tab. To move in the opposite direction, press Shift-Tab. If the insertion point is in the last cell in the table when you press the Tab key, Word inserts a new row below the last row and moves the insertion point to the first cell in the new row.

You can also use the keypad to move the insertion point from cell to cell within a table. The following key sequences (except for Tab and Shift-Tab) move between text areas in Page View, but they also work within a cell table in either Page View or Galley View:

To move	Press
Right	Option-Command-6
Left	Option-Command-4
Up	Option-Command-8
Down	Option-Command-2
To next cell	Option-Command-3, or Tab
To previous cell	Option-Command-9, or Shift-Tab

Each of these operations is represented by a command in Word's Command dialog box, and you could add them to a menu or change the key sequence assignment from the table above. (Refer to the table of commands at the end of this chapter for a complete listing of commands for working with tables.)

TIP

Decimal Tabs in Tables
Word's behavior with regard to decimal tabs in tables is interesting. If you set a decimal tab within a cell and then press the Tab key to move the insertion point to that cell, Word automatically moves the insertion point to that tab position. Moving to other types of tab stops in a table doesn't work in this way. When you set a decimal tab for an empty cell, Word moves the end-of-cell marker to that position to indicate that this is where the insertion point will move. Setting an alignment for a range of cells moves the end-of-cell marker in a similar fashion.

Copying, Cutting, and Pasting Cells

If you select a range of cells—a row, a column, a range of cells within the table, or the entire table—and then choose the Copy command, Word transfers both the text in the cells and the arrangement of cells selected to the Clipboard. Choosing the Cut command has the same result but empties the cells in the range you selected instead of actually removing the cells; to delete the cells, you must use the Table command, discussed below.

If you choose Show Clipboard from the Window menu, you'll see the copied material, as shown in Figure 11-14. If Show ¶ is on, Word displays the cell boundaries in the Clipboard window as well as in the document.

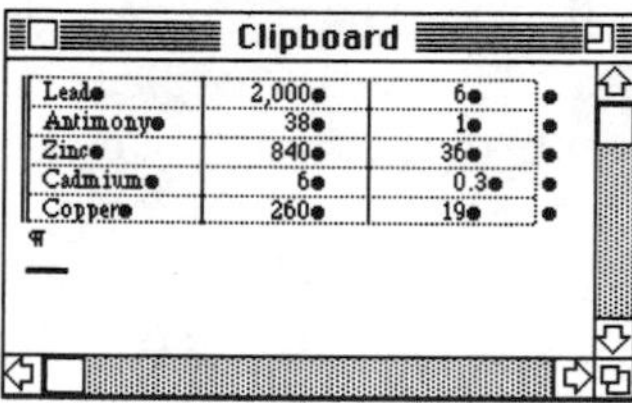

Figure 11-14
The Show Clipboard window after a range of cells has been copied.

When you paste the range of cells contained in the Clipboard, what happens depends on whether you're pasting into an area of the table or into an area outside the table. If you place the insertion point outside the table and choose the Paste command, Word inserts the actual arrangement of cells as well as their contents, as shown in Figure 11-15 on the following page. Notice that the width and border formats in the pasted material remain.

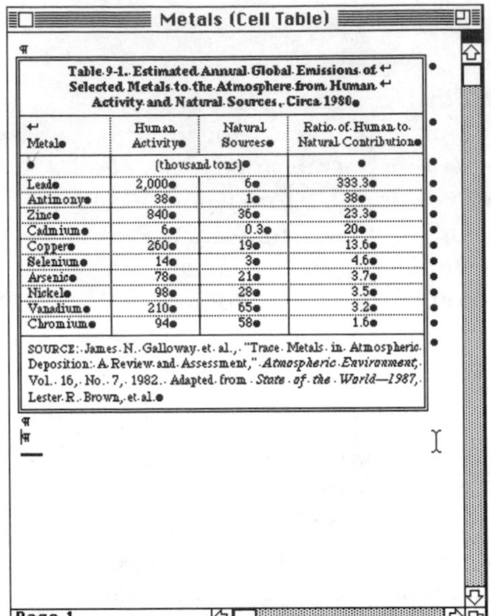

Table 9-1. Estimated Annual Global Emissions of Selected Metals to the Atmosphere from Human Activity and Natural Sources, Circa 1980

Metal	Human Activity	Natural Sources	Ratio of Human to Natural Contribution
	(thousand tons)		
Lead	2,000	6	333.3
Antimony	38	1	38
Zinc	840	36	23.3
Cadmium	6	0.3	20
Copper	260	19	13.6
Selenium	14	3	4.6
Arsenic	78	21	3.7
Nickel	98	28	3.5
Vanadium	210	65	3.2
Chromium	94	58	1.6

SOURCE: James N. Galloway et al., "Trace Metals in Atmospheric Deposition: A Review and Assessment," *Atmospheric Environment*, Vol. 16, No. 7, 1982. Adapted from *State of the World—1987*, Lester R. Brown, et al.

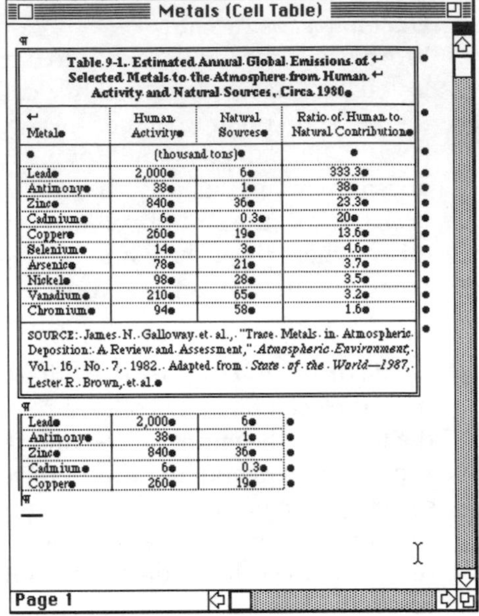

Table 9-1. Estimated Annual Global Emissions of Selected Metals to the Atmosphere from Human Activity and Natural Sources, Circa 1980

Metal	Human Activity	Natural Sources	Ratio of Human to Natural Contribution
	(thousand tons)		
Lead	2,000	6	333.3
Antimony	38	1	38
Zinc	840	36	23.3
Cadmium	6	0.3	20
Copper	260	19	13.6
Selenium	14	3	4.6
Arsenic	78	21	3.7
Nickel	98	28	3.5
Vanadium	210	65	3.2
Chromium	94	58	1.6

SOURCE: James N. Galloway et al., "Trace Metals in Atmospheric Deposition: A Review and Assessment," *Atmospheric Environment*, Vol. 16, No. 7, 1982. Adapted from *State of the World—1987*, Lester R. Brown, et al.

Lead	2,000	6
Antimony	38	1
Zinc	840	36
Cadmium	6	0.3
Copper	260	19

Figure 11-15
Inserting a block of cells by copying and pasting.

If, however, you place the insertion point in a cell or select a range of cells inside a table having the same number of columns and rows as the copied cells, and then choose Paste, Word replaces the contents of that range of cells with the material in the Clipboard and doesn't insert the actual cells. (See Figure 11-16.) If you paste into an area of selected cells that doesn't have the same number of columns and rows, you'll see the message *Copy and Paste areas are different shapes.*

When you paste a range of cells into a table, the cell formats in the pasted material are lost. This eliminates the need for extensive reformatting in the table after moving things around—the formats of the destination cells take precedence over the pasted material. Consequently, the cell widths in the pasted text in the figure are all the same, and the border formats have disappeared. The character and paragraph formats in the copied material remain.

You can also place the insertion point before an end-of-row marker. If you click in this area with the Ruler scale set to the Table scale, you'll see that the margins set for it are only about 1/8 inch wide. However, you can paste a range of cells into this area, but you can't enter text there. If you do, you'll see the message *Not a valid action for end of row.*

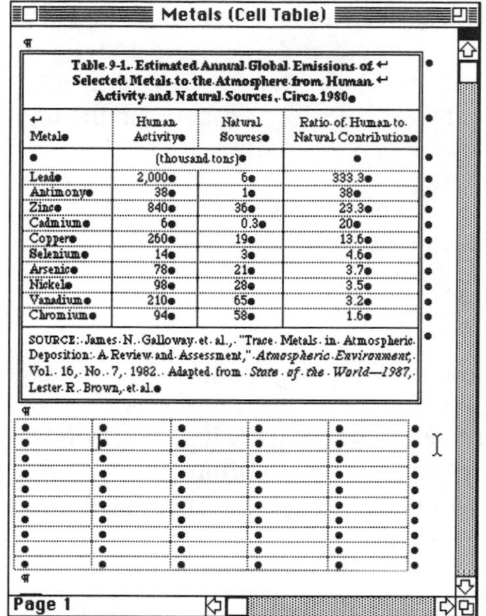

Table 9-1. Estimated Annual Global Emissions of Selected Metals to the Atmosphere from Human Activity and Natural Sources, Circa 1980

Metal	Human Activity	Natural Sources	Ratio of Human to Natural Contribution
	(thousand tons)		
Lead	2,000	6	333.3
Antimony	38	1	38
Zinc	840	36	23.3
Cadmium	6	0.3	20
Copper	260	19	13.6
Selenium	14	3	4.6
Arsenic	78	21	3.7
Nickel	98	28	3.5
Vanadium	210	65	3.2
Chromium	94	58	1.6

SOURCE: James N. Galloway et al., "Trace Metals in Atmospheric Deposition: A Review and Assessment," *Atmospheric Environment*, Vol. 16, No. 7, 1982. Adapted from *State of the World—1987*, Lester R. Brown, et al.

Lead	2,000	6
Antimony	38	1
Zinc	840	36
Cadmium	6	0.3
Copper	260	19

Figure 11-16
The effect of pasting a copied range of cells back into a table.

Editing Tables with the Table Command

The Cut, Copy, and Paste commands on the Edit menu allow you to move the text in a range of cells to another area in a table or to extend the table by copying and pasting sections of it. To work with the actual structure of the table apart from the material contained within it, however, you need to use the Table command, often in conjunction with Cut, Copy, and Paste. With it, you can add and delete rows and columns, reverse the order of rows and columns, and merge a collection of smaller cells into a larger cell.

When you choose Table from the Edit menu, you'll see the dialog box shown in Figure 11-17. Depending on the range of cells you've selected, some options in the dialog box might be dimmed or have different names. For example, Word permits splitting only those cells that have been previously merged—if you select a merged cell and choose the Table command, the Merge Cells button in the dialog changes to Split Cell.

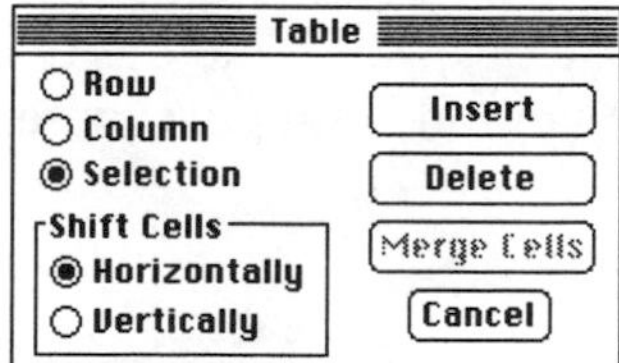

Figure 11-17
The Table dialog box.

Throughout the following discussion, as elsewhere, you might find it helpful to assign a key sequence to the Table command or even to add the commands for the various options in the Table dialog box to the Edit menu. This will make it easier to play with this feature of Word without having to use the mouse.

Inserting and deleting new rows, columns, and ranges of cells
To insert a new row or column in a table, do the following:

❶ Click anywhere in the row or column.

❷ Choose the Table command.

❸ Select the Row or Column option, and click the Insert button.

Word inserts the new row above the cell containing the insertion point. If you select the Column option, Word inserts the new column to the left of the cell. If you select an entire row or column before choosing the Table command, Word preselects the appropriate option for you. If you select a range of cells, Word preselects the Selection option in the dialog box.

To add more than one row, select the number of rows you want to insert and then use the Table command: Word inserts the number of rows you selected. New rows are inserted above the topmost row in the selected range. Similarly, you can insert more than one column by selecting the number of columns you want to insert before choosing the Table command. New columns are inserted to the left of the leftmost column in the selection.

If you've selected a range of cells instead of entire rows or columns, the Shift Cells group in the dialog box becomes active. You can use this group to insert one or more cells in a table, either by shifting previously existing cells to the right (horizontally) or by inserting the number of rows in the selected range and shifting the selected range down (vertically). Notice that shifting cells horizontally extends the table to the right by exactly the number of cells you selected, while shifting cells vertically inserts entire rows.

When you do insert or delete ranges of cells, the table usually changes from a rectangular shape to one having an irregular arrangement of cells, an example of which is shown in Figure 11-21 on page 354.

The process for deleting rows, columns, or ranges of cells is similar to that for inserting them; you simply select the cells you want to delete, choose the Table command, and click the Delete button. The remaining cells slide over to fill the gap. Be careful with this: If you've selected an entire column and then you select the Row option in the Table dialog box, you could delete the entire table! If you happen to delete something by mistake, simply choose Undo from the Edit menu.

TIP

Cell tables consisting of one cell
If you copy a cell and paste it into nontabular text, the result is a table consisting of only one cell. One-cell tables have a number of interesting uses. You can use styled text within the cell and change the width of the cell, in effect creating an exception to the established page margins or to the left and right indents, without having to add or subtract paragraph formats or change the page margins in the Document dialog box. The Table indention, position, spacing, and border formats are all independent of the paragraph formats of the text within the cell.

You can use one-cell tables to set up design elements that might occur only a few times in a document, when you don't want to spend extra time creating new styles. For example, if you want to put a special note in a box, yet have the text in the box retain its style and paragraph formats, you can put the text into a cell and then position and add borders to the cell rather than to the text in the cell.

Inserting a New Row at the End of a Table
One way to insert an arrangement of cells at the end of a table is to select and copy or cut the cells, enter an empty paragraph after the end of the table, and choose the Paste command. If you cut the cells, the cells are emptied of their contents, but the arrangement of empty cells remains. This method inserts not only the specific arrangement of cells you copied but the contents of the cells as well.

If, however, you want to continue the table with the same cell formats as the last row, simply click in the rightmost cell of the last row and press the Tab key.

Inserting a Normal Paragraph Above a Row
An interesting problem can occur if you've constructed a cell table at the very beginning of the document and then you want to insert a normal, nontabular paragraph before the table. You can't place the insertion point *before* the table—if you try to click there, the insertion point appears before the first character in the first cell of the table. And if you then press Return, the new paragraph appears inside the first cell. Similarly, you might want to break a table into two tables, with normal, nontabular text between them.

One way of inserting the normal paragraph would be to create a new blank row, select it, and choose Table To Text from the Document menu, but there is a better way. All you do is place the insertion point in any cell of the row above which you want the normal paragraph and then press Option-Command-Spacebar. The normal paragraph is inserted above the row containing the insertion point, breaking the table into two tables if the insertion point is anywhere in the table except the first row.

Inserting a Column Past the Rightmost Column

You can easily insert a new row beyond the last row in a table, but how do you insert a new column beyond the far right side of a table? Because Word inserts new columns to the left of the selected range of cells, you might think it impossible to select a range of cells past the rightmost column.

However, if you turn Show ¶ on in the Preferences dialog box, you'll see that each row of cells ends in a marker like the end-of-cell marker. Technically, the end-of-row marker marks a cell that cannot contain material or formats but is a cell nonetheless. You can see the limits of this cell by choosing Show Ruler from the Format menu. The indent markers are close together; if you try to change the width of the cell by dragging the indent markers, the markers simply pop back to their original positions. If you choose the Cells command, you see the message *Invalid selection to format cells.* If you try to enter text into it, you see the message *Not a valid action for end of row.* At other times, Word simply beeps or does nothing.

However, you can place the insertion point just before this marker to select this "pseudo-cell" and then choose the Table command to add the new rightmost column.

❶ Place the insertion point before the end-of-row marker at the end of any row, as shown in Figure 11-18. (Turn Show ¶ on first to see the end-of-row markers and the cell boundaries.)

❷ Choose the Table command.

❸ Select the Column option.

❹ Click the Insert button.

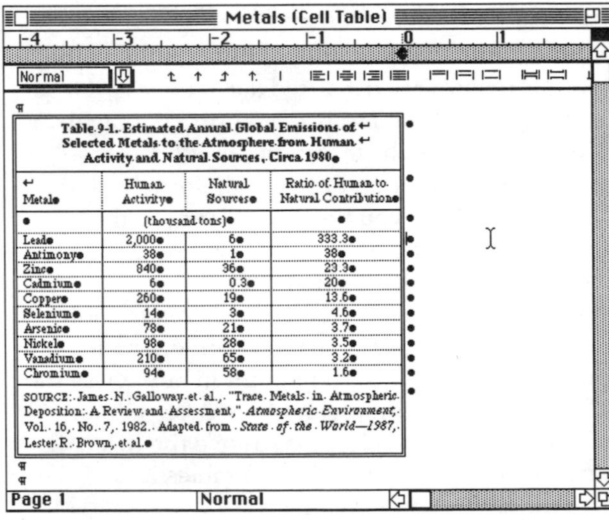

Table 9-1. Estimated Annual Global Emissions of Selected Metals to the Atmosphere from Human Activity and Natural Sources, Circa 1980

Metal	Human Activity	Natural Sources	Ratio of Human to Natural Contribution
	(thousand tons)		
Lead	2,000	6	333.3
Antimony	38	1	38
Zinc	840	36	23.3
Cadmium	6	0.3	20
Copper	260	19	13.6
Selenium	14	3	4.6
Arsenic	78	21	3.7
Nickel	98	28	3.5
Vanadium	210	65	3.2
Chromium	94	58	1.6

SOURCE: James N. Galloway et al., "Trace Metals in Atmospheric Deposition: A Review and Assessment," *Atmospheric Environment,* Vol. 16, No. 7, 1982. Adapted from *State of the World—1987,* Lester R. Brown, et al.

Figure 11-18
Placing the insertion point for inserting a new column beyond the rightmost edge of the table.

Word inserts the new column on the right edge of the table, as shown in Figure 11-19. Notice that, in this case, the widths of the new cells in the column aren't all the same and that the end-of-cell markers aren't located in the same place in every cell. The reason for this is simple: When you insert a new cell, Word usually copies the cell, paragraph, and character formats from the cell that is to the right. When you insert a cell at the end of a row, however, Word copies formats from the cell to the left. In the case of the first and last cells in the table, which have been merged (see the section on merging cells below), Word simply inserts a default cell that is one inch wide.

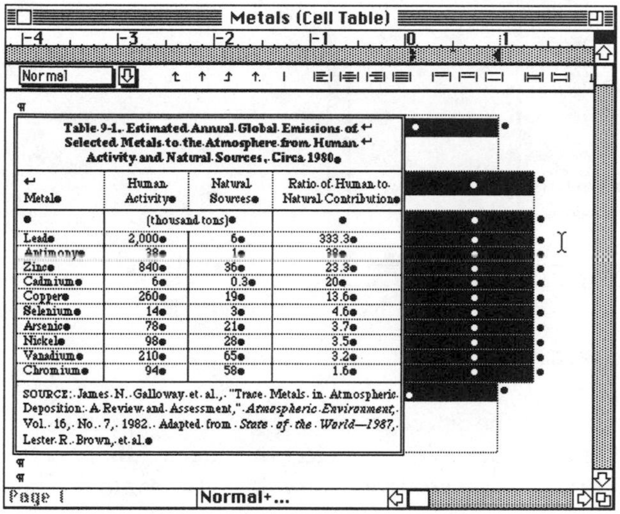

Table 9-1. Estimated Annual Global Emissions of Selected Metals to the Atmosphere from Human Activity and Natural Sources, Circa 1980

Metal	Human Activity	Natural Sources	Ratio of Human to Natural Contribution
	(thousand tons)		
Lead	2,000	6	333.3
Antimony	38	1	38
Zinc	840	36	23.3
Cadmium	6	0.3	20
Copper	260	19	13.6
Selenium	14	3	4.6
Arsenic	78	21	3.7
Nickel	98	28	3.5
Vanadium	210	65	3.2
Chromium	94	58	1.6

SOURCE: James N. Galloway et. al., "Trace Metals in Atmospheric Deposition: A Review and Assessment," *Atmospheric Environment*, Vol. 16, No. 7, 1982. Adapted from *State of the World—1987*, Lester R. Brown, et al.

Figure 11-19
After inserting the new column.

Word also copied the paragraph formats into the new cells from the cells to the left. In the figure, the placement of the end-of-cell markers in all but the first two and last rows of the last column of the table are determined by the decimal tab stops that have been set there.

If you want to insert more than one column, you can choose the Again command, or simply press Command-A.

Switching the Order of Rows and Columns

To delve deeper into the process of using the Cut, Copy, and Paste commands with the Table command, let's switch the order of two columns in a table. Let's say you want to switch the order of the *Human Activity* and *Natural Sources* columns in the Metals table, shown in Figure 11-20. Just to make it harder (and perhaps more realistic), we'll reverse only the range of cells containing the data, not the entire columns, because we want the merged cell containing the text *thousand tons* to be unaffected by the change.

To reverse the order of the two columns in the table, do the following:

❶ Select the range of data in the second column, as shown in Figure 11-20.

Metals (Cell Table)

Table 9-1. Estimated Annual Global Emissions of Selected Metals to the Atmosphere from Human Activity and Natural Sources, Circa 1980			
Metals	Human Activity	Natural Sources	Ratio of Human to Natural Contribution
	(thousand tons)		
Lead	2,000	6	333.3
Antimony	38	1	38
Zinc	840	36	23.3
Cadmium	6	0.3	20
Copper	260	19	13.6
Selenium	14	3	4.6
Arsenic	78	21	3.7
Nickel	98	28	3.5
Vanadium	210	65	3.2
Chromium	94	58	1.6

SOURCE: James N. Galloway et al., "Trace Metals in Atmospheric Deposition: A Review and Assessment," *Atmospheric Environment*, Vol. 16, No. 7, 1982. Adapted from *State of the World—1987*, Lester R. Brown, et al.

Page 1 Normal+...

Figure 11-20
After selecting the data in the second column.

❷ Choose the Table command. (The Selection and Horizontally options should be selected—if not, go back to ❶ and select the data again.) When you click the Insert button, a new range of cells in the same shape as the selection is inserted between the first and second columns, as shown in Figure 11-21.

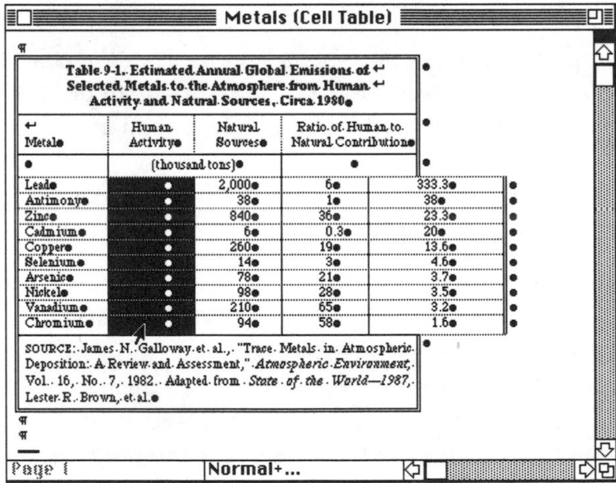

Metals (Cell Table)

Table 9-1. Estimated Annual Global Emissions of Selected Metals to the Atmosphere from Human Activity and Natural Sources, Circa 1980				
Metals	Human Activity	Natural Sources	Ratio of Human to Natural Contribution	
	(thousand tons)			
Lead		2,000	6	333.3
Antimony		38	1	38
Zinc		840	36	23.3
Cadmium		6	0.3	20
Copper		260	19	13.6
Selenium		14	3	4.6
Arsenic		78	21	3.7
Nickel		98	28	3.5
Vanadium		210	65	3.2
Chromium		94	58	1.6

SOURCE: James N. Galloway et al., "Trace Metals in Atmospheric Deposition: A Review and Assessment," *Atmospheric Environment*, Vol. 16, No. 7, 1982. Adapted from *State of the World—1987*, Lester R. Brown, et al.

Page 1 Normal+...

Figure 11-21
After inserting a blank range of cells.

Notice that the paragraph formats of the inserted cells are taken from the cells to the right of the new cells. In this case, the text in the first column is left-aligned, and the numbers in the second column are formatted with a decimal tab stop. (Remember that setting a single decimal tab stop in a cell doesn't require you to actually add a tab character within the cell to align the text: This is the only type of tab stop in tables that acts this way.)

❸ Select the range of cells containing both the *Human Activity* and *Natural Sources* numbers, and choose the Cut command. This leaves the arrangement of cells intact, clears the range of text, and transfers the range of cells to the Clipboard.

❹ Click the insertion point in the first cell of the empty range in the first column, and choose the Paste command. The table should look like Figure 11-22. (It's often easy to select the entire cell, highlighting the cell, rather than simply clicking the insertion point there. If you choose the Paste command with only one cell selected, Word reports *Copy and Paste areas are different shapes*.)

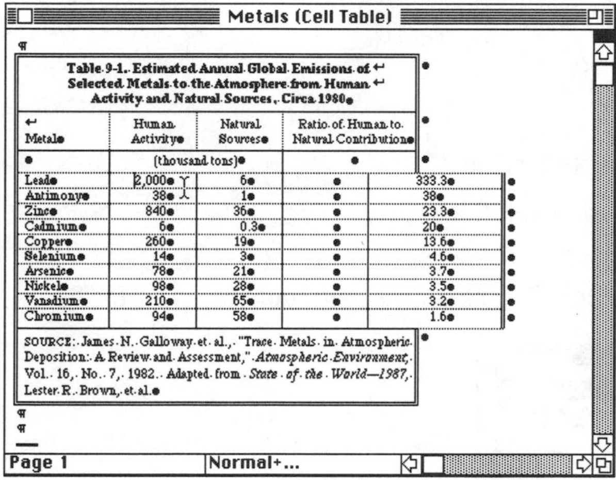

Figure 11-22
After pasting the *Human Activity* and *Natural Sources* columns.

❺ Select the empty range of cells in the fourth column, choose the Table command, and click the Delete button. The rightmost column containing the ratios slides to the left, returning to its original position.

All that remains is to exchange the contents of the cells containing the *Human Activity* and *Natural Sources* headings of the columns. You can do this in the way just described. However, for editing the text in single cells, it's often easier simply to cut the text in the cell and paste it into the new location, rather than adding and deleting cells.

Merging and Splitting Cells

In our last example, we worked around the merged cell beneath the headings of the second and third columns in the table, containing the text *thousand tons,* as shown in Figure 11-22. When you merge two cells, you create one cell which combines the contents and the area of both. There are two other examples of merged cells in the Metals table: One contains the title at the top of the table, and the other contains the attribution at the bottom of the table. Let's see how these were created. Figure 11-23 shows the table before merging the cells beneath the column headings.

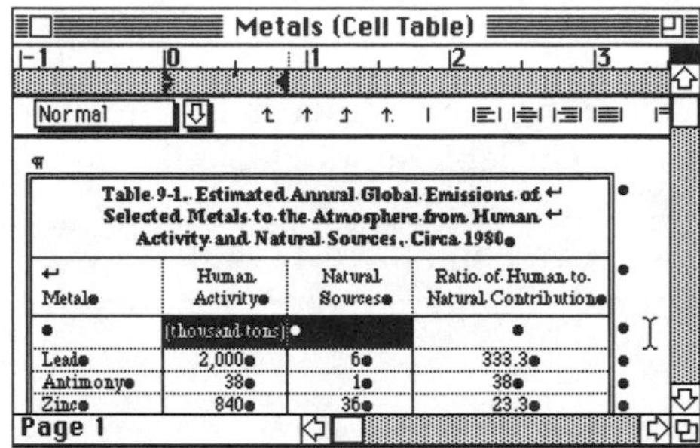

Figure 11-23
The two cells before merging.

To merge the two cells, do the following:

❶ Select the range of cells you want to merge.

❷ Choose the Table command.

❸ Click the Merge Cells button. The result is shown in Figure 11-24.

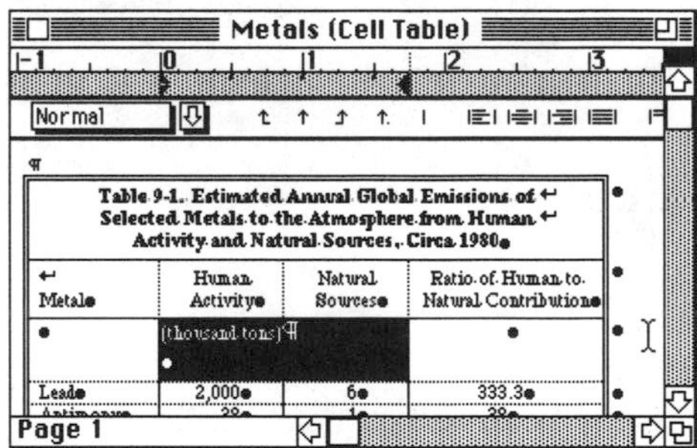

Figure 11-24
After merging the two cells.

As the figure shows, the merged cell stretches across two columns, but each cell has become one paragraph in the cell. If the Ruler is set to the Normal scale, you'll see that the new indents of the cell correspond to the left and right edges of the cell boundary. To finish, select and delete the paragraph mark, and apply the Centered paragraph format to the text in the cell.

Interestingly, once two cells are merged into one, you cannot merge the merged cell with yet another cell. If you do select them both and choose the Table command, you'll find that the Merge Cells button is dimmed.

To split a previously merged cell into two cells, the process is reversed:

1. Select the cell.
2. Choose the Table command. Notice that the Merge Cells button is now the Split Cell button.
3. Click the Split Cell button.

Word permits splitting only those cells that have been previously merged. The resulting number of cells equals the number of cells originally merged.

The text from the merged cell is distributed among the split cells in an interesting way. If the number of paragraphs in the original merged cell is greater than the number of resulting cells, Word works from the bottom of the list and begins by putting the bottom paragraph into the rightmost cell, the second-to-the-last paragraph in the cell second from the right, and so on. All the leftover paragraphs at the top of the list are placed in the leftmost cell. If, however, the original merged cell contains fewer paragraphs than resulting cells, Word works down from the top of the list and inserts each paragraph into a cell, working from left to right.

Formatting Tables

After you've established the basic structure of your table and entered the text or graphics you want in its cells, you can work on refining the appearance of the table. Of course, as elsewhere in Word, you can easily shift back and forth between editing a table and making it look better. For example, you'll probably find it useful to change the dimensions of cells immediately after entering the text, in order to make room for the text. Most of the formats you can add to tables are similar to formats that you can add to paragraphs, but you should keep in mind that they are two separate format domains. You can change table formats with the following features of Word:

- The Ruler—to change indention of rows and width of columns.
- The Cells dialog box—to change column width, space between columns, the indention of rows in the table, the height of rows in the table, and the alignment of rows relative to the page margins. You can also add borders to cells, columns, rows, and the entire table, either by clicking the Borders button in the Cells dialog box or by adding the Cell Borders command to the Format (or other) menu and choosing the command.

❑ The Position dialog box—to change the position of the table on the page, in much the same way you use the Position paragraph format to place one or more paragraphs on the page.

Ruler Formatting

If you've selected text that isn't in a table, clicking the Scale icon at the right end of the Ruler cycles between the Normal scale and the Page scale, as discussed in the Ruler Formatting section in Chapter 9, "Paragraph Formatting." If the insertion point is within a cell of the table and the Ruler is set to the Normal scale, the 0 point is set at the left edge of the cell boundary, and you see the paragraph formats—indents, tabs, alignment, and so on—attached to the selected paragraph in the cell. If the Ruler is set to the Page scale, you see the square brackets ([]), which correspond to the left and right page margins or to the edges of the current text column in a multiple-column section.

When the insertion point is within a table, however, the Table scale is added to the list. Place the insertion point in a table, and call up the Ruler. Click the Scale icon at the right end of the Ruler until you see the table formatting marks in the Ruler, as shown in Figure 11-25. We've indented the Metals table ½ inch from the left margin of the document, as indicated by the left-indent marker at that position in the Ruler. The edge of each column is marked by a T (T). The dotted line represents the right margin for one-column sections or the right edge of the current column for multiple-column sections. Notice that the icons representing the paragraph formats in the icon bar are dimmed—a reminder that you can apply these only when the Ruler is set to the Normal scale.

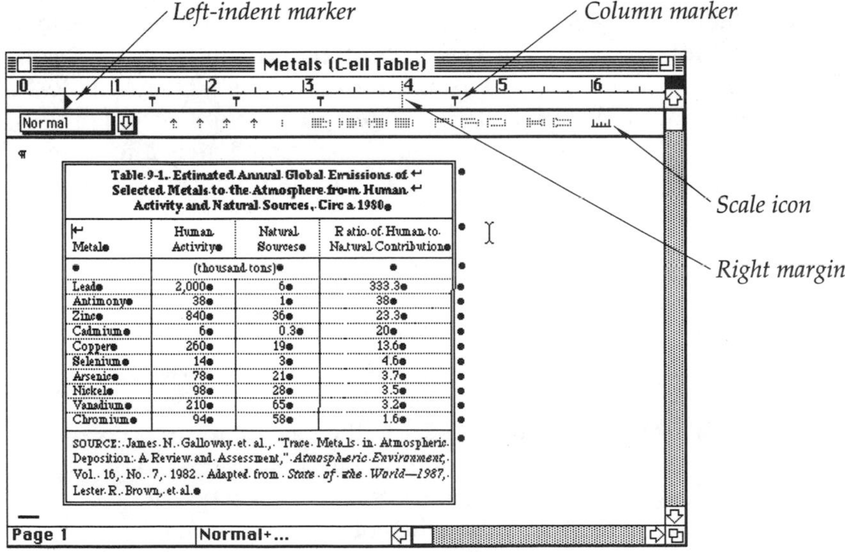

Table 9-1. Estimated Annual Global Emissions of Selected Metals to the Atmosphere from Human Activity and Natural Sources, Circa 1980

Metal	Human Activity	Natural Sources	Ratio of Human to Natural Contribution
	(thousand tons)		
Lead	2,000	6	333.3
Antimony	38	1	38
Zinc	840	36	23.3
Cadmium	6	0.3	20
Copper	260	19	13.6
Selenium	14	3	4.6
Arsenic	78	21	3.7
Nickel	98	28	3.5
Vanadium	210	65	3.2
Chromium	94	58	1.6

SOURCE: James N. Galloway et al., "Trace Metals in Atmospheric Deposition: A Review and Assessment," *Atmospheric Environment*, Vol. 16, No. 7, 1982. Adapted from *State of the World—1987*, Lester R. Brown, et al.

Figure 11-25
The Ruler showing the Table scale.

What you change from the Ruler is applied to all the cells in the currently selected rows; if you want to change the indention or column widths for an entire table, select the entire table. To change column widths or the left indent from the Ruler, do the following:

1. Select the rows you want to change.
2. Drag the left-indent marker to a new position to change the indention of the selected rows. Drag a column marker to change the position of the right edge of the cells in that column. The markers to the right of the dragged marker move with it. To prevent this, press the Shift key before you drag the marker.

The Cells Command

The Ruler presents an easy way to change the indention and width of cells in a table. You can also use the Cells command to change the same characteristics, as well as many others. When you select a range of cells in a table and choose the Cells command, Word displays the Cells dialog box, as shown in Figure 11-26.

As elsewhere in Word, the right side of the dialog box contains the OK button for setting cell formats and dismissing the dialog box, the Cancel button for canceling the operation, and the Apply button for applying formats without dismissing the dialog box. The Apply button works well with the Previous Column and Next Column buttons in the lower right corner of the dialog box. You can click the Apply button to set formats for the current column without dismissing the dialog box and then click the Next Column button to move the selection to the next column to the right: If you've clicked in or selected a cell, the selection moves by cells; if you've selected a column, the selection moves by columns. (Remember that you can easily select an entire column by pressing the Option key and clicking anywhere in the column.)

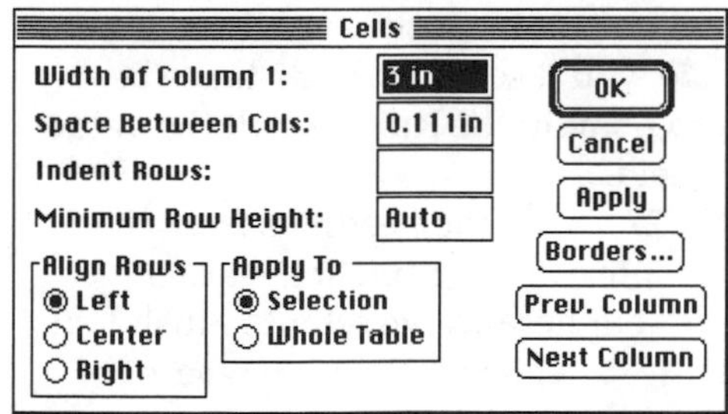

Figure 11-26
The Cells dialog box.

Through the Cells dialog box, you can change the following characteristics of tables, as discussed in the next several pages. Almost every option in the dialog box affects the entire set of rows containing the range of cells you've selected. For example, if you select three cells in one column of a cell table and enter a value in the Indent Rows field, every row that contains a selected cell becomes indented.

There are two exceptions to this. If you enter a number in the Width of Column field, the new column width is applied only to the cells you've selected. Applying border formats to cells works in the same way—you can draw a border around one cell, around the edge of a range of selected cells, and around the entire table.

Column Width

The first field in the Cells dialog box sets the width of the selected column or columns. Although the process is similar to setting column widths from the Ruler, with the Cells dialog box you can format more than column at a time. When you select a range of cells in a column and choose the Cells command, the actual name of the field changes to reflect the selection. For example, if you select a range of cells in columns 2 through 4, the name of the field reads *Width of Columns 2-4.* As just mentioned, the new column width is applied not to each cell in the selected rows, nor to entire columns, but solely to the cells you've selected.

Space Between Columns

The Space Between Columns field is similar to the Spacing option in the Section dialog box. You can use this setting to add space between the columns in a table. When you bring up the Cells dialog box and you haven't previously entered a value in the Space Between Columns field, Word sets a default of 0.111 inches. Word puts half the space entered in the field on the left side of each cell in the selected rows and half on the right side; the overall width of the cell doesn't change, but the room remaining for the text in the cell decreases. If you click in the cell and look at the position of the left and right indents in the Ruler in Normal scale, you'll see that the distance between the left cell boundary and the zero point in the Ruler is half the value entered in the Space Between Columns field.

Let's consider an example. Figure 11-27 shows the headings from the Metals table we've used earlier in this chapter; the alignment in earlier instances of the table was set to Centered, but here we've set it to Flush Left and set the left indents at the 0 point in the Ruler so you can see where the left edge of the text falls. We've also set the Space Between Columns value to *0 in,* so the left indent coincides with the left edge of the cell.

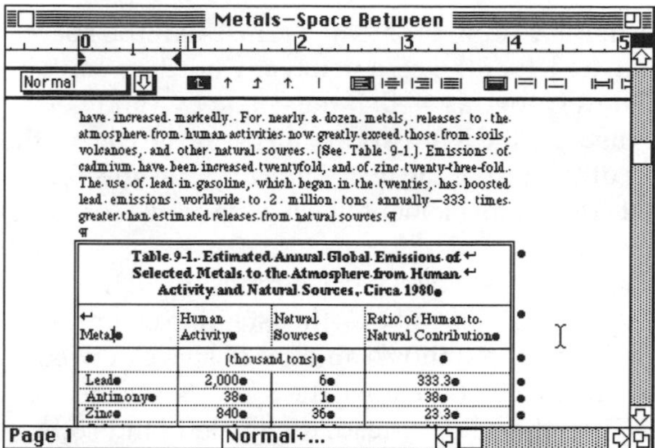

Figure 11-27
The headings in the Metals table, with the Space Between Columns value set to *0 in* and the alignment set to Flush Left.

If you set the insertion point in, say, the first cell of the row containing the headings and change the Space Between Columns setting to *0.25 in,* Word adds a gap of 0.125 inch on the left and right sides of each cell in the row, as shown in Figure 11-28.

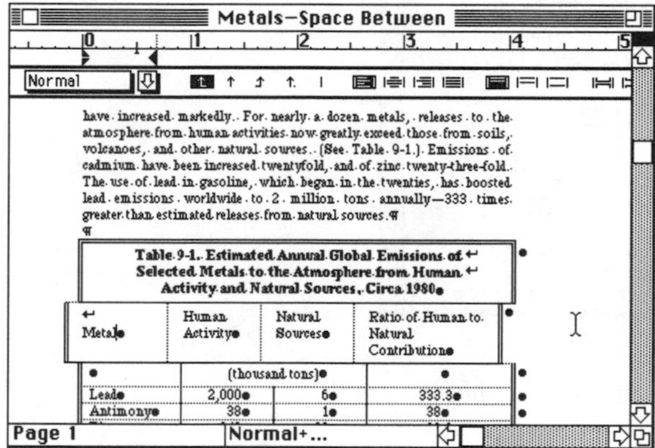

Figure 11-28
After setting the Space Between Columns value for the row to *0.25 in.*

The result of adding this space is that the 0 point of the text in the column aligns where it did previously, but the left edge of the cell moves to the left of the 0 point. Because the overall width of the cell doesn't change, you see the right edge of the cell moving to the left by 0.125 inch as well, but the space reserved for the text in the cell (indicated by the indent markers in the Ruler) decreases by 0.25 inch. Notice that the word *Contribution* in the last column wraps to the next line because the available width in the cell has decreased.

This behavior can lead to an interesting problem. Because half the space Word adds for this format is to the left of the zero point, any borders you've added to the cell (discussed below) move as well. If the text above and below the table aligns at the 0 point (usually the left margin), this seems to move the left edge of the table to the left of the rest of the text. Typically, designs for documents specify that the left edge of an element (such as a graphic or table) aligns cleanly on one or more edges.

Probably the best time to use the Space Between Columns format, therefore, is when you don't need to implement exacting standards for the design of a document and can live with a uniform amount of space between the columns in the table. You can effectively remove the Space Between Columns format by entering *0 in* in the field; instead, use the left (and right) indents belonging to the text in cells to add space between the columns. The first cell in the row that contains the headings in Figure 11-27 shows the cell with no space between columns, and the heading touches the left edge of the cell. Figure 11-29 shows the same table, but 1/16 inch indents are used instead, as indicated by the position of the left indent in the Ruler.

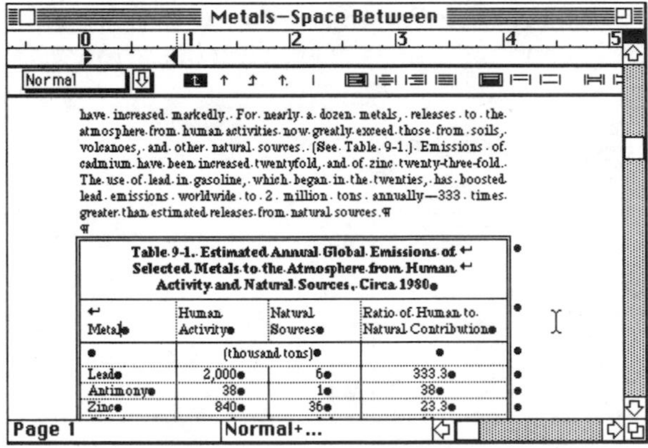

Figure 11-29
Using the indents to add space between columns.

Another point to consider when deciding whether to use the Space Between Columns format or paragraph indention for a particular table is whether you want to establish one or more styles for the text in the cells. If you want the control that styles afford, adding an indention format to the style probably won't cause additional work. However, if you would like all the text in the cells to have the same format as text outside the table, such as the *Normal* style, you might be better off using the Space Between Columns format in conjunction with Row indention, discussed next.

Row Indention

Entering a value in the Indent Rows field indents the entire row, in much the same way that paragraph indention works for paragraphs. You can indent rows through the Cells dialog box or by dragging the left-indent marker in the Ruler in the Table scale. The indention is measured from the 0 point in the Ruler's Normal scale—the left margin for single-column sections or the left edge of the column for multiple-column sections.

You can use this feature to counteract the effects of adding the Space Between Columns format discussed above or to create a special effect in a document. For example, it's relatively easy to create a "stair-step" structure for a table, such as that of the first table shown in Figure 11-30, by deleting cells on the right side of a rectangular table.

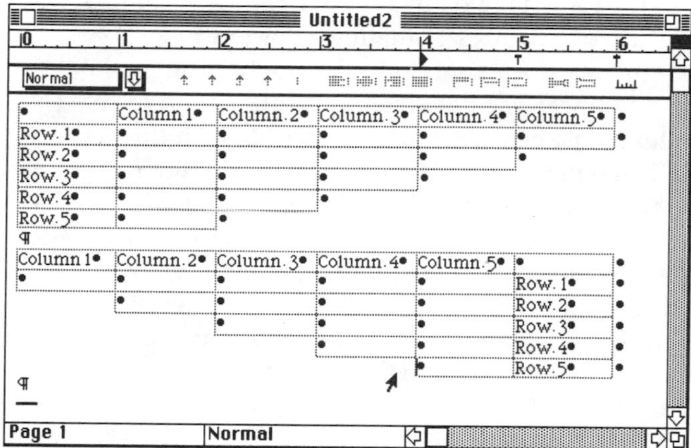

Figure 11-30
"Stair-step" table structure created by deleting cells.

However, if you'd like to begin the stair-step structure on the left side of the table, like that shown in the second table of Figure 11-30, you couldn't simply delete cells on the left side of the table—the cells on the right would then slide to the left. Instead, you could simply leave the cells on the left side of the table empty, and indicate the edges of the structure with border formats. Another way to accomplish the same result using row indention would be to indent each row by the width of one column, as you can see by the position of the indents in the Ruler in the figure.

Row Height

The Minimum Row Height field is similar to the Line Spacing field in the Paragraph dialog box. If the field contains the text *Auto,* the height of the row is determined by the height of the cell containing the "tallest" amount of text or graphics, either because the cell contains the most material or because you've set paragraph spacing formats for the text in the cell. (For example, the tallest cell could consist of less text than in other cells but be formatted with a large amount of Space Before and Space After.)

If you enter a measurement in the Minimum Row Height field, the value sets the height of the cells in the selected rows. If you enter more text in a cell than will fit within this cell height, Word increases the row height to accommodate the extra material.

Finally, in the same way that you can insert a minus sign before the measurement in the Line Spacing field of the Paragraph dialog box, you can insert a minus sign before the value entered in the Minimum Row Height field. In this case, a better name for the field might be Maximum Row Height, because Word does not increase the height of the cells in the row to accommodate the cell with the tallest material.

Setting an absolute row height for a cell can be very useful for creating forms, when the fields in the form should always have the same dimensions, or for creating regular gridlike structures. Sometimes, for example, it's desirable to set up a design for a document that requires "writing to the page." In such a design, no topic in the document can run over to the next page, and each piece of text must be placed on a specific area on the page. You can set up single cells having an absolute row height, and no matter how much text you enter in the cell, it will stay within the cell and remain on that one page. Unfortunately, the maximum number you can specify in the field is 6 inches, the same as for the Line Spacing field in the Paragraph dialog box.

Beware of entering too much text in such a cell, however, because the text can disappear past the bottom boundary of the cell. If you're using keyboard commands, the insertion point can travel into the undisplayed text. If the cell contains too much text and Show ¶ is on, Word reminds you that text exists "below the horizon" by drawing a thick bar across the bottom of the cell, as shown in Figure 11-31. (Don't confuse this bar with a thick border format.)

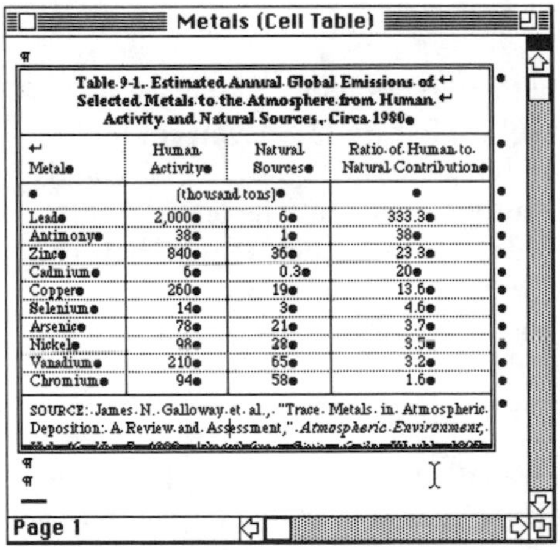

Metals (Cell Table)

Table 9-1. Estimated Annual Global Emissions of Selected Metals to the Atmosphere from Human Activity and Natural Sources, Circa 1980

Metal	Human Activity	Natural Sources	Ratio of Human to Natural Contribution
	(thousand tons)		
Lead	2,000	6	333.3
Antimony	38	1	38
Zinc	840	36	23.3
Cadmium	6	0.3	20
Copper	260	19	13.6
Selenium	14	3	4.6
Arsenic	78	21	3.7
Nickel	98	28	3.5
Vanadium	210	65	3.2
Chromium	94	58	1.6

SOURCE: James N. Galloway et al., "Trace Metals in Atmospheric Deposition: A Review and Assessment," *Atmospheric Environment,*

Page 1

Figure 11-31
The cell in the last row of the table has an absolute Minimum Row Height and contains too much text.

Alignment of Rows

Setting the alignment of rows works much like the process of setting alignments for paragraphs, except that you set the alignment of paragraphs through the Ruler and set row alignment through the Cells dialog box. Simply select the rows you want to realign, choose the Cells command, and click the appropriate option in the Align Rows group.

Cell Borders

You can invoke the Cell Borders command in two ways—either by clicking the Borders button in the Cells dialog box or by adding the Cell Borders command to the Format (or other) menu and choosing it instead. When you select a range of cells and call up the Borders dialog box (by either method), you'll see a dialog box like that shown in Figure 11-32.

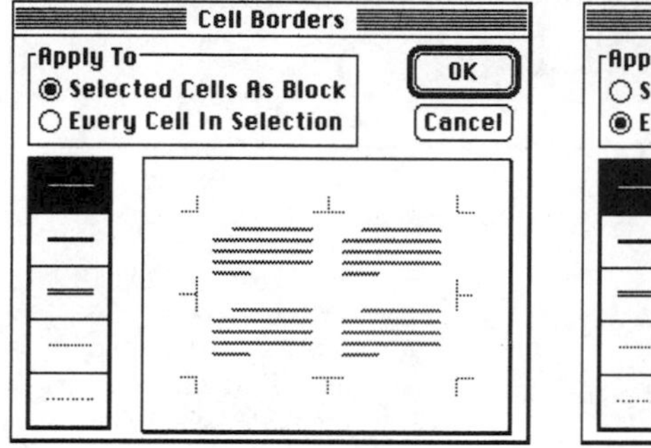

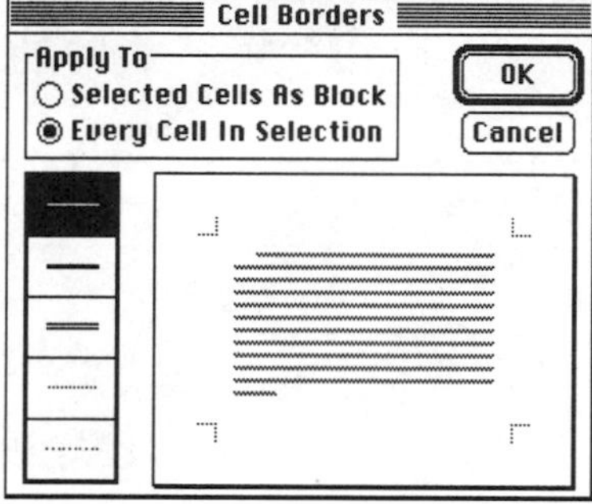

Figure 11-32
The Cell Borders dialog box, in its two versions.

The Cell Borders dialog box contains a schematic similar to that found in the Paragraph Borders dialog box. By clicking on the various boundaries in the schematic, you can draw lines around the perimeter of a range of cells or on one side alone. You can also click in the center of the schematic to draw lines between any two cells in the selected range.

You can add borders to individual cells, to columns, to any selected range of cells, or to the table as a whole, depending on what range you selected before calling up the dialog box. Specifically, what you add borders to depends on which of the two options you select in the Apply To group: If you select the Selected Cells As Block option, you see the schematic shown in the first version of the dialog box in Figure 11-32, and you add borders to the entire range of cells you selected as if it were one object. For example, you can draw a border around an entire table by selecting it and using this option.

If, however, you use the Every Cell In Selection option, the schematic changes to the second version of the Cell Borders dialog box shown in Figure 11-32. Note that the schematic represents only one cell with four boundaries;

the border formats you select are applied to each cell independently of the others in the range you selected.

Notice that the Cell Borders dialog box does not contain an edit field for border spacing, as does the Paragraph Borders dialog box. If you'd like to adjust the distance between a cell border and the text within the cell, you can do this by adding a Space Between Columns format, or by adding combinations of paragraph indention and Space Before and Space After. Of course, you can also ignore the Cell Border format completely and use paragraph borders to achieve much the same effect.

TIP

Spacing in Tables

Setting the spacing of elements in a table can involve a large number of parameters—it can get very complicated if you use many types of vertical and horizontal spacing in text at the same time. Here are the paragraph formats and table formats that influence spacing in tables:

Item	Horizontal	Vertical
Paragraph formats:		
Indents	Left, right, and first-line.	
Line Spacing		Space is added above each line. Otherwise, space is determined by the tallest character or graphic in each line.
Space Above and Space Below		Top and bottom.
Border spacing	Left and right.	Top and bottom.
Alignment	Left, right, and centered.	
Position formats	Text wraps around all sides of positioned paragraphs. You can also set the Distance From Text value, which is added to the border spacing.	
Table formats:		
Indention	Left indent.	
Column widths	Left and right.	
Space Between Columns	Space is added to both the left side and the right side of each column.	
Minimum Row Height	No effect.	Distance between top and bottom cell boundaries, determined by the tallest collection of text, graphics, and paragraph formats in the cell.
Alignment	Left, right, and centered.	
Position formats (see next section)	Text wraps around all sides of positioned tables. You can also set the Distance from Text value, which is not affected by table borders.	

Obviously, if you've combined many of these formats in a table, it might become difficult to determine what causes a certain spacing effect. One practice that can help you to discover what's going on with the character formats and the paragraph formats in a selected range of text is this: Pretend you're going to define a style for the selected text, and call up the Define Styles dialog box. In the definition area of the dialog box, you'll see the name of the style attached to the selected text and any additional formats the text might have. Because you can't assign table formats to styles, any spacing effect not specified in the style definition is probably caused by a table format.

Another practice that is very useful for unravelling knotty combinations of formats is to copy (not cut) the table and paste it at the end of the document. Select the entire table; then press Option-Command-P to return the paragraphs to the *Normal* style, and press Shift-Command-Spacebar to remove all character formats except those assigned to the *Normal* style. Any spacing effect left in the table must be either a table format or due to formats assigned to the *Normal* style.

In any case, the moral is this: Keep it simple—either by using the spacing numbers Word suggests (for quick-and-dirty work) or by restricting your use of spacing formats to a few types of formats. For example, you could set the Space Between Columns value for each row to *0 in* and use the first, left, and right indents to establish the distance between the text and cell boundaries. This adds the benefit of letting you set styles for the gaps in the table, rather than having to reformat the gaps manually.

Table Position

When you select one or more rows in a table and choose the Position command, Word presents the Position dialog box, shown in Figure 11-33. You can also click the Preview button or choose Print Preview from the File menu to drag positioned tables from one place to another on a page, just as you can with positioned paragraphs.

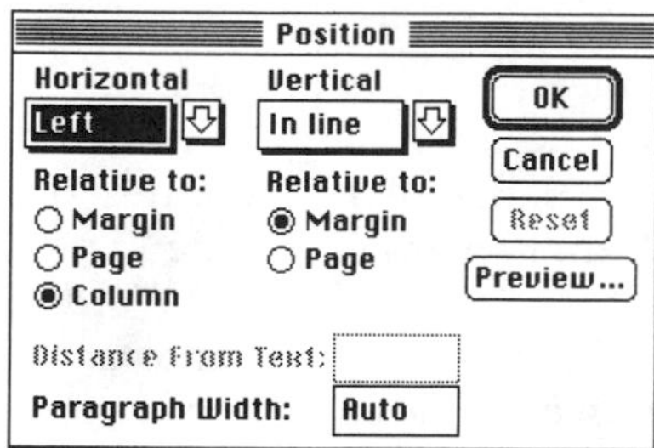

Figure 11-33
The Position dialog box.

The rules for placing tables are similar to the rules for positioning paragraphs, discussed in Chapter 9, "Paragraph Formatting," so we'll discuss only the peculiarities for positioned tables here. The Position command on the Format menu actually has two applications—one for Positioned paragraphs and one for Positioned tables. This can be a bit confusing because the Position format, when applied to paragraphs, becomes a paragraph format and obeys the rules for paragraph formats in general—you can add the format to a style definition, and so on.

When you apply the Position format to a table, however, it's applied to the text in the table you've selected—it's still a paragraph format, but its behavior changes. You can position an entire table, or you can position any selection of rows within the table. The position of the first cell takes precedence over the position of any other cell in the row.

As with paragraphs, adding a Position format to a row takes it out of the standard strict succession of paragraphs, which is the normal case in Galley View. For example, if you select a row and position it outside the margin in the upper right corner of the page, in Galley View the row appears to be part of the table, but in Page View the row moves to the position (in the upper right corner) it will have when printed.

■ *Making Side-by-Side Paragraph Tables*

When you enter a tabbed table of numbers into Word, you type lines, not columns, although the tab characters allow you to align the entries one above another. When you transfer numbers from an on-line service such as Dow Jones or CompuServe, however, you might get the numbers in a list—one per line. If you want to place the columns side by side, you have to rearrange the numbers, which can be quite time-consuming. One way to do this is to use the Option key to cut and paste blocks of text, as described earlier in this chapter.

Another way to format such data into columns is to use the Side-by-Side paragraph format. Each line in the column can end with either a paragraph mark or a newline mark. Select the lines that you want to put into one column, and set indents for that column in the Ruler. (See Figure 11-34.) Repeat this process for each column. Then select all the columns and turn on the Side-by-Side option. Check the format in Print Preview or in Page View. (As discussed in Chapter 9, "Paragraph Formatting," remember that Word might not be able to accurately display in Page View some arrangements of Side-by-Side paragraphs.) Figure 11-35 shows an example of columns formatted in this way. To set up separate groups of columns on a page, repeat this process for each new group.

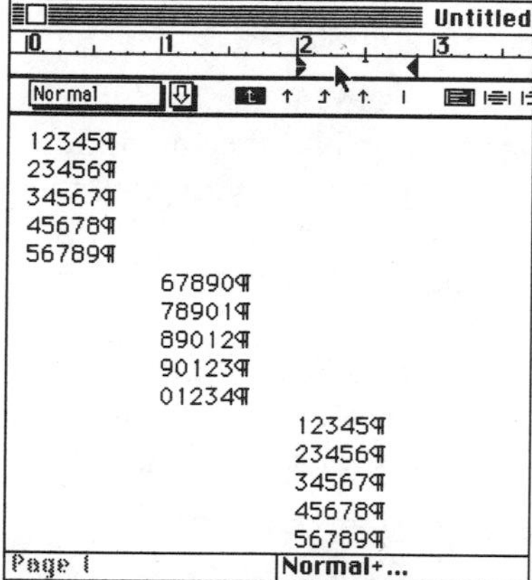

Figure 11-34
Setting Ruler indents for a column in Side-by-Side format, in Galley View.

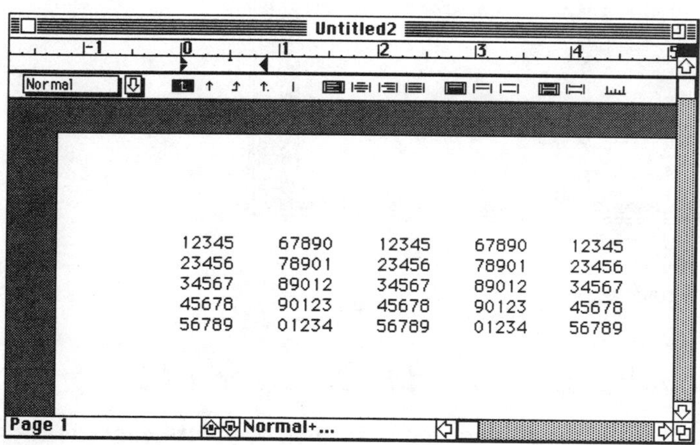

Figure 11-35
The formatted columns in Page View.

■ *Renumbering and Sorting Tables and Lists*

A list in Word is simply a series of items, each of which ends in a paragraph mark. An item can consist of one character or a string of characters on one line, or it can extend across several lines. If two or more successive lines on the screen do not end with a paragraph mark, Word considers them one list entry. After you've created a list, you can number its items either by using the Line Numbering paragraph format or by inserting numbers at the beginning of each paragraph. If you've inserted numbers, you can sort the items in the list alphabetically or numerically.

Using the Line Numbering Format to Number a List

If you only want to keep track of the number of entries in the list, and if none of the entries are longer than one line, try using the Line Numbering option in the Section dialog box. The line numbers appear only when you print the document or audition it with Print Preview (as shown in Figure 11-36). Be sure that your list is in a separate section unless you want to number all the lines in the document.

The Line Numbering format isn't affected by sorting; if you sort the list, the line numbering remains consecutive: The new first item will be number 1. For this reason, you can't use line numbers as the basis for sorting the list.

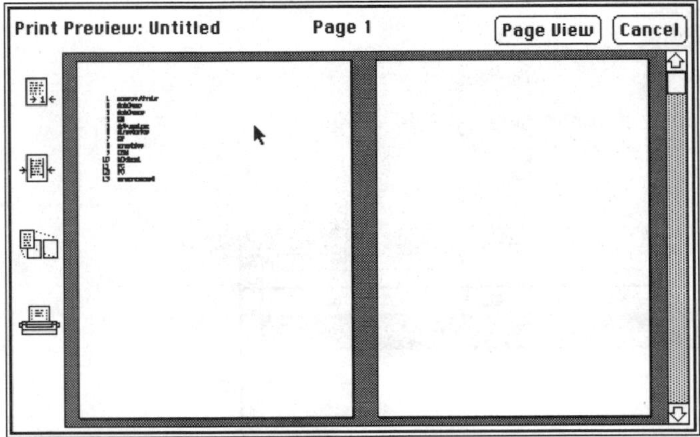

Figure 11-36
Line numbers in Print Preview.

Using the Renumber Command to Number a List

If some of the items in the list are longer than one line, or if you want to precede or follow the numbers with other characters or use letters instead of numbers, use the Renumber command. Numbers are inserted at the beginning of each paragraph and appear immediately on screen rather than becoming visible only when the document is previewed or printed. This command is discussed in Chapter 4, "Organizing Through Outlining"; following is a brief review of the process. To number a list:

❶ Select the items in the list.

❷ Choose the Renumber command. The dialog box shown in Figure 11-37 appears.

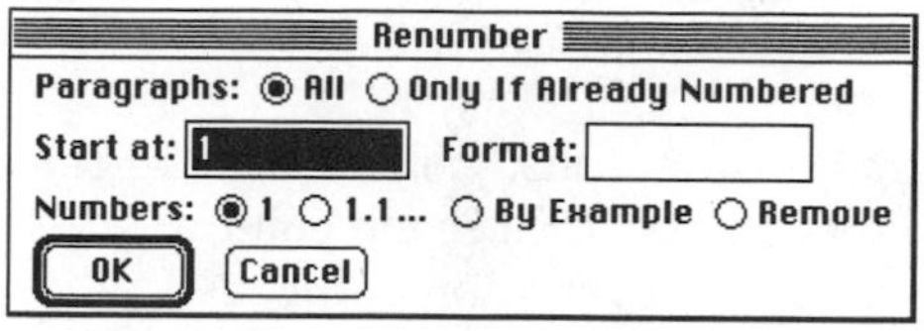

Renumber
Paragraphs: ◉ All ○ Only If Already Numbered
Start at: 1 Format:
Numbers: ◉ 1 ○ 1.1… ○ By Example ○ Remove
OK Cancel

Figure 11-37
The Renumber dialog box.

❸ Click the Only if Already Numbered option if you want to renumber only those entries that already have a number.

❹ Enter a number in the Start At field if you want to begin with a number other than 1.

❺ Enter a numbering or lettering format in the Format field, and click By Example or select one of the other Numbers options. Figure 11-38 provides some ideas for formats you can use when numbering lists.

❻ Click the OK button.

Word inserts a line number (or letter) and a tab character before each item in the list. Word doesn't insert numbers before empty paragraphs. If you subsequently add more items, or if you delete or rearrange some items, repeat this routine to have Word renumber the lines in the list.

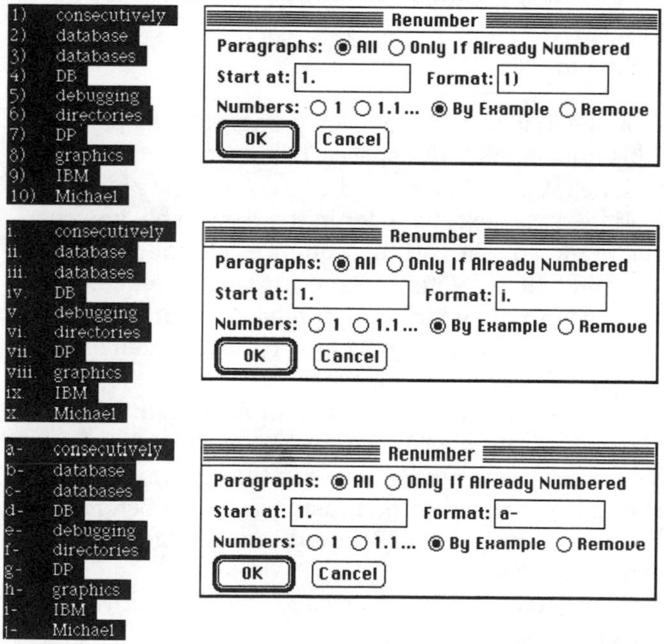

1) consecutively
2) database
3) databases
4) DB
5) debugging
6) directories
7) DP
8) graphics
9) IBM
10) Michael

Renumber
Paragraphs: ◉ All ○ Only If Already Numbered
Start at: 1. Format: 1)
Numbers: ○ 1 ○ 1.1… ◉ By Example ○ Remove
OK Cancel

i. consecutively
ii. database
iii. databases
iv. DB
v. debugging
vi. directories
vii. DP
viii. graphics
ix. IBM
x. Michael

Renumber
Paragraphs: ◉ All ○ Only If Already Numbered
Start at: 1. Format: i.
Numbers: ○ 1 ○ 1.1… ◉ By Example ○ Remove
OK Cancel

a- consecutively
b- database
c- databases
d- DB
e- debugging
f- directories
g- DP
h- graphics
i- IBM
j- Michael

Renumber
Paragraphs: ◉ All ○ Only If Already Numbered
Start at: 1. Format: a-
Numbers: ○ 1 ○ 1.1… ◉ By Example ○ Remove
OK Cancel

Figure 11-38
Numbering formats for lists.

TIP

Renumbering Columns in Tables

Because the renumbering feature acts upon paragraphs, you can't renumber only one selected column in a table. If you do select the second column in a table, for instance, Word inserts a number before every non-empty cell in every row containing a selected cell.

Instead, try copying the table, or that column of the table, and pasting it into a spreadsheet program such as Microsoft Excel. You can use the program's Series command to create a new column of numbers, combine the numbered column with the data you've transferred, and then transfer the numbered data back into Word. Alternatively, you could create a numbered series in Microsoft Excel and then copy the range and paste it into a new column to the left of the column that you want to renumber. Finally, use Word's Table command to merge the two columns, as described earlier in this chapter.

Sorting the List

You can sort the items in lists and tables alphabetically or numerically in either descending or ascending order. Each item in the list must end with a paragraph mark. To sort a list, follow these steps:

1. Select the list. Leave out any portions (such as headings) that you don't want to sort.
2. Choose the Sort command.

Word sorts the list by the first character of each paragraph. If a paragraph begins with double quotation marks, spaces, tabs, or diacritical characters (foreign accents alone rather than accented characters), the program ignores them and instead uses the next character in the paragraph; however, accented characters aren't ignored. The sorting sequence is as follows: punctuation marks, numbers, and letters. (Note: The specific sorting sequence used is customized for the country in which you purchased your copy of Word.) Word places an uppercase letter before a lowercase letter, all other things being equal; for example, *Fire* comes before *fire.*

Word sorts numbers by their value, rather than "alphabetically." For example, Word correctly puts the number *17* before *120*. Incidentally, you might have noticed that sorting filenames By Name in the Finder doesn't work this way: To sort numbers correctly, you must insert zeros before the number as placeholders. For example, *File 017* would come before *File 120* (but *File 120* would come before *File 17*).

The following table shows the sorting sequence for *single characters* in the visible ASCII character set for the Times font. Because the attachment of certain characters to ASCII numbers above 128 varies with the font used, Word reverts to sorting these characters in ASCII sequence. Finally, certain combinations of the Macintosh system software and internationalized versions of Word might sort in an order different from the one listed here. For example, the Swedish version of Word uses its own sort table. All other non-American systems use a third table; the French Canadian version alone uses a slightly different version of this table.

"	34	<	60	ë	145	p	112	°	161	⁄	218
^	94	=	61	F	70	Q	81	¢	162	¤	219
~	126	>	62	f	102	q	113	£	163	‹	220
!	33	?	63	G	71	R	82	§	164	›	221
¡	193	¿	192	g	103	r	114	•	165	ﬁ	222
«	199	@	64	H	72	S	83	¶	166	ﬂ	223
»	200	ß	167	h	104	s	115	®	168	‡	224
“	210	[	91	I	73	T	84	©	169	·	225
”	211	\	6	i	105	t	116	™	170	‚	226
#	35	\	92	í	146	U	85	´	171	„	227
$	36	]	93	ì	147	u	117	¨	172	‰	228
%	37	_	95	î	148	ú	156	≠	173	Â	229
&	38	`	96	ï	149	ù	157	∞	176	Ê	230
'	39	A	65	J	74	û	158	±	177	Á	231
‘	212	a	97	j	106	Ü	134	≤	178	Ë	232
’	213	á	135	K	75	ü	159	≥	179	È	233
(	40	À	203	k	107	V	86	¥	180	Í	234
)	41	à	136	L	76	v	118	µ	181	Î	235
*	42	â	137	l	108	W	87	∂	182	Ï	236
+	43	Ä	128	M	77	w	119	Σ	183	Ì	237
,	44	ä	138	m	109	X	88	Π	184	Ó	238
-	30	Ã	204	N	78	x	120	π	185	Ô	239
-	45	ã	139	n	110	Y	89	∫	186		240
.	46	B	66	Ñ	132	y	121	ª	187	Ò	241
/	47	b	98	ñ	150	ÿ	216	º	188	Ú	242
0	48	C	67	O	79	Z	90	Ω	189	Û	243
1	49	c	99	o	111	z	122	¬	194	Ù	244
2	50	Ç	130	ó	151	Å	129	√	195	ı	245
3	51	ç	141	ò	152	å	140	ƒ	196	ˆ	246
4	52	D	68	ô	153	Æ	174	≈	197	˜	247
5	53	d	100	Ö	133	æ	190	Δ	198	¯	248
6	54	E	69	ö	154	Ø	175	…	201	˘	249
7	55	e	101	Õ	205	ø	191	–	208	˙	250
8	56	É	131	õ	155	{	123	—	209	˚	251
9	57	é	142	Œ	206	|	124	÷	214	¸	252
:	58	è	143	œ	207	}	125	◊	215	˝	253
;	59	ê	144	P	80	†	160	Ÿ	217	˛	254

Sorting is normally done in ascending order—smallest to largest or A to Z. If you want to sort in descending order, press the Shift key while choosing the Sort command. If you do this, the Sort command changes to Sort Descending. Of course, you can also add the Sort Descending command to the Utilities menu.

Sorting Data in Tables

You can use the same basic procedure to sort the data in both tabbed tables and cell tables as to sort a list, but an added capability is available: You can sort the entire table by any selected column. If you want to alphabetize a list based on the contents of the third column of a tabbed table, for instance, hold down the Option key and drag over the third column to select it, and then choose the Sort command. (See Figure 11-39.) Word moves entire lines, not only the selected column, thereby keeping each row in the table intact. Each line is considered a complete entity.

One implication of this is that you can perform multiple sorts by sorting first on one column and then on another. For example, if the first column in a table contains last names, and the second column contains first names, you can alphabetize the first names of people having the same last name by sorting first by first name and then by last name. To sort only one column in a table and not the others, you must remove the column, sort it, and then replace the unsorted version.

Word normally sorts paragraphs by the first character in each line; however, when you use the Option key to select a column, you can end each line with a newline mark as well as with a paragraph mark. Similarly, you can select a column in a cell table and sort every row containing a cell of the selection.

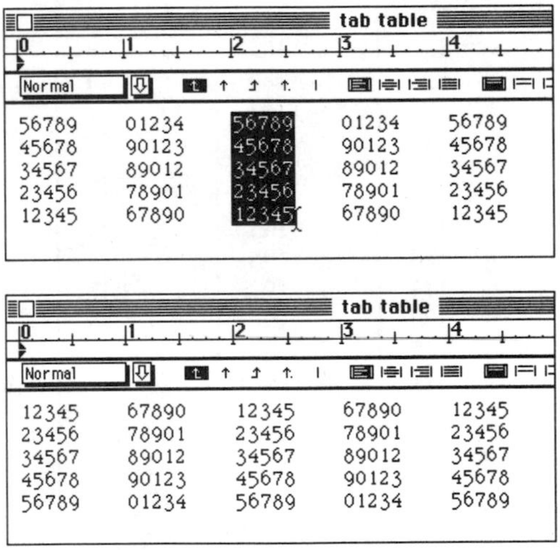

56789	01234	56789	01234	56789
45678	90123	45678	90123	45678
34567	89012	34567	89012	34567
23456	78901	23456	78901	23456
12345	67890	12345	67890	12345

12345	67890	12345	67890	12345
23456	78901	23456	78901	23456
34567	89012	34567	89012	34567
45678	90123	45678	90123	45678
56789	01234	56789	01234	56789

Figure 11-39
Sorting a table by one of its columns.

■ *Performing Mathematical Calculations*

Word's rudimentary electronic spreadsheet function allows you to add, subtract, multiply, and divide a set of numbers. It can also calculate percentages. You can use this feature to prepare invoices, statements, and inventory reports. Typically, addition is the most common operation; the program adds a column of numbers, and you insert the total at the bottom of the column. Figure 11-40 shows a simple tabbed table in which Word has calculated the total for each column. (Each column was added separately.)

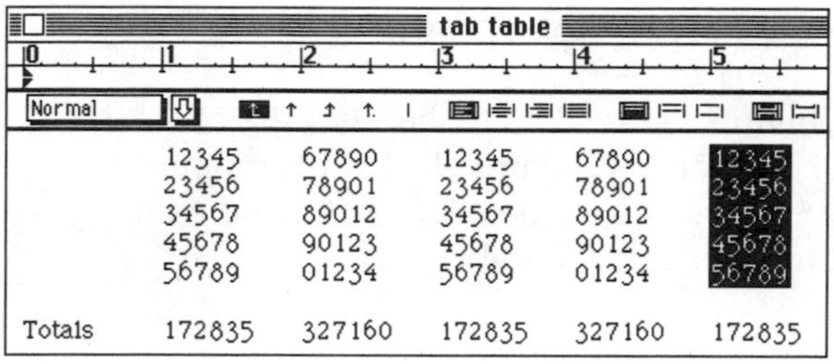

tab table

Normal

	12345	67890	12345	67890	12345
	23456	78901	23456	78901	23456
	34567	89012	34567	89012	34567
	45678	90123	45678	90123	45678
	56789	01234	56789	01234	56789
Totals	172835	327160	172835	327160	172835

Figure 11-40
Table with calculated totals.

With a bit of trickery, you can set up fairly complex working formulas for such tasks as calculating sales tax or figuring out a discount rate. Bear in mind, however, that Word isn't an electronic spreadsheet program; using the built-in calculator requires manual intervention, but it relieves you from reaching for your calculator or switching to a program like Microsoft Excel to prepare a mere expense report.

Doing Simple Addition

To add the numbers in a column or row, simply select them. If the numbers are in a tabbed table, you can select the column you want by pressing the Option key and dragging across the column. The same process works within cell tables as well—simply select the range of cells you want Word to calculate. Remember that you can select a column in a cell table by clicking in the selection bar at the top of the column or by holding down the Option key while clicking in the column you want to select. Blank lines or lines filled with text alone aren't included in the calculation; thus, you can even select a paragraph and have Word add the numbers it contains.

After the numbers are selected, choose the Calculate command. The sum of the numbers appears in the status box. Word also places the total in the Clipboard so that you can paste it where you want it. Set the insertion point where you want the total to appear and choose the Paste command.

Using Math Operators

To perform other types of calculations, use the following math operators:

To	Use
Add	+ (or no operator, because addition is assumed)
Subtract	– (or parentheses around the number)
Multiply	*
Divide	/
Find a percentage	% (divides the preceding number by 100)

Enter the +, –, *, and / operators before the number they are to act upon; type the percent sign (%) after the number. Figure 11-41 shows some examples. Characters such as $, #, and = have no effect, but avoid using parentheses unless you want to subtract the number.

```
7*4        Seven times four
2-5        Two minus five
-3-9       Negative three minus nine
25/5       Twenty-five divided by five
23*7%      Seven percent of twenty-three
12(7)      Twelve minus seven
114(-65)   One hundred fourteen minus negative sixty-five
```

Figure 11-41
Examples of using math operators.

Word calculates a formula from left to right and from top to bottom. Unlike an electronic spreadsheet program, no precedence of operations exists. Multiplication and division aren't carried out before the other operations, and calculations within parentheses aren't performed first. Instead, Word assumes that numbers enclosed in parentheses are negative. The percent sign is the only exception to this left-to-right sequence, because the preceding number is converted to a percentage before the number is used in the calculation (see the fifth example in Figure 11-41.)

The result that Word provides contains commas and decimal points only if one or more of the numbers in the formula contains them. The number of digits to the right of the decimal point is also determined in this way. If one of the numbers has five digits to the right of the decimal point, for example, the result is also shown with five decimal places.

If you don't want the math operators to appear in the printed copy, format them (including parentheses) as hidden text, as illustrated in Figure 11-42. The operators must be visible on the screen when you perform the calculation, so be sure that the Show Hidden Text option is on.

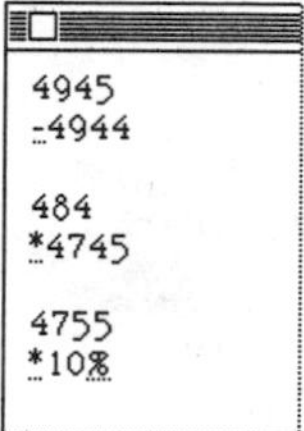

Figure 11-42
Math operators formatted as hidden text.

Constructing and Using Formulas

Figure 11-43 shows how you can use Word's calculation feature. The invoice consists of four major parts: the number of items and their base price, the total for each item and the subtotal, the sales tax, and the grand total. To arrive at the grand total, you must make several separate calculations.

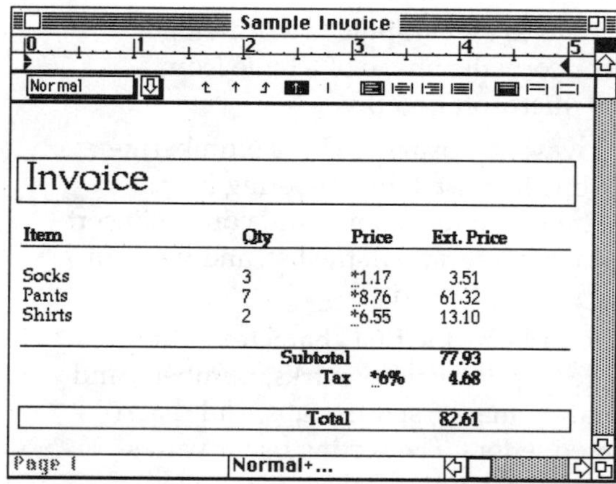

Figure 11-43
Sample invoice using Word's calculation feature.

You start by calculating the total price for each item—the base price multiplied by the quantity. After you paste in the item totals, you select them as a group and enter the sum as the subtotal. You then calculate the sales tax by multiplying the subtotal by a percentage—*6%* in the example—or by using the decimal form **.06;* using the percent sign is a little easier. Finally, to get the grand total, you add the subtotal and the sales tax.

Note that in the example the operators and the sales tax formula are hidden—they don't appear in the final printout.

For another example of using Word's calculator, see the invoice project in Chapter 18, "Blueprints."

Points to Remember

- Word supports three basic types of tables:

  A tabbed table consists of lines containing text or graphics. You use tab characters to separate the elements within each line and to align them vertically in columns. You can set the tab stops manually for a table, or you can define a style that has the tab stops you want.

  A cell table consists of rows and columns of cells. Each cell can contain one or more paragraphs of text or graphics. You can assign any paragraph format to the text in cells, but you can't assign paragraph formats to the table itself. (The end-of-cell marker can "hold" paragraph formats in the absence of a paragraph mark, however.)

  A Side-By-Side or Position paragraph format table uses either of the two paragraph formats to place blocks of text in a tabular arrangement. Word's new cell table structure makes Side-by-Side tables less useful than in earlier versions.

  In addition, you can construct tables as a graphic in a drawing program (such as MacDraw) or copy the image of a table from a spreadsheet program (such as Microsoft Excel).

- You can number items in two ways. By using the Line Numbering format, you can number each line in a list; the numbering isn't affected by sorting. By using the Renumber command, you can insert numbers at the beginning of each paragraph in the list, and you can alter the numbering format to suit your needs.

- The Sort command sorts paragraphs by the first character in the paragraph, in the following order: punctuation marks, numbers, and letters. It ignores double quotation marks, spaces, tabs, and diacritical characters, but not accented letters. The sorting order varies with the country for which your copy of Word was customized.

  The Sort command works on paragraphs in tabbed tables and in the rows in cell tables. You can sort a table in the order of a selected column by using the Option key to select a column of text within a tabbed table or by simply selecting the column in a cell table.

- Word's calculation feature allows you to add, subtract, multiply, divide, and calculate percentages. It operates on the numbers in the current selection, displaying the result in the status box and also placing it on the Clipboard. The calculation proceeds from left to right and from top to bottom; multiplication and division aren't given precedence, and numbers within parentheses are assumed to be negative. The result contains commas and decimal points only if one or more of the numbers in the selection has them, and is calculated to the same number of decimal places as the number in the selection having the most decimal places.

■ Techniques

Editing and Formatting Tabbed Tables

Select a column instead of entire lines

❶ Press the Option key before dragging over the column.

You can also use Shift-clicking with this method to extend the selection.

Move a column in a table

❶ Select the column to be moved. Include the Tab character after the column in the selection, but not the one before it.

❷ Press Command-X to cut the column, and place it on the Clipboard.

❸ Set the insertion point where the column is to appear, before the first character of the column that will be to the right of the pasted column.

❹ Press Command-V to paste the column in the specified location.

Add vertical lines between columns in a table

❶ Select the entire table.

❷ Using the Ruler, place a vertical line tab at each location where you want a line to appear.

Add horizontal lines to a table

❶ Select the lines that are to have underlines or overlines.

❷ Choose the Paragraph command.

❸ Click either the Below or the Above option in the Border group, depending on whether you want underlines or overlines or both, and then click OK.

Draw a box around a table

❶ End each line (except the last in the table) with a newline mark (Shift-Return); end the last line with a paragraph mark.

❷ Set the insertion point anywhere in the table.

❸ Choose the Paragraph command, and click the Borders button.

❹ Click either the Plain Box or Shadow Box option at the right side of the dialog box.

❺ Select a line type, if you want, and then click OK.

You can also select the Custom Box option, select line types and click on the various boundaries in the schematic to develop your own border designs.

Creating and Converting Cell Tables

Create a blank cell table

1. Place the insertion point where you want the table.
2. Choose Insert Table from the Document menu.
3. Enter the number of rows and columns you want. You can create tables of any number of rows and of up to 31 columns.
4. Word sets the initial width of each column to the width of the current text column divided by the number of columns. You can change the width of selected columns later, either from the Ruler or through the Cells command.
5. Click OK.

Convert a series of paragraphs to a table

1. Select a series of paragraphs, a tabbed table, or a series of paragraphs delimited by commas given the Side-By-Side format.
2. Choose the Insert Table command.
3. If the number of columns proposed is incorrect, enter a new value in the Number of Columns field. Word displays the corresponding number of rows, based on the number of selected paragraphs.
4. If the proposed width is incorrect, enter a new value in the Column Width field.
5. Word proposes an option in the Convert From option group based on the structure of the material selected. If incorrect, select the desired type of conversion.
6. Click OK.

Convert a range of rows to a series of paragraphs

1. Select a range of rows in the table. To select the entire table, press the Option and Command keys, and double-click anywhere in the table.
2. Choose the Table To Text command.
3. Select the type of paragraph to which you want to convert the table.
4. Click OK.

Editing Cell Tables

Select in tables

To select	Do this
A cell	Click in the cell's selection bar.
The text in a cell	Drag from the beginning to the end of the text.
A row	Double-click in any cell's selection bar in that row, or double-click to the left of the row.
A column	Press the option key, and click in the column.
A table	Press the option key, and double-click in any column.

As with paragraphs, clicking in a cell selects the cell for cell formatting operations as well as for paragraph formatting.

Move in tables

To move	Press
Right	Option-Command-6
Left	Option-Command-4
Up	Option-Command-8
Down	Option-Command-2
To next cell	Option-Command-3, or Tab
To previous cell	Option-Command-9, or Shift-Tab

Insert and delete new rows, columns, and ranges of cells

❶ Click anywhere in the row or column, or select a range of cells.

❷ Choose the Table command.

❸ Select the Row or Column option, and click the Insert button or the Delete button.

Word inserts new rows above, and new columns to the right of, the cell containing the insertion point. If you select an entire row or column before choosing the Table command, Word preselects the appropriate option for you. If you select a range of cells, Word preselects the Selection option in the Table dialog box and activates the Shift Cells group.

Inserting a new row at the end of a table

❶ Click in the rightmost cell of the bottom row.

❷ Press the Tab key.

Insert a normal paragraph above a row

❶ Place the insertion point in any cell of the row below which you want the normal paragraph.

❷ Press Option-Command-Spacebar.

Insert a column beyond the rightmost column

❶ Place the insertion point before the end-of-row marker at the end of any row. (Turn Show ¶ on first to see the end-of-row markers and the cell boundaries.)

❷ Choose the Table command.

❸ Select the Column option.

❹ Click the Insert button.

Merge cells

❶ Select the range of cells you want to merge.

❷ Choose the Table command.

❸ Click the Merge Cells button.

Split cells

❶ Select a cell that has been previously merged.

❷ Choose the Table command. The Merge Cells button changes into the Split Cell button.

❸ Click the Split Cell button.

Ruler Formatting

❶ Choose Show Ruler from the Format menu. Click the scale icon at the right end of the Ruler's icon bar until the Table scale appears. A **T** symbol marks each column boundary, and a triangle marks the selected row's left indent. (Tables don't have first-line indents.)

❷ Select the rows you want to change.

❸ Drag the left indent marker to a new position to change the indention of the selected rows. Drag a column marker to change the position of the right edge of the cells in that column. The markers to the right of the dragged marker move with it. To prevent this, press the Shift key before you drag the marker.

The Cells Dialog Box

Item	Action
Width of Column field	Sets the distance between cell boundaries for the columns within the selected range. The name of the field reflects the range of columns selected.
Space Between Columns field	Adds half of the space specified to the left edge and half to the right edge of every cell in the selected rows, even if one cell in each row is selected.
Indent Rows field	Sets the left indent of the selected rows.
Minimum Row Height field	Enter *Auto* if you want Word to adjust the height of rows to the cell having the "tallest" material. Enter a value to set the minimum row height. Precede the value with a minus sign to set the maximum row height.
Align Rows option group	Sets alignment relative to the left and right indents; for single-column text, the indents usually correspond to the left and right margins.
Apply To option group	Click the Selection option to apply the specified formats only to the currently selected cell range. Click the Whole Table option to apply formats to the entire table.
Borders Button	Click to bring up the Cell Borders dialog box.
Prev. Column	Moves the selection to the preceding column. Use this button with the Apply button.
Next Column	Moves the selection to the next column. Use this button with the Apply button.
OK button	Click to add the specified cell table formats.
Cancel	Click to dismiss the dialog box without adding the specified formats.
Apply	Click to add formats without dismissing the dialog box.

The Cell Borders Dialog Box

Item	Action
Apply To	Click the Selected Cells As Block option to apply border formats to the entire range as one object. Click the Every Cell in Selection option to apply borders individually to each cell in the selected range.
Line type group	Select a line type, and then click on the boundary in the schematic to have that border.

Renumbering and Sorting Tables and Lists

Number a list by using the Line Numbering format

❶ Be sure each item in the list consists of only one line of text.

❷ Place the list in its own section.

❸ Set the insertion point in the section.

❹ Choose the Section command.

❺ Turn on the Line Numbering option, and then click OK.

The line numbers do not appear until you preview or print the document.

Number a list by using the Renumber command

❶ Select the list to be numbered.

❷ Choose the Renumber command.

❸ Set the appropriate options in the dialog box that appears, and then click OK.

Word inserts the number before the first character in each paragraph and renumbers only those paragraphs containing text. If you try to renumber a single column in a cell table, Word renumbers every non-empty cell in each row that contains a selected cell.

Sort a list

❶ Select the list.

❷ Choose the Sort command to sort in ascending order, or press the Shift key and then choose the Sort Descending command to sort in descending order.

Sort a table based on any column

❶ Select the column that is to determine the sequence of the table. (Press the Option key as you drag within a tabbed table.)

❷ Choose the Sort command.

Word sorts entire lines of normal text and rows of cell tables, not only those in the selected column. To sort in descending order, press the Shift key as you choose the Sort command.

Perform calculations on selected numbers

❶ Enter math operators before each of the numbers in the calculation. The available operators are +, – (or parentheses), *, and /. For percentages, enter a percent sign (%) after the number. If you omit the operators, addition is assumed.

❷ Format the operators as hidden text if you don't want them printed. They must appear on the screen when you do the calculation.

❸ Select the numbers for the calculation. Any text or symbols included in the selection will be ignored.

❹ Choose Calculate from the Document menu.

Word places the result in the Clipboard and displays it in the status box.

■ *Commands*

Command name	Meaning, menu	Standard keyboard	Keypad	Extended keyboard
Calculate	Computes numerical expression in the selection and places result on the Clipboard.			
	Utilities	⌘=		
Cell Border:	Applies specified type of border to selected cells of a table.			
Cell Borders…	Applies and removes cell borders in a table.			
Cells…	Changes appearance of cells within a table.			
	Format			
Change Ruler Scale	Cycles among the three ruler scales: Normal, Page, and Table.			
Delete Cells, Shift Left	Deletes selected cells. Cells to the right of deleted cells are shifted left.			
Delete Cells, Shift Up	Deletes selected cells. Cells below deleted cells are shifted up.			
Delete Columns	Deletes selected columns of a table or the column containing insertion point.			
Delete Rows	Deletes selected rows of a table or the row containing insertion point.			
Hide Ruler	Toggles display of the Ruler. If the Ruler isn't visible, the command reads *Show Ruler* and appears in the list box after Show Menu Function Keys.			
		⌘R		
Insert Cells Down	Inserts empty cells above selected cells. Number of cells inserted is equal to the number of selected cells. Selected cells are shifted down.			
Insert Cells Right	Inserts empty cells to the left of selected cells. Number of cells inserted is equal to the number of selected cells. Selected cells are shifted right.			
Insert Columns	Inserts empty column(s) in a table to left of column containing insertion point or to left of selected columns.			
Insert Rows	Inserts empty rows in a table above row containing insertion point or above selected rows.			

(continued)

Command name	Meaning, menu	Standard keyboard	Keypad	Extended keyboard
Insert Tab	Inserts tab character, displayed as ➧ when Show ¶ is on.			
		⇥ or ⌥⇥		
Insert Table…	Inserts a table having specified number of rows and columns at insertion point.			
	Document			
Insert ¶ Above Row	Inserts a paragraph mark having *Normal* style above table row containing insertion point.			
		⌘⌥␣		
Merge Cells	Combines selected cells in a row into one cell.			
Move Down One Text Area	Moves insertion point to text area below text area containing insertion point (in Page View) or to cell below cell containing insertion point (within a table).			
			⌘⌥⌨2	
Move Left One Text Area	Moves insertion point to text area left of text area containing insertion point (in Page View) or to cell at left of cell containing insertion point (within a table).			
			⌘⌥⌨4	
Move Right One Text Area	Moves insertion point to text area right of text area containing insertion point (in Page View) or to cell at right of cell containing insertion point (within a table).			
			⌘⌥⌨6	
Move to First Text Area	Moves insertion point to first text area visible in window (in Page View) or to first cell visible in window (within a table).			
			⌘⌥⌨7	
Move to Last Text Area	Moves insertion point to last text area visible in window (in Page View) or to last cell visible in window (within a table).			
			⌘⌥⌨1	
Move to Next Cell	Moves insertion point to next cell (to right).			
Move to Next Text Area	Moves insertion point to next text area at right (in Page View) or to next cell (within a table).			
			⌘⌥⌨3	
Move to Previous Cell	Moves insertion point to preceding cell (to left).			
		⇧⇥		
Move Up One Text Area	Moves insertion point to text area above text area containing insertion point (in Page View) or to cell above cell containing insertion point (within a table).			
			⌘⌥⌨8	
Paste Cells	Inserts contents of cells on Clipboard into an equal number of table cells.			

(continued)

Command name	Meaning, menu	Standard keyboard	Keypad	Extended keyboard
Renumber…	Numbers or renumbers selected paragraphs in specified sequence.			
	Utilities			**⌘F15**
Show Ruler	Toggles display of ruler at top of document, footnote, or header/footer window.			
	Format	**⌘R**		
Show Table Gridlines	Toggles display of nonprinting gridlines in a table.			
Sort	Sorts entire document or selected paragraphs, columns, or lines in ascending order (A–Z or 1–9) according to leftmost character.			
	Utilities			
Sort Descending	Sorts entire document or selected paragraphs, columns, or lines in descending order (Z–A or 9–1) according to leftmost character.			
Split Cell	Splits a merged cell into separate cells.			
Table to Text…	Converts a table created with Insert Table command to text separated by paragraph marks, tabs, or commas.			
Table…	Adds and deletes rows, columns, and cells in a table and merges and splits cells.			
	Edit			

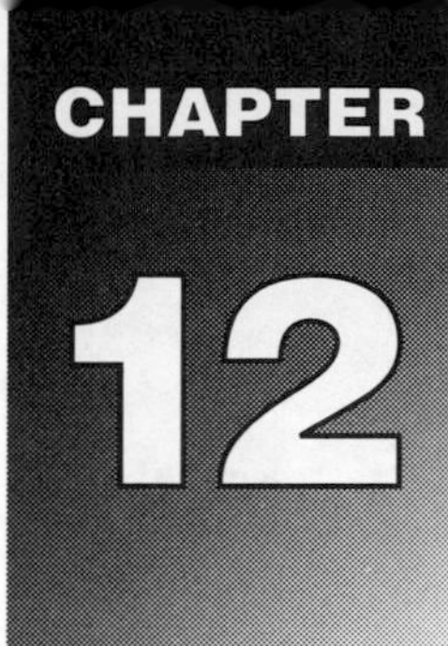

Section Formatting

So far, you've learned about two of the four format domains in Word: the character and paragraph domains. This chapter describes a third: the section domain. Sections are one of the least intuitive features of Word. A section can be as short as a single line or as long as your entire document. You decide where a section begins and ends. If you don't define sections, Word treats the entire document as one section. The flexibility that this feature affords you will become more apparent as you continue reading.

It helps to think of a section as a document within a document. A chapter in a book is a good example of a section, as is an article in a magazine or newsletter. Word lets you handle each section as a separate entity. Within each section you can control the following:

- The format and position of the page number on each page.
- The position and content of headers and footers.
- The location of footnotes.
- Line numbering.
- The number of columns and the spacing between them.
- Whether the section starts on the same page, in a new column, or on a new page.

■ *Dividing a Document into Sections*

Just as indents and tab settings affect an entire paragraph, section formats apply to a section—normally the entire document. If you divide a document into more than one section, you can reset these formats within each one. For example, you can change the headers in each section so that the title of the section appears at the top of each page. To create a new section, set the insertion point where you want the new section to start, and then press the Command and Enter keys simultaneously.

A double dotted line appears (see Figure 12-1), marking the division between the two sections. The status box in the lower left corner of the document window displays both the page number and the section number if the document contains more than one section. This is important when you are altering section formats because the insertion point must be inside the section you want to format. Note, however, that the status box displays the page number and section number of the topmost line in the window, not the section containing the insertion point. Newly created sections take on the section formats of the preceding section.

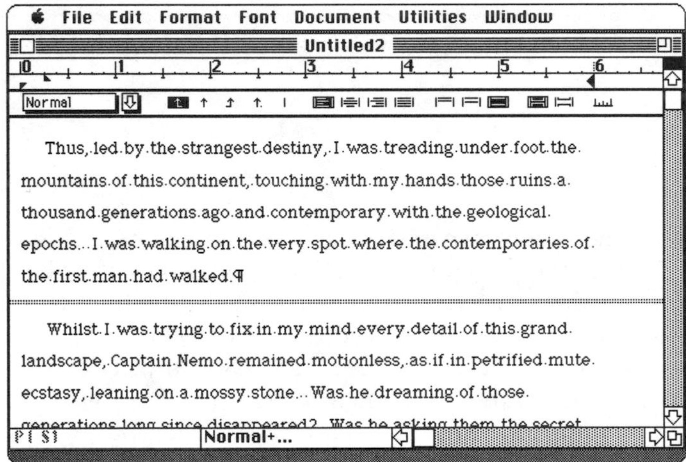

Figure 12-1
A section mark.

To apply section formats, you use the Section command, after first selecting the section mark at the end of the section, selecting any text within the section, or simply setting the insertion point anywhere in the section.

Choosing the Section command brings up the dialog box shown in Figure 12-2. The options in the box are divided into seven groups: Start, Page Number, Columns, Include Endnotes, Line Numbers, Header/Footer, and the standard buttons. You can use the Section command even if you are working with a one-section document.

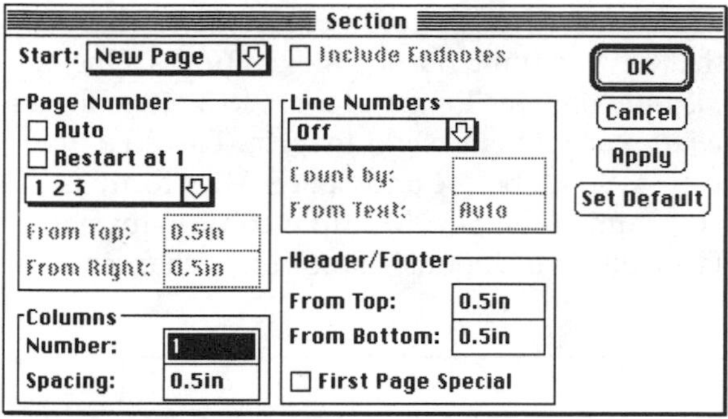

Figure 12-2
The Section dialog box.

To remove a section mark, click in the selection bar next to the mark and press the Backspace key. Just as the paragraph mark can be thought of as holding the paragraph formats of the preceding paragraph, the section mark holds the section formats of the preceding section. When you delete a section mark, the section formatting for the section that preceded the mark is replaced by the section formatting for the section that fell after the mark.

Let's take a tour of the section formats. As you read this chapter, refer to the multiple-column newsletter described in Chapter 18, "Blueprints."

TIP

Working with Section Marks
You can transfer section marks in many of the same ways that you can transfer paragraph marks. To promote the consistency of section formats within and between documents, you can select and cut or copy a section mark and paste it into another place in the document or into another document. You can even establish a range of specially formatted section marks in the glossary or archive them in your style template documents.

■ *The Start Options*

The Start options in the Section dialog box define how Word begins a new section. Normally, the New Page option is set, meaning that Word starts the section at the top of the next page. You can change this by selecting from the drop-down list one of the following options.

No Break

The No Break option starts the section without beginning a new page; the new section begins on the page on which the preceding section ended. A primary use for this option is to vary the number of columns within a page. Look at the section layout from the newsletter in Figure 12-3. This page contains three sections that have varying numbers of columns. One of the sections, the article's title, is only one line long and is set to a one-column format that stretches from the left margin to the right margin. To add a little space around the article's title area, Space Before and Space After formats were added to the paragraph containing the title. Multiple-column formatting is discussed further in "The Columns Options" later in this chapter and again in Chapter 18.

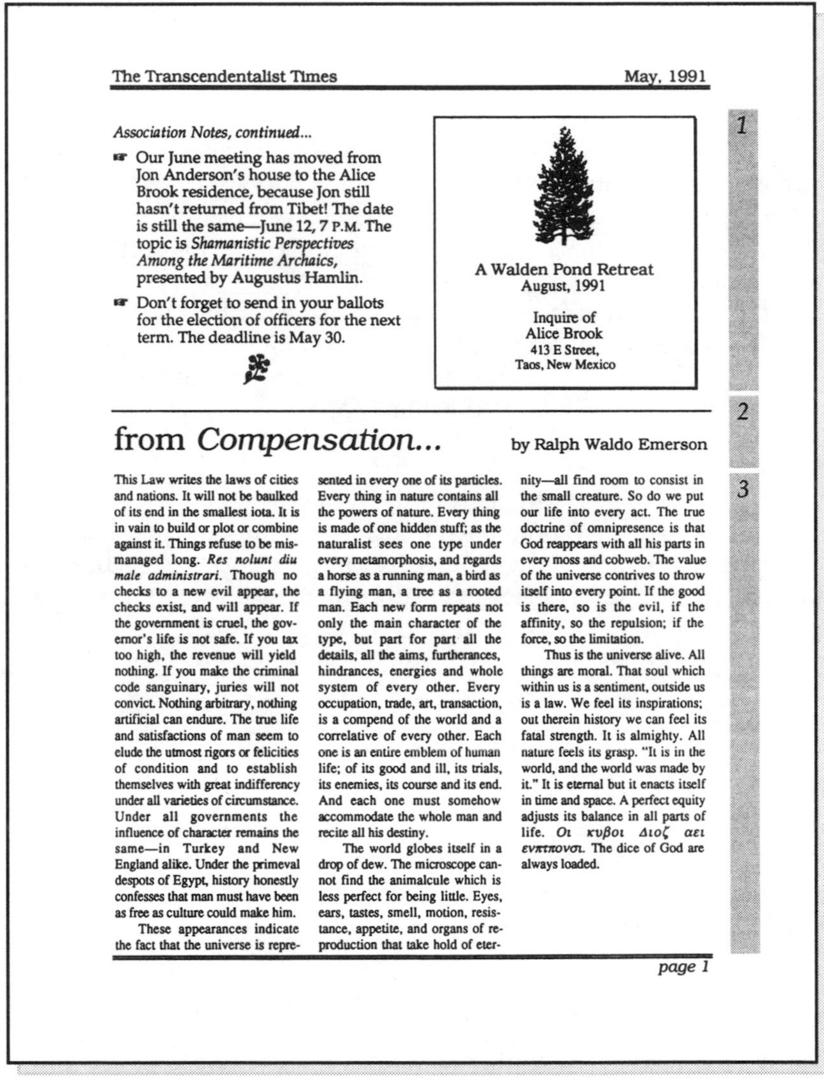

The Transcendentalist Times May, 1991

Association Notes, continued...

- Our June meeting has moved from Jon Anderson's house to the Alice Brook residence, because Jon still hasn't returned from Tibet! The date is still the same—June 12, 7 P.M. The topic is *Shamanistic Perspectives Among the Maritime Archaics*, presented by Augustus Hamlin.
- Don't forget to send in your ballots for the election of officers for the next term. The deadline is May 30.

A Walden Pond Retreat
August, 1991

Inquire of
Alice Brook
413 E Street,
Taos, New Mexico

1

2

3

from *Compensation...* by Ralph Waldo Emerson

This Law writes the laws of cities and nations. It will not be baulked of its end in the smallest iota. It is in vain to build or plot or combine against it. Things refuse to be mismanaged long. *Res nolunt diu male administrari*. Though no checks to a new evil appear, the checks exist, and will appear. If the government is cruel, the governor's life is not safe. If you tax too high, the revenue will yield nothing. If you make the criminal code sanguinary, juries will not convict. Nothing arbitrary, nothing artificial can endure. The true life and satisfactions of man seem to elude the utmost rigors or felicities of condition and to establish themselves with great indifferency under all varieties of circumstance. Under all governments the influence of character remains the same—in Turkey and New England alike. Under the primeval despots of Egypt, history honestly confesses that man must have been as free as culture could make him.

These appearances indicate the fact that the universe is represented in every one of its particles. Every thing in nature contains all the powers of nature. Every thing is made of one hidden stuff; as the naturalist sees one type under every metamorphosis, and regards a horse as a running man, a bird as a flying man, a tree as a rooted man. Each new form repeats not only the main character of the type, but part for part all the details, all the aims, furtherances, hindrances, energies and whole system of every other. Every occupation, trade, art, transaction, is a compend of the world and a correlative of every other. Each one is an entire emblem of human life; of its good and ill, its trials, its enemies, its course and its end. And each one must somehow accommodate the whole man and recite all his destiny.

The world globes itself in a drop of dew. The microscope cannot find the animalcule which is less perfect for being little. Eyes, ears, tastes, smell, motion, resistance, appetite, and organs of reproduction that take hold of eternity—all find room to consist in the small creature. So do we put our life into every act. The true doctrine of omnipresence is that God reappears with all his parts in every moss and cobweb. The value of the universe contrives to throw itself into every point. If the good is there, so is the evil, if the affinity, so the repulsion; if the force, so the limitation.

Thus is the universe alive. All things are moral. That soul which within us is a sentiment, outside us is a law. We feel its inspirations; out therein history we can feel its fatal strength. It is almighty. All nature feels its grasp. "It is in the world, and the world was made by it." It is eternal but it enacts itself in time and space. A perfect equity adjusts its balance in all parts of life. *Οι κυβοι Διοζ αει ενπτπονσι*. The dice of God are always loaded.

page 1

Figure 12-3
The No Break option used to start a new section on the same page.

The header or footer for a section is taken from the section that appears at the top of the page. If a section starts somewhere in the middle of a page and continues on to the top of the next page, its header or footer (if any) begins at the top of the next page. In fact, any section format you set in a section in which the No Break option is set (except for multiple columns and numbered lines) does not take effect until the following page. If a section doesn't start at the top of a page and doesn't continue on to the next, its header or footer is not printed at all.

New Column

The New Column option causes Word to start the new section at the top of a new column. This option works only in multiple-column documents if the preceding section has the same number of columns as the section having this format. Otherwise, sections with this format start at the top of the next page.

Even Page and Odd Page

The Even Page and Odd Page options are like Word's default New Page format, except that the section starts at the top of the next even-numbered or odd-numbered page. For example, if you set the Odd Page format for a section and the preceding section ends on an odd-numbered page, Word leaves the next even page blank and starts the new section at the top of the next odd page.

■ *The Page Number Options*

When you add page numbers to a document, you don't see them until you enter Print Preview mode or print the document. You can number the pages in a document in one of three ways:

- ❏ By inserting the page number into a header or footer. (This is discussed in Chapter 13, "Headers, Footers, and Footnotes.")
- ❏ By dragging the page number to the desired position on the page in Print Preview. (This is described in Chapter 14, "Document Formatting and Printing.")
- ❏ By specifying the page number location and format in the Section dialog box.

The page-numbering features in Print Preview and the Section command are linked; changes you make in one affect the other. Headers and footers have their own page-numbering method, as you will see in the next chapter, although you can alter the characteristics of page numbers through the Section dialog box. To avoid duplicate page numbers, choose one method.

The Page Number options in the Section dialog box let you:

- Turn page numbering on and off.
- Force page numbering to restart at 1 at the beginning of the section.
- Specify the numbering method: Arabic numerals (the default option), Roman numerals, or letters starting at A. Roman numerals and letters can be either uppercase or lowercase.
- Set the exact location of the page number on the page.

To set the page number for a section, do the following:

1. Select the section, if your document has more than one, and choose the Section command.
2. Click the Auto check box. Word activates the From Top and From Right edit fields.
3. If you want numbering to restart at 1 at the beginning of this section, click the Restart at 1 check box.

You can override the page numbering for the first section of a document with the Number Pages From field in the Document dialog box. This field allows you to start the first page of a document with a number other than 1, and it affects only the first section in the document. If the Restart At 1 option is turned on in subsequent sections, their page numbers begin with 1.

You might wonder why only the edit fields become activated when you click the Auto check box, whereas the Restart At 1 and number format options are always active. This happens because these options also set the numbering format for the page numbers that are inserted into headers and footers when you click the Page Number icon in a Header or Footer window.

4. Select the type of numbering you want; Figure 12-4 shows some examples. The default format is Arabic numerals. The front matter in a book, such as the preface, often uses lowercase Roman numerals. When you specify one of the letter options, Word numbers pages 1 through 26 as A through Z and then restarts on page 27 with AA, AB, AC, and so on.
5. Enter the position of the page number on the page in the From Top and From Right edit fields. The position (in inches, centimeters, or points) is measured from the top and right edges of the paper, not from the margins set in the Document dialog box. If you set the Mirror Even/Odd Margins option in the Document dialog box, Word orients the page-number placement from the upper left of left-hand (even-numbered) pages and from the upper right of right-hand (odd-numbered) pages. The Mirror Even/Odd Margins option is discussed in Chapter 14, "Document Formatting and Printing."

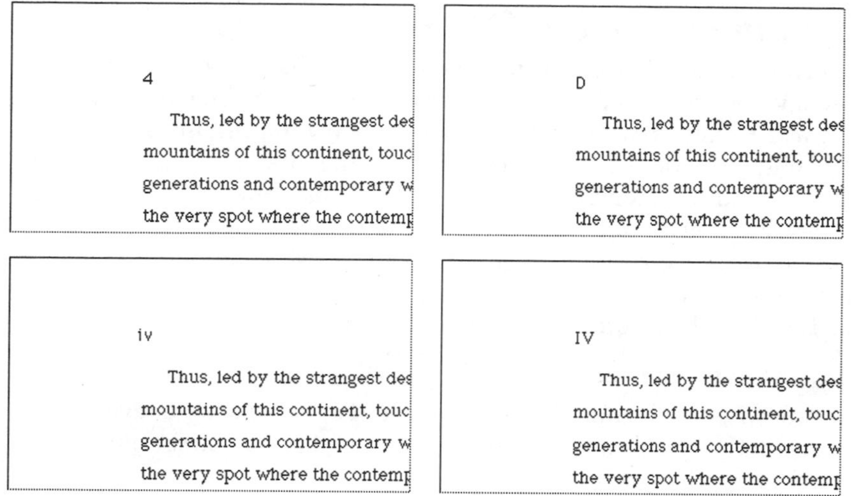

Figure 12-4
Page-numbering examples.

The Section page-numbering feature places only a number on the page. You cannot include any other characters with the number, such as hyphens on either side or the word *Page*. If you want to print additional characters with the page number, use headers or footers instead.

When placing the page number, be careful not to put it in the middle of text such as a header, footer, or the body of the document. Use Print Preview to check the position of the page numbers before printing the document. The default position of 0.5 inch from the top and right edges of the paper will usually not interfere with the rest of the document. If you have trouble getting it right, use Print Preview to position the number, as described in Chapter 14, "Document Formatting and Printing."

When you specify page numbers with the Section command, Word adds the automatic style named *page number* to the style sheet. You can set character formats for the page numbers by redefining this style, but Word ignores any paragraph formats you set. Even though the *page number* style pertains to all page numbers in the document, you can change the type of numbers used from section to section. You can also use the Restart At 1 and numbering options to change the page numbering in the header or footer.

Finally, suppose you've set the Page Numbering section format for a section, but later you decide you want to add a page number to a header or footer in that section instead. You only have to click the Page Number icon in the header or footer; when you close the window, Word removes the Page Numbering section format for you.

■ *The Line Numbers Options*

Many documents, such as legal briefs and contracts, have numbered lines. You can have Word insert line numbers at the left margin. The numbers do not appear in Galley view, but they show up when you print the document or audition it with Print Preview. You can't edit the numbers or delete them individually, and they don't apply to side-by-side paragraphs or in headers and footers, but you can redefine their automatic style, called *line number,* if you want to. As it does with the *page number* automatic style, Word ignores any paragraph formats you set for this style.

The Line Numbers options let you do the following:

- ❑ Turn line numbering on and off for the section.
- ❑ Indicate whether the numbers should restart at 1 at the top of every page or at the beginning of the section, or whether the numbering should be continuous.
- ❑ Number every line, or number lines at any interval you specify. Counting by 5, for example, numbers every fifth line.
- ❑ Indicate how far from the left margin of the text the rightmost digit of the line number is to be positioned.

To specify line numbering in a section, do the following:

❶ Select the section, if your document has more than one, and choose the Section command.

❷ Select the Line Numbering option: By Page if you want the numbers to restart at 1 at the top of each page, By Section if the numbers are to restart at the beginning of the section, and Continuous if the numbering is to continue across sections. Word activates the remaining options in the group.

❹ If you want to number lines at an interval other than 1, enter the desired interval number in the Count By field. Word counts an empty paragraph as a line but does not consider space added with the Space Before or Space After paragraph formats as lines.

❺ Position the line numbers relative to the left margin by entering a measurement in the From Text field (or use the Auto setting to specify a position of 0.25 inch for a single-column section format and 0.125 inch for multiple columns).

As was mentioned in Chapter 9, "Paragraph Formatting," when you turn on line numbering in a section, Word activates and sets the Line Numbering option in the Paragraph dialog box. You can specify that the lines in a paragraph not be numbered by selecting the paragraph, choosing the Paragraph command, and clicking the Line Numbering option.

■ The Header/Footer Options

The options in the Header/Footer group let you indicate the vertical position of the header and footer and let you instruct Word to use a different header for the first page of the section. To specify a position for the header, enter a position in the From Top field. The measurement is from the top edge of the paper. To specify a position for the footer, enter a position in the From Bottom field. That measurement is from the bottom edge of the paper. The horizontal position of the headers and footers is determined by the margins and by any indents you set in the Header and Footer windows.

Clicking the First Page Special check box creates a new header and footer for the first page of the section only, as illustrated in Print Preview in Figure 12-5. When you turn on this option, Word adds additional commands to the Document menu for the first-page header and footer, but only in Galley View: If Word is in Page View, the Open Header and Close Header commands refer only to the current page. You can leave the first-page header and footer empty for a title page, use the option to place a logo or return address on the first page of correspondence, or assign a different header or footer for the beginning of each chapter in a novel.

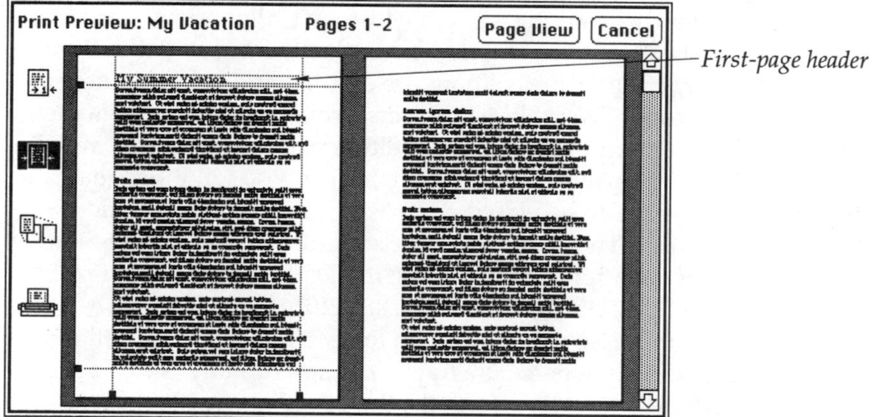

Figure 12-5
A first-page header.

If you want different headers for odd and even pages, you must set the Even/Odd Headers option in the Document dialog box. When you do this, you'll see a set of Open Header and Open Footer commands for both odd and even pages—but again, only in Galley View: In Page View you'll see only the Open Header and Close Header commands, which apply only to the current page. For more information on this and other aspects of using headers and footers, see Chapter 13, "Headers, Footers, and Footnotes."

■ *The Include Endnotes Option*

There is only one Footnotes option among the section formats: Include Endnotes. The option is active only if you have selected the End of Section option from the drop-down list in the Footnotes group of the Document dialog box. If you select the Include Endnotes option, Word places at the end of the section any footnotes that have accumulated.

If you don't want footnotes printed at the end of the section, turn off the Include Endnotes option. Word then collects the footnotes and prints them at the end of the next section in which the Include Endnotes option is set. If this option is turned off in every section, Word places the footnotes at the end of the document. See Chapter 13, "Headers, Footers, and Footnotes," for details on how to create footnotes.

■ *The Columns Options*

Word makes it easy to create multiple-column documents. You enter the number of columns you want in the Number field and the spacing between columns you want in the Spacing field (in inches, centimeters, or points). Word then calculates the resulting column width. In Galley View, text appears as one long column, but when you examine the document in Page View or Print Preview mode, the columns are divided and arranged next to one another on the page. The multiple-column format is different from the older Side-by-Side paragraph format, the Position paragraph format, and the Table format. When you use the Side-by-Side format, you tell Word that you want selected paragraphs to be placed next to one another in a specific horizontal arrangement. The Position format is similar to the Side-by-Side format but is broader in application. You use the Table format when text in your document needs a rectangular, gridlike structure.

When you set a multiple-column section format, however, you tell Word that you don't care exactly where paragraphs fall horizontally on the page, only that you want the text to flow from the bottom of one column to the top of the next. This type of format is illustrated in Figure 12-6, in which you can see three sections. In each section, the No Break format has been set and the Space Before and Space After paragraph formats have been changed to add space between the sections. The middle section on the page contains one entire three-column section, and the text flows from the bottom of one column to the top of the next within that section. Multiple-column formats are particularly useful for newsletters and magazines.

When you create a multiple-column section succeeded by a section having the No Break format, Word adjusts the lengths of the columns until they are approximately equal. This operation is called *column balancing*. If the text in a multiple-column section runs over to the next page, it flows from the end of the last column on the page to the top of the first column on the next page, and Word balances the text on that page as well. However, the columns at the end of the document are not balanced. If you want the text on the last page of a multiple-column document to be split evenly among the columns, insert one more section mark at the end of the document and set the No Break option for it.

For more information on how to format a two-column document, refer to the multiple-column newsletter project in Chapter 18, "Blueprints."

1

from *Compensation...*

by Ralph Waldo Emerson

2

This Law writes the laws of cities and nations. It will not be baulked of its end in the smallest iota. It is in vain to build or plot or combine against it. Things refuse to be mismanaged long. *Res nolunt diu male administrari.* Though no checks to a new evil appear, the checks exist, and will appear. If the government is cruel, the governor's life is not safe. If you tax too high, the revenue will yield nothing. If you make the criminal code sanguinary, juries will not convict. Nothing arbitrary, nothing artificial can endure. The true life and satisfactions of man seem to elude the utmost rigors or felicities of condition and to establish themselves with great indifferency under all varieties of circumstance. Under all governments the influence of character remains the same—in Turkey and New England alike. Under the primeval despots of Egypt, history honestly confesses that man must have been as free as culture could make him.

These appearances indicate the fact that the universe is represented in every one of its particles. Every thing in nature contains all the powers of nature. Every thing is made of one hidden stuff; as the naturalist sees one type under every metamorphosis, and regards a horse as a running man, a bird as a flying man, a tree as a rooted man. Each new form repeats not only the main character of the type, but part for part all the details, all the aims, furtherances, hindrances, energies and whole system of every other. Every occupation, trade, art, transaction, is a compend of the world and a correlative of every other. Each one is an entire emblem of human life; of its good and ill, its trials, its enemies, its course and its end. And each one must somehow accommodate the whole man and recite all his destiny.

The world globes itself in a drop of dew. The microscope cannot find the animalcule which is less perfect for being little. Eyes, ears, tastes, smell, motion, resistance, appetite, and organs of reproduction that take hold of eternity—all find room to consist in the small creature. So do we put our life into every act. The true doctrine of omnipresence is that God reappears with all his parts in every moss and cobweb. The value of the universe contrives to throw itself into every point. If the good is there, so is the evil, if the affinity, so the repulsion; if the force, so the limitation.

Thus is the universe alive. All things are moral. That soul which within us is a sentiment, outside us is a law. We feel its inspirations; out therein history we can feel its fatal strength. It is almighty. All nature feels its grasp. "It is in the world, and the world was made by it." It is eternal but it enacts itself in time and space. A perfect equity adjusts its balance in all parts of life. *Οι κυβοι Διοζ αει ενπτπονσι.* The dice of God are always loaded.

Figure 12-6
Using the No Break section format to change the number of columns within a page.

TIP

Starting Articles in a Newsletter

A common requirement for newsletters and similarly structured documents is the balancing of the columns on a page within both the ending of one article and the beginning of the next. For instance, if you set a two-column format for both articles and set the No Break format for both, you might see something like Figure 12-7. Notice that, in the absence of line spacing, Space Before, or Space After formats, the two sections run into one another.

Prudence, *continued from page 13*

There are all degrees of proficiency in knowledge of the world. It is sufficient to our present purpose to indicate three. One class lives to the utility of the symbol, esteeming health and wealth a final good. Another class live above this mark to the beauty of the symbol, as the poet and artist and the naturalist and man of science. A third class live above the beauty of the symbol to the beauty of the thing

from *Compensation...*

by Ralph Waldo Emerson

This Law writes the laws of cities and nations. It will not be baulked of its end in the smallest iota. It is in vain to build or plot or combine against it. Things refuse to be mismanaged long. *Res nolunt diu male administrari.* Though no checks to a new evil appear, the checks exist, and will appear. If the government is cruel, the governor's life is not safe. If you tax too high, the revenue will yield nothing. If you make the criminal code sanguinary, juries will not convict. Nothing arbitrary, nothing artificial can endure. The true life and satisfactions of man seem to elude the utmost rigors or felicities of condition and to establish themselves with great indifferency under all varieties of circumstance. Under all governments the influence of character remains the same—in Turkey and New England alike. Under the primeval despots of Egypt, history honestly confesses that man must have been as free as culture could make him.

These appearances indicate the fact that the universe is represented in every one of its particles. Every thing in nature contains all the powers of nature. Every thing is made of one hidden stuff; as the naturalist sees one type under every metamorphosis, and regards a horse as a running man, a bird as a flying man, a tree as a rooted man. Each new form repeats not only the main character of the type, but part for part all the details, all the aims, furtherances, hindrances, energies and whole system of every other. Every occupation, trade, art, transaction, is a compend of the world and a correlative of

signified; these are wise men. The first class have common sense; the second, taste; and the third, spiritual perception. Once in a long time, a man traverses the whole scale, and sees and enjoys the symbol solidly, then also has a clear eye for the beauty, and lastly, whilst he pitches his tent on this sacred volcanic isle of nature, does not offer to build houses and barns thereon, reverencing the splendor of the God which he sees bursting through each chink and cranny. 1

every other. Each one is an entire emblem of human life; of its good and ill, its trials, its enemies, its course and its end. And each one must somehow accommodate the whole man and recite all his destiny. 2

The world globes itself in a drop of dew. The microscope cannot find the animalcule which is less perfect for being little. Eyes, ears, tastes, smell, motion, resistance, appetite, and organs of reproduction that take hold of eternity—all find room to consist in the small creature. So do we put our life into every act. The true doctrine of omnipresence is that God reappears with all his parts in every moss and cobweb. The value of the universe contrives to throw itself into every point. If the good is there, so is the evil, if the affinity, so the repulsion; if the force, so the limitation.

Thus is the universe alive. All things are moral. That soul which within us is a sentiment, outside us is a law. We feel its inspirations; out therein history we can feel its fatal strength. It is almighty. All nature feels its grasp. "It is in the world, and the world was made by it." It is eternal but it enacts itself in time and space. A perfect equity adjusts its balance in all parts of life. *Οι κυβοι Διοζ αει ενπτπονσι.* The dice of God are always loaded.

Figure 12-7

Adjacent sections in two-column format without extra formatting.

You can achieve a better-looking break between the two sections by inserting between them a one-column section containing only one blank line. You can format this blank line as needed to separate the two sections. Figure 12-8 shows how this might look. To create this special section:

❶ Place the insertion point before the first character in the second section. Press the Return key and then Command-Enter to start a new paragraph and section.

Prudence, *continued from page 13*

There are all degrees of proficiency in knowledge of the world. It is sufficient to our present purpose to indicate three. One class lives to the utility of the symbol, esteeming health and wealth a final good. Another class live above this mark to the beauty of the symbol, as the poet and artist and the naturalist and man of science. A third class live above the beauty of the symbol to the beauty of the thing signified; these are wise men. The first class have common sense; the second, taste; and the third, spiritual perception. Once in a long time, a man traverses the whole scale, and sees and enjoys the symbol solidly, then also has a clear eye for the beauty, and lastly, whilst he pitches his tent on this sacred volcanic isle of nature, does not offer to build houses and barns thereon, reverencing the splendor of the God which he sees bursting through each chink and cranny. 1

2

---

from *Compensation...*

by Ralph Waldo Emerson

This Law writes the laws of cities and nations. It will not be baulked of its end in the smallest iota. It is in vain to build or plot or combine against it. Things refuse to be mismanaged long. *Res nolunt diu male administrari.* Though no checks to a new evil appear, the checks exist, and will appear. If the government is cruel, the governor's life is not safe. If you tax too high, the revenue will yield nothing. If you make the criminal code sanguinary, juries will not convict. Nothing arbitrary, nothing artificial can endure. The true life and satisfactions of man seem to elude the utmost rigors or felicities of condition and to establish themselves with great indifferency under all varieties of circumstance. Under all governments the influence of character remains the same—in Turkey and New England alike. Under the primeval despots of Egypt, history honestly confesses that man must have been as free as culture could make him.

These appearances indicate the fact that the universe is represented in every one of its particles. Every thing in nature contains all the powers of nature. Every thing is made of one hidden stuff; as the naturalist sees one type under every metamorphosis, and regards a horse as a running man, a bird as a flying man, a tree as a rooted man. Each new form repeats not only the main character of the type, but part for part all the details, all the aims, furtherances, hindrances, energies and whole system of every other. Every occupation, trade, art, transaction, is a compend of the world and a correlative of every other. Each one is an entire emblem of human life; of its good and ill, its trials, its enemies, its course and its end. And each one must somehow accommodate the whole man and recite all his destiny. 3

The world globes itself in a drop of dew. The microscope cannot find the animalcule which is less perfect for being little. Eyes, ears, tastes, smell, motion, resistance, appetite, and organs of reproduction that take hold of eternity—all find room to consist in the small creature. So do we put our life into every act. The true doctrine of omnipresence is that God reappears with all his parts in every moss and cobweb. The value of the universe contrives to throw itself into every point. If the good is there, so is the evil, if the affinity, so the repulsion; if the force, so the limitation.

Thus is the universe alive. All things are moral. That soul which within us is a sentiment, outside us is a law. We feel its inspirations; out therein history we can feel its fatal strength. It is almighty. All nature feels its grasp. "It is in the world, and the world was made by it." It is eternal but it enacts itself in time and space. A perfect equity adjusts its balance in all parts of life. *Οι κυβοι Διοζ αει ενπτπονσι.* The dice of God are always loaded.

Figure 12-8
Inserting a one-column section to add space between two multiple-column sections.

❷ Be sure to set the No Break option in all three sections. In the new middle section, set the number of columns to 1.

❸ Click in the single blank line in the new middle section and choose the Paragraph command. Set a double line above the paragraph, and set 18 points Space Before and 6 points Space After.

You can change the spacing formats and use graphics copied from a program such as MacDraw instead of using the boxed paragraph formats.

■ *The Command Buttons*

The Section dialog box has four command buttons: OK, Cancel, Apply, and Set Default. The OK, Cancel, and Apply buttons work as they do in the Character and Paragraph dialog boxes. You click OK to implement the format changes and close the dialog box, Cancel to close the dialog box without implementing the format changes, and Apply to implement the format changes without closing the dialog box.

When you use the Apply button to implement a section format, you can't undo the change by clicking the Cancel button. Should you decide to go back to the old format, reselect the original options and click OK (or choose the Undo Formatting command).

The Set Default button lets you record your new section formats as the defaults. If you always begin a new section on an odd-numbered page (as for chapters in a book, for example), you can save time by turning on the Odd Page option and clicking the Set Default button. Word stores the new choice in the current Word Settings file. This button does not apply the format to the currently selected section.

Points to Remember

- ❏ A section is any block of text that precedes a section mark (a double dotted line). If you don't divide your document into sections, any section formats you specify apply to the entire document.
- ❏ The section format domain controls page numbering, number of columns on the page and spacing between them, whether the section starts a new page or column, the position and content of headers and footers, whether footnotes are printed at the section's end, and line numbering.
- ❏ Section formats are tied to the section mark; deleting the section mark deletes the section formats for that section and merges it with the section that follows.
- ❏ You can select and copy section marks and their formatting in the same way that you select and copy paragraph marks.
- ❏ When you have more than one section in a document, the status box indicates the section number as well as the page number of the top line in the window. Word updates page numbers the next time the document is repaginated.
- ❏ The page numbers controlled by the Section dialog box are separate from any you include in a header or footer. The Restart at 1 and numbering options in the Section dialog box affect both types of page numbers.
- ❏ Page numbers and line numbers do not appear in Document view. You must enter Print Preview or print the document to see them.
- ❏ You can change the character formats of page numbers and line numbers through the automatic styles named *page number* and *line number*. Word adds these styles to the style sheet when you set their options.

Techniques

The Section dialog box

Item	Action
Start drop-down list	Determines where the section begins on the page.
No Break	Begins the section without starting a new page or column.
New Column	Begins the section at the top of the next column. The section must be in a multiple-column format, and the previous section must have the same number of columns as this one; otherwise, the section begins on a new page.

(continued)

Item	Action
New Page	Begins the section at the top of the next page; this is Word's default.
Even Page, Odd Page	Begins the section at the top of the next even-numbered or odd-numbered page, respectively, inserting a blank page if necessary.
Header/Footer option group	Specifies the vertical position of headers and footers within the section and indicates whether to use a first-page header or footer. Enter measurements in inches, centimeters, or points.
From Top	Specifies the distance between the top edge of the paper and the header.
From Bottom	Specifies the distance between the bottom edge of the paper and the footer.
First Page Special	Indicates whether the first page of the section uses a different header and footer.
Page Number option group	Adds page numbers to the section and controls their position and the type of numbering used.
Auto	Turns on page numbering in the section.
Restart at 1	Begins the page numbers for the section at 1.
Numbering drop-down list	Sets the page-numbering format.
1 2 3	Specifies Arabic numerals for the page numbers.
I II III	Specifies uppercase Roman numerals for the page numbers.
i ii iii	Specifies lowercase Roman numerals for the page numbers.
A B C	Specifies uppercase letters for the page numbers. After Z, the pages are numbered AA, AB, AC, and so on.
a b c	Specifies lowercase letters for the page numbers. The sequence is the same as for uppercase letters.
From Top	Specifies the distance between the top edge of the paper and the page number. The default is 0.5 inch.
From Right	Specifies the distance between the right edge of the paper and the page number. If the Facing Pages option is turned on in the Page Setup dialog box, this option specifies the distance from the left edge of the paper for even-numbered pages. The default is 0.5 inch.
Include Endnotes	Prints at the end of the section any footnotes that have accumulated. Active only if the End of Section option in the Footnotes group of the Document dialog box is selected.

(continued)

Item	Action
Include Endnotes, cont.	If Include Endnotes is not set, footnotes are printed at the end of the next section in which it is set or at the end of the document if the option is turned off in all subsequent sections.
Line Numbers option group	Controls line numbering.
Line Numbering drop-down list	Causes line numbers to be printed to the left of the text in the section.
Off	Turns off line numbering.
By Page	Starts the first line number of each page at 1.
By Section	Starts the first line number of the section at 1.
Continuous	Begins numbering lines where the previous section ended.
Count By	Specifies an interval for the line numbers. (To number every fifth line, for example, enter 5.)
From Text	Specifies the distance from the left margin to the line number. When Auto is set, a space of 0.25 inch for single-column text and 0.125 inch for multiple-column text is used.
Columns option group	Controls the number and spacing of columns. Word sets the column width based on the values of these options.
Number	Specifies the number of columns printed across the page.
Spacing	Specifies the space between columns.
Buttons	
OK button	Implements the selected formats and closes the dialog box.
Cancel button	Closes the dialog box without implementing the selected formats.
Apply button	Implements the selected formats without closing the dialog box.
Set Default button	Records the selected formats in the Word Settings file as the new defaults. Does not implement the formats in the current document.

Create a new section

❶ Set the insertion point where you want the new section to begin.

❷ Press Command-Enter.

Assign section formats to a section

❶ Set the insertion point in the section to be affected, or select the section mark.

❷ Choose Section from the Format menu.

❸ Make the desired changes in the section formats.

❹ Click OK to apply the formats and close the dialog box.

Create a multiple-column document

❶ Insert a section mark at each point in your document where you want to change the number of columns, begin a new column, or begin a new page.

❷ Set the insertion point in the first section you want to format.

❸ Choose the Section command.

❹ Specify the number of columns for this section and the spacing between columns in the Columns option group.

❺ Indicate where the section should begin on the page by clicking one of the Section Start options.

❻ Click OK to close the dialog box.

❼ Format the next section, following the same procedure.

❽ Choose Page View or Print Preview to see how the document looks.

■ *Commands*

Command name	Meaning, menu	Standard keyboard	Keypad	Extended keyboard
Alphabetic Page Numbers	Sets uppercase letters A–Z for page numbers of selected section.			
Arabic Page Numbers	Sets Arabic numerals for page numbers of selected section.			
Auto Page Numbering	Toggles automatic page numbering for selected section.			
Columns:	Formats current section with number of text columns you specify.			
First Page Special	Adds Open First Header and Open First Footer commands to Document menu in Galley View so that you can create first-page headers and footers for selected section. Turns off automatic page numbering for first page.			
Insert New Section	Inserts a section break at insertion point.			
		⌘⌤		
Line Numbers By Page	Turns on line numbering for selected section and restarts line numbering at 1 on each page.			
Line Numbers By Section	Turns on line numbering for selected section and restarts line numbering at 1 at beginning of section.			
Line Numbers Continuous	Turns on line numbering for selected section and continues numbering sequence from preceding section.			

(continued)

Command name	Meaning, menu	Standard keyboard	Keypad	Extended keyboard
Lowercase Alphabetic Page Numbers	Sets lowercase letters a–z for page numbers of selected section.			
Lowercase Roman Page Numbers	Sets lowercase Roman numerals for page numbers of selected section.			
No Line Numbers	Turns off line numbering for selected section.			
Restart Page Numbering at 1	Toggles option to start page numbering of selected section from 1.			
Roman Page Numbers	Sets uppercase Roman numerals for page numbers of selected section.			
Section Starts on Even Page	Starts selected section on next even-numbered page.			
Section Starts on New Column	Starts selected section in next text column on same page or, if selected section and preceding sections have different numbers of text columns, on next page.			
Section Starts on New Page	Starts selected section on a new page.			
Section Starts on Odd Page	Starts selected section on next odd-numbered page.			
Section Starts with No Break	Starts selected section on same page as preceding section.			
Section...	Brings up dialog box for changing page layout within the selected section.			
	Format			⌥F14

Headers, Footers, and Footnotes

This chapter provides the information you need to work with three special elements of your document: headers, footers, and footnotes. If you've ever written a research paper, you know what footnotes are, and you might already be familiar with headers and footers if you've worked with other word processors. For the uninitiated, here are some definitions:

- A header is repeating text that appears above the top of the body text on the page. (See Figure 13-1 on the following page.)
- A footer is repeating text that appears below the bottom of the body text on the page.
- A footnote provides more information about one or more statements in the text. Although footnotes can contain parenthetical asides, they usually list sources of information or provide additional comments that support assertions made in the body text. A footnote can appear at the bottom of the page containing its reference, at the end of a section, or at the end of the document.

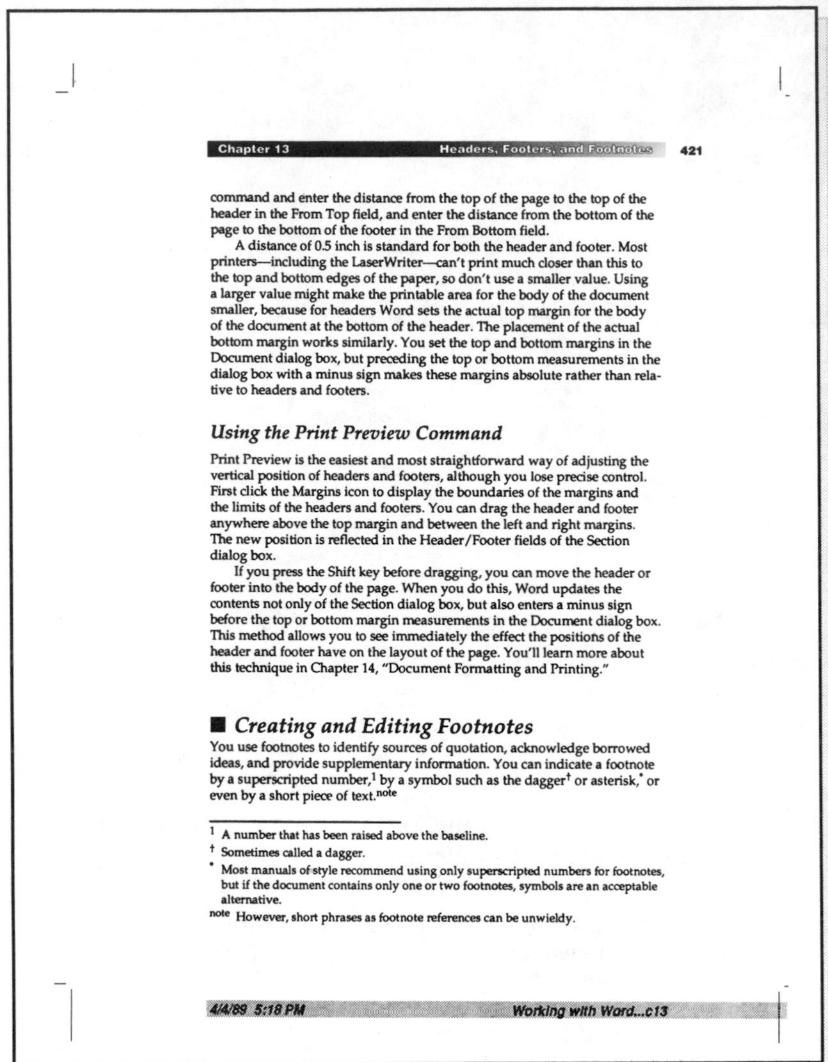

Chapter 13 Headers, Footers, and Footnotes 421

command and enter the distance from the top of the page to the top of the header in the From Top field, and enter the distance from the bottom of the page to the bottom of the footer in the From Bottom field.

A distance of 0.5 inch is standard for both the header and footer. Most printers—including the LaserWriter—can't print much closer than this to the top and bottom edges of the paper, so don't use a smaller value. Using a larger value might make the printable area for the body of the document smaller, because for headers Word sets the actual top margin for the body of the document at the bottom of the header. The placement of the actual bottom margin works similarly. You set the top and bottom margins in the Document dialog box, but preceding the top or bottom measurements in the dialog box with a minus sign makes these margins absolute rather than relative to headers and footers.

Using the Print Preview Command

Print Preview is the easiest and most straightforward way of adjusting the vertical position of headers and footers, although you lose precise control. First click the Margins icon to display the boundaries of the margins and the limits of the headers and footers. You can drag the header and footer anywhere above the top margin and between the left and right margins. The new position is reflected in the Header/Footer fields of the Section dialog box.

If you press the Shift key before dragging, you can move the header or footer into the body of the page. When you do this, Word updates the contents not only of the Section dialog box, but also enters a minus sign before the top or bottom margin measurements in the Document dialog box. This method allows you to see immediately the effect the positions of the header and footer have on the layout of the page. You'll learn more about this technique in Chapter 14, "Document Formatting and Printing."

■ *Creating and Editing Footnotes*

You use footnotes to identify sources of quotation, acknowledge borrowed ideas, and provide supplementary information. You can indicate a footnote by a superscripted number,[1] by a symbol such as the dagger[†] or asterisk,[*] or even by a short piece of text.[note]

[1] A number that has been raised above the baseline.

[†] Sometimes called a dagger.

[*] Most manuals of style recommend using only superscripted numbers for footnotes, but if the document contains only one or two footnotes, symbols are an acceptable alternative.

[note] However, short phrases as footnote references can be unwieldy.

4/4/89 5:18 PM Working with Word...c13

Figure 13-1
A page with a header, footer, and footnotes.

Headers and footers can be used in almost any document, even a letter. They can contain page numbers, the title of the document or chapter, and the current time and date, among other information. Once you've defined a header or footer for a section, Word applies it to all subsequent sections of the document until you change or delete it for a section.

Footnotes are generally used in academic and technical papers, journals, and books. They are rarely used in letters, casual business reports, and general-interest magazine articles.

■ *Creating a Standard Header or Footer*

Although headers and footers are independent entities, virtually no difference arises in the procedure you use to create either one. For the sake of simplicity, this section discusses headers only, but you use the same techniques to create and work with footers.

Think of a header that appears on every page of the document as a standard header, to distinguish it from the more specialized headers that you can define for the first page of the document, for odd pages only, and for even pages only. To create a standard header in Galley View for a document composed of one section, do the following:

1. Choose Open Header from the Document menu. (If you want to create a footer, choose the Open Footer command instead.) The Header window appears across the lower half of the window. (See Figure 13-2.)
2. Type some text, such as the title of the document, into the Header window. This window works like the main document window; Word wraps to the next line text you type that extends beyond the right indent.
3. Choose Show Ruler from the Format menu. Note that the tab stops for the Header window are not the same as the ones in the preset *Normal* style in the document window. The *Normal* style uses only the default tabs, but two tab stops are set in the Header window. The reason for this is that the text in the Header window defaults to the automatic style named *header*. This style contains two tab stops: a centered stop in the middle of the header area and a flush-right stop near the right indent. These tabs make it easy to position text in the header.
4. When you are finished typing the header, click the close box of the Header window.

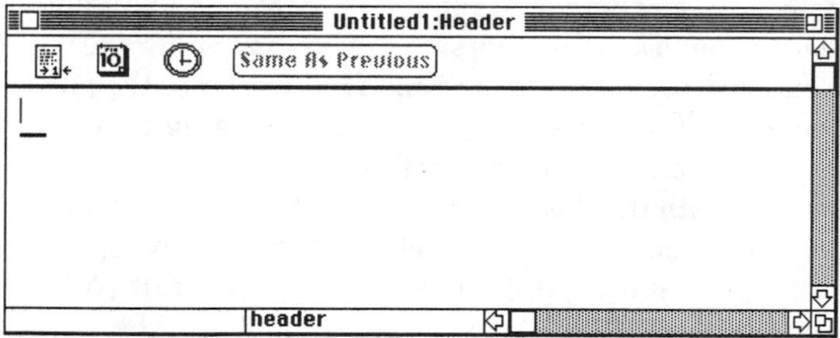

Figure 13-2
The Header window.

You can move the Header window by dragging it by the title bar, and you can resize it by dragging the size box, located in the lower right corner of the window. To quickly enlarge or reduce the window, click in the zoom box in the upper right corner, or double-click in the size box or title bar.

TIP

Keeping the Header Window Open
You need not close the Header window when you are finished with it, but doing so frees up memory and keeps screen clutter to a minimum. To return to the document without closing the Header window, click anywhere in the main document window in Galley View. The Header window drops behind it and is deactivated. To reactivate the Header window, click inside it, choose the Open Header command again, or choose the Header window from the Window menu.

The header text appears only when you print the document or audition it in Print Preview or in Page View. You can also create headers in Page View. When you choose the Open Header or Open Footer command in Page View, Word places the insertion point within the top or bottom margin of the currently visible page. Theoretically, a header can contain as many lines as you can fit on a page, but most headers consist of only one or two lines. If you enter more than a few lines in Page View, you can see that Word moves down the body text to accommodate large headers. Similarly, the body text is pushed up by large footers. If this weren't done, the text in the header or footer and the body text would overlap. (You might want to set the Background Repagination option in the Preferences dialog box to make screen updating proceed more quickly.)

At some point, however, you might need to have a header overlap with the body text in order to achieve a particular design effect. One example of this is shown in Figure 13-3. You can achieve this type of effect by specifying that the margin not be changed, regardless of the length of the header. To do this, choose Document from the Format menu, and insert a hyphen, or minus sign (–), before the Top margin measurement (or before the Bottom margin measurement for a footer). Doing this sets a fixed margin for the entire document, not only for a section. This technique is similar to the one of putting a minus sign in front of the line-spacing value in the Paragraph dialog box to specify a line spacing that never varies.

If you've experimented with the Position paragraph format, however, you might realize that you can achieve the same effect by giving one or more paragraphs in the Header an absolute position on the page. In fact, if you really wanted to complicate matters, you could place the contents of the header at the bottom of the page, and the contents of the footer at the top of the page!

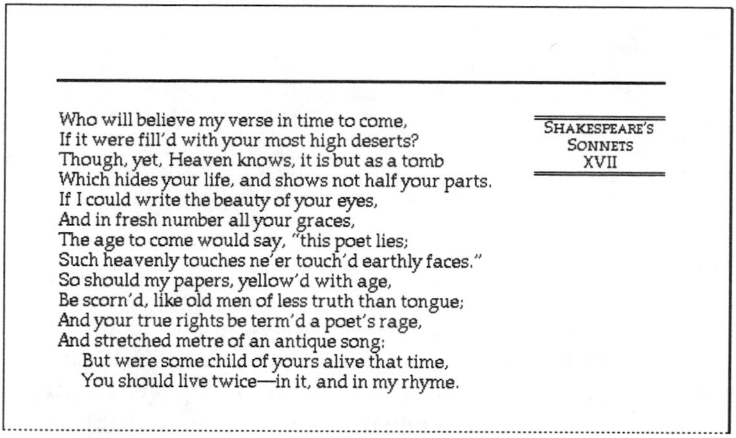

SHAKESPEARE'S
SONNETS
XVII

Who will believe my verse in time to come,
If it were fill'd with your most high deserts?
Though, yet, Heaven knows, it is but as a tomb
Which hides your life, and shows not half your parts.
If I could write the beauty of your eyes,
And in fresh number all your graces,
The age to come would say, "this poet lies;
Such heavenly touches ne'er touch'd earthly faces."
So should my papers, yellow'd with age,
Be scorn'd, like old men of less truth than tongue;
And your true rights be term'd a poet's rage,
And stretched metre of an antique song:
 But were some child of yours alive that time,
 You should live twice—in it, and in my rhyme.

Figure 13-3
A header overlapped with body text.

■ *Creating a First-Page Header or Footer*

Letters, title pages, and the first pages of reports and other documents generally do not contain a header, and the footer for the first page may be different from those in the rest of the document, containing a copyright notice, for instance. Word lets you remove the header or create a special header and footer for the first page of the document. To do this while in Galley View:

❶ Choose Section from the Format menu. However, if a header or footer window is in the foreground, the Section option is dimmed—if you want to keep the window open, simply click in the Galley View window to bring it to the front before choosing the Section command.

❷ Select the First Page Special option, located in the Header/Footer group, and click OK.

❸ Pull down the Document menu. It now contains two sets of header and footer commands. (See Figure 13-4 on the following page.)

❹ Choose the Open First Header or Open First Footer command to create a header or footer for the first page of the currently selected section. If you don't want a header on the first page, press Command-Option-M to select the entire header, and then press the Backspace key to delete it.

❺ Click the close box.

Figure 13-4
The Document menu after setting the the First Page Special option.

If you're in Page View, no new commands are added to the Document menu. The theory is that while you're working with a document in Page View, you're only interested in the header and footer for that page. To edit the header of the first page of a section while in Page View, go to that page first, then choose the Open Header or Open Footer command. When you choose the Open Header command, for instance, Word jumps to the position of the header at the top of the page, and places the insertion point before the first character in the Header. Remember that it's easier to determine where you are on the page by using the Show ¶ command (Command-Y) or by setting the Show Text Rectangles option in the Preferences dialog box.

Formatting Headers and Footers

You can change the character and paragraph formatting of headers and footers in the same way that you change them for text in the Galley View or Page View windows. As mentioned earlier, the text you enter in the Header window is assigned the *header* style; text in the Footer window uses an automatic style named *footer*. To display the definition for this style, choose Define Styles and click on the *header* entry. (See Figure 13-5.) The *header* style is based on the *Normal* style, to which a centered tab stop and a right-aligned tab stop have been added. You can also format headers by redefining the *header* style, or you can insert text having any other style you have created.

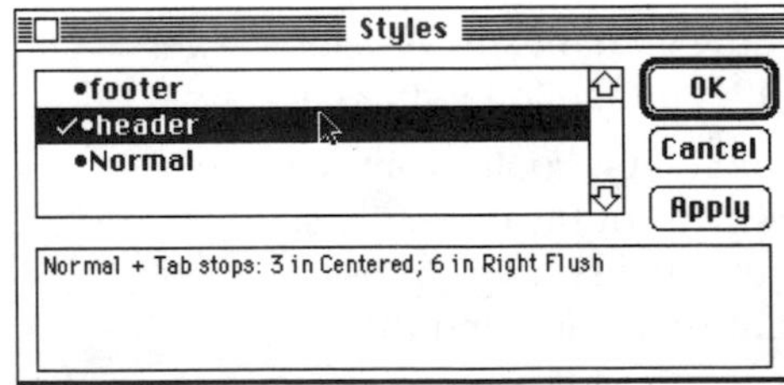

Figure 13-5
The default *header* style.

Adding Page Numbers and a Time or Date Stamp

The previous chapter described how to number pages through the Section dialog box, a method that is fine if all you need is an unadorned page number. However, if you want to include any text or symbols before or after the number, you must include the page number in a header or footer. For example, you can create a header that prints any of the following along the top of the page:

Report # 1 *Mac's Mad Movies* Page R1-103

Cascade Development Co. —43— April 15, 1991

My Summer Vacation **Page 1 of 4**

You add page numbers to a header while in Galley View as follows:

❶ Choose the Open Header command.

❷ Type the header text, and position the insertion point where you want the page number to appear.

❸ Click the Page Number icon in the Header window. The number of the current page appears. (See Figure 13-6.) Word places the correct number on every page when you print the document or view it in Print Preview.

To add page numbers to a footer, follow the same procedure, but choose the Open Footer command.

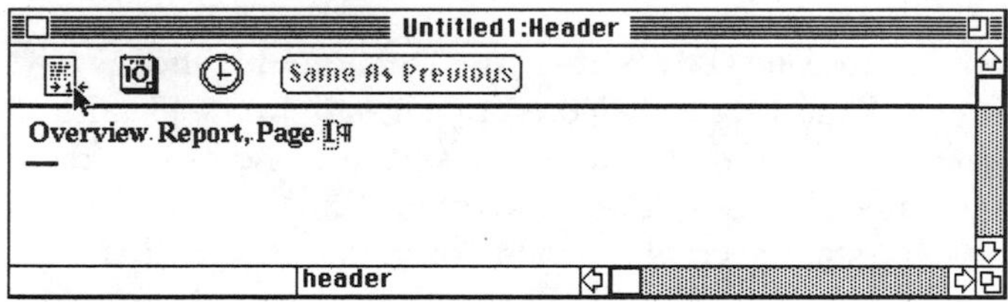

Figure 13-6
A page number added to a header.

You can readily identify a page number (or any of the other elements you insert by clicking icons in the Header or Footer icon bars) by choosing the Show ¶ command. Page numbers are then boxed with a dotted line, as shown in the figure. You can delete, cut, and paste page numbers as you would any other text, but you can't edit the number within the element.

The page number is formatted with the character formats currently in force in the header or footer. If no new character formats have been added, the number uses the formats specified in the *header* or *footer* style (not the *page number* style, used when you set page numbers through the Section dialog box). To change the format, select the page number and choose the formats you want from the appropriate menu.

TIP

Duplicate Page Numbers
You can enter as many page numbers as you like in the header and footer. In fact, both the header and footer can contain a page number. Page numbers created with the Print Preview or Section command are handled separately from the header and footer page numbers. You can use both concurrently, and Word increments both sets. There are few practical applications for this, but you should be aware of it in case you change from one numbering method to the other. However, when you click the Page Number icon and close the Header or Footer window, Word turns off the Section page numbering format for you.

You add the time and date in the same way that you add page numbers: Open the Header or Footer window, place the insertion point, and click the Clock icon for the time or the Calendar icon for the date. Word uses the current time and date as set by the Alarm Clock desk accessory. The time is in the form H:MM PM (or AM), and the date is in the form M/D/YY. The time and date change whenever you open or print the document, or when you open the header or footer window. If you want to add a fixed time or date that does not change, type it explicitly from the keyboard, or use one of Word's standard time or date glossary entries.

Like the page number, the time and date stamps each have a dotted box around them when Show ¶ is on and are considered one unit. You can neither edit the stamp nor delete a portion of it. If you backspace over any part of the stamp, it all disappears.

TIP

Entering a Page Number, Time, or Date Stamp in a Document Window
Because the Page Number, Time, and Date icons appear only in the Header and Footer windows, it might seem that you can't insert these items into the body text of your documents. However, the Glossary of Word 4 supports several versions of the same stamps created when you click the icons in a header or footer window. When you click the Page Number icon, Word inserts the standard *page number* entry from the glossary. When you click the Date icon, Word inserts the *date – print – short* entry. Clicking the Time icon inserts the *time – print – short* entry.

You can apply this principle in reverse, as well, by using the glossary to enter the time or date in formats other than those created by clicking icons in the header or footer window. Word updates each of these stamps in the body of the document in Galley View or Page View as it does when they are placed in a header or footer. Remember that the time and date are advanced only when you print, preview, or repaginate the document.

■ *Creating Headers for Facing Pages*

Word allows great flexibility in the use of headers and footers. You can set up special fonts, indents, and other formats for them as you would for the body text. As in the previous section, the focus here is on headers, but the same techniques apply to footers as well.

If the final document will be printed on both sides of the paper and bound into a book, you may want to use facing-page headers, in which the headers on the left and right pages (the even- and odd-numbered pages, respectively) are independent. How can you use this feature? You might place the page number and the name of the document on all the even-numbered pages and the name of your company on the odd-numbered pages. Figure 13-7 shows a variety of uses for facing-page headers.

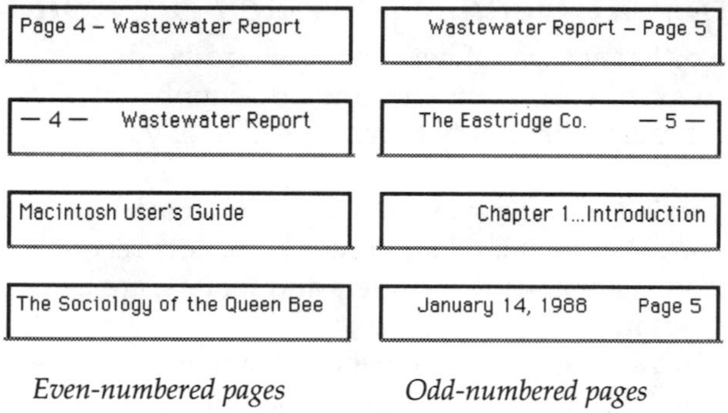

Even-numbered pages	*Odd-numbered pages*
Page 4 – Wastewater Report	Wastewater Report – Page 5
— 4 — Wastewater Report	The Eastridge Co. — 5 —
Macintosh User's Guide	Chapter 1...Introduction
The Sociology of the Queen Bee	January 14, 1988 Page 5

Figure 13-7
Examples of facing-page headers.

To create separate headers for even-numbered and odd-numbered pages, choose the Document command and select the Even/Odd Headers option. When you pull down the Document menu in Galley View after setting this option, you see two new sets of header and footer commands: one set for odd-numbered pages and one set for even-numbered pages. (See Figure 13-8.) Create each header as usual. You can test the layout of your headers by viewing them in Print Preview or Page View. As mentioned earlier when we discussed the First Page Special section format, Word lists only the Open Header and Open Footer commands when in Page View.

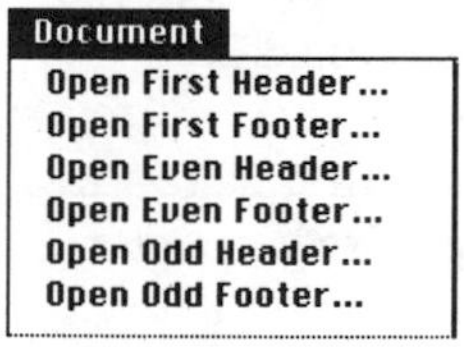

Document
- Open First Header...
- Open First Footer...
- Open Even Header...
- Open Even Footer...
- Open Odd Header...
- Open Odd Footer...

Figure 13-8
The Document menu after setting both Even/Odd Headers and First Page Special.

How did odd-numbered and even-numbered pages come to be the right and left pages, respectively? In conventional publication design, the first page of a manuscript is numbered 1 and is on the right-hand side. Therefore, all odd-numbered pages are on the right and all even-numbered pages are on the left. In Word, however, you can use the Start Pages From field in the Document dialog box to start your document on a page number other than 1. This is useful if your document is part of a larger set of documents that must be numbered consecutively. If you do this, Word still places even-numbered pages on the left and odd-numbered pages on the right. If you start a document on page 2, for example, the first page is formatted as a left-hand page.

Creating a Different Header for Each Section

You now know about three different types of headers: standard headers, first-page headers, and headers for even-numbered and odd-numbered pages. You can define these headers differently for each section of your document.

As you learned in the previous chapter, you enter a section mark (a double dotted line) by pressing the Command and Enter keys. Any section formats you define for a section, including the headers and footers, are tied to the section mark that follows it.

To create a new header in a section, scroll the window so that the desired section is in view; then click in that section to place the insertion point there. Remember that the status box shows the page and section number of the top-most line in the window, not the location of the insertion point. When you open the Header window, the title bar indicates the section number for which the header is defined; check to be sure it's the right one.

Word saves you typing if you want to use the same or similar text for a new header. When you press Command-Enter to start a new section, each new header (or footer), whether it be first, odd, even, or standard, is copied from the one immediately preceding it. You can then open any of the Header windows and edit, delete, or replace the text.

The Same As Previous Button

A useful tool for creating new headers is the Same as Previous button in the Header or Footer window, but it's a little complicated to describe. Let's consider three cases.

Suppose you create a standard header—not odd, even, or first page—in a document in which you have established three sections. Before you enter text into any of the three Header windows, each header is known as a *null header*. Now enter some text into the first section's Header window. If you open the Header windows for the second and third sections, you see the text you entered in the Header window for the first section. This happens because for every null header, Word scans back through the preceding sections and uses the contents of the first non-null header it finds.

Now open the Header window for the second section, select the default header text (which comes from the first header), and delete it. You might think that this action makes the header for the second section an empty header, but this is not the case. Instead, the second header remains a null header and contains only a single paragraph mark. (Every window in Word into which you enter text must have an ending paragraph mark, which you cannot delete.) If you close the header window for the second section and reopen it, you'll see that the previous contents have returned. In other words, paradoxically, deleting the contents of a header makes that header null, even if it was already null.

When you open the Header window for the third section, you still see the first header's contents because the second section's header is still null. Because you haven't entered anything in the Header window for the third section, it's still a null header, and so its contents are taken from the first section's header.

If you want to remove a header from a section, you must open the header, select its contents, and replace the contents with a space, a tab, or text given the Hidden character format—anything that takes up space in the header, but isn't visible when printed. Deleting the contents of a header makes the header null, and so it inherits the contents of the first preceding non-null header.

If you want to use the header for the first section again while leaving the header for the second section "empty" (having entered text which isn't visible when printed), you must open the first section's Header window and copy it, and then open the third Header window and paste it in.

Word supports the concept of the null header to make it easier to have a header default to the preceding header, yet allow you to "empty" a header and use that as the default as well. A good use for this feature is when you have a series of large graphs or tables in a section and want to reserve as much room on the page for them as possible by removing the headers or footers for that section.

What does the Same As Previous button have to do with all this? Clicking the Same As Previous button in a Header or Footer window clears that header or footer to the null state, and is equivalent to deleting the contents of the header window. When a header becomes null, Word takes its contents from the first preceding non-null header it finds. When you open a Header or Footer window and the Same As Previous button is dimmed, the header is null. When you change the contents of a null header, the button becomes active.

Now consider the second case. This time, suppose you create different Odd, Even, and First headers in only one section. If you create an Odd header but leave the Even and First headers null, you'll find that the Even header inherits its contents from the Odd header, but the First header remains empty. This happens because the Odd header has a special priority over the Even header in each section—entering text in the Odd header for a section creates a header for both odd- and even-numbered pages, until you explicitly enter text for the Even header. The First header does not inherit its contents from the Odd header, and so it remains empty. If you entered text into the Even header window, the Same As Previous button becomes active, indicating that it is no longer null.

In the third case, suppose you create three sections and enter different text into each of the three Header windows of the first section alone (all three headers in all other sections are null). If you open the headers in the second section, for example, you'll see that the Even header section is the same as the Odd header of the first section. This happens because the Even header inherits its text from the Odd header in the same section, but this Odd header inherits its text from the first preceding non-null Odd header.

If you enter text in the window for the Even header of the second section, the Same As Previous button becomes active, because it is no longer null. If you click the Same as Previous button, you get a copy of the contents of the Odd header from the same section because the Odd header has priority in that section. Again, the First header is outside this hierarchy and inherits from the first preceding non-null First header before it.

■ *Positioning Headers or Footers*

You use the same character and paragraph formatting operations that you use for the text in the document window to adjust the horizontal position of the header or footer relative to the document's page margins. As for vertical placement, Word normally places the header 0.5 inch from the top edge of the page and the footer 0.5 inch from the bottom edge of the page. You can change the vertical placement of a header or footer in one of three ways:

- ❑ By adding blank lines to the top or the bottom of the text in the header or footer window.
- ❑ By specifying its placement in the Header/Footer group of the Section dialog box.
- ❑ By adjusting its position in Print Preview.

As mentioned earlier, you can also format one or more paragraphs with the Position format to place the paragraphs anywhere on the page.

Vertical Positioning with the Section Command

For more precise control over the vertical placement of headers and footers, take advantage of the From Top and From Bottom edit fields in the Header/Footer group of the Section dialog box. Choose the Section command and enter the distance from the top of the page to the top of the header in the From Top field, and enter the distance from the bottom of the page to the bottom of the footer in the From Bottom field.

A distance of 0.5 inch is standard for both the header and footer. Most printers—including the LaserWriter—can't print much closer than this to the top and bottom edges of the paper, so don't use a smaller value. Using a larger value might make the printable area for the body of the document smaller, because for headers Word sets the actual top margin for the body of the document at the bottom of the header. The placement of the actual bottom margin works similarly. You set the top and bottom margins in the Document dialog box, but preceding the top or bottom measurements in the dialog box with a minus sign makes these margins absolute rather than relative to headers and footers.

Using the Print Preview Command

Print Preview is the easiest and most straightforward way of adjusting the vertical position of headers and footers, although you lose precise control. First click the Margins icon to display the boundaries of the margins and the limits of the headers and footers. You can drag the header and footer anywhere above the top margin and between the left and right margins. The new position is reflected in the Header/Footer fields of the Section dialog box.

If you press the Shift key before dragging, you can move the header or footer into the body of the page. When you do this, Word updates the contents not only of the Section dialog box, but also enters a minus sign before the top or bottom margin measurements in the Document dialog box. This method allows you to see immediately the effect the positions of the header and footer have on the layout of the page. You'll learn more about this technique in Chapter 14, "Document Formatting and Printing."

■ *Creating and Editing Footnotes*

You use footnotes to identify sources of quotation, acknowledge borrowed ideas, and provide supplementary information. You can indicate a footnote by a superscripted number,[1] by a symbol such as the dagger[†] or asterisk,[*] or even by a short piece of text.[note]

---

[1] A number that has been raised above the baseline.

[†] Sometimes called a dagger.

[*] Most manuals of style recommend using only superscripted numbers for footnotes, but if the document contains only one or two footnotes, symbols are an acceptable alternative.

[note] However, short phrases as footnote references can be unwieldy.

Footnotes always consist of two parts:

- A footnote mark, or reference. This is the superscripted number or symbol in the text.
- The footnote text, printed at the bottom of the page, at the end of the section, or at the end of the document.

Footnotes in Word are usually separated from the main text by a line 2 inches long, which you see when the document is printed or previewed. Footnotes are not the same as bibliographies, which do not have references in text but which follow a similar end-of-section or end-of-document style.

You can let Word do most of the footnote formatting for you, including the spacing and separator line. In fact, you can even have Word track the footnotes, numbering them for you as you go along. If you delete a footnote from the middle of the document, Word automatically renumbers the footnotes that follow it. If you want, however, you can edit and reformat any element in the complex structure of a footnote. We'll discuss this later in the chapter, after we've covered the basics.

Creating a Footnote

You can insert a footnote reference and its accompanying text when you enter the text or when you edit and format it. To create a footnote while in Galley View, place the insertion point where you want the reference mark to be. Then do this:

❶ Choose the Footnote command from the Document menu. The Footnote dialog box shown in Figure 13-9 appears.

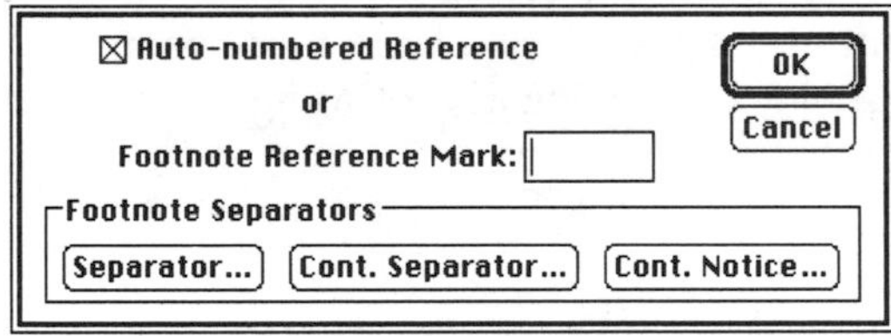

Figure 13-9
The Footnote dialog box.

❷ The Auto-numbered Reference option is already selected, so to insert a numbered footnote reference, simply press the Return key. If you want to use a footnote symbol (or up to 10 characters of text) instead of a number, type it into the Footnote Reference Mark field before pressing the Return key. Word inserts the reference number or mark, and the Footnote window opens, as shown in Figure 13-10.

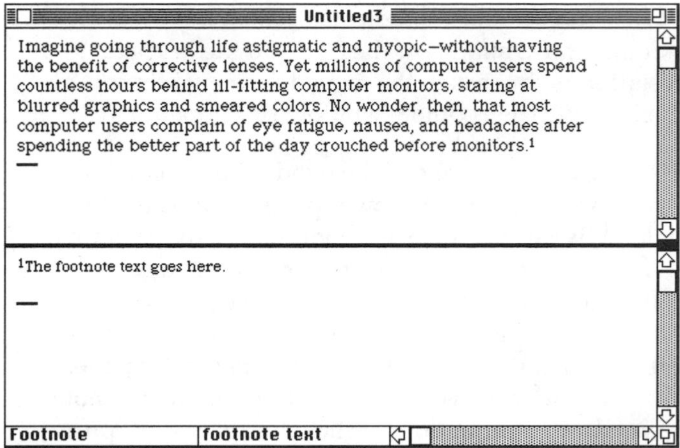

Figure 13-10
The Footnote window.

❸ Word inserts the same mark at the correct position in the Footnote window relative to the other footnotes. Type the footnote text after it, using any of the character and paragraph formats. Each footnote can be as long as you want; the Footnote window scrolls if you fill it with text. Word assigns the automatic style named *footnote text* to the text you enter, but you can change this style if you want.

❹ When you're finished entering the footnote, close the Footnote window by dragging the split bar down.

You can also enter footnotes while in Page View. If you choose the Footnote command while in Page View, Word moves the insertion point to the bottom of the page, the end of the section, or the end of the document, depending on which option is set in the Footnote Position drop-down list in the Document dialog box, discussed later in this chapter. You might set the Background Repagination option in the Preferences dialog box so that Word more promptly updates the screen image for the new footnotes you've added.

Speeding Up Footnote Entry

You can shorten this routine by using a few of Word's command-key shortcuts. If you're letting Word number the footnote references, you can do this:

❶ Press Command-E to open the Footnote dialog box.

❷ Don't wait for the box to appear to press the Return key. Press it while Word is drawing the Footnote dialog box on the screen, and you'll go right to the Footnote window. This cuts a second or two off the time. Many commands in this and other Macintosh programs act this way.

❸ When you've finished entering the footnote, use one of the Go Back key sequences—Command-Option-Z or the 0 key on the keypad. This places the insertion point back in the main document window at the exact place you left off. The Footnote window stays open.

The Footnote window opens in a pane of the window in Galley View. The upper pane contains the document; the lower pane contains the footnotes. You can scroll the active window up or down. (The active window is the one containing the blinking insertion point.) You can enlarge the Footnote window by dragging the split bar up, making the pane containing the document proportionally smaller. If the window is already split when you open the Footnote window, Word removes the original lower pane. You have to resplit the window when you're finished typing the footnote. To close the Footnote window, you can double-click the split bar or press Shift-Option-Command-S.

If you need to see the reference marks, choose the Show ¶ command to reveal all the formatting marks and special characters. The footnote references are shown boxed with a dotted line.

Automating Footnote Entry

You can enter a string of footnote references and then go to the Footnote window and type all the footnote text at once. To do this, create the first footnote as usual but don't type the footnote text yet. Instead, go back to the document and select the footnote reference number. Copy it to the Clipboard with the Copy command and close the Footnote window. Now go through the document and use the Paste command to insert any additional footnote references desired. Word increments each footnote number for you. Even if you return to the middle of the document and add more references, all the reference numbers will remain in the correct sequence in the document.

To type the text for all the footnotes, open the Footnote window, if it isn't already open. To do this, go back to the first reference number and double-click it. Alternatively, you can open the Footnote window directly by pressing the Shift key while dragging the split bar down. (You can also press Shift-Option-Command-S.) Word opens the Footnote window and places the insertion point at the end of the footnote text, if there is any.

Note that the reference numbers for the footnotes you just inserted are already in the window. Scroll the window until the footnote number to which you want to add text is uppermost in the pane; Word scrolls the upper document pane to the position of the corresponding reference mark. This is called synchronized scrolling; the outlining feature works similarly. Set the insertion point between the reference number and the following paragraph mark and type the footnote text, as shown in Figure 13-11.

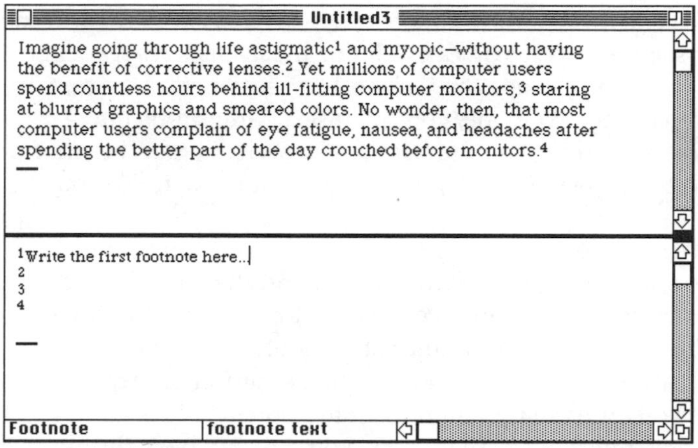

Untitled3

Imagine going through life astigmatic[1] and myopic–without having the benefit of corrective lenses.[2] Yet millions of computer users spend countless hours behind ill-fitting computer monitors,[3] staring at blurred graphics and smeared colors. No wonder, then, that most computer users complain of eye fatigue, nausea, and headaches after spending the better part of the day crouched before monitors.[4]

1 Write the first footnote here...
2
3
4

Footnote | footnote text

Figure 13-11
A string of footnotes.

TIP

The Special Footnote Character
Word uses a special character—ASCII code 5—to place and find auto-numbered footnote reference marks. You can verify this by selecting an auto-numbered footnote reference mark and pressing Option-Command-Q to see its ASCII equivalent. Note that you cannot find in this way other footnote reference marks you've entered in the Footnote dialog box.

You can quickly search for these references in your documents by typing ^5 in the Find What field of the Find or Change dialog box. However, you cannot create a footnote reference by inserting that character alone in a document because Word attaches a "buried" format to it that users cannot reproduce. Instead, you must copy the mark and paste it at each reference; you can also store it as a glossary entry.

Editing and Changing the Format of Footnotes

Editing a footnote is almost as easy as entering it in the first place. You can display a footnote for editing in any of four ways:

- Double-click the footnote reference mark.
- Select a footnote reference mark and press Command-E and then the Return key. Word takes you to the end of the footnote text associated with that mark.
- Press Shift-Option-Command-S to open the Footnote window. Scroll through the footnotes; Word scrolls in the document to show you the reference marks. Edit the text, then press Shift-Option-Command-S to close the footnote pane.
- Press the Shift key while dragging the split bar down.

You can change the format of the footnote reference mark and the text in the footnote itself in several ways. You can redefine the *footnote reference* and *footnote text* styles, or you can change the formats in a reference or the text in a footnote. Also, for footnote text alone, you can insert paragraphs into a footnote containing a style other than the *footnote text* style. Remember that both styles are based on the *Normal* style, so changes you make to *Normal* might affect them.

The *footnote reference* style is not a full-fledged style: You can set Line Spacing, Space Above, and the Border formats for it, but they aren't used; only the character formats are used. One result is that redefining this style doesn't automatically update the appearance of the footnotes in the document. For this reason, it's best to decide on the definition of the *footnote reference* style before you enter a large number of footnotes.

To change the appearance of the references, you must go back through the document, select each reference mark, and press Command-E to reenter it at that position. (A keyboard macro program such as Tempo from Affinity Microsystems or AutoMac III is good for automating this process.) Even though it seems as though replacing a reference mark might replace the footnote text attached to it, the footnote text is not lost. If you're using auto-numbered footnotes, it can help to search for the magic character Word uses to mark them, as described in the previous tip, "The Special Footnote Character."

Here's another way to change all the reference marks quickly to ensure that all the footnotes in a document have the same formatting:

1. After you've redefined the style, go to the first footnote in the document and reenter it as described earlier.
2. Select and copy that reference mark alone. Press the right arrow key a few times to move the insertion point a few characters to the right of the first reference mark.
3. Choose Change from the Search menu; enter ^5 in the Find What field and ^*c* in the Change To field.
4. Click Change All to replace every reference mark in the document with the reference mark you reentered.

Unfortunately, when you replace all the marks at once in this way, the footnote text is lost, so this method works best when you haven't entered any footnote text yet. Otherwise, try copying the text and pasting it into a new document to avoid losing the footnotes, then copy the footnotes back after you've replaced the reference marks in the body of the document.

TIP

Changing the Formats for References Preceding the Footnote Text
Often, you'd like to change the appearance of the references preceding the footnote text that correspond to the reference marks in the body of the document. A convenient way to do this is to select all the text in the Footnote window by pressing the Command key and clicking in the selection bar, and assigning the *footnote text* style (or any style in the document's style sheet) to everything in the Footnote window, including the reference marks. This brings the reference marks down to the baseline for the footnote text and brings together the formats for all the text in the Footnote window. When you do this, you may also have to press Shift-Command-Spacebar to return to the base character format any character formats you've given the text for the style you've just assigned.

Deleting Footnotes

When you are working with a typewriter, deleting a footnote also requires you to renumber all the following footnotes. Word does the renumbering for you, however, so deleting unnecessary footnotes is no longer a major chore. To delete a footnote:

1. Select the reference mark in the document for the footnote you want to delete.
2. Press the Backspace key.

This simple procedure erases the footnote reference, erases the footnote text in the Footnote window, and renumbers the auto-numbered references that follow.

Editing the Footnote Separators

Word places a single 2-inch line, known as the footnote separator, between the body text and the footnote text. You can make this line shorter or longer or do away with it altogether. You can even replace it with a double line, a row of pound signs (#), or a set of bullets. Figure 13-12 shows a few unusual footnote separators you might want to try.

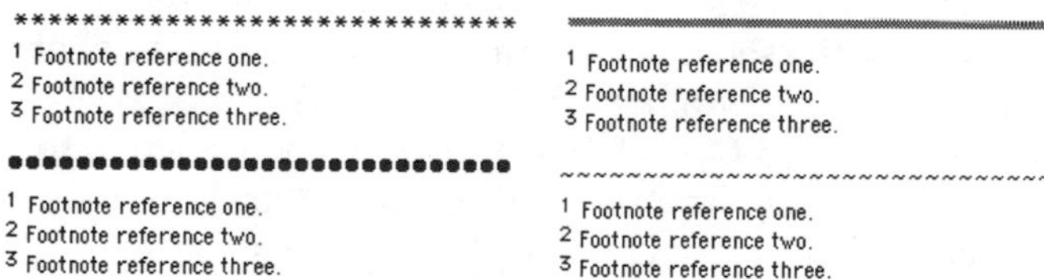

Figure 13-12
Some sample footnote separators.

When a footnote becomes too long to fit comfortably on the same page as the reference (assuming that you want it to appear on the same page), Word continues it on the next page. In such cases, Word inserts a single line that spans from margin to margin (called the continuing footnote separator) and can also provide a "continued" notice to help readers follow along. You can edit these as well; the changes affect the current document only and are not saved in the current Word Settings file. To edit the footnote separator, the continuing footnote separator, or the continuation notice:

❶ Choose the Footnote command.

❷ In the Footnote Separators option group, click the separator button for the feature you want to change. A special headerlike window appears, as shown in Figure 13-13. Edit the contents of the window. The Footnote Cont. Notice window is initially empty, but you can add text such as *continued on next page.*

❸ When you are finished, close the window by clicking the close box.

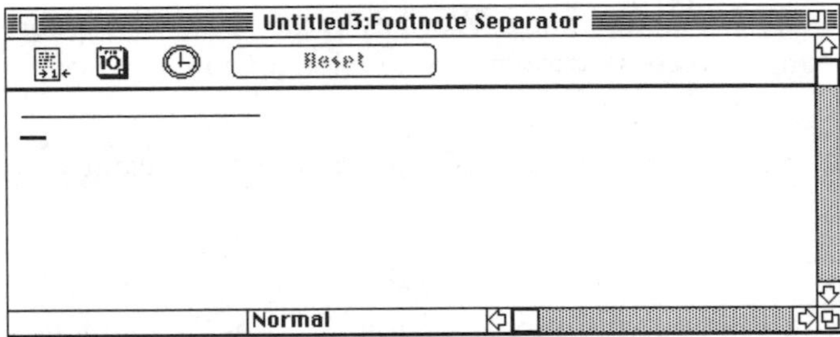

Figure 13-13
The Footnote Separator window.

Both separators are really special characters, as you can tell by turning on Show ¶ and clicking on the separator line. The line is shown surrounded by a dotted box, a telltale sign. Indeed, if you double-click on the line, all of it is selected, and pressing the Backspace key deletes all of it. If you delete one of the separators (intentionally or not), you can get it back by clicking the Reset button.

Because the separator characters are like the page number, time, and date characters discussed earlier, you can also create glossary entries for them beforehand. The ASCII code for the separator character is 6, and the code for the continuing separator is 7, but, as with the other special characters, you can't simply press Option-Command-Q, and then enter 6 to get the separator character. Instead, select and copy an instance of the character itself to paste or add to the glossary. Incidentally, if you create a glossary entry for the continuing separator, it becomes an easy margin-to-margin rule for use as a special design element.

TIP

Formats in the Separator Windows
Curiously, the footnote separator and continuation notice are contained in special "header" windows that have the familiar Page Number, Time stamp, and Date stamp icons in them, although there is usually little reason why you'd want to use these.

These windows share another feature with header windows: You can change the font, style, alignment, and position of characters within them. When editing the continuation notice, for example, you can display the Ruler to adjust the margins and alignment of the text. The footnote separator can be plain or bold, shadow or outline, 12 point or 48 point. Use restraint, however, so that the special effects in a document don't overshadow its content.

■ *Placing Footnotes in a Document*

You can have Word begin numbering footnote references at any number, not only at 1. To change the starting number, choose the Document command and enter a new number in the Number From field in the Footnotes group. This feature is handy if your manuscript spans several documents and you want the numbering sequence to continue where the numbering in the previous document left off. However, if you link documents through the Next File field, the process is not automatic—if you leave the Number From field blank, Word starts the count at 1.

You can also specify where the footnotes will be printed by selecting an option from the Position drop-down list in the Footnotes group. Normally, Word prints footnotes at the bottom of each page.

- ❏ To place footnotes at the end of the entire document, select the End of Document option from the Position drop-down list.
- ❏ To place footnotes at the end of each section, select the End of Section option. Then put the insertion point in each section, choose the Section command, and be sure the Include Endnotes option is set. To collect the footnotes at the end of a particular section, turn off the Include Endnotes option for all the sections which precede it.
- ❏ To place footnotes at the bottom of the page, near the bottom margin, select the Bottom of Page option.
- ❏ To place footnotes at the end of the text on the page, select the Beneath Text option.

The Bottom of Page and Beneath Text options are similar. If you select the Bottom of Page option, Word places the footnotes flush with the bottom margin, as shown in Figure 13-14 on the following page. If less than a full page of text is involved, a big gap can occur between the text and the footnotes. If you don't want a gap, select the Beneath Text option instead. This option causes the footnotes to be printed directly beneath the text.

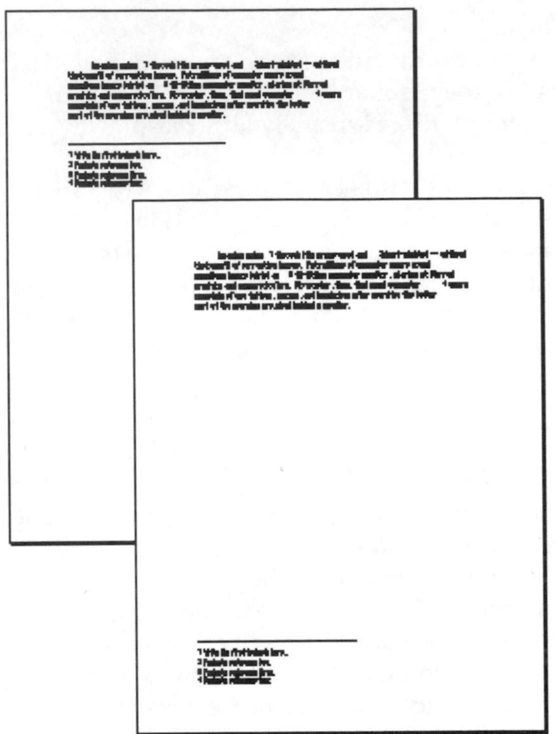

Figure 13-14
The difference between the Beneath Text and the Bottom of Page footnote options.

If you have occasion to use both the Bottom of Page option and the No Break section format, you might be surprised by the results. Because these two options can be contradictory (for example, it might be possible to get two footnotes numbered *1* at the bottom of the page), Word ignores the Bottom of Page option and places footnotes beneath the text.

The End of Section option in the Document dialog box tells Word to save footnotes until the end of each section, but only if you've set the Include Endnotes option in the Section dialog box. You can save footnotes across sections, and have Word "dump" the footnotes it has been saving at the end of a given section, by turning off the Include Endnotes option for every section except the one you want to contain the accumulated footnotes. Word saves its footnotes until it finds a section in which the Include Endnotes option is on and prints them at the end of that section.

Also, note that Footnote numbering is independent of the placement of the footnotes. To restart the numbering for each group, select the Restart Each Section option in the Document dialog box.

Points to Remember

- A header is text that is repeated above the top margin of the page. A footer is text that is repeated below the bottom margin of the page. These elements usually contain identifying text, such as page numbers, the section or document title, and so forth.
- Word provides three types of headers and footers: Standard headers and footers do not vary from page to page. First-page headers and footers are printed only on the first page of the document or section. Even and Odd headers and footers are printed only on even-numbered and odd-numbered pages, respectively.
- You can define a different set of headers and footers for each section in your document. If your document is not divided into sections, the headers and footers you create apply to the entire document.
- Word moves the top and bottom margins, if necessary, to accommodate the header and footer. To prevent this, enter a minus sign in front of the Top and Bottom margin measurement in the Document dialog box.
- If you include page numbers in a header or footer, be sure the Auto option in the Section dialog box is turned off. Otherwise, duplicate numbers will appear.
- A footnote provides supplementary information about one or more statements in the text. A footnote consists of a reference mark in the body text and the text of the footnote itself. Word can print footnotes at the bottom of the page on which their references appear, at the end of selected sections, or at the end of the document.
- Headers, footers, and footnotes don't appear in Galley View. You can see them by viewing your document in Print Preview or Page View.

Techniques

Working with Headers and Footers

Create a standard header or footer

1. Set the insertion point in the section to contain the header or footer.
2. Choose Open Header or Open Footer from the Document menu. The Header or Footer window appears.
3. Type the header or footer text. These windows have two preset tabs: one centered between the indents and one flush right against the right indent.
4. Click the close box of the Header or Footer window.

Add page numbers or the time or date to a header or footer

1. With the Header or Footer window open, set the insertion point where you want the page number, time, or date to appear.
2. Click the appropriate icon in the header or footer icon bar.

Change the formatting of a header or footer

1. Open the Header or Footer window.
2. Change any of the character or paragraph formats as you would those of body text.
3. You can also redefine the *header* and *footer* automatic styles or assign any style in your document to the header or footer.

Adjust the distance between the top or bottom edge of the page and the header or footer

1. Set the insertion point in the section to be affected.
2. Choose the Section command.
3. Enter the distance in the From Top or From Bottom field in the Header/Footer option group.

You can also drag the header or footer in Print Preview. (See Chapter 14, "Document Formatting and Printing.")

Create a header or footer for the first page of a section

1. Set the insertion point in the section for which you want to define the header or footer.
2. Choose the Section command.
3. Select the First Page Special option, and then click OK.
4. Choose Open First Header or Open First Footer from the Document menu.
5. Proceed as you would in a standard header or footer.

Create different headers and footers for odd and even pages

Even-numbered pages print on the left facing page, and odd-numbered pages print on the right facing page.

1. Choose the Document command.
2. Select the Even/Odd Headers option.
3. Choose Open Even Header, Open Even Footer, Open Odd Header, or Open Odd Footer from the Document menu.
4. Proceed as you would in a standard header or footer.

Define a header with the same text as the last nonempty header

This also applies to footers.

1. Open the Header window.
2. Click the Same as Previous button.

The text of the odd header for the section, if any, is used. If that header is empty, the text of the last nonempty header of the same type is used.

Working with Footnotes

The Footnote Dialog Box

Item	Action
Auto-numbered Reference option	Numbers footnotes sequentially. Word renumbers these reference marks when you add, rearrange, or delete footnotes. If you enter a symbol in the Footnote Reference Mark field, this option is turned off.
Footnote Reference Mark field	Sets the type of reference mark to be used. Word will not change this mark.
Footnote Separator button	Presents a window for changing the separator between body text and footnotes when the document is printed. The default is a 2-inch line.
Cont. Separator button	Presents a window for changing the separator between the text and a footnote carried over from the previous page. The default is a solid line from margin to margin.
Cont. Notice button	Presents a window for changing text printed when a footnote is carried over to the next page. The default is no continuation notice.
Buttons	
OK button	Inserts the footnote reference mark and opens the Footnote window.
Cancel button	Closes the dialog box without inserting a reference mark.

Create a footnote

1. Position the insertion point where you want the footnote reference. Choose the Footnote command.
2. Type a reference mark, or click OK for an auto-numbered footnote.
3. Type the footnote text in the Footnote window that appears.
4. Drag the split bar down to close the Footnote window.

Edit a footnote

❶ Open the Footnote window by double-clicking the footnote reference, pressing Shift while dragging the split bar down, or pressing Shift-Option-Command-S.

❷ Edit the footnote text, and close the footnote pane.

Delete a footnote

❶ Delete the footnote reference mark in the document text.

Word deletes the corresponding footnote text and renumbers the remaining footnotes.

Specify the location of footnotes

❶ Choose the Document command.

❷ Select one of the Position options.

Bottom of Page: Prints each footnote near the bottom margin of the page on which its reference appears.

Beneath Text: Prints each footnote just after the text on the page on which its reference appears.

End of Section: Prints footnotes at the end of sections in which the Include Endnotes option is selected, or at the end of the document if this option is not selected in any section.

End of Document: Prints footnotes at the end of the document.

Change the formatting of a footnote reference mark

❶ Choose Define Styles from the Format menu, and select the *footnote reference* style.

❷ Change the formats for the style. However, only the character formats are used in the style.

❸ Then, for each reference in the document, select the reference and reenter it. Entering ^5 in the Find What field of the Find dialog box helps to locate auto-numbered references.

Change the formatting of footnote text

❶ Choose Define Styles from the Format menu, and select the *footnote text* style.

❷ Redefine the style as needed.

Edit the footnote separators or continuation notice

❶ Choose the Footnote command.

❷ Click the button for the Footnote Separators option you want to change.

❸ In the window that appears, replace the separator or type text to be used as a continuation notice when a footnote is continued on the next page.

❹ Note that the preset separators are special characters; you can replace them, but you can't edit them.

❺ Click the close box for the window when you're through.

■ *Commands*

Command name	Meaning, menu	Standard keyboard	Keypad	Extended keyboard
Footnote Cont. Notice...	Opens footnote continuation notice window so that you can enter a continuation notice.			
Footnote Cont. Separator...	Opens footnote continuation separator window so that you can change what separates main text from footnotes continued from preceding page.			
Footnote Separator...	Opens footnote separator window so that you can change what separates footnotes from main text.			
Footnote...	Inserts a footnote reference mark at insertion point and opens footnote window. In Page View, moves insertion point into footnote text area.			
	Document	⌘E		
Include Endnotes in Section	Toggles option to print footnotes at end of selected section.			
Open Even Footer...	Opens footer window for even-numbered pages in selected section.			
Open Even Header...	Opens header window for even-numbered pages in selected section.			
Open First Footer...	Opens first-page footer window for selected section.			
Open First Header...	Opens first-page header window for selected section.			
Open Footer...	Opens standard footer window for selected section. In Page View, moves insertion point into footer text.			
	Document			
Open Footnote Window	Opens footnote window and displays footnotes related to footnote reference marks visible in document window.			
		⌘⇧⌥S		
Open Header...	Opens standard header window for selected section. In Page View, moves insertion point into header text.			
	Document			
Open Odd Footer...	Opens footer window for odd-numbered pages in selected section.			
Open Odd Header...	Opens header window for odd-numbered pages in selected section.			

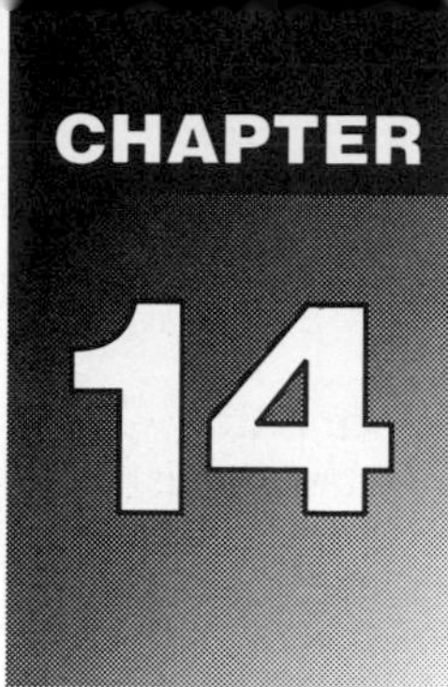

Document Formatting and Printing

This book presents a typical process for developing a document. First, you create the overall structure of the document with the outlining feature; then you enter the text, making use of glossaries (for boilerplate text) and the Spelling command. Next, you format the document at the character, paragraph, table, and section levels and add headers, footers, and footnotes. Of course, infinite variations on this theme are possible. If you're using styles, much of the formatting you do simply involves assigning styles. With Page View, you can better understand how the formats you've set influence the overall look of your document.

Now, you adjust the overall shape of your opus at the page and document level and then audition it in Print Preview. At this stage you often find room for further refinements and go back to change a few formats or adjust the margins. Finally, when everything is to your liking, you print the document. This part of the process is the subject of this chapter. It follows a standard sequence of steps for preparing your document for printing, including hyphenation, pagination, and page layout.

One of the topics covered in this chapter is Word's fifth formatting domain, the document domain, which controls the following characteristics, mostly through options in the Page Setup and Document dialog boxes:

- The size of the paper on which the document will be printed, as well as the reduction ratio for printing.
- The page margins, which determine the initial placement of major elements such as the left and right edges of the text, the left and right indents, and the headers and footers.
- Whether the document will be printed on both sides of the paper and therefore needs to be adjusted for left and right pages.
- The default tab-stop interval.
- Whether Word should control widows (stray lines at the top or bottom of a page).
- Where to print the footnotes.
- How footnotes, lines, and pages should be numbered.
- Whether to print another document after this one.

Let's go over the process of preparing a document for printing. First, you choose a printer. This is necessary because the actual size of the page and the position of margins, headers, footers, and so on, are affected by the printer used. The LaserWriter, for example, cannot print closer than 0.42 inch from the edge of the page. In addition, the ratio of screen pixels to printed pixels is different for the LaserWriter and the ImageWriter. You specify the printer in the Chooser dialog box, available from the Apple menu.

Next, you establish the overall shape of your document by setting formats in the Document dialog box. Once this is done, you can hyphenate the document. Hyphenation is optional, but it often enhances the appearance of a document, especially if you are using justified alignment.

The next step is to control where on the page each part of the document will be printed. For example, if you're writing a book, you probably want each chapter to start at the top of a page and on a right-hand (odd-numbered) page. You don't want a major section head to be printed alone at the bottom of a page, nor do you want to separate a figure and its caption. You can have Word take care of most of these page-layout decisions for you by using the Keep With Next ¶ and Page Break Before formats and the Section Start options in the Section dialog box. However, these methods aren't always sufficient, and you have to force page breaks at certain points to get the effect you want. One of the main reasons for doing this is to achieve a good visual balance among the elements on a page. You want to maintain the clarity and proportion of the design.

The process of calculating the depth of each element (that is, its vertical dimension on the page) and deciding where to break the text and start a new page is called *repagination*. Word repaginates a document when you specifically tell it to by choosing the Repaginate Now command, when you print the document, when you work with the document in Page View or in Print Preview, or during idle moments if the Background Repagination option in the Preferences dialog box is set.

The Print Preview command is an excellent way to see where Word has broken each page before you print the document. In Print Preview, you can move page breaks, the placement of headers and footers, add page numbers, adjust the margins and see the effect of these changes instantly.

After these final adjustments, you are ready for the *coup de grâce:* printing the document. This should present few surprises (although you need to know about several fine points). The following sections describe each of these steps in detail.

■ *Choosing a Printer*

The Chooser desk accessory lets you set the current printer. (Earlier versions of Word used an internal method for setting the printer.) Most people use either the ImageWriter or the LaserWriter, or they use the ImageWriter in the initial stages of writing, editing, and formatting and then switch to the LaserWriter for the final version. When you print a document, an application sends print commands to a special piece of Macintosh system software called a printer driver. The driver translates these commands into a form the printer can accept.

The driver for your printer must be in the System Folder of the System disk you use to start Word. If not, you must either copy it to the System Folder or use the appropriate Macintosh system software installer disk. Word supports the ImageWriter and LaserWriter printer drivers. (Remember to copy the Laser Prep file to the System Folder if you will be using the LaserWriter driver.) The versions of the LaserWriter and ImageWriter drivers must be compatible with the system file you are using; you can check with an Apple dealer for the most recent system software. Word also supports serial drivers for many popular serial printers: To get these drivers, send in the card accompanying the Word documentation.

To select a printer, choose Chooser from the Apple menu. The dialog box in Figure 14-1 on the following page appears. Icons for the available printers appear in the left side of the dialog box. Click the one you want.

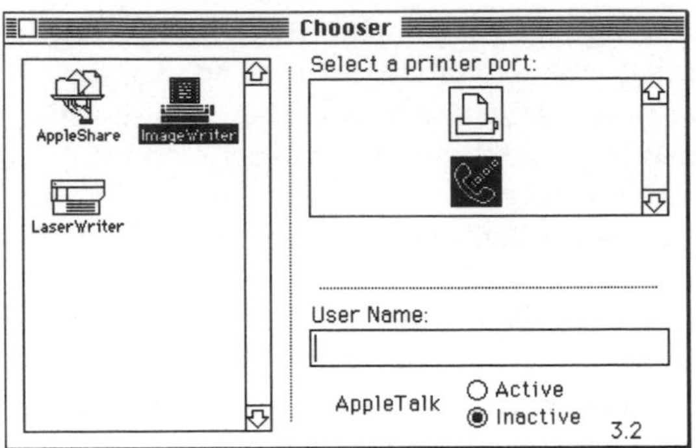

Figure 14-1
The Chooser dialog box.

Some Macintosh applications, such as for a Microsoft Mail server or AppleShare, are accompanied by their own drivers, the icons of which can also appear in the Chooser dialog box. Now do one of the following:

- ❑ If you selected the ImageWriter driver, the title of the list box to the right reads *Select a printer port*, and the Phone and Printer serial port icons appear in the list box. Click the icon for the port to which your printer is connected. If a hard disk is attached to the Phone port, don't select it—this might corrupt the information on the hard disk.
- ❑ If you selected the LaserWriter driver, the title of the list box to the right reads *Select a LaserWriter*, and the laser printers available on the network appear in the list box. Click on the name of the LaserWriter to which you'll be printing. Depending on the version of the Chooser that you're using (the version number is in the lower right corner of the window), the Chooser may present another dialog box telling you to be sure that AppleTalk is connected to the printer port. You might also have to click the AppleTalk Active button.
- ❑ Selecting the AppleTalk ImageWriter driver is like selecting the LaserWriter, except that you see a list of the AppleTalk ImageWriters on the network.

When you're finished choosing the printer, click the close box to close the Chooser dialog box. You're now ready to print.

TIP

Choosing the LaserWriter Even If You Don't Have One
If you will eventually print your document on a LaserWriter but have only the ImageWriter, you've probably discovered that the line lengths change when you go from one printer to the other. This happens because with the ImageWriter, Word maps 80 screen dots to every printed inch, whereas with the LaserWriter (and the Wide ImageWriter), Word maps 72 screen dots to every printed inch. Consequently, the intervals in the Ruler change size when you switch printers. This can cause problems when you're trying to print a rough draft on the ImageWriter so that you can polish the formatting in the document before printing it on the LaserWriter. You get the document the way you want it only to have everything change when you print it on the LaserWriter.

You can get around this problem in two ways. First, you can do all the writing and editing and most of the initial formatting (for instance, creating style definitions or setting italics and boldface formats where desired) using the ImageWriter to print drafts. Then, you can set the final formats when you have access to the LaserWriter. If you're renting time on the LaserWriter, however, this can be expensive.

The second way is to use the Chooser to select the LaserWriter driver, even though you don't have one connected to your Mac. When you click the LaserWriter icon, no LaserWriter names appear in the list box. Simply click the close box of the Chooser dialog box; Word sets the screen dimensions for the LaserWriter. You can then use Print Preview to fine-tune the formats in your document for the LaserWriter, temporarily switching back to the ImageWriter if you need to print a draft copy.

■ *Setting Document Formats*

The first phase in preparing your document for printing is to be sure that all the Document formats are set as you would like them. You might already have set some of them, such as for the page margins or the placement of footnotes, discussed in previous chapters. Word stores document formats with the document, as it does the character, paragraph, table, and section formats. As mentioned earlier, you can set certain document formats through the Page Setup dialog box, such as the page size, page orientation, and the printing reduction ratio for the document. If you select the Set Default option, these settings become the default for new documents. To change other document formats, such as the margins, numbering, and placement of footnotes, use the Document dialog box. When you click the Set Default button in the Document dialog box, you record these options in the current Word Settings file, and they become the defaults for new documents.

The Page Setup Dialog Box

To display the Page Setup dialog box, choose Page Setup from the File menu. The specific form this dialog box takes depends on whether you've chosen the ImageWriter or the LaserWriter as the current printer. Many of the options you can set from this dialog box, such as page size and orientation, have a direct relationship to the placement of text on the page. Other options, such as Smooth Graphics in the LaserWriter Page Setup dialog box, affect the appearance of text and graphics, but they have no effect on line breaks or page breaks.

The ImageWriter Page Setup Options

The ImageWriter Page Setup dialog box is shown in Figure 14-2. (In version 2.7, this box is labeled simply *ImageWriter*.) By setting options in this dialog box, you can set the page size and orientation and set certain special effects for the document.

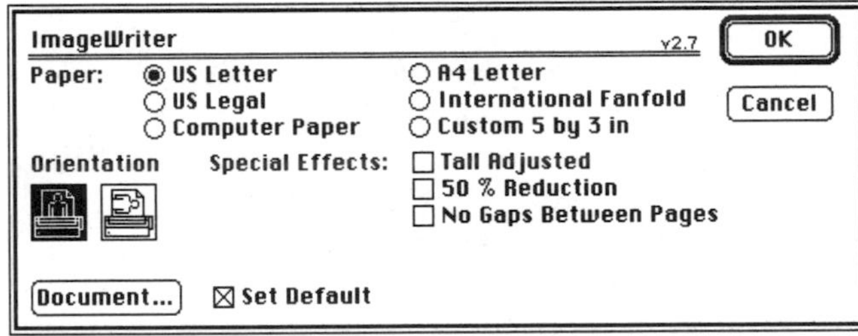

Figure 14-2
The ImageWriter Page Setup dialog box.

Paper Size Options

Setting a paper size option tells Word how large a canvas it has to work with. The options set the following dimensions, depending on the unit of measurement you've specified in the Preferences dialog box:

	Width x Height		
Paper	**Inches**	**Centimeters**	**Points**
US Letter	8.5 x 11	21.59 x 27.94	610 x 790
US Legal	8.5 x 14	21.59 x 35.56	610 x 1008
Computer Paper	14 x 11	35.56 x 27.94	1008 x 790
A4 Letter	8.27 x 11.69	21.01 x 29.69	595 x 842
International Fanfold	8.25 x 12	20.96 x 30.48	594 x 864

Notice the sixth entry among the options listed in the dialog box—the one starting with the word *Custom*. If you temporarily leave the Page Setup dialog box and choose Preferences from the Edit menu, you can enter the dimensions of a custom paper size in the fields at the bottom of the dialog box. This custom paper size then becomes an option in the Page Setup dialog box when you next call it up, and is stored in the current Word Settings file. Obviously, your printer must be able to accommodate these dimensions. Notice that these numbers are always listed width first: In Figure 14-2, we've set up a custom page size for a 3-by-5 index card which Word reports as *Custom 5 by 3 in.* You can set custom paper sizes only when the current printer is the ImageWriter—for any other printer, the Custom Paper Size fields are dimmed.

Orientation Options

By clicking one of the two page-orientation icons, you can specify whether the document is to be printed normally or sideways. The Tall option (sometimes called *portrait*), Word's preset default, prints the document in normal fashion, lines of text parallel to the short edge of the paper. By choosing the Wide option (sometimes called *landscape)*, you can print sideways, in order to generate documents that are wider than they are tall, as shown in Figure 14-3a and Figure 14-3b on the following page.

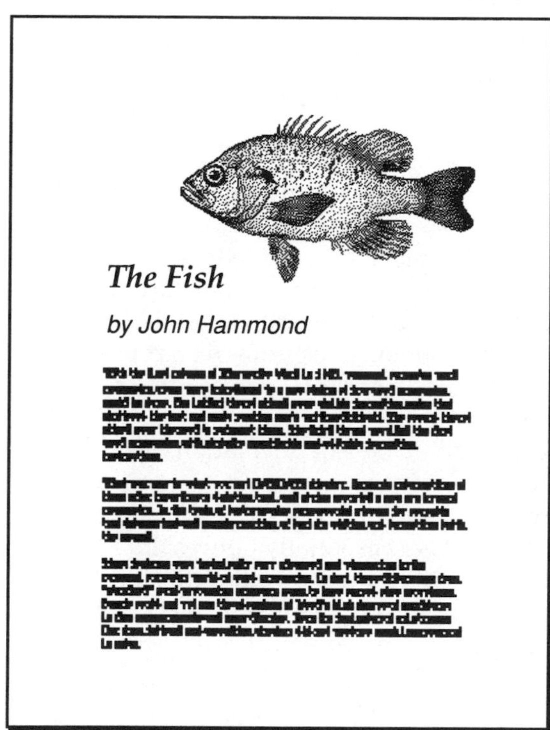

The Fish

by John Hammond

Figure 14-3a

Document printed using the Tall orientation option.

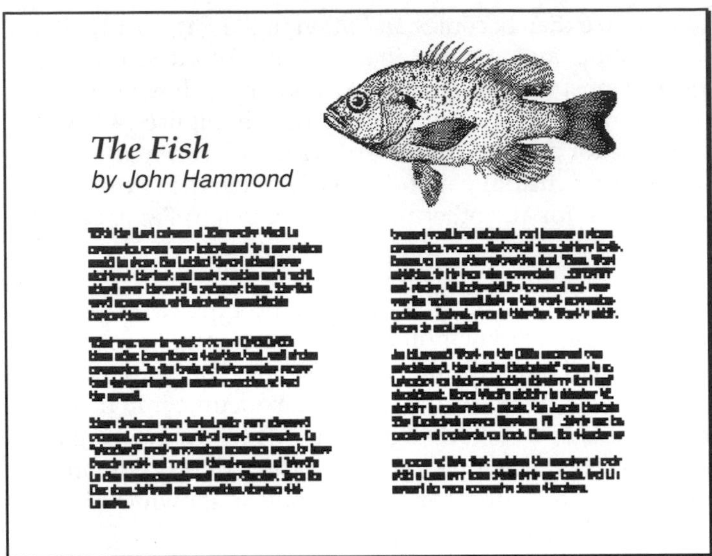

Figure 14-3b
Document printed using the Wide orientation option (formatted here for two columns).

Tall Adjusted
The Tall Adjusted option corrects the discrepancy between the horizontal resolution of the Mac's screen (72 dots per inch) and the horizontal resolution of the standard ImageWriter (80 dots per inch). (The Wide ImageWriter prints at 72 dots per inch.) This discrepancy is the reason the size of inches in the Ruler changes when you switch to the ImageWriter after using the LaserWriter. Without the Tall Adjusted option, circles onscreen print as ovals. With Tall Adjusted, a circle prints as a circle. Click the Tall Adjusted option whenever you must preserve the exact proportions of a graphic. This option works only in documents printed in the Tall orientation (the normal orientation).

You pay a slight price when you use this option. With Tall Adjusted, text is expanded slightly, although the effect isn't especially noticeable. You will notice, however, that because Word can fit less text on a line, the line breaks might not be the same as they were with Tall Adjusted turned off. This can have a domino effect, throwing off paragraph and page breaks.

50% Reduction
Setting the 50% Reduction option compresses the number of dots printed in both the horizontal and vertical dimensions by a factor of two. Interestingly, Word adjusts the reporting of measurements in the Ruler, Print Preview, and Page View by doubling what is reported. For example, for 8.5-by-11 inch

paper, the measurements in Word seem to indicate the page is really 17 inches wide and 22 inches tall. To compensate, halve the measurements you use to arrive at the corresponding printed values—18-point type becomes 9-point type on the paper, tabs set every 0.5 inch are printed every 0.25 inch, and so on.

No Gaps Between Pages

The primary use for the No Gaps Between Pages option is for printing mailing labels onto continuous stock. To do this, you would set the top and bottom margins for the mailing list document to 0 and set the No Gaps Between Pages option. If you didn't set the option, you would see ½-inch omissions in the printed material every 11 inches.

LaserWriter Page Setup Options

When you choose the LaserWriter driver and then choose the Page Setup command, you see the dialog box shown in Figure 14-4, which corresponds here to version 5.2 of the driver (which accompanies Macintosh System version 6.0 and later).

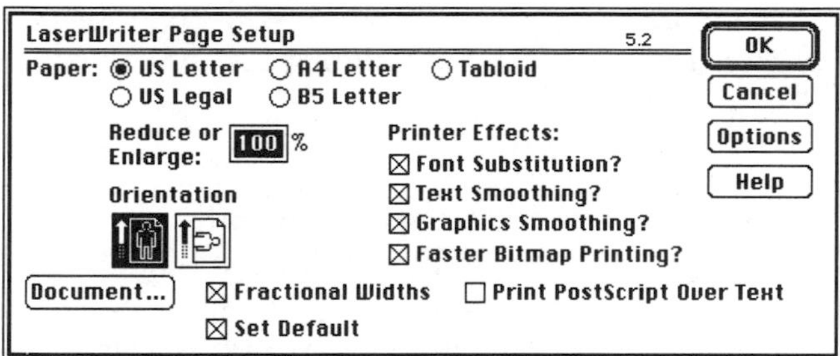

Figure 14-4
The LaserWriter Page Setup dialog box.

Paper Size

The Paper size options tell Word how large a canvas it has to work with. Clicking one of these options sets the following dimensions, depending on the unit of measurement you've set in the Preferences dialog box:

Paper	Width x Height Inches	Centimeters	Points
US Letter	8.5 x 11	21.59 x 27.94	610 x 790
US Legal	8.5 x 14	21.59 x 35.56	610 x 1008
A4 Letter	8.25 x 11.67	20.96 x 29.64	594 x 840
B5 Letter	7.2 x 10.1	18.28 x 25.65	518 x 727
Tabloid	11 x 17	27.94 x 43.18	792 x 1224

The fifth entry, Tabloid, is for desktop publishing on large-format PostScript printers that can handle 11-by-17-inch paper stock. Unlike the ImageWriter, you can't set up a custom page size for the LaserWriter: When the LaserWriter is the current printer, the Custom Paper Size fields in the Preferences dialog box are dimmed.

Orientation Options

As with the ImageWriter, you can click one of the two page orientation icons to specify whether the document is to be printed normally or sideways. Selecting the first icon sets the document for printing in normal fashion, with lines of text parallel to the short edge of the paper. Clicking the second icon sets the format for printing documents that are wider than they are tall.

Reduce/Enlarge %

The Reduce/Enlarge % option lets you specify the amount by which printed material is to be reduced or enlarged. You can specify a number from 25 percent (one-fourth the size of the original you see on the screen) to 400 percent (four times the size of the original). As with the ImageWriter, if you set a reduction factor other than 100 percent, Word multiplies on-screen distances by the corresponding factor. For example, if you specify a reduction ratio of 50% and set a tab stop of 0.5 inch in the Ruler, the resulting distance on paper will be 0.25 inch.

Fractional Widths

The Fractional Widths option causes Word to measure the widths of characters in PostScript fonts in a different way and improves the spacing of text when printed on a PostScript-compatible printer. When you set this option, the line breaks change because Word calculates different widths for the characters in each line of text. You might notice that the right edge of justified text on the screen is not precisely even with the right indent. This happens because the screen character widths and the printed character widths are now slightly different. Also, the spacing of characters on screen can vary slightly, because Word must convert the fractional widths of characters in memory to whole-pixel increments on screen. Some pairs of characters appear pinched and generally harder to read than when Fractional Widths is turned off. The advantage of this in Word 4 is that text is placed much more accurately on screen than in previous versions of Word.

Also, if you're using a Mac II with color, you'll find that turning on both color and Fractional Widths dramatically slows down scrolling speed in the document. The decrease in speed is proportional to the number of colors being displayed. To work around this, either decrease the number of colors displayed or turn off Fractional Widths until you need accurate character widths for working with line breaks, hyphenation, and page breaks and for printing the document.

Print PostScript Over Text
Normally, the special effects you add when inserting PostScript code into a document are all printed before any of the text in the document is printed. (See Appendix C, "Using PostScript.") The gray screen in the Tip sections of this book is an example of this process: First a gray rectangle is printed, and the text belonging to the tip is printed over it. When you select the Print PostScript Over Text option, however, PostScript special effects are printed over (rather than under) text and non-PostScript graphics. This trick is useful, for example, when you want to draw a PostScript-generated shape over a border created in Word.

Font Substitution
The Font Substitution option allows the LaserWriter to substitute one of its internal fonts when it encounters a bit-mapped font in your document. Printing of text formatted in a bit-mapped font is faster when Font Substitution is on, but you might notice unsightly gaps between letters and words. Don't use a bit-mapped font on the LaserWriter unless you have a real need for it. This option is set by default.

When this option is turned off, the Mac must send a complete specification for the font to a PostScript printer: the resulting increase in printing time is a leading source of what are called *timeout errors* on PostScript printers. If an error dictionary isn't resident on the printer (see Appendix C, "Using PostScript," for more information on error dictionaries), you might find that documents containing large numbers of bit-mapped fonts will stop printing, with no indication of what happened.

Text Smoothing and Graphics Smoothing
These options smooth the edges of bit-mapped fonts and graphics. This improves the appearance of some text and graphics, but blurs the appearance others. Printing is much slower with these options turned on; they are on by default.

Faster Bitmap Printing
The Faster Bitmap Printing option speeds printing by using memory in a PostScript printer more efficiently for bit-mapped graphics. The cost, however, is less available space for downloaded text and other types of graphics. Consequently, sometimes the printer runs out of memory and the page doesn't print. If this happens, deselect this option and try again.

LaserWriter Options Button
If you click the Options button, you see a dialog box like the one shown in Figure 14-5 on the following page. The features in this dialog box are most useful when your Word document contains bit-mapped graphic images that you want to print with as few distortions as possible.

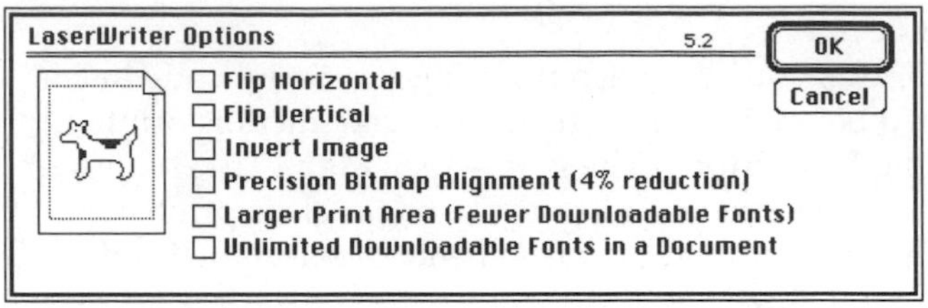

LaserWriter Options 5.2

OK

Cancel

- ☐ Flip Horizontal
- ☐ Flip Vertical
- ☐ Invert Image
- ☐ Precision Bitmap Alignment (4% reduction)
- ☐ Larger Print Area (Fewer Downloadable Fonts)
- ☐ Unlimited Downloadable Fonts in a Document

Figure 14-5
The LaserWriter Options dialog box.

- Flip Horizontal and Flip Vertical let you print a graphic upside down or reverse an image.
- Invert Image turns white to black and black to white. This is handy as a special effect or if you want to create a negative image (for example, to create an image for a silkscreen).
- Precision Bitmap Alignment is probably the most useful option in this dialog box. Almost every bit-mapped image created by scanners or paint programs on the Macintosh has a pixel density of 72 dots per inch. The LaserWriter prints at 300 dots per inch. Unfortunately, 72 doesn't divide into 300 evenly—if you used 4 LaserWriter dots to represent each Mac screen pixel, you'd get 288 dots per inch.

  You can deal with this inconsistency in two ways. One is to shrink the image a little (to 96 percent, which is 288 divided by 300) and retain the 4-to-1 pixel-mapping ratio. This leads to a 4 percent misalignment with the other elements on a page; the larger the bit-mapped graphic, the larger the error. The second way is to scale up the bit-mapped image by an extra 4 percent so that the dimensions of the image remain accurate and the image stays aligned. However, because the pixel-mapping ratio is not exactly 4 to 1, this method produces distortions in the printed image of the bit-mapped graphic—some Mac pixels are 4 LaserWriter pixels square, some are 4 by 5 LaserWriter pixels, some are 5 by 4, and some are 5 by 5.

  The Precision Bitmap Alignment option solves this problem by scaling down everything in the document to 96 percent, including the text elements around the graphic. In this way, the graphics retain the 4-to-1 ratio and alignment is maintained.
- The Larger Print Area option allows you to change the way in which the LaserWriter manages its memory. Normally, the printer reserves some memory for downloaded fonts. If you're printing very complicated pages with many elements and aren't downloading fonts, you can claim some of this memory so that the LaserWriter can store

larger images. This can be useful for printing onto legal-sized paper when feeding it manually, even though you have the standard-sized paper tray loaded in the LaserWriter.

- The Unlimited Downloadable Fonts in Document option is also very useful. Before the current version of the LaserWriter driver made it available, you had to limit the number of downloadable fonts in a document, because each font was stored in the printer's memory and a finite amount of memory is available on every printer. With this option, the printer purges an old font from memory to create room for the new font. However, this can slow down printing, because the Mac often must re-download fonts several times during the course of a print job.

The Document Dialog Box

When you choose Document from the Format menu, click the Document button in the Page Setup dialog box for the currently selected printer, or double-click inside the margin near the corner of a page in Page View, you'll see the dialog box shown in Figure 14-6. As mentioned earlier, the formats you set in this dialog box are stored with the document. If you click the Set Default button, the formats are stored in the current Word Settings file and become the default for all new documents.

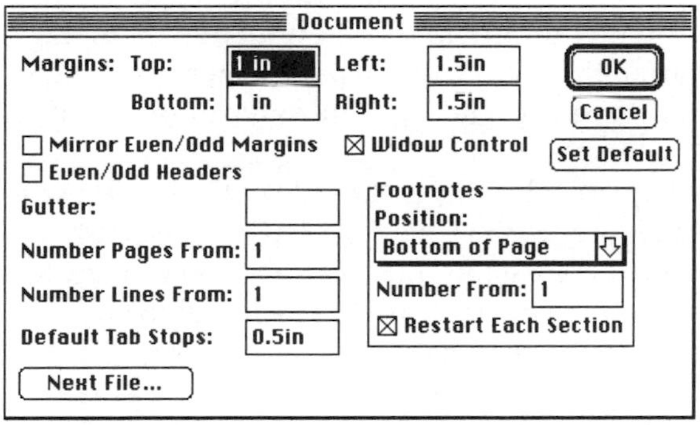

Figure 14-6
The Document dialog box.

The Margins Fields

Word measures the page margins from the edges of the page set in the Page Setup dialog box. The 0 point on the Ruler indicates the left margin for all but positioned paragraphs, the left edge of the cell containing the insertion point in a table, or the left edge of the current column in multicolumn documents.

A light dotted line on the right side of the Ruler shows the position of the right margin for text formatted in one column, the right edge of the cell containing the insertion point in a table, or the right edge of the current column of text. The indents are at the margins until you change them.

The Margins fields set the area for the body text of the document. (Page numbers, headers, and footers are usually printed outside this area.) To change a margin, click in the appropriate field and enter a measurement. You can use inches, centimeters, or points, but when you call up the dialog box, measurements are reported in the unit set in the Preferences dialog box.

As was discussed earlier, the left and right indents are measured relative to the margins. You can place the indents either inside the margins—the normal case—or outside them. When you drag the first-line indent marker to the left of the left indent, you create a hanging indent. When you drag a right indent marker to the right of the right margin, you create what is known as a breakthrough indent or a margin violation. When you change the left and right margins, the indents retain their positions with respect to the margins.

Setting a Fixed Top or Bottom Margin

As was mentioned in the previous chapter, if you create a header or footer that is more than a few lines deep, Word moves the top or bottom margin of the body text to accommodate it, if necessary, so that the header or footer text does not overlap the body text.

If you want to set a top margin that remains at a constant distance from the top of the page regardless of the size of the header, enter a negative number in the Top edit field. And if you want to set a bottom margin that remains at a constant distance from the bottom of the page, enter a negative number in the Bottom edit field. Word uses the absolute value of the number you enter to set the margin.

You could use this feature to place a header to the side of the body text rather than over it, as shown in Figure 13-3 in Chapter 13. (Of course, using the Positioned paragraph format works well for this, too.) Or you can create an "electronic letterhead" when you have established a stock design on a page and want the body text to appear within the limits of the design. The electronic letterhead project in Chapter 18, "Blueprints," shows an example of this. Finally, you could put a frame around the body text in a magazine or newsletter design, for example, as shown in Figure 14-7.

You'll learn more about how to set up these design elements in Chapter 16, which describes how to copy graphics into a Word document, and in Chapter 18, which presents projects you can adapt to your own documents.

The Transcendentalist Times
1243 Harrison Place, Duvall, WA 98702
Phone: 206-555-7532

Figure 14-7
A page frame for a magazine or newsletter.

Mirror Even/Odd Margins

Click the Mirror Even/Odd Margins check box if you'll be printing the document on both sides of the paper and assembling it in book form. When you do this, the names of the Left and Right margin fields change to Inside and Outside, respectively. When you give a paragraph the Outside Bar Border format, Word places the bar on the outside of the page, just to the left or right of the paragraph.

Even/Odd Headers

When the Even/Odd Headers option is set, Word creates separate headers and footers for the left-hand and right-hand pages (known as *even* and *odd* pages, respectively) and adds Even and Odd Header and Footer commands to the Document menu in Galley View. If you've set the Auto page numbering option in the Section dialog box, it also places page numbers in the outside corners of the paper—the upper left corner of even-numbered pages and the upper right corner of odd-numbered ones, according to the measurements entered in the From Top and the From Right fields in the dialog box.

The Gutter Field

Entering a number in the Gutter field lets you add space for the binding of the document, on the inside edge of the paper. (The inside edge is interpreted as being the left edge of odd-numbered pages, and the right edge of even-numbered pages.) The space you specify is added to the Inside margin if you selected the Mirror Even/Odd Margins option.

With Mirror Even/Odd Margins on, you can set a gutter margin, which increases the inner margin of each page to allow for the binding. Leave the Gutter field blank or enter a measurement in inches, centimeters, or points. A gutter of 0.5 inch, for example, shifts even-numbered pages ½ inch to the left and odd-numbered pages ½ inch to the right, as indicated by the gray area on the inside of each page shown in Figure 14-8, even if you're also using the Mirror Even/Odd Margins option. Word still sets the 0 point on the Ruler to the left margin.

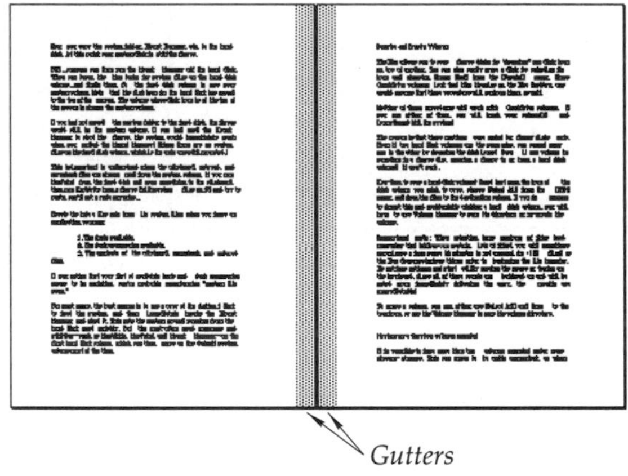

Figure 14-8
A page spread with 0.5-inch gutters.

The Widow Control Option

A *widow* occurs when the first line of a paragraph appears by itself at the bottom of a page. Widows are considered bad form because they are easy for a reader to lose. Word's Widow Control option prevents this from happening by moving the first line of a paragraph to the top of the next page. The option is normally set; click the box to turn it off. This option also causes Word to correct for *orphans*, which occur when the last line of a paragraph appears by itself at the top of a page: If an orphan occurs, Word brings over one more line from the bottom of the previous page.

The Number Pages From Field

Normally, you leave the starting page number at 1, unless the document is a unit in a larger series of documents (discussed later in this chapter in the section called "Chaining Files"). To have Word do the numbering for you, remove the number in the Number Pages From field, or enter a 0. If you haven't linked a series of documents through the Next File dialog box and still want the document to start on a specific page, enter the page number in the field. For example, if the last page of the previous document was page 24, enter *25*.

The Number Lines From Field

The Number Lines From option, similar to the Number Pages From option, lets you set the starting line number for paragraphs having the Line Numbering paragraph format in the document. See Chapter 9, "Paragraph Formatting," for more information on line numbering.

The Default Tab Stops Option

The Ruler contains default tab stops if you haven't placed any tab markers on it. Normally, Word places these at 0.5-inch intervals. Enter another measurement in the Default Tab Stops field to make the default tabs closer together or farther apart. Default tab stops appear as small upside-down Ts on the Ruler. If you don't want any default stops, enter *22 in*.

The Footnotes Options

As was discussed in the previous chapter, the Footnote Position drop-down list lets you specify where Word prints the footnotes:

- ❑ At the bottom of the page containing the footnote reference. The end of the last footnote on the page ends at the bottom margin.
- ❑ Directly beneath the text (even if the text only partially fills the page).
- ❑ At the end of a section.
- ❑ At the end of the document.

In documents with more than one section, you can collect footnotes at the end of certain sections by setting the End of Section option and then setting the Include Endnotes option in the Section dialog box for the section where the footnotes are to be collected. Word prints the accumulated footnotes at the end of each section in which this option is set.

Use the Number From field to set the number of the first footnote in the first section. Set the Restart Each Section option to restart footnote numbering at 1 in each section. If you selected the Beneath Text or Bottom of Page option in the Position drop-down list, the numbering starts with 1 on each page. If the End of Section option is selected, numbering starts at 1 at the beginning of each section. If you select the End of Document option, Word numbers the footnotes consecutively throughout the document regardless of the number of sections. See Chapter 13, "Headers, Footers, and Footnotes," for more details on these footnote options.

Chaining Files

Clicking the Next File button tells Word to link another document to the end of the current one. A standard dialog box appears, listing the files stored on the currently mounted disks. You use this feature to chain-print two or more documents, making it easier to print them all at once. You also use chained files when compiling a table of contents or an index (described in Chapter 15, "Creating a Table of Contents and Index").

If you're chaining more than two files, open each document in the series and select the name of the succeeding file in the Next File dialog box. For example:

Filename	**Enter into next file box**
Front Matter	*Part 1*
Part 1	*Part 2*
Part 2	*Appendixes*
Appendixes	(Leave blank)

When you set a chained file in this way, Word displays the name of the next file to the right of the button and changes the name of the button to Reset Next File. If you click this button, Word removes the link.

With chained files, even though Word continues the page numbers from one document to the next (if you've left the Number Pages From field blank or entered a 0), it doesn't continue line numbers or footnote numbers. Therefore, you must enter the correct starting line or footnote number in the appropriate field if you want to continue the numbering.

If you want to chain the currently opened document to a document that doesn't exist yet, temporarily close the Document dialog box, create a new, empty document, save it under the name of the document to be created or obtained later, and close the empty document. Having created an empty document with the desired name, reopen the Document dialog box and chain the first document to the second through the Next File dialog box.

A final note: If you want to chain files to extract an index or table of contents, but don't want to print all the documents in the series, deselect the Print Next File option in the Print dialog box (discussed later in this chapter).

■ *Hyphenation*

Once you reach a point where the line lengths in your document will no longer change, you can hyphenate it, if you want. Do this after you've chosen a printer, set the final page margins, and made final adjustments to the left and right indents. It's also a good idea to use the spelling checker and do your final editing first. Correcting spelling errors after hyphenation might change the lengths of words in a line of text, requiring you to do another hyphenation pass through the document.

As was mentioned earlier, hyphenation is optional. Some designers avoid it except where absolutely necessary, making the case that a hyphenated word is harder to read than an unbroken one. Most documents need only light hyphenation, especially those with ragged right (left-aligned) text. Hyphenation can improve the appearance of text, particularly when long words are placed on short lines, and in multiple-column documents. Justified text (text aligned at both the right and the left indents) and narrow columns often require heavier hyphenation because lines containing too few words tend to look stretched out, as Figure 14-9 illustrates.

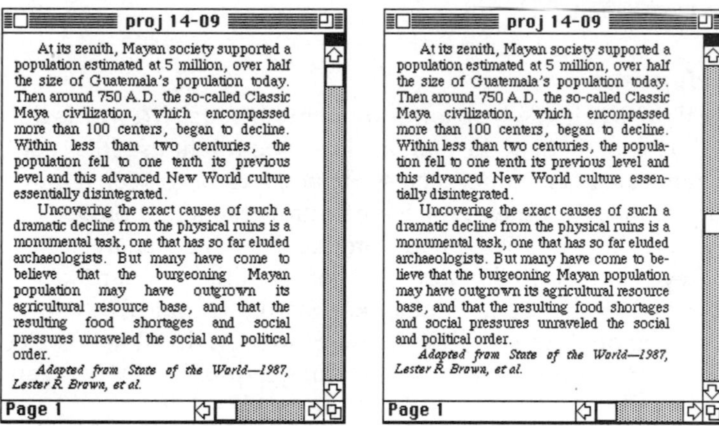

Figure 14-9
Spacing problems in justified text: unhyphenated (left) and hyphenated (right).

When hyphenating your document, keep the following guidelines in mind. Avoid hyphens at the end of more than two consecutive lines—too many hyphenated lines can be distracting. If more than two lines out of six or seven end with a hyphen, you're probably using text columns that are too narrow: Consider using a wider column or reducing the point size of the text. Don't hyphenate a word that is already part of a hyphenated compound. For example, don't hyphenate *ma-trix* in *dot-matrix*. Finally, acronyms, proper nouns, and addresses are seldom hyphenated.

Word lets you hyphenate in two ways: You can enter hyphens manually, or you can choose the Hyphenate command from the Document menu.

Hyphenating Manually

Word lets you manually enter three types of hyphens: normal, nonbreaking, and optional. (You can also enter em and en dashes, which are discussed in the next tip and in Chapter 5, "Writing and Editing Techniques.") Normal hyphens always appear in a line of text and can fall at the end of a line, whereas nonbreaking hyphens always appear in text but can't fall at the end of a line. Optional hyphens appear only when they fall at the end of a line.

Normal Hyphens

You enter a normal hyphen by pressing the hyphen, or minus, key (next to the = key). Word can break a line at a normal hyphen, as in the following:

They always thought he was a ne'er-do-
well, but he proved them wrong.

Nonbreaking Hyphens

You use a nonbreaking hyphen when you want to hyphenate two words but don't want Word to break them at the end of a line. You might use this type of hyphen in a hyphenated last name, such as *Smyth-Jones*, or to keep a unit such as an account number or other hyphenated number together on one line. To enter a nonbreaking hyphen, press Command- ~. The ~ character is called a *tilde;* the key is located in the upper left corner of the standard keyboard and to the left of the Spacebar on other keyboards. Technically, you press Command- `; you don't press the Shift key. However, the tilde is easier to remember because it appears above a nonbreaking hyphen (~̣) when you choose Show ¶.

Optional Hyphens

You enter optional hyphens manually when you don't want to hyphenate text extensively, but simply want to fix a few problem lines, or when you want Word to break a word at a different point than it would on its own. To enter this type of hyphen, press Command- – (hyphen). Optional hyphens are normally invisible; unless Show ¶ is in effect, they appear only if Word breaks the hyphenated word at the end of a line.

Suppose, for example, that the word *countermeasure* occurs at the end of a line, and that the last four characters of the word will not fit within the indents you've set. Normally, the word would be dropped to the next line. With Word's built-in hyphenation feature, *countermeasure* could be broken as follows: *countermea-sure* . However, you might prefer to divide the word at the prefix: *counter-measure*. Simply place the insertion point between the two parts and press Command- –.

This highlights an important property of Word's automatic hyphenation feature: Word uses a set of rules to divide words at syllables—sometimes it divides a word at other than the ideal location. When in doubt, consult a style manual, such as *The Chicago Manual of Style* from the University of Chicago Press. Such manuals exhaustively explain the fine points of word division in the English language.

If, after hyphenating a document, you make changes to it so that some words that you hyphenated with an optional hyphen no longer occur at the end of lines, Word rejoins the words and does not display the hyphens. When you choose Show ¶, Word marks the location of each optional hyphen, whether at the end of a line or not, by a normal hyphen with a dot under it (‐̣). If subsequent editing causes a word containing one of these special characters to again end a line, the word is broken at that point.

TIP

Other Kinds of Dashes

Some people use two hyphens together (--) to represent an em dash (—). This type of dash is often used to indicate a break in the flow of a sentence that isn't as extreme as that produced by parentheses. You can get this special character on your Mac keyboard by pressing Shift-Option- – (hyphen, or minus). Remember—if you want to use this character—that you leave no space on either side of the em dash.

Less common, an en dash is used to separate the beginning and end of a range, such as in *1988–91*, or in a compound, such as *Seattle–San Jose flight*. You enter this character by pressing Option- – (hyphen). Again, style manuals are good sources of information about the use of these special characters. Word treats both the em dash and the en dash as it does the normal hyphen.

Using Word's Hyphenation Feature

Word's hyphenation feature analyzes line lengths and splits words between syllables according to an internal set of rules. This set of rules is kept in a special file called Word Hyphenation. When the hyphenation feature breaks words, it inserts optional hyphens; however, if you edit the document or change the line lengths, the divided words are rejoined and the hyphens disappear. Using the hyphenation feature is easy; you set the insertion point where you want to start hyphenating, or you select a specific passage and choose Hyphenate from the Utilities menu. A dialog box like the one shown in Figure 14-10 appears after a short delay, so Word can load its hyphenation dictionary.

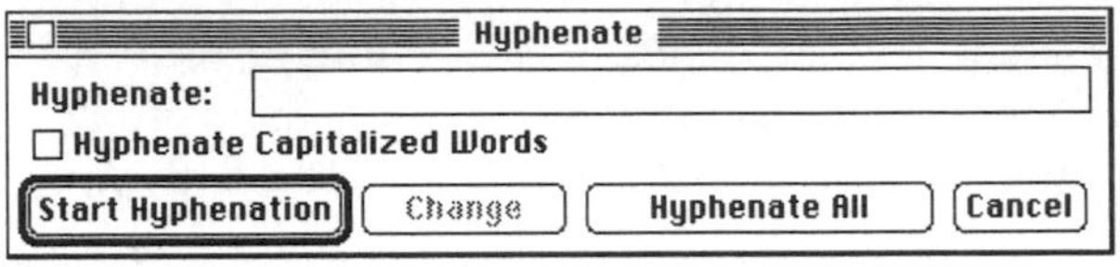

Hyphenate

Hyphenate: [ ]

☐ Hyphenate Capitalized Words

[Start Hyphenation] [Change] [Hyphenate All] [Cancel]

Figure 14-10
The Hyphenate dialog box.

You can choose to have the program hyphenate words automatically, or you can review and verify each candidate for hyphenation. If you've set an insertion point within a paragraph, Word starts hyphenating at the beginning of that paragraph, not from the insertion point. Be sure to turn off Show ¶ first: Word doesn't compensate for the width of characters that are visible only when Show ¶ is on, including the optional hyphen itself.

Automatic Hyphenation

To hyphenate words automatically, click the Hyphenate All button if you've set an insertion point or the Hyphenate Selection button if you've selected some text. Simply wait until the hyphenation process is complete. While Word is hyphenating, it pauses each time it inserts an optional hyphen so that you watch the progress. When the word is hyphenated, the part before the hyphen moves to the end of the preceding line.

If you set the insertion point anywhere but at the beginning of the document, Word presents a dialog box when it reaches the end of the document and asks if you want to start over from the beginning. It's a good idea to look over the document to be sure you agree with the way words are divided.

You can change a hyphen in one word by double-clicking on the word, choosing the Hyphenate command, and clicking Hyphenate Selection. Word presents a dialog box stating that it has hyphenated the word. However, for the hyphenation to work properly, the word you selected should be the first word on the line; otherwise, no part of the hyphenated word will move to the end of the preceding line.

You can also manually delete the existing optional hyphen; simply select it and press the Backspace key. If you edited or otherwise changed the line lengths, you can see the hyphen by turning on Show ¶. You can then enter an optional hyphen in a different place by placing the insertion point where you want the hyphen and pressing Command- – (hyphen).

Verifying Hyphenation

To verify each word before it is hyphenated, click the Start Hyphenation button. When Word finds a candidate for hyphenation, it displays it in the Hyphenate dialog box, with hyphens separating the syllables. Word highlights the hyphen it proposes to use, and in the document it highlights the hyphen that would split the word.

You'll want to pay careful attention to the dotted vertical line that appears in the Hyphenate field. (See Figure 14-11.) This line indicates where the word would break on the line if the rules for breaking between syllables were ignored. Adding optional hyphens to the right of the dotted line isn't helpful, because the word would still be too long to fit on the line.

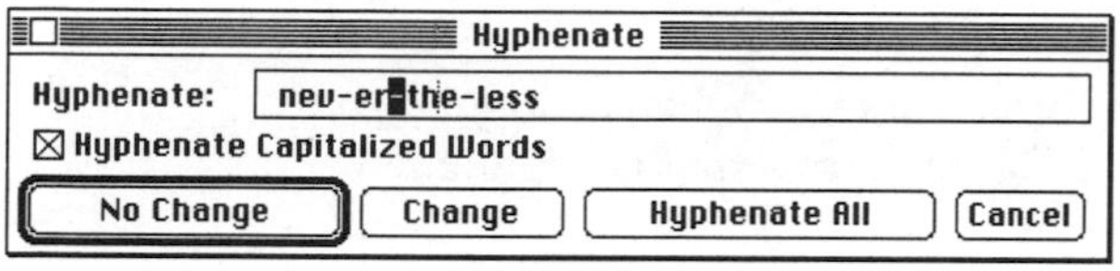

Hyphenate

Hyphenate: nev-er-the-less

☒ Hyphenate Capitalized Words

No Change | Change | Hyphenate All | Cancel

Figure 14-11

A candidate for hyphenation in the Hyphenate dialog box.

Once Word has displayed a candidate for hyphenation, you have several alternatives:

- Accept the suggested hyphenation by clicking the Change button.
- Do not hyphenate the word at all, by clicking the No Change button (or pressing the Return key).
- Choose one of the other hyphen points by clicking on it and then clicking the Change button.
- Choose an entirely new hyphenation point (one not shown by Word) by setting an insertion point between any two letters. After doing this, click the Change button.
- Stop hyphenation at any point by clicking the Cancel button.

Skipping Capitalized Words

Words in which the first letter or every letter is capitalized are usually not hyphenated. For example, proper nouns, such as names of persons or companies, are usually not hyphenated. It's also considered bad form to hyphenate the first word in a sentence or the last word in a paragraph. Acronyms should not be hyphenated unless absolutely necessary.

You can skip over capitalized words by turning off the Hyphenate Capitalized Words option (it's normally on) before you begin hyphenating. If you want to consider hyphenating capitalized words, leave the option checked and then review each candidate.

Searching for and Removing Hyphens

Unhyphenating a document is more difficult than hyphenating it. No "unhyphenate" command exists, although you can choose Undo Hyphenate immediately after you hyphenate a word. Sometimes, however, you might need to remove both optional and nonbreaking hyphens for any of these reasons:

- To conform to a certain format, such as when changing from a justified and hyphenated format to one that is left aligned and ragged right.
- If you decide that your document is too heavily hyphenated and you want to remove some of the hyphens.
- To make a Word document usable by some other word processor.

For an example of the last reason, suppose that you saved a document having optional and nonbreaking hyphens as a Text Only file and then opened the file in MacWrite. Each optional or nonbreaking hyphen would appear as a square, signifying an undefined character, as shown in Figure 14-12. The same thing happens when you open Word documents with other Macintosh word processors.

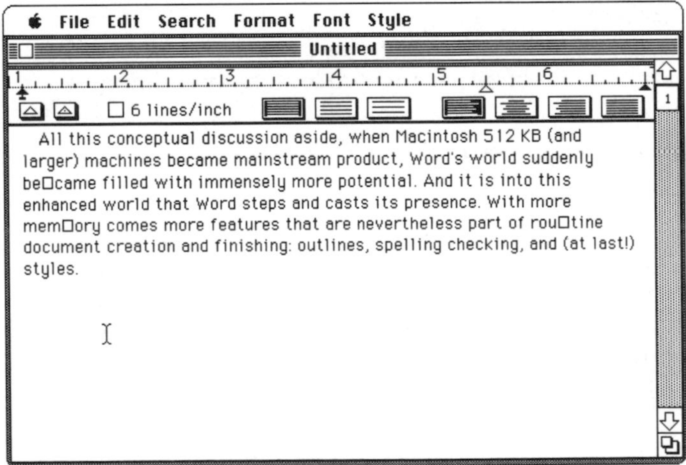

Figure 14-12
Optional hyphens as they appear in MacWrite.

You can use Word's search-and-replace feature to remove optional and nonbreaking hyphens. To start, position the insertion point at the beginning of the document. Then do the following:

1. Choose Change from the Search menu.
2. To remove optional hyphens, enter ^ - in the Find What field (the caret— Shift-6 —and the hyphen character). If you prefer, you can specify the ASCII equivalent of the optional hyphen by entering *^31*. To remove nonbreaking hyphens, use ^ ~. (The ASCII equivalent of the tilde is *^30*.)
3. Leave the Change To field empty.
4. Click the Start Search or Change All button, depending on whether you want to verify each change or have Word change every occurrence automatically.

Word finds all optional or nonbreaking hyphens and replaces them with nothing, thereby closing up each hyphenated word.

■ *Repagination, Page Breaks, and Page Layout*

When you enter text and copy graphics into a Word document, the result is similar to writing on a long scroll of paper. Most people use the vertical scroll bar to move up and down in a document, either a line at a time by clicking the scroll arrows, or one or more pages at a time by dragging the scroll box. Yet when you print the document, Word divides it into pages so that the text flows from the bottom of one page to the top of the next. The process of breaking a document into pages is called pagination.

Word paginates a document by adding up the line lengths, the point sizes of the text, the height of the graphics, the dimensions of the margins, and so on—a nearly endless list of factors—and calculating how much fits on each page. This calculation takes time. If Word repaginated dynamically—that is, every time you added text or made a formatting change—the amount of recalculation needed to handle the range of formatting features Word offers would cause an unacceptable degradation in performance. Therefore, Word repaginates only when necessary, as in the following instances:

- When you choose the Print or Print Merge commands. Word must do a repagination to generate an image for each page.
- When you choose Print Preview from the File menu. Word can't display the image of a page unless it repaginates the document up to the point where you chose the Print Preview command.
- When you're working with a document in Page View.

- When you choose Table of Contents or Index from the Utilities menu. Both of these commands need the correct page numbers of the headings or index references in the document.
- When you choose Repaginate Now from the Document menu.
- When the Background Repagination option in the Preferences dialog box is set. This feature is close to dynamic repagination; if this option is in effect, Word waits for idle moments when you're not entering, editing, or formatting text to update the line and page breaks in the document.

The page breaks that Word creates when repaginating are called automatic page breaks, and each appears as a light dotted line, as shown in Figure 14-13. When Word breaks the text into pages, each element falls on the page at the point determined by the dimensions of all previous elements combined. This arrangement is called the page layout. If the layout on a particular page isn't to your liking, you can adjust the position of the elements in a document in several ways:

- You can set the Page Break Before paragraph format for a paragraph that is to begin a new page. This is helpful when you want the title of a section to appear at the top of a page, especially when you are using styles to format the heads in a document.
- You can set the New Page, Odd Page, or Even Page formats for a section. This is good for starting a chapter in a book or an article in a magazine at the top of a new page, or for placing a large table on a page by itself.
- You can force a page break by clicking the insertion point where you want the page to end and pressing Shift-Enter. Word displays a manual page break as a heavy dotted line, as shown in Figure 14-13. To delete a manual page break, select it and press the Backspace key.
- You can force page breaks in Print Preview and convert an automatic page break to a manual one, but only for one-column text.
- You can add a Position format to paragraphs or tables you'd like to break out from the standard serial format as entered in Document view.

You can't delete automatic page breaks by selecting and deleting them, but you can "move" them by setting a manual page break earlier in the text. Word then recalculates automatic page breaks from the start of the new page.

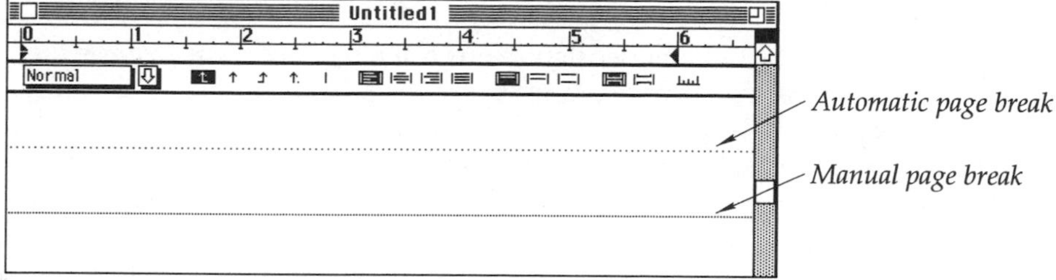

Figure 14-13
Types of page breaks, which appear on screen as dotted lines.

If you alter the text or insert manual page breaks, the length of one or more pages is affected. When you repaginate the document, Word places new automatic page breaks where appropriate but leaves your manual page breaks intact. You can use this rippling effect to change the layout for a particular page by making adjustments in the pages preceding it. Often, the resulting change in page breaks ripples through to the problem page and improves its layout. You can also alter the page layout by adjusting a multitude of other factors:

- Adding or removing lines by editing the text.
- Turning widow control on or off, through the Document dialog box.
- Changing the font or font size.
- Pressing Shift-Return to break lines in different places than where Word does automatically.
- Changing the spacing formats of paragraphs.
- Making small changes to the right indents of selected paragraphs, effectively changing the line lengths for certain paragraphs and causing lines to break in different places than previously. This trick works best in flush-left (ragged-right) paragraphs: If done with restraint, the reader seldom notices.

Word displays the current page and section number (if your document has more than one section) in the status area in the lower left corner of the document window. After repagination, these numbers appear in boldface and change as you scroll through the document. Word displays the number of the top line in the window. If you've made changes since the last repagination, the page numbers are dimmed, but you can still use them as an approximation (useful for traveling through the document). Also, don't forget that you can double-click in this area to bring up the Go To dialog box, useful for jumping to specific pages.

TIP

Full Repagination

As was mentioned earlier, many calculations must be done to determine the size of the elements in a document and where the page breaks should occur. In order to repaginate as quickly as possible, Word skips any paragraphs that haven't changed since the last repagination. This occasionally leads to problems if you changed printers or if a document specifies a font that isn't installed in your System file when you print the document. You can suspect an inaccurate repagination if page breaks seem to be in the wrong places; if lines are missing or overlap in Print Preview, in Page View, or on the printed page; or if objects aren't positioned accurately on the page.

To tell Word to leave no stone unturned (or to skip no paragraph) in its recalculation of page breaks, press the Shift key as you choose the Repaginate Now command. As you drag down the list of options on the Document menu, you'll see that the Repaginate Now command now reads Full Repaginate Now.

The Print Preview Command

Print Preview allows you to audition the page as it will appear on paper, manually set page breaks, adjust the margins, and move certain objects on the page (such as headers, footers, and positioned paragraphs and tables). To audition a document from the beginning, click at the start of the text and choose Print Preview from the File menu. You'll see small versions of the first two pages of your document, like the screen shown in Figure 14-14. Each page is scaled proportionally to the paper size specified in the Page Setup dialog box.

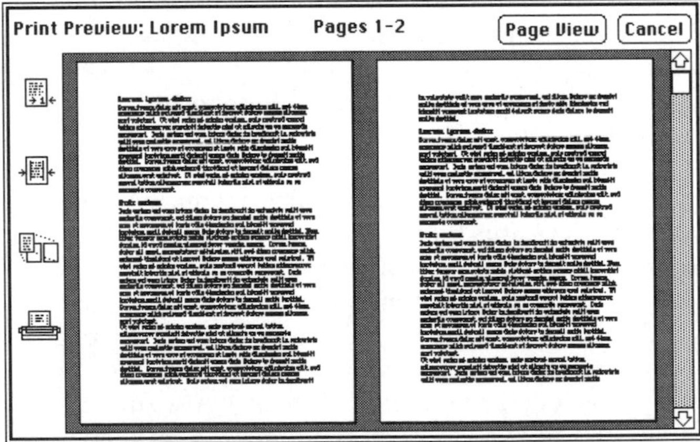

Figure 14-14
The Print Preview screen.

You can't edit the document while in Print Preview, and all the menu commands are inaccessible. You can display other pages in the document by using the vertical scroll bar or pressing the up or down arrow key on the keyboard. If you turned on the Even/Odd Headers option or the Mirror Even/Odd Margins option in the Document dialog box, the pages scroll two at a time, so the left-hand page is an even-numbered page and the right-hand page is an odd-numbered page. The four icons on the left side of the window let you manipulate the document. These will be discussed in a moment.

If you need to check the page layout for an entire document, possibly setting a few manual page breaks, do so with Print Preview. With Print Preview, the document is repaginated up to the page displayed and no further. If the document is a large one, you can both repaginate it and check the layout by starting at the beginning and scrolling through it page by page.

You can return to Galley View or Page View, whichever was the last mode selected, by clicking in the window's close box, clicking the Cancel button, or pressing Command-(period). When you do this, you are returned to the last page you displayed in Print Preview. This feature also works in reverse. If you want to preview a specific page, you can scroll there in Galley View or Page View and then choose the Print Preview command. You can also jump to Page View by double-clicking at a location on a page or by clicking the Page View button.

The following sections describe the icons on the left side of the Print Preview window.

The Page Number Icon

Clicking the Page Number icon lets you add page numbers to the document. Click the icon (the pointer turns into a 1 with arrows on either side), and click on the location where you want the number to appear. Or double-click the icon to put the number in the default location in the upper right corner of the page. The number is placed in that location on all pages. You can see the measurements corresponding to its location by displaying the Section dialog box. To see the position of the page number in Print Preview as you move it into place, click at any location on the page and hold down the mouse button as you drag the page-number pointer. The current position appears at the top of the dialog box.

If the Even/Odd Headers option is set in the Document dialog box, the position of the page number is symmetrical with respect to the inside edge of the page. For example, if the option is set and you double-click the Page Number icon, the number appears in the upper left corner of even pages and the upper right corner of odd pages.

The type of number used is determined by the Page Number options in the Section dialog box, and the automatic style named *page number* governs the character formats of the page numbers.

You can also include the page number in a header or footer, as described in the previous chapter. There is no relationship between the page numbers you specify in Print Preview and the ones placed in the header or footer.

The Margins Icon

When you click the Margins icon, guidelines for these page elements appear on the currently selected page. Click on the facing page to move the guidelines there. Figure 14-15 shows the various types of guidelines displayed. By dragging the guidelines you can change the position of the top, bottom, right, and left margins, automatic and manual page breaks, the header, the footer, and the location of positioned paragraphs and tables. You can also change the position of the page number if you've added one. The procedures for adjusting these will be described in a moment.

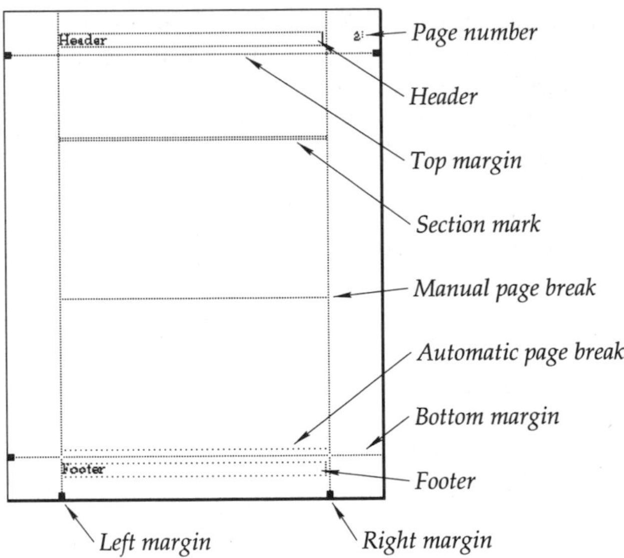

Figure 14-15
Guidelines showing elements that can be moved after you click the Margins icon. (However, you wouldn't see both the manual and automatic page breaks on the same page.)

The One-Page Display Icon

When you click the One-Page Display icon, only one page appears at a time. Click it again to return to the two-page display. Previewing your document one page at a time is useful for inspecting single pages on certain monitors, because the dimensions of the dialog box vary according to the monitor you're using. Also, it takes Word less time to create an image for one page than for two pages.

If you've set the Mirror Even/Odd Margins option, the Even/Odd Headers option, or set a gutter width in the Document dialog box, scrolling between pages proceeds by two facing pages at a time. Otherwise, when you scroll forward through the document, the right-hand page shifts to the left.

The Printer Icon

When you click the Printer icon, the standard Print dialog box for the currently chosen printer appears. This is most convenient for printing a page or two at a time, so you can check the placement of details too small to see well on screen.

Working in Print Preview

The Print Preview feature is the easiest and most straightforward way to adjust the placement of margins, page breaks, headers, footers, and page numbers in a document. It's not easy to create an extremely accurate design with it, however, especially on the small screen of the Mac Plus or Mac SE. This behavior becomes apparent when you click the Margins icon and drag an object—the current position displayed in the status box changes by increments, depending on the current unit of measure. Therefore, Print Preview is most helpful when you're first setting up a design for a document or when you don't have stringent requirements for the accuracy of a design.

Adjusting Margins

To move one of the margins in Print Preview, simply click the Margins icon and drag one of the four margins by its handle (the little black box at the end of the margin guideline). Word displays at the top of the dialog box the current position of the object you're dragging; the unit of measure is the one specified in the Preferences dialog box.

If you change the margins, the effect of the alteration won't appear until you either click the Margins icon again or click anywhere outside that page. The reason for this is that, again, it takes a little time to recalculate the position of each element on the page, and updating the screen every time you make an adjustment would slow down the program. However, if you've set the Background Repagination option, the screen updates automatically after a short delay. If you click the close box before updating the screen, the changes you've made will still take effect.

If you change the left or right margin after you hyphenate the document, you'll probably have to rehyphenate it. The margin change affects the entire document. You see the new margin measurement either when you next display the Document dialog box or in the Ruler after clicking the scale icon.

Adjusting Headers and Footers

To move the header or footer, simply click the Margins icon (you don't have to do this again if the guidelines are already displayed), place the pointer over the header or footer, and drag it to the new position. When you're done, click outside the page to update the screen.

Although you might notice a little horizontal play when you drag the header and footer, you can change only the vertical placement. In addition, the range of vertical movement for the header (for instance) is stopped by the top margin, unless you've set a "negative" top margin in the Document dialog box. If you have, you can move the header the full height of the page, or even into the area occupied by the footer at the bottom of the page. The Header/Footer options in the Section dialog box reflect the new positions and pertain only to the section in which you adjust the header.

Related to this is the behavior of headers and footers in Print Preview when you haven't set a negative margin in the Document dialog box and the header is more than a few lines deep. When you switch to Print Preview and click the Margins icon, you'll see that the outline for the header overlaps the body text. If you click on the header to adjust its position, it will pop up to a position over the body text, and you won't be able to move it back down into the text. (Usually you won't want to do this, but it can sometimes create an interesting effect.) Hold the Shift key down as you drag the header down into the body text. This also has the effect of automatically entering a negative margin in the Document dialog box. To reverse the effect, temporarily leave Print Preview, open the Document dialog box, and remove the minus sign preceding the number in the top margin field.

As you drag the header or footer, Word displays its vertical position at the top of the dialog box. For the header, the measurement shown is the distance from the top of the header to the top of the page. For the footer, the measurement shown is the distance from the bottom of the footer to the bottom of the page.

Adjusting the Page Number

To create a page number on a given page, you must click the Page Number icon and place the number somewhere on the page, double-click the icon to put the page number at the default position, or specify page numbering in the Section dialog box. To change the position of the page number, click the Margins icon and drag the page number to the new position. Click outside the limits of the page to have Word update the screen image. Also, if the document contains more than one section, the new position you set affects only that section. To find the precise position of the page number, place the insertion point in that section and look in the Page Numbering group of the Section dialog box. To remove the page number, drag its icon off the page.

Adjusting Positioned Paragraphs and Tables

If a paragraph or a table has a Position format, Word draws a dotted line around the object in Print Preview. When you move the pointer over it, the arrow pointer changes to a cross-hair pointer. As you drag the object, Word displays the position of the upper left corner of the object at the top of the dialog box. Click in the gray area outside the edges of the page to update the screen. If you return to Galley View or Page View, select the object, and choose the Position command, you'll see that Word has entered the new location of the object as a pair of absolute page locations in the two drop-down fields.

However, when an edge of the object you've relocated happens to coincide with one of the other options offered in the drop-down fields, Word often substitutes the option for the absolute number. For example, if you drag the object so that its right edge overlays the right margin in Print Preview, the Horizontal drop-down field changes from an absolute measurement to the Right option.

Working with Page Breaks

Print Preview really shines when you've already set the margins, the line lengths, and so on, and want to adjust the layout of each page before printing. Do this by scanning the document and checking each page layout. An automatic page break appears as a light dotted line; a manual break appears as a darker dotted line. If you click the Margins icon, drag an automatic page break up into the page, and then click outside the page, the line becomes darker, indicating that it's now a manual page break. When you convert an automatic break to a manual break, it is as though you had pressed Shift-Enter at that point. When you return to Galley View or Page View, the manual page break appears where you placed it in Print Preview.

To delete a manual page break, drag it into the bottom margin of the page. If you've set a manual break by pressing Shift-Enter in Document view, you'll see it in Print Preview.

Fortunately, Word also lets you change the column and page breaks in sections having more than one column of text. When a section has more than one column, pressing Shift-Enter starts a new column, not a new page, unless it's the end of the last column on the page. To set a column break from Print Preview, place the pointer at the bottom of the column that you want to break higher on the page. The arrow pointer changes to the cross-hair pointer. Drag the dotted line up from the bottom of the page. (Even though the dotted page-break line extends all the way across the page, from the left margin to the right margin, it affects only the column in which you originally placed the pointer.) When you release the mouse button, Word updates the screen, displaying the shorter column.

Unfortunately, once you've placed a manual column break in a column, you won't be able to select and drag it off the page with the pointer unless it's the lowest manual column break on the page. If you find a multiple-column page break that isn't to your liking, you can remove it manually as follows:

1. In Print Preview, identify the spot where you want to remove the column break, and then locate the same place in Galley View.
2. Select the dark dotted line representing the manual page break (in this case, it represents a column break), and delete it.
3. Switch back to Print Preview to verify that the column break is now gone, and add a different column break if you want.

■ *Printing*

After your document is the way you want it, you're finally ready to print it. The first part of this section describes how to set print options for the ImageWriter. Following that are instructions for using the LaserWriter.

To print a document on any printer, choose Print from the File menu, check the current settings in the dialog box, and click OK. What happens next depends on whether you're sending files across AppleTalk or printing them on a printer cabled directly into your computer. (LaserWriters connected to Macs use AppleTalk cabling and connectors.) If AppleTalk is not active, a dialog box appears, giving you the option of pausing or canceling. Clicking Pause stops the printer (the action is not immediate) until you click the Resume button. Clicking Cancel stops the printer and resets it to the top of the next page so that it's ready for another document. If you're using AppleTalk, you see a dialog box showing the status of the print job. The message in this box will change as the job progresses.

All options you set in the Print dialog box remain in effect until you change them (even if you quit Word), except for the Pages and Copies options. The following options appear in the Print dialog box regardless of the printer you've selected.

Specifying Page and Section Ranges

The Page Range option (called Pages for the LaserWriter's version of the dialog box) specifies the text you want to print. Normally, the All option is selected, which causes the entire document to be printed. You can also choose to print only the selected text or only certain pages and sections.

To print a selection, first select the text you want printed. It can be as little as one character or as much as the entire document. Then choose the Print command, click the Print Selection Only option, and click OK to print. When you print a selection, only those page numbers, headers, footers, or other elements that are part of the body text are printed.

To print a range of pages or sections, first repaginate the document, if necessary. Jot down the beginning and ending pages or section numbers for the pages you want to print. (They are displayed in the status box.) Then choose the Print command and enter the page numbers in the From and To fields. Enter the starting and ending section numbers in the Section Range fields. If the document has only one section, Word displays the number *1* in both Section Range fields. If your document is divided into sections with pages that are numbered separately, you should use both the page and section numbers for the range you want to print. Figure 14-16 shows some examples of page and section numbers you can enter. If you want to print from a particular page to the end of the document, leave the To field blank. If you want to print only one page, enter its number in both fields, and enter the relevant section number in both Section Range fields.

Copies: 1 Pages: ○ All ◉ From: 12 To:
Cover Page: ◉ No ○ First Page ○ Last Page
Paper Source: ◉ Paper Cassette ○ Manual Feed
Section Range: From: 1 To: 1 ☐ Print Selection

Copies: 1 Pages: ○ All ◉ From: 1 To: 5
Cover Page: ◉ No ○ First Page ○ Last Page
Paper Source: ◉ Paper Cassette ○ Manual Feed
Section Range: From: 1 To: 1 ☐ Print Selection

Copies: 1 Pages: ○ All ◉ From: 1 To: 9999
Cover Page: ◉ No ○ First Page ○ Last Page
Paper Source: ◉ Paper Cassette ○ Manual Feed
Section Range: From: 2 To: 2 ☐ Print Selection

Copies: 1 Pages: ○ All ◉ From: 2 To: 88
Cover Page: ◉ No ○ First Page ○ Last Page
Paper Source: ◉ Paper Cassette ○ Manual Feed
Section Range: From: 3 To: 5 ☐ Print Selection

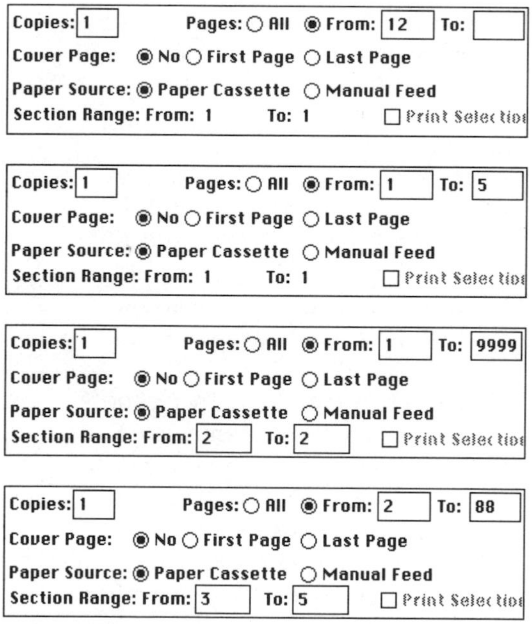

Figure 14-16
Sample ranges of page and section numbers for printing.

The Copies Option

The Copies option specifies the number of copies of the document to be printed. If you know you want three original copies of your document, it's faster to print them all at once rather than separately. Enter a number up to 99 in the Copies field. On PostScript printers, Word doesn't collate the copies but prints each page the specified number of times before moving on to the next. If you print on the ImageWriter, Word prints the entire document before printing the next copy.

The Print Hidden Text Option

Characters formatted as hidden can be displayed or hidden independently on the screen and on paper. You can choose to print hidden text (PostScript commands, index entries, notes to yourself, and so on) by clicking the Print Hidden Text option. When hidden text is printed, it doesn't have the gray underline you see when you display it on the screen.

The Print Next File Option

If you've linked a series of documents through the Next File button in the Document dialog box, you can print the next file or files in the series by setting the Print Next File option. If you haven't specified a following file, this option appears dimmed.

TIP

Printing Items That Are Not Documents

You can use the Print command to print Word style sheets, glossaries, and outlines as well as the contents of the screen. To print the style sheet for a document, choose the Styles or Define Styles command and then choose the Print command. You can get a full listing of the automatic styles by pressing the Shift key while choosing the Define Styles command. The automatic styles, each preceded by a bullet, print out with the others.

To print a glossary, choose the Glossary command and then choose Print. To print the outline for a document, choose the Outlining command and then choose Print. You can print the contents of the active window alone by pressing Shift-Command-4; to print the contents of the entire screen on an ImageWriter, press the Caps Lock key first. However, if you're trying to print the screen on a LaserWriter, press Shift-Command-3 instead to save a screen dump, and print the screen dump from a paint program such as MacPaint.

Printing with the ImageWriter

If you've already used the Chooser to select the ImageWriter printer driver, as described earlier, choosing the Print command displays the dialog box shown in Figure 14-17. For most printing tasks involving an ImageWriter loaded with continuous fanfold computer paper, you need only click OK to begin printing. Word prepares the document for printing and then, after a pause while Word creates a print file on disk, the printing commences. (Note that the program disk must have enough blank space on it to accommodate the print file generated by Word.)

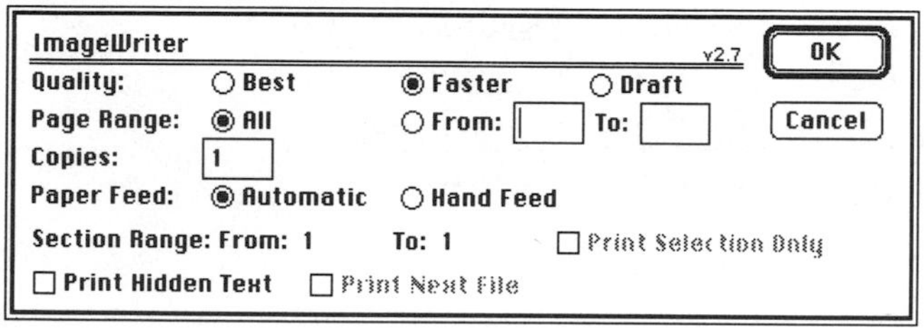

ImageWriter v2.7 OK
Quality: Best Faster Draft
Page Range: All From: To: Cancel
Copies: 1
Paper Feed: Automatic Hand Feed
Section Range: From: 1 To: 1 Print Selection Only
Print Hidden Text Print Next File

Figure 14-17
The ImageWriter Print dialog box.

The following additional options appear in the Print dialog box when you choose the ImageWriter.

The Quality Options

You can select the quality of printing with the Best, Faster, and Draft options. Examples of each are shown in Figure 14-18 on the following page.

- The Best option prints each character twice, giving the document a dark, neat appearance. If you've installed fonts that are twice the point size of those used in your document, Word uses these, compressing the pattern of bits that makes up each character into the point size you've chosen, which yields more detailed characters. Graphics, however, are printed in one pass. Using this option slows the printing speed and causes more wear on the printer's ribbon.
- The Faster option is the standard setting; it prints text and graphics as they appear on the screen, but in only one pass. This option prints about twice as fast as the Best option.
- The Draft option uses the fonts built into the ImageWriter to print your document, and it doesn't display fonts, graphics, or special paragraph formatting, such as lines and boxes. Different fonts, attributes, and point sizes affect the look of the print. (See Figure 14-18.) You get more reliable results in this mode when using a monospaced font such as Seattle, Monaco, Courier, or Dover.

Best	Plain	**Bold**	*Italic*	Shadow	Underlined
Best	Plain	**Bold**	*Italic*	Shadow	Underlined
Best	Plain	**Bold**	*Italic*	Shadow	Underlined
Faster	Plain	**Bold**	*Italic*	Shadow	Underlined
Faster	Plain	**Bold**	*Italic*	Shadow	Underlined
Faster	Plain	**Bold**	*Italic*	Shadow	Underlined
Draft	Plain	**Bold**	*Italic*	Shadow	Underlined
Draft	Plain	**Bold**	*Italic*	Shadow	Underlined
Draft	Plain	**Bold**	*Italic*	Shadow	Underlined

Figure 14-18
Samples printed with the Best, Faster, and Draft options.

The Paper Feed Options

You can tell Word to print nonstop from beginning to end or one page at a time. For nonstop printing in which paper is fed into the printer automatically, set the Automatic option. For page-at-a-time printing, when you need to hand-feed single sheets into the printer, click the Manual option. At the end of each page, a dialog box appears, telling you to insert the next sheet.

Printing with the LaserWriter

Apple's LaserWriter printer, probably more than any other factor, has fueled the development of high-powered word-processing programs such as Microsoft Word. Until the release of the Mac SE and the Mac II, it was said that the LaserWriter was the most powerful computer Apple made; it contains the same 68000 microprocessor as the Mac Plus but operates at a higher speed, has more internal programs (as well as fonts) stored in its 512 kilobytes of read-only memory (ROM), and has 1.5 megabytes of random-access memory (RAM). Now the newer LaserWriters, such as the Plus, II NT, and II NTX, have even more fonts and more memory than the standard LaserWriter. The benefits of using a LaserWriter with Word are many:

- ❑ The LaserWriter prints at 300 dots per inch instead of 72 or 80. You get higher-resolution text, clearer graphics, and faster text output.
- ❑ The fonts in the LaserWriter's ROM are stored in a form that makes use of this higher resolution. These fonts are registered with the International Typesetting Committee (ITC), which guarantees close

conformity with the standard fonts having the same names as those used by traditional typesetters. If you format a document in any of the LaserWriter fonts, such as Times or Bookman, and then take the document to a type service bureau that has a PostScript-compatible printer, the typeset version will look very much like the LaserWriter version.

- ❑ With the LaserWriter, you can reduce or enlarge pages from 25 to 400 percent of the normal size. You can reduce a large document to fit on a small piece of paper. (A document that is 22 by 22 inches is only 5.5 by 5.5 inches when reduced to 25 percent of its original size.)
- ❑ You can take advantage of all the benefits that PostScript offers—even if you don't know PostScript—because most of the newer graphics programs, such as Cricket Draw and Illustrator, are designed specifically to create high-quality images that can be printed only on PostScript printers. Appendix C, "Using PostScript," describes how you can insert PostScript graphics into your documents.

Since the LaserWriter's appearance, several other PostScript-compatible printers have been developed, such as the QMS-PS 810 and the Mergenthaler Linotronic 300. Although we cannot give specific recommendations for using these printers, the same issues that apply to the LaserWriter apply to most of them as well. For example, you use the LaserWriter driver to set options for PostScript-compatible printers, and many use the same fonts as the LaserWriter. The following discussion is oriented toward the LaserWriter, but it will also apply to the majority of PostScript printers.

What Happens When You Print with a LaserWriter

If you haven't already specified the LaserWriter as your printer, you should do so before setting the final margins and other document formats. Be sure that the LaserWriter is connected to the printer port of your Macintosh over AppleTalk. The LaserWriter printer driver (called LaserWriter) and the preparation program (called Laser Prep) must be in the System Folder. Choose the Chooser command, click the AppleTalk Active option, and select the LaserWriter icon. The names of the available printers are shown in the list box. Select the one you want, and then click the close box.

When you click OK in the Print dialog box, you see a dialog box that shows the status of the print job and a message that the Mac is looking for the LaserWriter on AppleTalk. If nothing has been printed on that LaserWriter before, another message states that the printer is being initialized. This means that the Mac has sent the Laser Prep file to the LaserWriter. This file consists of a set of PostScript instructions that the computer inside the LaserWriter uses to decode subsequent printing commands coming from the Mac.

Once the LaserWriter is initialized, Word repaginates the document and converts it to a sequence of PostScript commands, which it transmits to the LaserWriter over AppleTalk. Word translates the elements on each page in a particular order, whether printing on the ImageWriter or the LaserWriter:

❶ PostScript (for the LaserWriter only). However, if you've set the Print Postcript Over Text option in the LaserWriter's Page Setup dialog box, the PostScript commands are saved until last.

❷ Header.

❸ Footer.

❹ Automatic page numbers.

❺ The body of the text. (If you're using line numbering in a paragraph, the paragraph is printed first, then the line numbers.)

❻ Footnotes.

Knowing this printing order is useful when you want to achieve special effects such as printing text over a graphic, or a header behind the body of the text in a document. For example, this is why we can put the gray tint behind the tip elements in this book.

The LaserWriter then transforms these PostScript commands (with the aid of the Laser Prep file) into a fine-grained bit-mapped image that is transferred to the paper in the form of small piles of black toner powder. The toner is fused to the paper, and the page rolls out for you to see.

Fonts

Three types of fonts are available to you when you print on a LaserWriter: bit-mapped fonts, the high-resolution fonts stored in the LaserWriter's ROM, and special high-resolution fonts stored in the Mac and downloaded to the LaserWriter when specified in one of your documents. The latter two types we can lump together under the category of PostScript fonts.

Bit-mapped fonts, also called screen fonts, are the fonts you see on the screen. Each character consists of a pattern of bits; each point size has a different pattern. You can use these fonts in documents printed on the LaserWriter, but printing is much slower because only the 14-point version of the font is sent to the printer, which must scale that font to the point size specified in the document. In general, the quality of the text printed in a bit-mapped font is never as good as that achieved with the LaserWriter's own fonts. If you formatted text in a bit-mapped font, Word assumes that you did so unintentionally; therefore, the Font Substitution option in the LaserWriter Print dialog box is turned on by default. If you really want to print in a bit-mapped font on the LaserWriter, turn off the Font Substitution option.

The LaserWriter is most often used with its own internal fonts, such as Times, Palatino, and Symbol. This produces the fastest results because the fonts are built into the LaserWriter, and thus font information does not need to be transferred from the Mac to the printer. The Mac simply sends the commands to print the characters in the desired font and point size. A full page of text can be printed in less than 15 seconds.

Every font stored in the LaserWriter has a bit-mapped version, called its screen font, which you see on the screen while you're entering and formatting text in that font. If you've installed these fonts in your System file, you can use them to format a document even though a LaserWriter isn't attached to your Mac. You can print text formatted in one of these fonts on the ImageWriter as though it were any of the other bit-mapped fonts.

The third type of font is very much like the LaserWriter fonts, but the high-resolution patterns are stored in the Mac instead of the LaserWriter. These range from other ITC-registered fonts licensed by Adobe Systems to special-purpose and display fonts offered by companies such as Casady. These fonts are downloaded to the LaserWriter when needed. The downloaded font takes up memory in the LaserWriter, so you might find it impossible to print pages filled with complicated text and graphics if the LaserWriter runs out of memory.

TIP

Working with Fonts

You might have noticed that some character formats make text more difficult to read on the screen. Italics are an example of this—it often looks as if the space after an italicized word has disappeared, and it can be difficult to place the insertion point between characters correctly. Adobe Systems has released a set of screen fonts that are much easier to read.

Sometimes you need a special character that isn't available in any of the LaserWriter fonts. (Remember that you can use the Key Caps desk accessory to view the characters in a font.) You could search for the one character in the fonts offered by third-party suppliers. Instead, however, consider creating the character with a LaserWriter-compatible font editor such as Fontographer from Altsys Corporation.

The LaserWriter Print Dialog Box

The Print dialog box you see when you choose the LaserWriter is different from the one displayed for the ImageWriter. (See Figure 14-19 on the following page.) The additional options are as follows:

- ❏ Cover Page. Prints a page identifying your document. For use when more than one Mac shares a single LaserWriter. You can control whether the cover page is printed before the document or after it by selecting either the First Page or Last Page option.

- Print Back to Front. Printing begins with the last page of the document and ends with the first. This is a little slower than printing front to back because Word must repaginate all the way to the end of the document before beginning to print. If you're printing to a LaserWriter II or other printer that ejects pages printed side down, setting this option has the opposite effect, stacking sheets from back to front.

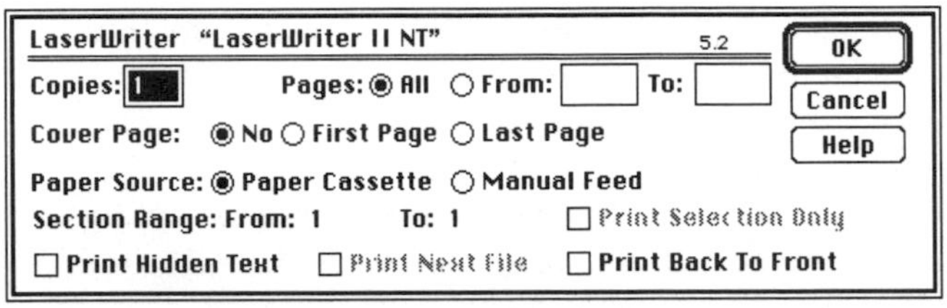

LaserWriter "LaserWriter II NT" 5.2 OK
Copies: 1 Pages: (•) All ( ) From: [ ] To: [ ] Cancel
Cover Page: (•) No ( ) First Page ( ) Last Page Help
Paper Source: (•) Paper Cassette ( ) Manual Feed
Section Range: From: 1 To: 1 [ ] Print Selection Only
[ ] Print Hidden Text [ ] Print Next File [ ] Print Back To Front

Figure 14-19
The LaserWriter Print dialog box.

The Paper Source Options

The Paper Source options are almost identical to the Paper Feed options for the ImageWriter. For nonstop printing in which paper is fed into the printer automatically, set the Paper Cassette option. For page-at-a-time printing, when you need to hand-feed single sheets into the printer, click the Manual Feed option. At the end of each page, a dialog box appears, telling you to insert the next sheet.

■ *Points to Remember*

- ❏ The document format domain represents the fifth and most global level of formatting. This domain controls the dimensions of the paper on which the document is printed, the location of the page margins, the default tab stop interval, whether even-numbered and odd-numbered pages are treated differently, where footnotes are printed and how they are numbered, whether widows should be allowed at the top or bottom of a page, and whether the document is part of a series. You set these formats through the Document dialog box and the Page Setup dialog box.
- ❏ Word repaginates a document automatically when you choose the Print, Print Merge, Table of Contents, Index, or Print Preview command. (With the last of these, it repaginates only as far as the page being viewed.) You can tell Word to repaginate the document by choosing Repaginate Now from the Document or by setting the Background Repagination option in the Preferences dialog box. Once a document has been repaginated, the page and section numbers in the status box are not dimmed.
- ❏ Repagination affects only the paragraphs that have changed since the last pagination. If you need to repaginate the entire document, including paragraphs that have not changed, press the Shift key while you choose the Full Repaginate Now command. This might become necessary if you have chosen a different printer, for example.
- ❏ Automatic page breaks appear as light dotted lines in the document. Manual page breaks appear as darker dotted lines. Word doesn't change manual page breaks when it repaginates a document.
- ❏ In addition to entering manual page breaks, you can set the Page Break Before format for paragraphs that must begin at the top of a new page and the New Page format for sections that must begin a new page.
- ❏ Word uses three types of hyphens. Normal hyphens always appear in text and can fall at the end of a line. Nonbreaking hyphens always appear in text but cannot fall at the end of a line. Optional hyphens appear only when they fall at the end of a line. The hyphenation feature inserts optional hyphens into the words it divides, or you can insert optional hyphens manually.
- ❏ Margin positions that you set in Print Preview appear in the Document dialog box. Positions you set in Print Preview for the page number, header, and footer appear in the Section dialog box.
- ❏ The Chooser desk accessory tells Word the type of printer to be used. The printer you choose may affect the appearance of your document, so it's best to choose the printer before final formatting.

■ Techniques

Choosing a Printer

Choose Chooser from the Apple menu. The dialog box lists the printer drivers in the System Folder. Click Active or Inactive to indicate whether or not your printer is connected to AppleTalk. Click the icon for your printer type; the box to the right of the icons asks for specific printer information:

- ❑ ImageWriter: Click the ImageWriter icon, and select a printer port, or click the AppleTalk ImageWriter icon, and select an available AppleTalk ImageWriter.
- ❑ LaserWriter: Click the LaserWriter icon, and select an available LaserWriter.

Click the close box when you are done.

Page Layout

The ImageWriter Page Setup Dialog Box

Item	Action		
Paper options	Sets a standard paper size for the document. When you click an option, the proportions of the page in Print Preview and Page View change correspondingly.		
	Inches	**Centimeters**	**Points**
US Letter	8.5 x 11	21.59 x 27.94	610 x 790
US Legal	8.5 x 14	21.59 x 35.56	610 x 1008
Computer Paper	14 x 11	35.56 x 27.94	1008 x 790
A4 Letter	8.27 x 11.69	21.01 x 29.69	595 x 842
International Fanfold	8.25 x 12	20.96 x 30.48	594 x 864
Custom	Enter the width and height of the page in the Custom Paper Size fields in the Preference dialog box. This paper size then becomes an option only in the ImageWriter Page Setup dialog box.		
Orientation options			
Tall	The default option; orients the page in the usual way; sometimes called portrait orientation.		
Wide	Rotates the page 90 degrees to print each line across the length of the page; sometimes called landscape orientation.		

Item	Action
Printer Effects	Sets various printing effects.
Tall Adjusted	Changes the horizontal printing pixel density from 80 to 72 dots per inch, which prints graphics in the correct proportions. Units on the Ruler change accordingly, as do line breaks.
50% Reduction	Compacts the number of dots printed in both the horizontal and vertical dimensions by a factor of two. Word adjusts measurements in the Ruler and in Page Preview by doubling what is reported.
No Gaps Between Pages	Removes the 0.5-inch omissions in the printed material at every page break if top and bottom margins are set to 0.

The LaserWriter Page Setup Dialog Box

Item	Action		
Paper options	Sets a standard paper size for the document. When you click an option, the proportions of the page in Print Preview and Page View change correspondingly.		
	Inches	**Centimeters**	**Points**
US Letter	8.5 x 11	21.59 x 27.94	610 x 790
US Legal	8.5 x 14	21.59 x 35.56	610 x 1008
A4 Letter	8.25 x 11.69	20.96 x 29.64	594 x 840
B5 Letter	7.2 x 10.1	18.28 x 25.65	518 x 727
Tabloid	11 x 17	27.94 x 43.18	792 x 1224
Orientation options			
Tall	The default option; orients the page in the usual way; sometimes called portrait orientation.		
Wide	Rotates the page 90 degrees to print each line across the length of the page; sometimes called landscape orientation.		
Printer Effects	Sets various printing effects.		
Reduce/Enlarge %	Specify a number by which printed material is to be reduced or enlarged, from 25 to 400 percent. Word multiplies distances on screen by the corresponding factor.		
Fractional Widths	Causes Word to measure the widths of characters in LaserWriter fonts in a different way and improves the spacing of text when printed on a PostScript printer.		
Print PostScript Over Text	PostScript special effects are printed over (rather than under) text and non-PostScript graphics.		

Item	Action
Printer Effects, cont.	
Font Substitution	Substitute one of its internal fonts when it encounters a bit-mapped font in your document.
Text Smoothing, Graphics Smoothing	Smooths the edges of bit-mapped fonts or graphics. Improves the appearance of some text and graphics, but blurs others.
Faster Bitmap Printing	Speeds printing by using memory in a PostScript printer more efficiently for bitmaps, but leaves less space for downloaded text and other types of graphics. Consequently, some documents might not print.
LaserWriter Options	Click the options button to select the following LaserWriter effects:
Flip Horizontal	Reverses the page image so that it prints backwards.
Flip Vertical	Prints the page image upside down.
Invert Image	Prints the page image as a negative. (Black is white and white is black.)
Precision Bitmap Alignment	Prints the page image at 96 percent of its original size so that bit-mapped images are mapped into the printer at a precise 4-to-1 ratio (288 dots per inch to 72 dots per inch).
Larger Print Area	Reallocates memory in the LaserWriter for storing more of the page image instead of storing fonts. Useful for printing pages larger than 8.5 x 11 inches.
Unlimited Downloadable Fonts in Doc.	The printer purges an old font from memory to create space for new fonts. This often slows down printing, because fonts often have to be re-downloaded several times during the course of printing.

The Document Dialog Box

Item	Action
Margins option group	Determines the area on the printed page occupied by the body text. Enter measurements from the edge of the page in inches, points, or centimeters.
Top	Sets the top margin. Enter a negative number to set a fixed margin that does not move to accommodate the header.
Bottom	Sets the bottom margin. Enter a negative number to set a fixed margin that does not move to accommodate the footer.
Left	Sets the left margin.
Right	Sets the right margin.

Item	Action
Mirror Even/Odd Margins	When set, replaces the Left and Right fields with Inside and Outside, respectively, letting you set different inside and outside margins for facing pages.
Even/Odd Headers	Causes even-numbered and odd-numbered pages to be treated differently. When this option is set, Word replaces the Open Header and Open Footer commands with Open Even Header, Open Odd Header, Open Even Footer, and Open Odd Footer commands; this option places page numbers in the upper left corner on even-numbered pages and in the upper right corner on odd-numbered pages; and Outside Bars assigned to paragraphs are placed on the left on even pages and on the right on odd ones.
Widow Control	Prevents the first line of a paragraph from appearing alone at the bottom of a page and the last line of a paragraph from appearing alone at the top of a page.
Gutter	Specifies extra margin space on the right edge of even-numbered (left-hand) pages and on the left edge of odd-numbered (right-hand) pages. Enter the measurement in inches, centimeters, or points.
Default Tab Stops	Sets default tab stops for the document. Word represents these tab stops with inverted Ts in the Ruler. These tab stops are overridden by any tabs you set for a paragraph. They remain beyond the rightmost paragraph tab stop you set.
Number Pages From	Sets the starting page number for the document. When you are chaining documents through the Next File dialog box, leave this field blank.
Number Lines From	Sets the starting line number for the document. This is useful when you are chaining documents with the Next File dialog box.
Next File button	If you want to print a series of documents or compile a table of contents or index for a series of documents, select the name of the next document in the Next File dialog box. To avoid printing linked documents, deselect the Print Next File option in the Print dialog box.
Footnotes options	Controls the placement and numbering of footnotes.
Position drop-down list	Determines where the footnotes are placed in the document.
Bottom of Page	Prints each footnote at the bottom of the page on which its reference appears.

Item	Action
Footnotes options, cont.	
Beneath Text	Prints each footnote immediately beneath the last paragraph on the page on which its reference appears.
End of Section	Prints accumulated footnotes at the end of the first section for which the Include Endnotes option is set in the Section dialog box, or at the end of the document if none of the sections have this option set.
End of Document	Prints accumulated footnotes at the end of the document.
Number From	Sets the starting footnote number. This is useful when you are chaining documents through the Next File dialog box.
Restart Each Section	Restarts footnote numbering at 1 at the beginning of each page or each section, depending on which Position option is set. If this option is not set, Word numbers all footnotes consecutively.

Previewing and Pagination

Preview a document

❶ Scroll to the page at which you want to begin previewing the document.

❷ Choose Print Preview from the File menu.

❸ Click in the vertical scroll bar or press the up or down arrow key to display other pages.

❹ When done, click the Cancel button.

Switch to a one-page display in Print Preview

❶ Click the One-Page Display icon. The display changes to show one page instead of two.

❷ Click the icon again to return to the two-page display.

Add page numbers in Print Preview

❶ Click the Page Number icon.

❷ Position the number on the page, and click to set the position. A page number is added to all pages.

Double-click the icon to place it at the default location. If the Even/Odd Headers option is set, the page number is placed symmetrically with respect to the inside edge of the document: in the upper left corner on even-numbered pages and in the upper right corner on odd-numbered pages.

Adjust the page margins in Print Preview

❶ Click the Margins icon. Margin guidelines appear on the current page.

❷ Drag the appropriate margin by its handle (the black box at the end of the margin) to the new location.

❸ Click anywhere outside the page to update the screen.

The change affects the entire document, not only the page you've altered. You must update the screen before returning to Galley View for the change to take effect.

Position a header, footer, page number, or positioned object in Print Preview

❶ Click the Margins icon. The elements you can move are shown surrounded by a dotted box.

❷ Drag the element you want to move to its new position. Word displays the current position at the top of the dialog box as you drag it. Press the Shift key before moving headers and footers to drag them into the body area of the document.

❸ Click anywhere outside the page to update the screen. You must update the screen before returning to Galley View for the change to take effect.

A change to a header or footer affects only the section containing the page you've altered. A change to the page number affects the entire document.

Insert or move a manual column or page break in Print Preview

❶ Display the page to be changed.

❷ Click the Margins icon.

❸ Drag the automatic page break from the bottom of the page to the new location. The automatic page break becomes a manual page break.

The page is updated when you release the mouse button. This also works for multiple-column sections, but you must begin dragging in the column within which you want to establish the column break.

Remove a manual page break in Print Preview

❶ Display the page to be changed.

❷ Click the Margins icon.

❸ Drag the page break into the bottom margin.

The screen is updated when you release the mouse button. To remove manual column breaks in multiple-column sections, select and delete them in Galley View.

Insert a manual page break in Galley View

❶ Set the insertion point where you want the page to break.

❷ Press Shift-Enter.

Remove a manual page break in Galley View

❶ Select the page break.

❷ Press the Backspace key.

Hyphenation

Enter a normal hyphen

❶ Press the – (hyphen, or minus) key.

Enter a nonbreaking hyphen

❶ Press Command- ~ (technically, Command-`). The character is displayed as ~ if Show ¶ is on.

Enter an optional hyphen

❶ Press Command- – (hyphen, or minus). The character is invisible unless it falls at the end of a line or Show ¶ is on. Then it appears as ¬.

Hyphenate the document and verify each hyphenated word

❶ Set the insertion point at the beginning of the document, and choose Hyphenate from the Document menu.

❷ To ignore capitalized words, turn off Hyphenate Capitalized Words.

❸ Click Start Hyphenation.

❹ For each candidate Word proposes for hyphenation, click No Change to leave the word unhyphenated; click Change to accept the hyphen Word suggests (the one that is highlighted).

To specify a different division for the word, click on another hyphen or between any two letters and then click Change. Place the division point to the left of the vertical dotted line.

Hyphenate the document automatically

❶ Set the insertion point at the beginning of the document, and choose Hyphenate from the Document menu.

❷ To ignore capitalized words, turn off Hyphenate Capitalized Words.

❸ Click Hyphenate All.

Hyphenate selected text only

❶ Select the text to be hyphenated, and choose Hyphenate from the Document menu.

❷ Click Hyphenate Selection to hyphenate the text automatically, or click Start Hyphenation to verify each word before it is hyphenated.

Printing

The Print dialog box

Item	Action
Pages options	
Pages	Prints the entire document. Enter the starting and ending page numbers.
Section Range	Enter the starting and ending section numbers; if the document has only one section, then you can't edit the Section fields.
Print Selection Only	Prints the currently selected text. No headers, footers, page numbers, and so forth will be printed. You can use this with page and section ranges; the shorter of the two passages is printed.
Copies	Sets the number of copies to print.
Print Hidden Text	Prints text formatted as hidden text regardless of whether you've set the Show Hidden Text option in the Preferences dialog box.
Print Next File	Prints the next file in a series of documents linked through the Next File dialog box.
ImageWriter options	
Quality Options	Specify the quality of the printing. The better the quality, the slower the printing.
Best	Prints at highest quality, compressing (if possible) installed fonts that are twice the point size you've chosen into that point size.
Faster	Prints at the standard quality.

Item	Action
ImageWriter options, cont.	
Draft	Prints at the lowest quality. Draft mode does not display fonts, graphics, or paragraph borders.
Paper Feed Options	Automatic: Indicates that the paper is fed automatically. Manual: Specifies that you'll be feeding individual sheets by hand. Word stops between pages and presents a dialog box asking you to insert the next sheet.
LaserWriter options	
Cover Page	Prints a cover page identifying your document. Select First Page or Last Page to print the cover page before or after the document.
Paper Source Options	Paper Cassette: Indicates that the paper is fed automatically from a cassette. Manual Feed: Specifies that you will be feeding individual sheets by hand. Word stops between pages and presents a dialog box asking you to insert the next sheet.
Print Back To Front	Prints documents from the last page to the first so that they appear in order in the output tray. Setting this option on printers that eject pages print-side down prints documents front to back.

■ *Commands*

Command name	Meaning, menu	Standard keyboard	Keypad	Extended keyboard
Background Repagination	Toggles option to automatically repaginate a document during pauses in typing and editing.			
Document…	Changes formats affecting the entire active document.			
	Format	⌘F14		
Fractional Widths	Turns on and off the LaserWriter fractional pixel width feature.			
Full Repaginate Now	Forces repagination of document even though no changes have occurred since last pagination. In Page View, forces repagination from beginning of document to currently displayed page.			
Hyphenate…	Scans document and hyphenates words to improve line breaks.			
	Utilities			⇧F15

(continued)

Command name	Meaning, menu	Standard keyboard	Keypad	Extended keyboard
Insert Line Break	Breaks a line of text without starting a new paragraph. Inserts newline character (displayed as ↵ when Show ¶ is on).			
		⇧↵		
Insert Nonbreaking Hyphen	Inserts a hyphen preventing a line break within a hyphenated word that occurs at end of a line. Hyphen is displayed as - when Show ¶ is on.			
		⌘`		
Insert Nonbreaking Space	Inserts a space preventing a line break on either side of space. Space is displayed as ~ when Show ¶ is on.			
		⌥␣ or ⌘␣		
Insert Optional Hyphen	Inserts a hyphen that is printed only when a word is broken at the hyphen. Hyphen is displayed as ¬ when Show ¶ is on.			
		⌘ -		
Insert Page Break	Inserts a manual page break at insertion point.			
	Document	⇧⌤		
Insert Page Number	Inserts automatic page number glossary entry.			
Page Break Before	Inserts a manual page break before selected paragraph.			
Page Setup…	Sets page size, print orientation, and certain printer effects for a document.			
	File			⇧F8
Page View	Toggles Page View.			
	Document	⌘B		F13
Print Preview…	Displays one or two pages at reduced size as they'll look when printed.			
	File	⌘I		⌥F13
Print…	Prints active document.			
	File	⌘P		F8
Repaginate Now	Repaginates entire document. In Page View, repaginates from beginning of document to currently displayed page.			
	Document	⌘J		

SECTION 4

Adding the Final Touches

Creating a Table of Contents and Index

Two of the most useful elements in any book are the table of contents and index. If you've ever had to create and compile your own, you know how time consuming and frustrating the job can be. And any last-minute changes in the pagination of the document mean that your original table of contents and index are off and that you have to redo all the entries. It wasn't fun the first time, and the second time isn't any better.

Once again, Word pitches in and saves you time and effort. The process of creating a table of contents and index for your documents is simple and straightforward; once you've identified the items you want to include, Word takes care of the rest.

■ *Making a Table of Contents*

If your document is longer than 10 to 15 pages and has several major topics, you'll probably want to add a table of contents at the beginning. Not only will this give the document a more professional look, but it will also help your readers find what they are looking for faster and more efficiently. You can create a table of contents in two ways: by extracting it from an outline you've created or by inserting a special code before each entry you want to include in the table of contents.

Generating a Table of Contents from an Outline

The levels in an outline can serve as the entries in a table of contents (TOC). The topmost level of the outline, consisting of topics formatted in the *heading 1* style, produces the main headings in the table of contents. Subordinate topics are subheadings formatted in styles *heading 2* through *heading 9*. When you create a table of contents in this way, Word repaginates the document and then uses each heading, along with its page number if you want, as an entry in the contents. Word formats each level of entry with the corresponding automatic style, *toc 1* through *toc 9*.

Figure 15-1 shows part of this section and the resulting entries in a table of contents. The title of the section is formatted in the *heading 1* style, which has been redefined to use bold, italic, 16-point text. The subheading uses the *heading 2* style, subordinate to the main heading, and has also been redefined. Word lists the headings in the table of contents and maintains the hierarchy of the levels of headings used in the body of the document.

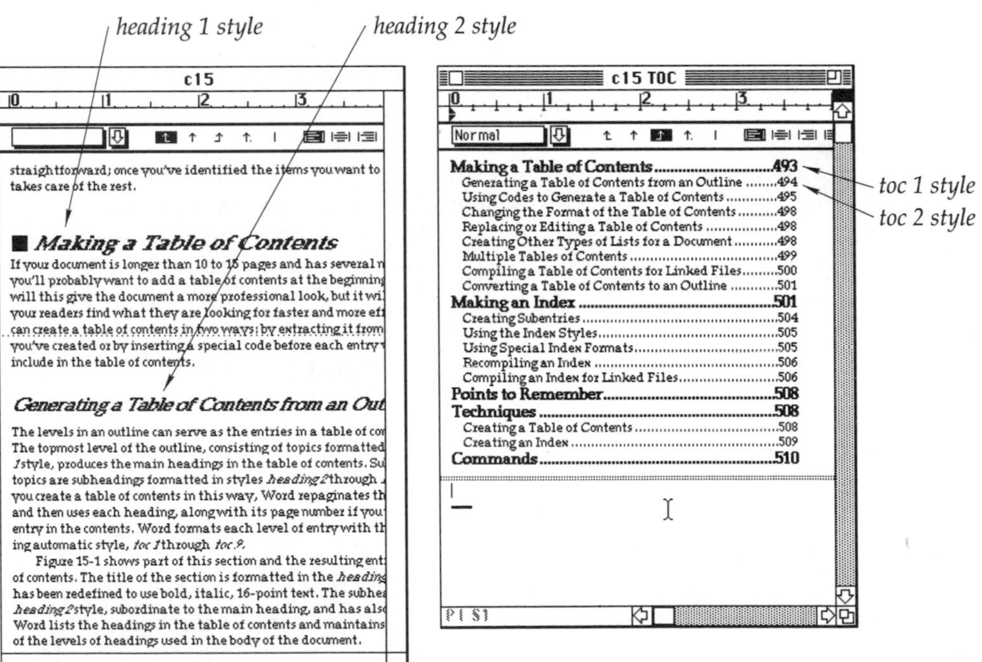

Figure 15-1
Generating a table of contents from headings in the document.

To compile a table of contents based on the headings in your document, do the following:

1. Choose Table of Contents from the Utilities menu. The dialog box in Figure 15-2 appears. The Outline and Show Page Numbers options should already be selected.
2. Enter the range of headings (levels 1 through 9) you want in the table of contents, or let the All option remain selected.
3. Click Start to begin.

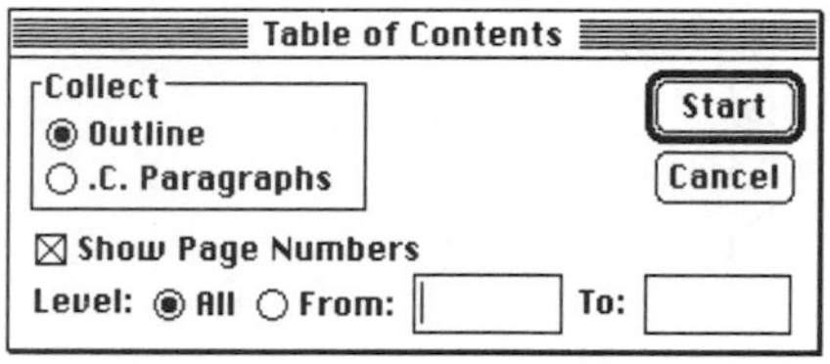

Figure 15-2
The Table of Contents dialog box.

Word first repaginates the document to ensure that the proper page numbers are used. It then goes through the document, collecting the various entries and assembling a complete table of contents. When it is finished, the table of contents is placed at the beginning of the document and is separated from the rest of the document by a section mark, so you can create a different page layout for it if you want.

The table of contents is like any other block of text; you can cut and paste it to another place in the document, and you can edit it, adding text before, after, or between the entries if you want. Most likely, you'll want to add a title page and other front matter before the table of contents. Simply set the insertion point at the beginning of the document and paste in or type the additional text.

Using Codes to Generate a Table of Contents

Another way to compile a table of contents is to insert a special code immediately before each entry that is to appear in the contents. This method gives you more control over the compilation at the expense of greater effort. By using codes, you can insert table-of-contents entries that aren't headings in the document or create entries from insertions having the Hidden character format. You can assign up to nine levels of entries, as you can with the outlining function (because there are nine levels of *toc* styles), but you'll probably use only the first two or three.

Type the code *.c.* just before each entry you want on the contents page. (The *c* can be uppercase or lowercase.) You must format the code as hidden text. That way, it won't appear in the final printout of the document. Word will generate a table of contents even if the hidden text is displayed (as it is in Figure 15-3), because it temporarily turns off Show ¶ in its internal representation of the document while generating the table of contents.

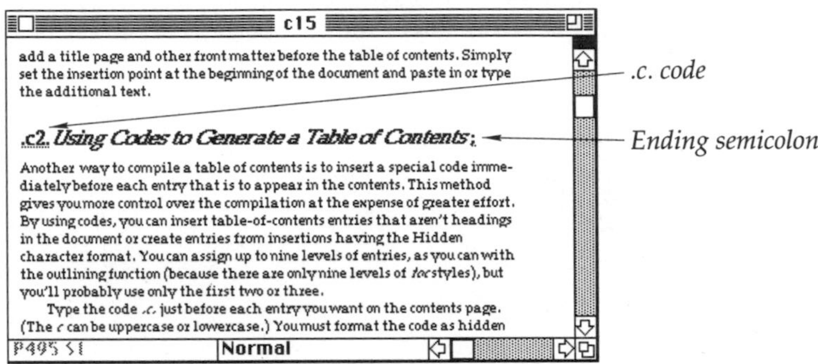

Figure 15-3
A table-of-contents entry. (Show Hidden Text is on.)

To assign different *toc* levels to entries, you insert a number within the contents code, as follows:

For	Type
1st level	*.c.* or *.c1.*
2nd level	*.c2.*
3rd level	*.c3.*
4th level	*.c4.*
5th level	*.c5.*
6th level	*.c6.*
7th level	*.c7.*
8th level	*.c8.*
9th level	*.c9.*

How does Word know where a table-of-contents entry ends? In most cases, you'll be using the headings in your document as entries, and headings almost always end in a paragraph mark. In such cases, the paragraph mark or newline character (entered by pressing Shift-Return) signals the end of the entry. However, many tables of contents contain entries that don't appear as headings in the document; an example of this is shown in Figure 15-4.

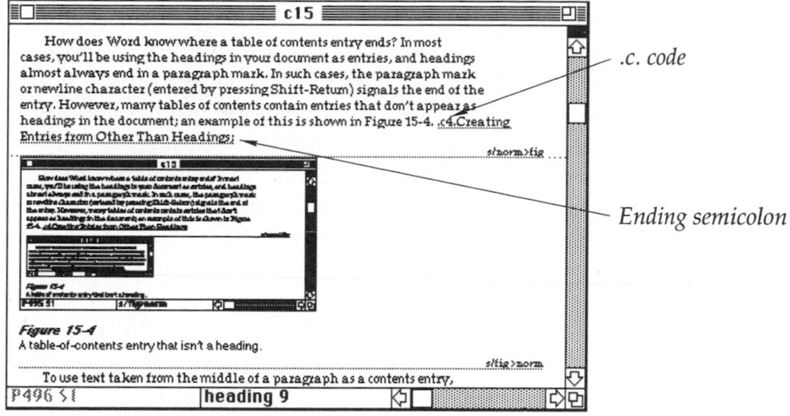

Figure 15-4
A table-of-contents entry that isn't a heading.

To use text taken from the middle of a paragraph as a contents entry, precede it with the .c. code and put a semicolon after it, both formatted as hidden text. Make sure the Show Hidden Text option is turned on in the Preferences dialog box before you do this, so that adding the Hidden format doesn't make the codes "disappear."

When you choose Insert TOC Entry from the Document menu, Word inserts both the .c. code and the ending semicolon for you, formatted as hidden text, placing the insertion point between them. Because the last period in the .c. is formatted as hidden text, the text you type will also have the Hidden format. (You can press Shift-Command-X to turn off the Hidden character format quickly.) This is useful, for instance, if you want to include a brief overview of each section in the contents.

If you want to use the actual text in the document as an entry, first select the passage, and then choose the Insert TOC Entry command. Word inserts the hidden-text codes before and after the selection. If, however, the entry already ends with a paragraph mark or a newline mark, Word doesn't add the ending semicolon (remember that you can also end an entry with either of these characters). After the codes are inserted, go back to insert the appropriate number within the .c. code.

If you need to place the codes around text, but you don't want the text to be hidden, you can also try using the glossary for storing and inserting all nine of the .c. codes as well as the ending semicolon, instead of using the Insert TOC Entry command. This has the advantage of making at least the entry of the numbered starting code a one-step process.

You can also create subentries in the table of contents by separating the main entry from a subentry by a colon. This convention is the same as that for creating subentries in indexes, discussed later in this chapter. If you need to include a semicolon or a colon within an entry, put single quotes on both sides of the entry, and format the quotes as hidden text.

After you've inserted the appropriate codes into your document, you're ready to compile the table of contents. You do not need to repaginate the document first; Word does it for you.

❶ Choose the Table of Contents command.

❷ Select the .C. Paragraphs option. The Show Page Numbers option should already be set.

❸ Enter the range of levels you want in the table of contents, or leave the All option selected.

❹ Click Start to begin.

Word prepares the table of contents and places it in its own section at the beginning of the document.

Changing the Format of a Table of Contents

Word's automatic *toc* styles establish the layout for nine levels of entries in the table of contents. This is the case regardless of how you generate the table of contents. You can redefine any or all of these styles. Chapter 10, "Working with Style Sheets," explains how.

Replacing or Editing a Table of Contents

After you've compiled a table of contents for a document, you can compile another at any time and use it to replace the old one. Before recompiling the table of contents, Word asks if you want to replace the old one. Click Yes in the dialog box that appears.

Because the table of contents is standard text, you can edit and reformat it in any way you want. These changes are lost, however, if you subsequently recompile and replace the table.

For example, if you set the Show Page Numbers option in the Table of Contents dialog box, Word adds a tab mark with leader dots and the page number to each entry in the table of contents. Some designs, however, call for the page number to appear for the major headings only and not for the subheadings. In this case, you would set the Show Page Numbers option and then manually remove the tabs and page numbers from the subheadings. You would have to do this each time you recompiled the table of contents.

Creating Other Types of Lists for a Document

You can use Word's table of contents feature to generate lists of other elements in a document as well. You can use it, for example, for a list of the illustrations and plates in a book or article. Word doesn't add the phrase *Table of Contents* before the table it creates, so you can type any title you like, such as *List of Illustrations*, *Projects*, or *Workshop Examples*. If the table or list doesn't require page numbers, you can easily omit them by turning off the Show Page Numbers option in the Table of Contents dialog box.

Your document can have more than one table created with the Table of Contents command, but you have to be careful that you don't erase an old table when you compile a new one. To extract an additional list, do the following:

❶ Generate the main table of contents from the headings, or by using the .c. codes, as was discussed earlier.

❷ Format the entries for the new table using .c. codes with a deeper level than any you used before—starting at .c4. or so, for example. Alternatively, you can format entries for the new table with deeper levels of headings. For example, you can reserve the *heading 1* through *heading 4* styles for the actual headings to be used in the main table of contents, and reserve *heading 5* through *heading 9* for the second table.

❸ When you have identified all the entries and specified the levels to be used in the resulting table of contents, choose the Table of Contents command.

❹ Click the .C. Paragraphs option.

❺ Enter the range of levels for the elements you want to list in the From and To edit fields. You must enter numbers in both fields even if you are extracting only one level of entry for resulting table of contents.

❻ Click the Start button.

If any of the levels are duplicated in another table, Word asks if you want to replace the existing table of contents. Click the Cancel button and edit the entries in the document, using new numbers to avoid any overlap. You can use this method to generate a collection of different lists, each using a different range of table-of-contents codes. For example, if the deepest level of entry in your document uses the .c4. code, you can use .c5. for figure numbers, .c6. for table numbers, and .c7. for hidden in-text editorial comments.

Multiple Tables of Contents

You can create multiple tables of contents simply by clicking No in the dialog box that asks if you want to replace the existing table of contents. If you have not moved the table, Word adds the new one before it. If you have moved the table of contents, Word leaves it where you put it. You can use this feature to generate additional tables when you have run out of outline or .c. levels or when you want to create an alternate table of contents. For example, you can create one table of contents comprising levels 1 through 3 for a student's study guide, and one comprising levels 1 through 5 for a teacher's reference.

TIP

Using Both Types of Tables in One Document
You can create tables of contents from the headings and from .c. codes in one document. This is useful in documents that have more than one type of list in the front matter, such as the table of contents proper, a list of figures, and a list of tables. Simply extract the main table of contents from the outline, and insert .c. codes for the figures and tables lists. Then extract each list separately by setting the correct options in the Table of Contents dialog box.

Compiling a Table of Contents for Linked Files

If your manuscript or other work spans several documents, you can link them together and have Word compile the table of contents from the whole group at once. The secret is in the Next File button in the Document dialog box. For each document that is followed by another in the sequence:

1. Choose Document from the Format menu.
2. Click the Next File button and select the following document.
   If you want Word to do the page numbering for you, delete the contents of the Number Pages From field in each document except the first in the series. Otherwise, be sure the starting page number in each document is correct.
3. Click the OK button.

When you start compiling the table of contents for the topmost document on the desktop, Word repaginates and scans each document, in order, and extracts its table. If Word can't find a file in the sequence, it prompts you to locate the folder or insert the disk that contains the document. Therefore, it's a good idea to have all the disks at hand when you assemble the table of contents.

A very useful application of this technique, even for smaller documents, is to put the table of contents in a "front matter" document file that precedes the main body of the document. To do this, create a new, blank document, open the Document dialog box, and specify the first file in the sequence through the Next File dialog box. When you compile the table of contents, Word places it in the new, first file. You can then put the other front-matter elements, such as the copyright page, the title page, and the acknowledgments, in the same file as the table of contents. This is a good way to set up special page layouts for the front matter without affecting the main body of the document.

TIP

Merging a Large Table of Contents
Another way to develop a table of contents for a large opus that spans many smaller documents—the chapters in a book, for example—is to use the method just described to generate a table of contents for each chapter, each in a separate document that is linked to that chapter alone. Then, create a new document which uses Word's INCLUDE merge language command to combine into one file the table of contents belonging to each chapter. For more information on Word's merge feature, see Chapter 17, "Merge Printing."

This trick is particularly useful when combined with the process of converting a table of contents back into an outline, discussed next.

Converting a Table of Contents to an Outline

Occasionally, you might want to play with an outline without having to deal with the body text that goes with each heading. For example, you might be dealing with a large document that is divided into many smaller files and want to work with an outline that covers all the files. Or you may want to format an outline in a different way than with the formats you get when printing a collapsed outline from Outline View with the Show Formats feature set.

To assemble one outline for a set of documents or to print a formatted outline without the body text, first extract a table of contents for the document or series of linked documents. It's best to put this table by itself in a blank document. Then choose Define Styles from the Format menu, select each *toc* style in turn, and change its name to the appropriate *heading* style. For each name change, Word asks you to verify that you want to reassign the text formatted in that style to the *heading* style. After you've converted all the *toc* style text to *heading* style text, you can work with the outline in Outline view or switch to Galley View or Page View to reformat the *heading* styles for printing.

■ *Making an Index*

If done skillfully, an index provides a way of navigating in a document that is as useful as the table of contents. Indexing is an art, but Word makes this art of creating and maintaining an index much more accessible to everyone.

Generating an index is only slightly more difficult than generating a table of contents with the .c. codes. Each index entry must begin and end with special hidden codes that don't appear when you print the document. You type the code .i. at the beginning of each index entry. Format the code as hidden text. The entry must end with an end-of-entry code, which can be a semicolon, a newline mark, or a paragraph mark. If you insert a semicolon to end an entry, format it as hidden text so that it won't be printed. Figure 15-5 shows a number of different index entries.

Untitled3	
index entry with semicolon	.i.first.entry;
index entry with paragraph mark	.i.second.entry¶
index entry with new line mark	.i.third.entry↵

Figure 15-5
Examples of formatted index entries.

If only the indexing codes are formatted as hidden text, the index entry will remain visible as text in the body of your document. However, if you want to link an index entry to a particular point in the document but prevent the entry from becoming part of the document, format both the indexing codes and the entry as hidden text.

When you choose Insert Index Entry from the Document menu, Word enters both the .i. code and the terminating semicolon and places the insertion point between them. The subsequent text you enter will have the Hidden format unless you remove the format. (Press Shift-Command-X to turn off the Hidden character format quickly.) If you want to turn existing, nonhidden text into an index entry, select it first, and then choose the Insert Index Entry command. Word inserts the codes before and after the selection, unless the selected text ends with a paragraph mark or a newline character. (Remember that these characters can end index entries, as does the semicolon.)

You can also take advantage of Word's glossary function to store the indexing codes. Create two index entries, one for the starting code and one for the ending semicolon. Give the glossary entries convenient names, such as *ind* and *end* (*end* because you can use it for ending table-of-contents entries as well). Insert the index starting code in text by pressing Command-Backspace, typing *ind,* and pressing the Return key.

After you've coded all the index entries, you can compile the index. As with generating a table of contents, it isn't necessary to hide all hidden text in the document by turning off the Show Hidden Text option. Now, do the following:

1. Choose Index from the Utilities menu. The Index dialog box, shown in Figure 15-6, appears.
2. Click the Nested or Run-in option, as desired. (A description of these is given next.)
3. Leave selected the All option in the Index Characters group.
4. Click the Start button.

Index
Format: (•) Nested
( ) Run-in
Index Characters:
(•) All
( ) From: [ ] To: [ ]
[Start]
[Cancel]

Figure 15-6
The Index dialog box.

Word's two basic index formats, nested and run-in, specify different ways of handling subentries, the subordinate entries that follow the main entry. With the nested format, subentries appear below the main entry and are indented. With the run-in format, Word places subentries on the same line as the main entry, using semicolons to separate them. Figure 15-7 shows both kinds of formats. Select the format you want by clicking the appropriate option in the Index dialog box.

INDEX – BUYING A COPIER
lease 1
ownership 2
Photocopier 10
  coated paper 12
  plain paper 10
  thermal 11
renting 2
Xerox 9
—
P11 S1 Normal

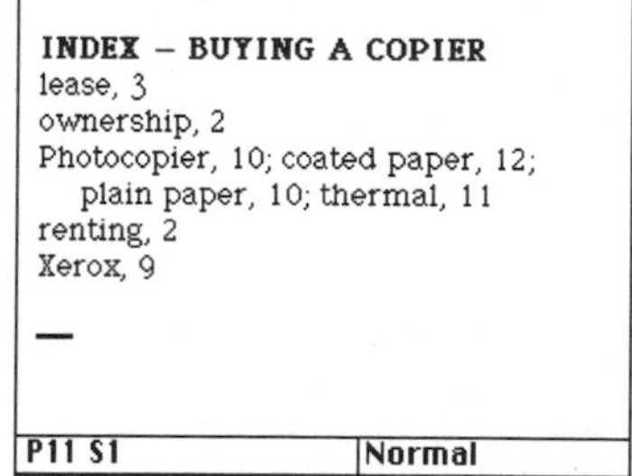

INDEX – BUYING A COPIER
lease, 3
ownership, 2
Photocopier, 10; coated paper, 12;
  plain paper, 10; thermal, 11
renting, 2
Xerox, 9
—
P11 S1 Normal

Figure 15-7
The two kinds of index formats.

When you click Start, Word repaginates the document and then searches through it to collect the entries you identified, along with the page number on which each entry falls. It assembles them in alphabetical order and places the index in a new section at the end of the document. The program also removes duplicate entries occurring on the same page and assembles a list of page numbers when the same entry occurs on different pages.

If you're working with a very large series of documents, you might find that Word doesn't have enough available memory to extract more than about 4000 index entries. If Word presents a dialog box such as *Not enough memory to complete operation,* try using the Index Character group in the Index dialog box to extract only a range of entries at a time. For example, if you want to extract entries beginning with the letters *A* through *F,* enter the letters in the From and To fields. Next, you might extract entries beginning with the letters *G* through *N,* and so on, until the index is complete.

After Word has compiled the index, you'll probably want to go over it and edit or combine entries that aren't exactly what you wanted. The most common type of change you're likely to make is to combine entries that are phrased differently at two or more locations in a document, such as *Formatting:italics* and *Character Formats:italics.* It's best to develop a consistent style for citing index entries; a manual such as *The Chicago Manual of Style* is a good place to learn about indexing conventions.

Creating Subentries

Word assumes that all entries are main entries unless you tell it otherwise. To create a subentry, you specify the main entry first and then the subentry, separated by a colon, as in *Word:using* or *Word:printing with.* Do not insert a space after the colon. You'll want to make the entire entry hidden, as shown in this example:

```
.i.Word:Using:Beginners;
```

You also use hidden text for expository index entries. Such entries consist of words and phrases that don't occur in the text but that more accurately reflect the subject matter of the entry. Format as hidden text both the starting and ending codes and the entry between them. Suppose, for example, that you are indexing the following paragraph:

The two main classes of cast iron are gray iron and white iron. Gray iron is inexpensive and easy to machine. It is, however, brittle and only about half as strong as steel. White iron is stronger and harder than gray iron but considerably more difficult to machine.

One way to index this paragraph might be to code the words *cast iron, gray iron,* and *white iron,* but those entries aren't very descriptive. A better way would be to create a new entry and format it as hidden text. Assigning the hidden format to the entry causes it to be omitted from the printed document. The entry you use might be something like the following:

cast iron, gray and white
    comparison of cost, strength, and machinability, 143

You would generate this entry by typing:

.i.cast iron, gray and white:comparison of cost, strength, and machinability;

You can create up to seven levels of subentries, corresponding to a maximum of seven *index* styles, by adding more subentries and more colons. An entry such as:

.i.Word:using:for beginners;

would appear like this in the index:

Word
    using
        for beginners, 174

You can skip a level by typing two colons with nothing between, as in:

.i.Word::for beginners;

In the index, you'd find:

Word
        for beginners, 174

Using the Index Styles

When you create an index, the character and paragraph formats attached to the entry are removed, and the entry is formatted with one of the seven *index* automatic styles. The *index 1* style is for main entries; *index 2* through *index 7* are for subentries. The only difference between these styles is the position of the left indent; it moves to the right 0.25 inch at each index level. You can redefine the index styles in any way you like. See Chapter 10, "Working with Style Sheets," for more information.

Of course, you can also edit and format the index manually after it is compiled, but any such changes will be lost if you recompile the index.

Using Special Index Formats

You can change the way that Word formats the page numbers or specify text to be used instead of a page number, by including certain characters in the index entry code. Many books use boldface or italic page numbers to indicate illustrations or definitions, for example. The following table shows examples of the various formatting options available.

Code	Format
.ib.*entry*;	Boldface page number; you can use either an uppercase or lowercase *b*.
.ii.*entry*;	Italic page number; you can use either an uppercase or lowercase *i*.
.i(.*entry*;	Start of multipage reference.
.i).*entry*;	End of multipage reference.
.i.*entry#text*;	*Text* replaces page number.

The following table gives some examples of how these codes might be used. As before, the dotted or gray underline signifies hidden text. If the entry is actually part of the text, don't format the entry as hidden text.

Index entry	Produces this index listing
.ib.Using Word;	Using Word **10**
.ii.Using Word;	Using Word *10*
.i(.Using Word; on the first page of the topic, and .i).Using Word; on the last page of the topic	Using Word 10-14
.iUsing Word#(See Word, Using);	Using Word (See Word, Using)

As with a table of contents, if you want to include a colon, semicolon, or other special character (such as the # character) in an entry, put single quotes around the entry and format the quotes as hidden text. For example, if you wanted to create an index entry which looks like this:

PRINT#, Using **127**

You would enter this text on page 127 of the document:

.ib.'PRINT#, Using';

Recompiling an Index

If you make changes to a document that affect the pagination, you'll want to recompile the index. When you do this, Word asks if you want to replace the old index. Click Yes if you do. Word then replaces the index, even if you moved it from the end of the document to some other location. Clicking No adds a second index without deleting the one that already exists. You can use this feature, for example, if you're designing the index and want to compare different formats. To recompile the index, choose the Index command again.

Compiling an Index for Linked Files

If your manuscript spans several documents, you can link them and have Word compile the index for the whole group all at once. You use the Next File button in the Document dialog box to link the files. For each document to be followed by another one in the sequence:

1. Choose the Document command.
2. Click the Next File button, and select the following document.
   If you want Word to do the page numbering for you, delete the contents of the Number Pages From field in each document except the first in the series. Otherwise, be sure the starting page number in each document is correct.
3. Click the OK button.

When you compile the index, Word assembles the entries for all documents and places the index at the end of the last document. If Word can't find a file in the chain, it prompts you to find the folder or insert the disk that contains the document. Also, as with tables of contents, you can compile an index into a blank document at the end of the chain of linked files.

Points to Remember

- Word's Table of Contents command generates a table of contents for your document, adding the page numbers automatically. You can base the contents on either the levels or headings in the document or on codes that you enter and format as hidden text.
- You can use the Table of Contents command to generate lists of figures and tables. Assign these elements levels of heading or .c. codes that are deeper than any used in the document; then enter the range of levels for the list in the From and To fields in the Table of Contents dialog box before compiling the table.
- Word's Index command generates an index for your document, adding the page numbers and alphabetizing the entries automatically. You must code each entry to appear in the index.
- To include an entry that isn't in the document in a table of contents or index, type it at the appropriate location and format the entire entry as hidden text, or use the Insert TOC Entry or Insert Index Entry command from the Document menu.
- Entries in the table of contents are assigned the automatic styles *toc 1* through *toc 9*; the number corresponds to the heading level or to the number in the .c. code for the entry. Entries in the index are assigned the automatic styles *index 1* through *index 7*, corresponding to the levels of subentries. You can redefine these styles in any way you like.
- Word places the table of contents in its own section at the beginning of the document and the index in its own section at the end of the document. You can edit and reformat these as you would any other text.
- You can create glossary entries for the table of contents and index codes to make the job of coding easier.

Techniques

Creating a Table of Contents

Generate a table of contents from the headings in the outline

1. Choose Table of Contents from the Document menu.
2. Be sure that the Outline option is on.
3. Be sure that the Show Page Numbers option is on if you want the contents to include the page numbers.

4. Specify the range of levels to appear in the contents, or leave All selected.
5. Click Start.
6. If a table of contents already exists for the document, Word asks if you want to replace it. Click Yes to replace it or No to generate a new table without deleting the old one.

Generate a table of contents from inserted codes

1. Before each entry to appear in the table of contents, insert the code *.c.* or *.c1.* for first-level entries, *.c2.* for second-level entries, and so on to the deepest level. Format these codes as hidden text. Each entry must end with a paragraph mark, a newline mark, or a semicolon. If you insert a semicolon, format it as hidden text. You can insert the codes with the Insert TOC Entry command, by typing them, or by inserting them from the glossary.
2. Choose Table of Contents from the Utilities menu.
3. Select the .C. Paragraphs option.
4. Be sure that the Show Page Numbers option is on if you want the contents to include the page numbers.
5. Click Start.

If the entry itself is formatted as hidden text, it is still compiled in the table of contents but doesn't become part of the printed document.

Creating an Index

Code index entries

1. To insert a new index entry, set the insertion point and choose the Insert Index Entry command. Word inserts the hidden-text codes and places the insertion point between them. To insert index codes around existing nonhidden text, first select the text, then choose the command. Word inserts the codes before and after the selection.

   You can vary the format of the page number by using the following codes:

Code	Format
.ib.*entry*;	Bold page number; you can use either an uppercase or lowercase *b*.
.ii.*entry*;	Italic page number; you can use either an uppercase or lowercase *i*.
.i(.*entry*;	Start of multipage reference.
.i).*entry*;	End of multipage reference.
.i.*entry#text*;	*Text* replaces page number.

❷ For subentries, type the usual index code; then enter the main entry, followed by a colon, and then the subentry. (Do not insert any space after the colon.) A subentry can be followed by a colon and a sub-subentry, to a maximum of seven levels.

❸ Format subentries and any other index entry that is not part of the document as hidden text.

If the entry itself is formatted as hidden text, it is still compiled in the index, but doesn't become part of the printed document.

Compile an index

❶ Choose Index from the Utilities menu.

❷ Select the Nested option to place each subentry on its own line with a suitable indent; select the Run-in option to place the subentries on the same line as the main entry. Enter a range of characters in the From and To fields to extract an alphabetic range of index entries.

❸ Click Start.

❹ If an index already exists for the document, Word asks if you want to replace it. Click Yes to replace it or No to generate a new index without deleting the old one.

Generate a table of contents or index for linked files

❶ Code the files as usual.

❷ For each file in the sequence that is followed by another file, specify the file to follow it through the Next File feature of the Document dialog box. If you want sequential page numbering throughout the files, delete the default number in the Number Pages From field in the Document dialog box.

❸ Open the first file in the sequence.

❹ Choose the Table of Contents or Index command, set the appropriate options, and click Start.

❺ Word places the table of contents in a new section at the beginning of the first document and places the index at the end of the last document.

Commands

Command name	Meaning, menu	Standard keyboard	Keypad	Extended keyboard
Index…	Compiles index based on index entries inserted in document. **Utilities**			
Insert Index Entry	Inserts index entry codes, formatted as hidden text, before and after selected text or on either side of insertion point. **Document**			
Insert TOC Entry	Inserts table-of-contents entry codes, formatted as hidden text, before and after selected text or on either side of insertion point. **Document**			
Table of Contents…	Compiles table of contents based on document outline or table-of-contents entries. **Utilities**			

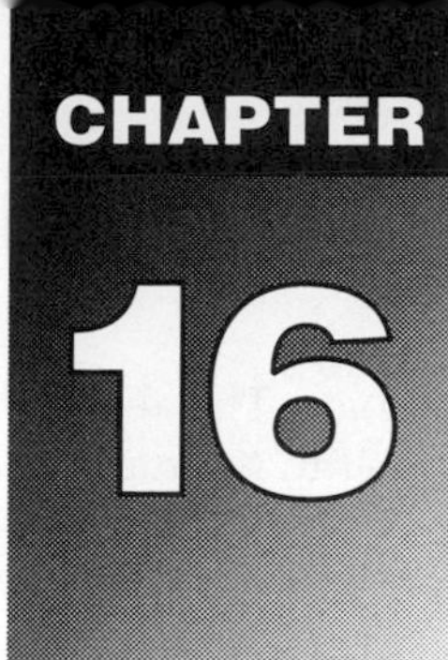

Transferring Text and Graphics

Word is a powerful program that can do much more than most people expect of word processors. You can extend this power by creating material in other programs and transferring it into a Word document. You can transfer three main classes of data to and from a Word document: raw text, graphics, and files from certain word processors such as MacWrite and Word for the IBM PC.

Raw text is any collection of characters without formatting such as boldface or underlining. You work with raw text when you want to incorporate into a Word document information taken from a bulletin board or information service such as CompuServe or DIALOG, tables of financial statistics from a spreadsheet, or text created with another program.

You can create illustrations and other visual elements in graphics applications, such as MacPaint, MacDraw, SuperPaint, Cricket Draw, or Adobe Illustrator, and move them into a Word document. You can also copy images from applications not ordinarily considered graphics programs. For example, you can create a chart in Microsoft Excel, copy the image of the chart to the Clipboard, and paste it into a report you're writing in Word.

Finally, Word can read and write files in a variety of formats. The ability to read and write files in MS-DOS Word format makes it easier to maintain common documents in an office where both Macs and PCs are used. Word can also read files containing graphics and formatted text created with MacWrite and Microsoft Works. You can even send a fully formatted Word document through an electronic mail system such as MCI Mail, first saving the document in the Rich Text Format (RTF), or by sending the document to another user of a Microsoft Mail server.

This chapter describes how to transfer text and graphics into and out of a Word document. You'll learn how to cut and paste data, manipulate text and graphics once they are in Word, and use Apple's MultiFinder for maximum efficiency.

■ *Transferring Text*

You can import and export text between Word and another program in two ways: by transferring selected text via the Clipboard or the Scrapbook and by opening and saving whole documents in a format that another program can read. Each of these will be discussed in turn.

Using the Clipboard and Scrapbook

The routines for cutting and pasting between programs are much the same no matter what program you are using. You select text or graphics in the source document and choose Cut or Copy from the Edit menu. This places the material, or a copy of it, in the Clipboard. Exit the application, and then start the program into which you want to move the material. Once you're in that application, place an insertion point and choose the Paste command.

When you cut and paste within an application such as Word, the Clipboard is maintained within an area of the Mac's memory. However, if you leave the application with something in the Clipboard, it saves the Clipboard's contents in a special file called *Clipboard File*, usually kept in the System Folder. A few programs store the Clipboard File on the disk that contains the application, and so to transfer information from one application to another, you might have to move the Clipboard File from the first disk to the second before you start the second program.

The Clipboard holds only one item at a time, but the Scrapbook can hold up to 256 items. Also, the contents of the Clipboard disappear when you copy another item to it, but items stored in the Scrapbook remain there until you remove them, allowing you to keep a collection of clip art, for instance. If you're cutting and pasting several items at a time, you can copy each item to the Clipboard and paste it into the Scrapbook before moving to the second program.

Just as the contents of the Clipboard are stored in the Clipboard File when you leave a program, the items in the Scrapbook are stored in the Scrapbook File, which is associated with the system files on the start-up disk. If the application you're pasting into is on another start-up disk, copy the current Scrapbook File on it. If that disk already has a Scrapbook File, change its name before you copy; otherwise, the existing file will be erased.

You can have many scrapbook files on a given start-up disk, but each must have a different name. You can maintain different scrapbook files for different purposes; simply give each a name that reflects its purpose, such as *Newsletter Scrapbook*, and change its name temporarily to *Scrapbook File* when you need to access its contents. The Mac always accesses the scrapbook file named Scrapbook File. If a file with that name doesn't exist on the current start-up disk, the Mac creates a new, empty one. You can also use a scrapbook desk accessory, such as SmartScrap from Solutions International, to easily switch from one scrapbook file to another.

When you select and copy something from a program to the Clipboard, the program determines what kind of material you've copied and attaches at least one four-letter *data type* code to the Clipboard. If you paste the clipping into the Scrapbook, you can see these codes in the lower right corner of the Scrapbook window, as shown in Figure 16-1.

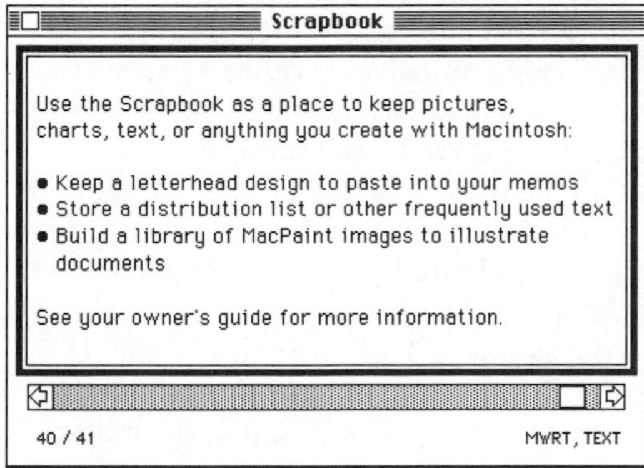

Figure 16-1
Data type codes attached to material pasted into the Scrapbook from MacWrite.

A data type code is like a message between the routines in a program or between programs; a program uses the codes to determine how to handle material stored in the Clipboard. For example, if you copy some boilerplate text from a program and store it in the Scrapbook, you'll undoubtedly see the code *TEXT* in the lower right corner of the Scrapbook window. If you paste this material into a Word document, Word checks the data type codes and determines that the material in the Clipboard should be inserted into the document as text (and not, say, as a graphic).

When you copy something, the program often transfers more than one version of the selected material to the Clipboard. If you're copying formatted text, for instance, the program doesn't know whether you intend to paste the material back into a document belonging to the current application (and therefore want to retain the formatting) or whether you intend to paste it into a document that belongs to another application. Because a given program can't depend on another program to be able to interpret the internal structure it uses to format text, the program might transfer to the Clipboard both its internal version of the formatted text as well as a copy of the raw, unformatted text. When this happens and you paste the material into the Scrapbook, you'll see two data type codes in the Scrapbook window—one code for the internal format and the *TEXT* code for the more standard format. When you paste this material into a document belonging to the receiving program, it nearly always is able to use the unformatted version of the copied material if it is not able to handle the formatted version.

For example, if you copy text in the MacWrite format to the Scrapbook, you'll see two data type codes in the Scrapbook window—*MWRT* and *TEXT*, as shown in Figure 16-1. If you start MacWrite again on another occasion and paste this material into a MacWrite document, the program uses the MWRT version of the text so that the formatting is retained. If, however, you paste this material into a document within a different program, the program uses the TEXT version of the material, and the formatting does not appear.

The discussion so far has centered on how most applications handle the Clipboard and the Scrapbook. Fortunately, Word works in almost the same way. Instead of using the standard Clipboard, Word maintains its own internal Clipboard to conserve space in memory. When you copy something, Word keeps only one version of the material—in its own internal data type—in its Clipboard. When you paste the material into the Scrapbook or switch to another application, Word converts its internal Clipboard to the standard, external Clipboard in two formats—the standard TEXT format and the RTF format (discussed below). If the receiving application can read material that is formatted in the RTF format, the formats are preserved. If not, the material is pasted as raw text. You can see this in the Scrapbook after pasting there text copied from Word: In the lower right corner of the Scrapbook, you see the data types TEXT and RTF (strictly, RTF and one space character, making four characters).

When you paste raw text (having the data type TEXT, and not RTF) copied from the Scrapbook or from another program into a Word document, Word assigns it the style of the surrounding text. If the pasted text contains paragraph marks, the text preceding each paragraph mark takes on the *Normal* style.

Transferring Tabular Data

As discussed in the previous chapter, tabular data consists of a series of lines in which each item is separated by tabs and each line ends in a paragraph mark. You can transfer raw text structured in this way between Word and spreadsheet and database programs, either by copying it from Word and pasting it into the other program or by saving the file in Text Only format (discussed in the next section).

Some programs, including Microsoft Excel, File, and Multiplan, can translate tabular data into their own file formats. In spreadsheets such as Microsoft Excel, each line of text is considered one row divided into columns by tabs. In database programs such as Microsoft File, each line of text is treated as a complete record. Commas or tabs in the table divide the items into fields. To export data from Word to a spreadsheet or database program:

❶ Select and copy the desired section of data from within Word.

❷ Quit Word and start the spreadsheet or file-management program.

❸ Set an insertion point in the spreadsheet (or start a new record in the database manager). Choose the Paste command.

Technically, the data in Word need not conform strictly to a rows-and-columns structure for it to be transferred into a spreadsheet or database program. For example, a series of lines with no tabs in Word will become a single column in a spreadsheet program, with one paragraph per cell.

Importing data from a spreadsheet or database program to Word works similarly: A row in Microsoft Excel translates to a paragraph in Word. When pasted into Word, the cells within each row are separated by tabs. With a database manager, each record becomes a paragraph, and the contents of the fields are separated by commas or tabs. To import data from a spreadsheet or database manager, do the following:

❶ Select and copy the desired area of data from within the spreadsheet or file-management program.

❷ Quit the program and start Word.

❸ Set an insertion point for the data and choose the Paste command.

❹ Select the data you pasted in, and set the tab stops in the Ruler to accommodate the columns. If necessary, adjust the right indent so that each row of data takes up only one line in the Word document.

If the imported data is separated by commas, you can use the Change command to replace all commas with tabs automatically:

❶ Select the text you pasted into the Word document.

❷ Choose Change from the Search menu.

❸ In the Change dialog box, type a comma in the Find What field and type ^*t* in the Change To field. Click the Change Selection button.

Alternatively, you can select the pasted text and use the Insert Table command to convert the pasted text to a table. See Chapter 11, "Formatting Tables and Lists," for more information on converting text delimited with commas and tabs to tables.

Some database managers allow you to copy only one record at a time or require that you use a conversion utility or save selected records to an ASCII-format document and then open the resulting document in Word. Once a file has been converted, Word can open it as a text-only document. See the instructions that accompany the database-management program for more details on the steps you must perform to import and export data.

Transferring Text Documents

If the block of text you want to transfer is large, it's often better to bypass the Clipboard and work with the text at the document level. Word can directly read and write documents created by a variety of other word processors and programs. You see a list of these formats when you choose Save As from the File menu and click the File Format button. The use of certain of these formats involves some interesting practical issues, however. The range of formats and document structures Word offers is extensive (multicolumn section formats, table structures, and footnotes, for example), and so Word translates formats to and from other applications as best it can.

The Text Only and Text Only with Line Breaks File Formats

You could call the Text Only format and the Text Only with Line Breaks format the generic options for transferring files from Word to any other Macintosh program. Both these formats save a Word document as raw text, but the Text Only with Line Breaks format puts a paragraph mark at the end of each line. This is helpful when you want to upload a Word document to an electronic mail or bulletin board service—simply format the lines for the length you want, and save a copy of the document in the Text Only With Line Breaks format.

Of course, all of the character and paragraph formats disappear from text saved in these formats. Word also converts newline marks, section marks, and page breaks to paragraph marks, and it converts optional hyphens to normal hyphens. If you intend to transfer the document to a computer other than a Macintosh, either through a modem or via a bulletin board service, be aware that other computers do not share many of the Mac's special characters (such as ¶, •, ™, —, and so on, almost all of which have ASCII codes from 128 to 255); you'll have to search for these and change them manually.

Word can also read files that have been saved in a text-only format with another program. Even if the program you are using can't save the document in any of the formats that Word can translate, it probably does have some type of text-only, file-saving option. When you choose Word's Open command, you see the names of all the standard Word documents, as well as the documents that Word is able to read and translate into a normal Word document: text only, those created with MacWrite, MacTerminal, Microsoft Write, Works, MS-DOS Word, and so on.

In Microsoft Excel, for instance, you can choose Save As from the File menu and select the Text file-format option. (Incidentally, Microsoft Excel saves either the values in the worksheet or the formulas, depending on which is visible when you choose the Save As command. Choose Display from the Options menu to switch between the two views.) Be sure to change the name so that you don't overwrite the original worksheet file. If a cell in the worksheet contains a comma, Microsoft Excel surrounds the text with quotation marks in the file saved on disk.

Once you've saved a file in this way, the name of the file appears in the list box when you choose Word's Open command. When you open the file, you can remove the quotation marks by searching for them and replacing them with nothing, but if you want to use the text in a data document for a merged form letter, you might want to keep these marks. (Read Chapter 17, "Merge Printing," for a complete discussion of form letters.)

Microsoft Word Formats

The File Format dialog box offers a number of options for saving documents in formats that can be read by other Microsoft products, and by applications that can read and write those formats.

Version 1.05 and Microsoft Works File Format

Some people who don't need the power of Word 4 prefer the ease of use and integration offered by Microsoft Works. Works is able to read the Word 1.05 format well, so there isn't a separate option for saving a document in Works format. Use the Microsoft Word 1.05 file format to store a Word 4 document in a format readable by Word 1.05 or Works. Again, not all of a Word 4 document's formats survive the translation. For example, Word 1.05 doesn't support style sheets, so if you save in Word 1.05 formatted text assigned a style, the text takes on the character and paragraph formats of the style without actually keeping the style.

The Word 3.0 and Microsoft Write File Format

If you want to send a version of a document to someone who has Word 3 or Microsoft Write, use this format. Certain other programs, such as PageMaker, read Word 3 files. Again, features peculiar to Word 4, such as colored text and tables, won't survive the transfer.

The MS-DOS Word File Format

Mac Word's conversion of files in the MS-DOS Word format is perhaps the most complete with respect to the actual structure of the document. This feature is helpful in offices that use computers from both the Macintosh and the IBM PC families, because it permits the sharing of standard documents between the two types of machines. Word-specific features such as headers, footers, footnotes, and so on, transfer well between the two versions of Word.

However, certain features that the programs don't share—such as graphics, character formats (such as outline and shadow), and paragraph formats (such as the border options)—are not translated. The transfer of style sheets depends on the direction of the transfer: You can transfer a style sheet for an MS-DOS document to the Mac, but you can't transfer the style sheet for a Mac document to the PC. Also, section styles from MS-DOS documents aren't converted. When you save a Mac Word document containing styles in the MS-DOS Word format, the styles are converted to individual character and paragraph formats.

Probably the main issue regarding the sharing of files is how to actually get the file from one machine to the other. One method is to use network software such as Sun Microsystems' TOPS to connect Macs and PCs via AppleTalk. Another is to connect a special drive to either the Mac or the PC that can read the other machine's formats. The most common way is to connect the two machines through modems or with an appropriate cable that connects their serial ports (the Phone, or modem, port on the Mac), run telecommunication software on each machine, and use an XModem communication protocol to manage the transfer of the file. Here are some suggested communication parameters for Microsoft Access on the IBM PC and for MacTerminal on the Macintosh:

Access	
Modify settings	9600 baud, half duplex, 8-bit word length, no parity, 1 stop bit, TTY terminal, XOn/XOff protocol, ^M end-of-line character.
MacTerminal	
Terminal settings	TTY, on line, local echo, auto wraparound, new line.
Compatibility settings	9600 baud, 8 bits, no parity, XOn/XOff protocol, connection via either modem or another computer (depending on how you've connected the machines), Phone port (also called the modem port).
File-transfer settings	No delays for pasting or sending text (but change the setting if the received text is missing characters), straight XModem protocol.

To transfer a document from MacTerminal to Access, do the following:

1. Save the document in MS-DOS Word format. It's helpful to use a filename that conforms to the MS-DOS Word file-naming convention, up to 8 characters, plus the *.DOC* extension. The name of the document doesn't change, because you're only saving a copy of it in the MS-DOS format.
2. Start both communications programs, and set the programs' communications parameters if you haven't already done so. (You can save these sets of parameters to make subsequent sessions easier.)
3. Establish a connection, and choose Send File from MacTerminal's File menu. A dialog box appears; find the name of the Mac Word file saved in the MS-DOS format and double-click on the name to open the file. A dialog box appears, saying *Sending the file "filename"*. At this point, MacTerminal waits for Access to respond to its attempts to send the file.
4. On the PC, press the F10 key to activate the command menu, and use the Transfer Protocol Receive command (type *T*, *P*, and *R*). Access prompts you for a filename; enter the name of the file you are transferring. Soon Access will tell MacTerminal that it's ready to receive the file: You'll see the gauge in MacTerminal's dialog box begin to move, and the Bytes Received field in Access increases by increments of 128 bytes at a time. (The XModem protocol transfers data in blocks of 128 bytes.)

To send an MS-DOS file to the Mac, the process is similar, but because MS-DOS Word does not keep the style sheets belonging to a document within the document, you have to transfer the MS-DOS Word document and its style sheet in separate steps.

1. In MS-DOS Word, save the document in the Formatted format, and quit the program.
2. Start both communications programs, and set their communications parameters if you haven't already done so. Establish a connection between the machines.
3. On the PC, press the F10 key to activate the command menu, and use the Transfer Protocol Send command (type *T*, *P*, and *S*). Access prompts you for a filename; enter the MS-DOS Word document's name. (You might also need to supply a pathname.) At this point, Access waits for MacTerminal to respond to its attempts to send the file.
4. In MacTerminal, choose Receive File from the File menu. A dialog box appears; enter the name of the MS-DOS file, and then click the Receive button. A second dialog box appears, saying *Receiving the file "filename"*. Soon MacTerminal will tell Access that it's ready to

receive the file: Instead of the gauge in MacTerminal's dialog box, you'll see the Blocks Received number begin to increase in blocks of 512 bytes; in Access, the Count field begins to increase as well. When the transfer is complete, MacTerminal presents a dialog box telling you that the transfer was successful.

5. When you've transferred the document, repeat steps 3 and 4 to transfer the style sheet for the document, if you have defined one.
6. Once both the document and its style sheet have been transferred to the Mac, start Mac Word and choose the Open command. Double-click on the filename of the MS-DOS Word document to open it. When Word opens the document, it discovers its source and presents a dialog box asking if there is a style sheet file for the document. If you click Yes, you'll see another dialog box containing a file list box. Simply double-click on the name of the style sheet file; Word then uses it to create a normal Word document. If you don't have a style sheet file for the document, click No; Word then uses its default style sheet.

The MacWrite Format

If you've moved up to Word from MacWrite, you'll find that it's easy to convert all your MacWrite documents into Word documents. Simply open the MacWrite file from within Word, and the file will be converted to the standard Word format and placed in an untitled window. Some programs are able to read and save documents in MacWrite format but not in Word format: If you need to transfer a file to or from such a program and preserve as much formatting as possible, and Word doesn't support the native format of the program, try saving the file in the MacWrite format.

The Interchange (Rich Text) Format

The Interchange format, commonly called Rich Text Format (RTF), might seem obscure, but can be very useful when you want to transfer a fully-formatted Word document to someone via an electronic communications medium that can't handle the binary transfer of Mac files. With MacTerminal, for instance, you can transfer any Mac document, associated icon and all, by using the MacBinary file-transfer protocol. However, many bulletin boards and communications services, such as MCI Mail, cannot store and transfer such files to their destination in this format and can only accept straight ASCII, raw text files.

If you save a Word document in RTF, Word converts everything in it to sequences of standard ASCII text characters—even complicated structures such as graphics and style sheets. Word also breaks paragraphs into lines of at most 255 characters so that the long lines that make up paragraphs will not confuse the computer system through which you're sending the document. Figure 16-2 shows an example of a text file resulting from this conversion.

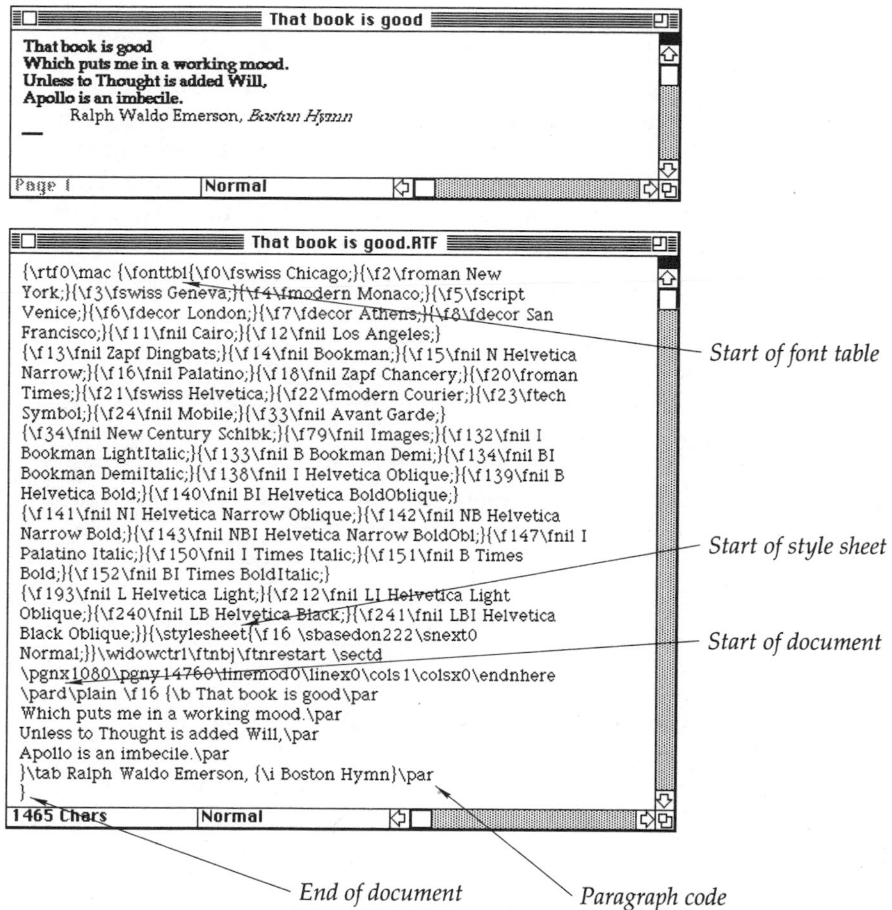

Figure 16-2
A document shown in Word format and in RTF format.

If you inspect this format, you might realize that its codes aren't impossible to decipher. For example, paragraph marks become *\par*, and **boldface text** becomes *{\b boldface text}*. You can upload a file in this format to an electronic mail service or a text-only bulletin board or transmit it directly to someone who doesn't have a communications program that can handle binary file formats.

When you receive an RTF file, you can capture the RTF text in two ways. The first way is to use the communication program's capture-to-disk feature (most of them have this) and save the RTF text on disk as a text file. The other way is to select and copy the RTF text within the communications program and paste it into a blank Word document. Save this document in the Text Only format, and close the document. The most important step in capturing and saving this text to a file is to be sure the actual beginning of the

RTF text, {*rtf*, starts within the first two characters in the file. This signals Word that the text in the file is in the RTF format.

Regardless of how you created the text file containing the RTF text, when you open the document in Word, the program presents a dialog box saying *Interpret RTF Text?* This gives you the option of opening the document as uninterpreted RTF codes if you want. If you click Yes, Word reassembles the formats in the document and creates a standard Word document in a new document window. After the conversion is complete, you can save it in the default format; from that point on, it's like any other Word document.

TIP

Advanced Uses for RTF Files

An earlier chapter mentioned that because Word knows a font by its internal identification number, rather than by its complete font name, text formatted in a font on one Mac sometimes appears in a different font when opened on another Mac. As you can see in Figure 16-2, however, when a document is encoded in RTF, the fonts in it are referred to by name as well as by font ID (FID) number. If you send a document in this format, when the receiving copy of Word on the destination Mac opens the RTF document, the fonts are mapped correctly, by name rather than by FID number. If you have problems with text changing fonts from one Mac to the next, try transferring the document as an RTF file.

Programmers find another interesting use for RTF files. Because in an RTF file the entire structure of the document, including graphics and styles, is encoded in a (for programmers) readable ASCII text format, it's much easier to write utility programs that manipulate RTF files to translate or otherwise operate on the internal structure of Word documents. Some examples follow:

- You can make global formatting changes by using the Change command to replace one format code with another. For example, to change every instance of boldface text in a document to underlined text, first save the document in RTF. Then, replace every instance of *b* with *ul*. Finally, close and reopen the document and convert it to standard Word format.
- You can write programs that automatically scale all the graphics in a document at once. To see how Word translates graphics into RTF, try pasting a simple MacDraw graphic (a circle, for instance) into a short Word document, save the document as an RTF file, and then open the file without interpreting it.
- You can perform complicated searches for combinations of text strings and formats, such as "replace all instances of *** with an incremented number that represents a bibliographic reference (from a list in another document), and put it in bold, 8-point, superscripted text." You could use this technique to number bibliographic references automatically across many chapters in a book at once.

- ❑ You can enforce one style sheet more easily across many documents by saving a document as an RTF file and then replacing its style sheet with the master style sheet. You could even extend this principle and develop document-level and section-level "style sheets" that standardize document and section properties, such as page size, margin settings, header and footer formats, and so on.

The possibilities are endless. For more information on the RTF specification, write Microsoft Corporation, RTF/Applications, 16011 NE 36th Way, Box 97017, Redmond WA 98073-9717.

The Document Content Architecture Format

The Document Content Architecture format (DCA, sometimes also called RFT or Revisable Format Text, not to be confused with RTF) was developed by IBM to provide a standard translation protocol between IBM mainframe and PC word processors.

The DCA format is not represented by an option in the Save As dialog box, but you can convert Word files saved in the RTF format to the DCA format (and back again) through the Apple File Exchange utility, which accompanies the Macintosh system software. (If you don't have this utility, ask your local Apple dealer.) The AFE utility uses a special translation file, called *DCA-RTF/Microsoft Word,* found on the Word Utilities 1 disk. Once you've converted a DCA file to RTF, you start Word and open the RTF file to convert it into a standard Word document. Conversely, to convert a standard Word document into a DCA format file, save the document as an RTF file; then quit Word and use the Apple File Exchange utility to translate it to the DCA format.

Most popular PC word processors also provide support for the DCA format, including DisplayWrite, Manuscript, MultiMate, WordPerfect, and WordStar. MS-DOS Word can use this format too, although for transfer to Mac Word, you'll generally save files in the default MS-DOS Word format instead. To convert files from the DCA format to the MS-DOS Word format and vice versa within the MS-DOS Word environment, use the RFTOWORD and WORDTORF programs that accompany the software. (Notice that the RF in these program names refers to Revisable Format text.)

Two-Step Conversions

As you can see, converting a standard Word document to a DCA-format file is a two-step process. Other combinations are possible. For instance, if you needed to convert an MS-DOS WordStar file to a Mac Word document, you could use the WordExchange utility, from Systems Compatibility Corporation (available by sending in a card that accompanies the MS-DOS Word 5.0 package), to convert the file into an MS-DOS Word file. Then, transfer the file to the Mac and convert it into a standard Mac Word document.

Using Shift-Open as a Last Resort

If the program from which you want to import text can't save the file in one of the formats that Word can translate (even Text Only), you can try using Word's ability to open just about any type of document, no matter what source program was used to create it. You can also use this feature when you need to get at the contents of a document but don't have access to the program that created it. Word will not, of course, recognize the internal codes used by the source program for special formatting or graphics. These formatting codes might appear in the opened file as gibberish, nontext or symbol characters, or squares denoting undefined characters, which you must manually remove.

To open an alien document in Word, first try to save it in an ASCII or text-only format from the source program; if one is not available, use a format that is as close to raw text as possible. If you want to preserve the original copy of the file, make a duplicate of it from the Finder's desktop by selecting it and choosing Duplicate from the File menu. Then do the following:

1. In Word, press the Shift key and choose the Open command. Word changes the name of the Open command to Open Any File. (Use the mouse to choose the command, not the Command-O keyboard shortcut. You can also add the Open Any File command to a menu through the Commands dialog box.)
2. In the Open dialog box, you'll see a list of all the documents on the current disk, regardless of whether or not they are in a format that Word can read. You might even see filenames you never knew existed; these might be hidden, temporary files used by some programs or by the Macintosh operating system. It's best to leave these files, programs, and system files alone, unless you're opening a copy of the file. When you find the document you want, open it.
3. Nine times out of ten, Word opens the document successfully; if it can't, Word presents a dialog box telling you this. For example, even though you can try to open files such as the MacPaint program as a "document," Word might not be able to make enough sense of what it finds to open the file at all. Some portions of the document might include squares, odd characters, and page and section marks. Remove these manually (but first read the next section for tips on doing this).
4. When you're finished editing the file, choose the Save As command, click the File Format button, select the Normal file format, and click OK. Use a new name for the opened, edited version. The document is now a standard Word document, and you can format and print it as usual.

Cleaning Up Imported Files

After you've brought text into a Word document, particularly after using Word's Shift-Open feature or after a conversion from another format, you'll often see strange characters sprinkled throughout the imported text. You can simply delete many of these characters. Others require a little more work because they're not visible when Show ¶ is off. Even when you've turned on Show ¶, you might see only empty boxes sprinkled throughout the document, denoting an ASCII code for which no corresponding character exists. To remove these characters, do the following:

❶ Choose Show ¶ from the Edit menu.

❷ Select one of the undesired characters in the document.

❸ Press Option-Command-Q. The status area displays the ASCII code of the character.

❹ Choose Change from the Utilities menu. Enter ^ and the character's ASCII number in the Find What field. Leave the Change To field blank (or replace the character with one space if necessary). Click the Change All, Start Search, or Change Selection button as needed.

❺ Repeat steps ❷ through ❹ for each undesired character.

For example, if you've transferred a PC file to the Mac, you might have linefeed characters as well as paragraph marks (otherwise known as carriage returns) at the end of each paragraph. If you follow these steps, you will find that the ASCII code for a linefeed character is 10, and so you would enter *^10* in the Find What field of the Change dialog box.

Using Microsoft Mail

Microsoft Mail is a new application that lets users of an AppleTalk network send messages and files through a Mac that has been set up as a Microsoft Mail server. Word supports this application by letting you open documents your Mac has received if they're compatible with Word. To use Microsoft Mail with Word, your Mac must be connected to a Mail server, and you must be logged on to the server. See the system administrator of the Mail server for more information about Microsoft Mail.

The File menu has two commands for sending and receiving messages. The Open Mail command lets you open one or more messages that are listed in a window, shown in Figure 16-3 on the following page. The messages that you haven't read yet are listed in boldface type. To open a message, you can either double-click its title or select one or more messages (hold down the Shift key to select more than one message) and then click the Open button. Each message you open appears in a separate document window and becomes a standard Word document. To delete a message, simply select it in the Open Mail dialog box and click the Delete button. If you try to delete a message you haven't read, Word presents a dialog box to verify your choice.

Mail Documents

From	Subject	Received
Chris Kinata	Puma, Puma	Wed Apr 19 4:57 PM
Bill Blake	Tyger, Tyger	Wed Apr 19 4:56 PM
David Laraway	Kitty, Kitty	Wed Apr 19 4:55 PM

Open | Comments | Delete | Cancel

Figure 16-3
The Open Mail dialog box.

To send a Word document as a Mail message, bring to the front the document you want to send, and then choose the Send Mail command. The Send Mail dialog box appears, as shown in Figure 16-4. Word suggests a title for the message, which you can edit if you want. If you click the Address button, Word presents the Address Mail dialog box. Select one or more recipients for the message, clicking the Add button for each, and then click the Close button. (You can also add recipients for complimentary copies by selecting the appropriate option in the Add As group.) The list appears in the To scroll box in the Send dialog box. If you want, you also can enter a short cover note for the document. Finally, click the Send button to send the document with its accompanying note.

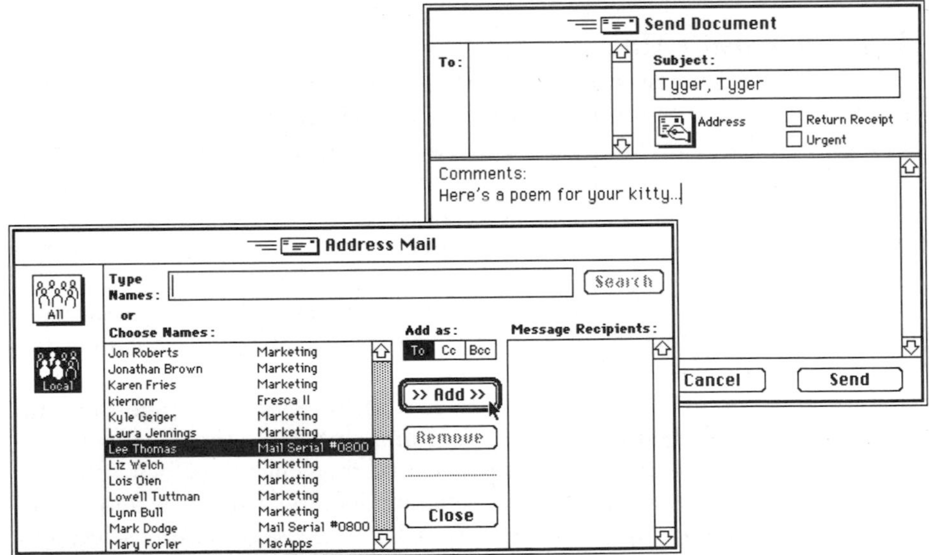

Figure 16-4
The Send Mail dialog box and the Address Mail dialog box.

To send and receive messages that aren't Word documents, use the Microsoft Mail desk accessory that has been installed if your Mac has been set up to communicate with the Mail server. For more information on Microsoft Mail, consult your Mail manual, or see the system administrator of the Mail server to which your Mac is connected.

■ *Transferring Graphics*

Word is almost as comfortable with graphics as it is with text. You can easily create images in any of the common graphics programs, such as MacPaint, FullPaint, SuperPaint, MacDraw, Cricket Draw, and Illustrator, and move them into a Word document. However, to achieve the highest quality possible from the combination of Word, the graphics program, and the printer you're using, you need to understand more about the kind of graphics you're transferring and some of the deeper issues involved in preparing and moving them into a Word document.

The Types of Graphic Elements

The Macintosh, and programs written for it, support a variety of formats for describing graphics. The developers of a program are, for the most part, free to represent a graphic within the program itself in any way they want in order to display it on the screen as patterns of pixels. On the other hand, the Mac environment is intrinsically an integrated system, one of the main advantages of which is the ability to share information more easily among programs than is possible with other computers.

To use an image you've created with a drawing program, for instance, in a Word document, the image must be represented in a standard format so that both programs can read it. The transfer of graphic data from one program to another usually happens so naturally in the Mac world that it's sometimes difficult to think of a graphic as anything other than simply a picture. This is a tribute to the vast amount of work the developers of the Mac have devoted to making this integration as seamless and intuitive as possible. However, every graphic image, after all, is still a complicated pattern of bits and bytes.

There are three common ways of representing a graphic for transfer between programs: as a bit map, as a QuickDraw graphic, or as a set of PostScript commands that describe the graphic object.

Bit-mapped Graphics

Bit-mapped graphics are represented as pixels. A program describes an image in this format as rows and columns of bits, with each bit representing a black or white dot, or pixel, in the image. (Newer programs which use the color capability of the Mac II can create pixels in colors other than black and white; such pixels are represented by more than one bit of information.) Programs that create bit-mapped graphics use a painting metaphor, in which you apply patterns of pixels with an image of a brush. Figure 16-5 shows a close-up of some objects having this format.

Figure 16-5
Several bit-mapped graphic objects, magnified by a factor of 2.

Bit-mapped graphics have many advantages. Most common graphics programs, such as MacPaint, FullPaint, and SuperPaint, handle bit-mapped graphics (although SuperPaint can work with object-oriented graphics as well). Word opens bit-mapped graphics saved in the MacPaint format directly; simply choose Open and double-click the name of the file. Often, the textures created by the patterns of bits you use in a painted image produce an artistic effect that can't be duplicated by any other means.

Another advantage is related to the fact that everything you actually see on the Mac's screen is a bit map, regardless of what that bit map represents (a circle or some text, say). For example, if you want to include a picture of a Mac screen in a document (as has been done throughout this book), you create a *screen dump* in this bit-mapped format by pressing Shift-Command-3. (This is described in more detail in "Creating a Screen Dump," a Tip that appears later in this chapter.)

Also, if you digitize a photograph using any of the scanners available, the program that drives the scanner can save the image as a bit-mapped graphic, in its own internal format (which often cannot be read by or transferred to any other program), or as a PostScript image (discussed later in this chapter). Bit-mapped graphics are the most compatible graphics interchange format in the Mac environment.

However, bit-mapped graphics have disadvantages as well. Most painting programs do not let you create an image based on independent objects; if you move an object in the foreground that covers something in the background, you have to reconstruct the part of the background that was hidden.

In addition, bit-mapped graphics have a lower resolution than other types of graphics because almost all bit maps are derived from the 72-dots-per-inch resolution of the standard Mac screen. Consequently, when you copy a graphic from a painting program into another program and print it, particularly on a PostScript printer such as the LaserWriter, the printed image is constructed of square pixels instead of smooth lines. You can use this to your advantage, however, as you will see a little later, because Word lets you squeeze a 72-dots-per-inch image into a smaller space, resulting in much higher resolution.

QuickDraw Object-Oriented Graphics

Object-oriented graphics consist of discrete elements—such as circles, squares, lines, and polygons—that together make up the image. The objects are created with QuickDraw, a graphics language and set of special routines built into the Mac's ROM. So-called drawing programs that create object-oriented graphics include MacDraw, Cricket Draw, and the drawing features in SuperPaint. You can also copy QuickDraw images from Adobe Illustrator, even though the program is designed to generate PostScript descriptions of graphics. Certain nondrawing programs, such as Microsoft Excel and Microsoft Chart, also provide QuickDraw graphics. Figure 16-6 shows the same objects as those in Figure 16-5, but shows them as QuickDraw graphic objects printed on the Linotronic 300 imagesetter.

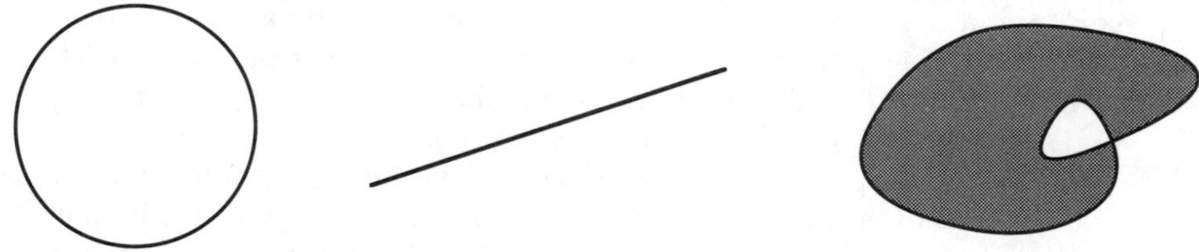

Figure 16-6
The same graphic objects as in Figure 16-5 shown in QuickDraw format.

You'll want to use object-oriented graphics if the document is to be printed with the LaserWriter or another PostScript-driven output device, such as a digital phototypesetter. These devices smooth the contours of object-oriented graphics much better than they do the contours of bit-mapped graphics. The result is a sharper image.

Printing quality is only one of the advantages of QuickDraw object-oriented graphics. Because each component of the graphic is encoded in QuickDraw commands instead of having every pixel in the image set explicitly, QuickDraw graphics take up much less space in memory and on disk than bit-mapped graphics. This can be a great help when you're working with large Word documents because it becomes more difficult to edit a document larger than a certain size, depending on the amount of memory installed in your Mac and the complexity of the document (the number of styles, paragraphs, and so on). Therefore, try to copy an image as a collection of QuickDraw objects rather than as a bit map whenever possible; charts, line drawings, diagrams, and tables are good candidates for this.

Another advantage of object-oriented graphics is that each component of such an image is independent of the others. Whereas moving the parts of a bit-mapped image usually requires repainting the uncovered areas in the image, with object-oriented graphics you can select, modify, and reposition each element without disturbing the others. For instance, let's suppose that you create an image in MacDraw, paste it into a Word document, and then discover you need to edit the graphic. Because the graphic is in QuickDraw format, you can cut the graphic from the Word document, paste it back into a MacDraw window, and then select and move each part of the image, as you did when creating it.

The PICT Graphic Format

The PICT graphic format is a special interchange format for transferring both bit-mapped graphics and object-oriented graphics between programs on the Mac. Technically, the PICT format is like a recording medium for calls that a program makes to the QuickDraw toolbox in the Mac ROM. The list of operations that construct an image in MacDraw, for instance, becomes a list of encoded instructions in the PICT format. You can see this when you copy a graphic from a painting or drawing program and paste it into the Scrapbook: The PICT data type code appears in the lower right corner. This format and the TEXT data type are used in the majority of data interchanges that occur through the Clipboard and Scrapbook.

When you copy an item from a document within a program that deposits two versions of the material into the Clipboard, and then paste the item into another program, if one of the data type codes attached to the Clipboard is either TEXT or PICT, you can usually count on the program's being able to interpret and use the material. For example, when you copy a chart from Microsoft Excel and paste it into MacDraw, every part of the chart becomes a separate object that you can move or alter as you want. Figure 16-7 shows a chart copied directly from Microsoft Excel and pasted into the document that eventually became this chapter. Figure 16-8 on page 534 shows the same chart after changes were made in MacDraw.

A graphic in the PICT format has all the benefits of both bit-mapped and object-oriented graphics. You can edit the object-oriented parts of the graphic in a program that uses the QuickDraw format, such as MacDraw or Cricket Draw, and then copy any bit-mapped elements it contains into a painting program such as MacPaint, FullPaint, or SuperPaint, edit it there, and copy it back into the drawing program. (Note that SuperPaint is able to handle both bit maps and a limited range of object-oriented functions.)

If you want to achieve the highest attainable level of quality from graphics programs on the Mac, the PICT format does have one drawback: The minimum resolution any object can have is one pixel, roughly equal to one point. This means that you can position any element in a PICT graphic only to the nearest point, and the thickness of lines must be in multiples of a point. This is fine for most documents but doesn't come close to the level of refinement attainable with traditional graphic arts techniques. To reach this level of quality, you need PostScript.

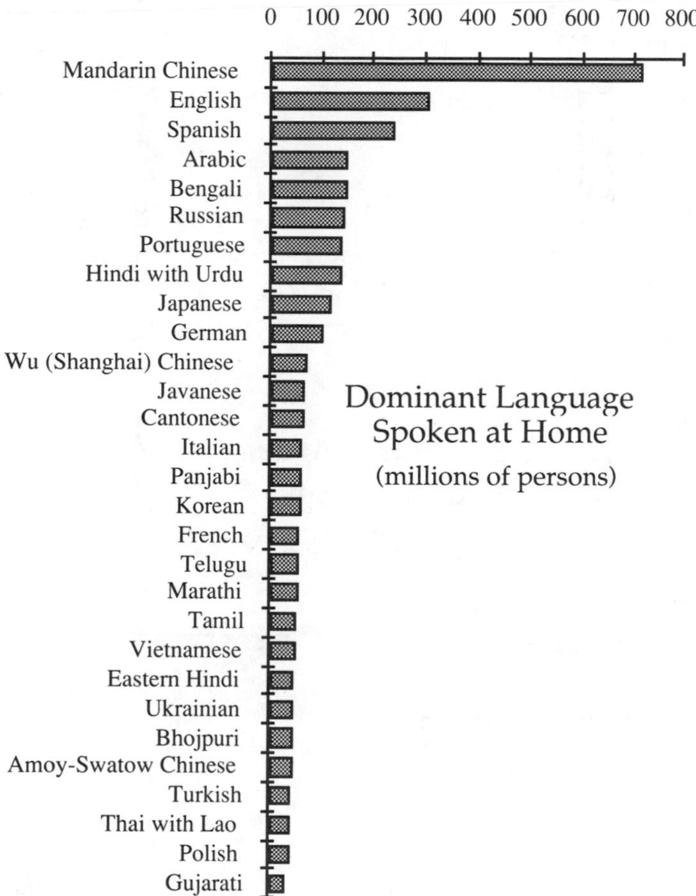

Figure 16-7
A graphic copied directly from Microsoft Excel.

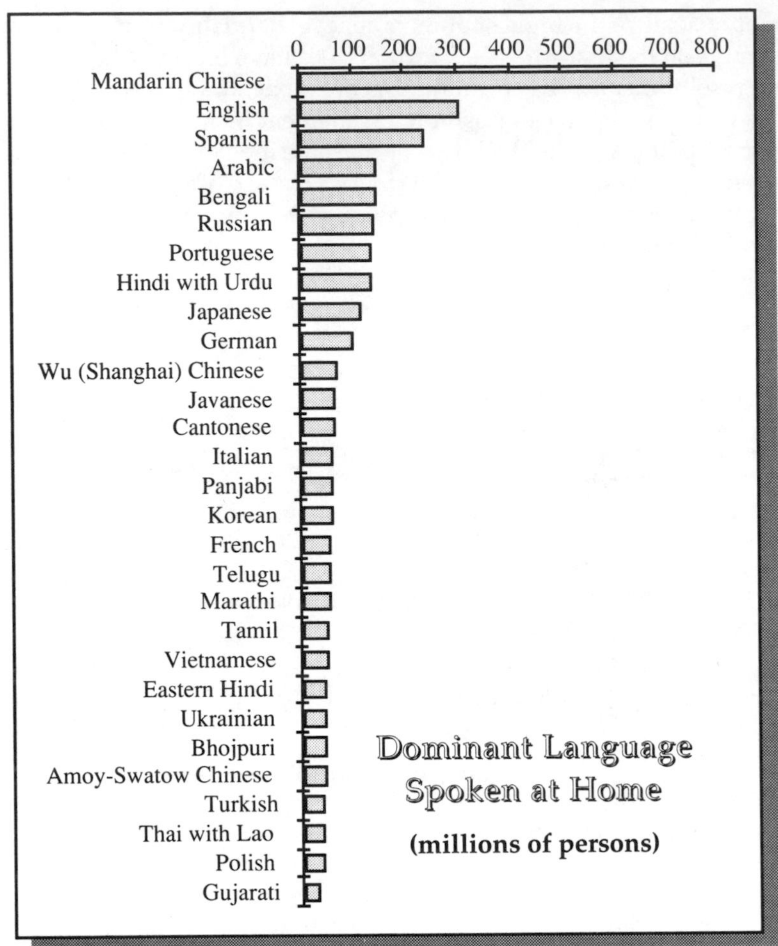

Figure 16-8
The same chart after being altered in MacDraw.

The PostScript and EPSF Formats

The third major format for encoding graphics in the Mac environment is the PostScript format. As both printers and programs become more powerful, software developers are finding it increasingly difficult to support the range of printer control codes offered by a large number of printers. John Warnock, Chuck Geschke, and others of Adobe Systems, Incorporated, developed PostScript to respond to this need for a standard *page-description language* to control printers. PostScript acts as an intermediary between a program and a PostScript-compatible printer; the program needs only to translate the elements in a document into a set of operators that describe those elements. PostScript is a powerful and extensive language, but you can use it to achieve a surprising range of effects without a deep understanding of the language. However, if you would like to write PostScript programs to create special effects in your documents, Appendix C presents enough of an overview for you to get started.

The set of PostScript routines for creating graphics is larger than that of QuickDraw. And whereas the lower limit of resolution for the description of graphic objects offered by QuickDraw and the PICT format is one pixel (1/72 inch), the lower limit of resolution supported by PostScript is the lower limit of the printer, not the screen, and can be as small as 1/2540 inch. For example, the thinnest lines you can create in QuickDraw are 1 point wide. Because of this, you can create PostScript graphics that are too detailed to be represented on the Macintosh screen. Therefore, programs that generate PostScript graphics usually create two forms of the graphic—one for the screen and one in PostScript. When you make changes to the screen version, which might not show all the detail of the printed result, the program changes both versions.

Programs that support PostScript directly, by explicitly encoding their graphic objects in PostScript code that you can save or transport to another program, do so in several ways. The first way is simply to generate a text list of the PostScript commands that create each graphic object on the printer. The data type of these PostScript commands is TEXT, and you can send them directly to a PostScript-compatible printer without using Word (via Adobe's SendPS program, for instance, or from the program itself in the case of Cricket Draw).

Some graphics programs, such as Cricket Draw and Illustrator, can save PostScript graphics in the Encapsulated PostScript File, or EPSF, format. This format is identical to the raw text version of the graphic, except that it saves a PICT version of the graphic in addition to the PostScript code. (For those who have a little more background, the PostScript code is stored in the data fork of the EPSF file, and the PICT image is stored as a resource in the resource fork.) Although Word cannot open these files directly, if you press the Shift key while choosing the Open command with the mouse, you'll see the names of files stored in this format among those listed in the Open dialog box. Simply double-click on the name of a file in the EPSF format; when Word opens it, you'll see the PostScript commands that correspond to the image, although you won't see the PICT-format image.

Once you get the PostScript code representing a graphic into a Word document, either by copying the PostScript code or by opening a file containing the PostScript code, select it and assign it the *PostScript* automatic style. When the document is printed, the PostScript code is interpreted to produce the graphic; you don't see the graphic until the document is printed. A few fine points are involved in copying PostScript graphics into a Word document; Appendix C goes into these in more detail.

There is another approach for those who want to get the benefits of PostScript without doing the work. When you copy a graphic from either Cricket Draw or Illustrator as a PICT image, the program uses a special feature of the PICT data format called a *PICT comment*. By using PICT comments, the program can bury the PostScript description of the object in the PICT image itself. If you paste this image into the Scrapbook, you'll see the PICT data type but no indication that PostScript commands are buried in the image. When you paste the image into a Word document, you see the PICT graphic, but when the document is printed, the PostScript version is printed, not the PICT version. Figure 16-9 shows a graphic created in Cricket Draw as you might see it in a Word document, and Figure 16-10 on page 538 shows the same graphic when printed on an ImageWriter, a LaserWriter, and a Linotronic 300 imagesetter.

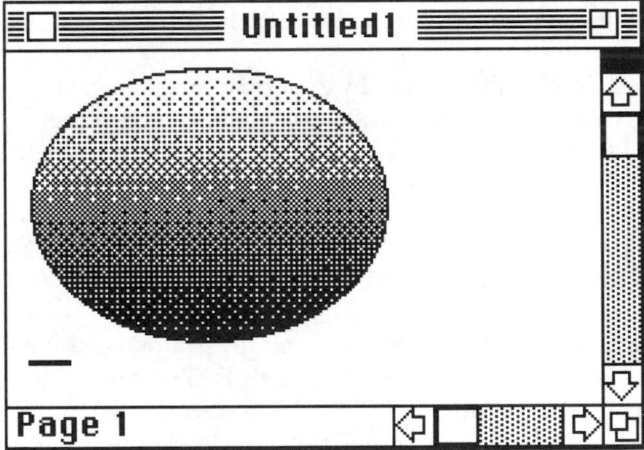

Figure 16-9
A PICT image as it appears on screen after being pasted into a Word document.

This approach has a drawback, however. When PostScript code is buried within a PICT image like this, the collection of PostScript operators that describe the graphic can often become very large. Oddly, most graphics programs that support this feature include in the copied graphic the entire set of PostScript routines which can create every effect possible in the program, even if you're using only one effect. A standard screen dump used in this book, for instance, is usually between 10 KB and 15 KB in size. The same image, with labels and other embellishments added in the form of buried PostScript comments, might exceed 50 KB.

To determine the size of a graphic containing buried PostScript, paste the graphic into an empty document, save the document, and check the size of the file in the Finder. If you're using many such images in a Word document, the size of the document may grow enormously—in fact, it can get so large that Word might no longer be able to handle the document effectively. Until new versions of graphics programs are developed that minimize the amount of PostScript code buried within a PICT graphic, you might need to either limit the number of such graphics in your Word documents or split up the document into smaller segments.

Printing Quality and the Format of a Graphic

To explore the differences between bit-mapped, QuickDraw, and PostScript graphics more fully, let's follow a simple graphic from conception to printed image. A circle, for example, is fundamentally a mathematical shape. You can describe the shape mathematically by stating the coordinates for its center and its radius, using a grid corresponding to a piece of paper or the screen.

A program can take that description and translate it into an image consisting of an arrangement of pixels, either on screen or on paper. It can do this either by painting bits or by encoding the image as a series of QuickDraw object-oriented graphics commands. When you print the graphic with the latter method, the program translates it into a list of QuickDraw operations that are fed to the driver for the printer you've set in the Chooser. If you are printing with the ImageWriter, the ImageWriter printer driver converts the QuickDraw commands into bands of bit-mapped graphic data and sends off each band to the ImageWriter. You see the image on the page grow from top to bottom not by lines of type, but by bands of bits.

In terms of the quality of the resulting image, if the ultimate destination of the graphic is the Mac screen or the ImageWriter alone, it doesn't matter whether the graphic is in bit-mapped, object-oriented, or PICT-with-buried-PostScript format. All you see is the image in pixels, and therefore the smallest detail you'll see will be pixel sized or larger.

The situation is different, however, if you're printing on a LaserWriter or other PostScript printer. When you send the graphic to a PostScript-compatible printer, the LaserWriter driver converts the QuickDraw commands to PostScript. If the document contains PICT images, it breaks them apart and converts each component, whether it's a bit-mapped graphic or an object-oriented graphic, to the appropriate PostScript commands. Although bit-mapped graphics cannot be translated into a higher resolution than their structure in pixels, the LaserWriter printer driver converts object-oriented graphics into PostScript commands that describe every object in the image. If the document contains any PostScript commands, either as text commands assigned the *PostScript* style or as PostScript code buried within a PICT image, they are passed on to the printer unchanged.

When all these PostScript commands reach the printer, they are drawn on the paper at the highest resolution the printer is capable of producing. The resolutions of the more common output devices, expressed in dots per inch, are as follows:

Device	Resolution
Mac screen	72 DPI
ImageWriter	72, 80, and 144 DPI (When you print at 50% reduction, you can compact the image's pixels to 144 DPI.)
LaserWriter	300 DPI (for the LaserWriter and most laser printers)
Linotronic 300	635, 1270, and 2540 DPI

Thus, depending on your printer and on the graphic format, a printed graphic might have a much higher level of detail than the same image when displayed on the screen. Figure 16-10 shows an image prepared in Cricket Draw and printed on different printers.

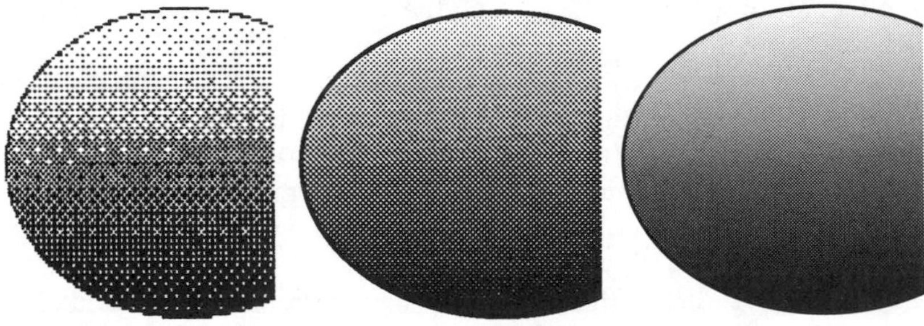

Figure 16-10
A Cricket Draw graphic printed on an ImageWriter, a LaserWriter, and a Linotronic 300 imagesetter.

Importing and Working with Graphics

The type of graphic format doesn't matter when you're importing an image to a Word document. You copy and paste both bit-mapped and QuickDraw graphics in the same way. To import a graphic:

1. Create the graphic, if necessary, in the graphics program. Select it and copy it to the Clipboard. (See the next section for specifics regarding various programs.)
2. Quit the graphics program and start Word.
3. Set an insertion point for the graphic, and choose the Paste command. You can insert the graphic either in a paragraph by itself or in a paragraph containing text or other graphics.

When you insert the graphic, the insertion point moves to the immediate right of the graphic; it is as tall as the graphic itself. If you click on the graphic to select it, you will see the graphic's *cropping box*. You can also display the limits of the graphic by choosing Show ¶ from the Edit menu. Also, you can greatly increase scrolling speed through the document by turning on the Use Picture Placeholders option in the Preferences dialog box—when the option is turned on, Word replaces graphics with a gray rectangle. (This option, incidentally, is a prime candidate for adding to a menu or assigning a key sequence through the Commands dialog box.)

Word can also directly open bit-mapped graphics saved in the MacPaint format. Simply save the graphic in the MacPaint format: In Word, choose the Open command; the Open dialog box lists the names of files saved in the format.

Copying from Various Applications

Transferring a graphic from an application is usually easy: You copy it from a document in the application and then paste it into the Word document. The graphic will be in the PICT format and will be made up of some combination of bit-mapped, object-oriented, and buried PostScript elements. In certain applications, however, transferring graphics can be a little more complicated. Keep in mind that most of the following programs transfer an object-oriented version of the copied graphic to the Clipboard. Consequently, if you want to modify the graphic before copying it again and pasting it into Word, do so in a drawing program that can accept PICT graphics, such as MacDraw, Cricket Draw, or the drawing portion of SuperPaint, if possible.

- ❑ In Microsoft Chart, choose Copy Chart from the Edit menu. A dialog box appears asking if you want the image to be copied as it appears on the screen or as it appears when printed. If you're pasting the graphic into MacPaint before it goes to Word, select the As Shown On Screen option, or the chart won't fit into MacPaint's window. Most other applications, including Word, can accept the As Shown When Printed option, which creates a chart sized to the dimensions of the printed page.
- ❑ Microsoft Excel works similarly for charts. To copy a PICT image of a range within a worksheet, select the range you want to copy, then press the Shift key while choosing Copy; the command changes to *Copy Picture*. Otherwise, you'll simply copy the text contained in the range. If you paste this graphic into MacDraw, each element—every line and piece of text—becomes a separate object. Figure 16-11 on the following page shows how this range looks as a PICT image and how it might look after being cleaned up in MacDraw and copied into Word.

	A	B
1	*Dominant Language Spoken at Home*	
2		
3	**Language**	**Millions**
4	Mandarin Chinese	720
5	English	305
6	Spanish	240
7	Arabic	150
8	Bengali	150
9	Russian	145
10	Portuguese	140
11	Hindi with Urdu	140
12	Japanese	120
13	German	105
14	Wu (Shanghai) Chinese	75
15	Javanese	66
16	Cantonese	66
17	Italian	65
18	Panjabi	63
19	Korean	61
20	French	60

Dominant Language Spoken at Home

Language	**Millions**
Mandarin Chinese	720
English	305
Spanish	240
Arabic	150
Bengali	150
Russian	145
Portuguese	140
Hindi with Urdu	140
Japanese	120
German	105
Wu (Shanghai) Chinese	75
Javanese	66
Cantonese	66
Italian	65
Panjabi	63
Korean	61
French	60

Figure 16-11
Graphic copied from Microsoft Excel; the same graphic after modifications in MacDraw.

- ❏ As was discussed earlier, when you select and copy a graphic from Cricket Draw, the program buries the PostScript commands for the graphic into the PICT image. Be aware that this can dramatically increase the size of the image in bytes. To copy the PICT image only, without the embedded PostScript code, save the image as a file in the PICT format and then open the file with another application that can read the format, such as MacDraw or SuperPaint. To copy only a bit-mapped version of the selected objects, press the Option key while choosing the Copy command; note that you'll lose quality in the resulting image.
- ❏ Illustrator doesn't permit the pasting of graphics into any other program and doesn't normally support the Scrapbook. However, you can copy a PostScript-embedded PICT image from an Illustrator document by pressing the Option key while choosing Copy with the mouse. As with Cricket Draw, however, the size of the copied graphic increases.

TIP

Creating a Screen Dump
You can send the contents of an entire screen, regardless of the current program, to a file on disk by pressing Shift-Command-3. If you're using color on a Mac II, turn it off first, unless you want color in the screen dump. The screen shots are saved as MacPaint files with the names *Screen 0* through *Screen 9*. (The icons might not look like MacPaint documents until you edit or print them with MacPaint.) The documents are placed on the same disk as the application. The Mac beeps at you when you've used up all 10 screen shots (or if you've run out of space on the disk).

The ROMs in all the newer Macs (the 512K Enhanced, the Mac Plus, the Mac SE, and the Mac II) don't allow you to create screen dumps of or print the contents of menus. If you press Shift-Command-3 while a menu is pulled down and then release the mouse button to start the screen dump, the menu disappears before the screen dump is sent to the disk. If you have to create a screen dump of a menu, you need what is called an FKEY resource, which is essentially a patch for the Mac's system software and is available from Macintosh users' groups.

Formatting Graphics

Interestingly, graphics pasted into Word are treated like characters. You can search for graphics by choosing the Find command and entering *^1* in the FindWhat field. You can also format graphics with many of the formats you can characters, but not all the character formats work when you apply them. You can select the graphic and give it an outline and a shadowed box, for instance, but to get a proper shadow you must use both formats, not the shadow by itself. On the other hand, the Bold format doesn't make the graphic itself bolder, but it does make an outline box thicker. The All Caps, Small Caps, font, and font size formats have no effect. The Position and Spacing formats do work, however, and are useful for making minor adjustments to the placement of a graphic, whether it is in a paragraph by itself or within the text of a paragraph. You can even hide graphics by giving them the Hidden character format.

If the graphic is in a paragraph by itself, you can adjust its horizontal position by moving the first-line indent. You can also place the insertion point before the graphic and press the Tab key to move it to the next tab stop, or you can choose one of the alignment icons in the Ruler.

To adjust the graphic vertically, you can add or remove lines above or below it or place it in a paragraph by itself and add a Space Before or Space After paragraph format. You can even give the paragraph a style, called *Graphic*, for instance, and change the formats for all such graphics at the same time by redefining that style. Giving the paragraph a Position paragraph format is very useful for "floating" a graphic between two columns of text in a newsletter, for example, because Word wraps the text around the space reserved for the paragraph. You can also select the graphic, cut it, and repaste it anywhere in that or another Word document, including into headers, footers, and footnotes.

TIP

Speed Scrolling by Using Picture Placeholders
Word takes longer to scroll through a document when graphics are in view because it redraws the image every time you scroll the window. To speed up scrolling during editing, hide the graphics temporarily. You can redisplay the graphics when you need to format them and just prior to final pagination and printing. To hide a graphic, simply choose Preferences from the Edit menu, and select the Use Picture Placeholders option. Word replaces every graphic in the document with a gray rectangle, retaining the character and paragraph formats it had previously. If you work with graphics frequently, it's also useful to add this command to the Edit menu (for instance) and give the command its own key sequence (such as Shift-Option-Command-P).

Cropping a Graphic

The term *cropping* refers to the process of removing the outer edges of a graphic, leaving only the portion that you want to have appear in the document. When you click on a graphic, the cropping box appears around it; this box has three handles, one each on the right edge, the bottom edge, and the lower right corner. The cropping box lets you either scale (magnify or reduce) the graphic to a particular size or crop off portions you don't want to show, although you can remove only the right and bottom edges of the graphic. For this reason, you should set the correct left and top edges for the graphic in the drawing or painting program from which it originated.

- ❑ To crop the graphic horizontally, drag the right handle, as shown in Figure 16-12. The status box displays the width of the graphic (in the unit of measurement set in the Preferences dialog box).
- ❑ To crop the graphic vertically, drag the bottom handle. The status box displays the depth of the graphic.
- ❑ To crop the graphic both horizontally and vertically while retaining its original proportions, drag the lower right handle. Note that the status box shows the percentage of reduction or enlargement of the frame around the graphic. If you size the frame larger than 100%, Word centers the graphic within the frame.

Figure 16-12
Cropping a graphic by dragging the right handle.

Scaling a Graphic

You can crop or scale a graphic in Word, but you can't do both at the same time. If you have demanding requirements for the arrangement and positioning of elements within a graphic, try doing the scaling in a program that can handle object-oriented graphics, such as MacDraw, SuperPaint, or Cricket Draw, and do the cropping (if necessary) in Word.

- ❑ To scale a graphic horizontally, hold down the Shift key and drag the right handle. The status box displays the current width of the graphic.
- ❑ To scale the graphic vertically, hold down the Shift key and drag the bottom handle. The status box displays the current depth of the graphic.
- ❑ To scale the graphic but retain its original proportions, press the Shift key and drag the handle in the lower right corner. (See Figure 16-13.) The status box gives the percentage of reduction or enlargement, rounded to the nearest whole number. The graphic is scaled by the percentage you see in the status box, even though it sometimes seems that you can drag the graphic's handles to positions between percentage points in the status box.

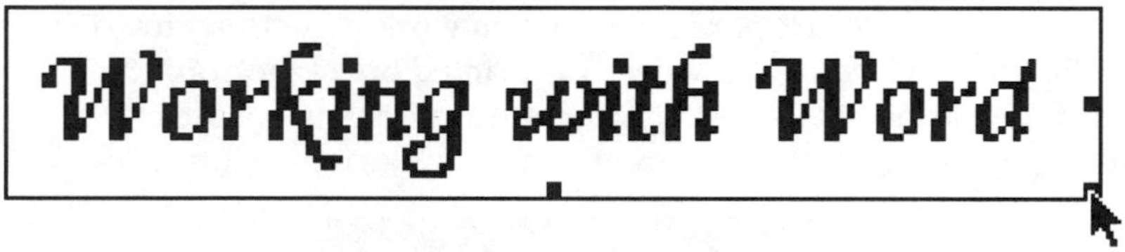

Figure 16-13
Scaling a graphic.

With both cropping and scaling, you can revert to the original size of the graphic by double-clicking on it.

Scaled object-oriented graphics typically look better than scaled bit-mapped graphics. If an object-oriented PICT image contains text, the text prints at the full resolution available on PostScript printers and isn't converted to the bit-mapped version of the text. If an object-oriented graphic contains text, the text will be scaled along with the rest of the graphic. This can yield some interesting effects. For example, you can stretch text when you scale the image of text pasted in as a PICT graphic, as shown in Figure 16-14 on the following page.

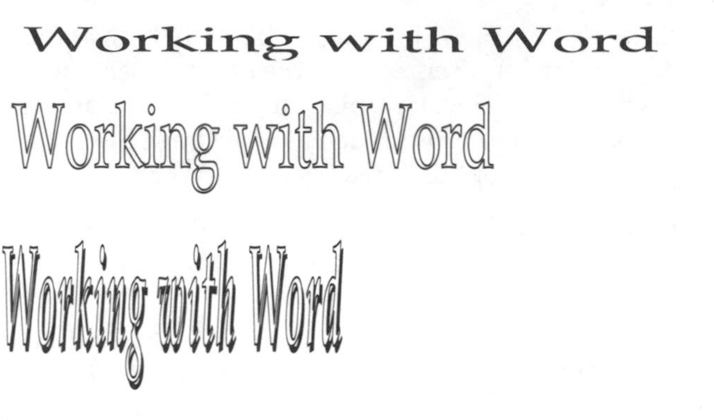

Figure 16-14
Distorted text resulting from a scaled object-oriented graphic.

When you scale down an image containing a bit-mapped component, either in a drawing program or in Word itself, the bits that make up the image are compressed into the smaller space, not lost. By using this feature, common to both drawing programs and Word, you can create an effect similar to that of a halftone image, particularly when working with scanned images, as shown in Figure 16-15, which was printed on a Linotronic 300 imagesetter. Because the pixels that make up the original image are compressed into a smaller space, the apparent quality of the image increases.

Figure 16-15
A bit-mapped graphic scanned with ThunderScan and scaled to 50%.

A scaled graphic looks considerably better when printed on a PostScript printer than when printed on the ImageWriter, due to the higher resolution. The correspondence between the scaling factor you apply to a graphic and its quality when printed depends on the ratio of the pixel density of the graphic to the pixel density of the output device.

For example, when you make a screen dump and use the resulting full-size image in a Word document, the pixels in the image have the same density as the Mac's screen—typically, 72 dots per inch, depending on the monitor you're using. The LaserWriter can print at a density of 300 dots per inch. Because 72 doesn't evenly divide into 300, some Mac pixels, when printed, are 4 LaserWriter pixels square, some are 4 by 5 LaserWriter pixels, some are 5 by 4, and some are 5 by 5. Normally this results in a peculiar type of distortion in the printed image known as a moiré pattern, as shown in Figure 16-16, which is copied from the same LaserWriter output that produced the graphic in Figure 16-15.

Figure 16-16
Moiré pattern caused by an inexact ratio of screen resolution to printer resolution.

If you pasted the image into Word and scaled it to 50 percent of its original size, the same situation exists because the pixel density increases to 144 dots per inch, which still doesn't divide evenly into 300. As mentioned in Chapter 14, "Document Formatting and Printing," when we discussed the Precision Bitmap Alignment option in the LaserWriter Page Setup dialog box, you can deal with this inconsistency in the ratio of pixel densities between the graphic and the printer resolution in two ways.

One is to shrink a full-size image to 96 percent (which is 288 divided by 300) to establish a 4-to-1 pixel-mapping ratio. This leads to a 4 percent misalignment of the graphic with the other elements on a page; the larger the bit-mapped graphic, the larger the error. The second way is to scale up the bit-mapped image by an extra 4 percent so that the dimensions of the image remain accurate and the image stays aligned. However, because the pixel-mapping ratio is not exactly 4 to 1, this method results in distortions in the printed image of the bit-mapped graphic.

The Precision Bitmap Alignment option solves this problem by scaling down everything in the document to 96 percent, including the text elements around the graphic. In this way, the graphics retain the 4-to-1 ratio and alignment is maintained.

When you're printing a scaled image with this option set, the ratio of image pixels to printed pixels can vary from this 4-to-1 ideal over the entire range of scaling, which leads to the same problem all over again. It turns out that the only reduction values that divide evenly into 288 pixels per inch result in 25 percent (1:1), 50 percent (2:1), or 75 percent (3:1) reductions.

If you're printing to a PostScript printer that is capable of more than 300 DPI, however, you should adjust your consideration of the ratios accordingly. At very high resolutions, moiré effects tend to disappear, because the printer can represent image pixels with many more pixels when the image is printed. For example, most of the illustrations in this book, printed with a Linotronic 300 imagesetter, were reduced to 50 percent of their original size, but because they were printed at 1270 dots per inch, the distortions due to bit-map scaling tend to be less noticeable: 72 DPI compressed to 144 DPI by scaling to 50%, and each image pixel at 144 DPI represented by either 8 or 9 printed pixels.

Inserting a Blank Graphics Frame

Sometimes it's useful to reserve space for a graphic without actually moving the graphic into a Word document. You might do this if you were in the process of writing or designing the document and didn't want to take the time to create and transfer the graphic. Also, because scrolling slows down noticeably when the graphics have been pasted into a document, you might find it convenient to do most of the writing and editing before incorporating the graphics. Finally, graphics in a document tend to increase its size dramatically; if a document is large (say, more than 100 KB), you might find it necessary to reduce its size for memory-intensive operations such as sorting and generating tables of contents.

You can insert a blank graphics frame anywhere in a Word document (including headers and footers). Do so as follows:

❶ Set an insertion point where you want the graphics frame to appear.

❷ Choose Insert Graphics from the Edit menu.

Word places a 1-inch-by-1-inch empty graphics frame at the insertion point. (It's easier to see this frame if you've chosen Show ¶.) You can leave the box empty until you're ready to paste a graphic into it. (See Figure 16-17.) If you want to resize the frame, click in it to display a cropping box, and drag the appropriate handles, as you would with a standard graphic. The size or percentage appears in the status box.

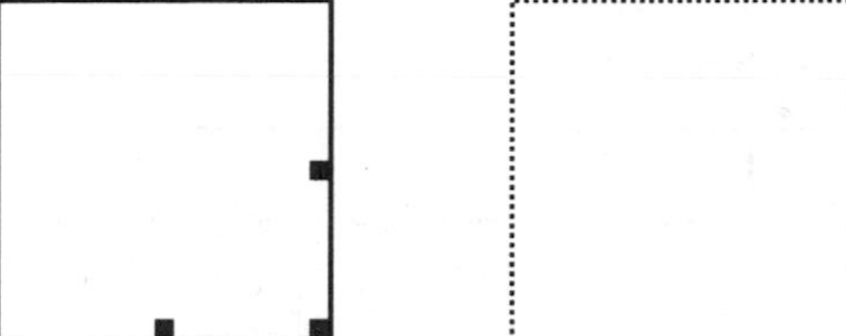

Figure 16-17
A graphics frame and the same frame with Show ¶ on.

You can also format the empty frame as you might if a graphic were actually pasted there. For example, you can assign the frame the outline character attribute to create a resizable box in your document. Simply select the box and choose Outline from the Format menu. An outline appears around the box, as shown in Figure 16-18, and remains even when the box is not selected and Show ¶ is off.

Figure 16-18
A graphics frame boxed with the Outline format.

You can use this handy trick to create small check boxes. Resize the blank box to the desired size, and give it the Outline format. Remember that the outline is always slightly larger than the box itself.

Choose various formats to see the effect they have. For example, you can create a box with a drop shadow by choosing both Outline and Shadow or make the box heavier by choosing Bold. You can even use the Strikethru format to draw a horizontal line through the graphic. You can add vertical lines within the frame by selecting the paragraph containing the frame, choosing the Show Ruler command, and then dragging a vertical-line icon in the Ruler to the desired position over the frame. The vertical lines show up over both text and graphics. Figure 16-19 on the following page shows some examples.

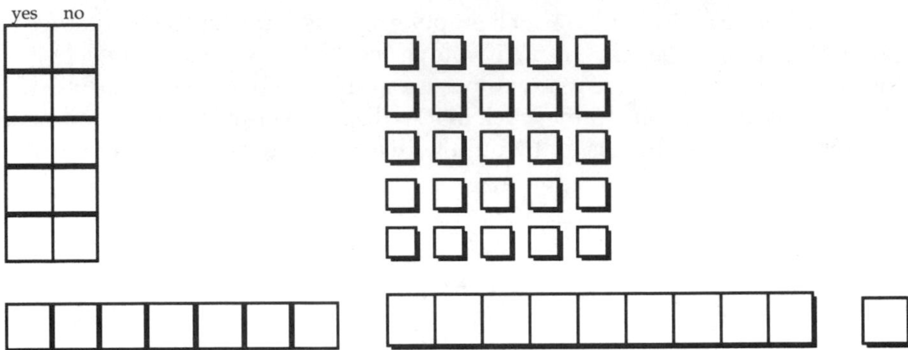

Figure 16-19
Boxes created from graphics frames.

TIP

Creating a Box Around a Group of Paragraphs
Setting one of the border paragraph formats is one way to draw a box around a single paragraph, but what do you do if you want to draw one box around more than one paragraph? The best way to do this is to use Word 4's Border formats to create simple borders composed of lines. Another way to do this involves inserting a graphics frame before the paragraphs and using the Side-by-Side or Position paragraph formats to lay the frame over them.

The following method uses the Side-by-Side format, but you could adapt it for the Position format easily. To overlay one set of paragraphs with another set of paragraphs, do the following:

❶ Insert an empty graphics frame before the paragraphs. Drag out the frame until it's approximately the size it would be if it surrounded the paragraphs. Format the frame as desired, usually by giving it the Box and/or Shadow character formats or one of the Border paragraph formats.

❷ Select the paragraphs and move their left or first-line indent (whichever is leftmost) to the right by a small amount, say ⅛ inch. Or, select the graphics frame and move its left or first-line indent ⅛ inch to the left. (Pressing the Shift key and clicking on the left scroll arrow is helpful for scrolling to the left of the left margin.)

❸ Select both the graphics frame and the relevant paragraphs and give them the Side-by-Side paragraph format. As discussed in Chapter 9, "Paragraph Formatting," you have to add the command for the Side-by-Side format to the Format or other menu through the Commands dialog box, because it isn't listed in the Paragraph dialog box.

❹ Finally, flipping between Galley View and Print Preview, adjust the dimensions of the graphics frame until it surrounds the paragraphs evenly.

Figure 16-20 shows how this might look in Galley View and in Print Preview. You can also use this same technique with a real graphic, rather than an empty frame. Figure 16-21 shows an example of this.

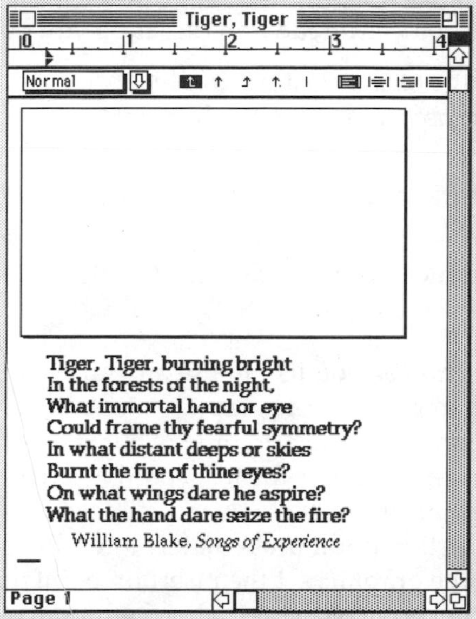

Tiger, Tiger, burning bright
In the forests of the night,
What immortal hand or eye
Could frame thy fearful symmetry?
In what distant deeps or skies
Burnt the fire of thine eyes?
On what wings dare he aspire?
What the hand dare seize the fire?
William Blake, *Songs of Experience*

Figure 16-20
Paragraphs boxed with a graphics frame and the Side-by-Side format in Galley View and as they appear when printed.

Tiger, Tiger, burning bright
In the forests of the night,
What immortal hand or eye
Could frame thy fearful symmetry?
In what distant deeps or skies
Burnt the fire of thine eyes?
On what wings dare he aspire?
What the hand dare seize the fire?
William Blake, *Songs of Experience*

Figure 16-21
A graphic placed behind some text with the Side-by-Side format.

Multiple Graphics on One Line

Microsoft Word is one of the few word-processing programs for the Macintosh that can place more than one graphic on the same line or successive lines within one paragraph. To insert a graphic alongside an existing one (assuming that the second graphic is already on the Clipboard):

1. Set the insertion point on the right edge of the existing graphic. You can do this by clicking on the graphic and pressing the right arrow key.
2. Press the Tab or spacebar key, if you want, to separate the two graphics.
3. Choose the Paste command. The graphic appears at the insertion point, and the insertion point moves to the right.

You can repeat the process as many times as you like to put any number of images on the same line. If you need to reposition the graphics along the length of the line, carefully set the insertion point and add or take out spaces. If a graphic is selected when you press a key on the keyboard, you'll delete it.

You can also place a graphic on the same line as text. To add a line of text after a graphic, for example, place the insertion point immediately after the image and type. To place the text before the graphic, set the insertion point at the front of the image and type. The bottom edge of the text aligns with the bottom of the graphic. You can use the Superscript and Subscript character formats to adjust the placement of graphics relative to the text on the line.

Exporting Graphics

Word is not a graphics program, and normally you wouldn't use it to draw pictures. Sometimes, however, it is useful to transfer an image of the text that you've formatted in Word to another program. The special formatting features of Word (such as boxes and columns) are not likely to be shared by the other program, and so the only way to transfer the material with the formats intact is to first convert it to an object-oriented picture. After the image of the formatted material is in the Clipboard, you can paste it into a document belonging to another application, or you could stay in Word and paste it to another location. Of course, the destination program must be able to accept PICT images from the Clipboard.

To transfer an image of the formatted text:

1. Select the desired material, and press Option-Command-D. The selection is copied to the Clipboard as an object-oriented graphic.
2. Quit Word and start the destination program.
3. Paste the contents of the Clipboard into a document belonging to the program. Manipulate the image as you would any other graphic. Note that font formatting is retained. (The font and point size you

used for the text in Word must also be present in the System file of the destination program; otherwise, the font will be scaled or it will be replaced with Geneva or New York.)

Word treats each line of text as a separate object. Each piece of text that changes in font, font size, or character attributes also becomes a separate object, as do any of the graphic formats, such as boxes and lines. Because the image copied to the Clipboard is a PICT image, you can transport it to an object-oriented graphics program, such as Cricket Draw, MacDraw, or SuperPaint. You can then manipulate the elements of the selection separately and copy the result to another program or even back into Word. The formatting boxes and lines are also transferred.

You can use this technique to create some interesting special effects with Word. Write and initially format the text, as usual. Select the font, size, character attributes, and margins you want to appear in the final version. Copy the text block to the Clipboard using Option-Command-D, as described. Quit Word and start the graphics program (let's say MacDraw). Once you're in MacDraw, paste the selection into the window, and then use the drawing tools to embellish it. Add extra boxes, charts, or other elements as desired. The technique is particularly helpful when you've used Word's mathematical typesetting feature to create a formula—you can convert the resulting image to QuickDraw format to "lock" the formula or copy it to a document in another program.

When you're finished, select the text and added graphics, copy them, and restart Word. Delete the old text and paste in the new image from the Clipboard. If all goes well, the revised version, which you handle as you would any other imported graphic, looks like the surrounding text but has the MacDraw flourishes you added.

TIP

Creating Boxed Text Elements from Formatted Text

It's sometimes difficult to use the border paragraph formats to position a box a specific distance from some text. Instead, try converting the text to a graphic and then formatting the graphic. First, format the text as you would like it to appear. Then, do the following:

1. Select the text and press Option-Command-D to transfer an image of it to the Clipboard.
2. While the text is selected, format it as Hidden text.
3. Paste the image of the text after the text itself. Draw a box around the graphic by giving it the Outline character format, or put the graphic in a paragraph by itself and use one of the Border formats.
4. You can drag the handles of the graphic to enlarge it; the graphic remains centered within the frame.

If you need to edit the text, set the Show Hidden Text option in the Preferences dialog box, edit the text, and repeat the process.

Linking Information with QuickSwitch

Word has a unique feature called QuickSwitch that lets you partially automate the transfer of text, data, and graphics between programs. With QuickSwitch, you establish a kind of pipeline from a source program to a location in a document belonging to Word. This process is almost identical to the manual process of running Word and another application under MultiFinder, creating material in the other program and copying it, switching back to Word, and pasting the material in a location in the Word document. If you need to change the pasted-in data or graphics, you can switch to the source program, edit the source material, copy it, and then replace the original in Word.

For most programs, the above procedure is what you must do to transfer material from another program to a Word document. If, however, you want to transfer information from the following list of programs, using Quick-Switch can make the transfer nearly automatic:

- Graphics copied from painting and drawing programs such as MacPaint 1.x, MacDraw 1.9, SuperPaint 1.1MS (which is included in the Word package), and SuperPaint 2.0.
- Tables prepared in Microsoft Excel. Once you've established the link between a table in a Word document and a range of cells belonging to a source spreadsheet in Excel, you can convert the table to Word's cell table structure, and Word will still be able to update it.
- Charts prepared in Excel. Using QuickSwitch, you can transfer an image of the chart from the source document and easily update the copy of it in a Word document.
- Links between a location in a Word document and other programs that support QuickSwitch. As of this writing, however, no programs other than those listed above support it.

To use QuickSwitch, you must also use MultiFinder—the extension to versions 5.0 and later of the Macintosh system software that lets you run as many applications at a time as memory permits. (Two megabytes of RAM is the minimum useful amount of memory for running most applications under MultiFinder.) For more information on MultiFinder, consult the MultiFinder manual, available from Apple or your local Apple dealer.

To turn on MultiFinder, choose Set Startup from the Finder's Special menu, and then select the MultiFinder option. If you want to automatically open certain documents or applications, select their icons on the Finder's desktop before choosing the Set Startup command and select the Selected Items option. If you want to reopen the currently open applications and desk accessories when you restart your Mac, select the Opened Applications And Desk Accessories option. Otherwise, select the MultiFinder Only option. Then click OK, and restart your Mac.

To turn off MultiFinder, choose the Set Startup command and select the Finder Only option. Then click OK, and restart your Mac.

When operating, MultiFinder allocates a specific amount of memory to each application you launch; the amount of memory is set in the application's Get Info dialog box. To change this amount, select the application's icon in the Finder and choose the Get Info command. In the lower right corner of the Get Info dialog box, enter in the Application Memory Size field the amount of memory you want to allocate to the application. Above the field is displayed a recommended minimum application size, usually 384 KB or more. The specific number you use depends on the application and the size of the documents with which you typically work. For example, Word needs a minimum of 384 KB to work well, but if you use this amount when working with large documents, Word might present messages telling you it's running out of memory. Setting Word's Application Memory Size to 512, 1024, 1536 or even 2048 KB of memory gives Word the room it needs to work optimally.

Three commands on the Edit menu enable you to easily update linked information. The Paste Link command lets you establish a link between a graphic in a document belonging to an application other than Word. You can use the Update Link command to locate, open, copy, and paste the updated version of something created in another program. Finally, you can use the Edit Link command to temporarily switch to the program so that you can copy the material and replace the original in the Word document—sort of a semiautomatic update. We'll explore the use of each of these commands through an example, creating a link between a chart in Microsoft Excel and a location in a Word document. Afterwards, we'll discuss the process of establishing links between a Word document and documents created with other applications.

The Paste Link Command

Let's say you want to prepare a report containing a chart. You've prepared the chart in Microsoft Excel but have done only the first-pass, rough work—just to get the report started. To establish a link between a document opened under Excel and a graphic in a Word document, you must first prepare the material to be linked. Figure 16-22 on the following page shows Excel running under MultiFinder, with a document containing the chart to be transferred, as well as the table used to create the chart behind it.

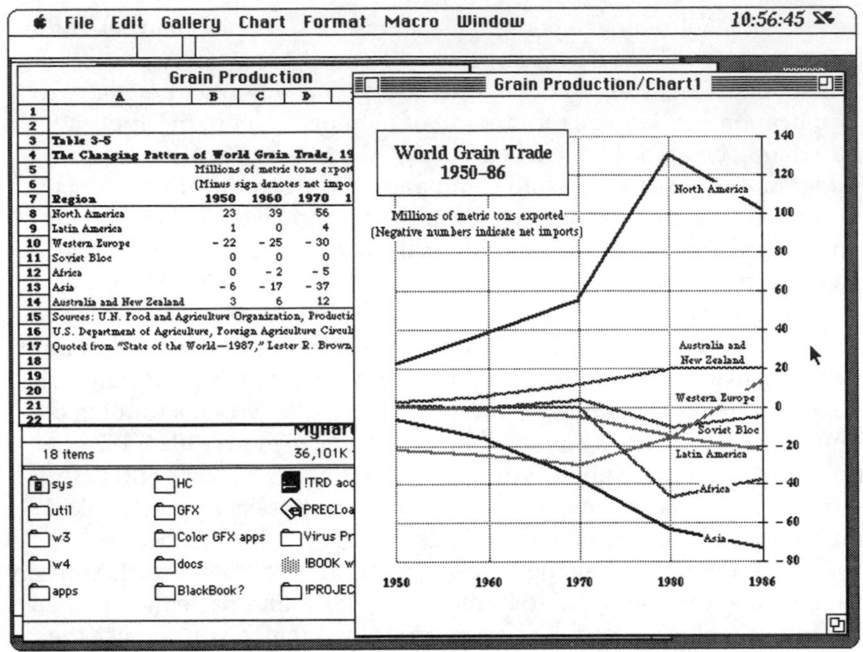

Figure 16-22

The open chart in Microsoft Excel running under MultiFinder, and its supporting spreadsheet.

After you've created the chart, use the Paste Link command to create a link between the document containing it and a location in a Word document. First turn on Show ¶, so you can see the result of creating the link more clearly. Then do the following:

1. Choose Copy Chart from Excel's Edit menu to copy the chart.
2. Use MultiFinder to switch to the Word document containing the report. If necessary, launch Word and open the report.
3. Place the insertion point where you want the chart to be, preceding an empty paragraph mark.
4. Choose Paste Link from Word's Edit menu. Word pastes the chart into the report, which has been converted to a graphic, as shown in Figure 16-23.

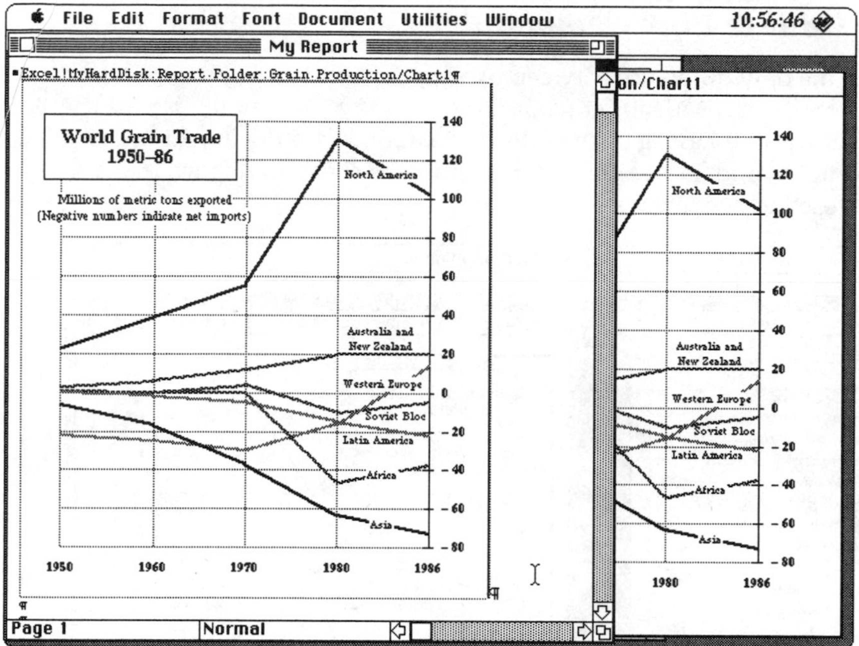

Figure 16-23
The chart linked into the Word document.

Notice the paragraph of text which Word has inserted before the chart graphic, called an identifier paragraph. It is *Normal* style text, except that Word has added the Keep With Next paragraph format (to ensure that the identifier paragraph is not separated from the graphic by a page break) and the Hidden character format (so that the identifier paragraph doesn't appear when the report is printed).

We'll discuss the characteristics of the identifier paragraph in more detail in a moment—for now, notice that the identifier paragraph has two parts, separated by an exclamation mark. The first part identifies the program that was used to create the source material; here we used Excel. Although the exact filename attached to the Excel program is usually different from this (for example, *Microsoft Excel 1.5*), the text *Excel* is all that's needed. The second part consists of "full pathname" of the source document: the name of the floppy disk or hard disk, a series of folder names, and the name of the document itself.

The Update Link Command

So far, the only difference between pasting a graphic and pasting a link is the insertion of the identifier paragraph. Let's say you edit the source chart in Excel without having opened the destination Word document under MultiFinder, and add a border, for example, as shown in Figure 16-24. You then close the document and quit Excel.

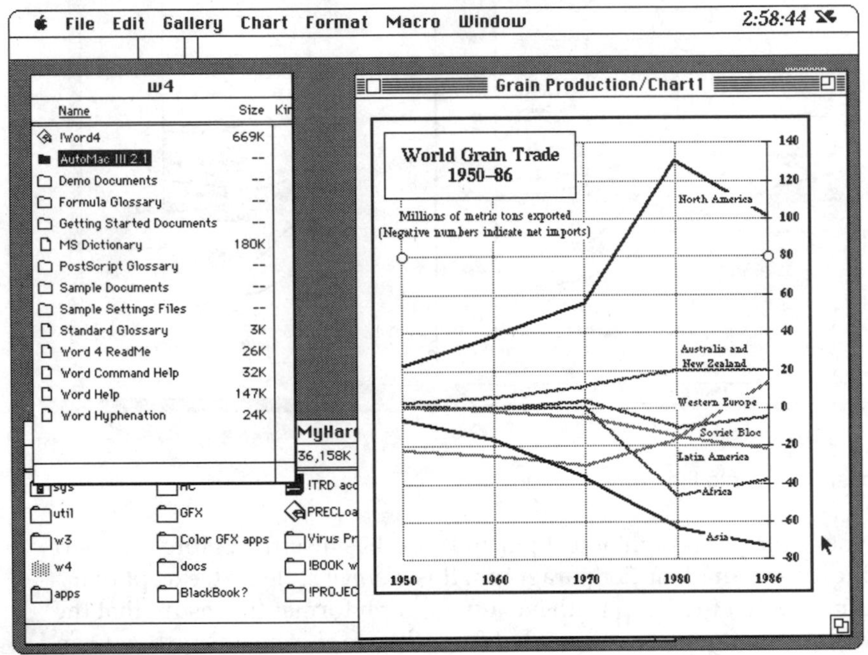

Figure 16-24
Adding a border to the source chart, in Excel.

Later, when you return to working with the report in Word, you can easily update the chart without having to go though the mechanics of manually switching to the program, copying it, and switching back again: The Update Link command does all this automatically. Assuming you've launched Word and opened the report document, do the following:

❶ Click on the chart graphic to select it.

❷ Choose the Update Link command. Word uses MultiFinder to switch to the application specified in the identifier paragraph—in this case, Excel. It doesn't matter if the source application isn't currently running under MultiFinder—if not, MultiFinder launches it. (The first time you try this, Word may ask you to locate the application; this location is then stored in the current Settings file). It also loads the specified document.

❸ After the source chart has been opened, Excel presents a dialog box asking if you want to update the chart from the table used to create it. Click Yes. (Earlier, you could have also edited the information in the table, independent of the formatting changes made to the chart, and the current version of the chart would use the new information from the table. You could consider this a two-step update.)

❹ The instant the source chart is updated, MultiFinder copies it, switches back to Word, and replaces the original chart in the report, as shown in Figure 16-25.

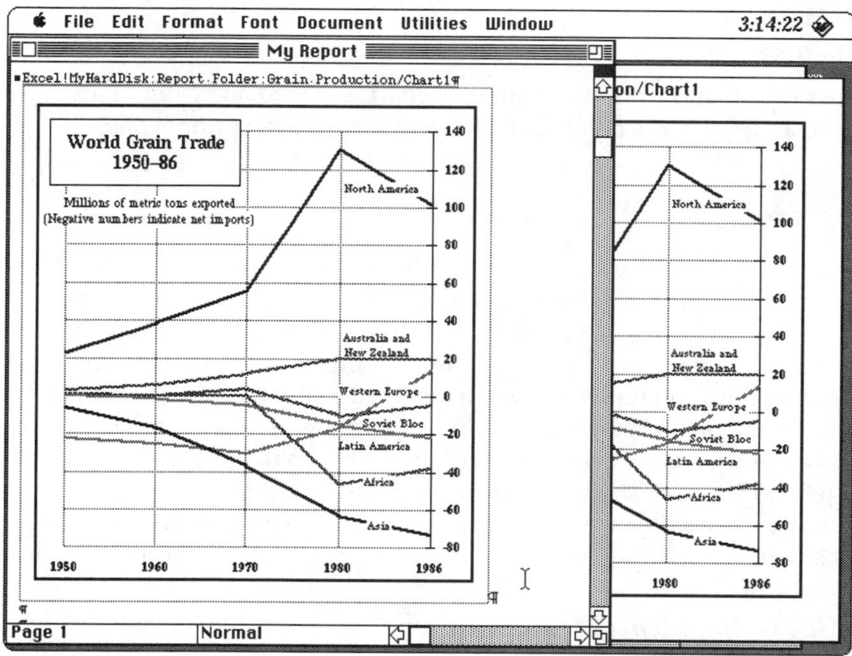

Figure 16-25
The updated chart graphic in Word.

Notice that the source chart in Excel is still open; after you've updated the report in Word, you can temporarily switch back to close the document and quit Excel.

The Edit Link Command

If you press the Shift key while dragging down the Edit menu, you'll see that the Update Link command changes to Edit Link. The two commands are similar, but Edit Link pauses in the source program rather than copying and immediately returning: You can edit the source material before MultiFinder transfers a copy of it back to Word.

If, for example, you decide that you want to add the border while the report is opened in Word, you could do the following:

1. Select the graphic of the chart in the Word document.
2. Hold down the Shift key and choose the Edit Link command, or simply press Command-(comma). You could also add the Edit Link command to the Edit menu through the Commands dialog box, discussed in Chapter 3, "The Word Environment."
3. Word uses the identifier paragraph to find the source document and passes the information to MultiFinder, which launches Excel and opens the document.
4. Edit the chart.
5. Press Command-(comma) again. The chart is copied and MultiFinder switches back to the report in Word, and replaces the prior version.

Notes on Using QuickSwitch

As you can see, the process of using QuickSwitch really isn't very different from simply opening both a Word document and a source document and then copying material from source to destination. The main advantage is speed and convenience. At the time of this writing the only applications incorporating support for QuickSwitch are MacPaint, MacDraw, SuperPaint, and Microsoft Excel. (Apple supports the programming internals of Quick-Switch as one way of interfacing with MultiFinder, so it's possible for other developers to add QuickSwitch to their products.)

Following is a collection of notes that will help you make the best use of QuickSwitch.

Specifics of the Identifier Paragraph

Word uses the identifier paragraph to keep track of up to three pieces of information, all of which are optional: the source program, the name of the document, and the location of the source material within the source document. Each item is separated from the others by an exclamation mark.

As mentioned earlier, the text is formatted as *Normal* style text, with the Keep With Next paragraph format and the Hidden character format. Interestingly, you could create a style for the text, for example called *QuickSwitch,* and add other formats you might want to the style, but if you use the Update Link or Edit Link commands to update the material, Word replaces the identifier paragraph and removes the style.

The Application Name

The first item in the identifier paragraph is the name of the application that created the source material. This part is optional—if the name is not supplied, Word assumes the source program is MacPaint or MacDraw. (See page 560 for specifics on using MacPaint and MacDraw with QuickSwitch.) Only Excel and SuperPaint need to be identified by name, and you don't have to type the name exactly. For example, the actual name of the version of SuperPaint that accompanies the Word package is *SuperPaint 1.1MS,* but you need only use *SuperPaint* in the identifier paragraph.

If and when other developers support QuickSwitch, you could also use a four-letter *creator code* here, instead of the name of the program. You can discover the creator code of a program by using a file utility such as ResEdit or the DiskTools II desk accessory from RainMaker Research. In ResEdit, for example, you select the name of the application and then choose Get Info from the Edit menu; the Get Info window for the application appears, as shown in Figure 16-26. Be certain you use the exact name, uppercase and lowercase, and spaces (if used). As shown in the figure, the creator type of the Canvas graphics program is "DAD "—three letters and a space character.

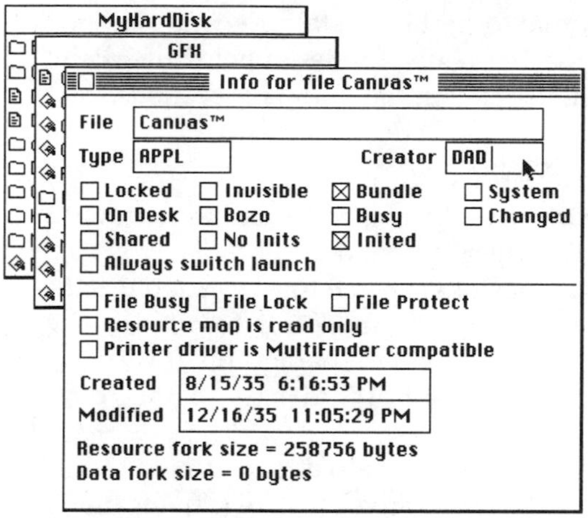

Figure 16-26
The Get Info window for Canvas, in ResEdit.

The Full Pathname of the Document

The second item in the identifier paragraph is the full pathname of the document, each element separated from the others by a colon:

- The volume name (name of the floppy disk or hard disk containing the document).
- Every intermediate folder name.
- The name of the document itself.

In Figure 16-25, the full pathname of the document is *MyHardDisk:Report Folder:Grain Production/Chart1;* the volume name is *MyHardDisk,* which contains the folder called *Report Folder,* which in turn contains the document entitled *Grain Production/Chart1.*

Interestingly, none of these names can include an exclamation mark. If one of them does, Word interprets this as an exclamation mark that separates the various parts of the identifier paragraph, and it either does something unexpected (such as opening a document you didn't want opened) or displays a dialog box containing an error message (such as *No reference area allowed for Microsoft Excel Chart*).

As mentioned earlier, if you use the Edit Link command (for example), and Word cannot find the document specified in the identifier paragraph, the application is launched anyway. A dialog box appears, asking you to find the document. When you switch back to Word, the pathname of the document is updated.

The Reference Area in the Source Document

The last item in the identifier paragraph specifies the location of the area in the source to be transferred. The actual form this can take depends on the application you're using, but this concern really applies only to SuperPaint and Excel. We'll discuss these in more detail in the following sections.

Using QuickSwitch with MacPaint and MacDraw

The way in which QuickSwitch works with MacPaint 1.x and MacDraw 1.9 is different from the way it works with SuperPaint and Excel. When you copy something from either MacPaint or MacDraw, switch to Word, and use the Paste Link command, you see the message *Clipboard does not contain linking information*, and Word doesn't produce an identifier paragraph. If you subsequently choose the Update Link command, Word acts as if the Edit Link command is being used.

Either or both of the graphics programs must already be running for the transfer to work. If either (but not both) of the programs are running and you select a graphic and press Command-(comma), Word copies the graphic and switches to the program, regardless of whether the graphic is an object-oriented graphic or one composed of bit maps. If both MacPaint and MacDraw are running, Word switches to MacPaint, even if the graphic originated in MacDraw.

If neither program is running and you select a graphic and press Command-(comma), Word reports *No painting or drawing program is active*, even if another graphics program (such as SuperPaint) is already running under MultiFinder.

As mentioned earlier, neither MacPaint nor MacDraw requires the identifier paragraph. In fact, the graphic doesn't even have to be in a paragraph by itself. For example, you could paste a graphic from MacDraw into the middle of a paragraph of text, then select it and press Command-(comma). If MacDraw is running, Word would copy the graphic and switch to MacDraw.

When you select the graphic and press Command-(comma), Word copies the graphic, switches to either MacPaint or MacDraw (depending on which program is running), pastes the material, and draws a box around it. If the destination is MacPaint, the rectangle tool is used to draw the box. If the destination is MacDraw, four lines are used. These lines mark the area you have to work in: You can draw outside the lines, but when you press Command-(comma) to transfer the edited graphic back to Word, only the area within (but not including) the box is transferred. Consequently, you should work only within the borders provided.

Using QuickSwitch with SuperPaint

For SuperPaint, the reference area of the identifier paragraph specifies both the coordinates of the rectangle containing the graphic and whether the graphic belongs to SuperPaint's drawing or painting layer. A typical identifier paragraph for a graphic copied from SuperPaint's drawing layer (for instance) might look like this:

```
SuperPaint!HardDisk:YourFolder:YourDoc:Draw(100, 200, 300, 400)
```

An important caveat: Do not resize or move the graphic from the position it has in the SuperPaint document. Because the reference area in the identifier paragraph specifies what part of the source document is to be transferred, moving the material outside that area might prevent QuickSwitch from finding it.

Using QuickSwitch with Microsoft Excel

QuickSwitch is compatible with Microsoft Excel versions 1.03 and above, but only versions above 1.5 generate the identifier paragraph. You can use the name *Excel* alone—you don't have to enter the full filename of the program as stored on disk.

If you're transferring a chart, as we've discussed in the example above, you don't use the reference area. If you're transferring a table from an Excel spreadsheet, the reference area can specify a range of cells in the source spreadsheet in either of two forms. In the first, you use the R1C1 format familiar to users of Excel, as follows:

```
Excel!MyDoc'sFullPathname!R1C1:R20C7
```

In this case, we've specified that the range of cells from rows 1 through 20 and columns 1 through 7 be transferred from Excel into the Word document.

In the second form, you specify a named range in the source spreadsheet that contains the data you want, as follows:

```
Excel!MyDoc'sFullPathname!MyTable'sAreaName
```

To assign a name to a range of cells in an Excel spreadsheet, select the range and choose Define Name from the Formula menu. Enter a name in the Define Name dialog box, and then click OK.

This method is advantageous because you can assign a name to the entire table in Excel and subsequently add and subtract rows and columns, without having to keep track of exactly which rows and columns you want to transfer back to Word. Interestingly, if you name the range first, then copy and paste the table into the Word document, Word gives priority to the name of the range over the R1C1 expression for that range.

After you've used the Paste Link command to both transfer a table and establish a link to an Excel spreadsheet, you can then use the Insert Table command to convert the initial tabbed data to Word's Table format. To update the table, first select it by pressing the Option key and then double-clicking anywhere in the table. Next, choose either the Update Link command or the Edit Link command if you want to edit the table before updating it. Word places each item of data from the source spreadsheet into the correct cell.

Unfortunately, if you then refine the table by merging cells or adding or deleting rows and columns, and if you subsequently update or edit the link, Word tries to put the new information into the table structure you've created, but it might put table elements in the wrong cells. For this reason, you would be wise to preserve the rectangular structure of the table as imported from Excel, and refrain from deleting or merging rows, columns, and cells in linked tables.

Points to Remember

- You can transfer raw, unformatted text and graphics to and from Word via the Clipboard and Scrapbook. Word can also read formatted files created by Word version 1.05, Microsoft Works, MacWrite, and MS-DOS Word; it can store files in all these formats except for the Works format, and it can't generate a style sheet for an MS-DOS format Word file.
- All items on the Clipboard and in the Scrapbook are assigned one or more four-character data type codes. The TEXT code means that the material consists of raw text; the PICT code means that the material is either a bit-mapped or object-oriented graphic. Other codes are assigned by application programs to mark material stored in the program's internal format.
- You can keep formatted Word text in the Clipboard and in the Scrapbook; Word clippings kept there are stored both in the RTF format and as raw text.
- If you'll be uploading a file to a bulletin board or on-line service, save it in the Text Only with Line Breaks file format. You can also use RTF (Rich Text Format), if the person or system receiving the file can convert RTF files.
- Saving in RTF stores a Word document, formatting and all, as an ASCII file. The formats are converted to text codes.
- Bit-mapped graphics are images typically represented as rows of white or black pixels. Object-oriented, or QuickDraw, graphics are images that are made up of discrete elements that can be moved independently of one another. The PICT format is used to transfer both bit-mapped and object-oriented graphics from program to program.

  PostScript graphics are images represented as PostScript commands. These can be printed only on PostScript-compatible printers. Some graphics programs bury PostScript code in PICT-format images; this is one form of encapsulated PostScript (EPS).
- Bit-mapped graphics are limited to 72 dots per inch, the resolution of the Macintosh, but you can compress bitmaps to higher pixel densities, both in Word and in most object-oriented graphics programs. When sent to a PostScript-compatible printer, object-oriented and PICT-format graphics are converted into PostScript code. PostScript graphics are printed at the resolution of the printer.
- The QuickSwitch feature allows you to update a chart or table in Microsoft Excel or a graphic in MacPaint, MacDraw, or SuperPaint, and then transfer the changes to a Word document automatically. QuickSwitch works only when Word is running under MultiFinder.

■ *Techniques*

Transferring Text

Transfer text with the Clipboard and Scrapbook

1. In the source program, cut or copy the text to be transferred to the Clipboard. From there, paste it into the Scrapbook, if you want.
2. In the destination program, set the insertion point where you want to insert the text.
3. Choose the Paste command to insert the text from the Clipboard, or open the Scrapbook, display the text clipping to be inserted, copy it to the Clipboard, and then paste it into the document.
4. Text inserted into a Word document from another program or from the Scrapbook is assigned the style of the surrounding text, but pasted paragraphs take on the *Normal* style.

Store a Word file for use by another program

1. Choose the Save As command, and click the File Format button.
2. Specify a file format in the dialog box that appears. If the destination program is not listed, specify Text Only.
3. Click OK, type a name for the new document, and then click Save.

Open a file created by another program

1. If the file was created in Word 1.05, Microsoft Works, MacWrite, or MS-DOS Word or was saved in the MacPaint format, simply open the file as you would a Word document. Files stored in the MacPaint format open in a new window containing the graphic.
2. Otherwise, in the source program, save the file in a text-only or ASCII format, if possible.
3. Quit the program and start Word.
4. Choose the Open command. If Word can read the file you want to open, its name will appear in the list box.

If the name of the file does not appear in the list box, try pressing the Shift key and choose the Open Any File command. This displays all the files on the disk, regardless of their format. Files opened in this way are likely to contain garbage characters, which you can remove manually. To save the file, choose Save As, click File Format, and click Normal. Give the file a new name before saving it.

Transfer a table in Word to a spreadsheet or database program

1. Set up the data in the Word document so that each paragraph contains a record (for a database program) or a row (for a spreadsheet) of data. Separate the fields or cells with tabs. (You can use tabs or commas if the destination is a database program.)
2. Select the data to be transferred and copy it to the Clipboard, or save it in the Text Only or Text Only with Line Breaks format.
3. Quit Word and start the destination program.
4. Set the insertion point and paste the data into a document in the program, or open the document saved in Text Only format.

Transfer spreadsheet data or database records to Word

1. In the source program, copy the desired data or records to the Clipboard, or save it in a text format, if available.
2. Quit the program and start Word.
3. Set the insertion point and choose the Paste command, or open the document saved in text format.
4. Each row or record in the resulting text is a paragraph, and the cells or fields are separated by tabs or commas.

If you wish, you can then convert the tabbed table into Word's cell table format, as discussed in Chapter 11, "Formatting Tables and Lists."

Transferring Graphics

Copy a graphic into a Word document

1. In the source program, create the graphic and copy it to the Clipboard.
2. Quit the program and start Word.
3. Set the insertion point and choose the Paste command.
4. Format the graphic, if you want, to adjust its position or to add an outline.

Crop a graphic

1. Click on the graphic. A cropping box with three handles appears.
2. Drag the right handle to crop the graphic horizontally; drag the bottom handle to crop the graphic vertically. To crop the graphic both horizontally and vertically while maintaining its original proportions, drag the corner handle.

Scale a graphic

1. Click on the graphic. A cropping box with three handles appears.
2. Press the Shift key while you drag the right, bottom, or corner handle. The right handle scales the graphic horizontally, the bottom handle scales it vertically, and the corner handle scales it but maintains the original proportions.

Insert a blank graphic frame into a Word document

1. Set the insertion point where you want the frame to appear.
2. Choose Insert Graphics from the Document menu. Word inserts a 1-by-1-inch frame.
3. To change the size of the frame, click in it to display a cropping box, and drag the handles to the desired size.
4. Format the frame, if you want, as you would a graphic.

Create a screen dump

1. Press Shift-Command-3. The contents of the screen are stored in a MacPaint file under the names *Screen 0* through *Screen 9*. If you're using a Mac II, set the display to black and white unless you want color in the screen dump.

Copy Word text to the Clipboard as an object-oriented graphic

1. Select the text to be copied.
2. Press Option-Command-D. The selection is copied to the Clipboard as a PICT-format graphic.
3. Quit Word and start the destination program. It must be able to accept PICT images.
4. Paste the Clipboard image into the program. You can paste it into a drawing program and alter it to achieve special effects.

Using QuickSwitch with SuperPaint or Excel

Paste a Link

1. Copy the material in SuperPaint or Excel that you want to transfer to Word. Both the source and the destination programs must be running under MultiFinder.
2. Switch to Word, and choose the Paste Link command.

Word inserts the material and an identifier paragraph that specifies the source program, the full pathname of the document, and the location of the linked material in the source document, if needed.

Update a Link

1. Select the linked material in the Word document.
2. Choose Update Link from the Edit menu. If the destination program isn't currently running, MultiFinder launches the program and opens the document.

The material is automatically copied from the source document and pasted at the location of the link in the Word document. The source document isn't automatically closed.

Edit a Link

1. Select the linked material in the Word document.
2. Press the Shift key and choose Edit Link from the Edit menu, or press Command-(comma). If the destination program isn't currently running, MultiFinder launches the program, opens the document, and returns control to you, so you can edit the file.
3. When you are done editing the file, press Command-(comma) to copy the source material, switch back to Word, and replace the previous version in the Word document.

■ Commands

Command name	Meaning, menu	Standard keyboard	Keypad	Extended keyboard
Copy	Copies selection to Clipboard.			
	Edit	⌘C		F3
Copy as Picture	Copies selection as a MacDraw graphic onto Clipboard.			
		⌘⌥D		
Edit Link (QuickSwitch)	Switches to the source application and file of the selected information in your Word document. After you revise the original file and return to Word, Word updates your document with the revised data or graphic. Available only when running under MultiFinder.			
		⌘,		⌥F2
Insert Graphics	Inserts an empty graphics frame at insertion point.			
	Document			
Open Any File…	Opens a document. Dialog box lists all files in current folder/drive. Files in formats not recognized by Word are opened as ASCII text.			
				⇧F6
Open File Name:	Opens indicated document.			

(continued)

Command name	Meaning, menu	Standard keyboard	Keypad	Extended keyboard
Open Mail…	Lists Word mail messages in your Microsoft Mail mailbox.			
	File			
Open…	Opens a document. Dialog box lists all Word files and files in formats recognized by Word.			
	File	⌘O		F6
Paste Link	Pastes contents of Clipboard into your document with an identifier paragraph linking pasted data or graphic to its source application and file.			
	Edit			⌥F4
Save	Saves active document under its current name.			
	File	⌘S		F7
Save As…	Renames document and saves it in a different format, or saves it in a different drive or folder.			
	File		⇧F7	
Send Mail…	Displays Microsoft Mail directory list window for selecting recipients of current Word message (active Word document).			
	File			
Show Clipboard	Displays contents of Clipboard.			
	Window			
Update Link	Updates selected information in your Word document to match current data or graphic in the original source application and file. Available only when running under MultiFinder.			
	Edit			⌥F3
Use Picture Placeholders	Toggles display of gray rectangles in place of graphics.			

Merge Printing

The form-letter feature in Word is commonly called merge printing. The concept involved is straightforward: Names, addresses, and other data in one document are inserted, or merged, into a template document. This template document can be a form letter, an invoice, or a set of mailing labels.

If your needs are simple, merge printing is easy to do. For example, setting up a basic form letter and having Word generate letters for a given set of names and addresses is a relatively simple task. However, if you're so inclined, you can also use this feature to achieve complex effects. You can include commands that specify that certain data be inserted only if a condition or set of conditions is met, that instruct Word to prompt you for data to be inserted, and that tell the program to include an entire file at a given point in the document. These instructions and advanced techniques are covered later in the chapter; first, you need to know the basics.

The document that contains the template—the text to appear in every letter of the mailing-list format—is called the *main document*. The document that contains the names, addresses, and other data to be inserted into the template is referred to as the *data document*. When you choose Print Merge from the File menu, Word inserts information from the data document into the appropriate locations in the main document and creates a series of form documents, which Word then sends to the printer, as shown in Figure 17-1.

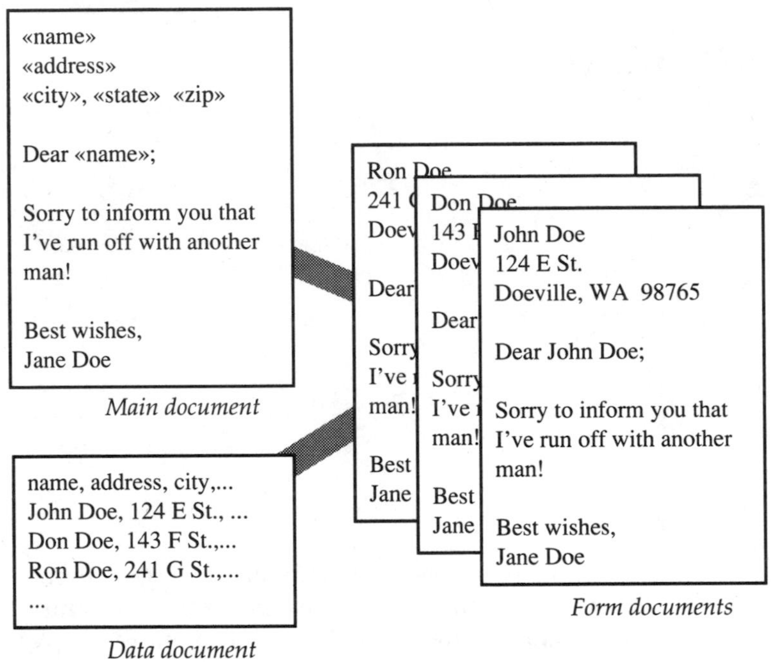

Figure 17-1
Merge printing.

Merge printing saves you the most time when many variables change from one letter to the next, or when you must prepare a large number of letters. If you have only a few letters to prepare, each with only a few variables, it is easier to type in the information directly. If you use the same data over and over again (such as the names and addresses of only a few major vendors), try storing the information in the glossary. Set it up so that you can call up a complete name and address by typing in a code name.

■ *Setting Up a Data Document*

The data document contains the sets of information to be plugged into the main document. In the example used throughout this discussion, the data document contains these items:

- ❑ First name
- ❑ Last name
- ❑ Address
- ❑ City
- ❑ State
- ❑ ZIP code

Of course, a data document can contain any kind of information, including account balances, phone numbers, and favorite foods. The idea is that a different set of information is provided for each person who will receive one of your form letters. The complete set of information for each person is called a *record*. Here are examples of two records:

```
Joe ➧        Smith ➧     123 Elm Ave. ➧        Gary ➧         IN ➧     46401¶
Mary Sue ➧   Ellison ➧   6703 Highland St. ➧   Santa Cruz ➧   CA ➧     95060¶
```

The data in a record is divided into *fields*. These example records consist of six fields: first name, last name, street address, city, state, and ZIP code.

The way the data is arranged is important: The arrangement tells Word the contents of each field. Each record consists of one paragraph and ends with a paragraph mark. You separate the fields in a record either by commas or by tabs. The fields must all be in the same order for each record, or Word might print a person's name where you expect to see the name of a town. Each record can have as many as 256 fields and take up as many lines as necessary, as long as the record contains only one paragraph mark that falls at the end.

You can enter the data for each record by hand, or you can copy data from another program, such as Microsoft File or Microsoft Excel. Excel, for example, has a file-saving option called Text Only, and you can open files saved in this format as Word documents. Each row of a spreadsheet file is a record; it ends with a paragraph mark, and its cells are separated by tab characters.

Each record should be followed by only one paragraph mark; otherwise, Word will display a dialog box saying *Missing comma in data record.* (It will say *comma* even if you use tabs to separate the fields.) Word assumes that a record exists for every paragraph mark, and it will treat extra paragraph marks as empty—and therefore faulty—records. This isn't a serious problem, but you can avoid the dialog box by deleting blank lines between records and extra paragraph marks at the end of the document.

Special Cases

If the data in a field contains one or more tabs, commas, or quotation marks, you must surround the entire field with quotation marks. Also, you must double every quotation mark in the field. This prevents Word from seeing two fields where there should be only one. Here are two examples:

```
"Joe ➧ Bob" ➧   Smith ➧     123 Elm Ave. ➧          Gary ➧          IN ➧    46401¶
""Mary Sue"" ➧  Ellison ➧   6703 Highland St. ➧     Santa Cruz ➧    CA ➧    95060¶
```

If you want to leave a field blank, simply leave the entry at that position empty. This tells Word to skip over the empty field and ensures that the contents of subsequent fields are associated with the correct field names. Here's an example:

```
➧               Resident ➧  6703 Highland ➧  Santa Cruz ➧    CA ➧    95060¶
```

The Header Record

After you have entered your data, you still have one small task to complete in the data document. Word needs to be told the name of each of the fields. You will then enter these names in the main document where you want Word to insert their data.

To assign field names, you enter a special record containing the field names, in the exact order in which they appear in the data records, at the very beginning of the data document. This special record is called the *header record* for the data document. Separate the field names in the header record with the same character you used to separate the fields in the data records—either a comma or a tab. Tabs are more useful because they arrange the data in easy-to-read columns. Each field name can be up to 65 characters long and doesn't have to be one word, unlike field names in most programming languages. For example, *first name* and *street address* are legal field names.

When the header record is complete, save the document under an easy-to-remember name. A complete data document, with a header record containing field names and one record, is shown in Figure 17-2.

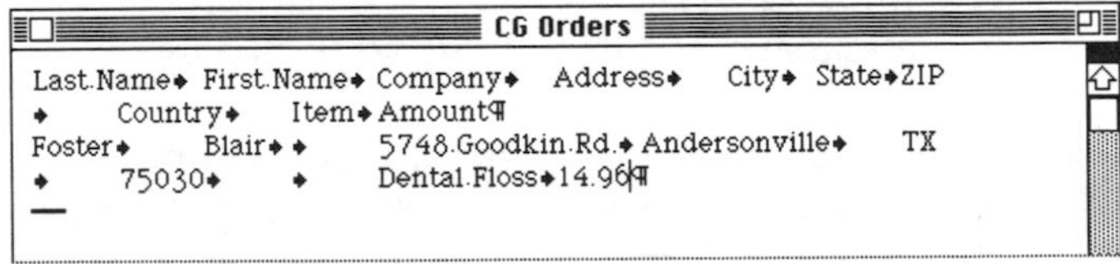

Figure 17-2
A sample data document.

TIP

Using a Cell Table in a Data Document
Separating records by commas or tabs is one way to structure the entries in a data document, but you can also enter data in the cells of a table. The cell table must be the first element in the data document. Enter the header record in the first row, entering one field name in each cell. Remember that you can enter more than one paragraph of text in each cell; Word transfers the entire contents of the cell into the form letter. Because cell tables are limited to a maximum of 31 columns, however, data documents set up in this way are limited to 31 fields. For more information on cell tables, see Chapter 11, "Formatting Tables and Lists."

Setting Up a Main Document

The main document can be almost any kind of document. In most instances, it will be a form letter of one type or another, so in this section we use a simple form letter to continue the discussion of merge printing. Main documents almost always contain these items:

- Field names inserted at various points throughout the body of the document.
- A print merge DATA instruction placed at the beginning of the document, which names the document holding the data to be inserted in each field name.

The body of the document consists of the standard text that everyone receives. It remains the same from letter to letter. You can give the body of the document any set of character, paragraph, table, section or document formats you want.

Field Names

You insert a field name wherever you want Word to insert a piece of information from the data document into the body of the main document. You can place a field name anywhere, even inside a paragraph of body text. The capitalization of field names must be the same in both the main document and the header record of the data document. Also, you must enclose each field name with the special characters « (Option-\) and » (Shift-Option-\). (See Figure 17-3 on the following page.) If a field name appears on a line of its own, you can end it with the paragraph mark instead of the final ».

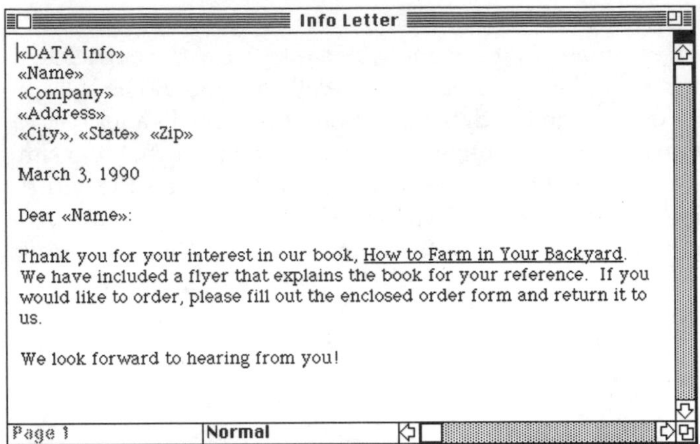

Info Letter

«DATA Info»
«Name»
«Company»
«Address»
«City», «State» «Zip»

March 3, 1990

Dear «Name»:

Thank you for your interest in our book, How to Farm in Your Backyard. We have included a flyer that explains the book for your reference. If you would like to order, please fill out the enclosed order form and return it to us.

We look forward to hearing from you!

Page 1 Normal

Figure 17-3
A sample form letter.

The DATA Instruction

The DATA instruction specifies the name of the data document containing the header and the data records that will be inserted in place of each field name in the main document. Other, more advanced merge instructions are available and are discussed later in this chapter, but the DATA instruction is all you need to create a form letter. The DATA instruction must be the first merge instruction in the document, and it must be enclosed by the same « and » bracket characters that enclose the field names. Specify the name of the data document after the word DATA, before the closing » character. (See Figure 17-3.) Be sure to type the name of the data document correctly.

Using a Separate Header Document

Word lets you keep the header record and the data records in two separate documents if you want. To do this, you must use a slightly different form of the DATA instruction:

«DATA header document, data document»

In place of *header document*, enter the name of the document containing the header; this document must contain only the header record. In place of *data document*, enter the name of the document containing the data records; it must contain only data records. Separate the two names with a comma. As in a regular data document, the field names in the header document must be in the same sequence as the fields in the data document.

In most cases, you'll keep your data records and header record in one file, and so the header document name is not necessary. Sometimes, however, it's helpful to keep the header record and the data records separate. You might want to use the same header record for more than one document, for example, or you might be using a data file created by saving database records from a program such as Microsoft Excel in Text Only file format. In such cases it can be more convenient to use a separate header document rather than opening the data file and inserting the header record.

TIP

Using Graphics in a Data Document
In addition to storing text in the fields of a data document, you can also store graphics. Because Word treats graphics like characters, you can insert a graphic within a paragraph and hence within a record in a data document. Here's an example:

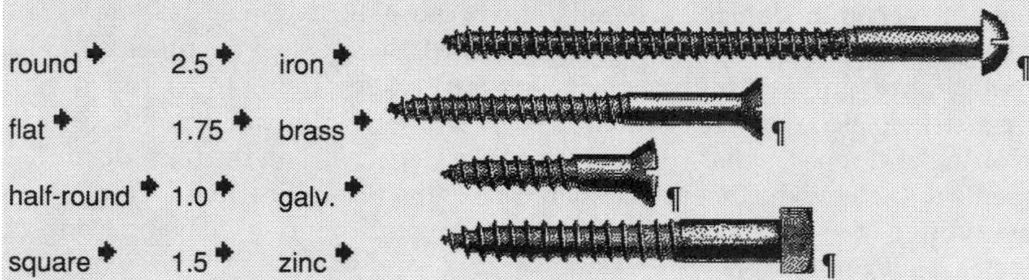

■ *Printing the Document*

To initiate printing, with the main document open choose Print Merge from the File menu. The dialog box shown in Figure 17-4 appears. Select the All option to print a form document for every record in the data document, or enter a range of record numbers in the From and To edit fields. The first data record is record 1, the second is record 2, and so on.

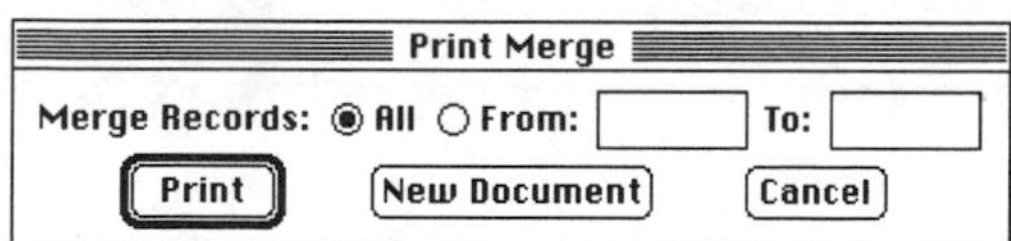

Figure 17-4
The Print Merge dialog box.

If you click the Print button, Word merges the data records into the main document according to the field names you've placed in the main document and sends each resulting form document to the printer. First, however, it presents the Print dialog box so that you can set the print quality, page range, number of copies of each form document, and so forth. Click OK when you are finished setting the options and are ready to print.

If you click the New Document button, Word opens a new, blank document and appends each merged form document to it. Section marks separate the documents. Placing the documents in a new document is useful when you want to see the results of the merge before printing or if you want to use the merge feature to synthesize new documents (from complicated sets of boilerplate text, for instance). Treat this file like any other Word document.

When merging very large files (containing more than 15 or 20 pages), Word might report that the editing session is too long and ask that you save your work. If this happens, some of the records in the data document might not be merged. To remedy this, divide the records in the data document into more sets of data documents, and merge them in more than one pass. Note that this error condition doesn't occur when you're sending the merged documents directly to the printer.

When you print the merged documents, each form document is repaginated to accommodate the inserted data. Because the length of the data in any given field can vary from record to record, the finished documents might look slightly different because their lines are broken differently. If you've set up a strict page layout involving forced page breaks, this can upset your formatting and repagination. If this is a problem, try merging the form documents into a new document and then correct the formatting there. Once everything is to your liking, you can print the document by choosing Print instead of Print Merge.

■ *Using the Merge Instructions*

The DATA instruction isn't the only instruction you can include in the main document when creating a main document for merging. You can instruct Word to interact with you during a merging session, set conditions and rules for merge printing, or insert entire files into the main document. Word supports six types of merge printing instructions. You've already encountered the first, the DATA instruction. The others are:

- ❑ IF, ENDIF, and ELSE—for changing what is inserted depending on whether a condition is met.
- ❑ NEXT—for skipping a record.
- ❑ SET—for creating temporary variables within a print merge. For example, you can store the name of a company in a variable, independently of the contents of the data document, and use the same company name in every form letter.
- ❑ ASK—which presents a dialog box on screen, for you to enter text which is inserted at that point in each form.
- ❑ INCLUDE—for including the entire contents of a file in the form letter.

The IF Instruction

"If it's foggy, I'll wear my mac." That's an example of conditional branching, a basic concept in daily life as well as in computer programming. You can break an IF instruction into two parts: a question and a result which depends on the question's answer. In our example, the question is: "Is it foggy?" If the answer is yes, you put on your overcoat; if the answer is no, you don't.

The question "Is it foggy?" can also be stated more completely as a condition: "Is the weather foggy?" Should the condition *weather = foggy* be met, you go off to the closet. But what do you do if it's not foggy? Then the condition isn't met, and nothing happens.

The IF instruction uses the same logic. You can use it to set up your form letter in such a way that it "asks" the records in the data document a set of questions. The text inserted in the merged document for that record varies—depending on whether or not the condition is met. You can set up three kinds of conditions within the IF instruction:

- ❏ Does this field contain anything at all?
- ❏ Does the text in this field match this text string?
- ❏ Does the text in this field match this number?

Checking for Text in a Field

One type of IF instruction checks to see if a particular field is empty and, if not, inserts text specified in the instruction at that location in the document. If the field contains any characters at all (including numbers, symbols, or even one blank space), then the condition is met. If the field is completely blank, the condition is not met. The syntax of this type of IF instruction is as follows:

```
«IF field name» text to insert «ENDIF»
```

You place this instruction in the main document at the point where you want to insert text if the field is not empty. In place of *field name* you enter the name of the field you want to test. In place of *text to insert* you type the text string you want inserted if the condition is met. The ENDIF element signals the end of the insertion text. Incidentally, the ENDIF element doesn't have to be on the same line or even in the same paragraph; you can insert whole paragraphs, graphics, or anything you like.

The first window in Figure 17-5, on the following page, shows a data document containing three data records; the second window contains the main document. The first line in the main document contains a DATA instruction specifying the name of the data document being used. The next five lines constitute the body of the document, with the field names used in the data document inserted at the appropriate places.

The last line in the main document consists of an instruction in Word's merge language that specifies: *If the field called Discount is not empty, print the text "Discount Given."* In the example, the field name is *Discount*. If the Discount field contains anything at all, as does the second record in the data document, the text *Discount Given* is inserted. If the Discount field is blank, no text is printed at that location.

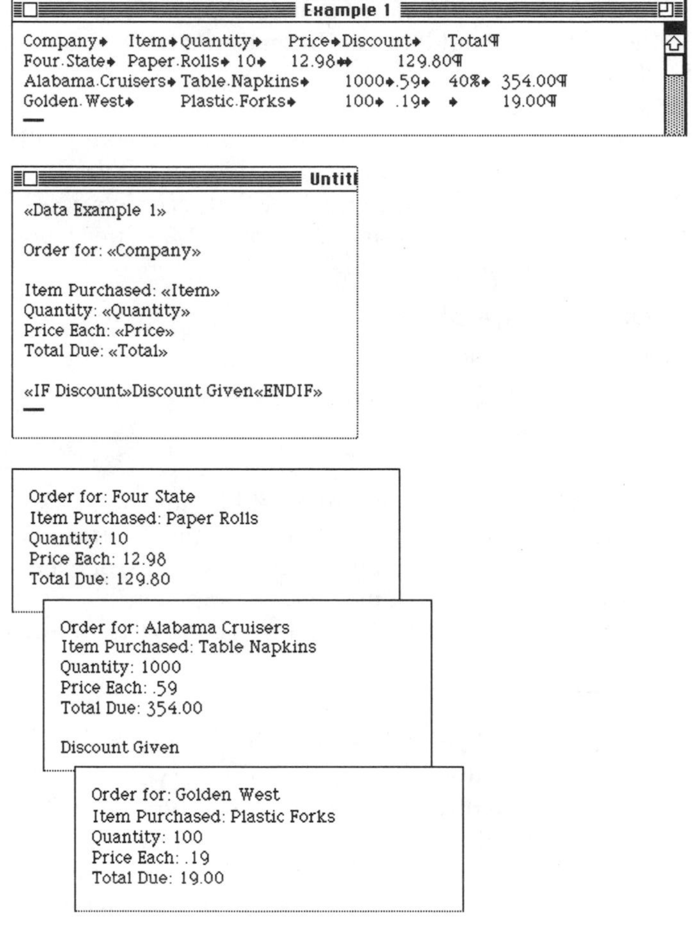

Figure 17-5
An IF instruction that inserts text if a field isn't empty.

Matching Text

Simply testing for the presence or absence of text in a field might not be enough. You might want to see whether a field contains certain characters and insert text if it does. The syntax for the IF instruction to accomplish this is as follows:

«IF field name = "text to match"» text to insert «ENDIF»

In place of *field name,* enter the name of the field you want to check. Replace *text to match* with the exact string for which you're checking. Don't forget the double quotation marks. Replace *text to insert* with the string that you want printed in each document for which the specified field meets the condition.

Figure 17-6 shows a set of records and part of a form letter containing an IF instruction that tests whether the Country field contains the text *Canada.* If this condition is met, the following text is printed: *Please refer to our sales office in Canada for your supply needs*. Note that the text to be inserted can be any length. Word stops when it reaches the ENDIF instruction.

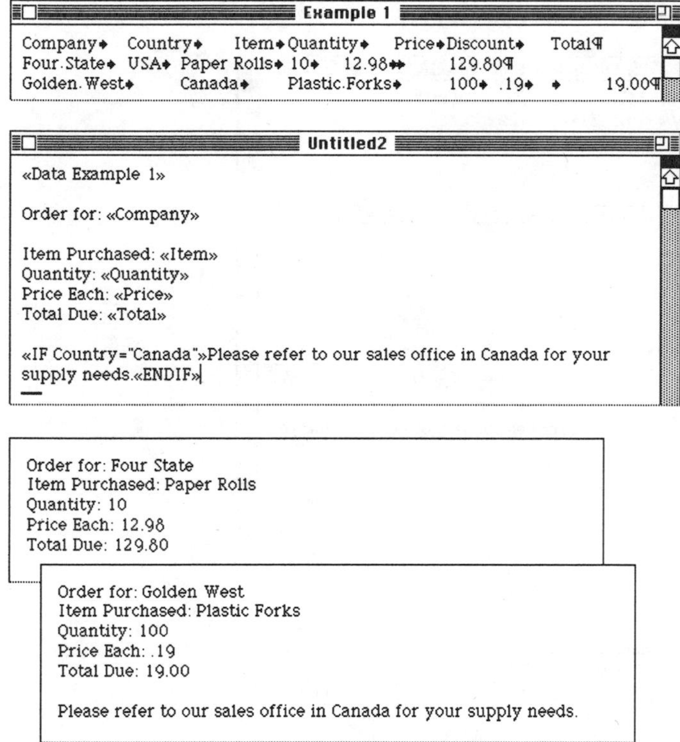

Figure 17-6

An IF instruction that inserts text if a field contains a certain string of characters.

Matching Numbers

Word provides some additional flexibility when you want to match numbers instead of text. You can test whether a field contains a specific number or a number that is higher or lower. The IF instruction for matching a number is:

«IF field name = number» text to insert «ENDIF»

In place of *field name*, you enter the name of the field to test, and in place of *number*, type the number to match. (It must be an integer.) Replace *text to insert* with the string you want printed in the merged document if the condition is met. Instead of an equal sign, you can use a greater-than sign (>) or a less-than sign (<) to determine whether the value in the field is higher than or lower than the test number.

Figure 17-7 shows a series of records and a main document containing an IF instruction that tests whether the number in the Total field is greater than 100. The condition is met when the number is 101 or greater. In the example, if Total is greater than 100, the text printed is: *We are enclosing a FREE gift as our way of saying thank you for your patronage.*

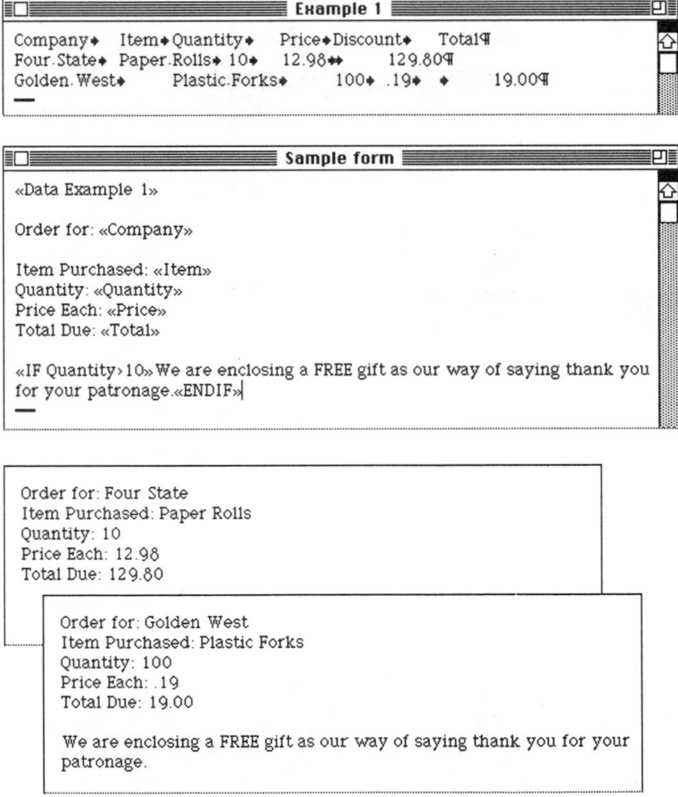

Example 1

Company◆ Item◆Quantity◆ Price◆Discount◆ Total¶
Four.State◆ Paper.Rolls◆ 10◆ 12.98◆◆ 129.80¶
Golden.West◆ Plastic.Forks◆ 100◆ .19◆ ◆ 19.00¶

Sample form

«Data Example 1»

Order for: «Company»

Item Purchased: «Item»
Quantity: «Quantity»
Price Each: «Price»
Total Due: «Total»

«IF Quantity›10»We are enclosing a FREE gift as our way of saying thank you for your patronage.«ENDIF»

Order for: Four State
Item Purchased: Paper Rolls
Quantity: 10
Price Each: 12.98
Total Due: 129.80

Order for: Golden West
Item Purchased: Plastic Forks
Quantity: 100
Price Each: .19
Total Due: 19.00

We are enclosing a FREE gift as our way of saying thank you for your patronage.

Figure 17-7

An IF instruction that tests a numeric value in a field.

Nesting IF Instructions

You can tuck IF instructions within other IF instructions. This is called *nesting*, and it provides a means of creating an elaborate tree of alternatives. Nesting allows you to refine the circumstances under which text will be inserted. Instead of having only one condition that must be met, you can specify that a record meet a number of nested IF conditions.

If you've done any programming, you'll recognize the nesting scheme as a way to implement the AND logical operator. It goes something like this: *IF condition 1 AND condition 2 AND condition 3 are met, insert the text.* Should a record fail to meet any of the three conditions, the text is not inserted. A typical nested IF instruction is as follows:

```
«IF Discount» «IF Total>100» You are a valued customer, and we would like to extend
open account privileges to you. Please contact our sales office to set up a new
account. «ENDIF» «ENDIF»
```

The syntax is simple: String all the IF statements one right after another, and then enter the text to be inserted. Finish by supplying an ENDIF for each of the IF instructions. If two IF instructions are used, for example, add two ENDIFs.

Using ELSE Within an IF Instruction

In the examples of the IF instruction that you've seen up to this point, nothing happened if the condition wasn't met. If the Discount field was blank, for example, no text was inserted. But what if you need a specific response if the condition isn't met? The ELSE instruction fulfills this need. You provide a condition in the IF instruction. (Any of the three types of condition will work.) You then enter the text to be inserted if the condition is met and another string to be inserted if the condition is not met. The syntax looks like the following:

```
«IF condition» text to insert «ELSE» alternative text to insert «ENDIF»
```

In place of *condition*, you enter the name of the field you want to test and also a conditional test if desired. If the condition is met, Word prints the *text to insert*. If the condition isn't met, Word prints the *alternative text to insert*. Figure 17-8 on the following page shows some examples that use the ELSE instruction.

You can also use ELSE within a set of nested IF instructions to provide an alternative when testing for more than one condition at a time. For example:

```
«IF Discount» «IF Total>100» You are a valued customer, and we would like to extend
open account privileges to you. Please contact our sales office to set up a new
account. «ELSE» Please contact our sales office for more information about open
account privileges.«ENDIF» «ENDIF»
```

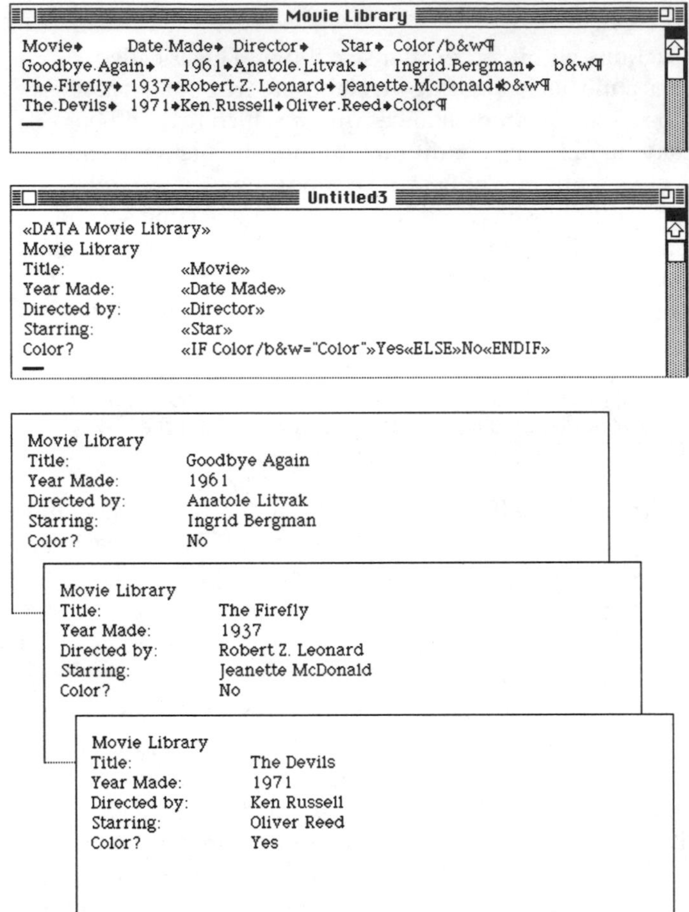

Figure 17-8
An ELSE instruction that inserts one item if a condition is met and inserts another item if the condition isn't met.

The NEXT Instruction

You can use the IF instruction to determine whether a form document for a certain record should be printed at all. If you know that you want to print only a certain range (from the third to tenth record, for instance), simply enter the appropriate values in the From and To edit fields in the Print Merge dialog box. If you want to print only those records that meet certain criteria, however, such as ones for past due accounts, use the NEXT instruction. You can think of the NEXT instruction as a filter: It passes (prints) only those records that meet the criteria specified in the IF instruction. The syntax for the NEXT instruction is as follows:

«IF condition» «NEXT» «ENDIF»

The *condition* can test for text in a field, matching text, or a matching number. If the condition isn't met, Word skips to the next record, as shown in Figure 17-9. If the condition is met, the record is merged into the main document and printed with the rest of the form documents. NEXT works when you're sending forms to the printer and also works when you're placing them in a new document.

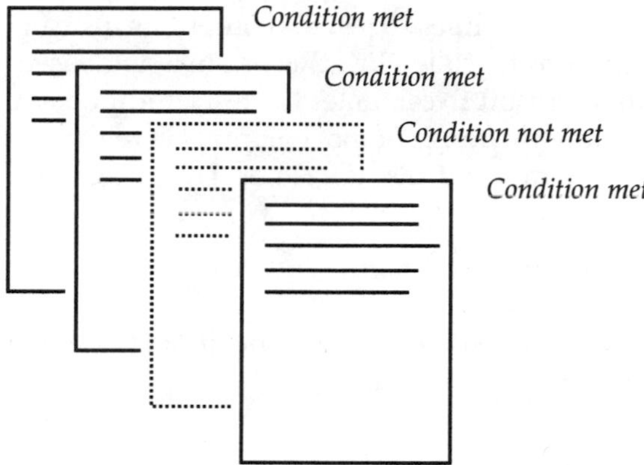

Figure 17-9
How the NEXT instruction works.

You can also use the NEXT instruction by itself. This is useful when you want to print more than one record in one document. For example, you can set up a merge document to print labels on an 8½ -by-11-inch sheet of labels by using a series of merge commands that look like this:

```
«name»¶
«address»¶
«city», «state»  «ZIP»¶
«NEXT»¶
¶
«name»¶
«address»¶
«city», «state»  «ZIP»¶
«NEXT»¶
¶
«name»¶
«address»¶
«city», «state»  «ZIP»¶
«NEXT»¶
¶
```

When you set up the merge document, you should create a single page of labels in this pattern and format the document for as many columns as the labels you're using. Also, use a font, line spacing, and margin measurements that position the addresses correctly with respect to each label. When you print merge the mailing list, each time the merge document is printed, it goes on to the next set of addresses. For example, if the labels you're using are arranged 3 across and 12 deep, you would set up the merge document for printing 36 records at a time.

TIP

Including a Condition Test in the Record
Setting up complicated conditions using Word's merge instructions can take some work. If you prepare data documents with a database or spreadsheet program, you can take advantage of its abilities to test for conditions instead. For example, you can create a new column called PrintRecord in a database worksheet that you've created in Microsoft Excel. Enter the test condition as a formula in the worksheet, throughout the range of that column. Have the formula return *true* if the condition is met and *false* if it is not. Then use the following instruction in the main document in Word:

```
«IF PrintRecord = "false"» «NEXT» «ENDIF»
```

In this way, you can have the data document tell the main document whether a form document should be created for that record.

The SET Instruction

The SET instruction lets you store information in a field that remains constant for every record merged. If, for example, you want to provide the current date in your monthly statements, you could include a SET instruction in the main document that asks you for the current date before merging and printing begin. Neither the data document nor the main document is physically altered by this.

You usually place the SET instruction right after the DATA instruction in the main document, although it can appear anywhere in the document as long as it falls before the field on which it acts. If you're using the SET instruction to enter the date, for instance, be sure to place the instruction before the date field, as shown in Figure 17-10.

The three ways to use the SET instruction are as follows:

```
«SET field name = text string»
«SET field name = ?»
«SET field name = ?prompt»
```

The field name you specify must not be one of the names specified in the header record for the data document.

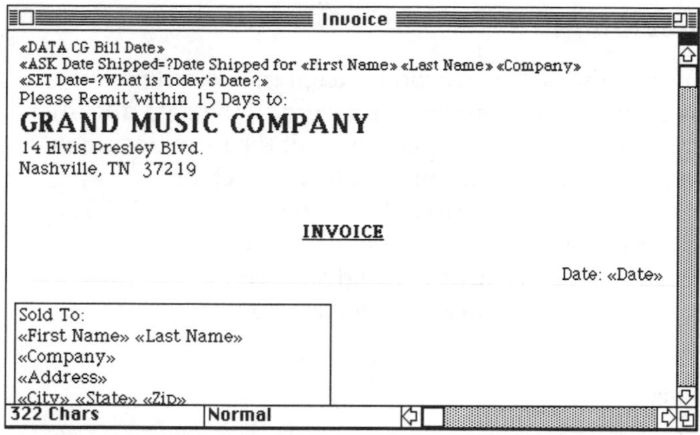

Figure 17-10
Storing data in a field with the SET instruction.

Use the first form to enter a text string into the field specified in *field name*. Word stores the characters indicated in *text string* in the field given in *field name*. Then, when you merge the document, Word replaces all occurrences of «*field name*» in the main document with the text string.

Use the second form of the instruction when you want to enter the text string for the field just before the documents are merged. When you begin merging, you'll see the dialog box shown in Figure 17-11.

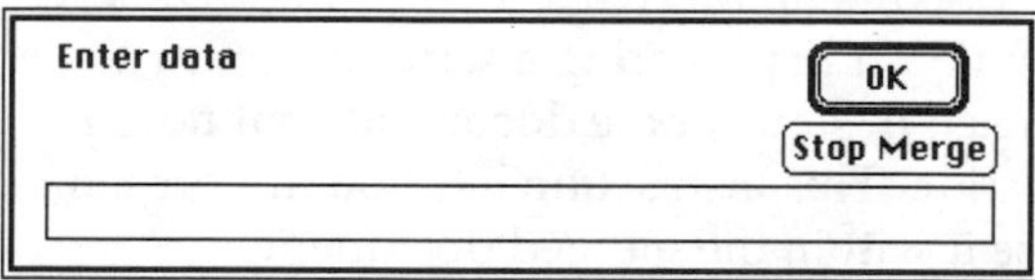

Figure 17-11
The standard SET dialog box.

If you want to provide a prompt in the dialog box, use the third form. Simply enter a message of up to 99 characters after the question mark, such as *What is the person's first name?* When Word encounters this type of SET instruction, it presents a dialog box like that shown in Figure 17-12.

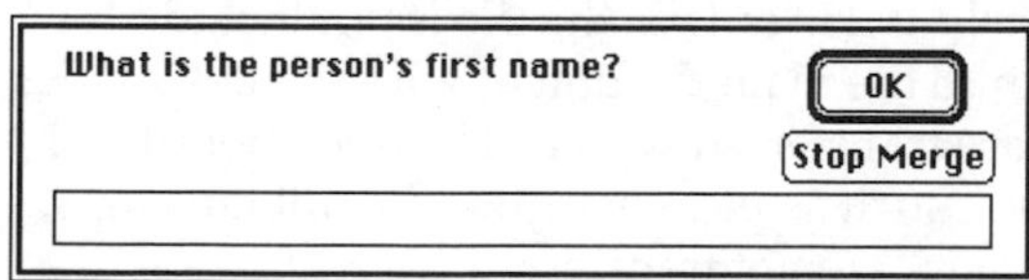

Figure 17-12
The SET dialog box with a user-specified prompt.

The ASK Instruction

The ASK instruction is like the SET instruction, except that Word presents a dialog box requesting new information for each record in the data document. Whereas the SET instruction plants the same text in all the form documents, the ASK instruction allows you to plant different text in each one.

Use the ASK instruction as you do SET: Place it right after the DATA instruction at the top of the document or anywhere before the field on which it acts. During the merge process, Word stops and asks you to enter the information for that record. The ASK instruction has two forms:

```
«ASK field name = ?»
«ASK field name = ?prompt»
```

Again, this field name must not be one of the fields in the data document.

As it does with the SET instruction, when Word encounters an ASK instruction, it presents a dialog box in which you enter the text to be placed in the field. In the first form, the dialog box lacks a prompt. So, if you have several SET or ASK instructions in the document, use the second form to have Word prompt you for the proper response.

The INCLUDE Instruction

Word's regular merge feature is useful when you want to insert individual words or sentences into the main document. But what if you want to merge entire paragraphs or pages? What if you're preparing a series of contracts in which certain paragraphs are used in some of the documents but not in others? Use the INCLUDE instruction. This instruction lets you import the contents of an entire file and place it within the merged document.

You can use INCLUDE by itself or with an IF instruction. When used by itself, INCLUDE inserts the contents of the specified document into the main document. You can place an INCLUDE instruction anywhere in the main document; Word then inserts the document at that point.

When used with an IF instruction, INCLUDE allows you to dictate which documents receive the included text and which do not. Figure 17-13 shows a main document in which the document that is entitled *Quantity Discount* is merged into the letter if the Quantity field contains a number greater than 250. If the value in the Quantity field is 250 or less, the file is not included.

When you copy a document into the main document with the INCLUDE instruction, not all of its formats are transferred with it. The document-level formats for the included document, such as page margins, default tab stops, and the contents of the Next File field, are not transferred.

In addition, if you've defined styles in the included document that have the same names as styles in the main document, the styles in the main document take precedence. This can be convenient because you can redefine styles in the main document without having to hunt for and redefine the styles in all the documents you might include in the main document.

If a DATA or INCLUDE instruction specifies a document that isn't in a disk drive when you choose the Print Merge command, Word presents a dialog box asking you to find it. Locate the folder or insert the disk that contains the document you need.

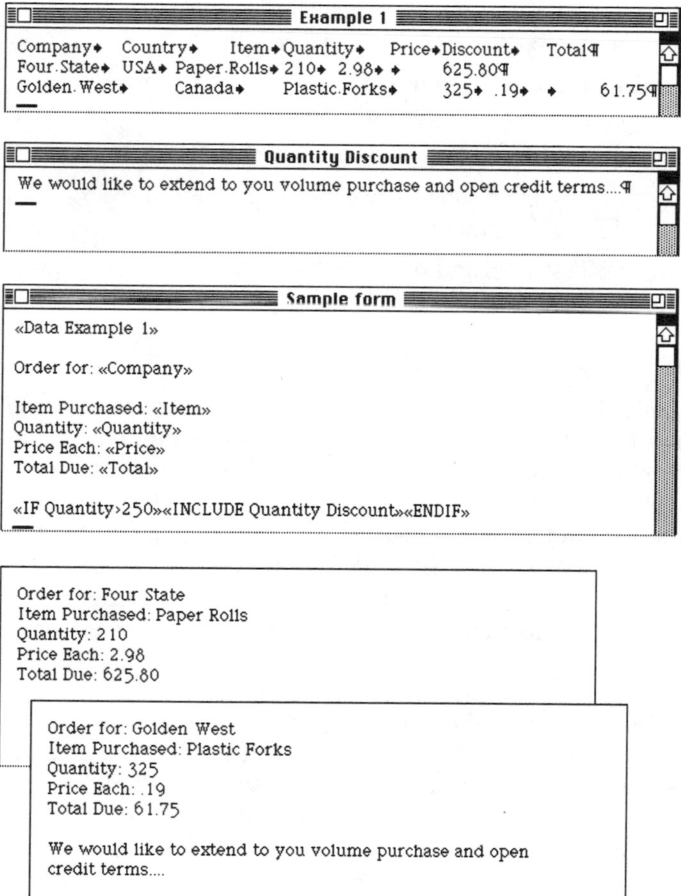

Figure 17-13
The INCLUDE instruction used with an IF instruction.

One further point: Word can open up to 22 documents at one time, and if you've added headers or footers and footnotes to a document, each counts as an additional document. Because Word opens every included document, a simple main document could therefore contain up to roughly 21 INCLUDE statements before running out of space. (Technically, Word can also keep "open" a document that you've opened, copied text from, and then closed, even though Word no longer shows a window for it on the desktop. You can "close" this document by either quitting and restarting Word, or by copying any text from a currently open document.)

Therefore, if you have many INCLUDE instructions in a document, close all unneeded documents. If you're using more INCLUDE instructions in the main document than Word can handle, you should do the merge in two or more passes, as follows:

1. Replace all « characters after, say, the twentieth INCLUDE instruction with a unique text string, such as @@@.
2. Do the merge printing and create a new document. This merges the first 20 included documents into the new document.
3. Replace the next set of 20 @@@ strings with one « character.
4. Do another merge printing from the newly created document to insert the next 20 included documents.
5. Continue replacing @@@ strings and merging from the new document until all the included documents are in place.

Nesting INCLUDE Instructions

Normally, only the main document has an INCLUDE instruction. However, Word allows you to put INCLUDE instructions in included documents, too. This can produce a waterfall effect in which Word includes document after document, each of which contains its own INCLUDE instructions.

A document named in an INCLUDE instruction can itself contain field names and an assortment of IF, ELSE, NEXT, SET, and ASK instructions. However, it can't contain the DATA instruction. All included documents retrieve records from the data document specified in the DATA instruction for the main document.

TIP

Using INCLUDE by Itself to Assemble New Documents

You don't have to create more than one form document to use the INCLUDE instruction effectively. The figures for this book, for example, could have been added not by copying and pasting them individually or by using QuickSwitch, but by moving each graphic into a Word file by itself and then merging all the graphics at once with the INCLUDE instruction. Each file might consist of one paragraph containing one graphic. Each graphic could be merged into a chapter document by inserting an INCLUDE command in this form:

```
«INCLUDE c16 f xx
```

where *xx* is the number of that figure in the chapter, and *c16 f xx* is the filename of the document containing that graphic. The final » character was omitted to avoid having an extra paragraph mark inserted when the merging was done. (See "Omitting the Closing Bracket," on page 591.)

You might choose this way to insert graphics in a document for two reasons. The first is that generally you don't need to have the figures in place until after the writing and editing is done, and having all the figures in the document would slow down scrolling, making it harder to move around and edit in the document. The second is that merging the graphics into a new document often doubles the size of the file. Working with very large files lessens the amount of memory left for processes such as editing and opening many documents at the same time.

■ *Formatting Fields*

The data placed into fields in data records doesn't keep its original formats when merged into a form document. For example, if a name in a data record is in boldface, it loses its formatting when merged with the main document and takes on the formats in effect where it is inserted.

You can, however, have character formats applied to merged text by specifying the formats in the field names in the main document. To do this, apply the character formats you want to at least the first letter of the field name. To make the ZIP code in a mailing list bold, for example, format the *z* in the *ZIP* field as boldface. (See Figure 17-14.) You can apply any other character format in the same fashion.

«Name»
«Address»
«City», «State» «**Z**IP»

John Anderson
1423 Evergreen St.
Kansas City, MO **64142**

Figure 17-14
Specifying a boldfaced ZIP code with a boldface *Z* in the *ZIP* field.

The only way to set paragraph formats for merged text is to insert the field into a paragraph of its own and assign the paragraph formats you want to the paragraph mark in the main document.

Controlling Blank Lines

For every paragraph mark in a main document, Word places a matching paragraph mark—which starts a new line—in the form documents. This isn't normally a problem, but sometimes you must control the number and placement of paragraph marks to prevent gaps in the text. You must be particularly wary of extra paragraph marks when printing mailing labels; if too many blank lines appear, the names and addresses won't fit correctly.

Even though the various merge instructions (such as DATA, SET, and ASK) don't appear in the final merged documents, blank lines will appear if you end these instructions by pressing the Return key. You can avoid these blank lines in one of three ways:

- By grouping instructions and text on the same line.
- By omitting the » character at the end of the instruction.
- By formatting the merge instruction as hidden text.

Grouping Instructions

You can put more than one instruction on a line, or you can surround an instruction with the text of the main document, as shown in Figure 17-15.

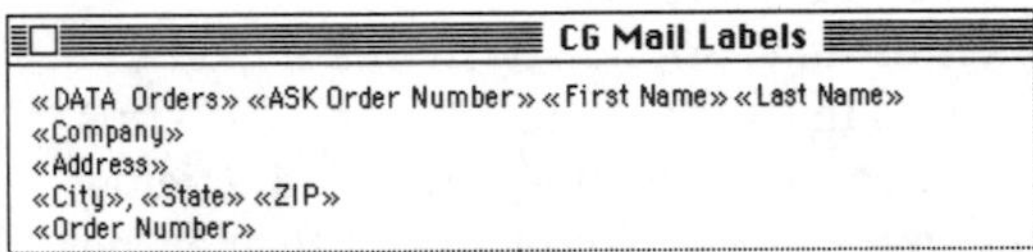

CG Mail Labels

«DATA Orders» «ASK Order Number» «First Name» «Last Name»
«Company»
«Address»
«City», «State» «ZIP»
«Order Number»

Figure 17-15
Grouped instructions and instructions with text.

You can position instructions (such as ENDIF) to suppress blank lines, as shown in Figure 17-16. By putting the ENDIF in the salutation, you avoid an extra line if the preceding paragraph doesn't print.

CG Late Complaint Response

response.to.our.book..Since.the.first.of.the.year,.we.have.had.to.
reprint.the.book.three.times,.and.it.looks.like.we'll.be.reprinting.it.
again.later.this.month..Fortunately,.we.have.caught.up.on.our.orders.
and.are.filling.them.within.48.hours.of.receipt.¶
¶
«IF.Late»You.may,.if.you.wish,.cancel.the.order.within.15.days,.and.
we.will.refund.your.remittance..A.postage.paid.envelope.is.included.
for.your.reply.¶
¶
«ENDIF»Sincerely,¶
¶
¶
¶
¶
Anderson.Book.Company¶
¶

Page 1 Normal

Figure 17-16
ENDIF positioned to avoid an extra blank line.

Omitting the Closing Bracket

If you end the instruction with a paragraph mark, you can avoid an extra blank line by omitting the final » symbol. Figure 17-17 shows a mailing-label document without and with the closing » character. Both documents produce the same labels, but the one with the paragraph mark and the closing bracket has an empty line at the top.

```
«DATA Orders¶                      «DATA Orders»¶
«First Name» «Last Name»¶          «First Name» «Last Name»¶
«Company»¶                         «Company»¶
«Address»¶                         «Address»¶
«City», «State» «ZIP»¶             «City», «State» «ZIP»¶
```

Figure 17-17
A mailing-label document without and with the closing bracket.

Hiding Merge Instructions

Because the DATA, SET, and ASK instructions don't appear when the merged documents are printed, you can make them invisible by formatting them as hidden text. As long as you also format the paragraph mark as hidden, it won't cause an extra blank line to appear in the printed document.

You can't format as hidden text the names of fields that you want to have printed in the final documents. If the fields are hidden, the merged text will be, too. You can use this to your advantage if you're using the Print Merge command to create a new document containing the merged form documents and you want to include special notes for each record. The hidden text will be merged into the documents, but unless you specify that hidden text be printed, the printed version of the document won't contain the notes. You can view the notes by opening the document and displaying the hidden text.

Points to Remember

- Word's Print Merge feature lets you create form letters and other items that combine standard text with text that is different for each document. The main document contains the standard text plus special instructions that tell Word when and where to insert the variable text. The data document contains the data to be inserted in the form documents.
- The set of data for a given form document is called a record. Each record ends with a paragraph mark. Records in the data document are divided into fields; each field contains text or data to be inserted at a certain point in the main document. A field can contain a word or even a sentence but cannot contain a paragraph mark. The fields in a record are separated by commas or tab characters. Each record can have up to 127 fields.
- A special record called the header record assigns names to each of the fields in a given data document. The header record can be either at the beginning of the data document or in a separate file.

Techniques

Create a data document

1. Type the header record at the beginning of a new document. Enter the name of each field you'll use, separated by commas or tabs. A field name can have up to 65 characters and can include spaces.
2. Type the data records. Separate the fields with the same character you used in the header record. End each record with only one paragraph mark. If a field contains tabs, commas, or quotation marks, enclose the entire field in quotation marks. To leave a field blank, enter an extra tab or comma.

Create a main document

1. Place the instruction «DATA filename» at the beginning of the document; replace *filename* with the name of the data document. (Press Option-\ to enter the « character; press Shift-Option-\ to enter the » character.)
2. Type the standard text for the form documents.
3. At each point where you want to insert a field from the data document, enter «field name», replacing *field name* with the appropriate name.

❹ If a field is to be inserted on its own line or at the close of a paragraph, omit the final » character to avoid generating an extra blank line.

Merge and print form documents

❶ With the main document open, choose Print Merge from the File menu.

❷ To merge a specific range of records, enter the beginning and ending record numbers in the From and To edit fields.

❸ Click Print.

❹ Choose the appropriate options in the Print dialog box that appears.

❺ Click OK.

Merge form documents into one file

❶ With the main document open, choose Print Merge from the File menu.

❷ To merge a specific range of records, enter the beginning and ending record numbers in the From and To edit fields.

❸ Click New Document. The form documents are placed one after another in a document. They are separated by section marks.

❹ When you are ready to print the form documents, choose Print.

The Print Merge Instructions

You include these instructions in the main document to specify conditions for the printing of text and so forth. Only the DATA instruction is required. You can use any combination of uppercase or lowercase for field names or for instructions, as long as the field names are consistent with each other. The italicized elements are optional.

«ASK field name = ?*prompt*»

Causes Word to present a dialog box requesting text for each form document. It stores the text you enter in the specified field. If you specify a prompt, Word displays it in the dialog box.

«DATA *header document*, data document»

Specifies the data document. If the header and data are in one file, you need only specify the name of that document.

«IF field name » text to insert *«ELSE» text to insert* «ENDIF»

If the specified field contains text, Word inserts the specified text at that point in the document. If you use the ELSE element and the field is empty, Word inserts the text after the ELSE element.

«IF field name = "text string"» text to insert *«ELSE» text to insert* «ENDIF»

Word inserts the text if the contents of the field match the text string enclosed in quotation marks. If you use the ELSE element and the field doesn't match the text string, Word inserts the text after the ELSE element. To include a quotation mark in the text string, enter two quotation marks.

«IF field name = number» text to insert *«ELSE» text to insert* «ENDIF»

Word inserts the text if the contents of the field equal the integer number. If you use the ELSE element and the field isn't equal to the number, Word inserts the text after the ELSE element. Instead of the equal sign, you can use the greater-than (>) or less-than (<) operator.

«INCLUDE document name»

Replaces the INCLUDE instruction with the file named. Omit the » character to avoid an extra paragraph mark. Styles in the main document take precedence over styles of the same name in the included document. An included document can itself contain an INCLUDE instruction, up to 64 levels deep. This instruction doesn't require a DATA instruction at the beginning of the main document.

«NEXT»

Causes Word to jump to the next data record without creating a form document for the current record. Usually used in an IF instruction, in place of text to be inserted.

«SET field name = text»

Specifies the contents of a field to remain constant in every form document.

«SET field name = ?*prompt*»

Displays a dialog box, with an optional prompt, requesting text that Word uses for that field in every form document.

■ *Command*

Command name	Meaning, menu	Standard keyboard	Keypad	Extended keyboard
Print Merge…	Merges specified data records with active main document. **File**			

SECTION 5

Blueprints for Projects

Blueprints

This chapter features sample documents that show you how the various features of Word work together in real situations. The examples are arranged in order of complexity, culminating in a description of some of the elements that went into the preparation of this book.

The first two sample documents are accompanied by a detailed description of the steps taken to construct each element in the design; you can re-create the design exactly or adapt parts of it to your own documents. As the documents progress in complexity, only the trickier parts will be highlighted; otherwise, a complete specification for a newsletter, for example, might take an entire chapter. If a procedure looks unfamiliar, take a moment to review the relevant material in the preceding chapters.

Once you've reproduced or adapted one of these models, be sure to save it in its original state so that you can use it as a template for further alterations. A good way to do this is to add a tag, such as *.template,* to the document's filename; that way you'll know it's the original.

Electronic Letterhead

You can use Word not only to print the text of your letters but to print your letterhead as well. You might want your letterhead to consist of formatted text alone. If so, you'll probably want to use a special font for it—or at least a unique font size or style. Your letterhead can also contain graphics in bit-mapped, object-oriented, or PostScript format or some combination of any of these. Remember that object-oriented and PostScript graphics reproduce better when printed on a PostScript printer such as the LaserWriter.

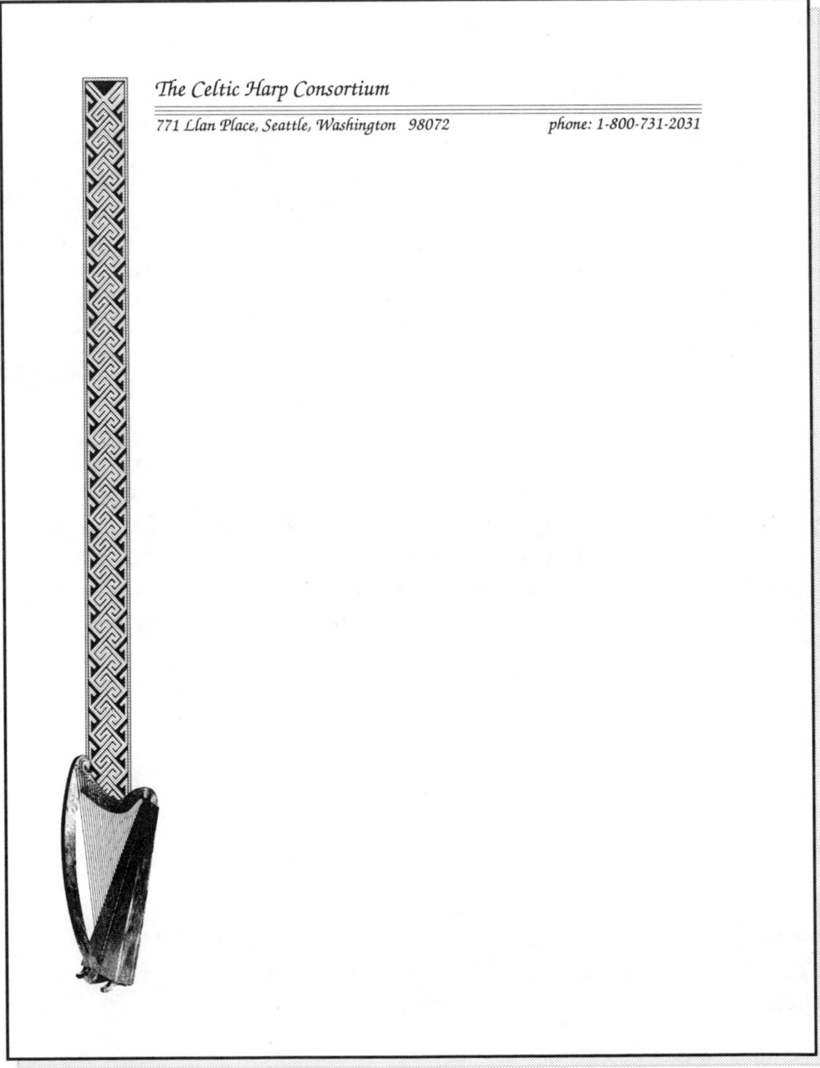

The Celtic Harp Consortium
771 Llan Place, Seattle, Washington 98072
phone: 1-800-731-2031

Figure 18-1
Sample electronic letterhead.

The letterhead shown in Figure 18-1 contains the image of a harp digitized by the MacVision video scanner (running under the control of MoreVision) and then combined with a border pattern in the form of object-oriented graphics (created with Cricket Draw). The combined image was copied from Cricket Draw into Word, and the name and address of the company were added at the top, next to the logo.

Both the graphic and the text are stored in the header of the document, leaving the body of the document blank. Thus, everything shown in the figure is actually the header of an otherwise blank document. Normally, a large header such as this would push the body of the document down below it on the page. To avoid this, set a negative top margin in the Document dialog box. This tells Word that you want the top margin to start at the specified location regardless of the size of the header.

The main reason for setting up the letterhead in this way is so that you can open the document and start typing a letter without having to pay much attention to the formatting of the header. You need only be sure that the left margin and left indent are set far enough to the right to avoid printing over the graphic.

Preparing the Letterhead

The first step is to create the graphic you want to use for your logo. You can, of course, use any program or method you like to get the effect you want; you're not limited to the programs used to create the sample. However, for the purposes of this discussion, it would be best to create a graphic of the same approximate dimensions as those of the example: roughly 1 inch wide and 9 inches tall.

When you're done, select and copy the graphic to the Clipboard and start Word. You'll see the usual blank document window.

Next, paste the graphic into the header of the blank document and add the name and address of the company, following the steps given here. (You could use the footer instead, setting a negative bottom margin rather than a negative top margin, but this project uses the header.)

❶ Choose Open Header from the Document menu, and then choose the Paste command. The insertion point should be blinking at the right edge of the pasted graphic in the Header window.

❷ Display the Ruler, if it isn't already visible. Press the Shift key and click the left arrow in the horizontal scroll bar twice to shift the Ruler and the graphic to the right in the Header window.

❸ Drag the left indent for the graphic to the left to place it 1.25 inches left of the left margin for the body of the document.

After you paste the graphic into the header, the next steps are to add the company's name and address and to format the text appropriately.

❶ The insertion point should still be at the right edge of the graphic. Press the Return key once to start a new line, and reset the line's left indent to the left margin (the 0 point on the Ruler).

❷ Enter the following text. Press the Return key where you see the ¶ mark and press the Tab key where you see the ➧ mark.

The Celtic Harp Consortium¶
¶
¶
¶
771 Llan Place, Seattle, Washington 98072➧ ➧phone: 1-800-731-2031¶

❸ Select the line containing the name of the company, and set the font to 18-point Zapf Chancery (or any other font you like).

❹ Select the line containing the address, and set it to 14-point Zapf Chancery. Notice that this line is still in the *Header* style, so the two tabs move the phone number past the center-aligned tab stop to the right-aligned tab stop at the right margin.

❺ To add the three rules below the company's name, select the three lines separating the company's name and address. Next, choose the Paragraph command, and enter *-3pt* in the Line Spacing edit field. Click the Borders button and, in the Borders dialog box, select the Hairline line weight and click on the middle and bottom horizontal boundaries of the paragraph schematic. Click OK to dismiss the Borders dialog box, and click OK again to dismiss the Paragraph dialog box.

❻ Select everything in the Header window. To do this, press the Command key and click in the selection bar, or press Option-Command-M. Next, choose the Commands command. Select the Side-by-Side command, and click the Do button. If you want, you can also add the Side-by-Side command to the Format menu and choose the new menu command instead of using the Commands command.

Because the left indent of the company's name and address is to the right of the left indent of the paragraph containing the graphic, the address aligns with the top of the graphic. The final step is to position both the letterhead and the body of the document on the page.

❶ Close the Header window, and then choose the Document command. Enter *-1.5* in the Top Margin field and enter *1.5* in the Left Margin field. Click OK, and close the Header window.

❷ Choose the Section command, and position the header vertically on the page by entering *1* in the From Top field.

Of course, if you're using a graphic with different dimensions, you'll have to experiment with these specifications until everything is arranged in the way you want it. You can use Print Preview to check the positions of the different elements.

Instead of using the Side-by-Side paragraph format to arrange both the graphic and the text containing the company's name, you could have placed them at absolute locations on the page with the Position format. This method has one advantage; you can move the objects around by dragging them in Print Preview, rather than through setting indents and specifying the header position in the Section dialog box. However, with the Position format, the text in the body of the document wraps around the graphic and letterhead, even though it's in the header. As discussed in Chapter 9, "Paragraph Formatting," one benefit of the Side-by-Side format is that it lets you overlay elements on the page, rather than wrapping them around each other.

Tips and Techniques

It's a good idea to keep the letterhead in a template file. When you need to create a letter, open the template and immediately save the document under a new name. You can then type the letter and print it or save it as you want. To avoid accidentally editing the template letterhead, you can lock the file. To do this, quit Word, select the file, and choose Get Info from the File menu. Click the Locked field in the Get Info box.

To prevent the letterhead from appearing on the second and subsequent pages, click the First Page Special option in the Section dialog box. Or you could create a variation of the letterhead to use on the subsequent pages.

The time required to print a letter on electronic letterhead stock varies with the complexity of the graphic you create. Graphics composed solely of QuickDraw objects require the least amount of time to print, whereas graphics containing PostScript or compressed bit-mapped images require considerably longer to print.

To avoid lengthy printing times, you can print many copies of the letterhead as blank stock, without any body text, and then later enter the body of the document into a blank window for printing on the letterhead stock. This is also more convenient if you have infrequent access to a LaserWriter or other PostScript printer and you would prefer the higher printing quality for the letterhead. If you use a letterhead like the one laid out in this blueprint, be sure to adjust the top and left margins of the document accordingly, to avoid printing over the design elements.

Reply Memo

With a reply memo like the one shown in Figure 18-2, you can quickly prepare memos for distribution to clients, customers, associates, and business prospects. It contains an area that the recipient can use, if necessary, to respond to the message.

Memo

From:
To:
Date:
Subject:

Reply Please respond ☐ No response needed ☐ Please telephone ☐

Date:

Figure 18-2
Sample reply memo.

The reply memo is divided into four areas:

- ❑ A heading, composed of the memo title and four spaces for the sender's name, the name of the recipient, the date, and the subject of the message.
- ❑ An area for the message.
- ❑ Another heading for the reply, with instructions for the recipient.
- ❑ An area for the reply.

In addition to the areas in the memo proper, the entire page has been surrounded with a box, entered into the Header window so that it overlaps the body of the memo. Now let's construct the document.

Building the Memo Form

The first step is to choose New from the File menu. Choose the Document command and set the page margins to 1 inch on all sides. Enter a minus sign (hyphen) in front of the Top margin measurement to overlap the contents of the Header window with the body of the document. Click OK. Then select a standard font and font size for the blank document, as follows:

❶ Choose the Define Styles command, and select the *Normal* style.

❷ Choose a font—Bookman, for example, and the 12-point font size. In the Define Styles dialog box, click Define and then Cancel.

Next, type the following text. (Don't enter the line numbers; they're for reference purposes only.) Where you see the ¶ mark, press the Return key; where you see the ➧ mark, press the Tab key.

```
Memo¶
¶
 ➧ From:¶
 ➧ To:¶
 ➧ Date:¶
 ➧ Subject:¶
¶
¶
¶
¶
¶
¶
¶
¶
¶
¶
¶
¶
¶
¶
```

```
21 Reply ➧ Please respond ➧ No response needed ➧ Please telephone¶
22 ¶
23  ➧ Date:¶
24 ¶
25 ¶
26 ¶
27 ¶
28 ¶
29 ¶
30 ¶
31 ¶
32 ¶
33 ¶
34 ¶
35 ¶
36 ¶
37 ¶
38 ¶
39 ¶
```

Next, format the header and the first few lines of the memo sheet:

❶ Select the first line by clicking in the selection bar to the left of the word *Memo*.

❷ Choose the Character command, change the font size to 24 points, and click the Italic option from the Character Formats group. Click OK.

❸ Choose the Paragraph command, and click the Borders button. In the Paragraph Borders dialog box, select the double line type and click the bottom horizontal boundary in the schematic. Click OK to dismiss the Borders dialog box, and click OK again to dismiss the Paragraph dialog box.

❹ Select lines 3 through 6 (the *From* through *Subject* lines).

❺ Choose Show Ruler from the Format menu, click the Right-aligned tab-stop icon (the third from the left), and drag a tab marker to 0.75 inch from the left margin. If you entered tab markers at the beginning of each of these lines as shown, each word is now right aligned at 0.75 inch.

Leave the second area unchanged. You can enter the message when you actually type a memo (or, as with the electronic letterhead, you can print many copies or take the form to a printer for offset printing). Next, format the Reply heading:

❶ Double-click on *Reply* to select it, and then press Shift-Command-> three times to increase its size to 24 points. Choose Italic from the Format menu.

❷ Add a double border as in ❸ above.

❸ Place the insertion point immediately after *Please respond*, and press the Spacebar once to add a space.

❹ Choose Insert Graphics from the Document menu. Select the resulting graphics frame by clicking on it, and choose Outline from the Format menu to create a resizable box. The graphics frame appears as a 1-inch-square box. Drag the right and bottom handles in the graphics frame until the box is 0.25 inch square.

❺ While the box is selected, copy it to the Clipboard. Place the insertion point after *No response needed*, press the Spacebar once, and paste in the box. Paste another box after *Please telephone*.

❻ Select the phrase *Please respond*, and choose Character from the Format menu. Change the font size to 10 points. Click the Superscript option, and enter *5pt* in the By field. This raises the phrase so that it's centered vertically with respect to the box. Repeat this for the phrases *No response needed* and *Please telephone*.

❼ To format line 23, which contains the reply date, select line 5, copy it, select line 23, and paste in the copied line, replacing the original.

The lines for the reply are simply a series of empty paragraphs having one hairline border between each pair of paragraphs and one border below the last paragraph:

❶ Select lines 23 through 39, choose the Paragraph command, and click the Borders button. The Paragraph Borders dialog box appears.

❷ Select the hairline line weight, and click the middle and bottom horizontal boundaries. Click OK to dismiss the Borders dialog box and OK again to dismiss the Paragraph dialog box.

All that remains is to add the box surrounding the text of the memo and then adjust the page dimensions so that the elements on the page are positioned correctly.

❶ Choose Open Header from the Document menu. If the Ruler isn't visible at the top of the Header window, choose the Show Ruler command.

❷ Choose the Insert Graphics command to insert an empty graphics frame. Select the frame and give it both the Outline and Shadow character attributes. Drag the frame out to 7.5 inches wide and 10 inches tall. (The current position appears in the status box when you drag a handle.) Unless your Mac has a large screen, you'll have to alternate between dragging the graphics frame and shifting the document by clicking the horizontal and vertical scroll arrows.

❸ Press the Shift key and click the left scroll arrow to shift the document ½ inch to the right until you can see the first ½ inch past the left margin in the Ruler. You need to do this before you can move the left edge of the graphics frame to the left of the left margin. If the graphics frame isn't selected, click in it to select it, and then drag the left indent marker in the Ruler to the left until it's ½ inch beyond the left margin. Click the Header window's close box.

Now you have the finished memo form. Be sure to save this form with a name that reflects its use, such as *Memo Form Template*. To avoid accidentally editing and resaving the template, lock the document from the Finder's desktop. (Use the Get Info box and click the locked check box.) Word won't let you alter a locked file.

Although the steps for constructing this document have been presented as though it was clear from the beginning how to get the desired result, in practice it's necessary to experiment and make many adjustments as you refine the design for a document.

Often, you can achieve a certain effect in many ways. For example, instead of using a graphics frame in the header, you could create a box of the proper dimensions in MacDraw and paste it into the Header window. The advantages of this approach include being able to create boxes with rounded corners and in patterns and different densities of gray. You could also create the entire form as a cell table, adding borders to cells instead of paragraphs. One advantage to this is that you can enter a "negative" Minimum Row Height in the Cells dialog box (chosen from the Format menu) to create a form that retains its structure regardless of the amount of text entered into cells. (See Chapter 11, "Formatting Tables and Lists," for more details on using cell tables to create forms.)

Using the Memo Form

To use the memo form, open the document and save it under a new name that describes the memo you want to write, such as *Memo to Clients, 900823.* Fill in the information at the top of the memo (From, To, Date, and Subject). You can easily enter text at these points by clicking immediately following the word *Date:*, for example, pressing the Tab key once to move to the next tab stop, and entering the current date. Because the next tab stop is a default left-aligned tab stop, the field names and the text you enter will stay correctly aligned. If you want, change the character format for the information you enter to distinguish it from the form itself.

To enter the message, type it in the sender's message area. Keep the message short, or the memo might spill onto a second page. If necessary, you can adjust the lengths of the message and reply areas by deleting lines or copying and pasting lines within the appropriate area. Save the completed memo if you want to keep a record of it.

Calculated Invoice

The blueprint provided in this section is an invoice template designed to let you enter the items and then have Word calculate the extended prices, subtotal, tax, and grand total for you. We'll use Word's cell table format to construct most of the form. Figure 18-3 shows a blank invoice, and a completed one is shown in Figure 18-4 on the following page.

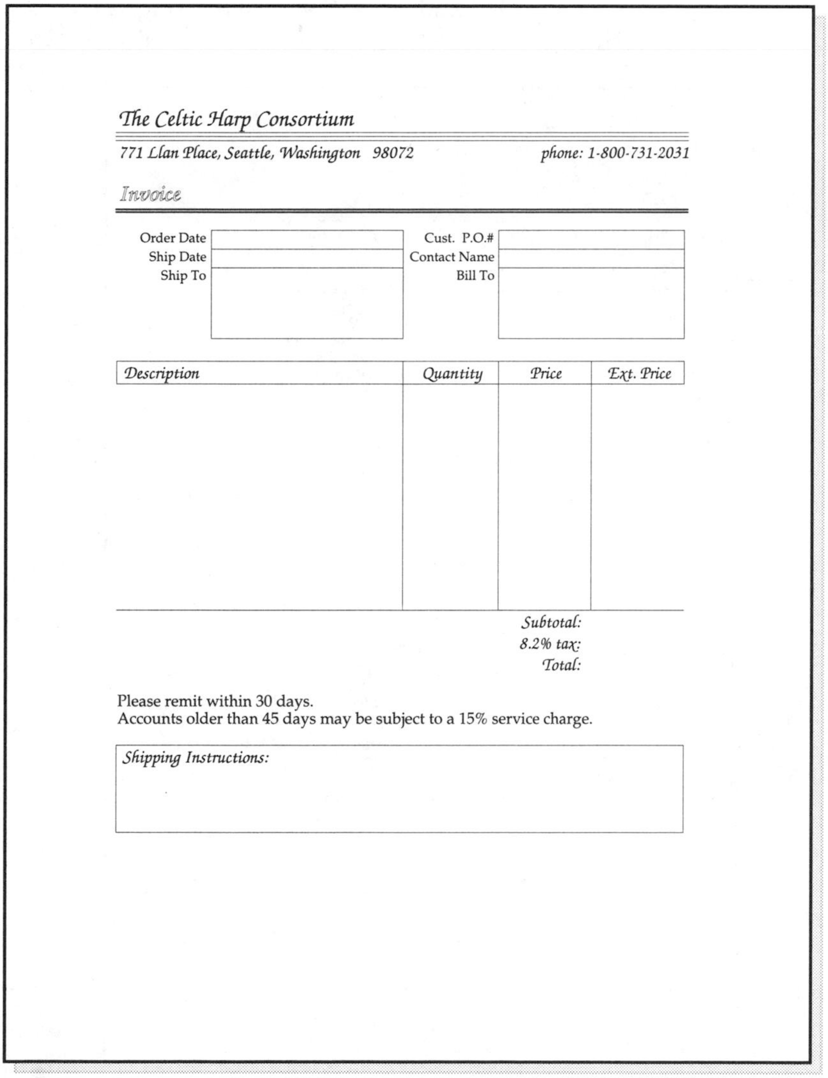

The Celtic Harp Consortium

771 Llan Place, Seattle, Washington 98072 *phone: 1-800-731-2031*

Invoice

Order Date		Cust. P.O.#	
Ship Date		Contact Name	
Ship To		Bill To	

Description	*Quantity*	*Price*	*Ext. Price*

Subtotal:
8.2% tax:
Total:

Please remit within 30 days.
Accounts older than 45 days may be subject to a 15% service charge.

Shipping Instructions:

Figure 18-3
Sample blank invoice.

Setting Up the Invoice

Instead of giving exhaustive directions for reproducing this template, we'll describe only the main features; use these as a starting point for your own invoice form. It's a good idea to set the margins at this point so that indents and column widths in the cell table have the correct dimensions. Choose the Document command and set 1-inch margins at the top and bottom of the page and 1.25-inch margins on the left and right. If you're printing to the LaserWriter, this leaves 6 inches between the margins for the invoice.

The Celtic Harp Consortium

771 Llan Place, Seattle, Washington 98072 *phone: 1-800-731-2031*

Invoice

Order Date	**3 Mar 1990**	Cust. P.O.#	**A1917**
Ship Date	**5 Mar 1990**	Contact Name	**George MacDonald**
Ship To	**Mr. & Mrs. Griffith 901 St. Cadfan's Way Chicago, IL 90823**	Bill To	**MacDonald's Music 728 Tywyn Lane Chicago, IL 90823**

Description	*Quantity*	*Price*	*Ext. Price*
Tara (Irish)	2	968.00	1936.00
Glensong (Scottish Clairseach)	3	1,264.00	3,792.00
Myrddin (Welsh 3-string)	12	1,350.00	16,200.00
		Subtotal:	21,928.00
		8.2% tax:	1,798.096
		Total:	23,726.096

Please remit within 30 days.
Accounts older than 45 days may be subject to a 15% service charge.

Shipping Instructions:

Send by Scotty's Transport Trucking

Figure 18-4
A completed invoice.

You can copy the title of the invoice from the electronic letterhead template described earlier. Or you can start over and enter the name of the company and the address and put it all in the Zapf Chancery font: use 18-point for the name and 14-point for the address. Use a right-aligned tab stop to position the phone number.

The three horizontal rules beneath the name of the company are actually two paragraphs with horizontal borders above, between, and below. To create the lines, do the following:

1. Press the Return key two times, select both empty lines, and choose the Paragraph command. Enter *-2pt* in the Line Spacing field to bring the lines close together.
2. Click the Borders button, select the hairline border type, and click at the top, middle, and bottom boundaries in the schematic. (After this, we'll assume that you've added both the Paragraph Borders and the Cell Borders commands to the Format menu through the Commands dialog box.) You could also use a tab stop with an underscore tab leader; these sometimes produce cleaner lines.

Skip a line after the address, enter the *Invoice* label in 18-point outline type, and add a double border line below the paragraph containing the label.

To set up the area for entering the order date, the shipping date, shipping address, and so on, as shown in Figure 18-5 on the following page, we'll use the Table format and format it as follows:

1. Choose the Insert Table command, and insert a table of 3 rows and 4 columns. Choose Show ¶ to make both the formatting marks and the table boundaries appear in Galley View.
2. Click the Scale icon at the right end of the Ruler until the table scale appears, as shown in the figure. Set the column boundaries at 1, 3, 4, and 6 inches.
3. Select the second column, and choose the Cell Borders command. Select the hairline border type, and then double-click in the schematic to add borders to every side of the second column. In the same way, add borders to the fourth column.
4. Enter the text shown in the figure in the cells of the first and third columns. Select the first column, and set the font to 10-point Palatino. Select the third column, and choose Format Again from the Edit menu (or press Command-A). Set the Ruler to the Normal scale to activate the alignment icons; select the first column again, and click the flush-right alignment icon in the Ruler. Select the fourth column, and choose Format Again. (If you want, you can also create a style for these labels and apply the style to all the labels at the same time.)

When you're done formatting the table containing the shipping information for the invoice, the document should look something like Figure 18-5.

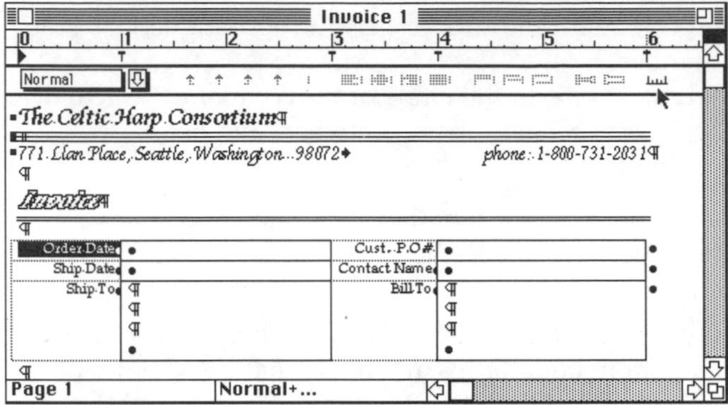

Figure 18-5
The boxed address areas as they appear on screen.

The area in the invoice that lists the items sold is almost as straightforward. This time, we'll insert another table and format it as follows:

❶ After the table containing the shipping information, press Return to skip a line, and choose Insert Table. Insert a table of 17 rows and 4 columns. Leave the Space Between Columns format set to *.111 in.*

❷ Word places half the Space Between Columns format, or approximately 1⁄16 inch, on each side of every column in the table, even to the left of the leftmost column. Because we want to add border formats to the cells in the first column, we should move the entire table 1⁄16 inch to the right, so the borders line up with the left margin. Select the entire table, by holding down the Option key while double-clicking anywhere in the table. With the Ruler set to the Table scale, drag the left indent marker to 1⁄16 inch. Also, set the column boundaries at 3, 4, 5, and 6 inches.

❸ In the cells of the first row, enter the table headings shown in Figure 18-6. In the last three cells of the third row, enter the labels for the subtotal, the tax, and the grand total, as shown in the figure.

❹ Select the first row, and format the table headings in 14-point bold Zapf Chancery. Choose the Cell Borders command, select the hairline border type, and double-click the schematic to add borders around every cell. Notice that the cell borders line up with the 0 point in the Ruler because we've indented the table 1⁄16 inch.

❺ Select the second, third, and fourth cells of the first row. In the Ruler, switch to the Normal scale, and click the Centered alignment icon.

❻ Format the cells containing the labels for the totals in the same way you did the table headings (14-point bold Zapf Chancery), but use flush-right paragraph alignment instead.

❼ Add a rule between the row containing the labels for the totals and the list proper. Select the third row from the bottom, and choose the Cell Borders command. Select the hairline border type, and click the top horizontal cell boundary in the schematic.

❽ Select the following range of cells in the area containing the listed items: from the second row to the fourth row from the bottom in columns 2, 3, and 4. Set the Ruler to the Normal scale, and place a decimal tab marker between the indents at 0.5 inch. When you do this, all the end-of-cell markers in the selected range jump to that position. To enter numbers in the table, you don't need to press the Tab key; simply clicking in a cell places the insertion point at the position of the decimal tab. (The decimal tab stop is the only tab stop that does this.) With the range still selected, choose the Cell Borders command, and select the hairline border type and the Every Cell In Selection option; the schematic changes to one displaying one cell. Click on the left cell boundary, and click OK.

At this point, the body of the invoice should look similar to Figure 18-6; if you've used other fonts, or added other borders, your results might be different.

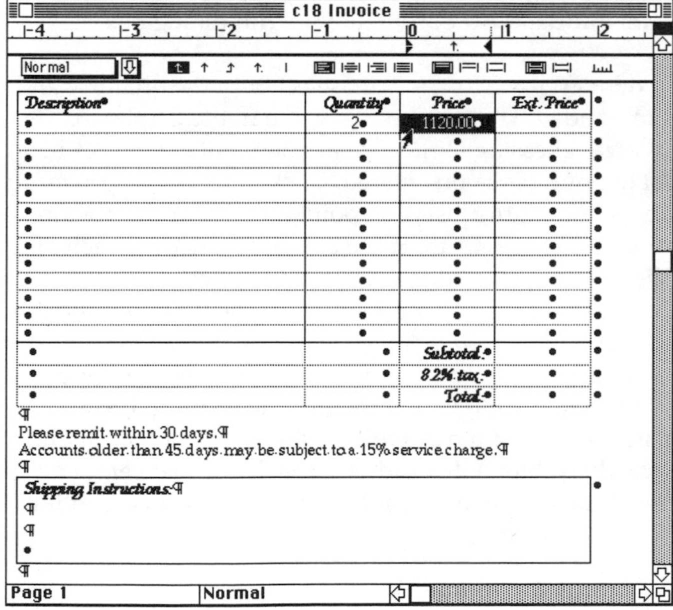

Figure 18-6
The lower portion of the invoice.

To finish the invoice, add the two lines citing the payment instructions in 12-point Palatino, as shown in Figure 18-6. The box that contains the shipping instructions is actually a one-cell table; you could create a similar border by using the Paragraph Border command, but here it's easier to simply copy the first cell of the first row and paste it at the end of the document. Set the Ruler to the Table scale, and then drag the right column boundary out to the right margin. Finally, change the text *Description* to *Shipping Instructions,* and press Return a few times to leave room for the instructions.

Using the Invoice

To use the invoice, enter the appropriate text in the cells to the right of the labels for the order date, the customer's purchase order number, and so on.

Next, enter the description, quantity, and price for each item on the invoice. If you need more lines, click in a row, choose Table from the Edit menu, and click the Insert button. If the list gets too long, however, you might need to extend the table to the next page by copying the row containing the headings and pasting it at the top of the next page.

You calculate the extended price by multiplying the quantity by the price, so when you enter the price, precede it with an asterisk and give the asterisk the Hidden character format. Word requires that hidden text be visible when you do calculations, but after the calculations are finished you can hide the text. Remember that Word won't print hidden text unless you tell it to, even if it's showing on the screen. To be sure that hidden text won't print, check that the Print Hidden Text option (in the Print dialog box) is turned off.

To determine the extended price for an item, select both the quantity and the price and press Command- =. Word stores the value in the Clipboard and displays it in the status area, guessing at the format you want for the result based on the formats of the numbers you entered. Click in the appropriate cell in the extended-price column; the insertion point appears at the position of the decimal tab stop. Continue to calculate the extended price for each of the other items in the list. When you're done, remove the asterisks if you want. (If you want, you could create a glossary entry for the hidden asterisk and give it a name such as *mul* for *multiplication.*)

To arrive at the subtotal, select only the numbers in the extended price column by dragging over the appropriate numbers in the column. Press Command- = to calculate the sum of the extended prices, and then paste the number in the cell for the the subtotal. Instead of using Zapf Chancery, you might want to format the totals in a more legible font. Palatino was used for the example in Figure 18-7.

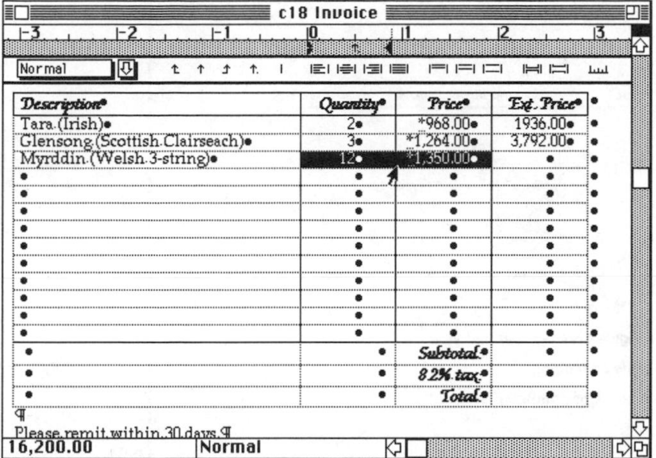

Figure 18-7
Calculating an extended price.

The invoice is also set up to calculate sales tax. The sales-tax percentage is included in the label for the tax line: *8.2% tax*. If you insert a hidden asterisk before this label, select the tax and subtotal lines, and press Command-=, Word calculates the percentage for you and puts the result in the Clipboard. Word understands the percent sign at the end of the tax rate; note also that you can "bury" a value in text instead of putting it in a column by itself. Paste the result after the label in the tax line, and format it as needed.

Calculate the grand total by selecting the cells containing the subtotal and the tax and then pressing Command-=. Paste the result into the *Total* line.

Tips and Techniques

Word ignores such symbols as $ and ¢, so even if you have them in the *Price* and *Ext. Price* columns, they won't be included in the result. If you want the symbols to appear in the result, you must type them yourself.

With Word's calculator, the value with the most decimal places determines the number of decimal places in the result, so some of your invoices might not be fully accurate unless the numbers in your calculations have enough decimal places. Applying the percent sign implies two decimal places in the result. For example, *75.90 * 6%* yields 4.55. On a floating-point calculator, the value is shown more accurately as *4.554*. Typing *75.900 * 6%* produces the correct result.

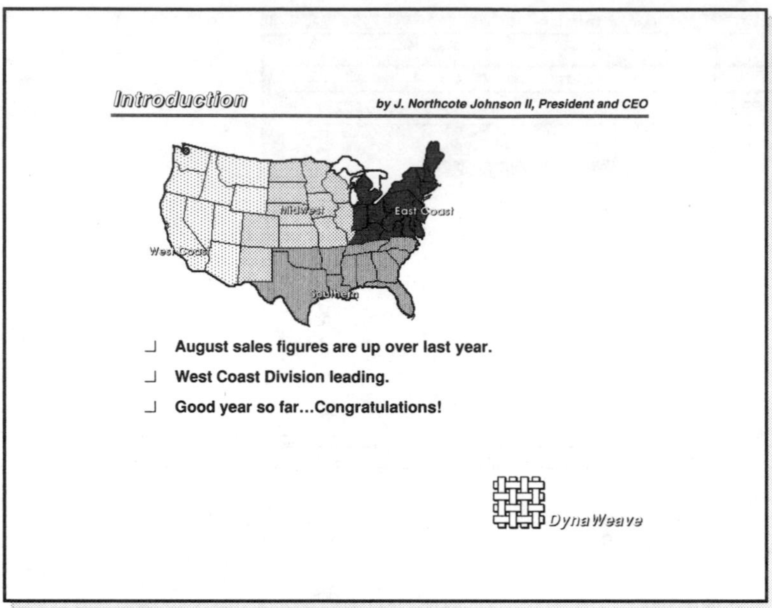

Figure 18-8a
First page of the presentation outline.

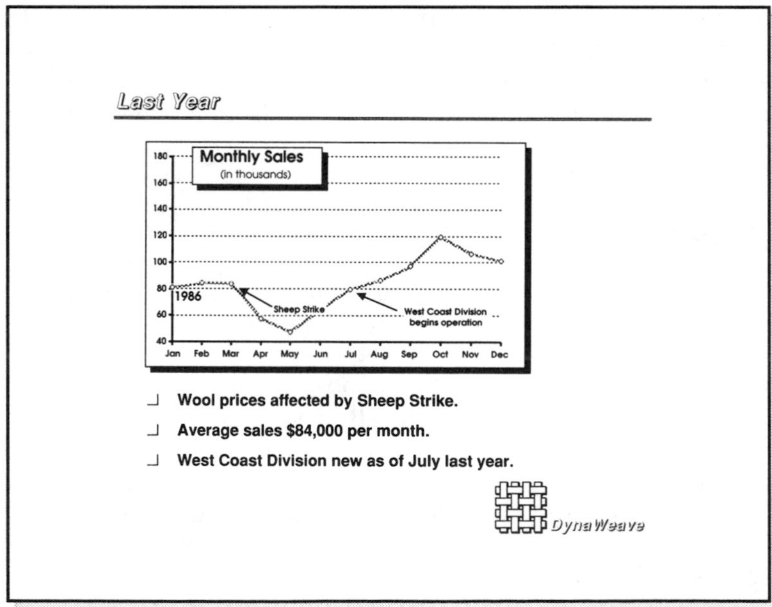

Figure 18-8b
Second page of the presentation outline.

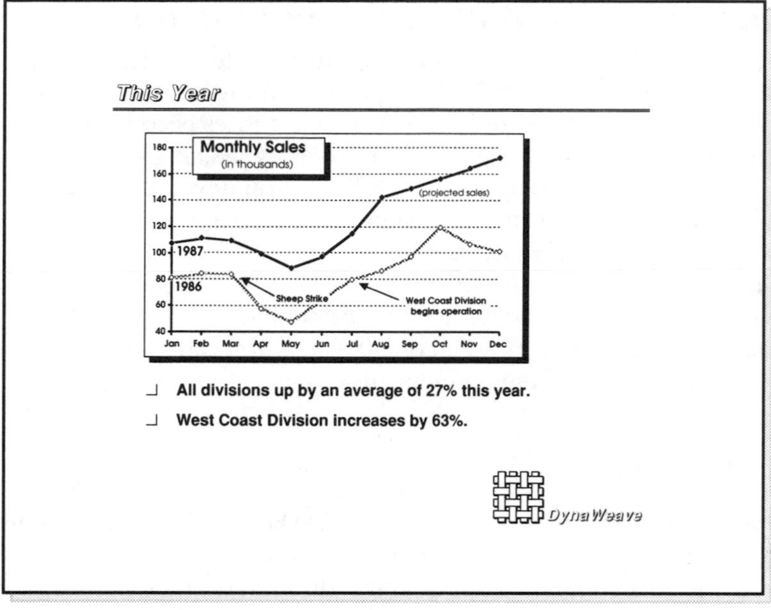

Figure 18-8c
Third page of the presentation outline.

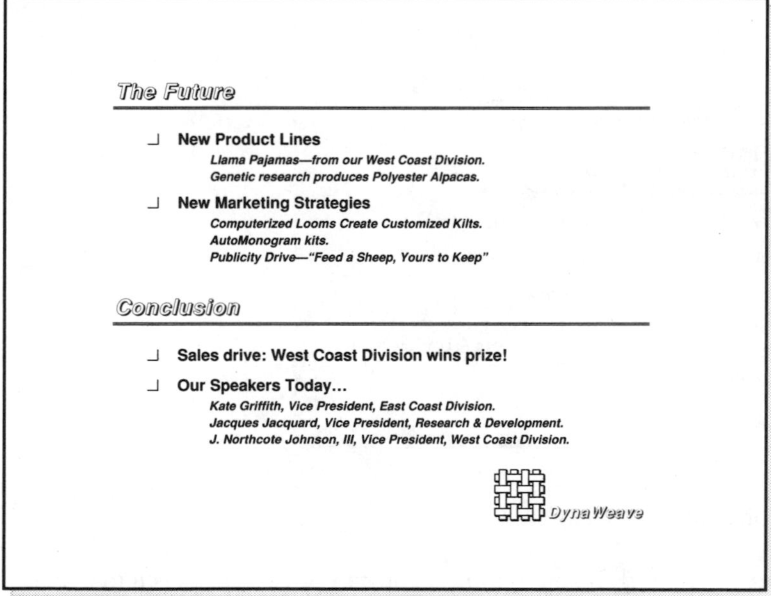

Figure 18-8d
Fourth page of the presentation outline.

■ *Presentation Graphics from an Outline*

You can use Word's outliner to order your thoughts by entering items in Outline View and then switching to Galley View to add the body of the text. When you switch to Galley View, all the *heading* style entries become headings in the document. You might later turn some of these *heading* style entries back into text in the *Normal* style or another style. As you develop the document, you can adjust the formats for the headings that remain by redefining their styles through the Define Styles dialog box.

This isn't, of course, the only way you can use Word's outliner. In this project, we've turned an outline prepared for a presentation into a set of transparencies to be used for the presentation itself, as you can see in Figures 18-8a through 18-8d on the previous two pages.

Preparing the Outline

This set of presentation transparencies had a humble beginning as the outline shown in Figure 18-9. Each topic in the speech has a level in the outline and is assigned one of the *heading* styles, from *heading 1* through *heading 3*.

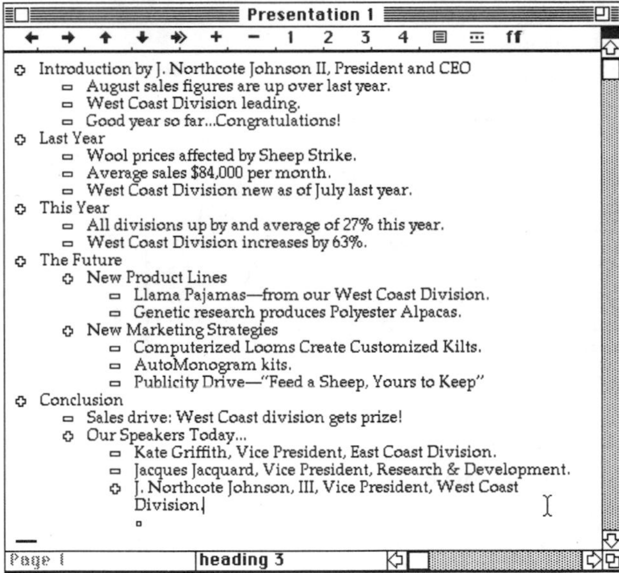

Figure 18-9
The outline of the speech in Outline View.

After you've entered the main topics, you can write the speech in Galley View. When you switch to Galley View, the outline should look something like Figure 18-10, depending on how you've customized your default style sheet.

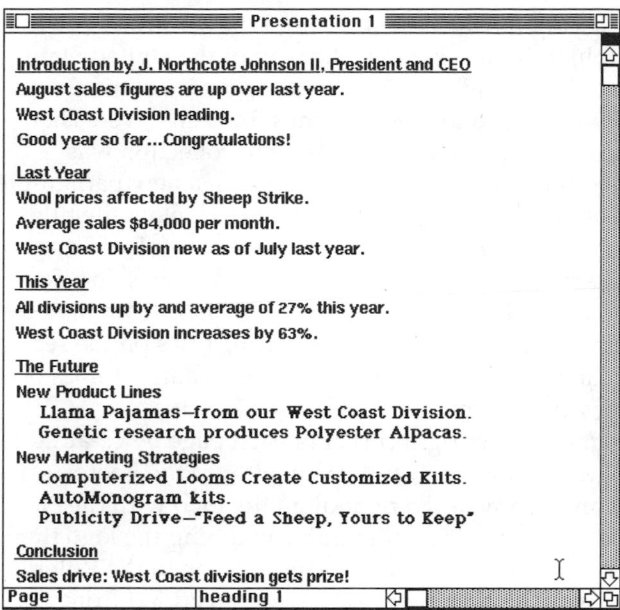

Figure 18-10
The outline of the speech in Galley View.

The next step is to transform this outline into a set of "screens," or pages, with each major topic on its own page. Start by choosing the Wide orientation option in the Page Setup dialog box so that the arrangement of the page looks more like a slide. Then redefine the styles for the document according to this table:

Style Name	Definition
footer	Normal + Tab stops: 3 in. Centered; 6 in. Right Flush
heading 1	Normal + Font: Helvetica 24 Point, Bold Italic Outline Shadow, Space After 12 pt., Page Break Before, Border: Bottom (Double)
heading 2	Normal + Font: Helvetica 18 Point, Bold, Indent: Left 0.5 in., Space Before 12 pt.
heading 3	Normal + Font: Helvetica 14 Point, Bold Italic, Indent: Left 1 in., Space Before 4 pt., Keep With Next

As the table shows, each of the major topics—those in the *heading 1* style—starts a new page and thus constitutes the title at the top of each slide. Each slide title has a double-line border beneath it to set off the title from the points to be covered in the slide. Also, each level of topic is indented ½ inch to the right of the one before it in the standard outline format.

After you finish redesigning the document through the style sheet, the next step is to add the graphics. In the example, the map of the United States is a bit-mapped image first altered in SuperPaint's paint layer to show the various sales regions and then copied to the program's drawing layer. Then the labels were superimposed on the map as text, and the collection was selected, copied, and pasted into the presentation outline, in a new paragraph inserted between the title on the first page and the first topic below the title.

The sales statistics were prepared first as a table in Microsoft Excel and then converted into two charts showing the company's growth in sales. To transfer the charts into the Word document, choose Copy Chart from the Edit menu, and then paste them into new paragraphs below the titles on the second and third pages. To make the graphics align with the *heading 2* topics on the page, select the graphics and assign them the *heading 2* style.

You can add the logo in the lower right corner of each page by creating the logo in a graphics program, copying it, and pasting it into the Footer window for the presentation document. To right-align the logo with the bar underneath the title on the page, give the paragraph containing the logo the Flush Right paragraph format by clicking the appropriate icon in the Ruler.

The name of the company, *DynaWeave*, could have been added from within the graphics program. However, Word does a better job of kerning the letters in the name (manually or by using the Fractional Widths option in the Print dialog box, or both), so we added the name in Word. To position the company's name, put the insertion point at the right edge of the logo, press the Spacebar twice, and then type the name. Format the name in 18-point Helvetica, shadow, and italic, and raise it 3 points (by giving it a superscript character format) to align it with the logo.

As you can see in Figure 18-8d, there are two *heading 1* titles on the screen. The *heading 1* style has the Page Break Before format, so we simply called up the Paragraph dialog box and removed the format to put both the topics in the same screen of the presentation.

Tips and Techniques

Generally, you would develop the presentation with a more comprehensive set of notes than was detailed in this example. A good way to go about this is to continue developing the outline, adding the charts and the body text for your speech, without redefining the styles. When everything is to your liking, print a copy of the presentation for you to use; the headings in your copy of the document will match those in the slides you'll use as visual aids.

After you've printed your copy of the document, format your comments under each topic as hidden text and turn off the Show Hidden Text option in the Preferences dialog box. Now that your part of the presentation is hidden, continue converting the document into the actual images you want the audience to see in the presentation.

Another way to achieve the same effect is to develop the full text for your presentation from the outline and then to use the Table of Contents command to extract the headings from your speech. Then, instead of redefining the *heading* styles, redefine the *toc* styles. This method has the advantage of separating the styles for your part in the presentation and those for the visual aids. You can even print both the slides and your speech from the same document.

■ *Screenplay Format*

Movie studios and producers expect screenplays to be in a specific format. Thanks to style sheets, Word is ideally suited for preparing scripts in this format. The example shown in Figures 18-11a and 18-11b on the following two pages is a simplified version of a Hollywood-format screenplay.

Setting Up the Screenplay

The sample screenplay uses automatic line numbering, so first choose Section from the Format menu, select the Line Numbering and Continuous options, and click OK. Next, choose the Document command. The screenplay uses standard 8½-by-11-inch paper with 1-inch margins on all sides except for the left, which uses a 1½-inch margin to accommodate the binding.

Six styles other than *Normal* are needed for the basic script format; all are based on the *Normal* style. This allows you to change the font for all the other styles simply by redefining the *Normal* style, even though *Normal*-style text isn't used anywhere in the document. The following table lists the styles used in the screenplay. The definitions in the table are precisely as Word lists them when you choose Print while the Define Styles dialog box is on screen, except that we have added periods after *pt* and *in* to enhance readability.

Style Name	Next Style	Definition
action,ax	*action,ax*	Normal + Space Before 9 pt., Not Line Numbering
actor,x	*dialogue,d*	Normal + Bold Caps, Centered, Space Before 12 pt., Keep With Next, Not Line Numbering
camera,c	*action,ax*	Normal + Bold Caps, Space Before 14 pt., Keep With Next
dialogue,d	*actor,x*	Normal + Indent: Left 1.25 in. Right 1.25 in., Not Line Numbering, Tab stops: 2 in.
footer	*footer*	Normal + Bold, Border: Top (Double), Tab stops: 3 in. Centered; 6 in. Right Flush
line number	*Normal*	Normal + Bold
Normal	*Normal*	Font: Palatino 12 pt., Flush left

1 **EXT. DARK STREETS—NIGHT**

SEVERAL SHOTS. Rex and Nixie are running down some streets. At first, only the SOUNDS of their FOOTSTEPS are heard. Gradually, SOUNDS of POLICE SIRENS can be heard approaching from the distance.

2 **STREET CORNER—NIGHT**

They spot a cab, its lights on and motor running. They jump in.

3 **INT. CAB—NIGHT**

Relieved, out of breath, they lean back, exhausted.

REX
(matter of factly)
Gotta go.

CARL
If you gotta go, you gotta go.

He puts the car in gear and they drive off.

NIXIE
We better hurry.

REX
You're following us. You were following us all day. Then you weren't there. Now we're here. How do you explain that?

CARL
(disinterestedly)
Coincidence.

Rex and Nixie sit back and look out the window of the moving cab. Lights reflect off their faces.

4 **INT. LARGE APARTMENT—NIGHT**

The apartment consists of a large loft, offering various possibilities for complex CAMERA SETUPS and a variety of LOCATIONS within the APARTMENT SCENES.

SAILOR, JOJO, SCOTT, and NADIA are gathered around a table on which are a bundle of dynamite sticks, some guns, hand grenades, alarm clocks, spools of wire, etc. They are listening intently to a shortwave radio.

RADIO
(sound of a prize fight)

Five Minutes to Doomsday **5/1/90** **page 1**

Figure 18-11a
First page of sample screenplay.

Notice that the only element in the template that actually uses line numbers is text assigned the *camera* style. All others have had line numbering turned off in the Paragraph dialog box (except for the *footer* style, whose text isn't numbered anyway). This allows you to number and refer to the camera shots in the screenplay without having to use the Renumber command. Also, the Next Style for each style has been set up so that it's easier to shift from one element to the one that logically follows.

One two three four five six seven eight nine ten
you're out.

SCOTT
They've got it backwards. Turn it off.

Jojo changes the station on the shortwave. After some noises, SOUNDS of a DEMONSTRATION are heard.

5 **EXT. INDUSTRIAL LANDSCAPES—DAY**

SEVERAL SHOTS of Rex and Nixie walking through desolate industrial settings: LARGE FACTORIES, AUTO JUNKYARDS, POWER PLANTS, DIRTY ALLEYS, and so on. They are the only ones in the SHOTS.

REX (VOICE OVER)
(whispering)
It all comes together. Each of us carries a stick of dynamite. That does several things. One. It forms a bond. Two. It makes you feel special. Three. It's how we live today. Not only us, but everyone. And it keeps you in touch with reality, the human condition...

NIXIE (VOICE OVER)
(whispering)
Never stop talking. Make words, make sounds. It's the connection between body and head. All you can do is keep track...

They keep walking.

6 **EXT. STREET CAFE—DAY**

A street scene, a sidewalk cafe, tables and EXTRAS sitting at the tables and walking on the sidewalk. In the distance down the street the DYNAWEAVE FACTORY emits columns of white steam. Rex and Nixie sit at a table on the street, nervously glancing down toward the factory.

NIXIE
We are only particles of change, floating in a beam of sunlight. Soon the sunlight fades, the wind moves, and no one sees us.

REX
Lighten up, OK?

In the distance, bursts of black cloud rise up through the steam rising from the factory. Flickers of orange FLAME in the clouds. In the distance, figures of small EXTRAS run from the factory. MUFFLED BOOM. Suddenly SUPERMAN

Five Minutes to Doomsday **5/1/90** **page 2**

Figure 18-11b
Second page of sample screenplay.

This is a simple document; the only step remaining is to add an appropriate footer showing the name of the screenplay, the date, and the page number, as shown in Figure 18-12 on the following page.

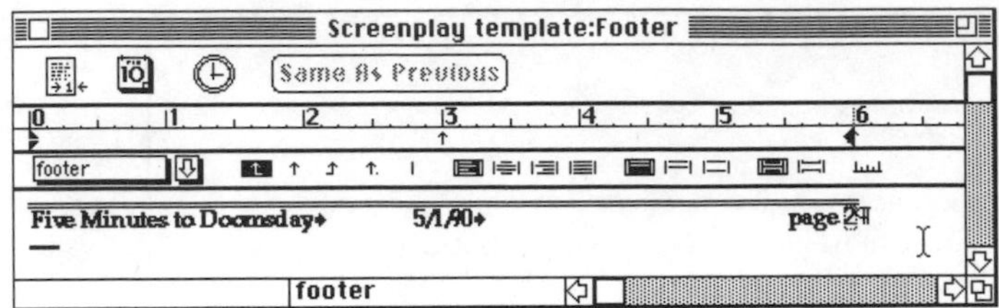

Figure 18-12
The footer for the screenplay format.

Using the Screenplay Format

Save the screenplay style sheet in a document named *Screenplay Template.* Open the document whenever you want to start a new screenplay, but save it immediately under a new name. You might want to lock the template document (call up the Get Info box from the Finder's desktop) so that you don't accidentally modify it.

When you start typing the screenplay, you can use the default *Normal* style for the title and introductory comments, if desired. To enter the first camera shot for the screenplay, press the Return key to begin a new line, and assign it the *camera* style. You can do this by choosing the style name from the Styles drop-down field in the Ruler, in the Styles or Define Styles dialog box, or by pressing Shift-Command-S and typing the name directly from the keyboard. With the latter method, you can type *camera* or the shortcut letter *c.* Then enter the text for the camera location. You don't need to capitalize the text; Word does it for you because the style has the All Caps character format.

When you press the Return key, Word switches to the *action* style, because after a camera shot you might want to describe what is happening in the scene. If you don't want to use the *action* style, choose another style.

When it's time for a character to speak, choose the *actor* style. Again, you don't need to capitalize the character name. When you press the Return key after typing the name, Word assumes that you want to enter dialogue, so it shifts to the *dialogue* style for you. If you need to indicate a manner of speech for the character, press the Tab key once to indent the text, and then press the Return key again to start the dialogue.

Word provides the required spacing between the elements of camera, action, actor, and dialogue; consequently, you usually don't need to add extra blank lines by inserting paragraph marks.

Both the *camera* and *actor* styles use the Keep With Next ¶ paragraph format. This keeps the camera direction and action together and the actor's name and dialogue together; Word won't separate them with a page break. However, if the dialogue or action description is more than two lines long, Word might break the page between the lines.

Multiple-Column Newsletter

Preparing a two-column or three-column document takes more time than preparing a single-column document, but the results are much more striking, especially if the text is printed on a PostScript printer such as the LaserWriter. The sample newsletter described here and depicted in Figures 18-13a and 18-13b on the following page is patterned after a page format in a typical news magazine.

The New Wave Times January, 1990

The Occult

Aliens Attack Writer

"They Came From Nowhere"

EUSTACE PODGRASS

Washington-state writer J. Steven York is visited by aliens from another planet—for the third time in the past six years. The latest visitors, York claims, attacked him and caused him bodily harm. Some UFO watchers believe York is sincere and telling the truth, but a growing number of experts think York is ready for the funny farm.

He sat on the chaise in the back yard and watched a shower of shooting stars descend on the Seattle, Washington twilight. The imagery was breathtaking, and his mind raced to put the image into words. ¶He liked words; all writers do. But few writers have the capacity for words of J. Steven York, three-time Yugoslavian Yugo Award winner for the Best Science Fiction Novel. ¶York rose to fetch a notepad, to jot down his mental image of the meteor shower. He stretched his six-foot-four frame and grabbed at the sheaf of paper resting on the patio table. ¶York began writing, but before he could dot his first i, his eyes were blinded by an intense flash of electric-blue light. He fell to his knees, covering his eyes in burning anguish. ¶Though York was temporarily blinded, he knew something was going on around him— something very big. He could feel heat rushing to his face, as if someone had opened a pizza oven in front of him (and if so, he hoped it would be a large sausage and mushroom, with extra cheese). Air hissed around his ears, and he felt a heavy thump shake the ground. ¶York knew: The aliens had landed. Again.

12

Figure 18-13a
First page of sample newsletter.

York's photograph of the spaceship that wanted to cart him off to another galaxy.

At least that's how J. Steven York, author of 17 best-selling books and three blockbuster movie scripts, claims he was visited by extra-terrestrials. "This time, they wanted more than just directions to the nearest In-N-Out Burger restaurant. They wanted me!"

A day after he was visited by the aliens from Tau Upsilon IV, York held a press conference and told reporters from around the globe that he was asked to accompany the green-faced aliens, but he had to disrobe before he could enter the space ship.

"I knew these guys could melt my brain if they wanted to, so I decided to go along with their request," York said. "But when my neighbor saw me taking my clothes off, she went into laughing hysterics, ran off into the street screaming at the top of her lungs, and finally was struck and killed by a dark green 1959 Bel Air."

At this, the aliens became nervous, York recounted, so they grabbed him with their giant pincher claws, apparently intending to wrestle him inside their intergalactic space ship. "See this?" York exclaimed, rolling up his right shirt sleeve. "I received this gift from their giant claws."

York's arm was completely bandaged, but no injury could be seen.

If York is indeed telling the truth, what did the aliens want from the hulking writer from Dothan, Alabama? Were they, as York insists, taking him back to their home planet for a bold repopulation experiment? And if so, would they give him Coke and peanuts along the way, as they do in airplanes?

"I think this Steven J. York (sic) has flipped," claimed noted parapsychologist Ephraim Schwartz. "I think this whole attack thing exists only in his twisted imagination."

University of Maryland film and literary criticism professor Trent Johansonn, agrees. "J. York Steven (sic) no longer has the ability to separate the worlds of reality and science fiction," Johansonn said after the press conference. Despite the criticism against him, York holds steadfastly to his account.

Shortly after the visitation, U.S. Air Force Colonel F. L. A. Hood investigated the sighting and made tests of the area surrounding the landing site. "Something was there," Hood told reporters, "but I can't be certain beyond doubt that it was a space craft."

York offered an artifact to Hood that he claimed was left by the aliens when they made their hasty retreat, immediately following the automobile death of the next-door neighbor and York's struggle to escape. "It's either an honest-to-goodness alien artifact," Hood said, "or a week-old pizza crust. Our lab is working on it right now. We should have the test results in a week or two."

This is not the first time York has been visited by aliens. His first "close encounter" occurred more than five years ago, in February 1981, while working as a sales clerk for Radio Shack. York claims he was visited by the same aliens two months later. ❍

Figure 18-13b

Second page of sample newsletter.

Preparing the Newsletter

Depending on the size and sophistication of the group publishing a newsletter, the person doing the writing might or might not be the person who transforms the articles into the formatted result. Typically, the people responsible for a newsletter first establish a design and then take articles from writers and format them according to the design specifications to construct each issue. It's best if the writer works on the content of the article first, either leaving the refinement of its appearance until later or letting others do it.

Therefore, we'll assume that a design for this newsletter has already been set up in a template document that contains a style sheet for the various elements. The style sheet that follows is for an article. A complete newsletter would use many more styles, of course, for such items as the table of contents, advertisements, the masthead, and so on. As you tour this document, refer back to this table to find exact specifications for each element.

Style Name	Definition
Byline	Display + Font: 14 Point, Bold Small Caps, Indent: Left 2 in., Space Before 36 pt. After 18 pt., Border: Bottom Between (Single)
Display	Font: Avant Garde 10 Point, Flush left
Drop Cap	Font: Bookman 14 Point, Indent: Left 1.944 in. Justified, Side-by-Side
Fig/caption	Normal + Font: 9 Point, Bold Italic, Space Before 2 pt. After 6 pt., Border: Bottom Between (Single)
Figure	Normal + Outline
First Page	Normal + Font: 14 Point, Indent: Left 2 in., Side-by-Side, Tab stops: 2.819 in.
footer	Normal + Tab stops: 3 in. Centered; 6 in. Right Flush
header	Display + Bold, Line Spacing -14 pt., Space After 2 pt., Border: Top (Single) Bottom (Single 2 pt. Spacing), Tab stops: 6.5 in. Right Flush
Normal	Font: Bookman 10 Point, Justified
Reading Line	Display + Font: 14 Point, Indent: Left 2 in.
Synopsis	Normal + Italic, Indent: Right 4.75 in. Flush left, Side-by-Side
Title	Display + Font: 36 Point, Bold, Indent: Left 2 in., Space Before 2 pt.
Title Bar	Display + Font: 36 Point, Bold Indent: Left 1.944 in. Right -0.5, Space Before 2 pt.

Because the newsletter uses a single-column format for the first page of an article and for figures and a two-column format for the remainder of an article, the design makes extensive use of sections and section formats. The template document contains a set of sample sections; the person composing the document would copy them and replace the text they contain with the actual contents for that part of the article. The sample shown in Figures 18-13a and 18-13b contains three sections: one for all of the first page, one for the graphic at the top of the second page, and one for the two-column text in the body of the article.

The measurements for the design elements in the template document depend on the settings in the Document dialog box. For this article, the following settings were used:

Option	Measurement
Top margin	-1.25 inches
Bottom margin	-1 inch
Left margin	0.75 inch
Right margin	0.75 inch
Even/Odd Headers	Set
Gutter	0.5 inch
Default tab stops	0.25 inch

The minus sign before the top and bottom margin measurements prevents any interaction between the size of the header in a section and the top and bottom margins for a page.

Section One: The First Page

The first page of the article comprises three main areas: the header and footer, the title area for the article, and the first few sentences of the article with the synopsis in the Side-by-Side format.

The Header and Footer

As you might remember, each section in a document can contain a separate header and footer for its odd and even pages (if you set the Even/Odd Headers option in the Document dialog box) and for its first page (if you set the First Page Special option in the Section dialog box). The newsletter uses two headers, one for odd pages and one for even pages. Because inflexible top and bottom margins have been set in the Document dialog box, the From

Top and From Bottom measurements specified in the Section dialog box are placed relative to the edge of the page; adjust these values so that the headers will be 1 inch from the top of the page and the footers will be 0.5 inch from the bottom.

Every sample section in the template document has the same set of odd and even headers, so the person composing the newsletter can assume that the headers will be there until they are explicitly removed (for example, on a page consisting only of one graphic or of advertisements). When you create a new section, its initial formats come from the section after it. Thus, if all or most of the sample sections in the template document use the standard headers, you have to adjust only the headers for pages that are different in some way.

The set of headers used in the article is shown in Figure 18-14. Because the article starts on a left-hand page, it uses the even header. The status area in the Header window indicates that the two lines of the header have the *header* style. You can see by referring to the table containing the style sheet that this style has a Border paragraph format, and the line spacing is set to -14 points so that the text in the header is evenly spaced with respect to the two lines.

Like the headers, the footers for each section consist of odd and even versions, but they contain only one line, which has the Border format.

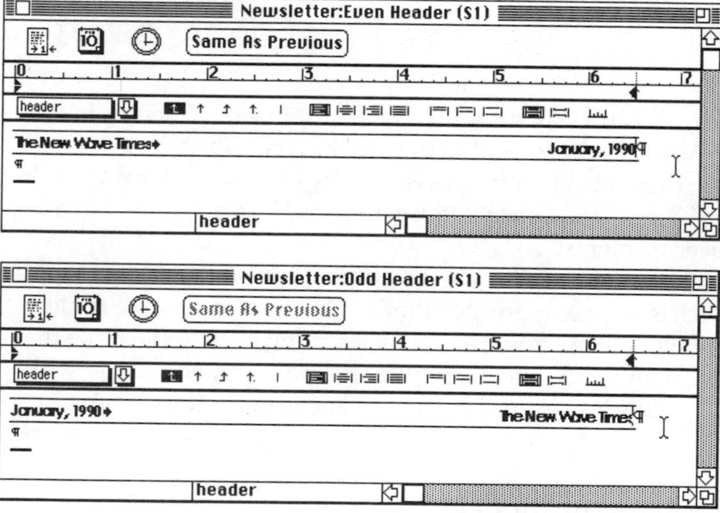

Figure 18-14
The set of odd and even headers for the newsletter.

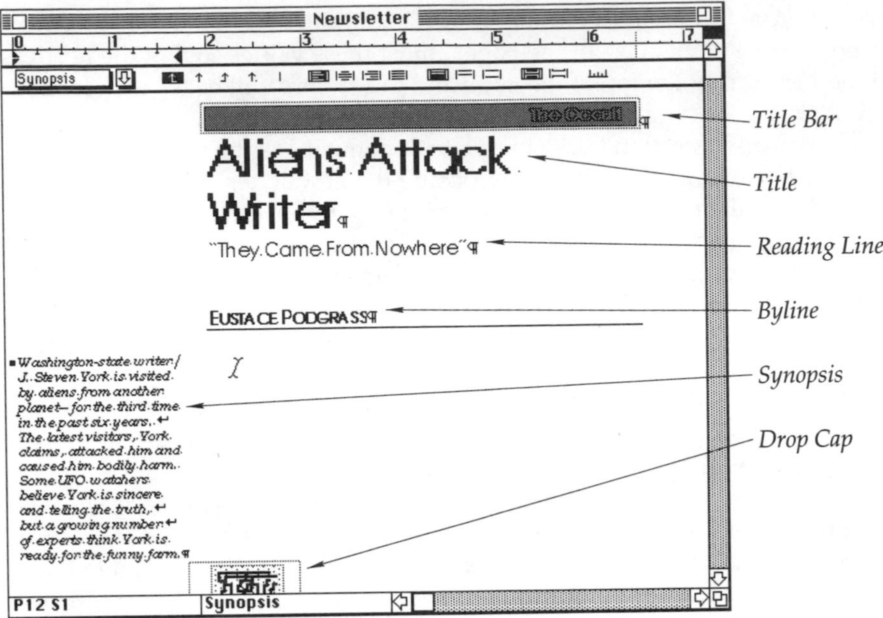

Figure 18-15
The article title in Galley View, and the names of the styles attached to the various elements.

The Title

Creating the title of the article is straightforward; Figure 18-15 shows how it looks in Galley View. Each element in the title has its own style so that all the corresponding elements in other articles will be consistent. Heavy use is made of the Space Before and Space After paragraph formats; there are no blank lines between elements.

Even though the bar above the title is a graphic copied from MacDraw, it has a style, which is used only for positioning the graphic relative to the running head and the title. As you can see by referring back to the table that describes the document's style sheet, the rule under the byline is done with a Border format, and the text for the author's name is in the Small Caps character format.

The Synopsis, Drop Cap, and First-Page Text

The synopsis of the article in the left margin, the drop cap that starts the article, and the decorative treatment for the first-page text are all single paragraphs having the Side-by-Side format. We could have used the Position paragraph format to place the drop cap and the text in the Synopsis, but the Side-by-Side format affords a little more control. It also permits overlapping the text on the first page and the drop cap, as the graphic frame surrounding the drop cap indicates. Figure 18-16 shows how they look on screen.

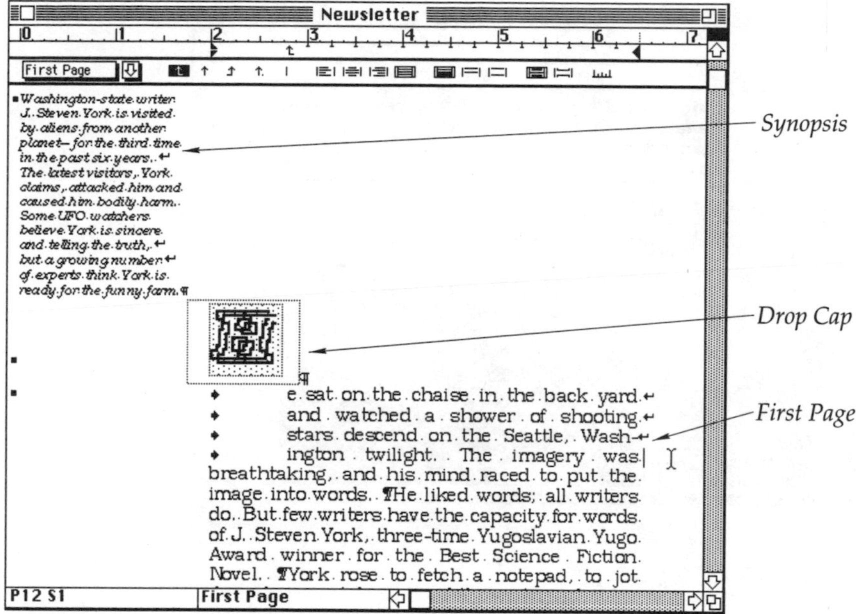

Figure 18-16
The three paragraphs in Galley View and their corresponding styles.

When the newsletter is printed, Word arranges the three paragraphs in one row because their styles contain the Side-by-Side format and the left indent of each is to the right of the one before it. The drop cap is another graphic created in MacDraw, although we could have used Word to create a large capital letter in a paragraph by itself.

Notice the space for the drop cap in the first paragraph. Even though the First Page style specifies a tab stop at 2.81 inches—just enough room for the superimposed drop cap—in practice you'd probably have to adjust the exact position of the tab stop manually for the width of the particular letter being used. Also, because the design for the newsletter specifies that the first paragraph be justified, newlines were added at the end of the first four lines; they cause Word to force each line to align at the right indent. If tab stops alone had been used, the first four lines would be ragged right, and the rest of the paragraph would be justified.

Section Two: The Figure and Caption

The graphic in the figure was digitized at 200 percent by MacVision from photographs of the alien spacecraft and the house and then squeezed down to 100 percent using the methods described in Chapter 16, "Transferring Text and Graphics." The graphic and its caption, two paragraphs, reside in a one-column section, as shown in Figure 18-17 on the following page.

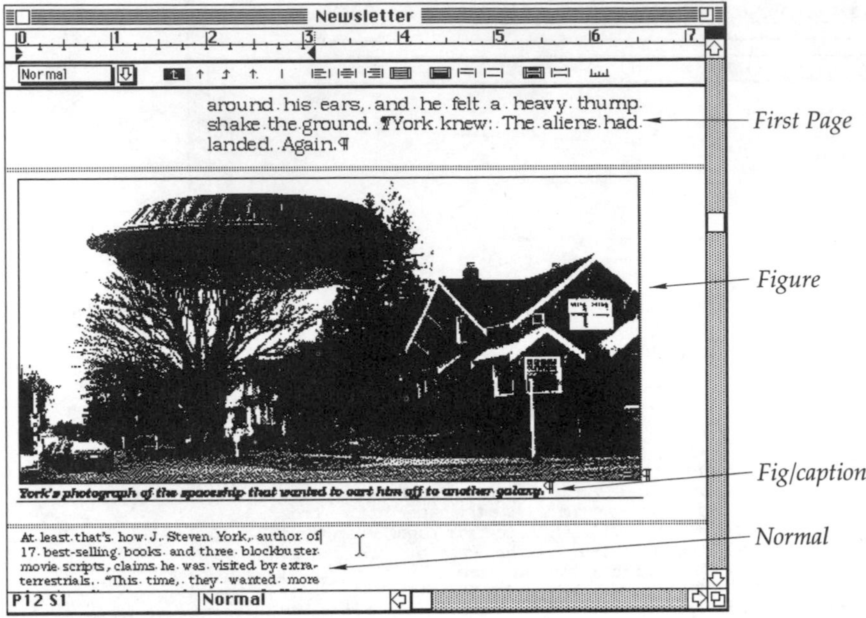

Figure 18-17
The graphic and its caption in Galley View, and their corresponding styles.

The style for the figure, simply named *Figure*, adds only two formats to those it inherited from the *Normal* style. The paragraph containing the graphic has 2 points of Space Before, which leaves a small gap between the top border of the graphic and the running head. It also has Outline character format, which creates a frame for the graphic.

In practice, instead of putting a box around the entire paragraph, you could select the graphic and give it a paragraph border format. The Outline character format was used here because it draws a black outline tightly around the graphic. However, it's difficult to generalize about what kind of graphic will be in the figure: a halftone picture, an object-oriented line drawing, or simply a graphic that you'll paste in after printing the document. A paragraph border format draws a box around the paragraph that goes from indent to indent at a given distance from the material in the paragraph, regardless of what's in the paragraph.

The caption underneath the graphic has its own style, the *Fig/caption* style, which uses a Border format below it to separate the figure from the text below it. It also uses the Space After format to leave a space between the figure and the two-column section beneath it.

Headers and Footers in the Second Section

The second section uses an interesting property of sections: namely that the headers and footers for a page are to be taken from the section at the top of the page. Because the section containing the figure is at the top of the second page of the article, the header and footer attached to it are the ones Word prints. Therefore, both the odd header and the odd footer on the second page belong to the second section. The structure of the odd header has already been discussed, but the odd footer for this section is special because it creates both the footer and the vertical line separating the two columns of the third section. Figure 18-18 shows this footer.

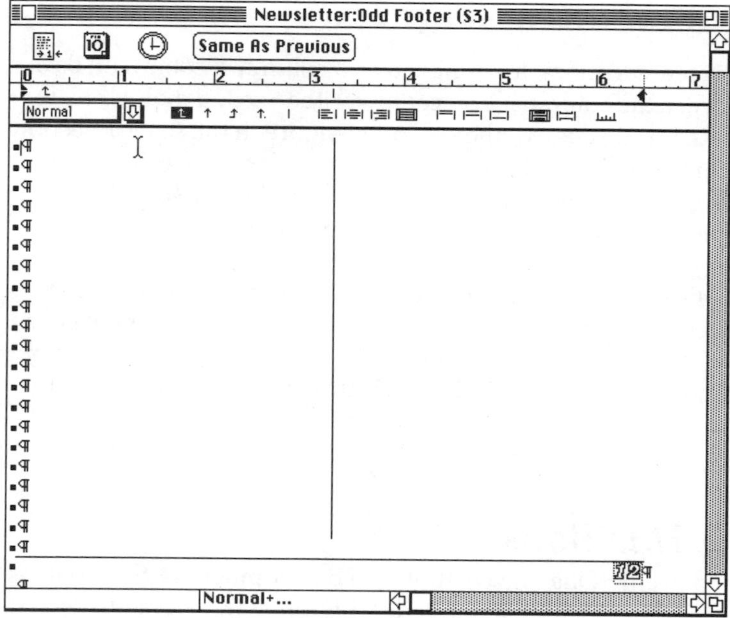

Figure 18-18
The footer for the second section.

This footer interleaves with the two-column section in the second half of the page. Every line in the footer has the *Normal* style, with a vertical-line tab stop set midway between the two columns. To adjust the length of the line between the two columns, simply add empty paragraphs in the Footer window until the length of the line matches the length of the column. You can work between Print Preview and the Footer window to do this.

Another way to do this would be to insert a paragraph mark at the bottom of the first column in the third section and add the vertical-line format for every line in the second column, but if you then had to edit or rearrange the article's text, rebreaking the column and reformatting the text in the second column would be unnecessarily time-consuming. By laying the contents of the Footer window over the text in the third section (remember that setting a negative bottom margin in the Document dialog box lets you do this), you can adjust the size of the figure so that the text in the third section fits exactly in the space provided.

If, however, you wanted to create something other than a 1-point line, you could could use a hairline border (set in the Paragraph Borders dialog box), or you could create a graphic in a program such as Cricket Draw, or insert a few PostScript commands in the header or footer of a section in the document. The latter method isn't difficult at all; for more information, see Appendix C, "Using PostScript."

Section Three: The Second-Page Text

This section offers few surprises; it's simply a two-column section with 0.25 inch of space between the columns. You could use the Section dialog box to set these values. As was discussed, the size of the figure in the second section determines how much space is left on the page for the text. The remaining text for the article doesn't go beyond the article's second page, so the figure was cropped vertically to adjust its size until the text filled out the bottom of the page exactly.

Incidentally, the moon symbol that ends the article is a Zapf Dingbat *m*. A few tab characters were inserted between it and the end of the sentence to right-align the symbols. This forces the text in the last line of a justified paragraph to align at both left and right indents. Ordinarily, it would align at the left indent alone.

■ *Creating This Book*

At last we come to the Big One: the creation and development of this book as a set of Word documents. In a sense, a full description of the methods used to produce this book fills a book itself—the one you're reading. However, many of the design elements used in this book are the result of a fair amount of work because we wanted not only to develop methods of achieving certain effects but also to achieve those effects in the easiest, most economical way possible in a publishing environment.

We believe that Word is preferable to any other desktop publishing program for large projects such as books because it lets you automate processes. Instead of hand-placing columns of text and graphics on a page-by-page basis, we simply pasted in each graphic and assigned it a style. Instead of finding and manually reformatting every instance of text elements, such as level headings and figure captions, every time we wanted to experiment with or refine the design, we simply adjusted the style sheet in one chapter and merged it into the other chapters. This allowed us to play with the design until quite late in the production cycle for the book.

Because we could print proofs for the chapters on the LaserWriter before final output on a Linotronic 300 imagesetter, we could fold the production of the book into the editorial cycle and do both the editing and the design development concurrently. We like to call this method a *sculptural paradigm* for developing a document, because both the design and the text are refined in small increments until the result is ready to be printed; at every stage the document is readable and is continuously better looking.

We call the standard method of document production a *transformational paradigm* because the writers and production people are separated from one another in their approach to the document, and the process of taking the document from the draft to the printed version requires what often seems like a miraculous conversion that consumes much time and energy.

With Word, everyone involved in a project works only at the level of training and expertise required for his or her role. For example, a writer's understanding of styles needn't extend much beyond using the outlining feature. The persons implementing the design, on the other hand, can exercise style sheets, import graphics, and use PostScript to achieve the look they want for the document. And they all work within the same environment.

Now let's take a tour of some of the prominent features of this project.

The Style Sheet

The style sheet for a typical chapter in this book follows:

Style Name	Definition
**body*	Normal +
**chap.Num*	*disp.helv + Font: 60 Point, Outline, Superscript 3 Point, Space Before 6 pt., Tab stops: 0.625 in. Centered
**chapD1*	*chap.Num + Side-by-Side, Tab stops: 0.375 in. Centered; Not at 0.625 in.
**chapD2*	*chap.Num + indent: 0.028 in., Side-by-Side, Tab stops: 0.819 in. Centered; Not at 0.625 in.
**disp.helv*	Normal + Font: LB Helvetica Black 12 Point, Line Spacing: 0 pt.
**display*	Font: Helvetica 18 Point, Bold, Flush left
**Spacing*	Font: Times 9 Point, Flush left, Line Spacing: -10 pt., Tab stops: 4.875 in.
dropcap18	Normal + Line Spacing: -13 pt., Tab stops: 0.569 in.
footer	*display + Font: 10 Point, Italic, indent: Right -1.25 in., Line Spacing -13 pt., Tab stops: 4.75 in. Right Flush
header	*disp.helv + Font: 9 Point, Outline, Line Spacing: 12 pt., Side-by-Side, Tab stops: 0.083 in.
header/even	header + Tab stops: 4.75 in. Right Flush

Style Name	Definition
header/odd	header + Tab stops: 4.861 in. Right Flush
heading 1, 1, chapHead	*display + Space Before 110 pt. After 148 pt.
heading 2, 2, aHead	*display + Font: Palatino 16 Point, Italic, Space Before 30 pt., Keep With Next, Tab stops: 0.25 in.
heading 3, 3, bHead	*display + Font: Palatino 14 Point, Italic, Space Before 20 pt. After 5 pt., Keep With Next
heading 4, 4, cHead	*display + Font: Palatino 12 Point, Italic, Space Before 15 pt., Keep With Next
heading 5, 5, tip	*display + Font: Palatino 10 Point, Line Spacing: -13 pt., Side-by-Side, Keep With Next
heading 6, 6, note	*display + Font: Times 9 Point, Not Bold, indent: Left 4.875 in. Right -1.25 in., Side-by-Side Border: Top Bottom Left Right Between (Single)
heading 7, 7, figGfx	*display + Font: Palatino 10 Point, Not Bold, indent: Right -1.25 in., Side-by-Side, Keep With Next
heading 8, 8, figNum	*display + Font: 9 Point, Italic, Line Spacing: -10 pt., Space Before 10 pt., Keep With Next, Tab stops: 5 in.
heading 9, 9, figCap	*display + Font: 9 Point, Not Bold, Line Spacing: 11 pt., Side-by-Side
L/bull	*body + indent: Left 0.25 in. First -0.25 in., Right 0.25 in., Space Before 3 pt.
Normal	Font: Palatino 10 Point, Flush left, Line Spacing: -12 pt.
page number	header + Not Outline, indent: Left -1 in., Tab stops: -0.167 in. Right Flush; 4.931 in.; Not at 0.083 in.
PostScri pt., ps	Font: Courier 9 Point, Hidden, indent: Right -1.292 in. Flush left, Side-by-Side, Keep With Next, Tab stops: -0.111 in. Vertical Line; -0.083 Vertical Line; -0.056 in. Vertical Line; 0.25 in.; 0.5 in.; 0.75 in.; 1 in.; 3.5 in.
s/fig>fig, s/ff	*Spacing + Space Before 12 pt.
s/fig>lev1, s/f1	*Spacing +
s/fig>lev2, s/f2	*Spacing +
s/fig>lev3, s/f3	*Spacing +
s/fig>lev4, s/f4	*Spacing +
s/fig>norm, s/fn	*Spacing + Space Before 2 pt.
s/fig>num, s/f#	*Spacing +
s/lev4>norm, s/4n	*Spacing +
s/norm>fig, s/nf	*Spacing +
s/norm>lev4, s/n4	*Spacing +
s/norm>norm, s/nn	*Spacing +

Style Name	Definition
s/norm>num, s/n#	*Spacing + Line Spacing: -3 pt.
s/norm>user, s/nu	*Spacing +
s/num>fig, s/#f	*Spacing +
s/num>lev4, s/#4	*Spacing +
s/num>norm, s/#n	*Spacing +
s/num>user, s/#u	*Spacing +
s/user>norm, s/un	*Spacing +
s/user>num, s/u#	*Spacing +
*T/**	Normal + Font: Times 9 Point, Line Spacing: -10 pt., Space After 3 pt.
T/2 col	T/* + Tab stops: 0.125 in.; 2.25 in.; 2.375 in.
T/2 col/wrap	T/2 col + indent: Left 2.375 in. First -2.375 in.
T/3 col	T/* + Tab stops: 0.125 in.; 1.875 in.; 2 in.; 3.375 in.; 3.5 in.
T/3 col/wrap	T/3 col + indent: Left 3.5 in. First -3.5 in.
T/4 col	T/* + Tab stops: 0.125 in.; 1.75 in.; 1.875 in.; 2.75 in.; 2.875 in.; 3.75 in.; 3.875 in.
T/cmds	T/* + indent: Left 1.625 in. First -1.625 in., Space Before 2 pt. After 2 pt., Tab stops: 2.375 in.; 3.125 in.; 3.875 in.
T/cmds/head	Normal + Font: Times 9 Point, Bold, Line Spacing: -10 pt., Space Before 2 pt. After 2 pt., Tab stops: 1.625 in.; 2.5 in.; 3.25 in.; 4 in.
T/keys	T/cmds + Font: Word Chicago, indent: First 0 in., Space Before 1 pt. After 1 pt., Tab stops: 2.5 in.; 3.25 in.; 4 in.; Not at 2.375 in., 3.125 in.; 3.875 in.
Tab	*disp.helv + Font: 14 Point, Outline, Superscript. 3 Point, Line Spacing: -18 pt.
Tab/chap	Tab + indent: Left -0.5 in., Tab stops: 0.667 in. Centered
Tab/summary	Tab + indent: Left -0.25 in., Tab stops: 0.653 in. Centered; 4.222 in. Centered
Tip	Font: LB Helvetica Black 10 Point, Outline, indent: Left -1 Flush left, Space Before 3 pt., Side-by-Side, Keep With Next, Tab stops: -0.25 in. Right Flush; 5.028 in.
User Entry	Normal + Font: Helvetica 9 Point, Line Spacing: -10 pt.

Probably the most noticeable aspect of the style sheet is the large number of styles devoted to spacing, all of which begin with *s/*, such as *s/fig>norm*. Because Word doesn't measure the space before and after a paragraph from baseline to baseline, we created these special styles to get the most control over the elements in the book. Many of these styles are simply based on the

**spacing* style, but we added them in case we wanted to adjust globally the spacing between certain pairs of elements. A single line having one of these styles goes between each element in the book and the next; for example, *s/fig>norm* would go between a figure caption and body text having the *Normal* style.

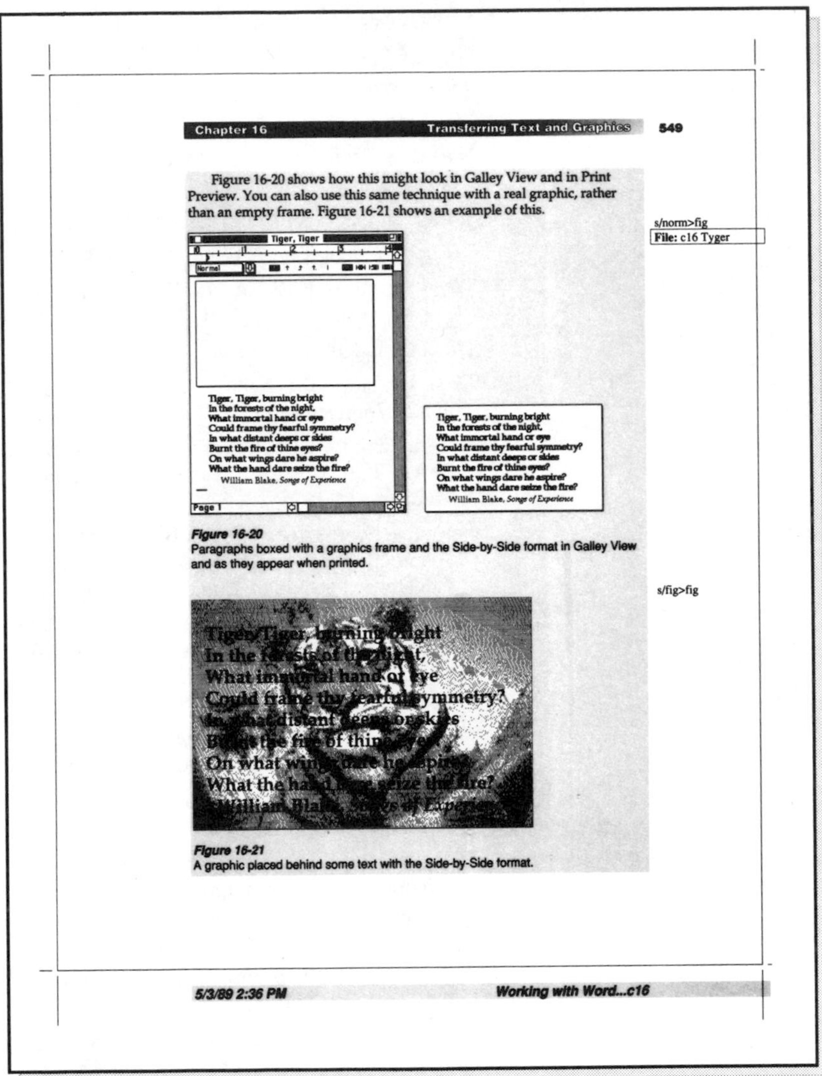

Chapter 16 Transferring Text and Graphics 549

Figure 16-20 shows how this might look in Galley View and in Print Preview. You can also use this same technique with a real graphic, rather than an empty frame. Figure 16-21 shows an example of this.

s/norm>fig

File: c16 Tyger

Tiger, Tiger, burning bright
In the forests of the night,
What immortal hand or eye
Could frame thy fearful symmetry?
In what distant deeps or skies
Burnt the fire of thine eyes?
On what wings dare he aspire?
What the hand dare seize the fire?
William Blake, *Songs of Experience*

Figure 16-20
Paragraphs boxed with a graphics frame and the Side-by-Side format in Galley View and as they appear when printed.

s/fig>fig

Figure 16-21
A graphic placed behind some text with the Side-by-Side format.

5/3/89 2:36 PM Working with Word...c16

Figure 18-19
A typical page from this book.

Figure 18-19 shows how a typical page looks, including the crop marks, spacing elements, and margin notes. Each line that has a spacing style contains a label formatted with the hidden character attribute, making it easy to verify that the spacing elements have been placed correctly. We added one line for each of the spacing styles to the Standard Glossary so that it would be easy to insert them where needed.

Preparing the Graphics

All the images of screens in the book were produced by using the Shift-Command-3 key sequence to create screen dumps on disk. SuperPaint was used to clean up the images, reduce them to 50 percent of their original size, and add labels where needed. We could have added lines running from each label to the item it references, but because 1 point is the smallest increment that the PICT data format represents for object-oriented graphics, we decided instead to use special arrows drawn with PostScript commands. (For a discussion of the commands you can use to create arrows and other special effects, see Appendix C, "Using PostScript.")

In order to present high-quality samples for Word's formatting options, we prepared many of the full-page graphics by printing them on the LaserWriter, photographically reducing the result, and pasting them by hand into appropriately sized boxes on the final L300 output.

Design Elements

The design elements for the running heads, the Tip tabs, the chapter opening headings, and the section openers were prepared by a designer who used FreeHand from Aldus. These elements were then converted to PostScript, and a PostScript programmer modified them so that they could be printed from a Word document. This was done more as a feasibility study than because it was the only way to create sophisticated effects in this book. For example, you can create graphics in Cricket Draw and copy them into a Word document with much the same effect, because PICT-type graphics copied from Cricket Draw carry embedded PostScript commands, as was discussed in Chapter 16, "Transferring Text and Graphics."

Much of the custom PostScript developed for this book was added to the Word program itself, using the method described in Appendix C, "Using PostScript."

Word's table-of-contents feature was used to create the table of contents. We didn't use the indexing feature extensively, however, because indexing at Microsoft Press is done by freelancers who don't use Mac Word.

Statistics

For the curious, some statistics on the size of this book as a set of files:

- The source material used to research this book, including specifications, bug reports, recommendations from the developers of Word, and project management files, comes to 1,157 KB.
- The test documents we used to explore every feature of Word we could manage total 4,262 KB.
- In the first edition of this book, each screen dump in the book was stored in its original, cleaned-up, and final form—once for each of these three forms. These figures took up 4,900 KB. In the second edition, we decided that this was unnecessary, and stored final graphics in the chapters themselves.

  The actual text of the book totals about 1,300 KB of written text in 18 chapter files, 5 appendix files, 6 section opener files, and 7 other files for items such as the index, the table of contents, and the introduction.
- The total size of one "electronic" copy of this book, including text, figures, PostScript, and so on, comes to 4,507 KB.

The full-time team that produced the first edition of this book consisted of two writers, an editor, and a copy editor. We also used a designer, a PostScript programmer, a layout person, and two part-time proofreaders, for short-term projects. The team for the second edition (which corresponds to Word version 4) consisted of one writer, one editor, one technical/graphics editor, and two part-time proofreaders. The final page proofs were printed on a LaserWriter II NT; after each chapter was finished, it was printed on a Linotronic 300 Laser Imagesetter by a typographic specialist in the production department of Microsoft Press.

SECTION 6

Appendixes

Setting Up Word

Before you start working with Word, you should prepare working copies of the Word Program and Word Utilities disks. You can optimize these working copies for the type of Mac you have and the size of your disk drives. You can use Word on any Mac except the 128 KB Mac and the unenhanced 512 KB Mac, which don't provide enough random-access memory (RAM). Your Mac must have at least two double-sided 800 KB disk drives because the Word 4 program no longer fits on one 400 KB disk and you should use the internal disk drive for the system disk. The Word program and its associated files come on double-sided disks, which a single-sided drive cannot read.

Also, the Word 4 package doesn't include the Macintosh system software, known as the Macintosh System Tools, as did earlier versions of the program. With rare exceptions, you should always use the most current version of the System Tools software—check with an Apple dealer for the most recent versions. Remember that all the components of the System Tools package are designed to work together. You should use the Installer program from the System Tools disks to install the most recent versions of the System, Finder, Control Panel, and printer drivers such as the ImageWriter, LaserWriter, and Laser Prep files.

■ *Preparing Working Copies of Word*

You should make copies of the Program and Utilities disks because you can then store the original disks in a safe place—and use the copies for your everyday work. Using a copy reduces the chance of a serious loss of data if something catastrophic should ever happen to a disk. If you have a hard disk, you'll probably prefer copying the files you need from the originals to the hard disk. Making working copies of Word and its support files is easy; because they aren't copy-protected, you won't ever have to insert a master disk to start the program.

It's a good idea to begin by sliding open the write-protect tabs in the corners of the Word Program and both Word Utilities disks. This prevents accidental modification of the disks' contents when inside the Macintosh.

After you prepare working disks (or copy the files you need to your hard disk), store the original disks until you need them again. Word and its support files come on three 800 KB disks. The following is a list of the files on the Word distribution disks:

Disk and Files	Size	Contents
Word Program		
Microsoft Word	668 KB	The Word application itself.
Word 4 ReadMe	26 KB	Last-minute information.
Utilities 1		
MS Dictionary	180 KB	Word's main dictionary.
Word Help	147 KB	Word's help file.
Word Command Help	32 KB	Help messages that appear when you select a command in the Commands dialog box and click the Help button. These messages are listed in the Commands sections at the end of each chapter and in Appendix E, "Word's Preset Defaults."
Word Hyphenation	24 KB	Word's hyphenation rules.
Standard Glossary	3 KB	Word's default glossary.
AutoMac III 2.1	108 KB	The AutoMac III macro-recording utility.
Demo Documents	39 KB	Documents for creating dropcaps, legal stationery, résumés, and macros for redlining.
Formula Glossary	36 KB	A glossary containing entries for creating formulas, and a Settings file specifying a list of these glossary entries on the Work menu.
Getting Started Documents	27 KB	The documents used in "Getting Started and Learning Word."
Sample Documents	113 KB	The documents used in the "Microsoft Word Sampler."
Sample Settings Files	10 KB	Settings files that configure Word so that it works like other products.
PostScript Glossary	12 KB	Sample PostScript code you can add to your documents, and notes on using PostScript.

Disk and Files	Size	Contents
Utilities 2		
UK Dictionary	164 KB	British spellings: To use this dictionary, name this file *MS Dictionary*.
SuperPaint	188 KB	SuperPaint version 1.1MS.
Word Finder	147 KB	The Word Finder thesaurus desk accessory.
Conversions	168 KB	Apple File Exchange modules that convert files between the Microsoft Rich Text Format (RTF), DCA-RFT, and Word Perfect for the PC version 4.x formats.
Mailing Labels	79 KB	Folder containing merge documents for preparing mailing labels: two sample data documents and a collection of form documents.

Of course, you don't need to transfer all these files to your working disks or to your hard disk. At a minimum, to write with Word you need only the Word program file and the Word Settings file. (Even though it isn't included on any of the distribution disks, Word itself creates the Settings file and puts it in the System folder when you first quit the program.) The other files, including the dictionaries, Help files, Standard Glossary file, and so forth, are required only when you specifically access them. When Word needs to access these supplementary files, it will prompt you to insert into the drive the disk that contains them.

In the next sections we'll discuss how to best arrange the files you need in the space you have. If you have two floppy drives and no hard disk, read the next section: even though it's theoretically possible to run Word on a system that has only one 800 KB drive, in practice you would be swapping the system and Word disks too often for it to be a useful way to work. If you're installing Word on a hard disk, you can safely skip the next section.

Mac with Two 800 KB Drives

In practice, you cannot use Word 4 unless you have at least two 800 KB disk drives. Because it's impossible to fit both Word and your system files on one disk, your only option is to spread them across two or more disks and swap disks where necessary. This table shows a disk layout for two 800 KB drives, assuming you're using three or more disks:

Disk	Drive	Files on disk
System disk	Internal drive	System Folder containing any printer drivers needed, such as the Image-Writer or LaserWriter and Laser Prep files, and your documents (depending on the size of your System Folder).

Disk	Drive	Files on disk
Program disk	External drive	Word program, Standard Glossary, Word Hyphenation. Roughly 90 KB left for your documents.
Utilities disk	External drive	MS Dictionary, Help files, custom glossaries and user dictionaries, and SuperPaint 1.1MS. Roughly 250 KB free.
Data disks	External drive	Copy documents from the external drive to the System disk, and work with the copies on the System disk.

When setting up your System files, you should look for every available economy, so that as much room as possible is left for your documents. Use the Font/DA Mover to remove from the System file all fonts and desk accessories except those you really need. Fonts in particular consume a large amount of disk space.

If you want to strip your System file to the bare minimum, you can remove all fonts but 9-point Monaco, 9- and 12-point New York, and 9-point Geneva (the only fonts the Macintosh operating system requires), and all DAs but the Control Panel, the Chooser, and perhaps the Scrapbook. In the System Folder retain only the System, Finder, General, Keyboard, Mouse, Startup Device, Clipboard, and Scrapbook files.

Also keep in the System Folder only the printer drivers you need. For example, if you rarely use the LaserWriter, remove the Laser Prep and the LaserWriter drivers, which together count for more than 50 KB.

If you keep many items in the Scrapbook, consider copying the Scrapbook file in the System Folder onto another disk and removing everything in the first Scrapbook. You can replace the Scrapbook desk accessory with one that can open a Scrapbook from a disk other than that containing the System Folder, such as SmartScrap from Solutions International.

Of course, you can also prepare more than one type of system disk, each optimized for different requirements. For example, you can create system disks containing different collections of fonts, or you can create one disk for printing on the ImageWriter and one for printing on the LaserWriter.

A good strategy for using the extra space on the system disk is to copy your documents from a data disk to the system disk to work on them and then to copy them back to the data disk when you're done. Eject the program disk and load the data disk to transfer the document to the system disk, and then replace the program disk to use Word with the copy of the document on the system disk. If you need to access the Dictionary, Hyphenation, or custom glossaries, swap the Program and Utilities disks.

To use Word more effectively with small documents, choose Preferences from the Edit menu and select either the Now or Always option in the Keep File in Memory group. If you select the Always option, it becomes the default the next time you start Word, and you won't have to call up the Preferences dialog box again. Then, when you open a file, Word loads as much of it as possible into memory.

If your Mac has 1 MB or more of memory, it might be more effective to start Word (this might require a few disk swaps) and select either the Now or Always option in the Keep Program in Memory group. This loads almost all of Word into memory, so you can eject the Program disk and insert a Utilities disk. When you're using a dictionary, accessing Help, or hyphenating the document, eject the Utilities disk and reinsert the Program disk.

Any Mac with a Hard Disk

You can load all 2,171 KB of files from the three Word disks onto your hard disk if you want, but you really don't need to use every file that's distributed with Word. For example, you might load the collection of sample documents until you've browsed through them and then delete them, retaining the copies on the masters until you need them again.

The best way to install Word on a hard disk is to create a new folder called, for instance, *Word Folder*, and then copy Word and its support files into it. If you keep the Standard Glossary, Word Help, and Word Hyphenation files in the same folder as Word, Word will open them without presenting a dialog box asking you to find them. However, if you want to split up Word's files, read the information in the next section.

It's also a good idea to keep your documents in a folder other than the one containing the Word files. This makes it easier to keep track of documents. The following table shows a sufficient arrangement of files for a hard disk:

Folder	Files in Folder
System Folder	Normal system files plus any printer drivers needed, such as the ImageWriter or LaserWriter and Laser Prep files.
Word Folder	Word program, Word Help, Word Command Help, Standard Glossary, MS Dictionary, Word Hyphenation, custom glossaries and user dictionaries, SuperPaint 1.1MS (or put it in the folder containing your other graphics programs).
Word documents folder(s)	Your documents.

Some people don't like to put their applications in a folder because they don't want to have to open a folder to start an application. Also, the first folder you see after choosing the Open command is the folder containing Word, which typically shouldn't contain document files. They prefer placing their applications at the topmost level on their hard disks. Word works well with this arrangement; if you do this, however, put the files which would otherwise reside in the Word Folder in the System Folder instead, to make it easier for Word to find them.

■ *How Word Finds Files*

Word must be able to find its files when it needs to access one of them. You open the vast majority of files in Word by choosing the Open command and locating the file on a disk or in a folder. However, Word opens the Standard Glossary, the User 1 dictionary, the Help file, and the Word Hyphenation file by following a search path through a list of certain folders on the disks that you've mounted. If Word can't find the file, it presents a dialog box asking you to find the file by inserting a disk or opening the correct folder.

If you have more than one file named *Standard Glossary*, for example, Word opens the first one found, and it might be difficult to determine exactly which of the files was opened. This issue is important if you have a hard disk, because with the extra space it's easier to develop a multiplicity of files and folders and therefore easier to lose track of their names and locations.

The following list shows the search path Word uses to find files. If you keep this list in mind when saving the Standard Glossary or User 1 files, you can avoid creating secondary version of these files. You can't as easily modify the Help or Hyphenation files as you can the Standard Glossary and User 1 files, but you can avoid the dialog box asking you to find them if you ensure that Word can find them. Word searches through disks and folders in the following order:

❶ The folder containing Word.

❷ The root, or topmost, folder of the disk containing Word.

❸ The System folder.

❹ The root, or topmost, folder of all other disks.

❺ The last folder that was displayed in an Open or Save dialog box.

When you do a print merge, however, Word looks first in the folder containing the main document before it looks in the folders listed above. If Word can't find a file it needs, it displays a dialog box asking you to find the folder or insert the disk that contains the file. Also, Word 4 can remember where many of its files are—after you've indicated their location. This information becomes part of the current Settings file, and Word remembers the information the next time you start the program.

Table of Character Sets

Appendix B presents a table of the complete character sets for six common Macintosh fonts. The character sets for three different types of fonts are represented:

- ❑ Two standard Mac screen fonts—Geneva and New York.
- ❑ Two standard LaserWriter fonts—Times and Courier.
- ❑ Two special LaserWriter fonts—Zapf Dingbats and Symbol.

Each font contains several types of characters, and the way you enter a character depends on its type. You can look up the key sequence for a given character in the Keystrokes column in the table. To save space, we condensed the words *Shift*, *Option,* and *Command* to single letters. For example, we represent the keystrokes for creating an em dash (Shift-Option- –) as *SO-*. For clarity, we represent an uppercase letter or symbol as Shift-*letter*.

Often, you can enter a character in more than one way. You can enter its key sequence from the Keystrokes column in the table. Or you can place an insertion point, press Option-Command-Q, enter its ASCII code from the table, and press the Return key. You can enter a paragraph mark, for example, either by pressing the Return key or by pressing Option-Command-Q, entering *13*, and then pressing the Return key (although this is a roundabout way to enter a simple paragraph mark).

Neither method works for all characters. For example, Word represents a graphic (or an empty graphics frame) with a character that has the ASCII value 1. You can insert a graphics frame by choosing Insert Graphics from the Document menu, but you cannot get the graphics frame by pressing Option-Command-Q, entering *1*, and then pressing the Return key. On the other hand, you could remove every graphic from a document at one time by searching for *^1* and replacing it with nothing.

Normal characters: Those you use in everyday writing—the uppercase and lowercase letters from A through Z, the numbers, and the punctuation marks. You enter one of these in the expected way, by pressing a key on the keyboard or by pressing the Shift key at the same time as you press the key for the character. For example, in the table we represent an *A* as *Sa*.

Dingbat and symbol characters: Supported in many Macintosh character sets, such as the standard bullet • (Option-8) or the paragraph symbol ¶ (Option-7). You enter these by pressing the Shift or Option key in conjunction with a key. In the table, Option-8 is represented as *O8*.

Accented characters: Normal characters with added accents, such as *é* and *ö*. You enter these by first pressing, at the same time, the Option key and a key for the type of accent you want, and then pressing, alone, the letter you want accented. For example, to enter *ö*, first you press Option-u, and then press *o*. This sequence is represented in the table as *Ou,o*.

Control characters: Assigned to ASCII characters between 0 and 30, such as the tab, paragraph, and newline marks. You can enter only a few of these from the keyboard. For example, enter a tab mark by pressing the Tab key, a paragraph mark by pressing the Return or Enter key, and a newline mark by pressing Shift-Return. In the table these keys are spelled out in a small point size, such as *SReturn* for a newline mark.

Word's reserved characters: Set aside for marking some of the internal structures in a document, such as section marks, page breaks, and graphics. Some you can enter with a key sequence, such as Command-Enter for a section mark or Shift-Return for a newline mark. Others, such as the character produced when you click the Page Number icon in a Header window, can't be entered from the keyboard, because even though Word uses a character to represent a component of a document, it also adds other internal attributes that you can't add from the keyboard. If you want to enter one of these special characters, start by entering it in the normal way (by clicking an icon, for instance), and then create a glossary entry for it that you can enter by pressing Command-Backspace and a code you have chosen.

Many of the special characters Word uses to place items such as graphics, paragraph marks, and so on, are visible only when Show ¶ is turned on. The

Comments column in the table identifies some of these special characters by name and offers some other notes where needed. Some ASCII characters in a given font are undefined and have no unique shape. When you turn on Show ¶, you see either a box (□) or nothing at all. Because PostScript printers don't print these boxes, we've added boxes to the table as graphics to show you which are visible and which are not.

Finally, it should be mentioned that the shapes attached to certain ASCII numbers in certain fonts vary with the point size. In Geneva, for example, Shift-Option-` can be a fish, a sheep, a rabbit, or a Mac. (We spelled these out rather than showing you the images associated because the 12-point size of a font is downloaded to a PostScript printer, and the printer scales that size to whatever size is needed in the document. Therefore, a PostScript printer will always represent Shift-Option-` as a 🐇.)

ASCII	Times	Geneva	New York	Courier	Zapf Dingbats	Symbol	Keystrokes	Comments
0	□	□	□	□		□		
1	□	□	□	□				Graphic (either an Insert Graphic box or an actual graphic)
2	□		□	□				Page number in header or footer
3	□		□	□				Short date in header or footer
4	□		□	□				Short time in header or footer
5	□		□	□				Footnote reference
6	\	\	\	\	✻	∴		Formula character (^\) and footnote separator
7	□	□	□	□				Footnote continued separator
8	□	□	□	□				
9							Tab	Tab (^t), also long form of date.
10								Linefeed, also abbrev. form of date.
11							SReturn	Newline (^n), also HH:MM:SS form of time.

ASCII	Times	Geneva	New York	Courier	Zapf Dingbats	Symbol	Keystrokes	Comments
12							SEnter CEnter	Page-break mark and Section mark (^d)
13							Return	Carriage return or paragraph mark (^p)
14	□	□	□	□				
15	□	□	□	□				
16	□	□	□	□				
17	□	□	□	□				
18	□	□	□	□				
19	□	□	□	□				
20	□	□	□	□				
21	□	□	□	□				
22	□	□	□	□				
23	□	□	□	□				
24	□	□	□	□				
25	□	□	□	□				
26	□	□	□	□				
27	□	□	□	□				
28	□	□	□	□				
29	□	□	□	□				
30	-	-	-	-	✍	–	C~	Nonbreaking hyphen
31							C-	Optional hyphen (^_)
32							Spacebar	Normal space
33	!	!	!	!	✁	!	S1	
34	"	"	"	"	✂	∀	S'	Double quote, inches, or seconds (see also ASCII 210–213)
35	#	#	#	#	✃	#	S3	
36	$	$	$	$	✄	∃	S4	
37	%	%	%	%	☎	%	S5	
38	&	&	&	&	✆	&	S7	
39	'	'	'	'	✇	∋	'	Single quote, feet, or minutes (see also ASCII 210–213)
40	(	(	(	(	✈	(	S9	
41	)	)	)	)	✉	)	S0	(zero)

ASCII	Times	Geneva	New York	Courier	Zapf Dingbats	Symbol	Keystrokes	Comments
42	*	*	*	*	☛	∗	S8	
43	+	+	+	+	☞	+	S=	
44	,	,	,	,	✌	,	,	Comma
45	-	-	-	-	✍	−	-	Normal hyphen
46	.	.	.	.	✎	.	.	Period
47	/	/	/	/	✏	/	/	
48	0	0	0	0	✐	0	0	Zero
49	1	1	1	1	✑	1	1	
50	2	2	2	2	✒	2	2	
51	3	3	3	3	✓	3	3	
52	4	4	4	4	✔	4	4	
53	5	5	5	5	✕	5	5	
54	6	6	6	6	✖	6	6	
55	7	7	7	7	✗	7	7	
56	8	8	8	8	✘	8	8	
57	9	9	9	9	✙	9	9	
58	:	:	:	:	✚	:	S;	(semicolon)
59	;	;	;	;	✛	;	;	
60	<	<	<	<	✜	<	S,	(comma)
61	=	=	=	=	✝	=	=	
62	>	>	>	>	✞	>	S.	(period)
63	?	?	?	?	✟	?	S/	(slash)
64	@	@	@	@	✠	≅	S2	
65	A	A	A	A	✡	Α	Sa	
66	B	B	B	B	✢	Β	Sb	
67	C	C	C	C	✣	Χ	Sc	
68	D	D	D	D	✤	Δ	Sd	
69	E	E	E	E	✥	Ε	Se	
70	F	F	F	F	✦	Φ	Sf	
71	G	G	G	G	✧	Γ	Sg	
72	H	H	H	H	★	Η	Sh	
73	I	I	I	I	✩	Ι	Si	
74	J	J	J	J	✪	ϑ	Sj	
75	K	K	K	K	✫	Κ	Sk	
76	L	L	L	L	✬	Λ	Sl	

ASCII	Times	Geneva	New York	Courier	Zapf Dingbats	Symbol	Keystrokes	Comments
77	M	M	M	M	✭	M	Sm	
78	N	N	N	N	✮	N	Sn	
79	O	O	O	O	✯	O	So	
80	P	P	P	P	✰	Π	Sp	
81	Q	Q	Q	Q	✱	Θ	Sq	
82	R	R	R	R	✲	P	Sr	
83	S	S	S	S	✳	Σ	Ss	
84	T	T	T	T	✴	T	St	
85	U	U	U	U	✵	Y	Su	
86	V	V	V	V	✶	ς	Sv	
87	W	W	W	W	✷	Ω	Sw	
88	X	X	X	X	✸	Ξ	Sx	
89	Y	Y	Y	Y	✹	Ψ	Sy	
90	Z	Z	Z	Z	✺	Z	Sz	
91	[	[	[	[	✻	[	[	
92	\	\	\	\	✼	∴	\	Backslash
93	]	]	]	]	✽	]	]	
94	^	^	^	^	✾	⊥	S6	Caret (^^)
95	_	_	_	_	✿	_	S-	Underscore
96	`	`	`	`	❀	‾	`	Grave accent; however, in the Symbol font pressing ` produces a NOT operator over the succeeding character. For example, pressing ` and then *a* in Symbol results in α.
97	a	a	a	a	❁	α	a	
98	b	b	b	b	❂	β	b	
99	c	c	c	c	❃	χ	c	
100	d	d	d	d	❄	δ	d	
101	e	e	e	e	❅	ε	e	
102	f	f	f	f	❆	ϕ	f	
103	g	g	g	g	❇	γ	g	
104	h	h	h	h	❈	η	h	
105	i	i	i	i	❉	ι	i	
106	j	j	j	j	❊	φ	j	
107	k	k	k	k	❋	κ	k	
108	l	l	l	l	●	λ	l	
109	m	m	m	m	❍	μ	m	
110	n	n	n	n	■	ν	n	

ASCII	Times	Geneva	New York	Courier	Zapf Dingbats	Symbol	Keystrokes	Comments
111	o	o	o	o	❏	ο	o	
112	p	p	p	p	❐	π	p	
113	q	q	q	q	❑	θ	q	
114	r	r	r	r	❒	ρ	r	
115	s	s	s	s	▲	σ	s	
116	t	t	t	t	▼	τ	t	
117	u	u	u	u	◆	υ	u	
118	v	v	v	v	❖	ϖ	v	
119	w	w	w	w	◗	ω	w	
120	x	x	x	x	❘	ξ	x	
121	y	y	y	y	❙	ψ	y	
122	z	z	z	z	❚	ζ	z	
123	{	{	{	{	❛	{	S[	
124	|	|	|	|	❜	|	S\	(backslash)
125	}	}	}	}	❝	}	S]	
126	~	~	~	~	❞	~	S`	(tilde)
127	□							
128	Ä	Ä	Ä	Ä	❨		Ou,Sa	Zapf Dingbats and Symbol characters from ASCII 128 through 160 are undefined. However, even though characters in Zapf Dingbats from 128 through 141 are undefined (i.e., have no screen image), when printed on a PostScript printer they produce the images shown here.
129	Å	Å	Å	Å	❩		SOa	
130	Ç	Ç	Ç	Ç	❪		SOc	
131	É	É	É	É	❫		Oe,Se	
132	Ñ	Ñ	Ñ	Ñ	❬		On,Sn	
133	Ö	Ö	Ö	Ö	❭		Ou,So	
134	Ü	Ü	Ü	Ü	❮		Ou,Su	
135	á	á	á	á	❯		Oe,a	
136	à	à	à	à	❰		O`,a	
137	â	â	â	â	❱		Oi,a	
138	ä	ä	ä	ä	❲		Ou,a	
139	ã	ã	ã	ã	❳		On,a	
140	å	å	å	å	❴		Oa	
141	ç	ç	ç	ç	❵		Oc	
142	é	é	é	é			Oe,e	
143	è	è	è	è			O`,e	
144	ê	ê	ê	ê			Oi,e	
145	ë	ë	ë	ë			Ou,e	

ASCII	Times	Geneva	New York	Courier	Zapf Dingbats	Symbol	Keystrokes	Comments
146	í	í	í	í			Oe,i	
147	ì	ì	ì	ì			O`,i	
148	î	î	î	î			Oi,i	
149	ï	ï	ï	ï			Ou,i	
150	ñ	ñ	ñ	ñ			On,n	
151	ó	ó	ó	ó			Oe,o	
152	ò	ò	ò	ò			O`,o	
153	ô	ô	ô	ô			Oi,o	
154	ö	ö	ö	ö			Ou,o	
155	õ	õ	õ	õ			On,o	
156	ú	ú	ú	ú			Oe,u	
157	ù	ù	ù	ù			O`,u	
158	û	û	û	û			Oi,u	
159	ü	ü	ü	ü			Ou,u	
160	†	†	†	†			Ot	Dagger
161	°	°	°	°	❡	ϒ	SO8	Degree
162	¢	¢	¢	¢	❢	′	O4	Cent
163	£	£	£	£	❣	≤	O3	Pound sterling
164	§	§	§	§	❤	⁄	O6	Section symbol
165	•	•	•	•	❥	∞	O8	Standard bullet
166	¶	¶	¶	¶	❦	ƒ	O7	Paragraph mark (the symbol itself, not the Word marker)
167	ß	ß	ß	ß	❧	♣	Os	
168	®	®	®	®	♣	♦	Or	Registration mark
169	©	©	©	©	♦	♥	Og	Copyright mark
170	™	™	™	™	♥	♠	O2	Trademark symbol
171	´	´	´	´	♠	↔	Oe,Oe	Acute accent
172	¨	¨	¨	¨	①	←	Ou,Ou	Umlaut or diaeresis
173	≠	≠	□	≠	②	↑	O=	
174	Æ	Æ	Æ	Æ	③	→	SO'	(single quote)
175	Ø	Ø	Ø	Ø	④	↓	SOo	
176	∞	∞	□	∞	⑤	°	O5	Infinity symbol
177	±	±	□	±	⑥	±	SO=	
178	≤	≤	□	≤	⑦	″	O,	(comma)

ASCII	Times	Geneva	New York	Courier	Zapf Dingbats	Symbol	Keystrokes	Comments
179	≥	≥	□	≥	⑧	≥	O.	(period)
180	¥	¥	¥	¥	⑨	×	Oy	Japanese yen symbol
181	µ	µ	□	µ	⑩	∝	Om	
182	∂	∂	□	∂	❶	∂	Od	
183	∑	∑	□	∑	❷	•	Ow	
184	∏	∏	□	∏	❸	÷	SOp	
185	π	π	□	π	❹	≠	Op	
186	∫	∫	□	∫	❺	≡	Ob	Integral
187	ª	ª	ª	ª	❻	≈	O9	
188	º	º	º	º	❼	…	O0	(zero)
189	Ω	Ω	□	Ω	❽	⏐	Oz	
190	æ	æ	æ	æ	❾	—	O'	(single quote)
191	ø	ø	ø	ø	❿	↵	Oo	
192	¿	¿	¿	¿	①	ℵ	SO/	(slash)
193	¡	¡	¡	¡	②	ℑ	O1	Inverted exclamation point
194	¬	¬	□	¬	③	ℜ	Ol	
195	√	√	□	√	④	℘	Ov	
196	ƒ	ƒ	□	ƒ	⑤	⊗	Of	
197	≈	≈	□	≈	⑥	⊕	Ox	
198	∆	∆	□	∆	⑦	∅	Oj	
199	«	«	«	«	⑧	∩	O\	(backslash) European open parenthesis, math *much less than,* and the symbol starting a merge language command
200	»	»	»	»	⑨	∪	SO\	(backslash) European close parenthesis, math *much greater than,* and the symbol ending a merge language command
201	…	…	…	…	⑩	⊃	O;	Ellipsis
202					❶	⊇	Ospace	Nonbreaking space
203	À	À	À	À	❷	⊄	O`,Sa	

ASCII	Times	Geneva	New York	Courier	Zapf Dingbats	Symbol	Keystrokes	Comments
204	Ã	Ã	Ã	Ã	❸	⊂	On,Sa	
205	Õ	Õ	Õ	Õ	❹	⊆	On,So	
206	Œ	Œ	Œ	Œ	❺	∈	SOq	
207	œ	œ	œ	œ	❻	∉	Oq	
208	–	–	–	–	❼	∠	O-	En dash
209	—	—	—	—	❽	∇	SO-	Em dash
210	“	“	“	“	❾	®	O[	Open double quote
211	”	”	”	”	❿	©	SO[	Close double quote
212	‘	‘	‘	‘	➔	™	O]	Open single quote
213	’	’	’	’	→	∏	SO]	Close single quote
214	÷	÷	□	÷	↔	√	O/	
215	◊	◊	◊	◊	↕	·	SOv	
216	ÿ	ÿ	ÿ	ÿ	➘	¬	Ou,y	
217	Ÿ	[illegible]	~	Ÿ	➙	∧	SO`	
218	/	□	□	/	➚	∨	SO1	
219	¤	□	□	¤	➛	⇔	SO2	
220	‹	□	□	‹	➜	⇐	SO3	
221	›	□	□	›	➝	⇑	SO4	
222	fi	□	□	□	➞	⇒	SO5	
223	fl	□	□	□	➟	⇓	SO6	
224	‡	□	□	‡	➠	◊	SO7	
225	·	□	□	·	➡	〈	SO9	
226	‚	□	□	‚	➢	®	SO0	(zero)
227	„	□	□	„	➣	©	SOw	
228	‰	□	□	□	➤	™	SOe	
229	Â	□	□	Â	➥	∑	SOr	
230	Ê	□	□	Ê	➦	⎛	SOt	
231	Á	□	□	Á	➧	⎜	SOy	
232	Ë	□	□	Ë	➨	⎝	SOu	
233	È	□	□	È	➩	⎡	SOi	
234	Í	□	□	Í	➪	⎢	SOs	
235	Î	□	□	Î	➫	⎣	SOd	
236	Ï	□	□	Ï	➬	⎧	SOf	
237	Ì	□	□	Ì	➭	⎨	SOg	
238	Ó	□	□	Ó	➮	⎩	SOh	

ASCII	Times	Geneva	New York	Courier	Zapf Dingbats	Symbol	Keystrokes	Comments
239	Ô	□	□	Ô	⇨	|	SOj	
240		□	□				SOk	
241	Ò	□	□	Ò	⇨	〉	SOl	(letter "el")
242	Ú	□	□	Ú	➲	∫	SO;	
243	Û	□	□	Û	➳	⌠	SOz	
244	Ù	□	□	Ù	➴	⎮	SOx	
245	ı	□	□	ı	➵	⌡	SOb	
246	ˆ	□	□	ˆ	➶	⎞	SOn	
247	˜	□	□	˜	➷	⎟	SOm	
248	¯	□	□	¯	➸	⎠	SO,	
249	˘	□	□	˘	➹	⎤	SO.	(period)
250	˙	□	□	˙	➺	⎥	Oh	
251	˚	□	□	˚	➻	⎦	Ok	
252	¸	□	□	¸	➼	⎫		No keyboard equivalent
253	˝	□	□	˝	➽	⎬		No keyboard equivalent
254	˛	□	□	˛	➾	⎭		No keyboard equivalent
255	□	□	□	□				No keyboard equivalent

Using PostScript

PostScript is a deep and beautiful language. In some ways, however, it shares the reputation of languages based on the syntax of FORTH, namely, that it's difficult to read and to learn. Some have said that you can tell a program in FORTH is well written if you can't read it at all!

But nothing could be further from the truth. Programs written in PostScript can be as clear and self-documenting as those in any other computer language. While the depths of PostScript require as much study as any language, you can achieve many special effects in your Word documents, such as thin lines, gray-scale text, and boxes, without great effort. This appendix is by no means a complete introduction to the language, but it should give you enough background to get started. We assume that you've had some exposure to at least one other programming language. For further study, the *PostScript Language Reference Manual* and *PostScript Language Tutorial and Cookbook*, by Adobe Systems Incorporated and published by Addison-Wesley, are highly recommended. (It might be a good idea to review the material on printing with the LaserWriter in Chapter 14, "Document Formatting and Printing," especially the section entitled "What Happens When You Print on a LaserWriter.")

■ *Understanding PostScript Syntax*

The PostScript language is easy to understand, once you become accustomed to its inverted syntax. If you've ever used a Hewlett-Packard calculator, you've already had a taste of this syntax, in which you enter the numbers for the calculation first, and then enter the operator for the calculation. When you enter the numbers, they go into a special structure within the calculator called a *stack*—the last number entered becomes the topmost entry on the stack. When the operation is performed, it acts upon one or more of the topmost entries in their order of entry and puts the result on the stack for the next calculation. Here's an example of some PostScript:

```
2 3 add       % This enters two numbers and then adds them together
```

The two numbers precede the *add* command. (Most commands, known as *operators* in PostScript, are spelled for ease in reading rather than being represented by symbols. Other math operators include *sub* for subtraction, *mul* for multiplication, *div* for division, and *neg* for reversing the sign of a number.) Here, the two numbers are pushed onto the stack, and the *add* operator adds them, putting the result—*5*—back on the stack. Finally, the % character signifies that whatever follows on the same line is a comment and is to be ignored by the PostScript interpreter.

■ *Writing a Simple Program*

PostScript operators in a Word document act upon one of five rectangular areas: a page, a paragraph, a graphics frame, a cell in a table, or a row of cells in a table. The drawing commands that your program issues are measured relative to the lower left corner of one of these areas, depending on which you specify. The coordinate system PostScript uses sets the origin at the lower left corner and measures positive distances in points (1/72 inch) to the right and in an upward direction from the origin. For example, the coordinates of the origin are (0,0), and the coordinates of a point one inch to the right and two inches upward from the origin are (72,144). Where this origin is placed on a page depends on which area you set in your PostScript program.

Let's create a simple shape and show how it looks when printed. Here's a short program for drawing a box in the lower left corner of a page:

```
.page.              % Draw relative to the page rectangle
newpath             % Start the path to be drawn
72 72 moveto        % Move to bottom left corner of box
72 144 lineto       % Draw to top left corner of box
144 144 lineto      % Draw to top right corner
144 72 lineto       % Draw to bottom right corner
closepath           % Close path (draw back to first point)
.5 setgray          % Set a 50% gray level for the box
stroke              % Draw lines on the path just defined
```

To experiment with this PostScript, enter these lines into a blank document window. (You don't have to type the comments.) Then select all the lines from beginning to end, choose the Styles command, and give the lines the *PostScript* automatic style. If the style doesn't appear in the dialog box, press the Shift key while choosing the Styles command to make all the automatic styles appear. Because the definition of the *PostScript* style contains the Hidden attribute, you need to select the Show Hidden Text option in the Preferences dialog box so that you can see code assigned to the style. If you click the Set Default button while the *PostScript* style is selected, the style will appear in the Define Styles dialog box for any new document you create.

Word knows that any text in the *PostScript* style is to be sent on to a PostScript printer, such as the LaserWriter, as PostScript code instead of document text. When the PostScript interpreter inside the printer receives this series of operators, it executes each in the order received, creating patterns of pixels, which are then printed on paper or transferred to film.

The final step is to choose the Print command, ensure the Print Hidden Text option is not selected, and Click OK. The printed page should look like Figure C-1 (allowing for the 75% reduction in size that was used to represent the image of the page).

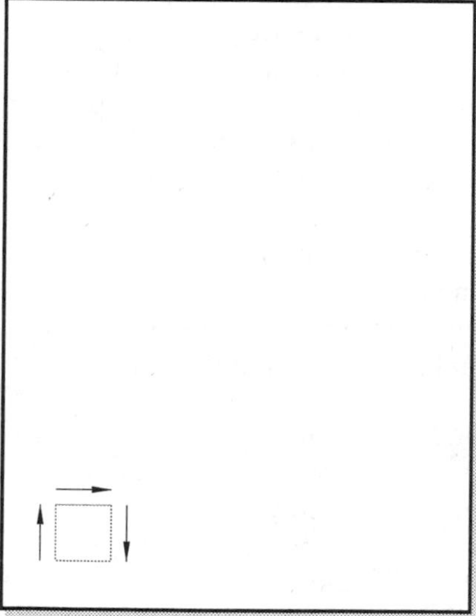

Figure C-1
The PostScript code as it looks when printed. (This figure is reduced to 25% and adds arrows to show the order of drawing.)

Let's look at this code more closely. The first PostScript operator, *.page.*, tells Word that the PostScript that follows is to be drawn relative to the rectangle of the page. The next operator, *newpath*, expresses a peculiarity of PostScript relative to other languages that contain graphics commands.

In other languages, when you draw a line, that line is drawn immediately. In PostScript, however, you create a *path* first, and then your code tells the PostScript interpreter in the printer what to do with the path. It's as if the PostScript interpreter first outlines a pattern with an empty pen, creating a template, and then waits for subsequent commands to draw the pattern in the way you want.

Here, the *newpath* operator tells PostScript to create a new, empty path, and the *moveto* operator moves the location of the imaginary pen to the first point in the new path. The *lineto* operators add line segments to the path after the last point specified in the path. The program contains three of these *lineto* operators, which create the left, top, and right edges of the box. The arrows in Figure C-1 show the direction of this path. The *closepath* operator is a convenience; it tells the PostScript interpreter to add a line segment to the current path leading from the last point in the path back to the first point, without requiring that you specify the coordinates of the path. The line not marked by an arrow is the line segment created by the *closepath* operator.

Because PostScript uses the point system to set measurements, these instructions specify a path for a box that is 1 inch square and starts 1 inch up from and to the right of the lower left corner of the page. The *setgray* operator sets the gray level of any subsequent drawing. It takes the number that precedes it on the stack; this can go from 0 (black) to 1 (white), so this box is drawn in 50% gray.

Finally, the *stroke* operator tells the PostScript interpreter to draw the path as a series of lines. This can be confusing at first, because you might have thought that this is what the program was doing all along—the use of the *lineto* operators seems to imply that actual lines are being drawn.

TIP

Turn Off Background Printing when Using PostScript
If the lower left corner of the box in this example seems to start roughly ½ inch lower and to the right than described above, you probably have Background Printing turned on. Macintosh system software versions up to 6.0.2 contain a bug that displaces PostScript on the first page of a Word document down and to the right by roughly ½ inch. To turn off Background Printing, choose Chooser from the Apple menu, and select the LaserWriter icon. To the right appears a list of the available LaserWriters in your AppleTalk network; below it is a pair of radio buttons for turning Background Printing on and off.

Modifying the Program

To understand the difference between a path and the lines drawn on the path with the *stroke* operator, let's repeat the program but replace the *stroke* operator with another, the *fill* operator:

```
.page.              % Draw relative to the page rectangle
newpath             % Start the path to be drawn
72 72 moveto        % Move to bottom left corner of box
72 144 lineto       % Draw to top left corner of box
144 144 lineto      % Draw to top right corner
144 72 lineto       % Draw to bottom right corner
closepath           % Close the path back to first point
.5 setgray          % Set a 50% gray level for the box
fill                % Fill the path with a gray level
```

When you change the one line in the program above that's different from the previous example (which we've indicated in boldface) and print the document, the page you'll see should look like Figure C-2.

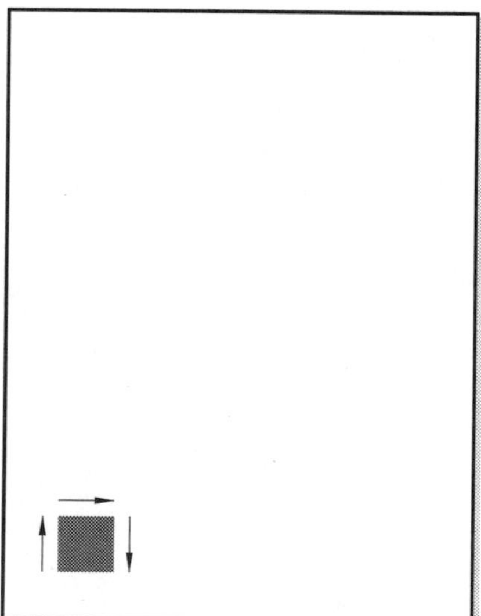

Figure C-2
The same path drawn with the *fill* operator instead of the *stroke* operator.

Now let's write a new program and define a new operator called *squarePath*, which we can use to draw a both filled and stroked box.

```
.page.              % Draw relative to the page rectangle

/squarePath
   {                % Start the definition of the operator
   newpath          % Start the path to be drawn
   72 72 moveto     % Move to bottom left corner of box
```

```
   72 144 lineto      % Draw to top left corner of box
   144 144 lineto     % Draw to top right corner of box
   144 72 lineto      % Draw to bottom right corner
   closepath          % Close the path back to first point
   } def              % Define the operator

.5 setgray            % Set a 50% gray level for the box
squarePath fill       % Draw the box as a filled path
0 setgray             % Set the color to black
squarePath stroke     % Draw the box as a series of stroked lines
```

We pulled out the part of the PostScript that sets the path for the box and defined it as an operator. When you do this, you must precede the name for the new operator with a slash and surround the operators that define it with curly braces. Finally, end the definition with the *def* operator. When you print the page containing this code, it should look like Figure C-3.

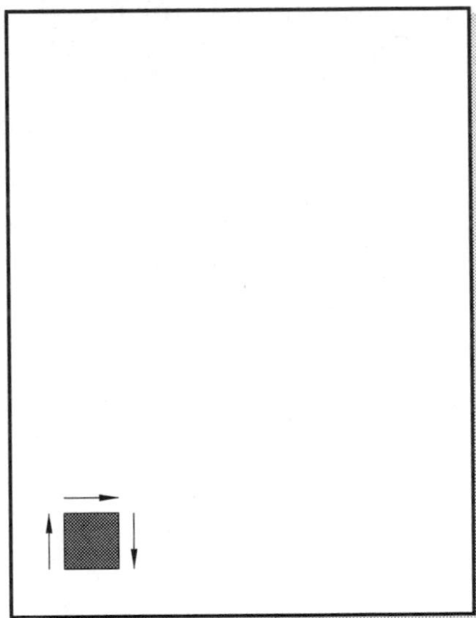

Figure C-3
Using both *fill* and *stroke* with the new *squarePath* operator.

■ *If an Error Occurs*

If your PostScript program contains an error, your LaserWriter or other PostScript printer usually does the worst thing possible (other than blowing up)—nothing. The yellow light blinks as the page is processed, and when the error happens, the blinking stops. You might get a partially completed page, letting you determine where in the page the problem occurred, but it's likely that you won't even get this. Errors that occur in the PostScript sent to the printer might not be reported to you by Word or by the printer.

Fortunately, there are steps you can take. If either a blank page or nothing at all appears instead of the results you expected, first check your typing. Also, in the last program, notice the blank lines between the groups of code. All the lines in a group of PostScript code must have the *PostScript* style, with no lines inadvertently assigned another style such as the *Normal* style—even the blank lines. This misassignment can happen easily, because the Next Style set in the definition for the *PostScript* style is the *Normal* style, which means that whenever you press the Return key after entering a line of PostScript, the next line reverts to the *Normal* style. To prevent this from happening, redefine the *PostScript* style, setting the contents of the Next Style field to *PostScript.*

Also, it's easier to read your code if you remove the Bold character attribute and set the font to Courier so that the spaces between operators are easier to see. In fact, you can change the *PostScript* style to anything you want, but leave the Hidden attribute set—it's not necessary in Word 4, but typically you want to print the PostScript effect, not the PostScript code *and* the effect.

You can also use a set of routines, called an *error dictionary,* which runs to about 30 lines of PostScript. (Groups of programs in PostScript are called dictionaries because you define operators that act like words in a sentence.) Error dictionaries, when sent to the printer ahead of your code, tell the printer to eject a page containing text describing what kind of error occurred and what was on the stack at the time of the error. From this you can usually discover the bug. You can get error dictionaries from user groups or from CompuServe; some are included with graphics programs that support PostScript.

You can use an error dictionary in two ways. First, you can download the dictionary to the PostScript printer before starting Word, making the dictionary *resident* on the printer until you reset it or turn it off. Cricket Draw has this ability, as does the SendPS utility from Adobe Systems. Using a resident error dictionary is handy because once you've sent it to the printer, you don't have to worry about including it before every piece of PostScript code you place in a document.

Second, you can include the dictionary in your Word document before the PostScript code you're writing and want to test. This type of dictionary is called a *nonresident* dictionary because it is cleared from the printer's memory after the printing is done. When your code works, remove the preceding error dictionary; including the error dictionary before every occurrence of your PostScript in a document can become unwieldy. (Later in this appendix we'll describe a method that lets you add your own PostScript dictionaries to the Word program itself.)

TIP

Saving a Printed Document's PostScript to a File
When you begin to plumb the depths of using PostScript in Word, you may find it useful to take a look at exactly what PostScript code is being sent to the printer. As discussed in Chapter 14, "Document Formatting and Printing," when you print a document on a PostScript printer, Word sends the document to the LaserWriter driver, which translates the graphics commands that comprise it into PostScript commands and sends them on to the printer. It precedes this stream of PostScript with a file called the Laser Prep file, consisting of about 25 KB of PostScript definitions for many of the operators used by the LaserWriter driver when it translates the document.

You can intercept this translation process and send the PostScript to a file rather than to the printer. This file can take two forms. If you choose the Print command and immediately press Command-K, the PostScript is sent to a file called PostScript0 (or PostScript1, and so on) beginning with the 25 KB of PostScript in the Laser Prep file. However, if you press Command-F instead, the file is saved without the Laser Prep header. The file is saved in the same folder as the Word program, and you can open it as a text file from Word to see the PostScript commands it contains. Finally, this technique works only if Background Printing is turned off.

■ *Working with Operators and Variables*

Earlier we defined a new operator by giving a group of operators a name. You can define other objects in the PostScript environment as well. For example, consider this operator for converting inches to points:

```
/inch
   { 72 mul } def
```

The *inch* operator takes a number from the stack and multiplies it by 72, returning the result to the stack. You could use it in this way to change the definition of the *squarePath* operator:

```
/inch
   { 72 mul } def

/squarePath
   { newpath
   1 inch 1 inch moveto
   1 inch 2 inch lineto
   2 inch 2 inch lineto
   2 inch 1 inch lineto
   closepath
   } def
```

The number of inches to be converted precedes each instance of the *inch* operator in *squarePath*. When the PostScript interpreter encounters the number, it puts the number on the stack. When the interpreter reads the *inch* operator, it looks up the definition and executes its code. The code in the definition first puts the number 72 on the stack, pushing the number representing the inches to the second position on the stack. The *mul* operator multiplies the first two numbers on the stack and puts the result on the stack.

Defining Variables

In PostScript, variables are almost identical to operators. If you wanted, you could define the number of points per inch as a constant, as in this code:

```
/pointsPerInch
   { 72 } def

/inch
   { pointsPerInch mul } def

/squarePath
   { newpath
   1 inch 1 inch moveto
   1 inch 2 inch lineto
   2 inch 2 inch lineto
   2 inch 1 inch lineto
   closepath
   } def
```

In the above code, *squarePath* uses, or calls, the *inch* operator and passes it the number to be converted on the stack. The *inch* operator in turn calls *pointsPerInch* to find its value and puts that number on the stack. The *mul* operator multiplies the numbers and puts the result on the stack. When control returns to *squarePath,* the number returned becomes a value passed to either the *moveto* or *lineto* operators. By defining values as constants in this way, you can make your code easier to read and to change.

Setting Values Outside a Routine

You can make a routine more useful, and therefore more general, by passing it values, which the routine uses internally. You can make the *squarePath* operator more general, allowing you to specify the coordinates of the lower left corner and to draw the sides of the square relative to that point. The complete code you need to draw a square in this manner is as follows:

```
.page.
/inch
   % Usage: number inch
   % Take: number in inches to be converted to points
   % Return: number converted to points
   { 72 mul } def
```

```
/squarePath                  % Draws a 1-inch square
   % Usage: xLeft yBottom squarePath
   % Take: coordinates of lower left corner
   % Return: nothing
   { newpath                 % Start new path
   moveto                    % Move to x and y coordinates on stack
   0 inch 1 inch rlineto     % Draw up 1 inch
   1 inch 0 inch rlineto     % Draw right 1 inch
   0 inch -1 inch rlineto    % Draw down 1 inch
   closepath                 % Draw back to beginning of path
   } def

1 inch 1 inch squarePath stroke
3 inch 3 inch squarePath fill
.5 setgray
5 inch 5 inch squarePath stroke
7 inch 7 inch squarePath fill
```

These lines of PostScript code might seem heavily commented for such short routines, but the style presented here is good for maintaining your work in as understandable a format as possible. Notice that *lineto* has been replaced with *rlineto*; whereas *lineto* adds a line to the current path in absolute coordinates, *rlineto* adds a line relative to the preceding point specified. In this version of the *squarePath* routine, you specify the first point in the path—the lower left corner of the square, outside the *squarePath* routine. The first *rlineto* operator measures from that first point 0 inches in the *x* dimension and 1 inch in the *y* dimension. Figure C-4 shows how these squares look when printed.

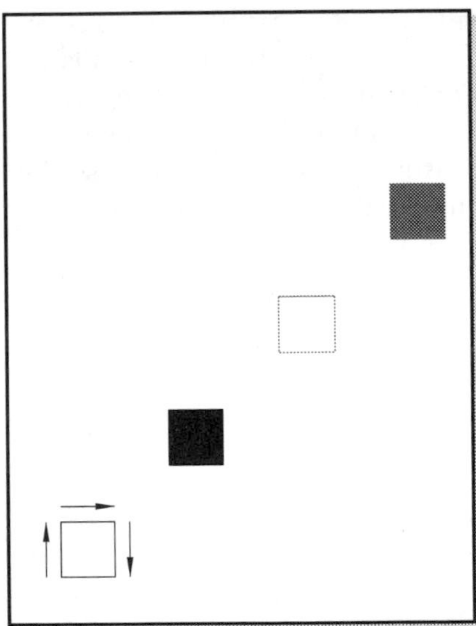

Figure C-4
Specifying the starting point of the square outside the *squarePath* routine.

Defining Variables Within a Routine

Often, it's helpful to give names to the values passed to a routine, making them variables to be used within the routine itself. You can make *squarePath* even more useful by passing it the size of the square as well as the position of its lower left corner.

```
.page.
/inch
   % Usage: number inch
   % Take: the number in inches to be converted to points
   % Return: the number converted to points
   { 72 mul } def

/squarePath                   % Draws a variable-sized square
   % Usage: xLeft yBottom size squarePath
   % Take: coordinates of lower left corner and size
   % Return: nothing
   {
   /size exch def             % Store first number on stack
                              %  in variable size
   newpath                    % Start new path
   moveto                     % Move to x and y coordinates on stack
   0 size rlineto             % Draw up size points
   size 0 rlineto             % Draw right size points
   0 size neg rlineto         % Draw down size points
   closepath                  % Draw back to beginning of path
   } def

1 inch 1 inch 3 inch squarePath stroke
3 inch 3 inch 2 inch squarePath fill
.5 setgray
5 inch 5 inch 1 inch squarePath stroke
7 inch 7 inch .5 inch squarePath fill
```

In this version, *squarePath* takes three values—two numbers representing the coordinates of the lower left corner and one number for the size of the square in points. Because the size value is the last one set before *squarePath*, it's the first value on the stack when the routine is executed.

Notice the first line in the *squarePath* routine: */size exch def*. This is a special construction in PostScript; first the label */size* is pushed onto the stack, making the size the second value. The *exch* operator exchanges the positions of the first two values on the stack, and the *def* operator then assigns the value representing the size to the label *size*. Subsequently, every instance of the variable *size* is replaced with the number the label contains.

Creating variables in this way is very useful because you can use values over again or set a variable to a value at the beginning of a routine and alter the value at various points within the routine. In the *squarePath* routine, the *size* variable sets the amount by which all the relative movements are added to the current path through the *rlineto* operators. Figure C-5 shows how this code looks when executed.

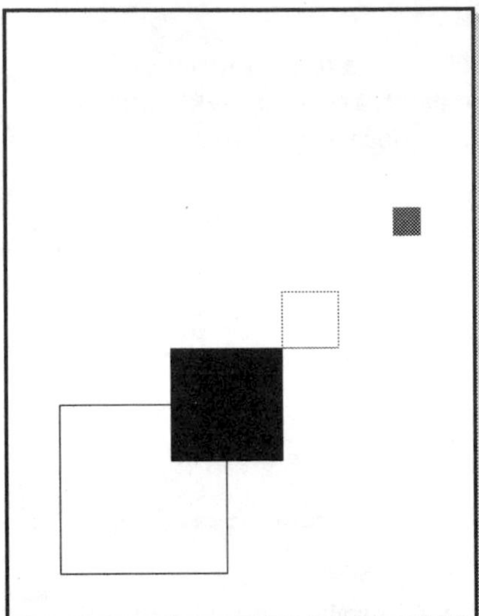

Figure C-5
Specifying both the starting point and size of the square outside the *squarePath* routine.

Word's Drawing Rectangles

Earlier we mentioned that the PostScript operators that you group at one place in a document are drawn on the page relative to one of five areas, called drawing rectangles. The distances you specify are measured from the lower left corner of one of these areas. You've already encountered one of them—the page. Each group of PostScript operators that you insert in a document should be preceded by one of the following group operators, to specify the area you want to draw in:

Group operator	Applies to
.page.	The limits of the printable area on the page. If you don't specify a group operator, Word defaults to this area. Applies to the page containing the PostScript.
.para.	Vertically, from the top of the Space Before value for the paragraph to the bottom of the Space After value. Horizontally, from either the first-line or left indent (whichever is leftmost) to the right indent. Applies to the first non-PostScript paragraph following the group.
.pic.	The limits of a graphics frame within the first non-PostScript paragraph following the group. The first .pic. group applies to the first graphics frame in the following paragraph, the second .pic. group applies to the the second, and so on.

Group operator	Applies to
.cell.	The limits of the cell containing the PostScript.
.row.	The limits of the entire row containing the PostScript.

As shown in the table, you place the group of PostScript operators that you want to apply to an area either inside the area or immediately before it. With pages, cells, and rows, you can place the PostScript anywhere within the area. With paragraphs you place the PostScript immediately before the paragraph. Applying PostScript to graphic frames is like applying it to paragraphs, with a minor difference we'll discuss in a moment.

Let's look at a few examples of how you might apply PostScript to these areas. We've already discussed drawing within the page. You might use *squarePath* within a paragraph to create an interesting effect in this way:

```
.para.
/inch
   % Usage: number inch
   % Take: the number in inches to be converted to points
   % Return: the number converted to points
   { 72 mul } def

/squarePath  % Draws a variable-sized square
   % Usage: xLeft yBottom size squarePath
   % Take: coordinates of lower left corner and size
   % Return: nothing
   {
   /size exch def        % Store first number on stack
                         %  in variable size
   newpath               % Start new path
   moveto                % Move to x and y coordinates on stack
   0 size rlineto        % Draw up size points
   size 0 rlineto        % Draw right size points
   0 size neg rlineto    % Draw down size points
   closepath             % Draw back to beginning of path
   } def

0 setgray
0 inch 1 inch .5 inch squarePath fill
.25 setgray
.25 inch .75 inch .5 inch squarePath fill
.5 setgray
.5 inch .5 inch .5 inch squarePath fill
.75 setgray
.75 inch .25 inch .5 inch squarePath fill
```

Figure C-6
Using *squarePath* within the rectangle of the paragraph.

The paragraph in Figure C-6 containing the text was indented from the left margin and has 1 inch of Space After; all the *x* values are measured from the left margin of the paragraph, and all the *y* values are measured from the bottom of the Space After format. We added a Border format above the paragraph after the one the PostScript was applied to, providing a reference point. Notice that the squares were drawn behind the text; the PostScript on a page is drawn before any Word text is printed, regardless of where on the page it is placed or which drawing rectangle it applies to. However, if you want to draw the PostScript effects over all the Word's text, select the Print PostScript Over Text option in the Page Setup dialog box.

Applying PostScript to graphics frames is similar to applying it to pages and paragraphs, but there is one difference. To draw within a graphics frame that is itself within a paragraph, place the code before that paragraph. If more than one graphics frame exists in the paragraph, you can apply PostScript to each in sequence by preceding each group of PostScript operators with a *.pic.* operator, as shown below. You can see the resulting output in Figure C-7. (However, as of this writing, Word 4.0 puts each PostScript effect in the first of a series of graphics frames instead of placing one effect in each graphics frame, as shown in the figure, which was printed from Word 3.02.)

```
.pic.        % graphics frame 1
/squarePath
   {/size exch def
   newpath moveto
   0 size rlineto size 0 rlineto 0 size neg rlineto
   closepath
   } def
0 setgray 0 0 9 squarePath fill
.pic.        % graphics frame 2
/squarePath
   {/size exch def
   newpath moveto
   0 size rlineto size 0 rlineto 0 size neg rlineto
   closepath
   } def
.25 setgray 9 9 9 squarePath fill
```

```
.pic.        % graphics frame 3
/squarePath
   {/size exch def
   newpath moveto
   0 size rlineto size 0 rlineto 0 size neg rlineto
   closepath
   } def
.5 setgray 18 18 9 squarePath fill
.pic.        % graphics frame 4
/squarePath
   {/size exch def
   newpath moveto
   0 size rlineto size 0 rlineto 0 size neg rlineto
   closepath
   } def
.75 setgray 27 27 9 squarePath fill
```

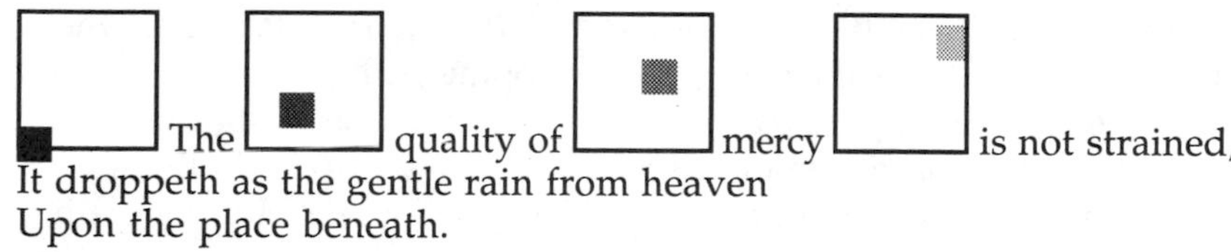

The quality of mercy is not strained,
It droppeth as the gentle rain from heaven
Upon the place beneath.

Figure C-7
Using *squarePath* within the rectangle of four graphic frames.

As you can see, you must repeat the definitions of every operator used for each instance; to shorten the resulting code, we reverted to the point system instead of using the *inch* operator. We also removed the comments and compacted the remaining code. Each graphics frame has the Outline attribute, so you can see the position of the squares relative to the frame.

One benefit of being able to specify drawing areas with the group operators is that you can nest effects. For example, if you wanted you could nest a graphics frame within a paragraph, within a cell, within a row, within the page, and give each area a different type of PostScript effect.

Word's Drawing Rectangles and Clipping

Word's drawing rectangles have an additional property that can be both a help and a hindrance, depending on the effect you want to achieve. Whenever you draw within one of Word's five types of drawing rectangles, the images drawn on the page are limited to the edges of that area. The perimeter of the rectangle within which your commands are drawn is often called its *bounding box*. The path of the box that clips the image beyond its borders is called its *clipping path*.

This behavior is useful when you want to limit, for example, the extent of a PostScript effect you're adding to a certain paragraph. But what do you do if you want to draw something immediately outside a paragraph? For example, if you want to place a shaded square to the left of a paragraph by using the *squarePath* operator described earlier, you might use code such as the following:

```
.para.
/inch { 72 mul } def
/squarePath
   {/size exch def
   newpath moveto
   0 size rlineto size 0 rlineto 0 size neg rlineto
   closepath
   } def

.5 setgray
-.5 inch 0 inch .25 inch squarePath fill
```

The last line in this code will start the lower left corner of the square 1 inch to the left of the left indent. Because the width of the square is 0.25 inch, the square is positioned outside the paragraph's clipping path.

You can empty the clipping path that Word automatically attaches to the drawing rectangle for the region associated with a group of PostScript commands by using the *initclip* operator. This reinitializes the clipping path, allowing you to draw anywhere on the page relative to the lower left corner of the drawing rectangle you've specified. To draw the square in the last example correctly, you would use code such as this:

```
.para.
/inch { 72 mul } def
/squarePath
   {/size exch def
   newpath moveto
   0 size rlineto size 0 rlineto 0 size neg rlineto
   closepath
   } def

initclip
.5 setgray
-.5 inch 0 inch .25 inch squarePath fill
```

The .dict. Group Operator

There's actually a sixth group operator, called the *.dict.* operator, new in Word 4. It doesn't specify an area on the page, but solves a problem associated with defining routines in your documents. Let's say that you want to use the *inch* and *squarePath* operators as defined in the last example to the left of the following paragraph, but didn't use the *.dict.* group operator. If you wanted to draw the grey square to the left of several locations on a page, you'd have to redefine both routines at every location. This happens because Word forgets the operators defined in each group of code after the group has been sent to the printer.

This behavior is both beneficial and problematic. It's beneficial because usually you don't want the effects of the PostScript you send to the printer to accumulate or to affect subsequent PostScript. If Word remembered every change made from one group to the next, some characteristic you've set in one group could affect the results specified in another. If, for example, you set the grey level to 50% in one group, and didn't set it to another level in the next group, the grey level would remain at 50%. Unless controlled, the combination of possible effects among groups could make it very hard to write, debug, and predict the effects of your PostScript routines.

On the other hand, having to redefine effects at every instance can be cumbersome, because it clutters your document with text that has nothing to do with its actual content. Having a large amount of code distributed throughout a document makes it much easier to damage code inadvertently, particularly in work-group situations, where writers and formatters have to work together. Also, if you want to adjust an effect, you have to find and edit or replace every instance of the code in the document.

The *.dict.* group goes far to solve the problem of redundant PostScript in a document. With it you can define operators that hold for an entire page, not solely for one group. When you want to use a routine defined in a *.dict.* group, you need only use the name of the routine, not redefine it. To continue our example mentioned above, you can isolate the definitions for the inch and squarePath operators in a .dict. group, and use them many times on a page without having to redefine the operators:

```
.dict.
/inch { 72 mul } def
/squarePath
   {/size exch def
   newpath moveto
   0 size rlineto size 0 rlineto 0 size neg rlineto
   closepath
   } def
.
.
.
```

(non-PostScript text in the document)

```
.
.
.
.para. initclip .5 setgray
-.5 inch 0 inch .25 inch squarePath fill
```

(following non-PostScript paragraph to have the special effect)

```
.
.
.
.para. initclip .5 setgray
-.5 inch 0 inch .25 inch squarePath fill
```

(following non-PostScript paragraph to have the special effect)

When you use the *.dict.* group operator, the operators in the group shouldn't actually draw anything on the page. Instead, use the operators you've defined here within the other groups of PostScript on the page.

It's "beyond the scope of this book," as they say, to go into a detailed explanation of the reason why the definitions in *.dict.* groups last only for one page. Technically, it's because the Macintosh Printing Manager, which is responsible for converting the Toolbox commands used to create the document into a series of PostScript operators, inserts several levels of *save* and *restore* operators between one page and the next. These operators "protect" the PostScript which creates one page from the PostScript on the next by saving the state of the printer's memory before executing the PostScript on the page. When the PostScript that creates the image of the page has been executed, the saved memory state is restored. Because the operators you define are defined within the page-level PostScript, the operators are forgotten when the page is done.

However, you can use a trick to get around this limitation. As we discussed in Chapter 14, "Document Formatting and Printing," Word prints the contents of a page's header before anything else on the page. If you put the *.dict.* group in the header belonging to a section, the definitions are sent automatically before each page in the section. In this way, you can hide a definition as a routine in the header, and use it at one or more locations in the body of the document. If the document has only one header, you can define PostScript routines that hold for the entire document in only one place.

Word's Variables

Word makes it easier to position PostScript effects relative to the current drawing rectangle by passing certain variables to the PostScript printer before each group of code you place in a document. Some of these variables contain the same information regardless of which drawing rectangle is being used, and some change. The following table lists these variables.

Variable	Type and unit	Applies to	Contains
Variables that remain constant for all drawing rectangles			
wp$page	number	all	Current page number.
wp$fpage	string	all	Current page number in the format set in the Section dialog box.
wp$date	string	all	Current date.
wp$time	string	all	Current time.

Variable	Type and unit	Applies to	Contains
Variables that change depending on the drawing rectangle specified			
wp$yorig *wp$xorig*	number in points	all	Location of the lower left corner of the drawing area, expressed in page coordinates (e.g., for the *.page.* group, both variables are set to zero).
wp$y	number in points	all	Height of the drawing rectangle.
wp$x	number in points	all	Width of the drawing rectangle.
wp$box	path	all	Defines a path containing the current drawing rectangle.
wp$style	string	*.para.* only	Full style name of the paragraph following.
wp$top	number in points	*.page.*	Top margin.
		.para.	Space Before value.
		.cell.	Space Before value of the first paragraph in the cell.
		.row.	Space Before value of the first paragraph in the row.
wp$bottom	number in points	*.page.*	Bottom margin.
		.para.	Space After value.
		.cell.	Space After value of the first paragraph in the cell.
		.row.	Space After value of the first paragraph in the row.
wp$left	number in points	*.page.*	Left margin, including the gutter.
		.para.	Distance between left margin and left indent.
		.cell.	Distance between left margin and left indent of the first paragraph in the cell.
		.row.	Distance between left margin and left indent of the first paragraph in the row.
wp$right	number in points	*.page.*	Right margin, including the gutter.
		.para.	Distance between right margin and right indent.
		.cell.	Distance between right margin and right indent of the first paragraph in the cell.
		.row.	Distance between right margin and right indent of the first paragraph in the row.
wp$first	number in points	*.para.* only	Width of the first-line indent.
wp$col	number	*.page.* only	Number of columns.
wp$colx	number in points	*.page.* only	Width of each column.
wp$colxb	number in points	*.page.* only	Space between columns.

Notice that in the second section of the table the four entries *wp$top*, *wp$bottom*, *wp$left*, and *wp$right* contain measurements that are defined for either pages or paragraphs—but not graphic frames. Using a variable in a group of code for an area in which the variable isn't defined creates an error.

Also, there are no entries for the *.dict.* group in the table, because Word doesn't generate variables when you use this group. You can use the variable names in your definitions, however, because the PostScript interpreter in the printer looks up the definitions of the routines in the *.dict.* group only when it encounters the name of the routine in one of the other five groups. Because the code you include in any of the other groups is preceded by variable definitions which pertain to that group, those variables will be used in the routines you defined in the *.dict.* group.

Let's look at a few examples of how you might use these variables in your PostScript code. If you want to put a gray box behind the text in a paragraph, as we've done with the tip design elements in this book, use this code:

```
.para. .9 setgray wp$box fill
```

Here, the *wp$box* variable defines a path for the *fill* operator, in much the same way that we used the *squarePath* operator above.

If you want to draw a box around a paragraph, use this code:

```
.para. wp$box stroke
```

This produces an effect much like using the Box Border paragraph format. However, whereas the Box format does not take into account the Space before and Space After values, the PostScript version does. If you want to change the width of the line used to draw the box, use the *setlinewidth* operator, which takes a value in points:

```
.para. .5 setlinewidth wp$box stroke
```

Finally, if you want to draw a 0.5-point line around a paragraph that takes into account both the Space Before and Space After formats and starts at the margins rather than at the left and right indents, you might use code such as this:

```
.para.
initclip                          % Reset the clipping path
.5 setlinewidth                   % Draw half-point-wide lines
newpath                           % Start a new path
wp$left neg 0 moveto              % Move to first point
wp$left neg wp$y lineto           % Draw left side of box
wp$x wp$right add wp$y lineto     % Draw top of box
wp$x wp$right add 0 lineto        % Draw right side of box
closepath                         % Return to beginning
stroke                            % Draw the path as a series of lines
```

The possibilities for PostScript in your Word documents are limitless, and this book can only hint at the range of the effects you can produce. The two books cited at the beginning of the chapter are great aides for extending your knowledge of PostScript.

■ *Adding PostScript Operators to Word*

You can add your own PostScript operators to Word by modifying the Word program itself. This isn't difficult, but you should take a few preliminary steps. First, make a copy of Word to use in your experiments. Next, find the SerialPrinter driver file; if it isn't in your System Folder already, copy it there from the Word Utilities disk.

If you're using a hard disk, put a copy of ResEdit on the hard disk. If you're using floppies, put a copy of the ResEdit program on the startup disk. ResEdit1.2b2.2 is about 264 KB, so you might have to remove or rearrange some files to get the System Folder and ResEdit to fit on one disk.

Finally, you'll need the definitions for the PostScript operators you want to add to Word. For this example, suppose you've developed the following code, inventing two new operators. The PostScript in boldface contains the operators you want to add.

```
.para.
/inch
   % Usage: num inches
   % Take: a number in inches
   % Return: the number converted to points
   { 72 mul } def

/grayBoxFill
   % Usage: num grayBoxFill
   % Take: the graylevel, from 0 (black) to 1 (white)
   % Return: nothing
   {
      setgray              % Takes the graylevel from the stack
      wp$box fill          % Fills the path with that graylevel
   } def
.5 grayBoxFill
0 setgray
0 0 moveto 2 inch 1 inch lineto stroke
```

A good way to go about developing this code is to first write and debug it as text given the *PostScript* style in a Word document. When everything works the way you want, select and copy every line of the code between the *.para.* operator and the commands that execute the operators you've defined. Then paste them into the Scrapbook where they'll remain until needed. Also, save the Word document you used to develop the code so that you can make further refinements later.

The following procedure describes a method for adding our PostScript to a special resource called the PREC 103 resource within the Word program. Word doesn't come with a PREC having this ID number, but it does have one called PREC 4, which we can duplicate and convert to a PREC 103 resource.

❶ Start ResEdit. You'll see a small window for each volume you have open. Scroll in the list box, and double-click the name of the folder which contains Word. Another window opens which lists all the files in the folder, as shown in Figure C-8.

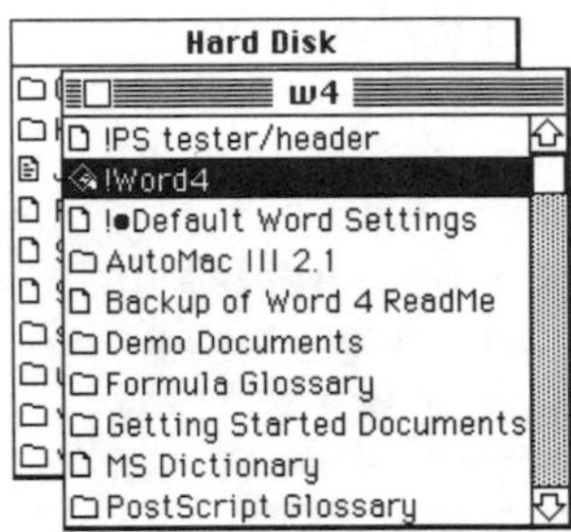

Figure C-8
The window listing the files contained in the Word folder.

❷ Find the entry for the Word program and double-click its name. Another window opens, listing Word's resources. Scroll in the list box until you find the PREC resource, as shown in Figure C-9.

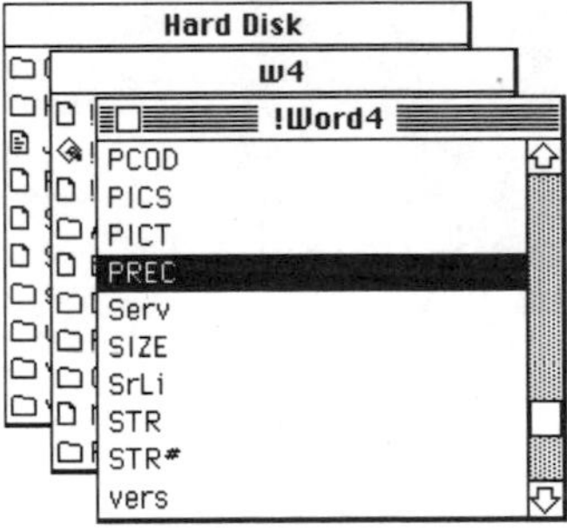

Figure C-9
The window listing all the resources attached to the Word program.

❸ Find and double-click the entry containing Word's PREC resources. Yet another window opens, listing Word's PREC resources, as shown in Figure C-10. Only one entry should be listed—the PREC 4 resource.

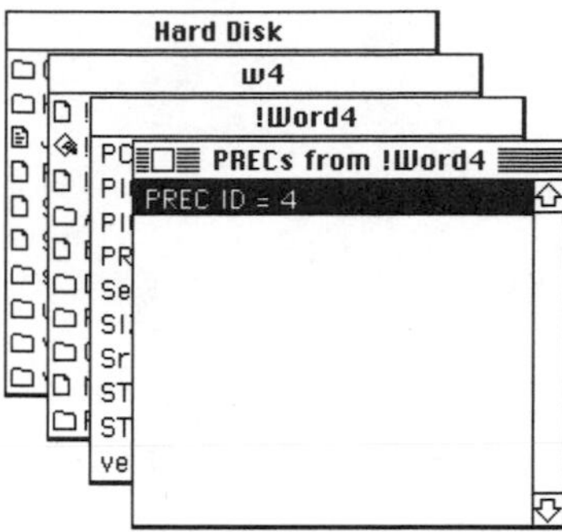

Figure C-10
The window listing the PREC 4 resource in the Word program.

4. Select the PREC 4 resource and choose Duplicate from the Edit menu to create another copy of the PREC 4 resource. The new resource has the same contents as the PREC 4 resource, but ResEdit assigns it a random ID number. (When you do this step, you'll likely get a different ID number.)

5. Select the new resource and choose Get Info from the File menu. The window shown in Figure C-11 appears. Change the contents of the ID field to *103,* and close the Get Info window. Now the resource has the correct ID number, but retains the same contents as the PREC 4 resource.

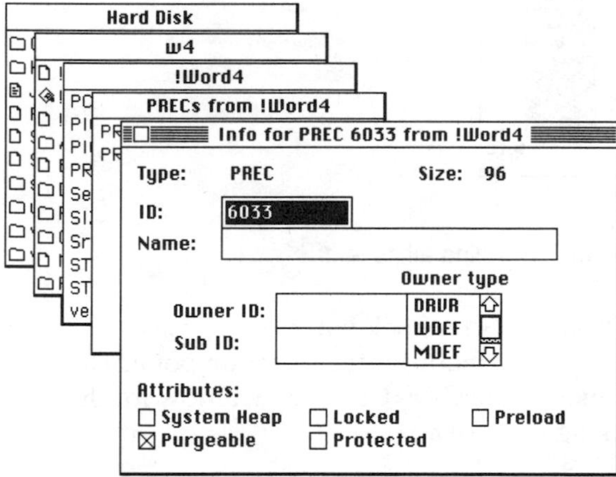

Figure C-11
The Get Info window for the new resource.

6. Double-click the entry for the PREC 103 to see what it contains. Another window opens, as shown in Figure C-12, displaying the contents of the resource in both hexadecimal and text format.

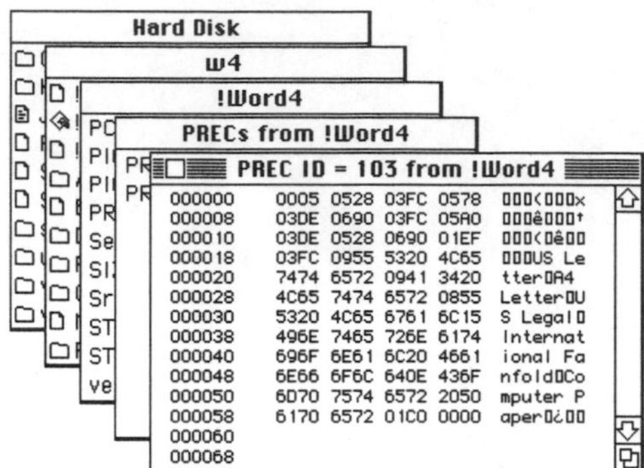

Figure C-12
Word's new PREC 103 resource, in both hexadecimal and text formats.

❼ Select all the text in the text area of the resource by dragging from just before the first character to beyond the last character, as shown in Figure C-13. Choose Clear to delete the text, leaving only the insertion point.

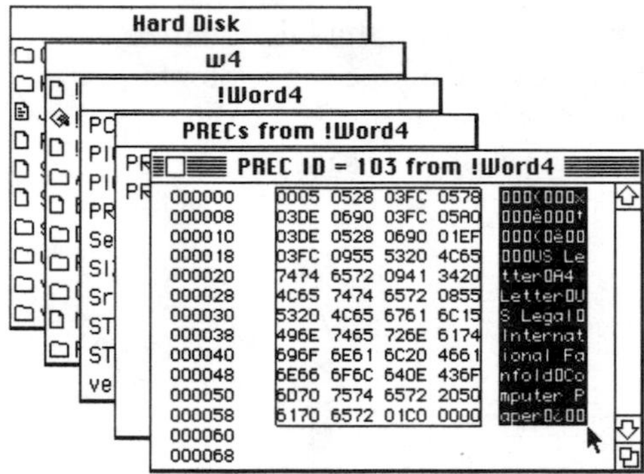

Figure C-13
How the PREC 103 window looks after selecting all its text.

❽ Copy the PostScript code from the Scrapbook where you pasted it earlier. Paste it into the PREC 103 window at the insertion point. The window should now look like Figure C-14. Close the window for the PREC 103 resource by clicking its close box.

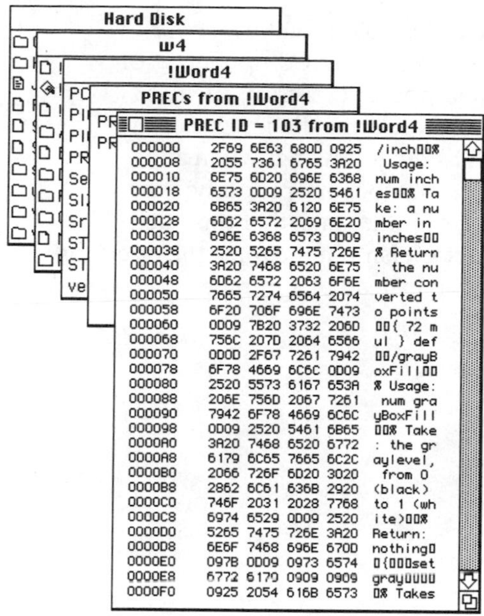

Figure C-14
The PREC 103 resource after pasting in the PostScript code.

❾ Quit ResEdit. A dialog box appears asking if you want to save the edited copy of Word. Click Yes.

To verify that you've successfully added new PostScript commands to Word, start the copy of Word to which you've added the PREC 103 resource, and enter the same PostScript code as before, but this time leave out the definitions for the commands you've added:

```
.para.
.5 grayBoxFill
0 setgray
0 0 moveto 2 inch 1 inch lineto stroke
```

If the operators you've added don't work correctly or don't seem to work at all, try the following suggestions:

- ❑ Be sure you've fully debugged the code in the Word document you first used to develop the code.
- ❑ Even though you've moved the definitions for the new PostScript commands into the PREC 103 resource, you still need to precede each group of PostScript code in your document that uses the commands with a group operator. If you don't use one, *.page.* is assumed.

- Make the first block of code in the PREC 103 resource an *error dictionary,* which you can get from user groups, CompuServe, or from some software packages that support PostScript, such as Cricket Draw. The various forms of these error dictionaries can report certain types of errors, such as the following: when an operator needs more values on the stack to work properly; when a procedure generates so many entries on the stack that the stack overflows; or when a value on the stack isn't in the form the operator needs (for example, a character string instead of a number).

Mathematical Typesetting

If you work with mathematical formulas frequently, you'll appreciate Word's math typesetting feature. However, it's a feature that requires study and a fair amount of practice to master, because it diverges from the philosophy of What You See Is What You Get. To use this feature, you encode mathematical terms in a special language instead of entering text and arranging the terms with the mouse. For example, to express the equation for the length of the hypotenuse of a right triangle, you could create an equation such as this:

$$r = \sqrt{x^2 + y^2}$$

It's easy to superscript the number *2* in this example and to change the point size from 9 to 8. But how do you create the square root, or radical, symbol? For effects like this, you must use the math typesetting feature. The same equation expressed in math typesetting code looks like this:

r = .\R(x^2 + y^2)

This equation has only one component that isn't part of the text of the formula: the backslash with a dot under it, called the *formula character*, and the capital *R* that follows it. The *R* command draws a radical around whatever is enclosed in the parentheses. Word's typesetting commands typically use one or more *arguments*, listed inside parentheses; in the example above, the text $x^2 + y^2$ is an argument used by the *R* command. You can format the contents of an argument as you would any other text in Word.

You enter the formula character by pressing Option-Command-\. You must have Show ¶ on, or you'll see only a normal backslash. Each typesetting command begins with.\ and a letter specifying the command. After you construct the formula, press Command-Y again to turn Show ¶ off. Word converts the typesetting codes into the actual formula; the formula characters, typesetting codes, and the parentheses surrounding the arguments disappear. You can select parts of the formula to format when Show ¶ is off, but remember that the placement of the parts is determined by the typesetting codes and not by Word's standard routines for arranging text, so the results can be unpredictable. Do all your formatting and editing within the typesetting code, when Show ¶ is on, or format an entire line containing the formula at once.

Most of the typesetting commands have options that alter their effects. You enter an option immediately after a command and precede each option with the formula character. For example, if you want to draw brackets around the name of a variable, you might use typesetting code such as this:

.\B.\BC.\{(X)

to create this:

{X}

Some additional points to remember:

- ❑ When typesetting formulas, avoid putting a minus sign in front of the Line Spacing measurement in the Paragraph dialog box, because this might cause parts of a formula that extend beyond the limits of the line spacing to be cut off. Often, however, the text will reappear when the document is printed.
- ❑ Use a glossary to store fragments of formulas. Give each entry a name you can remember. Select only the fragment you want to record—not an ending paragraph mark, for instance—because you want the fragment inserted from the glossary to take on the character and paragraph formats of the surrounding text. When you insert the glossary item, use it as a template, replacing its parts as needed. The distribution disks for Word contain a glossary file that you can customize for your own needs.
- ❑ You can use many of the characters in the Symbol font to represent special characters in formulas. For example, to get the symbol for pi (π), switch to the Symbol font and type the letter *p*. A special key sequence exists for using the Symbol font: Press Shift-Command-Q,

and the next letter you type will be in the Symbol font. Text you enter after the first character returns to the base character format for the style.

- Often, it's easier to use Word's standard character formatting features to create an effect, rather than construct complex arrangements of typesetting code. For example, you can superscript by using the \S command, but you can also superscript by using the Character command.
- Once you create a formula, you can prevent changes to it. To do this, select the formula, press Option-Command-D to copy an image of the selection to the Clipboard as a PICT graphic, and paste the image over the original selection. Or you can keep the original formula in a separate place and transfer only the finished image of the formula to the main document. Also, you can transfer images of formulas to programs other than Word by copying the PICT version and pasting it into a document opened from within the other application.
- If you rarely need to create formulas, remember that you can create the image of a formula as an arrangement of text objects in an object-oriented drawing program such as SuperPaint and then copy the image into Word.
- You can also use the typesetting commands to create other effects besides mathematical formulas. For example, you can position characters with the D, or Displace, command, as shown below.

The codes and options for each command and some examples showing their use are listed below:

A, Array

The A command creates a two-dimensional array from a series of arguments.

Usage \A*options*(*argument1*, ...)

Options	AL, AR, AC	Alignment: left, right, or centered.
	CO*n*	Formats for *n* columns.
	VS*n*	Sets line spacing to *n* points.
	HS*n*	Sets column spacing to *n* points.

Examples

$$\begin{pmatrix} 1\,2\,3 \\ 4\,5\,6 \\ 7\,8\,9 \end{pmatrix}$$

Draw a 3-by-3 matrix.

\B\BC\((\A\AC\CO3(\S\AI4(1),\S\AI4(2),\S\AI4(3), 4, 5, 6 , 7, 8, 9))

$$\begin{bmatrix} x_{11} & \cdots & x_{1n} \\ \cdot & & \cdot \\ \cdot & & \cdot \\ \cdot & & \cdot \\ x_{n1} & \cdots & x_{nn} \end{bmatrix}$$

Create an *n*-by-*n* array.

\B\BC\[(\A\AC\CO5(x\S\DO3(11) , ., ., .,
x\S\DO3(1n) , . , , , , . , . , , , , , . , . , , , , , . . ,
x\S\DO3(n1), ., ., ., x\S\DO3(nn)))

B, Brackets

The B command places brackets on one or both sides of an argument.

Usage \B*options*(*argument*)

Options LC*c*, RC*c*, BC*c* Sets brackets on left, right, or both sides with character *c*. If *c* is {, [, (, or <, the corresponding closing character is used on the right side.

Example

| f(x) | Absolute value of f(x).

\B\BC\ | (f(x))

D, Displace

The D command positions the next character horizontally. It doesn't take an argument, but you must supply the parentheses anyway.

Usage \D*options*()

Options

FOn	Moves to the right *n* points.
BAn	Moves to the left *n* points.
LI	Draws a line from the end of the first specified character to the starting position of the second specified character.

Examples

X Y — Draw *Y* 30 points to the right of *X*.

X\D\FO30()Y

Y X — Draw *Y* 40 points to the left of *X*.

X\D\BA40()Y

X——Y

Draw *Y* 30 points to the right of *X*, and draw a line between them.

X.\D.\LI.\FO30()Y

Y X

Draw *Y* 40 points to the left of *X*, and draw a line between them.

X.\D.\LI.\BA40()Y

F, Fraction

The F command creates a fraction from two arguments (numerator and denominator) centered above and below the line.

Usage .\F(*argument1*, *argument2*)

Example

$\frac{a + b}{c + d}$

Fraction *a* + *b* over *c* + *d*.

.\F(a + b,c + d)

I, Integral

The I command creates integral, product, and summation symbols from three arguments: In the case of the integrand, the first sets the lower limit; the second sets the upper limit; the third sets the integrand.

Usage .\I*options*(*argument1*, *argument2*, *argument3*)

Options

SU, PR	Changes the integral symbol to a summation symbol (SU) or the product symbol (PR).
IN	Inline format, with the limits printed to the right of the symbol.
FC.*c*, VC.*c*	Changes the integral symbol to *c*. FC creates a fixed-height character, and VC creates a variable-height character that matches the height of the integrand.

Examples

$\int_a^b f\, d\alpha$	Integral of *f* from *a* to *b*. \I\IN (\S\DO5(a),\S\UP15(b),*f*) dα The symbol *f* is Option-7 in the Symbol font. The symbol α is the letter *a* in the Symbol font.
$\prod_{i=1}^{n} x_i$	Product of x_i from 1 to n. \I\PR (i =1,n, x \S\DO3(i))

L, List

The L command creates a list of values from any number of arguments, without requiring the use of \ before each value.

Usage \L(*argument1, ...*)

O, Overstrike

The O command draws arguments over each other, in the order given by the arguments.

Usage \O(*argument1, argument2, ...*)

Options AL, AR, AC — Aligns the characters on their left or right edges, or centers them (the default option).

Example

\	Simulate the formula character. \O\AL(.,\)

R, Radical

The R command draws a radical symbol. If one argument is supplied, it appears under the radical. If two arguments are supplied, the first appears over the radical.

Usage \R(*argument1, argument2*)

Examples

$\sqrt{x}$	Square root of x. .\R(x)
$\sqrt[n]{x}$	*N*th root of x. .\R(n, x)

S, Superscript or Subscript

The S command positions vertically one or more arguments.

Usage .\S(*argument1, argument2, ...*)

Options

UP*n*, DO*n*	Moves the argument up or down *n* points.
AI*n*, DI*n*	Adds space in points above the ascender or below the descender of the argument. You can use this with the X command to adjust spacing around bordered elements. These options are affected by "negative" line spacing measurements.

Example

f_1	Function *f* sub 1. *f*.\S.\DO3(1) The subscript is in 7-point Palatino font. The *f* symbol is Option-7 in the Symbol font.

X, Box

The X command draws borders around an argument. If you don't supply an option, it draws borders on all four sides.

Usage .\X(*argument*)

Options

TO	Top border.
BO	Bottom border.
LE	Left border.
RI	Right border.

Example

$\boxed{\text{abc}}$	Draw a box around *abc*. .\X(abc)

Word's Preset Defaults

The tables in this chapter present the defaults stored in the Word Settings (4) file, which comes with the Word Program disk and is normally kept in the System Folder of the startup disk. As you add commands to Word's menus, assign key sequences to commands, set preferences, and so on, the new settings become the defaults stored in the current Settings file. This Settings file is either the Word Settings (4) file itself or one you've created by clicking the Save As button in the Commands dialog box. To return the current Settings file to the preset state:

1. Open the Commands dialog box.
2. Press the Shift key while clicking the Reset button. Word responds with a dialog box asking, "Are you sure you want to revert to default settings?"
3. Click OK. Word returns the current Settings file to its preset defaults.

For more information about commands, defaults, and storing defaults in Settings files, see Chapter 3, "The Word Environment."

Settings Stored in a Word Settings File

Following is a table describing what is stored in a Word Settings file and showing the preset state (indicated in italic type) of the Word Settings (4) file from your original Word Program disk.

Where and What Set	Options
Preferences dialog box	
Unit of measurement	*Inch,* Centimeter, Points, or Picas
Show Hidden Text	*On* or off
Use Picture Placeholders	On or *off*
Show Table Gridlines	On or *off*
Show Text Boundaries in Page View	On or *off*
Open Documents in Page View	On or *off*
Background Repagination	On or *off*
"Smart" Quotes	On or *off*
Keep Program in Memory	Now and/or Always; *neither*
Keep File in Memory	Now and/or Always; *neither*
Custom Paper Size	Length and width, or *no custom paper size*
Menu configuration and Commands dialog box	
Full/Short Menus	Either *Short Menus* or Full Menus
Menu configurations	You can assign almost any of Word's commands to any menu. *See the Commands table later in this appendix.*
Key sequences for commands	You can assign almost any Shift, Option, and Command key sequences to all of Word's commands. *See the Commands table later in this appendix.*
Work menu	Document, glossary, command, and style names. *No entries.*
Document formats	
Document dialog box	When you click the Set Default button, Word records the state of every option in the dialog box. When you choose New from the File menu, Word uses the new defaults. (See Chapter 14, "Document Formatting and Printing.") *1 in. top and bottom margins, 1.25 in. left and right margins, 0.5 in. default tab stops, Widow Control, Footnotes at Bottom of Page, Number Pages from 1, Number Lines from 1.*
Page Setup dialog box	Options are stored in the document, not in the Settings file.

Where and What Set	Options
Document formats, cont.	
Print dialog box	Print Hidden Text (On or *Off*), Print Back to Front (On or *Off*), Print Quality (ImageWriter only—Best, *Faster,* Draft), Cover Page (LaserWriter only—First Page, Last Page, or *No*).
Section formats	
Section dialog box	When you click the Set Default button, Word records the state of every option in the dialog box. When you choose New from the File menu, Word uses the new defaults. (See Chapter 12, "Section Formatting.")
Style formats	
Define Styles dialog box	When you click the Set Default button, Word records the definition of the selected style. When you choose New from the File menu, Word adds all recorded styles to the document. (See the table below for the preset style definitions; see also Chapter 10, "Working with Style Sheets.")
Other defaults	
Hide/Show ¶	Either *Hide ¶* or Show ¶
Dialog box placement	If you move a dialog box, Word remembers the new position.
File locations	Help, MS Dictionary, up to three user dictionaries, Hyphenation, and the location of the Excel and SuperPaint programs (for QuickSwitch, covered in Chapter 16, "Transferring Text and Graphics"). If Word can't find one of these files in an expected folder (see "How Word Finds Files" in Appendix A, "Setting Up Word"), it presents a dialog box asking you to find the file. This location is stored in the Settings file.
Outline View	*Show Formats,* Show Body Text.
Print Preview	Number of pages displayed.
Index	*Run-in* or Nested style.
Table Of Contents	*Outline* or .i. method of table-of-contents extraction, and whether page numbers are extracted.
Word Count	*Characters, Words,* Lines, and *Paragraphs.*
Spelling	*Ignore Words in All Caps.*
Hyphenation	Hyphenate Capitalized Words.
Find/Change	Match Case, and Find Whole Words.

■ *Preset Style Sheet Definitions*

Below is a list of Word's automatic styles and their preset definitions. As with the other settings stored in the current Settings file, you can reset the default definitions for the automatic styles by pressing the Shift key while clicking the Reset button in the Commands dialog box. However, when you do this, you lose the other styles you've added to the current Word Settings file as well as the other preferences you've set.

Name	Definition
footer	Normal + Tab stops: 3 in. Centered; 6 in. Right Flush
footnote reference	Normal + Font: 9 Point, Superscript 3 Point
footnote text	Normal + Font: 10 Point
header	Normal + Tab stops: 3 in. Centered; 6 in. Right Flush
heading 1	Normal + Font: Helvetica, Bold Underline, Space Before 12 pt.
heading 2	Normal + Font: Helvetica, Bold, Space Before 6 pt.
heading 3	Normal + Bold, Indent: Left 0.25 in.
heading 4	Normal + Underline, Indent: Left 0.25 in.
heading 5	Normal + Font: 10 Point, Bold, Indent: Left 0.5 in.
heading 6	Normal + Font: 10 Point, Underline, Indent: Left 0.5 in.
heading 7 through *heading 9*	Normal + Font: 10 Point, Italic, Indent: Left 0.5 in.
index 1	Normal +
index 2 through *index 7*	Normal + Indent: Left (in multiples of 0.25 in.)
line number	Normal +
Normal	Font: New York 12 Point, Flush left
page number	Normal +
PostScript	Normal + Font: 10 Point, Bold Hidden
toc 1	Normal + Indent: Right 0.5 in, Tab stops 5.75 in. …; 6 in. Right Flush
toc 2 through *toc 9*	Normal + Indent: Left (in multiples of 0.5 inch), Right 0.5 in., Tab stops: 5.75 in …; 6 in. Right Flush

Word's Commands and Key Sequences

Following is a table listing the complete range of commands, dialog box options, and actions that are available through Word's Commands dialog box. A few actions available in Word are not represented in this list, and you cannot add them to menus or assign key sequences to them; for example, the key sequences you can use to navigate in dialog boxes have no equivalent commands. (Navigation in dialog boxes is discussed in Chapter 3, "The Word Environment.") Accompanying each entry is a description of the meaning of each command, compiled from the messages Word itself presents when you click the Help button in the Commands dialog box, as well as the preset key sequence assignments stored in the Word Settings (4) file. A few notes:

- *Italicized entries* in the table are not generated when you click the List button in the Commands dialog box in the preset configuration. Only those entries that have been placed on a menu or have been given a key sequence are listed when you click the List button.
- *Toggle* in the table means *turns on and off*. For example, to put text in boldface, you use the Bold command in some form, either from the command on the Format menu, through the Character dialog box, or by using the Shift-Command-B key sequence. To remove the bold attribute, use the command again.
- As discussed in Chapter 3, commands followed by an ellipsis (...) call up the relevant dialog box, within which you can set one or more options.
- When you select a command in the Commands dialog box followed by a colon, Word presents a dropdown list or dropdown field in the dialog box for selecting further options. For example, when you select the Apply Style Name command, Word displays a dropdown list presenting the names of all style names that are defined for the current document as well as the names of all automatic styles. Similarly, when you select the Font Size command, Word displays a dropdown field listing a range of font sizes. You can select a font size from the list to add to the Font menu or enter a new font size in the field.
- Many commands take effect even though you might not see the effect on screen. For example, you can use the Show Heading 5 command in Page View and see no change on screen. However, when you switch back to Outline View, you'll see that the command actually does display the outline to heading 5.
- Even though the rest of this book references the command key from left to right (i.e., Shift-Option-Command-A), this table lists them in the order they appear in the list generated when you click the List button in the Commands dialog box.

- ❑ When you generate your own list of commands and key sequences, Word also adds the names of documents you've added to the Work menu, and the names of fonts and font sizes you've added to the Format (or other menu).

Command Key Icons

Following is a table of the icons associated with various keys as represented on Word's menus, in the Commands dialog box, and in the Commands table on the next page:

Icon	Meaning
⌘	Command
⌥	Option
⇧	Shift
⇥	Tab
←	Left arrow
→	Right arrow
↑	Up arrow
↓	Down arrow
⌫	Delete or Backspace
⌦	Delete forward, on the extended keyboard
▦	Keypad (another key follows the icon)
⌤	Enter
↵	Return; not the newline character entered when you press Shift-Return
␣	Spacebar
⌧	Clear, or NumLock key, on the keypad

Also, many of these keys in the Key group of the Commands dialog box are spelled out instead of being represented by an icon. Function keys for use on the Extended keyboard are noted with an *F* followed by the number of the function key.

Command name	Meaning, menu	Standard keyboard	Keypad	Extended keyboard
1 1/2 Line Spaced	Sets one-and-one-half-line spacing (18 points) for selected paragraphs.			
About Microsoft Word	Identifies version of Word and provides access to online help.			
	****			
Activate Keyboard Menus	Activates menu bar so that you can choose menu commands using keys.			
		⌘⇥	⌨.	
Add to Menu	Adds the selected command to its predefined "home" menu. Mouse pointer changes to +.			
		⌘⌥= or ⌘⇧⌥=		
Again	Repeats latest command or editing action.			
	Edit	⌘A		
All Caps	Toggles the All Caps character format.			
		⌘⇧K		⇧F10
All Styles...	Applies a selected style to selected paragraph(s). Dialog box lists defined styles and all automatic styles.			
Alphabetic Page Numbers	Selects uppercase letters A–Z for page numbers of current section.			
Apply Style Name:	Applies indicated style to selected paragraph.			
Arabic Page Numbers	Selects Arabic numerals for page numbers of current section.			
Assign to Key	Assigns a key combination to a command. Mouse pointer changes to ⌘.			
		⌘⌥←	⌘⌥⌨+	
Auto Page Numbering	Toggles automatic page numbering for current section.			
Background Repagination	Toggles option to automatically repaginate a document during pauses in typing and editing.			
Backspace	Deletes selection or character left of insertion point.			
Black	Toggles black character color.			
Blue	Toggles blue character color.			
Bold	Toggles bold character format.			
	Format	⌘⇧B		F10
Calculate	Computes numerical expression in the selection and places result on the Clipboard.			
	Utilities	⌘=		
Cancel	Stops current command action.			
		⌘.	⌧ (clear)	
Cell Border:	Applies specified type of border to selected cells of a table.			
Cell Borders...	Applies and removes cell borders in a table.			
Cells...	Changes appearance of cells within a table.			
	Format			

Command name	Meaning, menu	Standard keyboard	Keypad	Extended keyboard
Centered	Centers text of selected paragraph between left and right indents.			
		⌘⇧C		
Change Font	Changes current font to font you indicate by typing font name and pressing Return.			
		⌘⇧E		
Change Ruler Scale	Cycles among the three ruler scales: normal, page, and table scales.			
Change Style	Changes style of selected paragraphs to style you indicate by typing style name and pressing Return.			
		⌘⇧S		
Change…	Finds and replaces text with replacement text you specify.			
	Utilities	⌘H		
Character…	Changes character formatting of current selection.			
	Format	⌘D		F14
Clear	Deletes selection from document without placing it on Clipboard.			
	Edit			
Close	Closes active document.			
	File	⌘W		
Close Spacing	Removes vertical space before selected paragraphs.			
Collapse Selection	In Outline View, hides selected outline headings and/or body text regardless of heading level.			
Collapse Subtext	In Outline View, hides all subordinate levels or the next higher level subordinate to the selected outline heading, depending on whether the entire heading is selected.			
Columns:	Formats current section with number of text columns you specify.			
Commands…	Creates and opens customized keyboard and menu configurations.			
	Edit			
Condensed:	Reduces space between characters by specified number of points.			
Context Sensitive Help	Displays Help information for open command dialog box or a command you subsequently select from a menu.			
		⌘/		*help*
Copy	Copies selection to Clipboard.			
	Edit	⌘C		F3
Copy as Picture	Copies selection as a MacDraw graphic onto Clipboard.			
		⌘⌥D		

Command name	Meaning, menu	Standard keyboard	Keypad	Extended keyboard
Copy Formats	Copies character or paragraph formatting of selection (depending on whether entire paragraph is selected) and applies it to subsequently selected text.			
		⌘⌥V		⇧F4
Copy Text	Copies current selection to new location or copies subsequent selection to current position of insertion point.			
		⌘⌥C		⇧F3
Cut	Deletes selection from document and places it on Clipboard.			
	Edit	⌘X		F2
Cyan	Toggles cyan character color.			
Define All Styles…	Defines, modifies, and applies styles. Dialog box lists defined styles and all automatic styles (even if you haven't explicitly defined them).			
Define Styles…	Defines, modifies, and applies styles. Dialog box lists defined styles and automatic styles used in your document.			
	Format	⌘T		
Delete Cells, Shift Left	Deletes selected cells. Cells to the right of deleted cells are shifted left.			
Delete Cells, Shift Up	Deletes selected cells. Cells below deleted cells are shifted up.			
Delete Columns	Deletes selected columns of a table or column containing insertion point.			
Delete Forward	Deletes character to right of insertion point.			
		⌘⌥F		⌦
Delete Next Word	Deletes word (or part of word) to right of insertion point.			
		⌘⌥G		
Delete Previous Word	Deletes word (or part of word) to left of insertion point.			
		⌘⌥⌫		
Delete Rows	Deletes selected rows of a table or row containing insertion point.			
Delete…	Deletes an unopened document.			
	File			
Demote Heading	Lowers selected heading paragraph to next lower outline level.			
Document…	Changes formats affecting the entire active document.			
	Format	⌘F14		
Dotted Underline	Toggles dotted underlining.			
		⌘⇧\		⌥F12
Double Space	Sets double-spacing (24 points) for selected paragraphs.			
		⌘⇧Y		
Double Underline	Toggles double underlining.			
		⌘⇧[		⇧F12

Command name	Meaning, menu	Standard keyboard	Keypad	Extended keyboard
Edit Link (Quickswitch)	Switches to the source application and file of the selected information in your Word document. After you revise the original file and return to Word, Word updates your document with the revised data or graphic. Available only when running under MultiFinder.			
		⌘,		⌥F2
Expand Subtext	In Outline View, displays all subordinate levels or the next lower level subordinate to the selected outline heading, depending on whether the entire heading is selected.			
Expanded:	Increases space between characters by specified number of points.			
Extend to Character	Extends selection (highlighted area) to character you type.			
		⌘⌥H	⌨-	
Fast Save Enabled	Toggles option to save a file more quickly but with less efficient use of memory.			
Find Again	Repeats search for text or format you specified when you last chose Find or Find Formats command.			
	Utilities	⌘⌥A		
Find Formats	Searches for character or paragraph formats matching that of selected text, depending on whether an entire paragraph is selected.			
		⌘⌥R		
Find…	Searches for text and/or special characters.			
	Utilities	⌘F		
First Line Indent	Indents first line of selected paragraph to first default tab stop to right.			
		⌘⇧F		
First Page Special	Adds Open First Header and Open First Footer commands to Document menu so that you can create first-page headers and footers for current section. Turns off automatic page numbering for first page.			
Flush Left	Aligns text of selected paragraph flush with left indent.			
		⌘⇧L		
Flush Right	Aligns text of selected paragraph flush with right indent.			
		⌘⇧R		
Font Name:	Applies specified font to selected text or to text typed at insertion point. A drop-down list appears at the top of the dialog box, where you can select a font to add to the Font menu. You can also assign a key command to the selected font.			
	Font			

Command name	Meaning, menu	Standard keyboard	Keypad	Extended keyboard
Font Size:	Applies specified font size to selected text or to text typed at insertion point. A drop-down field appears at the top of the dialog box, where you can select a font size to add to the Font menu or enter an unlisted font size. You can also assign a key command to the selected font size. **Font**			
Footnote Cont. Notice…	Opens footnote continuation notice window so that you can type continuation notice.			
Footnote Cont. Separator…	Opens footnote continuation separator window so that you can edit characters separating main text from footnotes continued from preceding page.			
Footnote Separator…	Opens footnote separator window so that you can edit characters separating footnotes from main text.			
Footnote…	Inserts a footnote reference mark at insertion point and opens footnote window. In Page View, moves insertion point into footnote text area. **Document**	⌘E		
Fractional Widths	Toggles the fractional character width option in the LaserWriter dialog box.			
Full Repaginate Now	Forces repagination of document even though no changes have occurred since last pagination. In Page View, forces repagination from beginning of document to currently displayed page.			
Glossary Entry:	Inserts indicated glossary entry at insertion point.			
Glossary…	Inserts or defines a glossary entry. **Edit**	⌘K		
Go Back	Displays previous selection or returns insertion point to its previous position. **Utilities**	⌘⌥Z	⌨0	
Go To…	Displays indicated page if document has been paginated. **Utilities**	⌘G		
Green	Toggles green character color.			
Hanging Indent	Indents lines after first line of selected paragraph to next default tab stop to right.	⌘⇧T		
Help…	Displays list of on-line Help topics. **Window**			
Hidden Text	Toggles hidden text character format.	⌘⇧U	⌘⇧H	⌥F9
Hide Ruler	Toggles display of the Ruler. If the Ruler isn't visible, the command reads *Show Ruler* and appears in the list box after Show Menu Function Keys.	⌘R		

Command name	Meaning, menu	Standard keyboard	Keypad	Extended keyboard
Hide ¶	Toggles display of Word's normally invisible characters, such as spaces, tabs, and paragraph marks. If the characters aren't visible, the command reads *Show ¶* and appears in the list box after Show Text Boundaries.			
		⌘R		
Hyphenate…	Scans document and hyphenates words to improve line breaks.			
	Utilities			⇧F15
Include Endnotes in Section	Toggles option to print footnotes at end of current section.			
Include RTF in Clipboard	Toggles option to include RTF code when something is copied to the Clipboard for pasting into another program.			
Index…	Compiles index based on index entries inserted in document.			
	Utilities			
Insert Cells Down	Inserts empty cells above selected cells. Number of cells inserted is equal to the number of selected cells. Selected cells are shifted down.			
Insert Cells Right	Inserts empty cells to the left of selected cells. Number of cells inserted is equal to the number of selected cells. Selected cells are shifted right.			
Insert Columns	Inserts empty column(s) in a table to left of column containing insertion point or to left of selected columns.			
Insert Date	Inserts current date glossary entry (m/d/y).			
Insert Formula	Inserts formula code (\ ).			
		⌘⌥\		
Insert Glossary Text	Prompts you to type a glossary entry name and inserts glossary entry text at insertion point or in place of selection.			
		⌘*delete* or ⌘*backspace*		
Insert Graphics	Inserts an empty graphics frame at insertion point.			
	Document			
Insert Index Entry	Inserts index entry codes, formatted as hidden text, before and after selected text or on either side of insertion point.			
	Document			
Insert Line Break	Breaks a line of text without starting a new paragraph. Inserts newline character (displayed as ↵ with Show ¶ on).			
		⇧↵		
Insert New Paragraph	Terminates current paragraph and inserts a paragraph mark.			
		↵ or ⌅		
Insert New Section	Inserts a section break at insertion point.			
		⌘⌅		

Command name	Meaning, menu	Standard keyboard	Keypad	Extended keyboard
Insert Nonbreaking Hyphen	Inserts a hyphen preventing a line break within a hyphenated word that occurs at end of a line. Hyphen is displayed as ⌐ when Show ¶ is on.	⌘`		
Insert Nonbreaking Space	Inserts a space preventing a line break on either side of space. Space is displayed as ˜ when Show ¶ is on.	⌥␣ or ⌘␣		
Insert Optional Hyphen	Inserts a hyphen that is printed only when a word is broken at the hyphen. Hyphen is displayed as ¬ when Show ¶ is on.	⌘ -		
Insert Page Break	Inserts a manual page break at insertion point. Document	⇧⌤		
Insert Page Number	Inserts automatic page number glossary entry.			
Insert Rows	Inserts empty rows in a table above row containing insertion point or above selected rows.			
Insert Tab	Inserts tab character, displayed as ➧ when Show ¶ is turned on.	⇥ or ⌥⇥		
Insert Table…	Inserts a table having specified number of rows and columns at insertion point. Document			
Insert Time	Inserts print time glossary entry.			
Insert TOC Entry	Inserts table-of-contents entry codes, formatted as hidden text, before and after selected text or on either side of insertion point. Document			
Insert ¶ Above Row	Inserts a paragraph mark having *Normal* style above table row containing insertion point.	⌘⌥␣		
Italic	Turns italic character format on and off. Format	⌘⇧I		F11
Italic Cursor	Toggles slanted insertion point and mouse I-beam pointer in italic text.			
Justified	Justifies text of selected paragraph between left and right indents.	⌘⇧J		
Keep Lines Together	Prevents a page break within selected paragraph.			
Keep with Next ¶	Prevents a page break between selected paragraph and following paragraph.			
L Thick Paragraph Border	Adds a thick border on the left side of the selected paragraphs.	⌘⌥2		

Command name	Meaning, menu	Standard keyboard	Keypad	Extended keyboard
Larger Font Size	Increases font size to next larger size.	⌘⇧. or ⌘⇧>		
Line Numbers By Page	Turns on line numbering for current section and restarts line numbering from 1 on each page.			
Line Numbers By Section	Turns on line numbering for current section and restarts line numbering from 1 at beginning of section.			
Line Numbers Continuous	Turns on line numbering for current section and continues numbering sequence from preceding section.			
List All Fonts	Lists all installed fonts on Font menu.			
Load File into Memory	Toggles option to load as much as possible of open file into memory for current session.			
Load Program into Memory	Toggles option to load as much as possible of Word program into memory for current session.			
Lowercase Alphabetic Page Numbers	Selects lowercase letters a–z for page numbers of current section.			
Lowercase Roman Page Numbers	Selects lowercase Roman numerals for page numbers of current section.			
Magenta	Toggles magenta character color.			
Make Backup Files	Toggles the option to make a backup file when the document is saved.			
Make Body Text	Makes selected paragraph the body text of preceding outline heading.			
Merge Cells	Combines selected cells in a row into one cell.			
More Keyboard Prefix	Amplifies extent of subsequent keyboard action; e.g., right arrow key moves to next paragraph instead of next character.	⌘⌥'		
Move Down One Text Area	Moves insertion point to text area below text area containing insertion point (in Page View) or to cell below cell containing insertion point (within a table).		⌘⌥▦2	
Move Heading Down	Moves selected outline heading or body text below next visible paragraph in outline.			
Move Heading Up	Moves selected outline heading or body text above preceding visible paragraph in outline.			
Move Left One Text Area	Moves insertion point to text area left of text area containing insertion point (in Page View) or to cell at left of cell containing insertion point (within a table).		⌘⌥▦4	

Command name	Meaning, menu	Standard keyboard	Keypad	Extended keyboard
Move Right One Text Area	Moves insertion point to text area right of text area containing insertion point (in Page View) or to cell at right of cell containing insertion point (within a table).		⌘⌥⌨6	
Move Text	Moves current selection to new location or moves subsequent selection to current position of insertion point.	⌘⌥H		⇧F2
Move to Bottom of Window	Places insertion point after last character visible in window.			*end*
Move to End of Document	Places insertion point after last character in document.		⌘⌨3	⌘*end*
Move to End of Line	Moves insertion point to end of current line.		⌨1	
Move to First Text Area	Moves insertion point to first text area visible in window (in Page View) or to first cell visible in window (within a table).		⌘⌥⌨7	
Move to Last Text Area	Moves insertion point to last text area visible in window (in Page View) or to last cell visible in window (within a table).		⌘⌥⌨1	
Move to Next Cell	Moves insertion point to next cell (to right).			
Move to Next Character	Moves insertion point right one character.	→ or ⌘⌥L	⌨6	
Move to Next Line	Moves insertion point down one line.	↓ or ⌘⌥,	⌨2	
Move to Next Page	In Page View, moves insertion point to top of next page.	⌘*page down*		
Move to Next Paragraph	Places insertion point at start of next paragraph.	⌘↓ or ⌘⌥B	⌘⌨2	
Move to Next Sentence	Places insertion point at start of next sentence.		⌘⌨1	
Move to Next Text Area	Moves insertion point to next text area at right (in Page View) or to next cell (within a table).		⌘⌥⌨3	
Move to Next Window	Activates next document window, based on order in which you opened windows.	⌘⌥W		
Move to Next Word	Places insertion point after current word or next word.	⌘→ or ⌘⌥;	⌘⌨6	

Command name	Meaning, menu	Standard keyboard	Keypad	Extended keyboard
Move to Previous Cell	Moves insertion point to preceding cell (to left).			
		⇧⇥		
Move to Previous Character	Moves insertion point left one character.			
		← or ⌘⌥K	▤4	
Move to Previous Line	Moves insertion point up one line.			
		↑ or ⌘⌥O	▤8	
Move to Previous Page	In Page View, moves insertion point to top of preceding page.			
		⌘*page up*		
Move to Previous Paragraph	Places insertion point at start of current paragraph or preceding paragraph.			
		⌘↑ or ⌘⌥Y	⌘▤8	
Move to Previous Sentence	Places insertion point at start of current sentence or preceding sentence.			
			⌘▤7	
Move to Previous Text Area	Moves insertion point to preceding text area at left (in Page View) or to preceding cell (within a table).			
			⌘⌥▤9	
Move to Previous Word	Places insertion point before current or preceding word.			
		⌘← or ⌘⌥J	⌘▤4	
Move to Start of Document	Places insertion point before first character in document.			
			⌘▤9	⌘*home*
Move to Start of Line	Moves insertion point to beginning of current line.			
			▤7	
Move to Top of Window	Places insertion point before first character visible in window.			
			⌘▤5	*home*
Move Up One Text Area	Moves insertion point to text area above text area containing insertion point (in Page View) or to cell above cell containing insertion point (within a table).			
			⌘⌥▤8	
Nest Paragraph	Shifts left indent of selected paragraph to next default tab stop to right. First-line indent is relative to new left indent position.			
		⌘⇧N		
New	Opens a new untitled document.			
	File	⌘N		F5
New Window	Opens a new window for active document.			
	Window			⇧F5
New ¶ After Ins. Point	Inserts a paragraph mark after insertion point without moving insertion point to next line.			
		⌘⌥↵		

Command name	Meaning, menu	Standard keyboard	Keypad	Extended keyboard
New ¶ with Same Style	Starts a new paragraph with same style as current paragraph. Overrides Next Style indicated in Define Styles dialog box.			
		⌘↵		
No Line Numbers	Turns off line numbering for current section.			
No Line Numbers in Paragraph	Turns off line numbering for selected paragraph. Available if line numbering option is on for current section.			
Normal Paragraph	Applies *Normal* style to paragraph.			
		⌘⇧P		
Normal Position	Applies normal character position (relative to text baseline) to selected text or text you type at insertion point.			
Normal Spacing	Applies normal character spacing to selected text or text you type at insertion point.			
Numeric Lock	Toggles Num Lock so that you can type numbers using numeric keypad.			
			▦⌫	
Open Any File...	Opens a document. Dialog box lists all files in current folder/drive. Files in formats not recognized by Word are opened as ASCII text.			
				⇧F6
Open Documents in Page View	Toggles option to open documents in Page View rather than Galley View.			
Open Documents with Ruler	Toggles option to automatically display Ruler when documents are opened.			
Open Even Footer...	Opens footer window for even-numbered pages in current section.			
Open Even Header...	Opens header window for even-numbered pages in current section.			
Open File Name:	Opens indicated document.			
Open First Footer...	Opens first-page footer window for current section.			
Open First Header...	Opens first-page header window for current section.			
Open Footer...	Opens standard footer window for current section. In Page View, moves insertion point into footer text.			
	Document			
Open Footnote Window	Opens footnote window and displays footnotes related to footnote reference marks visible in document window.			
		⌘⇧⌥S		
Open Header...	Opens standard header window for current section. In Page View, moves insertion point into header text.			
	Document			
Open Mail...	Lists Word mail messages in your Microsoft Mail mailbox.			
	File			

Command name	Meaning, menu	Standard keyboard	Keypad	Extended keyboard
Open Odd Footer…	Opens footer window for odd-numbered pages in current section.			
Open Odd Header…	Opens header window for odd-numbered pages in current section.			
Open Spacing	Adds 12 points of vertical space before selected paragraphs.			
		⌘⇧O		
Open…	Opens a document. Dialog box lists all Word files and files in formats recognized by Word.			
	File	⌘O		F6
Outline	Toggles outline character format.			
	Format	⌘⇧D		F11
Outline Command Prefix	Sets the prefix enabling you to promote, demote, and move outline paragraphs in Galley View or Page View by pressing a key.			
		⌘⌥T		
Outlining	Toggles Outline View.			
	Document	⌘U		⇧F13
Page Break Before	Inserts a manual page break before selected paragraph.			
Page Setup…	Sets page size, print orientation, and certain printer effects for a document.			
	File			⇧F8
Page View	Toggles Page View.			
	Document	⌘B		F13
Paragraph Border:	Applies specified type of border to selected paragraph.			
Paragraph Borders…	Applies and removes paragraph borders.			
Paragraph…	Changes paragraph formatting of selected paragraph(s).			
	Format	⌘M		⇧F14
Paste	Inserts Clipboard contents at insertion point or in place of current selection.			
	Edit	⌘V		F4
Paste Cells	Inserts contents of cells on Clipboard into an equal number of table cells.			
Paste Link	Pastes contents of Clipboard into your document with an identifier paragraph linking pasted data or graphic to its source application and file.			
	Edit			⌥F4
Paste Special Character	Inserts a special font character indicated by decimal code you type.			
		⌘⌥Q		
Plain For Style	Removes all character formatting not defined in the current style from selected text. Restores font, font size, and other character formats defined for style of a paragraph.			
	Format	⌘⇧␣		F9

Command name	Meaning, menu	Standard keyboard	Keypad	Extended keyboard
Plain Text	Removes character formatting that can be turned on and off, such as bold, italic, and underlining.			
	Format	⌘⇧Z		⇧F9
Position…	Positions selected paragraphs on current page.			
	Format			
Preferences…	Brings up the Preferences dialog box.			
	Edit			
Print Merge…	Merges specified data records with active main document.			
	File			
Print Preview…	Displays one or two pages at reduced size as they'll look when printed.			
	File	⌘I		⌥F13
Print…	Prints active document.			
	File	⌘P		F8
Promote Heading	Raises selected heading paragraph to next higher outline level.			
Quit	Quits Word and prompts you to save changes to open documents, glossaries, and dictionaries.			
	File	⌘Q		
Red	Toggles red character color.			
Redefine Style From Selection	Redefines the style attached to the selected paragraph based on the formats in the selected text.			
Remove From Menu	Removes a selected command from a menu. Mouse pointer changes to ▬.			
		⌘⌥-		
Renumber…	Automatically numbers or renumbers selected paragraphs in specified sequence.			
	Utilities			⌘F15
Repaginate Now	Repaginates entire document. In Page View, repaginates from beginning of document to currently displayed page.			
	Document	⌘J		
Reset Spelling	Clears list of spelling corrections Word remembers for current session.			
Restart Page Numbering at 1	Toggles option to start page numbering of current section from 1.			
Roman Page Numbers	Selects uppercase Roman numerals for page numbers of current section.			
Save	Saves active document under its current name.			
	File	⌘S		F7
Save As…	Renames document, saves it in a different format, or saves it in a different drive or folder.			
	File		⇧F7	

Command name	Meaning, menu	Standard keyboard	Keypad	Extended keyboard
Screen Test	Displays graphics to test display monitor. Click the mouse to stop.			
Scroll Line Down	Scrolls first line in window out of view, displaying one more line at bottom of window.			
		⌘⌥/	▦*	
Scroll Line Up	Scrolls last line in window out of view, displaying one more line at top of window.			
		⌘⌥[	▦+	
Scroll Screen Down	Displays next screenful (based on window size) of document.			
		⌘⌥.	▦3	*page down*
Scroll Screen Up	Displays preceding screenful (based on window size) of document.			
		⌘⌥P	▦9	*page up*
Section Starts on Even Page	Starts current section on next even-numbered page.			
Section Starts on New Column	Starts current section in next text column on same page or, if current and preceding sections have different numbers of text columns, on next page.			
Section Starts on New Page	Starts current section on a new page.			
Section Starts on Odd Page	Starts current section on next odd-numbered page.			
Section Starts with No Break	Starts current section on same page as preceding section.			
Section…	Changes page layout within the current section.			
	Format			⌥F14
Select Whole Document	Selects entire document. Same as pressing the Command key while clicking in the selection bar.			
		⌘⌥M		
Select Window:	Activates indicated document window.			
Send Mail…	Displays Microsoft Mail directory list window for selecting recipients of current Word message (active Word document).			
	File			
Shadow	Turns shadow character format on and off.			
	Format	⌘⇧W		⌥F11
Short Menus	Switches between Full Menus and Short Menus.			
	Edit			
Show All Headings	In Outline View, displays headings of all levels and body text.			
Show Clipboard	Displays contents of Clipboard.			
	Window			
Show Heading 1	In Outline View, displays only heading level 1.			
Show Heading 2	In Outline View, displays only heading levels 1 and 2.			
Show Heading 3	In Outline View, displays only heading levels 1–3.			
Show Heading 4	In Outline View, displays only heading levels 1–4.			
Show Heading 5	In Outline View, displays only heading levels 1–5.			

Command name	Meaning, menu	Standard keyboard	Keypad	Extended keyboard
Show Heading 6	In Outline View, displays only heading levels 1–6.			
Show Heading 7	In Outline View, displays only heading levels 1–7.			
Show Heading 8	In Outline View, displays only heading levels 1–8.			
Show Heading 9	In Outline View, displays heading levels 1–9.			
Show Hidden Text	Toggles display of hidden text, indicated with a dotted underline.			
Show Menu Function Keys	Toggles display of extended keyboard function keys assigned to menu commands.			
Show Ruler	Toggles display of ruler at top of document, footnote, or header/footer window.			
	Format	**⌘R**		
Show Styles on Ruler	Displays list of styles from ruler style selection box.			
Show Table Gridlines	Toggles display of nonprinting gridlines in a table.			
Show Text Boundaries	Toggles display of nonprinting boundary lines of text areas in Page View.			
Show ¶	Displays screen symbols such as ¶ (paragraph mark).			
	Edit	**⌘Y**		
Show/Hide Body Text	In Outline View, switches between display of all body text or first line only.			
Show/Hide Formatting	In Outline View, turns on and off display of character formatting.			
Side by Side	Applies side-by-side format to selected paragraphs.			
Single Line Spaced	Sets single-spacing (12 points) for selected paragraphs.			
Small Caps	Turns small capitals character format on and off.			
		⌘⇧H		**⌥F10**
Smaller Font Size	Decreases font size to next smaller size.			
		⌘⇧<	**⌘⇧,**	
Smart Quotes	Toggles option to use “ ” and ‘ ’ instead of " " and ' ' when you press the standard quote key.			
Sort	Sorts entire document or selected paragraphs, columns, or lines in ascending order (A–Z or 1–9) according to leftmost character.			
	Utilities			
Sort Descending	Sorts entire document or selected paragraphs, columns, or lines in descending order (Z–A or 9–1) according to leftmost character.			
Spelling...	Checks a document or selected text for incorrect spelling.			
	Utilities	**⌘L**		**F15**
Split Cells	Splits a merged cell back into separate cells.			
Split Window	Splits active window.			
		⌘⌥S		

Command name	Meaning, menu	Standard keyboard	Keypad	Extended keyboard
Strikethru	Turns strikethrough character format on and off.			
		⌘⇧/		
Styles…	Applies a selected style to selected paragraph(s). Dialog box lists defined styles and automatic styles used in your document.			
	Format			
Subscript:	Lowers characters below baseline by specified number of points and reduces font size to next smaller size.			
Subscript 2 pt	Subscripts by 2 points and decreases the font size.			
		⌘⇧-		
Superscript:	Raises characters above baseline by specified number of points and reduces font size to next smaller size.			
Superscript 3 pt	Superscripts by 3 points and decreases the font size.			
		⌘⇧=		
Symbol Font	Applies Symbol font to current selection.			
		⌘⇧Q		
Table of Contents…	Compiles table of contents based on document outline or table-of-contents entries.			
	Utilities			
Table to Text…	Converts a table created with Insert Table command to text separated by paragraph marks, tabs, or commas.			
Table…	Adds and deletes rows, columns, and cells in a table and merges and splits cells.			
	Edit			
Tabs…	Sets and clears tabs for selected paragraph(s). Controls tab alignment and type of tab leader.			
Underline	Turns single continuous underlining on and off.			
	Format	⌘⇧U		F12
Undo	Reverses latest command action if possible.			
	Edit	⌘Z		F1
Unnest Paragraph	Shifts left indent of selected paragraph to next default tab stop to left. First-line indent is relative to new left-indent position.			
		⌘⇧M		
Update Link	Updates selected information in your Word document to match current graphic or data in the original source application and file. Available only when running under MultiFinder.			
	Edit			⌥F3
Use Picture Placeholders	Toggles display of gray rectangles in place of graphics.			
White	Toggles white character color.			
Word Count…	Displays number of characters, words, paragraphs, and lines in a document or selection, excluding headers and footers.			
	Utilities			⌥F15

Command name	Meaning, menu	Standard keyboard	Keypad	Extended keyboard
Word Underline	Toggles word underlining.			
		⌘⇧]		⌘F12
Yellow	Toggles yellow character color.			
Zoom Window	Switches active window between its full size and an alternate size.			
		⌘⌥]		
---Separator---	Inserts a dashed line at bottom of selected menu (used to separate groups of commands).			

Index

Symbols

■ *A*

■ *B*

D

E

F

■ *G*

H

I

■ *K*

L

M

N

O

■ P

■ *Q*

■ *R*

S

■ *T*

U

V

W

Z

Chris Kinata

Chris Kinata graduated from the University of California at Irvine with a degree in psychology and a minor in computer science. He joined Microsoft Press as a technical editor in 1984. He alternates between writing about Microsoft Word and helping User Education groups in the Applications Division of Microsoft Corporation use Word to publish manuals for Microsoft products.

The manuscript for this book was prepared and submitted to Microsoft Press in electronic form. Text files were processed and formatted using Mac Word on an Apple Macintosh II.

Graphics were prepared on a Macintosh II and modified in SuperPaint, Cricket Draw, ThunderScan, MacVision, FreeHand, and Canvas. Certain effects were produced by custom PostScript routines. Graphics were printed on the ImageWriter, LaserWriter, and Linotronic 300 laser imagesetter.

Cover design by Williams & Helde, Inc.
Interior text design by the staff of Microsoft Press
Typographer: Chris Kinata

Text composition by Microsoft Press in Palatino with display in Palatino Italic and Helvetica Black. The book was typeset from a Macintosh SE to a Linotronic 300 laser imagesetter.

Printed on recycled paper stock.